Financing Residential Real Estate

15th Edition

Megan Dorsey
David Rockwell

Rockwell Publishing Company

Contents

Chapter 1
Finance and Investment

Borrowing Money to Buy a Home

Investments and Returns

Types of Investments
- Ownership investments
- Debt investments
- Securities

Investment Risk
- Safety, liquidity, and yield
- Diversification
- Lending risks
  - Risk of default
  - Risk of loss
  - Interest rate risk
  - Prepayment risk
- Misjudging risk

Market Interest Rates

Introduction

Financing—lending and borrowing money—is fundamental to the real estate business. If mortgage financing weren't available, buyers would have to pay cash for their homes, something few people can afford to do.

This book has a practical focus; it explains the basic process of obtaining a loan to purchase a home and discusses the financing options available to home buyers. The opening chapters present background information about the U.S. financial system and mortgage industry, including how government fiscal and monetary policy affects mortgage lending, the relationship between the primary and secondary mortgage markets, the different types of mortgage lenders, and the various sources of loan funds. All of these factors directly or indirectly affect whether home buyers can get the financing they need, and if so, on what terms.

From an economic perspective, mortgage loans are a type of investment, one of many types that compete for a share of the available investment funds. This chapter provides an overview of investing and explains some of the underlying investment considerations that determine what kinds of loans mortgage lenders are (and are not) willing to make.

Borrowing Money to Buy a Home

In the United States, owning a home has long been considered an essential part of a middle-class lifestyle. It's seen as a mark of achievement, and also as part of the groundwork for future prosperity and security. Exactly how beneficial home ownership actually is may be open to debate—especially in the current economic crisis, when home values are falling in many parts of the country. Nonetheless, most Americans will buy a home if they can afford to do so.

Whether an individual or a family can afford a home depends on many factors, including housing prices, income level, tax considerations, and so on. Among the most important factors is the availability of mortgage financing. A home is the most expensive purchase most people ever make, and nearly everyone needs to borrow a large amount of money to do it.

In a typical mortgage loan transaction, the lender loans the home buyers a large portion of the purchase price and requires them to pro-

Factors that affect whether someone can afford to buy a home:
- Housing prices
- Income
- Tax considerations
- Availability of financing

vide the rest out of their own resources, as a downpayment. In return for the loan, the buyers must execute a mortgage or a deed of trust in the lender's favor. This creates a **lien**, giving the lender a security interest in the property being purchased, so that the property serves as **collateral** for the loan.

Typical mortgage financing:
- Loan covers much of price
- Downpayment is from buyer's own resources
- Purchased property serves as collateral

The buyers agree to pay back the **principal** (the amount borrowed) by means of monthly payments over a specified period (the repayment period or **loan term**). In addition, as long as part of the debt is outstanding, the buyers must pay the lender a specified percentage of the remaining principal balance as **interest**. From the buyers' point of view, the interest is the cost of borrowing money; it's the amount the lender charges them for the temporary use of the principal.

Principal: the original amount borrowed, or the part of the loan that remains to be repaid

Interest: the cost of borrowing money

When the full amount borrowed and all of the interest owed have been repaid, the lender releases the property from the lien. This might not happen until the end of the loan term, when all of the scheduled monthly payments have been made. Or the loan could be paid off earlier—for example, out of the sale proceeds if the home is sold.

On the other hand, if the loan isn't repaid as agreed, the lien created by the mortgage or deed of trust gives the lender the right to foreclose. In a **foreclosure**, property is sold against the owner's will, so that a debt can be repaid from the proceeds of the forced sale.

Foreclosure: forced sale of property to pay off a debt secured by a lien

Home buyers need loans, and lenders generally want to make loans—after all, that's the business they're in. But from a lender's point of view, a loan is an investment. The interest paid by the borrower will be the lender's primary **return** (profit) on its investment. When evaluating a prospective borrower's loan application, a lender considers whether the proposed loan is likely to be a profitable investment under current (and foreseeable) economic conditions. If not, the lender won't make the loan.

Loan is an investment; lender is an investor

Interest is lender's return on the loan/investment

Because loans are investments, the availability of affordable mortgage financing fluctuates with general economic conditions. To understand mortgage lending, it's necessary to look at it in the broader context of investing and the economy as a whole.

Investments and Returns

The national economy—the system of businesses, industries, and trade that provides us with jobs, income, places to live, and goods and services—is driven in part by **investment capital**. Investment capital

Investment capital: accumulated wealth (savings) made available to fund enterprises

is simply money (accumulated wealth, or savings) that's used to fund business enterprises and other ventures, projects, and transactions.

An investor supplies capital for an enterprise or a project in the expectation (or the hope) that it will generate additional wealth for the investor—a return on the investment. Depending on the type of investment, the investor's return may take various forms, including interest, appreciation, rents, or dividends.

Return of investment: recapture of amount originally invested

A return *on* an investment is distinguished from a return *of* the investment. A return of the investment, also called **recapture**, refers to getting back the full amount originally invested. A return on the investment, by contrast, is a profit over and above the amount originally invested.

Return on investment: investor's profit

Sometimes an investor only breaks even, receiving a return of the investment without a return on the investment. And sometimes an investor may lose part or even all of the money originally invested. In other words, if an investment turns out badly, the investor might not even receive a return of the investment, much less a return on the investment.

Types of Investments

There are two general categories of investments: ownership investments and debt investments.

Ownership Investments

Ownership investment: investor purchases an asset or a property interest in an asset

When an investor uses his investment funds to purchase an asset or an interest in an asset, it's an ownership investment. If the asset is income-producing, the net income it generates during the investor's period of ownership is a return from the investment.

Return on ownership investment may be:
- Net income, and/or
- Appreciation

The investor will also get a return in the form of **appreciation** if the asset increases in value (appreciates) over time. An asset may appreciate because of **inflation**, a general increase in prices due to economic forces, or because the demand for that type of asset increases, or as a result of both inflation and increased demand. A return that takes the form of appreciation ordinarily isn't **realized**—actually received by the investor—until the asset is sold.

Real Estate Investment. The purchase of real estate is an example of an ownership investment. If the real estate is an income-producing property such as an apartment building, the net income from the property (rents paid by the tenants, minus the operating expenses) provides a return for the investor/owner.

Whether or not the property is income-producing, when the property is sold the investor may receive a higher price than she paid for it. The appreciation—the difference between the price paid (the amount invested) and the price received—is a return on the investment. On the other hand, if the property has lost value (depreciated) since it was purchased, when it's sold the investor won't even receive a return of the full amount originally invested.

Ownership investment examples:
• Real estate purchases
• Stock purchases

Corporate Stock. The purchase of shares of corporate stock is another example of an ownership investment. The shares represent an ownership interest in the corporation. The corporation uses the funds invested by the stockholders to help its business grow and generate profits. If the corporation pays **dividends** (a share of its profits) to the stockholders, the dividends are one type of return they receive from their investment. They can also receive a return in the form of appreciation: if the corporation is successful, the value of the corporation's stock goes up, and stockholders can sell their shares at a profit.

Debt Investments

With a debt investment, the investor lends money to an individual or a company. In exchange for the temporary use of the funds, the investor/lender charges the borrower interest, a specified percentage of the amount owed, until the debt is repaid. The investor acquires no ownership interest in whatever the borrower is using the money for. The investor is involved only as a creditor, and the investor's main return is the interest the borrower pays.

Debt investment: investor provides money to an entity that will eventually repay it

Loans. Any form of loan that will earn interest for the lender is a debt investment, including the residential mortgage loans that we're concerned with in this book. When a bank loans a couple money so that they can buy a home, the loan represents a debt investment for the bank. The borrowers agree to repay the bank's invested capital in monthly installments over a period of years, and also to pay interest on the capital.

Note that at the same time the bank is making a debt investment, the home buyers are making an ownership investment. They're investing their own savings (the downpayment) plus the money they're borrowing, in order to purchase an asset (the home). Their primary reason for buying the home may be to have a place to live, but if the home appreciates while they own it, they'll get a return on their investment when they sell it.

Bonds. Another example of a debt investment is the purchase of bonds. A **bond** is a certificate of indebtedness issued by a governmental body or business entity. An investor who buys bonds (a bondholder) is essentially loaning the price paid for the bonds to the entity that issued them.

With most bonds, the issuer makes periodic payments of interest to the bondholder. The rate at which interest accrues on the bond is called the coupon rate. On the bond's maturity date, the issuer pays the bondholder a lump sum called the face amount (or face value) of the bond, which is usually the same as the original purchase price.

Debt investment examples:
- Loans
- Bonds
- Savings accounts

> **Example:** If you purchased a ten-year bond for $50,000 with a coupon rate of 5%, you'd receive interest payments amounting to $2,500 each year (5% of $50,000) for ten years. At the end of that period, on the maturity date, the issuer would pay you the face amount, $50,000.

Savings Accounts. An ordinary savings account is also a debt investment. A depositor puts his money into a savings account for safekeeping and so that it will earn interest. The financial institution uses its depositors' funds to make loans to home buyers and other borrowers. In effect, the depositors are loaning their money to the financial institution (and receiving interest as a return on their investment) to enable the financial institution to make debt investments of its own (loans to customers). To make a profit, the financial institution must charge a higher interest rate on the loans it makes than the rate it pays on its savings accounts.

A debt investment similar to a savings account is the **certificate of deposit**, or CD. With a CD, in return for interest payments the investor/depositor agrees to keep funds on deposit (and available for use by the financial institution) during a specified period, such as 6, 12, or 24 months. If the depositor withdraws the funds before the end of the commitment period, the financial institution charges a penalty. As a general rule, CDs with longer commitment periods have higher interest rates than shorter-term CDs.

Fig. 1.1 Types of investments

Ownership Investments
- Investment capital used to purchase an asset or a property interest in an asset or company
- Stocks, real estate, mutual funds
- Possible returns: appreciation, rental income, and/or dividends

Debt Investments
- Investment capital provided temporarily, subject to withdrawal or eventual repayment
- Loans, bonds, savings accounts, CDs
- Returns take the form of interest

Securities
- Investment instruments
- Ownership interest or right to repayment, without managerial control
- Traded in established financial markets
- Stocks and bonds

Securities

Certain types of investments are categorized as **securities**. A security is an investment instrument (such as a share certificate) that grants the holder an interest or a right to payment, without giving the holder any direct managerial control over the enterprise in question. Securities may be either ownership investments or debt investments; stocks and bonds are the most prominent examples.

A key characteristic of securities is that they can be bought or sold easily in financial markets established for that purpose. Stocks may be traded on a stock exchange, bonds may be traded in the bond market, and so on. Thus, securities are **liquid assets**—assets that can quickly be converted into cash.

Mutual Funds. A simple way for individuals to invest in securities is through a **mutual fund**. A mutual fund is a company that buys and sells stocks and bonds on behalf of its investors. The investors purchase shares in the company, which then uses the investors/owners' capital to invest in securities. The fund managers, who are investment

Securities are investment instruments that:
- Give the holder an interest or right to payment
- Do not give the holder any direct managerial control

Securities: liquid assets that can be sold easily in established financial markets professionals, choose which securities to buy and when to sell them. This makes it much simpler for an individual with limited knowledge of the financial markets to invest in a variety of securities and benefit from diversification (discussed later in this chapter).

Securities Regulation. To protect investors, both the issuance and the trading of securities are regulated by the federal Securities and Exchange Commission (SEC). The SEC requires companies to disclose certain financial information to the public, in order to help prospective investors judge which securities are likely to be good investments. The SEC also enforces the rules against insider trading. It's illegal for "insiders" such as company executives and stockbrokers to reap profits or avoid losses in the securities markets by taking advantage of information that isn't yet available to the public.

Securities and the Mortgage Industry. Securities trading affects mortgage lending in two main ways. First, it has an impact on mortgage interest rates and the availability of funds for home loans, since mortgage lending competes with other types of investments. Second, mortgages themselves can be pooled together and "securitized" for sale to investors. These **mortgage-backed securities** have played a crucial role in the mortgage industry. We'll look at mortgage-backed securities in Chapter 3, when we discuss the secondary market.

Investment Risk

The pool of funds available for investment is large but not unlimited, and all of the different investment opportunities in the economy are in competition for those funds. When deciding where to put their money, investors have to weigh the benefits of particular investments against the risks they entail.

Key Investment Characteristics

Investors consider any investment opportunity in terms of three potential advantages: safety, liquidity, and yield.

Safety. An investment is considered safe if there's little risk that the investor will actually lose money on it. Even if the investment doesn't generate the profit hoped for, the investor will at least be able to recover the money originally invested. In other words, the investor

Margin notes:

SEC regulates securities trading to protect investors
- Financial disclosures required
- No insider trading

Investment opportunities compete for available investment funds

Safety: low risk of losing amount originally invested

can probably count on a return *of* the investment, if not a return *on* the investment.

Liquidity. An investment is liquid if it can be converted into cash (liquidated) quickly. Liquidity is important in case the investor suddenly needs cash for unexpected expenses, or perhaps for better investment opportunities. With an investment that's **illiquid** (not liquid), the investor's funds are effectively "locked up" and unavailable for other purposes.

> **Example:** Two investors each have $20,000 to invest. Investor A uses his $20,000 to buy stock, a liquid asset. Investor B uses her $20,000 to buy real estate, an illiquid asset.
>
> Six months later, both investors decide they want to use the funds they've invested for some other purpose. Investor A can sell his stock—cash in his investment—without delay. It will be much more complicated and time-consuming for Investor B to sell her real estate. Depending on B's situation, the delay may merely be an inconvenience, or it could result in financial difficulties or a missed opportunity.

Liquidity: investment can quickly be converted to cash

While real estate and other illiquid assets can be excellent investments, their lack of liquidity has consequences that prospective investors should take into account.

Yield. An investment's yield is its rate of return. Investments that are both safe and liquid typically offer the lowest yields.

Yield: investor's rate of return

> **Example:** Patterson deposits $5,000 in an ordinary savings account. This investment is very safe, because the deposited funds are federally insured against loss. It's also very liquid, because the funds can be withdrawn at any time without penalty. However, the investment's yield (the annual interest rate that the bank pays to Patterson) is only 1.15%.

In a sense, investors "pay" for safety and liquidity with low yields. For a high yield, an investor must be willing to take the risk of losing some (or possibly even all) of the original capital if the investment turns out badly. It may also be necessary to sacrifice liquidity, allowing the capital to be tied up for a while.

As a general rule, the greater the risk, the higher the potential yield needs to be; otherwise, investors won't be willing to make the investment. The higher yield compensates the investors for the additional

Safe, liquid investments offer comparatively low yields

9

Investors expect higher yields for greater risks

Yield isn't necessarily fixed when an investment is made

Portfolio: investor's mix of investments plus cash reserves

Diversification: putting money into a variety of different investments to reduce the risk of loss

risk. Investors generally also expect higher yields for long-term investments, those that will take longer to achieve the desired yield.

Of course, the yield from a particular investment isn't necessarily fixed at the time the investment is made. The yield may change with market conditions, such as a rise or fall in interest rates. In the case of ownership investments, the enterprise or property invested in may turn out to be either more or less successful or valuable than anticipated, making the actual yield higher or lower than the projected yield. In the case of debt investments, a bond default or loan default may result in a sharply reduced yield.

Diversification

An investor's mix of investments, plus any cash reserves, is referred to as a **portfolio**. To reduce risk, investors are advised to **diversify** their portfolios, putting their money into a variety of different types of investments. A diversified investment portfolio is more likely to match the growth of the economy overall, instead of being subject to fluctuations in one particular sector of the economy. Thus, an investor with a diversified portfolio is less likely to face a serious net loss; if one investment does poorly, there's a fair chance that the other investments will offset that loss with good returns.

Lending Risks

The particular risks involved in mortgage lending, from the lender/investor's point of view, include the risk of default, the risk of foreclosure loss, interest rate risk, and prepayment risk.

Risk of Default. The degree of risk associated with a particular loan depends largely on how likely it is that the borrower will default. A **default** occurs when the borrower fails to make the payments as scheduled.

When deciding whether to approve a loan application, a lender evaluates the risk of default. Through the underwriting process (see Chapter 8), the loan applicants are screened to determine whether they are likely to pay off the proposed loan on schedule. If the prospective borrowers look like a good risk—that is, if the risk of default is low—the lender will probably agree to make the loan. If the risk of default is somewhat higher, the lender might make the loan but charge a higher interest rate to compensate for the extra risk. If the risk of default is too great, the lender will decline to make the loan.

Risk of Loss. In addition to screening prospective borrowers to evaluate the risk of default, lenders take steps to limit the risk of loss in the event that a borrower eventually does default. These steps include appraising the property to make sure that it's worth enough to serve as collateral for the loan, in case foreclosure becomes necessary, and in some cases requiring mortgage insurance on the loan. (Appraisal is covered in Chapter 9; mortgage insurance in Chapter 10.)

Borrowers are also required to keep the collateral property adequately insured against fire and other natural hazards, to protect the lender from losses that might otherwise result from the impairment of the collateral.

Interest Rate Risk. Another type of risk that a lender may face in connection with a loan is interest rate risk. This is the risk that after the lender has loaned money to a borrower at a certain interest rate, market interest rates will rise.

> **Example:** A lender makes a $200,000 mortgage loan to a home buyer. Based on market interest rates, the lender agrees to make the loan at a fixed interest rate of 5%. That interest rate represents the lender's return on its $200,000 investment.
>
> Shortly after the loan closes, market interest rates begin a steep climb. A year later, they've reached 7.25%. The lender would prefer to reinvest its $200,000 now, to get a 7.25% return instead of a 5% return. But the loan agreement allows the borrower to repay the lender over a 30-year term. The lender's money is tied up and can't be reinvested until it's repaid.

Interest rate risk increases with the length of the loan term. The longer the loan term, the longer the lender's funds could be tied up. This makes interest rate risk a particular concern for mortgage lenders, because home purchase mortgages have very long repayment periods compared to other types of loans. (In the U.S., 30-year repayment periods are common for mortgages. See Chapter 6.)

Mortgage lenders have devised a number of ways of dealing with interest rate risk, including adjustable-rate mortgages (see Chapter 6) and selling loans on the secondary market (see Chapter 3).

Prepayment Risk. It isn't only rising interest rates that can cause trouble for a mortgage lender. When market interest rates fall, a lender often has to worry about borrowers **prepaying** their loans—paying back all or part of the principal balance sooner than expected. This might not sound like a problem for the lender, but it can be one.

Lenders face:
- Risk of default (borrower)
- Risk of loss (collateral)
- Interest rate risk
- Prepayment risk

Prepayment: paying back all or part of the principal before it's due

Refinancing:
- Home owners get new mortgage at lower rate
- Use proceeds of new mortgage to pay off old mortgage

Example: The Henrys financed the purchase of their home when market interest rates were quite high. They got a 30-year mortgage from Acme Savings at 9% interest.

Now it's four years later, and the outstanding balance on the mortgage is $192,400. Market interest rates have dropped to 6% since the Henrys bought their house, so they decide to refinance. They borrow $193,000 from Widget Bank at 6% interest and use the new loan to pay off their old 9% loan.

When the Henrys prepay the old mortgage, Acme Savings has to reinvest the $192,400 they've paid back. It's unlikely that loaning that money to other borrowers will provide Acme with a 9% return, like the Henrys' mortgage did. When the mortgage was prepaid, that effectively reduced Acme's yield on the investment.

As in the example, a significant decline in interest rates typically leads to a great deal of refinancing and loan prepayment.

Because prepayment can work to a lender's disadvantage, some loan agreements allow the lender to charge the borrower a penalty if the loan is prepaid. The penalty prevents the prepayment from reducing the lender's yield to the extent it otherwise could. (Prepayment penalties are discussed in more detail in Chapter 5.)

Misjudging Risk

Unfortunately, whatever steps investors take before making an investment to evaluate how risky it is, investors may turn out to be wrong—perhaps very wrong. Various factors contribute to poor investment decisions.

Naturally, poor decisions often involve a failure to correctly predict future events.

Example: Home prices have been going up rapidly and steadily for many years. Jan Dillon wants to buy a rental house, and Acme Savings agrees to loan her the money she needs for the purchase. Both the buyer and the lender are making investment decisions, and both are basing their decisions partly on the assumption that home prices will continue to rise for a long time to come. They're also both assuming that Dillon, who has been earning a good salary at her job for a long time, will continue to have that steady income.

If those predictions turned out to be correct, both investments might be very profitable. Instead, not long after the lender makes the loan and Dillon buys the rental house, economic forces cause home prices to start dropping suddenly, and a general economic downturn ensues. Dillon loses her job. She defaults on the loan, and Acme forecloses. The property doesn't sell for nearly enough to cover the amount Dillon owes Acme. Dillon loses all the money she invested in the house, and Acme takes a substantial loss on the loan.

Predicting future events is never easy, but it can be made much more difficult by inaccurate information. Sometimes a person who stands to benefit will deliberately provide an investor with false or misleading information. For example, a loan applicant might lie to the lender about his financial situation; or a lender might conceal unfair loan terms or charges from a prospective home buyer. Of course, investment decisions based on false information often turn out badly for the investor.

On the other hand, in many cases an investor has no one to blame for a loss but herself. Poor investment decisions were certainly among the factors that led to the subprime mortgage crisis, which we'll discuss in Chapter 4. Incorrect predictions, inaccurate information, deception, and recklessness all played a role, along with bad luck.

Market Interest Rates

We've referred more than once to "market interest rates," a concept that will come up repeatedly throughout the book. Market interest rates are the typical rates that lenders are currently charging borrowers for particular types of loans. The going rate for a residential mortgage may depend on the size of the loan, whether it has a fixed or adjustable interest rate, how long the loan term is, and certain other factors. A prospective borrower's credit score also affects the rate lenders are willing to offer. A borrower with a mediocre credit score can generally expect to pay a considerably higher interest rate than one with a good score. (Credit scoring is covered in Chapter 8.)

Market interest rate: typical rate charged for a certain type of loan in the current market

To attract business, some lenders offer borrowers an interest rate below the going market rate. But in most cases lenders with dramatically lower rates make up for it by charging higher loan fees (see Chapter 7). On the other hand, lenders won't charge much more than the market rate, to avoid losing customers to competing lenders.

At one time, market interest rates for mortgages varied significantly from one area of the country to another. That's no longer true; now

Mortgage rates affect real estate activity:
- High rates cause a slowdown
- Low rates spur the market

Mortgage "prices" (interest rates) respond to changes in supply and demand

the regional variations tend to be relatively slight. This is largely a result of the growth of the secondary market (see Chapter 3).

Of course, market interest rates for mortgage loans have a considerable impact on real estate activity. If mortgage rates rise extremely high, as they did in the 1980s, that can bring real estate activity to a standstill. On the other hand, low rates stimulate home sales (and also spur lots of refinancing).

The forces that cause market interest rates to rise and fall are very complex. But basically, like other kinds of prices, market interest rates for mortgage loans are affected by supply and demand: if supply exceeds demand, prices (rates) go down; if demand exceeds supply, prices (rates) go up. We'll discuss some of the factors that affect the supply of and demand for mortgage funds in Chapters 2 and 3.

Outline: Finance and Investment

I. Borrowing Money to Buy a Home

    A. Buyer's ability to afford a home depends in part on the availability of mortgage financing.

    B. From lender's point of view, a loan is an investment.

        1. Interest is lender's primary return on the investment.

        2. Lender will make a loan only if it appears to be a profitable investment under prevailing economic conditions.

II. Investments and Returns

    A. Investment capital: accumulated wealth (savings) made available to fund enterprises, projects, and transactions.

    B. Investor supplies capital in the expectation that it will generate additional wealth for the investor.

    C. Returns

        1. Return *on* investment: a profit over and above the amount originally invested.

        2. Return *of* investment: recapturing the amount originally invested (breaking even).

III. Types of Investments

    A. Ownership investments: investor buys a property interest in an asset.

        1. Ownership investments may generate net income, pay dividends, and/or appreciate.

        2. Examples: purchase of real estate, purchase of corporate stock.

    B. Debt investments: investor provides money that is to be paid back.

        1. Debt investments generate interest income.

        2. Examples: loans, bonds, savings accounts, certificates of deposit.

    C. Securities: may be either ownership investments or debt investments.

        1. Examples: stocks, bonds, mortgage-backed securities.

        2. Designed to be liquid investments, easily bought and sold in established markets.

        3. Mutual funds: investor purchases shares in a mutual fund company; fund managers use the capital to buy and sell securities.

        4. Federal Securities and Exchange Commission (SEC) regulates issuance and trading of securities to protect investors.

IV. Investment Risk

    A. Key investment characteristics

        1. Safety: low risk of losing part or all of original investment amount.

        2. Liquidity

            a. Liquid asset can be converted into cash (sold) quickly.

            b. Liquidity tends to increase safety (reduce risk of loss).

        3. Yield: rate of return.

            a. Investor usually pays for safety and liquidity with lower yield.

            b. Generally, the greater the risk, the higher the yield investors will demand.

            c. Investment's yield is not necessarily fixed at outset; may change with economy, success or failure of enterprise, etc.

    B. Diversified investment portfolio reduces overall risk of loss.

    C. Lending risks

        1. Risk of default: borrower might not repay loan.

        2. Risk of loss: property might depreciate; foreclosure proceeds might not cover loan balance.

        3. Interest rate risk: market rates may rise while loan funds are tied up at low rate.

        4. Prepayment risk: loan may be paid off sooner than expected if market rates decline.

V. Market Interest Rates

    A. Market rates are typical rates paid for a particular type of loan in the current market.

    B. Factors that may affect market rates for mortgages include size of loan, fixed or adjustable rate, length of loan term, region of country, and/or borrower's credit score.

    C. Real estate activity increases with low rates, and decreases with high rates.

    D. Market interest rates go up when demand for mortgage funds exceeds supply, and go down when supply exceeds demand.

Key Terms

Mortgage loan: A loan secured by a mortgage or deed of trust that creates a lien against real property; especially, a loan used to purchase real property when that same property serves as security for the loan.

Lien: A nonpossessory interest in real property, giving the lienholder the right to foreclose if the owner does not pay a debt owed to the lienholder.

Collateral: Property (personal or real) accepted by a lender as security for a loan. The lender has the right to keep or sell the collateral if the borrower fails to repay the loan as agreed.

Principal: The original amount of a loan, or the remainder of that amount after part of it has been repaid.

Interest: A periodic charge that a lender requires a borrower to pay in exchange for the temporary use of the borrowed funds, usually expressed as an annual percentage of the remaining principal balance. Sometimes referred to as the cost of borrowing money.

Investment: When someone (an investor) makes a sum of money (investment capital) available for use by another person or entity, in the expectation that this will generate a return (a profit) for the investor.

Investment capital: Accumulated wealth (savings) made available to fund business enterprises or other ventures, projects, or transactions.

Return on investment: A profit that an investment generates for an investor, over and above the amount of money that he originally invested in it.

Return of investment: When an investment generates enough money for an investor to replace the amount of money she originally invested in it. Also called recapture.

Ownership investment: An investment in which the investor's funds are used to purchase an asset or a property interest in an asset.

Debt investment: An investment in which temporary use of the investor's funds is exchanged for interest payments, pursuant to an agreement that requires repayment of the funds or allows withdrawal of the funds.

Appreciation: An increase in the value of an asset over time; the opposite of depreciation.

Dividend: A share of a company's profits paid to a stockholder as a return on the investment.

Certificate of deposit (CD): A savings arrangement in which a depositor agrees to leave money on deposit for the use of the financial institution for a specified period, or pay a penalty for earlier withdrawal.

Securities: Investment instruments that confer an interest or a right to payment, without allowing any direct managerial control over the enterprise invested in.

Stock: A share of a corporation's stock represents a fractional ownership interest in the corporation; a shareholder may receive a return on the investment in the form of dividends and/or appreciation of the share's value.

Bond: A certificate of indebtedness issued by a governmental body or a corporation; it will generate a return for the bondholder in the form of periodic payments of interest until the principal is repaid in a lump sum.

Mutual fund: A company that invests its capital in a diversified portfolio of securities on behalf of its investors, who own shares in the fund.

Liquid investment: An investment that can be quickly and easily converted into cash.

Yield: The rate of return that an investor receives on an investment, usually stated as an annual percentage of the amount invested.

Portfolio: The mix of investments and cash reserves held by an investor.

Diversification: The practice of investing in a variety of different ways and/or in a variety of different sectors of the economy, to make a portfolio safer.

Interest rate risk: The risk that, after a loan is made for a specified term at a fixed interest rate, market interest rates will rise and the lender will miss the opportunity to invest the loaned funds at a higher rate.

Prepayment risk: The risk that a loan will be paid off sooner than expected (often because market interest rates have dropped), reducing the lender's anticipated yield.

Market interest rates: The rates that, under current economic conditions, are paid on particular types of investments or charged for particular types of loans.

Chapter Quiz

1. In connection with a loan, the term "principal" refers to the:
   a. amount borrowed
   b. lender
   c. property purchased
   d. repayment period

2. Stocks and bonds are the primary examples of:
   a. ownership investments
   b. securities
   c. collateral
   d. All of the above

3. All of the following are debt investments, except:
   a. savings account
   b. government bond
   c. certificate of deposit
   d. purchase of real estate

4. A company that invests in a diversified portfolio of stocks and bonds on behalf of its investors/owners is called a:
   a. mutual fund
   b. security fund
   c. insider trading firm
   d. liquidity firm

5. Stevenson borrowed money from Acme Savings to buy a rental house. He paid 15% down. Which of the following is true?
   a. Acme has made a debt investment
   b. Stevenson has made an ownership investment
   c. Both of the above
   d. Neither of the above

6. The return that a mortgage lender receives on its typical investments takes the form of:

   a. appreciation
   b. dividends
   c. rental income
   d. interest

7. The phrase "return on an investment" refers to:

   a. recapture of the amount originally invested
   b. an annual yield of at least 10%
   c. an investor's profit over and above the amount originally invested
   d. net income after deducting dividends

8. As a general rule, the safer the investment:

   a. the less liquid the yield
   b. the less certain the yield
   c. the lower the yield
   d. the higher the yield

9. When market interest rates are rising, a lender making a 30-year loan at a fixed interest rate will probably be most concerned about:

   a. prepayment risk
   b. liquidity risk
   c. mutual fund risk
   d. interest rate risk

10. An investor who might need to cash in investments to cover unexpected expenses is likely to be especially concerned about:

    a. bond yields
    b. liquidity
    c. prepayment risk
    d. insider trading

Answer Key

1. a. A loan's principal is the money that was borrowed—the amount originally borrowed, and once repayment has begun, the amount that remains to be paid—as opposed to the interest that accrues on the principal.

2. b. Stocks and bonds are examples of securities, investment instruments that are traded in established financial markets. (Stocks are ownership investments, but bonds are debt investments.)

3. d. The purchase of real estate is an ownership investment, not a debt investment.

4. a. A mutual fund invests the capital provided by its shareholders in a diversified portfolio of securities; the fund managers who make the decisions are investment professionals.

5. c. Acme's loan to Stevenson was a debt investment, and Stevenson's real estate purchase was an ownership investment.

6. d. A mortgage lender's typical investments (mortgage loans) provide a return in the form of interest payments.

7. c. A return *on* an investment is a profit for the investor. (A return *of* the investment is the recapture of the amount originally invested.)

8. c. The safer the investment, the lower the yield. High-yield investments tend to be high-risk investments.

9. d. The lender will be most concerned about interest rate risk, the risk that market rates will rise significantly while the lender's funds are tied up in long-term loans at lower rates.

10. b. If an investor might need to cash in an investment on short notice, it's better if the investment is a liquid one—one that's easily converted into cash.

Chapter 2
Federal Fiscal and Monetary Policy

Fiscal Policy

- Spending and debt financing
- Taxation
  - Deduction of mortgage interest
  - Exclusion of gain on the sale of a home
  - Cost recovery deductions for investors

Monetary Policy

- Federal Reserve System
- Economic growth and inflation
- Tools for implementing monetary policy
  - Reserve requirements
  - Interest rates
  - Open market operations
- Changes in monetary policy

Introduction

The federal government has many ways of influencing the economy as a whole, and real estate finance in particular. We're going to take a look at some of them here. For instance, the government oversees the secondary mortgage market (see Chapter 3) and regulates lending institutions (see Chapter 4). It also influences the cost of borrowing money through fiscal and monetary policy, the subject of this chapter.

As you might expect, the factor that has the biggest impact on the cost of borrowing money is the interest rate charged by the lender. As we discussed in Chapter 1, market interest rates represent the current cost of money: the price that a borrower will have to pay to get a loan today. The cost of money, like the cost of other things in our society, is controlled primarily by the law of supply and demand. If the supply of money is large—if there is a large amount of money in circulation—interest rates tend to fall. The lower interest rates encourage more people to borrow money for both business and personal purposes, including borrowing to finance the purchase of homes. Then, as the money supply tightens, interest rates tend to rise, and fewer people can afford to borrow.

Government influences
interest rates through:
- Fiscal policy
- Monetary policy

The cost of borrowing money is influenced by the federal government in two ways:

1. with its **fiscal policy**, and
2. with its **monetary policy**.

Fiscal policy refers to the government's actions in raising revenue (through taxation), spending money, and managing its debt. These activities can indirectly affect the nation's money supply, and therefore the cost of money. Monetary policy refers to the government's direct efforts to control the money supply and the cost of money.

Fiscal Policy

Fiscal policy:
- Government spending
- Debt financing
- Taxation

Fiscal policy is determined by the government's executive branch (the president and the administration) and legislative branch (Congress). The two branches establish the federal tax laws, which generate the government's largest source of income, and the federal budget, which determines how the money will be spent. The U.S. Treasury Department carries out the fiscal policy; it is responsible for managing the federal government's finances, including the national debt.

Spending and Debt Financing

When the federal government spends more money than it takes in (through taxation and other income sources), a shortfall known as the **federal deficit** results. A deficit has occurred in most years since the Great Depression in the 1930s.

When there is a deficit, the Treasury obtains funds to cover the shortfall by issuing interest-bearing securities for sale to investors. Depending on their term, these securities are referred to as Treasury bills (one year or less), Treasury notes (two to ten years), Treasury Inflation-Protected Securities (five to twenty years), or Treasury Bonds (thirty years). In issuing these securities, the federal government is actually borrowing money from the private sector. And when the government borrows to cover the deficit, less money is available for private borrowers.

Federal deficit absorbs investment funds from private sector

Some economists believe the federal deficit has little, if any, effect on interest rates. Others believe large-scale federal borrowing pushes interest rates upward, as private borrowers are forced to compete for the limited funds remaining. It's true that not long after the deficit soared in 2003, interest rates began a gradual but steady climb. Yet by the end of 2008, when the deficit reached a record high, interest rates were relatively low. Whatever impact the deficit has on interest rates, it's clear that it is only one of several forces that affect them.

Taxation

The other element of fiscal policy is taxation. When taxes are low, taxpayers have more money to lend and invest. When taxes are high, taxpayers not only have less money to lend or invest, they are also more likely to invest what money they do have in tax-exempt securities instead of taxable investments. Since real estate and mortgage-backed securities are taxable investments, this has a significant impact on residential finance.

When taxes are high, taxpayers:
- Have less money to lend or invest
- Tend to prefer tax-free investments

Taxation also affects mortgage financing and the real estate industry in other ways. While the primary purpose of taxation is to raise revenue, some provisions of the income tax laws are used to implement social policy. This is accomplished through tax exemptions, deductions, and exclusions. We'll take a brief look at some provisions in the federal tax code that affect the demand for real estate, and therefore have an indirect impact on the cost of mortgage funds.

Deduction of Home Mortgage Interest. Taxpayers who own a home are allowed to deduct the interest they pay on their mortgage from their taxable income, which ultimately reduces the amount of taxes they have to pay. (Interest on other forms of consumer debt is not deductible.) By making it less expensive to own a home, the mortgage interest deduction implements the government's social policy of encouraging home ownership.

Limits on deductibility. There are some limits on the mortgage interest deduction. A taxpayer generally can deduct all of the interest paid on loans for buying, building, or improving first and second residences, as long as the loans don't add up to more than $1,000,000 ($500,000 for a married taxpayer filing separately).

The rules are a little more complicated for home equity loans. A taxpayer can deduct the interest paid on the smaller of the following amounts: 1) up to $100,000 ($50,000 for a married taxpayer filing separately), without regard to the purpose of the home equity loan, or 2) the fair market value of the property reduced by the amount of acquisition (purchase) debt still remaining.

> **Example:** Julio has $95,000 of his original mortgage still outstanding, plus another $22,000 in debt from an equity loan taken out three years ago. Because of declining property values, Julio's home is currently worth $110,000. At this point, the fair market value of his house exceeds the purchase mortgage balance by $15,000. Thus, only the interest on $15,000 of Julio's equity loan is deductible.

Tax benefits for homeowners:
- Mortgage interest deduction
- Exclusion of gain on sale of principal residence

Exclusion of Gain on the Sale of a Home. Another tax code provision that benefits homeowners allows a gain or profit on the sale of a principal residence to be excluded from taxation. A taxpayer who sells her principal residence may exclude a gain of up to $250,000, or up to $500,000 if the taxpayer is married and filing a joint return. If the gain on the sale exceeds the $250,000 or $500,000 limit, the excess is taxed at the capital gains rate. (The maximum capital gains tax rate is lower than the maximum tax rate on ordinary income.)

Note that if a taxpayer converted a home to his principal residence after 2008 (previously holding it as a vacation residence or a rental, for example), the amount of excludable gain may be lower. However, if the taxpayer lives in the residence for a long enough period of time, the full exclusion will become available.

Eligibility. To qualify for the exclusion, the taxpayer must have both owned and used the property as a principal residence for at least two years during the five-year period before its sale. Because of this rule, the exclusion is available only once every two years.

If the sellers are married and filing a joint return, only one spouse has to meet the ownership test, but both spouses must meet the use test. If only one spouse meets both the ownership test and the use test, the maximum exclusion the married couple can claim is $250,000, even if they file a joint return.

In special circumstances, taxpayers who owned and used a principal residence for less than two years may be able to claim a reduced exclusion. A reduced exclusion would be allowed if a home was sold after only a year because of a change in the taxpayer's health or place of employment, or because of some other unforeseen circumstances.

The deductibility of mortgage interest and the exclusion of gain on the sale of a principal residence both make a big difference to homeowners. Together, they are quite effective in helping to fulfill the government's social policy of encouraging homeownership.

Cost Recovery Deductions for Investors. Many other provisions in the federal tax code also have an impact on real estate investment. To take one example, owners of income property, such as apartment buildings and rental homes, are allowed to take cost recovery deductions (also called depreciation deductions). In other words, they can deduct some of the cost of buildings and other property improvements that eventually will wear out and have to be replaced. The cost is spread out over a number of years (for residential rental properties, usually 27½ years), rather than deducted all at once. When the government changes the rules for these cost recovery deductions—for example, by requiring them to be stretched out over a greater number of years—it can affect the profitability of investing in real estate.

Cost recovery (depreciation) deductions affect real estate investment

Thus, how the federal government raises revenue—how much it taxes income, how it taxes different kinds of income, and what tax deductions and exclusions it allows—can stimulate or dampen the demand for real estate and increase or decrease the availability of mortgage funds.

Monetary Policy

The federal government exercises considerable control over the nation's money supply (how much money is in circulation). Monetary policy refers to the government's efforts to use its control over the money supply to keep the national economy running smoothly. Monetary policy is set and implemented by the Federal Reserve System, commonly called "the Fed."

The Federal Reserve System

The Federal Reserve System regulates commercial banks, and its responsibility for monetary policy grew out of that function.

Historical Background. In the early nineteenth century, there was very little government regulation of depository institutions in the United States. The security of bank deposits depended primarily on the integrity of bank managers. Not surprisingly, serious problems sometimes developed. For example, a bank might loan out nearly all of its deposits and keep almost no funds in reserve. When a depositor tried to make a withdrawal, the bank might not have enough cash on hand to fulfill the request. To protect the public against this kind of mismanagement, in 1863 Congress passed the National Bank Act, which established basic banking regulations and procedures for supervising commercial banks.

In spite of the 1863 law, certain problems persisted, and the public lacked confidence in the banking industry. Economic downturns periodically led to financial panics involving "a run on the bank," in which most of a bank's depositors would suddenly doubt the security of their money and withdraw it all at once. This could cause even a financially sound bank to fail, and the depositors who had not withdrawn their money would be left empty-handed.

To strengthen the financial system and improve public confidence, support grew for the creation of a central bank for the U.S., similar to the central banks of other countries. The American public had long resisted the idea of a central bank; average citizens tended to be hostile toward banks, Wall Street interests, and centralized authority

The Fed:
- Regulates commercial banks
- Sets and implements monetary policy

Federal Reserve was established to strengthen the financial system and improve public confidence

28

Fig. 2.1 The organization of the Federal Reserve System

The Federal Reserve System

Board of Governors
(Seven appointed members)

- Sets reserve requirements and approves discount rates as part of monetary policy
- Supervises and regulates member banks and bank holding companies
- Establishes and administers protective regulations in consumer finance
- Oversees Federal Reserve Banks

Exercises general supervision →

Federal Reserve Banks
(Twelve districts)

- Propose discount rates
- Hold reserve balances for depository institutions and lend to them at the discount window
- Furnish currency
- Collect and clear checks and transfer funds for depository institutions
- Handle U.S. government debt and cash balances

Advise

Consumer Advisory Council

Federal Advisory Council

Thrift Institutions Advisory Council

Compose

Federal Open Market Committee
(Board of Governors and five reserve bank presidents)

- Directs open market operations (buying and selling U.S. government securities), which are the primary instrument of monetary policy

Source: The Federal Reserve

29

in general. However, huge losses suffered by depositors in a series of bank panics in 1907 finally overcame public resistance.

In the Federal Reserve Acts of 1913 and 1916, Congress created the Federal Reserve System and established the modern banking system. The Fed would regulate commercial banks, perform periodic bank examinations, and impose **reserve requirements**, specifying what proportion of a bank's deposits had to be held in reserve, available for immediate withdrawal on demand by depositors. In addition, the Federal Reserve would serve as a "lender of last resort," providing short-term backup loans to banks that ran low on funds.

The creation of the Federal Reserve improved the financial system in many ways, but it did not entirely solve the problem of financial panics and bank runs. A more direct solution, federal deposit insurance, was developed in the 1930s, during the Depression. The Federal Deposit Insurance Corporation and the Federal Savings and Loan Insurance Corporation were created as part of the New Deal.

Organization. To prevent the centralization of too much power, Congress included checks and balances in the Federal Reserve System. Its structure was designed to spread power three different ways: 1) geographically; 2) between the private and government sectors; and 3) among bankers, businesses, and the public. The Federal Reserve System includes:

- twelve regional Federal Reserve Banks in twelve Federal Reserve Districts,
- the Federal Reserve Board,
- the Federal Open Market Committee,
- several advisory councils, and
- over 2,500 member banks.

The system is controlled by the seven-member Board of Governors, known as the Federal Reserve Board (see Figure 2.1). The governors are appointed by the U.S. president and confirmed by the Senate for 14-year terms. To prevent one area of the country from having disproportionate power on the board, the governors must be chosen from different Federal Reserve Districts. The board's chairman is chosen from among the governors for a four-year term, and may be reappointed repeatedly. Some Fed chairmen have served under several presidents.

The Board of Governors controls the Fed's monetary policy. All seven governors are on the Federal Open Market Committee, which we'll discuss shortly. The governors set reserve requirements for commercial banks and, through the process of review and approval, effectively control the discount rate set by the Federal Reserve Banks. (We'll discuss the discount rate shortly, too.) The governors also have substantial control over regulations affecting the activities of commercial banks and bank holding companies.

Each of the twelve Federal Reserve Districts has one main Federal Reserve Bank, and some districts have branch banks as well. Technically, each Federal Reserve Bank is an incorporated banking institution owned by the member commercial banks in the district. (The member banks are required to purchase stock in their reserve bank.) Each reserve bank has a nine-member board of directors. Six of the directors are elected by the stockholders and three are appointed by the Fed's Board of Governors. The nine directors appoint the president of their reserve bank, subject to the approval of the Board of Governors.

All of the Federal Reserve Banks are involved to some degree in monetary policy. Each reserve bank has a staff that conducts research on economic conditions in its district, and each reserve bank selects one banker to be a member of the Federal Advisory Council. The Advisory Council meets and consults with the Board of Governors regarding monetary policy.

Economic Growth and Inflation

The Federal Reserve's ultimate goal in setting and implementing monetary policy is a healthy U.S. economy. The economy is considered healthy when there is sustainable economic growth with low unemployment, stable prices, and reasonable interest rates.

Sustainable economic growth is neither too weak nor too strong, and neither too slow nor too fast. If growth is too strong and too fast, it's usually accompanied by **inflation**, a trend of general price increases throughout the economy. Uncontrolled inflation eventually chokes off economic growth. The ideal is for the economy to grow steadily, but at a moderate pace that won't trigger severe inflation.

When the economy is stagnating, the Fed takes action to stimulate growth. But if the economy starts booming and inflation threatens to gain momentum, the Fed takes action to slow down growth and keep inflation in check.

Fed chairman and Federal Reserve Board make decisions concerning monetary policy

12 regional Federal Reserve Banks:
- Owned by member banks
- Make discount loans
- Set discount rates (with Board approval)
- Appoint bankers to Federal Advisory Council

Inflation: prices increasing throughout the economy

Goal is sustainable growth with inflation in check

Tools for Implementing Monetary Policy

The Fed relies on three main tools to implement its monetary policy and influence the economy:

- reserve requirements,
- interest rates (the discount rate and federal funds rate), and
- open market operations.

Reserve Requirements. A commercial bank's reserve requirement is the percentage of its deposits the bank is required to maintain on reserve, either in its own vaults or on deposit at the Federal Reserve Bank in its district. The requirements are set by the Federal Reserve Board and may reach 10%, depending on the amount of deposits at the institution. It used to be that only member banks were required to keep reserves at the reserve banks. But the Depository Institutions Deregulation and Monetary Control Act of 1980 subjected all commercial banks to the same reserve requirements as members of the Federal Reserve, and also imposed reserve requirements on savings banks, savings and loans, and credit unions. The same act also gave all commercial banks access to some Federal Reserve benefits such as check clearing and discount loans. As a result, there are now fewer differences between member and nonmember banks.

As explained earlier, the original purpose of reserve requirements was to help avert financial panics by giving depositors confidence that their deposits were safe and accessible. The requirements protect depositors by helping to ensure that their bank will have enough funds available to meet unusual customer demand.

At the same time, reserve requirements also enable the Fed to exercise some control over the growth of credit. By increasing reserve requirements, the Fed can reduce the amount of money that banks have available to lend. On the other hand, a reduction in reserve requirements frees more money for investment or lending by banks. Thus, an increase in reserve requirements tends to decrease available loan funds and increase interest rates. Conversely, a decrease in reserve requirements tends to increase funds available for lending and decrease interest rates.

Interest Rates. The Fed has control over two key interest rates: the federal discount rate and the federal funds rate.

The **discount rate** is the interest rate charged when a bank borrows money from one of the Federal Reserve Banks to cover a shortfall in

Fig. 2.2 By changing the funds rate target, the Fed affects other interest rates and the economy as a whole

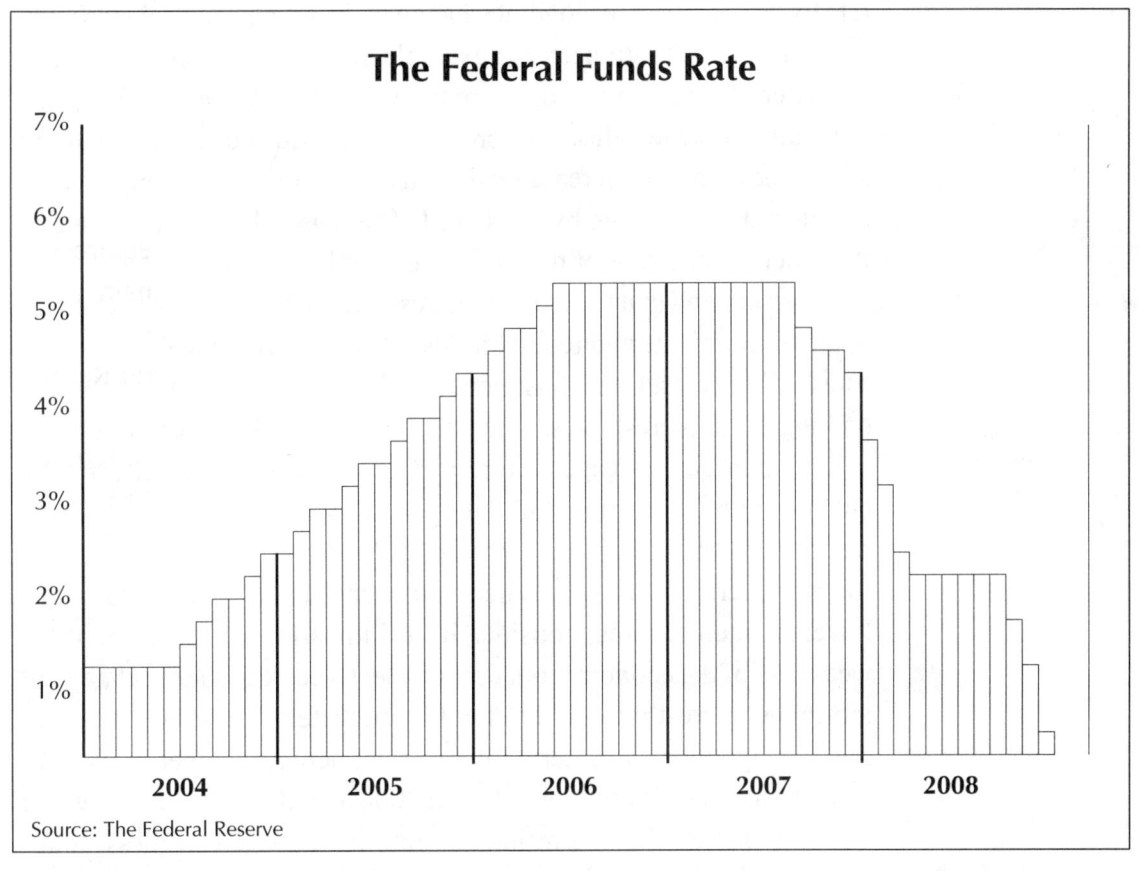

The Federal Funds Rate

Source: The Federal Reserve

funds. The discount rate is set by the Federal Reserve Banks with the approval of the Fed's Board of Governors.

The **federal funds rate** is the interest rate banks charge each other for overnight loans. A bank that doesn't have enough funds to meet its reserve requirements may borrow the money needed from a bank that has excess reserves. Unlike the discount rate, the federal funds rate is not set directly by the Fed; the banks themselves can determine how much they'll charge each other for overnight loans. However, when the Federal Open Market Committee meets, it sets a target for the federal funds rate. It also issues a directive indicating what open market operations will be conducted in an effort to achieve the target rate.

When the Federal Reserve raises or lowers the discount rate or the target for the federal funds rate, it's regarded as an indication of the Fed's overall view of the economy. For example, if either or both of these interest rates are lowered, that's seen as a signal that the Fed feels the economy needs a boost, since lower interest rates usually stimulate economic activity.

Federal discount rate: interest rate charged banks that borrow from the Fed

Federal funds rate: interest rate banks charge each other for overnight loans

Lower interest rates stimulate economic activity

Lenders often respond to a change in the funds rate or the discount rate by making a corresponding change in the interest rates they charge on loans to their customers. For example, if the federal funds rate drops a quarter of a percentage point, market interest rates are likely to follow suit. However, this relationship is complicated by anticipation; sometimes lenders increase or decrease their rates in anticipation of an interest rate change by the Fed. In that case, the actual change in the federal funds rate or discount rate may have little impact.

Keep in mind that the market interest rates most affected by changes in the discount rate and federal funds rate are short-term interest rates. The Fed's interest rate adjustments don't have such a direct influence on long-term interest rates, which include the market interest rates for home purchase mortgages. Mortgage rates are, of course, affected by changes in the economy, but they generally don't go up or down in response to an increase or decrease in the discount rate or the target for the federal funds rate. When you hear that the Fed has raised or lowered interest rates, consider it an indication of the strength or weakness of the economy, but don't expect a corresponding change in mortgage interest rates, at least not immediately. There was a period not long ago when long-term interest rates actually moved counter to short-term rates. Throughout most of 2004 and 2005, the Fed provided a steady diet of short-term interest rate increases; regardless, long-term rates declined during that time. With the increased globalization of financial markets, it may be harder for the Fed to influence U.S. long-term rates.

Open Market Operations. The Fed also buys and sells government securities. These transactions are called open market operations. They are conducted by the Securities Department of the Federal Reserve Bank of New York (often referred to as "the Trading Desk," or just "the Desk"), following directives from the **Federal Open Market Committee** (FOMC). Open market operations are the most important tool for controlling the money supply, so the FOMC is the most important policy-making organization in the Fed.

The FOMC has eight regularly scheduled meetings per year. It consists of twelve members: the seven members of the Federal Reserve Board, the president of the New York Federal Reserve Bank, and four other Reserve Bank presidents (chosen on a rotating basis from the other eleven Reserve Banks).

Long-term interest rates like mortgage rates don't respond directly to Fed's interest rate adjustments

Open market operations: the Fed buys and sells government securities

Open market operations are the Fed's primary method of controlling the money supply (which in turn affects inflation and interest rates). Only money in circulation is considered part of the money supply, so actions by the Fed that put money into circulation increase the money supply, and actions that take money out of circulation decrease the money supply.

When the Fed buys government securities, it increases the money supply. The Fed may pay for the securities in cash, by check, or if purchasing from a bank, simply by crediting the bank's reserves with the Fed. Any of these actions puts more money into circulation. On the other hand, when the Fed sells government securities, the money the buyer uses to pay for the securities is taken out of circulation, decreasing the money supply.

Money supply:
- Increases when Fed buys government securities
- Decreases when Fed sells government securities

Other things being equal, an increase in the money supply is supposed to lead to lower interest rates. But other things are seldom equal, and several factors may apply upward pressure to interest rates at the same time that an increase in the money supply is exerting downward pressure. For example, an increase in the money supply is often associated with an increase in inflation, and when inflation is anticipated, interest rates tend to rise. The Fed uses open market operations and its other tools to balance these complicated forces. It tries to manage the money supply to adequately serve the growth of the economy at reasonable interest rates, without fueling inflation or fears of inflation that could lead to higher interest rates.

Changes in Monetary Policy

In the years since its creation, the Fed has frequently modified its monetary policy, both in terms of primary objectives and in the choice of tools employed to reach those objectives. Since the Fed really has no direct control over inflation or market interest rates, it works toward its goals by tracking certain economic indicators and by taking action to influence those indicators. At various times, the Fed has focused on the discount rate, reserve requirements, general money market conditions, the federal funds rate, and changes in one or more of its measures of the money supply. Its actions are more or less experimental, and when a particular experiment does not seem to be working, the Fed may try a different one.

Monetary policy is experimental, and Fed changes strategies from time to time

We can illustrate this by looking at Fed moves in recent decades. During the 1970s, the Fed's practice was to moderate interest rates by increasing the money supply whenever interest rates started to rise. Although this succeeded in keeping interest rates down, inflation worsened as money was pumped into the economy to satisfy the demands of borrowers. Concerned about inflation, the Fed then adopted a different approach. It stopped its efforts to control interest rates by increasing the money supply, and instead tried to control inflation by restricting the growth of the money supply. In the months that followed, interest rates soared. (The high rates caused problems for savings and loans, which led to their deregulation. See Chapter 3.)

By 1982 the Fed had again shifted course. The inflation rate had fallen sharply, but interest rates remained high and variable. The Fed once again put more emphasis on preventing large fluctuations in interest rates. The result was positive. Over the next couple of decades, the inflation rate remained relatively moderate, and interest rates were much lower and comparatively stable.

In the early years of the new century, however, the economy began slowing and the Fed tried to spur growth by lowering interest rates to levels that hadn't been seen since the early 1960s. When the economy began improving, inflation once again became a concern. This led to a series of incremental increases in the key interest rates. From mid- 2004 to mid-2006, the federal funds rate target rose from 1.00% to 5.25%; the discount rate also went up steadily, from 2.00% to 6.25%.

Rates then remained flat for a year or so, until credit began to tighten and general economic growth faltered. In August 2007, the Fed began lowering rates again, hoping to encourage the flow of lending to businesses. By late 2008, the funds rate had fallen back down to 1.00%. Nonetheless, the "credit crunch" continued. (We will discuss the mortgage and credit crisis in Chapter 4.) With a recession underway, some analysts predicted a period when the Fed would charge no interest at all on overnight funds.

Outline: Federal Fiscal and Monetary Policy

I. Government Influences on Finance

    A. The federal government influences real estate finance by influencing the cost of mortgage funds.

    B. Market interest rates represent the cost of borrowing money, which is subject to the rules of supply and demand.

    C. The federal government affects the cost of borrowing through fiscal policy and monetary policy.

II. Fiscal Policy

    A. Federal government fiscal policy is determined by both the legislative and executive branches, and is carried out by the U.S. Treasury Department.

    B. If the federal government spends more money than it receives in a year, a deficit occurs.

    C. To finance the shortfall, the government sells interest-bearing securities to investors.

    D. When private investors lend money to the government to cover a deficit, less money is available to private borrowers.

        1. Some economists believe federal deficits have little effect on interest rates.

        2. Other economists believe deficit spending pushes interest rates up because government borrowing takes funds out of the money market and increases demand for funds.

III. Taxation

    A. Taxation affects mortgage rates by affecting how much money taxpayers have available to lend or invest.

    B. Taxation also affects mortgage rates through tax exemptions, deductions, and exclusions, which may affect demand for mortgages.

    C. Taxpayers are allowed to deduct interest paid on home mortgage loans from their taxable income, which reduces the amount of taxes they pay.

        1. Interest on loans for the purchase, construction, or improvement of a home is deductible; if the loans total more than $1,000,000 (or $500,000 for a married taxpayer filing separately), interest paid on the excess is not deductible.

        2. Interest on home equity loans totaling up to $100,000 ($50,000 for a married taxpayer filing separately) is also deductible.

D. Taxpayers may exclude from taxation the gain received from selling a principal residence.

1. A gain of up to $250,000 for an individual or $500,000 for a married couple filing jointly may be excluded.

2. To qualify for this exclusion, the taxpayers must have owned the property and used it as a principal residence for at least two of the previous five years.

E. Investors may take deductions for cost recovery, meaning that depreciation of investment property may be deducted.

IV. Monetary Policy

A. Federal government monetary policy refers to the government's control over the money supply, which is implemented by the Federal Reserve System (or "Fed").

B. Historical background

1. Banks were first regulated in 1863 through the National Bank Act, which created basic procedures for supervising banks.

2. The Federal Reserve Acts of 1913 and 1916 created the modern banking system.

3. The Federal Reserve System imposes reserve requirements, specifying what amount of a bank's deposits must be kept in reserve to be available for withdrawal.

4. The Federal Reserve acts as a lender of last resort, providing short-term loans to banks running low on funds.

5. The stability of the banking industry was bolstered in the 1930s with the creation of the Federal Deposit Insurance Corporation.

C. Organization of the Federal Reserve

1. The Federal Reserve System is decentralized into twelve regional Federal Reserve Banks.

2. The system is controlled by the seven-member Board of Governors, each chosen for 14-year terms from different Federal Reserve Districts.

3. Each regional Federal Reserve Bank is an incorporated bank owned by the member commercial banks in its district.

4. Each regional bank is controlled by a nine-member board of directors.

D. Economic growth and inflation

1. If economic growth occurs too quickly, inflation results, causing price increases that hamper further growth.

2. If inflation appears to be a possibility, the Fed will take action to slow growth and limit inflation.

V. Tools for Implementing Monetary Policy

A. Reserve requirements: a percentage of deposits that each bank must maintain either in its own vaults or on deposit with the Federal Reserve Bank.

1. Reserve requirements were originally intended to avert financial panic by making sure that depositors were always able to withdraw deposits.

2. Reserve requirements also allow the Fed to control the money supply.

3. An increase in reserve requirements reduces the amount of money banks have available to lend and therefore increases interest rates.

B. Interest rates: the Fed controls two key interest rates, the federal discount rate and federal funds rate.

1. The discount rate is the rate charged to member banks when they borrow money from the Fed to cover a shortfall in funds.

2. The federal funds rate is the rate banks charge each other for loans to cover shortfalls.

3. Lenders' market interest rates will usually rise or fall in response to changes in the federal rates, although long-term rates (such as mortgages) are not immediately affected.

C. Open market operations: the Fed controls the money supply by buying and selling government securities.

1. If the Fed buys government securities, it puts more money into the money supply, which by itself will decrease interest rates.

2. If the Fed sells government securities, it takes money from investors out of the money supply, which will increase interest rates.

VI. Changes in Monetary Policy

A. The Fed will modify its monetary policy in response to changing economic indicators.

B. In recent years, the Fed has tried to spur economic growth by lowering interest rates without allowing inflation to become a problem.

Key Terms

Fiscal policy: Government actions in raising revenue through taxation, spending money, and financing budget deficits.

Monetary policy: Government action in controlling the money supply and therefore the cost of borrowing money.

Federal deficit: A shortfall in funds that occurs when the federal government spends more money than it collects in a particular year.

Home mortgage interest deduction: Interest paid on mortgage loans secured by the taxpayer's home or homes is deductible, up to certain limits.

Exclusion of gain on sale of home: A taxpayer may exclude from taxation any gain on the sale of a principal residence, up to a limit of $250,000 (or $500,000 if married and filing jointly).

Cost recovery deductions: Owners of income property are allowed to deduct the cost of assets that will wear out and eventually have to be replaced. Also called depreciation deductions.

Federal Reserve System: The Federal Reserve System regulates commercial banks and implements the nation's monetary policy. Often referred to as "the Fed."

Reserve requirements: The Fed requires commercial banks to hold a certain portion of their deposits on reserve for immediate withdrawal by depositors.

Federal Reserve Bank: There are twelve Federal Reserve Banks, one for each Federal Reserve District, owned by the commercial banks within that district.

Federal Reserve Board: The Federal Reserve System is controlled by a seven-member Board of Governors, known as the Federal Reserve Board. Each of the seven members is appointed from a different district to a 14-year term.

Inflation: A trend of general price increases throughout the economy.

Discount rate: The interest rate that a Federal Reserve Bank charges on short-term loans to member banks; the Fed sets this rate directly.

Federal funds rate: The interest rate that banks charge one another for overnight loans; the Fed sets a target for this rate.

Open market operations: The Fed adjusts the money supply by engaging in open market operations; as it buys and sells government securities, it changes the amount of money available in circulation.

Federal Open Market Committee: The Federal Open Market Committee is a board that makes decisions regarding open market operations by the Fed.

Chapter Quiz

1. The government controls the money supply and cost of money through:

   a. fiscal policy
   b. monetary policy
   c. budgetary policy
   d. fiduciary policy

2. In a given year, the federal government spends more money than it receives as revenue. The result is a:

   a. federal deficit
   b. federal debt
   c. federal surplus
   d. federal default

3. Which item may be excluded from taxation, rather than simply taken as a deduction?

   a. Home mortgage interest
   b. Home equity loan interest
   c. Gain on the sale of a principal residence
   d. Depreciation of investment property

4. The gain from the sale of which of the following properties would be excluded from taxation?

   a. A residential rental owned for the last ten years
   b. A residential property used as a primary residence from ten years ago until five years ago
   c. A vacation home owned for the last five years
   d. A residential property used as a primary residence from four years ago until one year ago

5. Which of the following is the best definition of reserve requirements?

   a. Buying and selling government securities on the open market
   b. Setting interest rates for loans to banks facing cash shortfalls
   c. Requiring banks to make a certain percentage of deposits available for immediate withdrawal
   d. Controlling inflation by raising interest rates (to slow growth)

6. How many Federal Reserve Districts and Federal Reserve Banks are there?

    a. 7
    b. 9
    c. 12
    d. 14

7. Inflation occurs when:

    a. rapid economic growth causes prices to increase
    b. the Fed raises interest rates
    c. the Fed decreases the pool of available funds by selling government securities
    d. economic stagnation causes higher unemployment

8. The interest rate charged by the Federal Reserve when a member bank borrows money to cover a shortfall in funds is the:

    a. federal funds rate
    b. federal discount rate
    c. federal key rate
    d. market interest rate

9. The Federal Reserve decides to decrease the supply of money available. It will:

    a. buy government securities and increase reserve requirements
    b. buy government securities and decrease reserve requirements
    c. sell government securities and increase reserve requirements
    d. sell government securities and decrease reserve requirements

10. In the early 1980s, the Fed tried to control inflation by restricting growth of the money supply. What happened?

    a. Interest rates shot up
    b. Interest rates plunged
    c. Inflation got worse
    d. The government bought back most of its government securities

Answer Key

1. b. Monetary policy refers to the government's efforts to control the money supply and thus the cost of borrowing money.

2. a. A federal deficit results if, in a particular year, the government spends more than it takes in.

3. c. Gain on the sale of a principal residence of up to $250,000 (or $500,000 for a married couple filing jointly) may be excluded from taxation.

4. d. To qualify for exclusion of gain, the taxpayer must have owned and used the property as a principal residence for at least two years during the five-year period before its sale.

5. c. Reserve requirements specify what percentage of a bank's deposits must be kept in reserve, available for immediate withdrawal by depositors.

6. c. There are twelve Federal Reserve Districts, each of which has its own Federal Reserve Bank.

7. a. Inflation occurs when economic growth is too rapid and prices throughout the economy shoot up. The Fed may take action to limit inflation—by raising interest rates, for example.

8. b. The federal discount rate is the interest rate charged by the Fed when a bank borrows funds to cover a shortfall in funds on deposit.

9. c. Both selling government securities on the open market and increasing reserve requirements take money that would otherwise be available to lend out of the money supply. A reduced money supply will increase the demand for funds and increase the cost of borrowing money.

10. a. The result of the Fed's efforts to decrease the money supply in the early 1980s was a decline in inflation, but also a sharp increase in interest rates.

Chapter 3
The Primary and Secondary Markets

The Two Mortgage Markets

- Primary market and funds for mortgage lending
  - Local financing
  - Real estate cycles
  - National forces affect local markets
  - Addressing the problem of cycles
- Secondary market
  - Buying and selling loans
  - Mortgage-backed securities
  - Effects of the secondary market

The Secondary Market Agencies

- Creation of the agencies
  - Fannie Mae
  - Ginnie Mae
  - Freddie Mac
- GSE status
- MBS programs
- Standardized documents and underwriting
- The GSEs and the economic crisis
  - Conservatorship
  - Federal guaranty

Introduction

The residential mortgage industry is made up of the financial institutions, private companies, agencies, and other investors that make investment funds available to people who want to finance (or refinance) the purchase or construction of a home. The industry is divided into two "markets" that supply the funds for mortgage loans: the primary market and the secondary market.

In this chapter, we'll explain the two markets and the relationship between them. We'll also discuss the major secondary market agencies, Fannie Mae, Freddie Mac, and Ginnie Mae, and the mortgage-backed securities that are traded in the secondary market. (The different types of lenders in the primary market and other aspects of the mortgage industry will be covered in Chapter 4.)

Both the primary market and the secondary market are undergoing fundamental changes as part of the fallout from the subprime mortgage crisis. The ultimate impact of the crisis is very uncertain at the time of this writing. We'll discuss some of the changes that are taking place at the end of this chapter; the crisis itself is covered in Chapter 4.

The Two Mortgage Markets

Home buyers borrow the money they need from banks and other mortgage lenders. Those loan transactions take place in the financial arena known in the mortgage industry as the **primary mortgage market**. To obtain money to make more loans, lenders often sell their loans to investors. These transactions take place in another arena, the **secondary mortgage market**. As you'll see, the secondary market has come to play an extremely important role in making financing available to home buyers in the primary market.

Primary market: where lenders make loans to home buyers

Secondary market: where lenders sell loans to investors

The Primary Market and Funds for Mortgage Lending

In the primary mortgage market, home buyers apply for mortgage loans and residential mortgage lenders **originate** them. Loan origination includes processing the application, deciding to approve the loan, and then funding the loan. Where do lenders get the funds they use to make mortgage loans? The answer to that question has changed significantly over the course of the twentieth century.

Loan origination:
- Processing application
- Approval decision
- Funding the loan

Local Financing. At one time, the primary market was purely a local market, consisting of the various financial institutions in a community—the local banks, savings and loan associations, and so on. Although the primary market is considerably more complicated than that today (as a result of interstate banking, Internet lenders, and other developments), it will be easier to explain the relationship between the primary market and the secondary market if we start with a simple example along traditional lines.

Primary market was originally a local market, made up of local lending institutions

> **Example:** The Browns live in a small city called Seacliff. When the Browns want to borrow money so that they can buy a house, they apply for a loan from one of the local financial institutions, Vault Savings Bank. Vault is a mortgage lender in the primary market.
>
> Vault Savings Bank's primary source of funds for making mortgage loans is the savings of its depositors, who are individuals and businesses in the Seacliff area. Vault uses the savings deposits to make loans to residents of that same community. It pays depositors 2% interest for the use of their savings, and it charges borrowers 6% interest on their mortgage loans. The difference between the interest rate charged to borrowers and the rate paid to depositors (less the bank's operational costs) is Vault's profit.

In the past, the basic model of mortgage financing presented in the example worked well: local lenders had an adequate supply of mortgage funds to meet the community's demand, enabling most people who wanted to finance the purchase of a home to do so. The residential real estate market was essentially local, and mortgage financing was originally a local matter, too.

Real Estate Cycles. Unfortunately, a local mortgage financing system doesn't always function smoothly; supply and demand aren't always in balance. Local real estate markets go through active periods followed by slumps. These periodic changes are called **real estate cycles**. They may be dramatic or moderate, short-term or long-term. They may be affected by economic, political, or social factors, such as changes in employment levels, in tax policy, or in lifestyles.

Availability of local funds for lending may be disrupted by local real estate cycles

Real estate cycles can create problems for local financial institutions and for potential home buyers.

> **Example:** A new industry recently started up in Seacliff, and the local economy is booming. As a result of this new prosperity, the residents are saving somewhat more, but they're also

spending more, and many people want to buy or build homes in the area.

Vault Savings Bank and the other local financial institutions don't have enough funds on deposit to meet the increased demand for mortgage loans. This might prevent some members of the community who want to finance the purchase of a home from doing so. It might also prevent local lenders from doing as much business as they otherwise could.

On the other hand, sometimes a community's demand for mortgage funds is weak. If the local economy goes into a slump, many people who might otherwise buy homes can't afford to. Local banks may have funds available for mortgage loans, but no one wants to borrow. This reduces the banks' main source of income (interest on loans), so that the institution also suffers from the local economic woes.

National Forces Affect Local Cycles. Local conditions are not the only factor that affects a community's supply of and demand for mortgage funds. National economic and political forces and social trends may also have an impact on local real estate cycles.

Disintermediation: when depository institutions lose funds to higher-yielding investments

For example, a phenomenon known as **disintermediation** can reduce the supply of funds that local financial institutions have available for mortgage lending. Disintermediation occurs when depositors withdraw their funds from savings accounts and put them into competing investments that offer higher returns, such as stocks and bonds. The changes in interest rates and investment yields that lead to disintermediation take place on a national level.

Disintermediation can affect the local supply of mortgage funds; other national factors can affect local demand. For example, if Congress changes the federal tax code in a way that favors home ownership, that encourages more people nationwide to purchase homes. The demand for mortgage financing in a local real estate market such as Seacliff's is likely to increase as a result.

Addressing the Problem of Cycles. At one time, there wasn't very much that local financial institutions—lenders in the primary market— could do about real estate cycles in their community. If the demand for mortgage funds exceeded the supply, some of the demand would go unmet; potential home buyers would have to wait, and the banks would miss out on opportunities to make money. If supply exceeded demand, the banks would have to make relatively unprofitable investments until demand picked up again, or they might even have to let funds on deposit sit uninvested.

What local financial institutions needed was a source of additional funds to lend when demand exceeded supply, and a place to invest their surplus funds when supply exceeded demand. The creation of a secondary mortgage market helped meet both of these needs.

The Secondary Market

The primary mortgage market is where lenders make mortgage loans; the secondary mortgage market is where lenders sell those loans to investors. The secondary market is a national market in which mortgages secured by residential real estate all over the country can be bought and sold.

Buying and Selling Loans. The idea of buying or selling a loan may be unfamiliar. But a loan is an investment and, like other investments (stocks, bonds, and so on), mortgage loans can be bought and sold.

Valuing loans. The purchaser of a loan pays the lender the present value of the lender's right to receive payments from the borrower over the life of the loan. The present value is determined by comparing the rate of return on the loan to the rate of return available on other investments.

> **Example:** A bank makes a home loan of $190,500 at 5.5% interest. One year later, approximately $187,900 of principal remains to be paid on the loan. But if market interest rates have gone up to 7% for investments of similar quality, then the present value of the loan is less than $187,900. The present value is the amount of money it would take to generate the same amount of income at a 7% rate of return. A 5.5% return on $187,900 would be $10,335 per year. This same return could be achieved by investing $147,640 at 7% interest. So (all other factors being equal) the present value of the loan is $147,640 rather than its face value of $187,900. If the bank decided to sell the loan at this point, the buyer would pay only $147,640.

Many factors affect the value of a loan; the degree of risk associated with it is especially important. In the example, the loan was being compared to "investments of similar quality," which means investments involving approximately the same degree of risk as the loan. Of course, investors may overestimate or underestimate the riskiness of a loan or other investment, and therefore under- or overvalue it. A severe underestimation (or disregard) of risk played a central role in creating the subprime mortgage crisis. (See Chapter 4.)

Secondary market activities:
- Buying and selling loans
- Issuing mortgage-backed securities

Fig. 3.1 The two mortgage markets

Primary Market	Secondary Market
• Local market • Mortgage lenders such as banks and mortgage companies make loans to home buyers	• National market • Lenders from all over the country sell loans to the secondary market agencies and other investors

Who buys loans? A lender that decides to sell some of its mortgage loans may sell them directly to another lender in a different part of the country. For example, a bank in Arizona might get cash to make more loans by selling some of its loans to a bank in New York.

More often, a lender sells mortgage loans to one of the three **secondary market agencies** created by the federal government:

Loans are purchased on the secondary market by the secondary market agencies and other investors

- the Federal National Mortgage Association (FNMA or "Fannie Mae"),
- the Federal Home Loan Mortgage Corporation (FHLMC or "Freddie Mac"), and
- the Government National Mortgage Association (GNMA or "Ginnie Mae").

The federal government created these agencies in order to establish a strong secondary market for mortgage loans. They are the major purchasers of loans on the secondary market.

A lender can "package" a group of similar loans together for sale to one of the secondary market agencies. To be accepted for purchase, the packaged loans must meet standards of quality set by the agency that's going to buy them. We'll discuss the agencies and their standards in more detail later in the chapter.

After loans have been sold to a secondary market agency, they may be serviced by the lender that originated them, or by another entity acting as a servicer. Loan servicing includes tasks such as processing borrowers' payments, dealing with collection problems, and working with borrowers to prevent default.

Loan servicing:
• Processing payments
• Collections
• Preventing default

Mortgage-backed Securities. In addition to buying mortgages from lenders around the country, the secondary market agencies also issue mortgage-backed securities. A mortgage-backed security (MBS) is an investment instrument that has mortgages as collateral; it's a type of bond. A secondary market agency creates mortgage-backed securities by buying a large number of mortgage loans, "pooling" them together, and pledging the pool as collateral for the securities. This is called **securitizing** loans.

Investors who buy mortgage-backed securities receive a return on their investment in the form of monthly payments from the secondary market agency that issued the securities. As the mortgage loans in the pool are repaid by the borrowers, the agency passes the payments of principal and interest on to the MBS investors.

For investors, buying mortgage-backed securities is much more convenient than buying the actual mortgage loans. The securities are more liquid than the mortgages, and they can be purchased in relatively small denominations.

Although most mortgage-backed securities are issued by the major secondary market agencies, private firms can also buy and pool mortgage loans and issue securities based on the pools. These are referred to as "private-label" mortgage-backed securities.

Effects of the Secondary Market. The development of the secondary market transformed the mortgage industry in the U.S. The secondary market gave primary market lenders a way to address an imbalance in a community's supply of and demand for mortgage funds. This moderated the adverse effects of local real estate cycles and provided a measure of stability in local markets.

> **Example:** Acme Savings & Loan has a long list of prospective borrowers who need funds for the purchase of homes. Acme's problem is that all of its savings deposits are already tied up in mortgage loans. But by selling its existing mortgage loans on the secondary market, Acme can get the funds it needs to make new loans and satisfy its customers. The effects of a tight money market in Acme's local community are moderated because Acme can get funds in the national secondary market.
>
> If Acme Savings & Loan had a surplus of deposits instead of a shortfall, it might have a difficult time finding enough local investments to absorb its funds. In this case, Acme could buy mortgages or mortgage-backed securities on the secondary market—in essence, investing in real estate located all over the country, without ever seeing the properties it is helping to finance or meeting the borrowers who are buying them.

Mortgage-backed securities: investment instruments with pools of mortgage loans as collateral

MBS purchases may be made directly from secondary market agencies or on Wall Street

Secondary market functions:
- *Promotes home ownership and investment*
- *Provides funds*
- *Stabilizes primary market*

The secondary market also drew investment funds into the mortgage industry and into real estate, substantially increasing the availability of mortgage funds nationwide and promoting home ownership.

The availability of funds in the primary market now depends to a great extent on the secondary market. Figure 3.2 shows how mortgage funds flow between the primary and secondary markets: first, mortgage funds are given to the home buyer by a lending institution in the primary market; then the mortgage is sold to a secondary market agency; then, the agency may pool the mortgage with many others to create mortgage-backed securities, which it will sell to investors. As mortgage-backed securities are sold by the agency, more funds become available to the agency for the purchase of new mortgages from the primary market. As the agencies purchase more mortgages, more funds become available for primary market lenders to make loans to borrowers.

If a lender does not sell a loan on the secondary market (either by choice or because no one wants to buy it), the lender keeps the loan **in portfolio**—that is, it holds onto the loan and receives the principal and interest payments from the borrower. But the secondary market has become such an important source of funds that most residential lenders sell the majority of their mortgage loans, keeping comparatively few in portfolio. In 2008, for example, lenders sold about 80% of all new home loans they made to Fannie Mae and Freddie Mac. This dominance has made those agencies tremendously influential. As we'll discuss shortly, their underwriting guidelines have shaped lending practices throughout the mortgage industry.

Fig. 3.2 Mortgage funds flow from the secondary market, to lenders, to borrowers

The Flow of Mortgage Funds

The Secondary Market Agencies

Now that we've provided an overview of the secondary market, let's take a closer look at the major secondary market agencies: Fannie Mae, Ginnie Mae, and Freddie Mac.

Creation of the Agencies

The federal government created the three secondary market agencies at separate points during the course of the twentieth century.

Fannie Mae. The Federal National Mortgage Association was created in 1938. It eventually became better known by the nickname Fannie Mae (based on its acronym, FNMA).

Fannie Mae: Federal National Mortgage Association (FNMA)

Fannie Mae was part of the federal government's efforts to fix unprecedented credit problems during the Great Depression (see Chapter 4). The government had earlier established the Federal Housing Association and the FHA-insured loan program to help make home financing affordable again, and Fannie Mae's original purpose was to provide a secondary market for FHA-insured loans.

By 1948 the agency was purchasing FHA-insured loans on a large scale. That same year, Congress authorized Fannie Mae to start buying loans from the new VA-guaranteed loan program, which had been established in the wake of World War II.

Two decades later, Congress took steps to increase the size and scope of the secondary market, hoping to moderate the disruptive economic effects of local and regional real estate cycles. In 1968, Fannie Mae was reorganized as a **government-sponsored enterprise** (GSE). That meant it became a private corporation owned by stockholders, although it was still chartered by Congress and supervised by the Department of Housing and Urban Development (HUD).

Government-sponsored enterprise (GSE):
- Created and supervised by the federal government,
- But owned by private stockholders

Ginnie Mae. At the same time that it turned Fannie Mae into a private corporation, Congress created a new wholly owned government corporation, the Government National Mortgage Association (or Ginnie Mae), as an agency within HUD. Ginnie Mae managed and eventually liquidated mortgages that had been purchased by Fannie Mae before the change-over.

Ginnie Mae: Government National Mortgage Association (GNMA)

Today, Ginnie Mae buys FHA and VA loans. Ginnie Mae is also involved in a variety of other activities, such as helping to finance urban renewal and housing projects.

Freddie Mac: Federal Home
Loan Mortgage Corporation
(FHLMC)

Freddie Mac. The Federal Home Loan Mortgage Corporation, nick-named Freddie Mac, was created in 1970 by the Emergency Home Finance Act. From the outset, Freddie Mac was a government-sponsored enterprise—a private corporation owned by its stockholders but chartered by Congress and supervised by HUD. Thus, the secondary mortgage market now had two GSEs, Fannie Mae and Freddie Mac, while Ginnie Mae remained a government agency.

Freddie Mac's original purpose was to assist savings and loan associations, which were hit particularly hard by a recession in 1969 and 1970. Savings and loans (S&Ls) mostly made **conventional loans**—loans that aren't insured or guaranteed by the government—and there wasn't a dependable secondary market for conventional loans at that time. As a result, S&Ls had kept most of their loans in portfolio. By purchasing their conventional loans, Freddie Mac enabled S&Ls to acquire additional funds for lending. The Emergency Home Finance Act also permitted Fannie Mae to start buying conventional loans.

Conventional loans make up a substantial portion of the residential mortgage market in the United States. Because Fannie Mae and Freddie Mac buy conventional loans, they have a much greater impact on the mortgage industry than Ginnie Mae, which buys only FHA and VA loans. That's why most discussions of the secondary market (including this one) focus mainly on Fannie Mae and Freddie Mac.

Fig. 3.3 Secondary market agencies

Fannie Mae and Freddie Mac
- Government-sponsored enterprises (GSEs)
- Buy conventional, FHA, and VA loans from all types of lenders
- Issue mortgage-backed securities based on pools of conventional, FHA, or VA loans

Ginnie Mae
- Wholly owned government corporation
- Agency within HUD
- Buys FHA and VA loans (not conventional loans)
- Issues mortgage-backed securities based on FHA and VA loans

GSE Status

As government-sponsored enterprises, Fannie Mae and Freddie Mac were given certain advantages over ordinary private corporations. For example, by the terms of their congressional charters, the GSEs were exempted from certain types of taxes and from some of the registration and disclosure requirements of the Securities and Exchange Commission.

On the other hand, GSE status also imposed certain restrictions and responsibilities on Fannie Mae and Freddie Mac. They were restricted by charter to investment in residential mortgage assets (essentially, mortgage loans and mortgage-backed securities). They have also had to meet affordable housing goals set annually by HUD. This requirement has led the GSEs to develop and promote programs that help provide affordable home financing and rental housing to low- and middle-income families and in areas that have historically been underserved by lenders, such as inner city neighborhoods.

GSEs must meet affordable housing goals set by HUD

MBS Programs

The first mortgage-backed securities program was started by Ginnie Mae in 1970. It offered investors securities backed by pools of FHA and VA loans. Both Fannie Mae and Freddie Mac eventually followed in Ginnie Mae's footsteps. They established MBS programs of their own, issuing securities backed primarily by pools of conventional mortgages.

In the 1980s, Congress changed how mortgage-backed securities were taxed and removed certain statutory restrictions to make the securities more competitive with corporate bonds. Mortgage-backed securities became steadily more popular, fueling the expansion of the secondary market.

Mortgage-backed securities could be purchased directly from Fannie Mae, Freddie Mac, or Ginnie Mae. These direct purchases were typically made by large institutional investors such as life insurance companies, pension funds, and charitable endowments. Smaller companies and individual investors tended to buy and sell the securities on Wall Street, through securities dealers.

One feature of mortgage-backed securities that investors found particularly attractive was that the securities were guaranteed by the secondary market agency that issued them. Under the terms of the guaranty, investors receive full payment from the secondary market agency each month even if borrowers default on some of the mortgages in the pool backing the securities. (Guaranty fees and servicing fees are subtracted before payments are passed along to investors.)

Standardized Documents and Underwriting

Among the key factors that have enabled the secondary market to function as it has are standardized loan documents and underwriting rules.

Quality Control. For conventional loans, Fannie Mae and Freddie Mac publish uniform loan application forms, appraisal forms, and mortgage documents, and they also issue their own underwriting guidelines. Underwriting guidelines are the rules lenders apply when they're qualifying loan applicants and deciding whether or not to make particular loans (see Chapter 8). Conventional loans sold to Fannie Mae or Freddie Mac must comply with the agency's underwriting rules, not just the lender's own rules.

If a lender makes a conventional loan that doesn't conform to an agency's underwriting guidelines or fails to use the uniform documents, the agency generally won't buy the loan from the lender. Not only that, if an agency buys a loan and later discovers that the lender violated the guidelines, the lender can be required to buy the loan back.

The standardized documents and underwriting guidelines are intended to ensure that loans purchased by the secondary market agencies are of a minimum quality. Quality control is important for the agencies and for MBS investors who are, in effect, investing in real estate sight unseen. They depend on primary market lenders to adequately evaluate borrowers and properties and make sound lending decisions.

Influencing Lending Practices. The underwriting guidelines set by Fannie Mae and Freddie Mac have strongly influenced lending practices in the primary market. For example, once the secondary market agencies began accepting adjustable-rate mortgages (ARMs) and 15-year fixed-rate mortgages, those types of financing became readily available in the primary market. Lenders were much more willing to make those types of loans after they were assured the loans could be sold on the secondary market.

The GSEs and Subprime Loans. Loans made to borrowers with the highest credit rating (an A rating) are called **prime loans**; loans made

Underwriting guidelines: rules lenders apply when deciding whether to approve a loan to less creditworthy buyers are **subprime loans** (see Chapter 4). At one time, Fannie Mae and Freddie Mac bought only prime loans, at least as a general rule. Subprime loans generally weren't eligible for purchase because they didn't meet Fannie Mae and Freddie Mac's underwriting standards. In a sense, Fannie Mae and Freddie Mac's underwriting standards came to define the boundary between prime and subprime lending.

Subprime loans: loans made to less creditworthy buyers

But that boundary began to blur around 2005, when Fannie Mae and Freddie Mac began buying significant numbers of subprime and less than prime loans (for example, "no doc" loans where the borrowers may or may not be subprime). HUD encouraged them to do this to help meet their affordable housing goals, since many of the people affordable housing programs are intended to help can't qualify for prime loans. The GSEs loosened their underwriting guidelines and started purchasing the very top layer of subprime loans, referred to as A-minus loans. This step was controversial at the time, and it eventually had undesirable consequences, as we'll discuss shortly.

The GSEs and the Economic Crisis

The federal government gave Fannie Mae and Freddie Mac the mission of increasing the overall availability of home mortgage funds throughout the country and limiting the adverse effects of local economic conditions on real estate markets. For decades, the GSEs were considered very successful in fulfilling that mission. In addition, they have been credited with helping to dramatically increase home ownership rates, reduce mortgage interest rates, make underwriting practices in the mortgage industry sounder and fairer, and provide mortgage lenders access to global capital markets as a source of funds.

Of course, Fannie Mae and Freddie Mac were also subject to criticism. Some critics contended that claims about how much the GSEs benefited the public were exaggerated. Many argued that they had grown too large and wielded too much power in the mortgage industry, limiting opportunities for other investors and enterprises. (For example, when the GSEs began gradually expanding into the subprime market, some businesses already involved in the market saw it as an unfair encroachment on their territory.) There was also criticism of how the GSEs were being run. In 2004, Fannie Mae's reputation was seriously tarnished by a massive accounting scandal, which eventually led to the resignation of top executives and payment of a $400 million fine.

In spite of the accounting scandal, Fannie Mae and Freddie Mac continued to play a major role in the mortgage industry. But only a few years later, as the subprime mortgage crisis began to unfold with home prices plunging and mortgage default rates soaring, the two GSEs stumbled badly. While the agencies had only a comparatively small share of their assets invested in the subprime market, by 2007 almost one-third of the GSEs' new purchases and guarantees were of low-doc, interest-only, and other relatively risky loans. This left the agencies badly exposed when these risky loans went into default in mounting numbers. Investors took note of the agencies' crumbling portfolios, and the prices of Fannie Mae and Freddie Mac stocks plunged, further undermining their financial stability.

Federal Conservatorship. By the summer of 2008, the foreclosure crisis was taking such a toll on Fannie Mae and Freddie Mac that insolvency loomed. This was an alarming prospect; if the GSEs failed, many economists thought it would have a devastating impact on the U.S. economy as a whole. In late July, Congress passed the Housing and Economic Recovery Act of 2008 (HERA). In addition to measures addressing other aspects of the subprime mortgage crisis that we'll discuss in Chapter 4, HERA included provisions concerning Fannie Mae and Freddie Mac.

The Federal Housing Finance Agency (FHFA) regulates Fannie Mae and Freddie Mac

HERA created a new regulator for the two GSEs, the **Federal Housing Finance Agency** (FHFA). The previous regulator, the Office of Federal Housing Enterprise Oversight, was part of HUD, but the FHFA is an independent agency.

The statute authorized the FHFA to take control of both Fannie Mae and Freddie Mac if that step appeared necessary to maintain the agencies' solvency. In early September, a little more than a month after HERA's enactment, the FHFA placed both agencies into conservatorship. The conservatorship had no termination date and was to continue until agency solvency was restored.

The conservatorship was essentially a government takeover. The FHFA immediately replaced top management at Fannie Mae and Freddie Mac and removed voting power from their shareholders and directors. However, the most important steps taken were financial. The FHFA stated that it would buy mortgage-backed securities from Fannie Mae and Freddie Mac as needed to maintain solvency, and that it would also directly infuse capital into the two companies by purchasing up to $100 billion of stock in each.

Despite its plan to restore the GSEs' financial health by buying their stock and mortgage-backed securities, the FHFA's longer-term goal was to sharply reduce the economic size and power of Fannie Mae and Freddie Mac. The FHFA stated that the mortgages and securities held by each company were to be capped at $850 billion by the end of 2009 (down about 40% from 2008 levels). The holdings would decline by 10% each year thereafter until the relatively modest size of $250 billion was reached.

Federal Guaranty. As mentioned earlier, Fannie Mae and Freddie Mac guarantee their mortgage-backed securities. The GSEs promise to pay the MBS purchasers even if borrowers default on the underlying mortgages. However, a guaranty usually becomes worthless if the guarantor goes bankrupt. Until recently, the U.S. government had no legal obligation to stand behind Fannie Mae or Freddie Mac's securities if either GSE failed. (In contrast, Ginnie Mae's securities have always been backed by the government, since Ginnie Mae is a federal agency.) Even so, it was widely believed that Fannie Mae and Freddie Mac's securities carried an implicit federal guaranty, based on the assumption that the government would almost certainly come to the rescue of MBS investors in the event that Fannie Mae or Freddie Mac became insolvent.

With the 2008 takeover of Fannie Mae and Freddie Mac, the government removed any doubt about a federal guaranty. The risk that a GSE's default on payments owed to MBS investors would devastate the entire economy seemed too great. The Federal Housing Finance Agency, under its conservancy power, announced that the government would now guarantee all of the mortgage-backed securities sold by both Fannie Mae and Freddie Mac.

This guaranty put the U.S. Treasury behind about five trillion dollars worth of agency debt. It was a dramatic and potentially drastic step. However, the actual cost to taxpayers of the guaranty, and the investments in the agencies, depends on the future of the housing market. A housing recovery could actually make the investment profitable and the guaranty irrelevant. On the other hand, if residential loan defaults do not abate within a few years, the Treasury could face some enormous bills.

As for what will happen with the FHFA's longer-term plan to scale down the size of Fannie Mae and Freddie Mac, only time will tell. These secondary market agencies have historically proved quite beneficial. Evolving market and political conditions will determine whether lessening the role of these players is realistic or even desirable.

Outline: The Primary and Secondary Markets

I. The Two Mortgage Markets

  A. Primary market: financial arena in which home buyers apply for loans and lenders originate them.

    1. Traditionally a local market, made up of local lending institutions.

    2. Problem: local market is subject to real estate cycles.

      a. When business is booming, local community's demand for mortgage funds may exceed local lenders' supply.

      b. In an economic slump, local lenders' supply of mortgage funds may exceed local demand.

      c. Secondary market helps cure problem of real estate cycles.

  B. Secondary market: national market in which mortgage loans are bought and sold.

    1. Mortgage loans can be sold like other types of investments.

      a. Present value of loan based on yield currently available on investments of similar quality (same degree of risk).

      b. Lender may sell loans to other lenders or investors in another part of the country, or to a secondary market agency.

    2. Mortgage-backed securities

      a. Secondary market agency buys many mortgages and pools them together; pool is pledged as collateral for the securities.

      b. Investors who buy mortgage-backed securities receive monthly payments of principal and interest from agency as pooled loans are repaid.

      c. Agency guarantees full payment to investors, even if borrowers miss payments on underlying loans.

    3. Functions of the secondary market

      a. Makes funds available for mortgage loans nationwide.

      b. Promotes home ownership and real estate investment.

      c. Moderates adverse effects of local real estate cycles.

      d. Flow of mortgage funds

        i. Agency uses funds from sale of securities to buy more mortgage loans from primary market.

        ii. Primary market lender uses funds from sale of loans to make more loans to borrowers.

II. Secondary Market Agencies

   A. Creation of the agencies

      1. Fannie Mae (Federal National Mortgage Association)

         a. U.S. government created Fannie Mae in 1938.

         b. Original purpose: buying FHA-insured loans from lenders.

         c. Reorganized as a private corporation in 1968, but remains a government-sponsored enterprise (GSE) supervised by FHFA.

      2. Ginnie Mae (Government National Mortgage Association)

         a. Created in 1968 as a wholly owned government corporation to take Fannie Mae's place.

         b. Buys FHA and VA loans (not conventional loans).

         c. 1970: Started first mortgage-backed securities program, based on pools of FHA and VA loans.

      3. Freddie Mac (Federal National Mortgage Corporation): GSE created in 1970 to help savings and loans by buying conventional loans.

   B. GSE status

      1. Fannie Mae and Freddie Mac limited to residential mortgages and mortgage-backed securities.

      2. Required to meet annual affordable housing goals set by HUD.

   C. MBS programs

      1. First mortgage-backed securities program started by Ginnie Mae in 1970, backed by pools of FHA and VA loans.

      2. Fannie Mae and Freddie Mac soon followed, issuing MBSs backed by pools of conventional mortgages.

      3. Attractive to investors because MBSs were guaranteed by secondary market agency that issued them.

   D. Standardized documents and underwriting

      1. Loans sold to GSE must meet GSE's underwriting guidelines, which are standardized across the country.

      2. GSE's rules give MBS investors confidence in loan quality.

      3. Lenders are more willing to make specific types of loans once Fannie Mae and Freddie Mac have decided to purchase them.

      4. GSEs and subprime loans

         a. GSEs used to purchase only prime loans.

         b. HUD encouraged looser underwriting standards and the purchase of A-minus subprime loans to meet affordable housing goals.

E. Fannie Mae and Freddie Mac today

1. In general, Fannie Mae and Freddie Mac credited with increased homeownership rates, reduced loan processing times, sounder and fairer underwriting, and reduced mortgage interest rates.

2. Federal conservatorship

    a. In 2008, Congress put GSEs under regulation of Federal Housing Finance Authority (FHFA) as part of plan to address fallout of subprime mortgage crisis.

    b. Later that year, FHFA took control of both GSEs and put them under federal conservatorship until both are financially stable again.

    c. Plans for solvency include: FHFA will purchase mortgage-backed securities from Fannie Mae and Freddie Mac, buy $100 billion in stock, and systematically decrease holdings over several years.

3. Federal guaranty

    a. Previously, Fannie Mae and Freddie Mac guaranteed their MBSs, but federal government had no legal obligation to back up those guaranties.

    b. Under conservancy power, federal government now guarantees all mortgage-backed securities sold by Fannie Mae and Freddie Mac.

Key Terms

Primary mortgage market: The financial arena in which mortgage loans are originated, where lenders make loans to home buyers.

Secondary mortgage market: The financial arena in which investors buy mortgage loans from lenders throughout the country.

Loan origination: Processing a loan application, deciding whether to approve or reject the application, and funding the loan.

Real estate cycles: Ups and downs in the level of activity in a local real estate market, where a boom may be followed by a slump, or vice versa.

Law of supply and demand: A basic rule of economics which holds that prices (or interest rates) tend to rise when supply decreases or demand increases, and tend to fall when supply increases or demand decreases.

Disintermediation: When depositors withdraw their savings from financial institutions and put the money into other types of investments that have higher yields.

Secondary market agency: One of the three government-created entities that buy loans and issue mortgage-backed securities: Fannie Mae, Ginnie Mae, or Freddie Mac.

Government-sponsored enterprise (GSE): An entity that is privately owned but created, chartered, and supervised by the government. A GSE functions as a private corporation but must fulfill special legal responsibilities imposed by the government. The GSEs discussed in this chapter are Fannie Mae and Freddie Mac.

Mortgage-backed security (MBS): An investment instrument that has a pool of mortgage loans as collateral; usually, issued by one of the secondary market agencies.

MBS guaranty: A guaranty offered by an issuer of mortgage-backed securities, which provides that the MBS investors will receive the expected payments of principal and interest from the issuer, even if borrowers fail to make their payments on some of the pooled mortgage loans.

Loan servicing: Processing loan payments, keeping payment records, and handling collection problems and defaults. The entity that services a loan is not necessarily the lender that originated it.

Securitizing: When a secondary market agency creates mortgage-backed securities by buying a large number of mortgage loans, "pooling" them together, and pledging the pool as collateral for the securities.

Portfolio loan: A mortgage loan that the lender keeps in its own investment portfolio until the loan is repaid (instead of selling the loan on the secondary market).

Conventional loan: A loan that is not insured or guaranteed by a government agency.

Chapter Quiz

1. The Cantors just borrowed money from Seacliff Savings to finance the purchase of a home. This transaction took place in the:

   a. national market

   b. primary market

   c. secondary market

   d. None of the above

2. The federal government created the secondary market agencies in order to:

   a. originate residential mortgage loans nationwide

   b. help moderate the adverse effects of real estate cycles

   c. bring inflation under control at the local level

   d. stimulate disintermediation

3. A lending institution with more mortgage loan applicants than available loan funds would be likely to:

   a. buy mortgage-backed securities from another lender

   b. buy mortgage-backed securities from a secondary market agency

   c. buy mortgages from a secondary market agency

   d. sell mortgages to a secondary market agency

4. A lender cannot sell a mortgage loan to Fannie Mae unless:

   a. it followed the agency's underwriting guidelines

   b. it is a federally certified primary market agency

   c. it is a federally insured savings and loan association

   d. the loan is either FHA-insured or VA-guaranteed

5. A mortgage-backed security is a type of:

   a. mortgage loan

   b. corporate debt certificate

   c. investment instrument

   d. guaranty

6. Taking a home buyer's loan application is a step in the:

   a. loan servicing process

   b. loan origination process

   c. loan guaranty process

   d. MBS process

7. Investors prefer to buy mortgage-backed securities instead of mortgages because the securities are:

   a. less liquid, and therefore safer

   b. serviced by the federal government

   c. guaranteed

   d. None of the above

8. Most residential mortgage loans are:

   a. kept in portfolio

   b. sold on the secondary market

   c. sold on the primary market

   d. None of the above

9. An investor's return on mortgage-backed securities usually takes the form of:

   a. monthly servicing fees

   b. annual dividends from the mortgage pool

   c. monthly payments of principal and interest

   d. annual installment bonds

10. As government-sponsored enterprises, Fannie Mae and Freddie Mac are:

    a. private corporations owned by stockholders

    b. government agencies financed with taxpayer dollars

    c. regulated by the Federal Housing Finance Agency (FHFA)

    d. Both a) and c)

Answer Key

1. b.   Loan transactions take place in the primary market.

2. b.   Moderating the negative effects of local real estate cycles and stabilizing the primary market were among the government's goals in creating Fannie Mae, Ginnie Mae, and Freddie Mac.

3. d.   A mortgage lender with more loan applicants than funds could raise the money to make more loans by selling some of its existing loans to a secondary market agency.

4. a.   A loan that's going to be sold to one of the secondary market agencies must comply with that agency's underwriting guidelines (not just the lender's own guidelines).

5. c.   A mortgage-backed security is a type of investment instrument.

6. b.   Loan origination refers to processing the loan application, making the decision to approve the loan, and funding the loan.

7. c.   Mortgage-backed securities are usually guaranteed by the agency that issues them. Under a 2008 conservatorship, MBSs issued by Fannie Mae and Freddie Mac are also guaranteed by the federal government.

8. b.   Nowadays, mortgage lenders tend to sell most of their loans on the secondary market.

9. c.   MBS investors usually receive monthly payments of principal and interest from the agency that issued the securities.

10. d.   The government-sponsored enterprises are private corporations owned by their stockholders, but supervised by the Federal Housing Finance Agency, an independent agency.

Chapter 4
The Mortgage Industry

Description of the Mortgage Industry

- Basic steps in the mortgage process
- Loan origination
- Types of loan originators
- Government regulation

Mortgage Lenders

- Depository institutions
- Mortgage companies
- Government regulation of mortgage lenders
- Alternative sources of financing

Government Intervention in Mortgage Lending

- The Depression
- Savings and loan crisis
- Mortgage and financial crisis
  - Housing bubble
  - Government bailouts and oversight

Introduction

The previous chapter explained the relationship between the primary market and the secondary market. These two markets give the mortgage industry its basic structure. In this chapter, we'll take a closer look at how the mortgage industry works, with an emphasis on the primary market. We'll also explain how actions and activities in one market can have a significant impact on the other market.

We'll start the chapter with an overview of the different types of entities that play a role in the primary market. As you will see, those entities may be involved in some or all of the steps in the mortgage lending process. The second half of the chapter describes how major economic crises have periodically led the federal government to intervene in the mortgage industry. In addition to the Great Depression in the 1930s and the savings and loan crisis in the 1970s, we'll discuss the mortgage and economic crisis that's been developing in recent years.

Description of the Mortgage Industry

We'll begin our examination of the mortgage industry with a basic overview of residential mortgage transactions. We'll touch on the basic steps in the mortgage process, define "loan originator," and explain retail versus wholesale lending.

Basic Steps in the Mortgage Process

In its most basic form, the residential mortgage process will involve:

1. a home buyer, who needs a mortgage loan;
2. a loan originator, who works with the buyer to complete the loan application and gather supporting documentation and other material to get the loan application approved; and
3. a mortgage lender, who reviews the completed application and provides funding for the loan (if the application meets its underwriting standards).

Once the mortgage has been funded, there is still more to be done. Just like other loans, a mortgage requires servicing: ongoing administration that includes payment processing, loan modifications (if any), and other duties. A lender may choose to keep loan servicing in-house or it can transfer these duties to a separate entity, called a **loan servicer**.

Loan servicing involves processing payments and generally dealing with the borrower

Further, as we discussed in earlier chapters, the mortgage lender may also decide to sell the loan to one or more mortgage investors. This transfer of loan ownership could have an impact on the borrower later on if she has trouble making payments or has some other problem with the loan.

Loan Origination

Loan origination refers to the processing of a loan application, including collecting all the necessary information about the borrowers and submitting the required documentation to the lender for review. In the past, nearly all mortgage loans were originated in basically the same way. Each stage of the process was handled by a lender who was sought out by the prospective home buyers. An employee of the lender (typically called a **loan officer**) would help the buyers decide what type of financing they wanted and help them prepare their application. The application would be submitted to the lender's in-house underwriting department, where the borrower's financial situation and the value of the property serving as collateral would be reviewed. If the loan application was approved, the lender would fund the loan.

Transactions like this are sometimes referred to as **retail loans** or **direct lending**. Retail transactions are still common, but they are no longer the only type of mortgage transaction. As a result of several developments (including the growth of the secondary market, the emergence of national financial institutions, the rise of mortgage companies, and the speed of technological advances), many loan originations are much more complicated now.

Retail lending: the lender deals directly with the borrower

Today, the person who helps buyers apply for a loan—the **loan originator**—may or may not be the lender's employee, and the lender may or may not be the ultimate owner of the loan. If asked, many buyers may not be able to identify exactly who is providing the money they're using to purchase their house. To understand how the role of a loan originator has evolved, we need to take a moment to discuss some historical developments in the financing industry.

The Growth of Wholesale Loans. In the 1990s, federal regulations were loosened to allow interstate bank mergers, which led to the development of very large lenders doing business nationwide. These large lenders came to dominate the mortgage industry. For example, in 2007 the 25 largest mortgage lenders in the U.S. originated about 90% of single-family home loans. (In 1992, only 30% of single-family loans were originated by the top 25 lenders.) These large lenders are often **wholesale lenders**: lenders who have vast quantities of funds available for lending, but who use outside entities to find their borrowers.

As we have already noted, a retail lender works directly with customers (the buyers) and usually handles the entire origination process from the application through closing. In contrast to the retail lender, the wholesale lender is much more removed from the buyer, working through an intermediary to handle the loan application process. Intermediaries in a wholesale lending transaction are usually referred to as **loan correspondents** or **mortgage brokers**.

Using loan correspondents or mortgage brokers to handle loan origination reduces the lender's overhead. For example, a wholesale lender can save on the cost of local office space and employees. On the other hand, if mistakes occur during the loan application process, a wholesale lender is less likely to know about it or have the ability to prevent similar mistakes from being made in the future.

Perhaps in response to some of the problems that have surfaced during the recent mortgage crisis, there appears to be a shift by several large lenders back to the retail lending model. Regardless of whether this trend continues, it's important to keep in mind that several different entities can play a role in the mortgage process: one entity may underwrite the loan, another may fund the loan, yet another may service the loan, and still another may end up owning the loan.

Types of Loan Originators

Now let's take a look at the two main types of loan originators: loan officers and mortgage brokers.

Loan Officers. As was explained earlier, if a home buyer is applying directly to the lender for a mortgage loan, the loan originator for that

Wholesale lending: the borrower deals with a loan correspondent, who represents the lender

Mortgage brokers and loan correspondents find borrowers for wholesale lenders kind of transaction will be the lender's loan officer. The loan officer will help the buyers complete the loan application and make sure all the necessary financial documents and supporting information have been submitted and verified. The loan officer will then pass the completed application on to the lender's underwriting department, for further review and a funding decision. While you may encounter some confusion surrounding the use of the term "loan officer," it generally refers to a loan originator who is processing loan applications for a specific mortgage lender.

Loan officer: a loan originator working for a particular lender

Mortgage Brokers. In contrast to a loan officer, a mortgage broker is usually an independent contractor who often works with multiple lenders. A mortgage broker is not an actual lender but rather an intermediary, a go-between who brings borrowers together with lenders in exchange for a commission. Home buyers go to a mortgage broker for help in finding a loan; the broker informs the buyers about various financing options that are offered by different lenders. It's important to note that in some states, a mortgage broker does not have a fiduciary duty to find the best financing option for a particular home buyer. In other words, no agency relationship exists between the mortgage broker and the borrower unless they have entered into a written agency contract.

Mortgage brokers work with multiple lenders

After the buyers have decided which type of loan they want to apply for, the mortgage broker helps them complete a loan application. Although the mortgage broker has access to the underwriting standards for each lender he represents, a mortgage broker can give the buyers only a preliminary loan approval. The actual underwriting decision and formal loan approval must be issued by the lender.

Table-funded loans. As we have pointed out, mortgage brokers are intermediaries for mortgage lenders, and usually don't use any of their own assets to fund the loan. However, certain kinds of transactions—table-funded loans—may create the impression that the mortgage broker is acting as both the loan originator and the lender, when in fact the true lender is another entity.

In a **table-funded loan**, a mortgage broker stays involved in the lending process all the way to closing, even naming itself as the originating lender. However, the broker assigns the rights to that loan to the true mortgage lender during the closing process. Federal regulators have ruled that table-funded loans are never really "funded" by the mortgage broker, as the actual loan funds are carefully timed to be delivered at closing by the true lender. (A mortgage broker who arranges this kind of loan receives a **service release premium**, her commission for originating the loan.) In this type of transaction, it's easy to understand how a borrower might think the mortgage broker is acting as the initial mortgage lender. And whether someone is a mortgage broker or a mortgage lender may have important consequences when it comes to certain consumer protection laws (see Chapter 14).

Government Regulation of Loan Originators

Recognizing the important role loan originators play in the mortgage industry and the potential for predatory practices, Congress passed the Secure and Fair Enforcement for Mortgage Licensing Act as part of the 2008 Housing and Economic Recovery Act. This law is often called the S.A.F.E. Mortgage Licensing Act. S.A.F.E. is designed to prevent abusive practices during loan origination by:

- requiring all loan originators to be either state-licensed or federally registered (they must obtain a unique federal identifying number before performing any origination duties);
- requiring all states to comply with standard reporting requirements and use uniform license application forms for state-licensed loan originators;
- increasing the tracking and reporting of loan originator information (background checks and fingerprinting, employment history, and disciplinary actions) across state lines;
- imposing fiduciary duties on all loan originators; and
- enhancing consumer protection and anti-fraud measures.

As defined in S.A.F.E., a **registered loan originator** is a loan originator employed by a depository institution or its subsidiary. **State-licensed loan originators** are all other loan originators. Even if a person performs only clerical or support duties (i.e., loan processing or underwriting duties), they must still be licensed or registered. Although a real estate agent is generally excluded from the requirements of this law, she will be considered a loan originator (and thus need to be licensed) if she is compensated by a lender or a mortgage broker for helping to arrange a loan.

Mortgage Lenders

Once a loan originator has helped a home buyer complete a loan application, the next step in the process is submitting that application to a mortgage lender for review. If the lender approves the application, it will fund the loan.

Types of Lenders

There are several types of mortgage lenders in the primary market. These include:

- commercial banks,
- thrift institutions,
- credit unions, and
- mortgage companies.

The majority of home buyers obtain financing from one of these four types of lenders.

Commercial Banks. As their name suggests, commercial banks originally developed to serve commercial enterprises: merchants and other businesses. At first banks just provided a secure place for keeping money. Later they began paying interest on deposits and using those deposited funds to make loans. Later they began offering what are now called checking accounts to facilitate commercial transactions.

Commercial banks have always emphasized commercial lending, supplying capital for business ventures and construction activities. Originally, residential mortgages weren't a significant part of their lending business. Various developments in the twentieth century, including regulatory changes and the expansion of the secondary market, helped make residential mortgage lending more attractive to commercial banks.

Traditionally, commercial banks didn't make many home mortgage loans

Commercial banks accept deposits and make loans

In the U.S., commercial banks are either national banks (chartered by the federal government) or state banks (chartered by a state government).

Commercial banks should be distinguished from **investment banks**. Investment banks are securities firms, commonly known as stock brokerages. They raise capital for corporations, arrange for the issuance of government and corporate bonds, manage corporate finances, and handle mergers and acquisitions. They also provide

Investment banks: securities firms involved in corporate finance

investment advice to clients and manage their investments. Investment banks don't accept deposits from individuals or make loans to individuals, and they aren't regulated in the same way that commercial banks and other depository institutions are.

In the past, banks were required to choose between commercial banking services and investment banking services; a bank was prohibited from offering a combination of these services. With the passage of the **Financial Services Modernization Act** (also called the Gramm-Leach-Bliley Act), it became legal for a holding company to have a bank, a securities firm, and an insurance company as subsidiaries. (A holding company is basically a corporate entity created for the purpose of owning other companies.)

Thrift Institutions. Savings banks and savings and loan associations are generally grouped together and referred to as thrift institutions, or simply as **thrifts**. Like commercial banks, thrifts are governed by either a federal or a state charter.

Thrift industry: savings and loans and savings banks

Savings banks started out in the early nineteenth century by offering financial services to small depositors, especially immigrants and members of the new industrial working class. They are sometimes called mutual savings banks, because many were originally organized as mutual companies, owned by and operated for the benefit of their depositors rather than stockholders.

Savings and loan associations (S&Ls) also developed in the nineteenth century. Originally called building and loan associations, S&Ls were formed in local communities to finance the construction of homes. An association was designed to serve only its members, who would pool their assets and then take turns using the money to build houses for themselves. After all the members had satisfied their financing needs, the association would be dissolved. Over the years, however, savings and loan associations began to make some loans to nonmembers, and they eventually became permanent institutions.

The institutions' traditional emphasis on home mortgages and savings accounts was the basis for the name "thrifts," and for much of their history they were restricted by law to providing only a limited range of services. Regulatory changes in the 1970s and early 1980s allowed thrifts to become more like commercial banks. For example, they began offering checking accounts as well as savings accounts, and they got involved in other types of lending besides home mortgages. Deregulation in this arena was one of the factors that led to the savings and loan crisis, discussed later in this chapter.

Today thrifts offer essentially the same consumer services as commercial banks: checking accounts, savings accounts, credit cards, and so on. In addition to home mortgage loans, thrifts make consumer loans, providing financing for the purchase of furniture, appliances, and cars. They also offer financial services to businesses, but typically on a much smaller scale than commercial banks.

Thrifts make mortgage loans and other consumer loans

Credit Unions. Credit unions got their start in the U.S. in the early twentieth century. They are nonprofit cooperative organizations designed to serve the members of a particular group, such as a labor union or a professional association, or the employees of a large company. Like other depository institutions, credit unions may be organized under either a federal or state charter.

Credit union: a nonprofit depository institution that serves the members of a particular group

Originally, credit unions didn't make mortgage loans. They specialized instead in small, personal loans that were often unsecured. (In other words, no collateral was required.) This type of loan generally wasn't available from banks or savings and loans at that time, and small borrowers had previously turned to pawn shops and loan sharks. Credit unions provided an alternative.

Later on, many credit unions emphasized home equity loans. A **home equity loan** is a mortgage on the borrower's equity in the home she already owns. These are generally short-term loans. The legislation deregulating financial institutions in the early 1980s allowed credit unions to begin offering their members long-term home purchase loans.

As nonprofit organizations, credit unions are generally exempt from taxation. That advantage, along with certain others, enables credit unions to loan money to their members at interest rates that are slightly below market rates. They can also offer interest rates on deposits that are slightly higher than market rates. Credit unions have been significantly increasing their involvement in mortgage loans in recent years.

Mortgage Companies. The types of mortgage lenders we've looked at so far—banks, thrifts, and credit unions—are depository institutions: government-regulated entities that hold customers' deposits and provide a wide range of financial services in addition to offering mortgage loans. In contrast, **mortgage companies** are not depository

Mortgage companies (aka mortgage bankers) are not depository institutions

institutions, and their business is focused exclusively on mortgage lending and affiliated services.

Mortgage companies are also called mortgage banking companies or mortgage bankers. The first ones in the U.S. were established in the 1930s. Today, some mortgage companies are direct subsidiaries or affiliates of large banks or thrifts, but there are still many that aren't. Mortgage companies that aren't associated with a bank or a thrift are called **independent mortgage companies**. As we'll discuss below, independent mortgage companies aren't as strictly regulated or supervised as depository institutions and their affiliates and subsidiaries.

Note that some mortgage companies engage in mortgage brokerage activities as well as mortgage banking. A business called "Acme Mortgage" might be strictly a mortgage banker, strictly a mortgage broker, or a combination of the two. And mortgage companies often engage in mortgage loan servicing activities as well.

Since mortgage companies aren't depository institutions, they can't use customers' deposits to fund loans. They have to raise the necessary capital in other ways. For example, a mortgage company may have a line of credit with a financial institution, draw on its line of credit for funds to make mortgage loans, and then sell the mortgages to secondary market investors. The mortgage company then uses the proceeds of those sales to repay its own creditor and to make more loans. Alternatively, a mortgage company may simply act as a loan correspondent, making loans on behalf of large investors such as pension funds or insurance companies. (Banks and thrifts may also act as loan correspondents, but mortgage companies specialized in that role early on.)

Fig. 4.1 Mortgage companies can act as mortgage bankers or as mortgage brokers

Mortgage Banker	**Mortgage Broker**
• A type of lender	• An intermediary, not a lender
• Takes buyer's application, makes underwriting decision, and funds loan	• Helps buyer choose and apply for a loan

Government Regulation of Mortgage Lenders

Depository institutions are subject to a complicated system of regulation. There are state regulators for state-chartered institutions and federal regulators for federally chartered institutions. Not only that, different types of institutions are regulated by different state or federal agencies. On the federal level, the regulatory agencies include the Federal Reserve System, the Federal Deposit Insurance Corporation, the National Credit Union Administration, the Office of the Comptroller of the Currency, and the Office of Thrift Supervision.

Depository institutions are required to undergo periodic examinations by government regulators to make sure their operations comply with the law. The Federal Financial Institutions Examination Council is an interagency body that prescribes standardized examination procedures for federal regulators.

Regulators periodically examine depository institutions

In addition to enforcing financial regulations concerning capital requirements, reserve requirements, accounting procedures, and so on, regulators enforce mortgage lenders' compliance with consumer protection laws and fair lending laws. In Chapter 14, we'll discuss some of the federal consumer protection laws, including the Truth in Lending Act, the Real Estate Settlement Procedures Act, the Equal Credit Opportunity Act, the Home Mortgage Disclosure Act, and the Community Reinvestment Act.

As we mentioned earlier, independent mortgage companies aren't subject to the same regulations as depository institutions and their affiliates and subsidiaries. Neither are they systematically examined in the way that depository institutions are, in terms of their risk assumption, capitalization, and general business practices. An independent mortgage company's operations are ordinarily investigated only if a complaint is filed with the Federal Trade Commission or a state agency. (However, independent mortgage companies are required to report data under the Home Mortgage Disclosure Act, discussed in Chapter 14.)

Alternative Sources of Financing

Most home buyers obtain financing from one of the four types of lenders we've discussed so far—from a bank, a thrift, a credit union, or a mortgage company. But there are other sources of financing.

Sometimes an individual with capital to invest will make mortgage loans to home buyers on a small scale. This type of private lending business is legal in some places and not in others, depending on state licensing laws and various other restrictions. **Usury** laws (limits on interest rates for certain types of loans), disclosure laws, and predatory lending laws also may apply to this type of transaction.

Private investment groups such as real estate limited partnerships and real estate investment trusts put a great deal of money into real estate. They generally don't offer loans directly to buyers, however.

Probably the most important alternative for buyers is seller financing. Home builders and residential developers frequently offer financing to buyers who purchase homes or lots from them. And ordinary home sellers sometimes provide part or even all of the financing necessary for the purchase of their property. Home sellers are an especially important source of financing in periods when institutional loans are hard to come by or market interest rates are high. Seller financing is covered in Chapter 13.

Sellers are an important source of financing when institutional loans are expensive

Government Intervention in Mortgage Lending

In addition to regulating mortgage lenders, from time to time the federal government has intervened in the mortgage industry more directly. The creation of the secondary market agencies, discussed in Chapter 3, is an example of this type of intervention. There are some other government interventions that you should be aware of, because of their long-term effects on the industry. These have occurred in response to the Great Depression in the 1930s, the savings and loan crisis in the 1980s, and more recently in response to the mortgage and financial crisis.

The Depression and the Mortgage Industry

The nineteenth century was a period of rapid growth in the United States, as the country expanded westward. Money poured into investments that promised high returns, including real estate. In addition to depository institutions, many private investors got involved in mortgage lending. The mortgage business remained prosperous through the first decades of the twentieth century, up until the Depression.

The economic collapse of the 1930s had a severe impact on housing and mortgage lending in the U.S. As unemployment rose to staggering levels, hundreds of thousands of homeowners throughout the country defaulted on their mortgages. At the worst point, about half the outstanding home mortgage debt was in default. Foreclosures became commonplace; government officials estimated that in 1933 nearly one thousand homes were foreclosed on every day. Some states declared a moratorium on foreclosures, allowing defaulting borrowers to stay in their homes. Many financial institutions failed, and mortgage lending and home construction came to a standstill. As part of the New Deal, a broad plan to pull the nation out of the economic crisis, the federal government stepped in to try to revive the mortgage industry.

Mortgage lending and home construction virtually ceased during the Depression

Several of the agencies and programs that were instituted at this point long outlasted the Depression. These include the Federal Housing Administration (FHA), which encouraged residential lending by offering mortgage insurance to protect against foreclosure losses; the Federal Home Loan Bank Board (FHLBB), which assisted savings and loans; and, as we discussed in Chapter 3, the Federal National Mortgage Association (Fannie Mae), which provided a secondary market for FHA-insured loans.

One important reaction to the Depression foreclosures was the introduction of long-term, fixed-rate, amortized home purchase loans. The mortgages offered through the FHA-insured loan program could be paid off over a 20- or 30-year term at an unchanging rate of interest. They were also fully amortized: each monthly payment included a share of the principal as well as interest, and the regular monthly payments were sufficient to pay off the principal in full by the end of the term. (Amortization is covered in Chapter 6.)

These features of FHA-insured mortgages made it much easier for home buyers to avoid default and foreclosure. Once that advantage was well-established, lenders began to offer long-term, fixed-rate, fully amortized loans outside of the FHA program. By the early 1940s, these longer-term loans had become standard. They became even more common after World War II, when many returning veterans bought homes with financing obtained through the Veterans Administration's new guaranteed loan program.

Depression foreclosures led to the introduction of long-term, fixed-rate, amortized mortgage loans

In the last few years, many home buyers were attracted to adjustable-rate mortgages with low teaser rates, loans with interest-

Fig. 4.2 Mortgage loans changed dramatically after the Depression

Standard Loan, circa 1930	**Standard Loan, circa 1940**
• Renewable at lender's discretion, and interest rate may go up • Interest-only payments; full principal amount still owed at end of term	• Thirty-year term • Fixed interest rate • Amortized so that regular payments pay off all principal and interest by end of term

only payments, or loans with terms of less than 30 years. As we will discuss later in this chapter, this shift to "nontraditional" mortgage loan products, combined with lax underwriting standards, contributed significantly to the current mortgage crisis. As a result, there now appears to be a shift back to the standard 30-year, fixed-rate loan.

The Savings and Loan Crisis

Another chapter in the history of mortgage lending that had far-reaching effects was the savings and loan crisis in the 1980s. Savings and loans dominated the U.S. residential mortgage industry in the 1950s, yet 30 years later many S&Ls faced insolvency.

Government regulations limited the amount of long-term lending that commercial banks could engage in, but did not restrict savings and loans in the same way. The main reason for this distinction was that in those days S&Ls held only savings and time deposits, whereas commercial banks primarily held demand deposits. **Demand deposits** can be withdrawn on demand, anytime the depositor wants the funds, so the amount a commercial bank has on deposit may change frequently. An example of a demand deposit would be a checking account. In contrast, **time deposits** can be withdrawn without penalty only after giving notice to the financial institution, or after a specific period has elapsed; certificates of deposit are an example. **Savings deposits** may be withdrawn without notice, but are generally intended to remain on deposit for a long time (not used for day-to-day transactions).

Because time and savings deposits are less susceptible to withdrawal than demand deposits, they're more stable and easier to use for long-term loans. So government regulations gave savings and loans,

From the 1950s until the 1980s, savings and loans were the largest source of mortgage financing

S&Ls had long-term deposits well suited to making long-term loans

82

with their long-term deposits, free rein to make long-term mortgage loans. However, in response to changes in the national economy, market interest rates soared to unprecedented heights in the late 1970s and early 1980s. (In the early 1960s a typical mortgage rate was 4.5%; by the mid-1970s 10% was common, and by 1982 18% was not unusual.) Rates were also extremely unstable, changing by as much as 3% in the course of a single year.

As a result, lending institutions—especially savings and loan associations—began experiencing financial difficulties. Regulations imposed a decade earlier limited how much interest savings and loans could pay their depositors, so S&Ls now found themselves unable to offer attractive returns. They ended up losing a large portion of their deposits to competing investments such as money market funds and government bonds. (See the discussion of disintermediation in Chapter 3.) Making matters much worse, the S&Ls had most of their funds tied up in long-term mortgages at what were now considered very low interest rates.

Congress addressed these problems by passing several bills that loosened regulatory restrictions on savings and loan associations. That deregulation is now seen as one of several factors that led the savings and loan industry into a much worse crisis. Some S&Ls tried new types of investments that were much riskier than single-family home loans, and often the risks didn't pay off. When insolvency loomed, the officers of some S&Ls took even greater risks, gambling to see if they could get back into black ink. Since the deposits were insured by the federal government, they felt they had little to lose.

The result was a sharp increase in the failure rate of savings and loans. Hundreds of federally insured S&Ls became insolvent, and eventually the Federal Savings and Loan Insurance Corporation could not meet all of the liabilities. Finally, to protect S&L depositors, the federal government stepped in. The bailout of the savings and loan industry ultimately cost taxpayers about $124 billion.

In response to the savings and loan crisis, Congress passed the **Financial Institutions Reform, Recovery, and Enforcement Act,** or **FIRREA** in 1989. The act imposed new rules on the lending activities of savings and loans to prevent high-risk transactions, and it reorganized the federal agencies that supervise and insure financial institutions. The Federal Home Loan Bank Board was replaced by the Federal Housing Finance Board and the Office of Thrift Supervision.

Market interest rates skyrocketed in the late 1970s and early 1980s

Deregulation allowed S&Ls to pay depositors higher interest rates, charge higher rates on mortgage loans, and branch out from residential lending

Hundreds of S&Ls became insolvent, leading to a government bailout of the industry

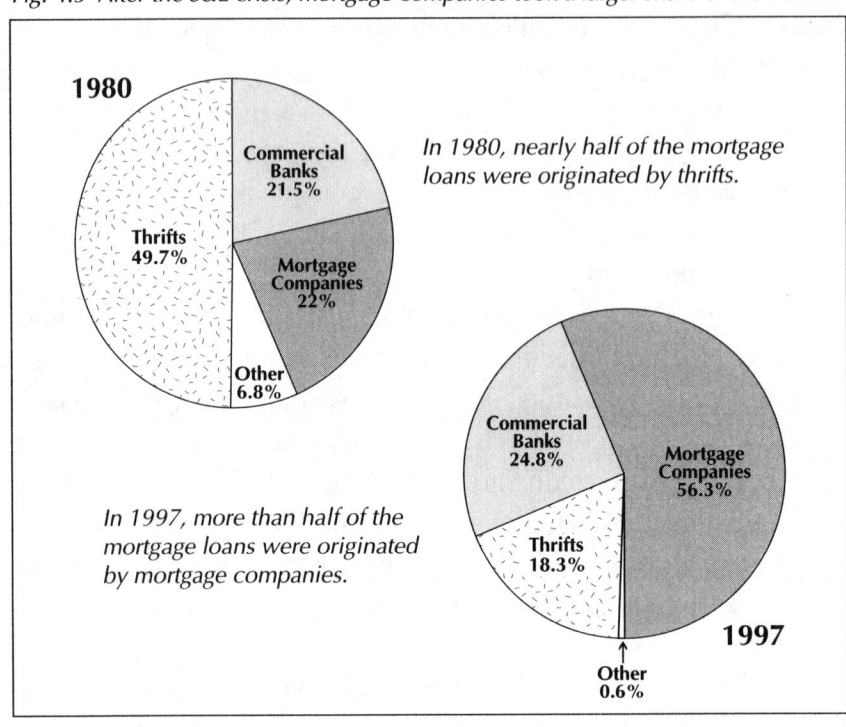

Fig. 4.3 After the S&L crisis, mortgage companies took a larger share of the market

The Federal Savings and Loan Insurance Corporation was eliminated, and the Federal Deposit Insurance Corporation (FDIC) was reorganized to cover S&L deposits as well as bank deposits. FIRREA also formed the Resolution Trust Corporation to manage insolvent S&Ls, selling them or closing them and disposing of their assets.

The savings and loan industry recovered from its crisis, but because of insolvencies and mergers, there are far fewer savings and loan associations now than there were in the 1970s. In the wake of the savings and loan crisis, the composition of the primary mortgage market changed. Where S&Ls had once dominated, mortgage companies and credit unions came to the forefront.

A number of forces came together to cause this shift in the residential mortgage market. Clearly, one factor was the savings and loan crisis and the decline in the number of savings and loans. The growth of the secondary market (see Chapter 3) was another important factor, because it made much more capital available for mortgage companies to work with. It's possible that market shares will shift again in response to the most recent crisis and government interventions in the residential mortgage industry.

The Mortgage Market and Financial Crisis

It is difficult to pinpoint the exact causes of the most recent mortgage and financial crisis, and as events continue to unfold, more information comes to light. But one thing is clear: an action or event in one segment of the economy has a ripple effect in other areas. What began with rising numbers of subprime mortgage foreclosures ended up crippling the entire economy. Here, we'll briefly describe the events leading up to the economic crisis and the government's reaction.

Housing Bubble. Most economists agree that the bursting of the housing bubble (the artificial inflation of property values) was a primary cause of the mortgage crisis. There were several factors that contributed to the creation of the housing bubble. An important one was the ongoing quest to bring the American dream of homeownership to increasing numbers of people.

Housing bubble: an artificial increase in property values

Expanding access to homeownership has been a top priority of policymakers for decades. A prime example is the Community Reinvestment Act, which was passed in 1977 to increase homeownership for low- and moderate-income people. Under this law, banks were required to begin reporting the number of mortgage loans issued to low- and moderate-income home buyers living in the communities served by those banks. This program has been so successful in achieving its goal of making homeownership more attainable for these borrowers that some policymakers want to expand the law's scope to include independent mortgage companies and other financial institutions.

Government actions that encouraged homeownership played a role in rising prices

Tax breaks that make the purchase and sale of homes more financially attractive have been introduced as well. For example, in 1997, Congress (at the urging of the Clinton Administration) increased the tax benefits of homeownership. Taxpayers who sold their principal residence could now exclude a large portion of the gain from that sale from taxation. This change resulted in a surge of interest in real estate as an investment option, not just as a place to live.

Other government actions included the 1999 passage of the Financial Services and Modernization Act, which removed barriers between the commercial banking industry, Wall Street investment firms, and the very wealthy insurance industry. Extremely large institutions now had greater access to substantial pools of capital, and real estate became one of the top choices for investors looking for high-yield profits. The Bush Administration also promoted policy initiatives designed to make homebuying easier and more affordable.

This was also a time in which free market principles were encouraged, and there was little, if any, regulation or oversight of the financial markets. Relaxed borrowing standards for borrowers and high profits for investors became the norm. As investors, lenders, and mortgage professionals developed new and increasingly complex ways to make (and sell) mortgage loans, the housing market boomed and profits soared. Loan originators competed aggressively for a larger share of the home loan market.

Home buyers and mortgage professionals alike gave little or no thought to what might happen if the bubble burst and housing prices started to decline. Homeowners who viewed their homes as investment opportunities wanted mortgage loans with minimal downpayment requirements and low monthly payments in the early years of the loan. They expected ever-increasing home prices to allow them to sell or refinance their home easily, before the larger mortgage payments inevitably became due.

Many lenders promoted mortgage products specifically tailored to this new type of customer. Borrowers were allowed to buy homes using **piggyback loans**: primary and secondary loans from the same lender that equaled the total purchase price of the home—meaning no downpayment was required. (Piggyback loans are also discussed in Chapter 10.) And many borrowers received these loans with little or no documentation of their ability to actually repay the loan amounts. Traditional underwriting standards and verification practices were discarded in the rush to originate more home loans. Many of these risky loans were immediately sold to investors, so lenders could—at least temporarily—escape accountability for poor underwriting decisions. A compensation structure that rewarded mortgage originators for the volume of loans originated (rather than the quality of the loans) meant an unprecedented number of high-risk mortgage loans were issued between 2005 and 2007.

Many of these high-risk mortgages were **subprime loans**, loans issued to home buyers with low credit scores or other financial problems. (See the discussion of subprime loans in Chapter 8.) The secondary market for subprime loans reached peak levels in 2006. From 1994 to 2006, subprime lending increased from 4.5% of all

The risky subprime market grew rapidly between 1994 and 2006 home mortgage originations to 20% of originations, and accounted for an estimated $600 billion in mortgage loans. (The GSE involvement with these loans is discussed in Chapter 3.)

Regulators became concerned about the increasing numbers of subprime and other nontraditional mortgages, especially those that allowed negative amortization (see Chapter 6). In 2007, key federal regulators issued a joint Statement on Subprime Lending, describing their concerns about the products being offered and emphasizing the importance of consumer awareness. Particularly worrisome to the regulators were ARM products that offered low introductory rates that lasted only a short period of time. These artificially low interest rates were slated to adjust fairly quickly to much higher rates, a scenario likely to cause payment shock. Many home buyers thought they could easily refinance these loans, or sell their property at a profit, before the higher interest rates kicked in. However, by the time many of the interest rates adjusted upwards, the housing crisis had begun and home prices were falling. Refinancing or selling were no longer viable options.

As more and more borrowers found themselves trapped in homes they could no longer afford, the number of foreclosures surged. The Mortgage Bankers Association estimated that more than one million home loans were in foreclosure proceedings in 2007. As the housing market crumbled, the financial losses quickly spilled into other areas of the economy, because so many institutional investors had purchased securities based on home loans. (Mortgage-backed securities are covered in Chapter 3.) As the crisis continued to grow, financial institutions went bankrupt, the government took control of Fannie Mae and Freddie Mac, and lenders cut back sharply on lending. A recession was formally declared in 2008.

Government Bailouts and Oversight. One of the first government interventions to address the financial crisis took place in July of 2008, when Congress passed the **Housing and Economic Recovery Act** (HERA) to shore up the housing market. HERA:

HERA: federal law passed to strengthen the housing market

- established a tax credit for first-time home buyers,
- provided neighborhood revitalization funds that communities could use to purchase foreclosed homes,
- reformed the FHA lending program by increasing FHA loan limits,

- strengthened the regulation of and provided more capital to Fannie Mae and Freddie Mac,
- set out new rules for mortgage disclosures, and
- established the HOPE for Homeowners Program.

The HOPE for Homeowners Program, effective from October of 2008 through September of 2011, allows struggling homeowners to refinance their current mortgages with new affordable 30-year fixed-rate mortgages insured by the FHA. The program is only available to owner-occupants who can show that they are good loan risks. Further, the new loan cannot exceed 90% of the new appraised value of the home, which means that lenders who choose to participate in this program must accept the proceeds of the HOPE loan as full settlement of outstanding debts and be prepared to write off the difference.

Unfortunately, few borrowers took advantage of the HOPE for Homeowners Program, and housing and economic conditions continued to worsen. As more financial institutions floundered, the credit markets began to dry up, leaving businesses in the U.S. and around the world without access to essential capital. In early September, a little more than a month after HERA's enactment, the federal government placed both Fannie Mae and Freddie Mac into conservatorship. (See Chapter 3.)

TARP: $700 billion bailout law

Investors and consumers alike began to panic. In October 2008, Congress passed an emergency bailout bill known as the **Troubled Asset Relief Program**, or TARP, to bolster confidence in the economy and help ease credit. Among the key provisions in the $700 billion law was unfettered authority for the Treasury Department to purchase stock in and assets of the country's largest financial institutions, in order to make more funds available for lending. (Ultimately, non-financial institutions were given access to the funds as well.) In addition, the FDIC cap on insurance for savings deposits was raised from $100,000 to $250,000, to alleviate concerns about the safety of depositor accounts.

As the economy continued to suffer, several government initiatives were discussed that would provide direct assistance to homeowners facing foreclosure as well as to help other economic sectors. However, at the time of this writing, no real solution to the myriad economic problems has yet been found. There is little doubt, though, that the financial crisis will have implications for the residential mortgage industry for many years to come.

Outline: The Mortgage Industry

I. Basic Steps in Mortgage Process

    A. The residential mortgage process involves:

        1. a home buyer,

        2. a loan originator (who arranges the loan), and

        3. a mortgage lender (who funds the loan).

    B. The loan originator and the lender may or may not be the same entity.

    C. Often someone other than the lender services the loan (processing the payments, etc.).

II. Loan Origination

    A. Retail lenders

        1. Retail lenders deal directly with borrowers; the borrower doesn't apply for the loan through a mortgage broker or other intermediary.

    B. Wholesale lenders

        1. With a wholesale lender, the borrower applies for the loan through an intermediary—a mortgage broker or a loan correspondent (not an employee of the lender).

        2. Most wholesale lenders are large financial entities: in 2007, 25 wholesale lenders handled 90% of all home loans; however, some of these lenders are moving back towards the retail model.

    C. Types of loan originators

        1. Loan officers: loan officers work for a retail lender; they help borrowers complete loan applications and supporting materials and pass this material on to the underwriting department.

        2. Mortgage brokers: most mortgage brokers are independent contractors working with various lenders; they bring the borrower and lender together in exchange for a commission.

        3. Mortgage brokers rarely provide funds for loans; although in a "table-funded" loan, the broker names herself as the originating lender, the loan proceeds are actually brought to the table at closing by the true lender.

    D. Government regulation of loan originators

        1. In 2008, Congress took aim at abuses by loan originators with the Secure and Fair Enforcement for Mortgage Licensing Act (also called the S.A.F.E. Mortgage Licensing Act).

2. The act requires all originators to be either state-licensed or federally registered.

3. Real estate agents who receive commissions for helping arrange loans must be licensed.

III. Mortgage Lenders

    A. The four main types of residential lenders are commercial banks, thrift institutions, credit unions, and mortgage companies.

    B. Commercial banks

        1. Commercial banks were originally oriented toward commercial lending for activities like business ventures and construction; residential mortgages were a small part of their business.

        2. Regulatory changes made residential lending more attractive to commercial banks.

        3. Commercial banks are either chartered by the federal government or the state government.

        4. Commercial banks are different from investment banks; investment banks focus on selling securities and underwriting offerings of stocks and bonds; they don't accept deposits from, or make loans to, individuals.

    C. Thrift institutions

        1. Savings banks: traditionally oriented toward small depositors, offering savings accounts and making mortgage and consumer loans; today, savings banks offer the same services as commercial banks.

        2. Savings and loan associations: originally created to finance home construction with services only available to members; later however, S&Ls began issuing loans to nonmembers and taking deposits from small depositors; deregulation in the 1970s allowed S&Ls to become more like banks.

    D. Credit unions

        1. Credit unions are nonprofit cooperatives that serve members of a particular group, such as a labor union or employees of a large company.

        2. Credit unions originally specialized in small, unsecured loans; they later began emphasizing home equity loans and issuing residential loans.

E. Mortgage companies

1. Mortgage companies, also known as mortgage bankers, are not depository institutions and focus entirely on mortgage loans.

2. Mortgage companies may borrow money, use it to originate mortgages, and sell the mortgages to secondary market investors.

3. Mortgage companies may also act as loan correspondents, originating loans on an investor's behalf and servicing the loans in order to receive servicing fees; typical loan correspondent clients are national-scale investors such as life insurance companies and pension funds, which don't have the resources to deal with local real estate markets or day-to-day loan servicing.

4. Some mortgage companies are strictly a broker or strictly a banker, while others may do both; a mortgage banker originates loans, while a mortgage broker is an intermediary who brings a borrower and a lender together for a commission.

F. Government regulation of mortgage lenders

1. Regulators of federally chartered depository institutions include the Federal Reserve System, the Federal Deposit Insurance Corporation, the National Credit Union Administration, the Office of the Comptroller of the Currency, and the Office of Thrift Supervision.

2. The Federal Financial Institutions Examination Council prescribes examination procedures for regular inspection of federally chartered depository institutions.

3. Independent mortgage companies (not subsidiaries or affiliates of banks or thrifts) aren't subject to the same federal regulations as banks or S&Ls, and aren't systematically examined.

G. Alternative sources of financing

1. The most important source of alternative financing for home buyers is home sellers, either through primary or secondary financing.

2. Real estate investment trusts and real estate limited partnerships are another alternative source for financing capital; generally only for builders, not individual home buyers.

IV. Government Intervention in Mortgage Lending

A. The Depression

1. The Depression brought about a wave of defaults and foreclosures; the government enacted a number of reforms during the Depression to fix the mortgage industry, including creation of the Federal Housing Administration.

2. The FHA provided insurance that protected lenders against default, so that lenders were more confident about issuing long-term (20- or 30-year) fully amortized loans.

3. Reforms also included the creation of the Federal National Mortgage Association (Fannie Mae).

B. The savings and loan crisis

1. Savings and loans came to dominate the residential lending market in post-World War II years.

2. S&Ls were able to meet the need for deposit stability required for long-term residential lending, since they only accepted time deposits and savings deposits rather than demand deposits.

3. Deregulation in the early 1980s allowed S&Ls to engage in new investments, many of which were risky and didn't pay off, causing many S&Ls to fail.

4. Congress reformed the S&L industry through the Financial Institutions Reform, Recovery, and Enforcement Act (FIRREA), but fewer S&Ls remained and mortgage companies wound up with a much larger part of the residential lending market.

C. The mortgage market and financial crisis

1. The housing bubble: an artificially high run-up in house prices that peaked around 2006.

2. Various government policies played a role in the housing bubble, mainly by making credit more available and subsidizing some of the costs of ownership.

3. Government actions included the Community Reinvestment Act (a 1977 statute designed to help low- and moderate-income people buy houses), various tax code changes (e.g., the exclusion of gain on sale of principal residence rules), and regulatory changes that helped make more financial institution capital available for lending in the housing market.

4. Lenders fueled the housing bubble by lending aggressively to risky "subprime" borrowers and by allowing underwriting standards to deteriorate—for example, funding borrowers who provided little or no documentation of income.

5. Lenders also made home loans with dangerous features, such as little or no downpayment, low initial interest rates, and negative amortization; many borrowers mistakenly believed that rising house prices would help them escape these onerous loans through a sale or refinance.

D. Government bailouts and oversight

1. In July 2008, the government reacted to the housing bubble collapse with the Housing and Economic Recovery Act (HERA); HERA provisions included funding neighborhood revitalization, reforming FHA lending, and increasing Fannie Mae and Freddie Mac capitalization.

2. In September 2008, the government placed Fannie Mae and Freddie Mac into conservatorship, hoping to shore up investor confidence in these agencies.

3. In October 2008, the government passed a bailout bill called the Troubled Asset Relief Program (TARP), which authorized spending up to $700 billion to buy troubled loans that present a high risk of default from financial institutions, with the goal of stabilizing the mortgage lending industry.

Key Terms

Loan origination: The processing of a loan application from the initial submission of information to the funding of the loan.

Commercial bank: A type of financial institution that traditionally has emphasized commercial lending, but which also makes many residential mortgage loans.

Investment bank: A firm that handles corporate finances, arranges for the issuance of government and corporate bonds, and provides investment advice to clients. Also called a securities firm or stock brokerage.

Savings bank: A type of financial institution that has traditionally emphasized consumer loans and accounts for small depositors, and which also makes mortgage loans. Also called a mutual savings bank or thrift.

Savings and loan association: A type of financial institution that has traditionally specialized in home mortgage loans; also called a savings association or a thrift.

Thrift industry: Savings banks and savings and loan associations.

Credit union: A type of financial institution that serves the members of a particular group, such as a professional organization or labor union. Credit unions have traditionally emphasized consumer loans, and now also make residential mortgage loans.

Mortgage banker: A type of real estate lender that originates loans on behalf of investors or with it's own line of credit; may service loans as well. Also called a mortgage company.

Mortgage broker: An intermediary who brings real estate lenders and borrowers together and negotiates loan arrangements between them.

Loan correspondent: An intermediary who originates or arranges loans on behalf of a wholesale lender or a large investor, and may also service the loans.

S.A.F.E. Mortgage Licensing Act: A federal law enacted in 2008 to implement a national system of licensing and registration for all loan originators.

Federal Housing Administration (FHA): An agency within the Department of Housing and Urban Development that provides mortgage insurance to encourage lenders to make more affordable home loans.

Time deposit: A deposit in a financial institution that is not supposed to be withdrawn until a certain period has elapsed, unless the depositor pays a penalty.

Demand deposit: A deposit in a financial institution that a depositor can withdraw at any time, without notice, such as a deposit in a checking account.

Financial Institutions Reform, Recovery and Enforcement Act (FIRREA): A federal law enacted in 1989 in response to the savings and loan crisis; it reorganized the federal agencies that oversee financial institutions.

Wholesale lending: Loans made by large lenders or investors through loan correspondents or mortgage brokers.

Retail lending: Loan transactions in which the borrower applies directly to the lender, rather than to a loan correspondent or mortgage broker.

Subprime lending: Making riskier loans to borrowers who might otherwise be unable to qualify for a loan, often requiring higher interest rates and fees to make up for the increased risk of default.

Housing and Economic Recovery Act (HERA): A federal law enacted in 2008 to strengthen the housing market by funding neighborhood revitalization, providing capital to the secondary market agencies, adding mortgage disclosure requirements, and offering lower-cost financing to struggling homeowners.

Troubled Asset Relief Program (TARP): A federal law enacted in 2008 to address the U.S. economic crisis, authorizing the expenditure of up to $700 billion in taxpayer funds to buy loans that present a high risk of default from financial institutions, and also to provide financial aid to other sectors of the economy.

Chapter Quiz

1. The 30-year fully amortized loan is now the "standard" loan type. This:

   a. was brought about in the Financial Institutions Reform, Recovery, and Enforcement Act (FIRREA) in 1989

   b. was imposed on lenders by the Garn–St. Germain Act in 1982

   c. occurred as a response to the large numbers of foreclosures that took place during the Depression

   d. happened as a result of the deregulation of financial institutions

2. As a general rule, mortgage companies do not:

   a. keep any loans in portfolio

   b. sell their loans on the secondary market

   c. service loans

   d. accept any type of deposits except demand deposits

3. FIRREA:

   a. deregulated financial institutions

   b. established the secondary market

   c. abolished the Federal Reserve System

   d. was enacted in response to the S&L crisis

4. A depository institution that limits its membership to members of a particular group, such as employees of a large company, is a:

   a. commercial bank

   b. credit union

   c. savings and loan association

   d. savings bank

5. An intermediary that brings together lenders and borrowers and arranges loans for a commission is a:

   a. mortgage banker

   b. mortgage broker

   c. loan servicer

   d. subprime lender

6. In the 21st century, the majority of residential loans are made by:

    a. commercial banks
    b. credit unions
    c. mortgage companies
    d. savings and loan associations

7. A wholesale lender:

    a. originates and services loans
    b. issues loans to high-risk individuals
    c. issues short-term lines of credit to retail lenders
    d. makes loans through a loan correspondent

8. Which of the following borrowers would NOT use the services of a subprime lender?

    a. A person with a low credit rating
    b. A developer needing financing to build a subdivision
    c. A buyer of a nonstandard property that may not provide acceptable collateral
    d. A buyer of an expensive house needing a "jumbo" loan

9. A subprime lender is likely to:

    a. charge higher interest rates because of the greater risk
    b. charge higher interest rates because of the lower risk
    c. charge lower interest rates because of the greater risk
    d. charge lower interest rates because of the lower risk

10. Which type of lender is oriented toward short-term deposits and short-term loans to big business clients, although it may have significant investments in residential mortgages?

    a. Commercial bank
    b. Savings bank
    c. Credit union
    d. Savings and loan association

Answer Key

1. c. The 30-year, fully amortized loan became standard after the Depression, in reaction to the high failure rate for the short-term loans that were common before the Depression.

2. a. Mortgage companies typically do not keep loans in portfolio, but sell them on the secondary market. Mortgage companies are not depository institutions.

3. d. FIRREA was a federal law passed in 1989 in response to the savings and loan crisis, which reformed the thrift industry to provide greater oversight and prevent high-risk transactions.

4. b. A credit union is a depository institution with membership limited to members of a particular group, such as a labor union or professional organization.

5. b. A mortgage broker is an intermediary who helps lender and brokers find each other, in exchange for a commission. By contrast, a mortgage banker originates loans with its own line of credit, usually for the benefit of investors.

6. c. In the wake of the savings and loan crisis and the growth of the secondary market, the majority of residential loans today are made by mortgage companies.

7. d. A wholesale lender is a large investor that makes loans through many loan correspondents, who specialize in local real estate markets and originate loans on the investor's behalf.

8. b. A subprime lender may lend to a person with poor credit, a borrower with an unusual property, or a "jumbo loan" borrower. A real estate developer would probably seek financing from a private investment group, such as a real estate investment trust.

9. a. A subprime lender charges higher interest rates and fees because of the greater risk of default and more intensive servicing associated with such loans.

10. a. A commercial bank is oriented toward demand deposits and short-term commercial loans, although most commercial banks also have large investments in residential mortgages.

Chapter 5
Finance Instruments

Promissory Notes
- Basic provisions
- Negotiability
- Types of notes

Security Instruments
- Purpose
- Historical background
- Mortgages
- Deeds of trust
- Foreclosure
- Alternatives to foreclosure

Finance Instrument Provisions
- Subordination clauses
- Late charge provisions
- Prepayment provisions
- Partial release clauses
- Acceleration clauses
- Alienation clauses and assumptions

Types of Real Estate Loans

Introduction

The "instruments" discussed in this chapter are the legal documents used in real estate finance transactions: promissory notes, mortgages, and deeds of trust. We'll give an overview of how these instruments work, and also explain the provisions commonly found in them.

This chapter is only an introduction to finance instruments, to give you a basic understanding of their purpose and the differences between them. The information presented here should not be used as the basis for personal action or to advise clients or customers. The laws governing creditor-debtor relations vary substantially from one state to another, and they are also subject to change by judicial or legislative action. As a result, it is important to consult an attorney for current, state-specific advice concerning real estate loans and the effect of finance instruments.

Finance instruments:
- Promissory notes
- Mortgages
- Deeds of trust

Promissory Notes

A promissory note is a written promise to pay money. The one who makes the promise (the debtor) is called the **maker** of the note; the one to whom the promise is made (the creditor) is called the **payee**. In a typical real estate loan transaction, the maker is the buyer, who is borrowing money to finance the purchase of property, and the payee is the lender. (Or if the seller is extending credit to the buyer, the payee is the seller.) The promissory note is the basic evidence of the debt; it shows who owes how much money to whom.

Promissory note:
- Maker is borrower
- Payee is lender
- Note is evidence of debt and promise to repay

Basic Provisions of a Note

A promissory note can be a very brief and simple document, as you can see from the example in Figure 5.1. The note states the names of the parties, the amount of the debt (the principal), the interest rate, and how and when the money is to be repaid. It may also specify the maturity date, which is the date by which the loan should be repaid in full.

In addition, the note may include provisions dealing with other rights held by the parties. For example, the note might address the maker's right to prepay the loan, or the payee's remedies if the money is not repaid according to the terms of the agreement. Real estate lenders often protect themselves with late charges, acceleration clauses, and

Fig. 5.1 Simple promissory note

PROMISSORY NOTE

FOR VALUE RECEIVED, Maker promises to pay to the order
of _____ , or to Bearer,

THE SUM OF $_____

PAID AS FOLLOWS: $_____ OR MORE per
month starting _____ , including interest
at _____% per annum.

ACCELERATION: In the event of default, Payee or Bearer
can declare all sums due and payable at once.

Maker/Borrower_____

Date _____

similar provisions, which we'll discuss later in this chapter. Other provisions of the financing agreement between the borrower and lender are found in the mortgage or deed of trust instead of the note.

A promissory note must be signed by the maker, but the payee's signature isn't required. A legal description of the property also isn't required, because the note concerns only the debt, not the property. The legal description appears instead in the mortgage or deed of trust.

Negotiability

Promissory notes used in real estate financing are usually **negotiable instruments**. The Uniform Commercial Code (UCC), which every state has enacted into law in some form, sets forth the requirements for negotiable instruments. Under the UCC, a negotiable instrument is a written, unconditional promise to pay a certain sum of money, on demand or on a certain date; it must be payable "to the order of" a specified person or to the bearer, and it must be signed by the maker. An ordinary check is the most familiar example.

A negotiable instrument is freely transferable. That means the payee can transfer the instrument—and the right to payment that it represents—to a third party. For example, if the payee on a check

A negotiable instrument is
freely transferable

endorses the check and gives it to someone else, the right to cash the check is transferred to that person. Real estate lenders use negotiable promissory notes so that they have the option of selling their notes (and their loans) on the secondary market to obtain immediate cash. (See Chapter 3.)

Without Recourse. If a promissory note or other negotiable instrument is endorsed "without recourse," it means that the issue of future payments is strictly between the maker and the third party the instrument is being endorsed to. The original payee will not be liable if the maker fails to pay as agreed.

Holder in Due Course. If a third party buys a negotiable promissory note from the payee for value, in good faith, and without notice of defenses against it, the third party purchaser is referred to as a holder in due course. The maker of a note is required to pay a holder in due course the amount owed even if there are certain defenses that the maker might have been able to raise against the original payee.

Types of Notes

Promissory notes are sometimes classified according to the way in which the principal and interest are to be paid off. With a **straight note**, the required periodic payments are interest only, and the full amount of the principal is due in a lump sum on the maturity date. With an **installment note**, the periodic payments include part of the principal as well as the interest that has accrued. If an installment note is fully amortized, the periodic payments are enough to pay off all of the principal and interest by the maturity date. Amortization is explained in Chapter 6.

Whether the payments required by the promissory note are interest-only or amortized, the interest paid on a real estate loan is virtually always simple interest. This means that the interest is computed annually on the remaining principal balance. (By contrast, compound interest is computed on the principal amount plus the accrued interest.)

Security Instruments

In a real estate loan transaction, the promissory note is accompanied by a security instrument—either a mortgage or a deed of trust against the borrower's property.

Types of notes:
- Straight note
- Installment note

Note is accompanied by security instrument

The Purpose of Security Instruments

While the note establishes the borrower's obligation to repay the loan, the security instrument makes the property the collateral (the security) for the loan. The security instrument gives the lender the right to foreclose on the property if the borrower doesn't repay the loan as agreed, or fails to fulfill any of the other obligations contained in the security instrument. In a foreclosure, the lender forces the sale of the property and collects the debt out of the sale proceeds.

Security instrument (mortgage or deed of trust) gives lender the right to foreclose

A lender can enforce a promissory note even if it is unsecured—in other words, even if the borrower has not executed a security instrument in the lender's favor. In that situation, if the borrower doesn't repay the loan as agreed in the note, the lender can file a lawsuit and obtain a judgment against the borrower. But without a security instrument and without collateral, the lender (now the judgment creditor) may have no way of collecting the judgment. The borrower might have already sold her property and spent the proceeds, leaving little or nothing for the lender.

A secured lender is in a much better position than an unsecured lender. Since a real estate loan involves a large amount of money, real estate lenders always require borrowers to sign a security instrument to back up the promissory note.

Historical Background

To understand how security instruments work, it may be helpful to know how they developed.

Possession of Collateral. In the earliest forms of secured lending, personal property was used as collateral. A borrower was expected to give the lender some form of valuable personal property (such as jewelry, or perhaps a herd of goats) to hold until the loan was repaid. The lender would actually take possession of the collateral pending repayment. If the loan was not repaid, the lender would keep the collateral. This type of secured lending still exists; pawnshops are the most obvious example.

Hypothecation. Transferring possession of personal property to a lender was a relatively straightforward matter. But when land was used as collateral, a transfer of possession to the lender could be complicated and inconvenient. It was also unnecessary, since the borrower could not move the land or conceal it from the lender. As a result, a practice called hypothecation developed. **Hypothecation**

means pledging property as collateral without giving up possession of it. It became a standard arrangement for a borrower to remain in possession of his land and merely transfer the title to the lender. Once the loan had been repaid, the lender was required to return title to the borrower.

When title to property is transferred only as collateral, unaccompanied by possessory rights, the lender's interest in the property is referred to as **legal title**, or sometimes as naked title. The property rights the borrower retains (without legal title) are referred to as equitable rights or **equitable title**. The original function of mortgages and deeds of trust was to transfer legal title to land from borrower to lender.

Liens. Eventually, in many jurisdictions, a transfer of legal title was no longer considered necessary for the lender's protection. Instead, it became established that a mortgage or deed of trust simply created a **lien** against the borrower's property in favor of the lender. A lien is a financial encumbrance on a property owner's title that allows the lienholder to foreclose on the property to collect a debt.

In some states, referred to as "title theory" states, a security instrument is still considered to transfer legal title to the property to the lender until the loan is paid off. Most states, however, are "lien theory" states, where a security instrument creates a lien and doesn't transfer title. Nowadays, this theoretical distinction has little, if any, practical effect; either way, the security instrument enables the lender to foreclose.

The rights of the lender and the borrower under the terms of a security instrument vary according to the type of instrument used and according to the laws of the state where the property is located. We will look first at the difference between a mortgage and a deed of trust, and then at foreclosure procedures.

Mortgages

Mortgage:
- Mortgagor is borrower
- Mortgagee is lender
- Foreclosure by judicial process

A mortgage is a two-party security instrument in which the borrower (called the **mortgagor**) mortgages his property to the lender (the **mortgagee**). The document must include the names of the parties and an accurate legal description of the mortgaged property, and it must identify the promissory note that it secures.

Covenants. In the mortgage, the mortgagor promises to pay the property taxes, to keep the property insured against fire and other hazards, and to maintain any structures in good repair. These promises are intended to protect the property, so that the mortgagee's security does not lose its value. The mortgagee is allowed to inspect the property periodically to make sure that the mortgagor is maintaining it.

If the mortgagor fails to fulfill these or any other obligations imposed by the mortgage, or fails to pay as agreed in the promissory note, he is in default, and the mortgagee can foreclose.

Recording. After a mortgage is executed, the mortgagee has the document recorded in order to establish the priority of the mortgagee's security interest in the property. As we will discuss shortly, the priority of the mortgagee's security interest will become very important in the event of a foreclosure.

Satisfaction. When a mortgage has been paid off, the mortgagee is required to give the mortgagor a document that releases the property from the mortgage lien. This document is called a satisfaction of mortgage, or sometimes a "satisfaction piece." The mortgagor has the satisfaction document recorded, to provide public notice that the property is no longer encumbered by the mortgage.

Deeds of Trust

The deed of trust (sometimes called a trust deed) is used for the same purpose as a mortgage: to secure the debtor's obligations under a loan agreement. The deed of trust involves three parties rather than two. The borrower is called the **grantor** or **trustor**; the lender is called the **beneficiary**; and there is an independent third party called the **trustee.** The trustee's role is to arrange for the property to be released from the deed of trust when the loan is paid off, or to arrange for foreclosure if necessary.

Deed of trust:
- Grantor is borrower
- Beneficiary is lender
- Trustee is independent third party with power of sale
- Nonjudicial foreclosure

A deed of trust usually includes all of the same basic provisions that are found in a mortgage: the parties, the property, and the promissory note are identified; the grantor promises to pay the taxes and to insure and maintain the property; and the beneficiary has the right to inspect the property. Like a mortgage, a deed of trust should be recorded immediately to establish the priority of the lender's security interest.

When a deed of trust loan has been paid off, the trustee executes a **deed of reconveyance**, releasing the property from the lien. Like a satisfaction of mortgage, the deed of reconveyance is recorded to provide public notice that the property is no longer encumbered by the deed of trust.

Note that the terminology connected with a deed of trust—the fact that the instrument is called a deed, and that the trustee "reconveys" the property to the trustor—reflects its roots in title theory.

Foreclosure

The key difference between mortgages and deeds of trust concerns the procedures the lender must follow in order to foreclose. Since foreclosure procedures vary considerably from state to state, this section will provide only a very general overview.

As you know, lenders frequently sell their loans to other lenders, investors, or secondary market agencies. By the time a borrower goes into foreclosure, the party holding the mortgage or deed of trust may not be the original lender. However, in our discussion of foreclosure, we'll simply refer to the foreclosing party as the "lender."

Traditionally, to foreclose on a mortgage, the lender was required to file a lawsuit against the borrower. If the lender proved that the borrower was in default, a court-ordered auction of the property (called a **sheriff's sale**) was held. The borrower's property was sold to the highest bidder at the auction, and the lender was entitled to the proceeds of the sale. This type of foreclosure process is called **judicial foreclosure**, and it is still used today.

Eventually, in many jurisdictions, an alternative to judicial foreclosure was developed. **Nonjudicial foreclosure** is generally associated with deeds of trust rather than mortgages. When the borrower defaults, the lender is not required to file a lawsuit and obtain a court order to foreclose. Instead, the trustee appointed in the deed of trust arranges for the property to be sold at a **trustee's sale**. Like a sheriff's sale, a trustee's sale is a public auction. The trustee sells the property to the highest bidder on the lender's behalf.

Power of Sale. Because court supervision is not required, nonjudicial foreclosure is generally less expensive and faster than judicial foreclosure. But nonjudicial foreclosure proceedings are permitted only if the security agreement contains a **power of sale** clause. This provision, which is standard in a deed of trust, authorizes the trustee to sell the property if the borrower defaults. In some states, a power of sale clause may also be included in a mortgage, enabling the mortgagee to foreclose nonjudicially.

A typical power of sale clause might read as follows:

> Upon default by Grantor in the payment of any indebtedness secured hereby or in the performance of any agreement contained herein, and upon written request of Beneficiary, Trustee shall sell the trust property, in accordance with the Deed of Trust Act of this state, at public auction to the highest bidder.

In many states, deeds of trust are now more widely used than mortgages, but in many other states mortgages remain the standard real estate security instrument. In some of the states that use mortgages, state law does not permit nonjudicial foreclosure.

In states that do allow nonjudicial foreclosure, a lender may choose to foreclose a deed of trust or mortgage judicially even though the instrument contains a power of sale clause. We'll explain why a lender might prefer judicial foreclosure under certain circumstances after we've discussed the procedures in more detail.

Judicial Foreclosure Procedures. In this section, for simplicity's sake, we'll describe the foreclosure of a mortgage. Keep in mind, however, that the same general procedures would be used for the judicial foreclosure of a deed of trust, if the lender chose judicial foreclosure.

Acceleration. When a mortgagor defaults—either by failing to repay the loan or by breaching covenants in the mortgage—the mortgagee notifies the mortgagor that the entire outstanding loan balance

Judicial foreclosure:
- Acceleration of debt
- Foreclosure lawsuit
- Equitable right of redemption
- Order of execution
- Public notice of sale
- Sheriff's sale
- Statutory right of redemption

Fig. 5.2 Security instruments and foreclosure procedures

Mortgage without power of sale clause
Judicial foreclosure only

Mortgage with power of sale clause
May be foreclosed either judicially or nonjudicially

Deed of trust
Always includes power of sale clause
May be foreclosed either judicially or nonjudicially

(not merely any delinquent payments) must be paid off at once, or the mortgagee will foreclose. This is called **accelerating** the loan; in effect, the due date of the debt is moved up to the present, speeding up repayment. A provision in the mortgage known as an acceleration clause gives the mortgagee the right to demand immediate payment in full in the event of default.

Lawsuit. Not surprisingly, the defaulting mortgagor is usually unable to pay off the entire debt as demanded. (This payoff is especially unlikely if home prices have fallen, since refinancing or selling will net less than the amount owed.) The mortgagee's next step is to initiate a lawsuit, called a foreclosure action, in the county where the property is located. The purpose of this legal proceeding is to ask a judge to order the county sheriff to seize and sell the property. The defendants in the lawsuit are the mortgagor and any junior lienholders—other creditors who have liens against the property that have lower priority than the foreclosing lender's mortgage. The junior lienholders are included in the lawsuit because their security interests are likely to be affected by the foreclosure.

At the same time that the lawsuit is started, the mortgagee has a document called a **lis pendens** recorded. A lis pendens states that the property is subject to a foreclosure action. By recording the lis pendens, the mortgagee provides constructive notice to anyone who might consider buying the property from the mortgagor (or acquiring some other interest in it) that the title may be affected by the pending lawsuit.

Reinstatement vs. equitable redemption. In some states, the mortgagor has a right to "cure" the default during the period when the lawsuit is pending. (In most states, this period is three or four months, though legal filings and scheduling delays can lengthen the time to a year or more.) If the default was a failure to make payments on the loan, the mortgagor can cure it by paying the delinquent amounts, plus interest and whatever costs have been incurred because of the foreclosure (such as court costs and attorneys' fees). If the mortgagor cures the default, the foreclosure is terminated and the loan is reinstated; the parties are back to where they were before the default.

In other states, however, a defaulting mortgagor doesn't have a right to cure and reinstate the loan. But the mortgagor does have an **equitable right of redemption.** This is the right to redeem the property by paying off the entire outstanding loan balance (not just the

Some states allow mortgagor to cure the default and reinstate the loan

Equitable right of redemption: mortgagor can redeem the property before sheriff's sale

Fig. 5.3 Steps in a judicial foreclosure

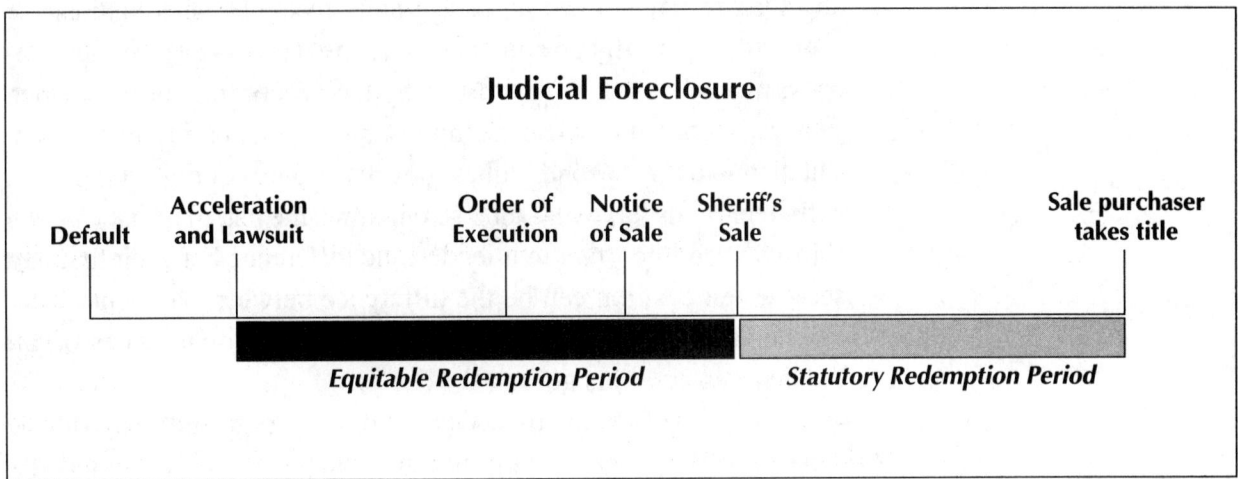

delinquent payments), plus costs incurred as a result of the foreclosure. Redemption stops the foreclosure, satisfies the debt, and terminates the mortgagee's interest in the property. (This is in contrast to a cure, in which the lender and borrower continue their financial relationship.)

Court order and notice of sale. Unless the mortgagor redeems the property (or in those states that allow it, cures and reinstates the loan), the scheduled court hearing in the foreclosure action is held. In most cases, after reviewing the note and mortgage and the facts concerning the default, the judge issues a court order directing the sheriff to seize the property and sell it. This type of court order is often called a **writ of execution**.

Acting under the court order, the sheriff notifies the public of the place and date of the sale. This usually requires posting notices at the property and the courthouse and running an advertisement of the sale in a newspaper circulated in the county. The number of times the ad must be published depends on state law, but the process generally takes several weeks.

In those states where the mortgagor has the right to cure the default and reinstate the loan, that right typically ends as soon as the judge orders the property sold. But the equitable right of redemption lasts until the sheriff's sale is held. The mortgagor can still prevent the sale and redeem the property by paying off the debt, plus costs.

Sheriff's sale. The sheriff's sale (sometimes called an execution sale) is a public auction. It is usually held at the county courthouse, and anyone who wants to bid on the property can attend. The property is sold to the highest bidder, who is given a **certificate of sale.**

Sheriff's sale:
- Public auction
- Foreclosed property sold to highest bidder
- Purchaser gets certificate of sale

The proceeds of the sale are used to pay for the costs of the sale, and then to pay off the mortgage and any other liens against the property. The mortgage and other liens are paid in order of their priority, which is usually established by their recording dates: the lien that was recorded first has the highest priority, and it is paid off first. The lien with the second highest priority is paid off only if there are sufficient funds left over—and so on, down the list. (This is why lien priority is so important to a lender: the difference between first and second lien position can be the difference between payment in full and no payment at all.) If the sale proceeds are enough to pay off all the liens, any surplus goes to the debtor.

If the property sale proceeds are not enough to fully pay off the foreclosed mortgage (usually because the property's value has declined since the loan was made), the shortfall—the difference between the sale proceeds and the amount owed to the lender—is referred to as a deficiency. The court may award the lender a personal judgment against the debtor for the amount of the deficiency. This is called a **deficiency judgment.**

Many states place restrictions on the right of the mortgagee to obtain a deficiency judgment against the mortgagor. For example, some states prohibit a deficiency judgment if the mortgage secured a loan on homestead property (the mortgagor's personal residence). And some states prohibit a deficiency judgment on a purchase money mortgage (a mortgage given by a buyer to a seller).

Post-sale redemption. Following the sale, the debtor (the former mortgagor) will often have an additional period of time to save or redeem the property. To redeem it at this stage, the debtor usually must pay the sale purchaser the amount paid for the property plus accrued interest from the time of the sale. This right to redeem the property following the sheriff's sale is called the **statutory right of redemption**. It's called a statutory right because it was established by the state legislature in a statute. By contrast, the pre-sale right of redemption is referred to as an equitable right because it was originally created by the courts as a matter of equity (fairness).

The length of the statutory redemption period varies from state to state, of course, but it is generally at least six months and sometimes as long as two years. In many states the length of the period may change according to such factors as whether the property is agricultural land, or whether the mortgagee is willing to waive the right to a deficiency judgment.

If sheriff's sale proceeds do not cover the debt, lender may be entitled to deficiency judgment

Statutory right of redemption: mortgagor can redeem the property after the sheriff's sale

Rights of purchaser. The purchaser at the sheriff's sale may be entitled either to take possession of the property or to collect rent from the debtor during the statutory redemption period. However, in some states if the property is homestead property, the debtor is permitted to remain on the property without paying rent. At the end of the statutory redemption period, if the property has not been redeemed, the sheriff's sale purchaser receives a **sheriff's deed** to the property.

Depending on state law concerning notice requirements and redemption, and also on factors such as the number of legal motions filed by the debtor, court congestion, and the availability of the sheriff for foreclosures, judicial foreclosure of a mortgage may take anywhere from a few months to a few years from the time of default until a sheriff's deed is delivered to the purchaser, finally divesting the debtor of title.

Nonjudicial Foreclosure. In this section we'll describe the foreclosure of a deed of trust. But essentially the same procedures would apply to a mortgage with a power of sale clause, if the mortgagee chose nonjudicial foreclosure.

To foreclose a deed of trust nonjudicially, the trustee must follow steps similar to those taken by the sheriff in a judicial foreclosure. The trustee must give notice of the default to the trustor (and in some states must also record the notice of default), and then give notice of the impending sale to the public. As with judicial foreclosure, most states require that this notice of sale be posted at the property and published in a newspaper circulated in the county, so that the greatest number of potential buyers will have an opportunity to attend and bid at the trustee's sale.

Nonjudicial foreclosure:
- Notice of default
- Public notice of sale
- Cure & reinstatement
- Trustee's sale
- No post-sale redemption

After giving the trustor notice of default, the trustee must allow at least a certain length of time to expire before issuing the notice of sale (in most states, the minimum period is between three and six months). There is also a minimum period between the time the notice of sale is issued and the date of the sale (for example, one month). The grantor is allowed to cure the default and reinstate the loan by paying only the delinquent amounts plus costs. The right to cure and reinstate ends shortly before the trustee's sale is held (for example, five days before the sale).

The statutory right of redemption that follows the sheriff's sale in a judicial foreclosure does not apply to a trustee's sale. When the property is sold at the trustee's sale, a **trustee's deed** is given to the

Fig. 5.4 Steps in a nonjudicial foreclosure

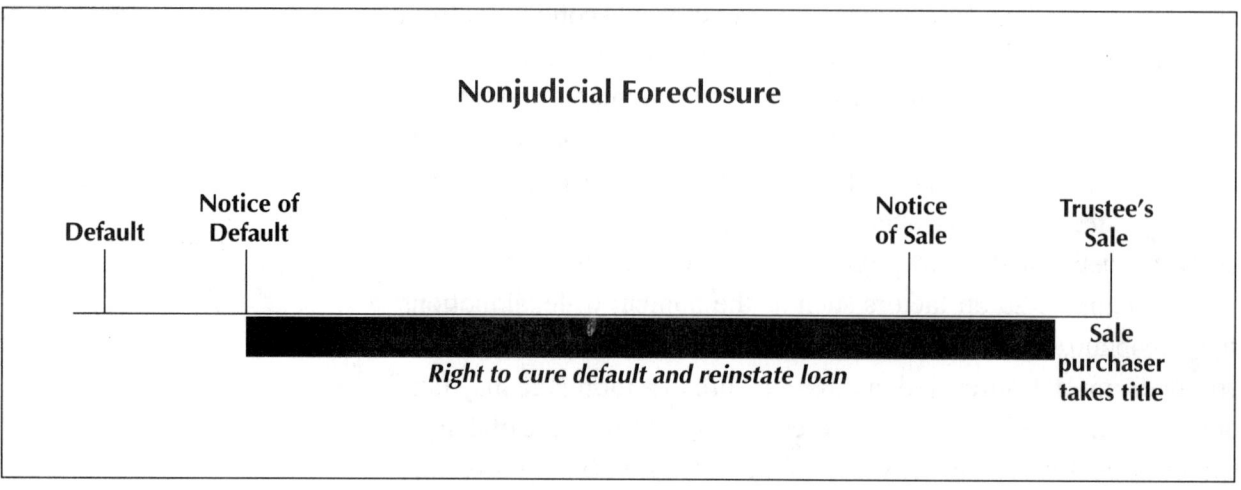

successful bidder. The debtor is immediately divested of title and may have only a short period of time (perhaps 20 or 30 days) to vacate the property. As in a sheriff's sale, the trustee's sale proceeds are first applied to the sale costs, then to the debt and other liens in order of priority, and any surplus is then given to the debtor.

The entire nonjudicial foreclosure process may be accomplished in most states in well under a year (usually around six or seven months) and usually without many of the expenses involved in court proceedings. Naturally, there are expenses connected with a trustee's sale, but they tend to be substantially less than those connected with a court-ordered sheriff's sale. However, the debtor may be entitled to challenge the nonjudicial foreclosure in court, just as with a judicial foreclosure.

Restrictions. Even in states that allow it, a variety of restrictions may be placed on the use of nonjudicial foreclosure; for example, a post-sale redemption period might be required for agricultural property. One standard restriction is that the beneficiary is not allowed to obtain a deficiency judgment after a trustee's sale, even if the sale proceeds were far less than the amount of the debt. However, if the beneficiary chooses to foreclose the deed of trust judicially (just like a mortgage), then all of the procedures and rights relating to judicial foreclosure apply.

Comparing Judicial and Nonjudicial Foreclosure. From a lender's point of view, judicial foreclosure can have two main advantages over nonjudicial foreclosure. The first advantage concerns the difference between the equitable right of redemption and the right to cure and

No deficiency judgment after nonjudicial foreclosure

reinstate. In a nonjudicial foreclosure, the borrower generally has the right to cure the default and reinstate the loan even after the lender has accelerated it. But in a judicial foreclosure, some states do not give the borrower the right to cure and reinstate; the borrower can stop the foreclosure only by exercising the equitable right of redemption and paying off the entire debt. Thus, with judicial foreclosure the lender is not required to continue its relationship with a borrower who has proved unreliable.

The second advantage of judicial foreclosure for the lender is the right to obtain a deficiency judgment against the borrower if the property does not bring enough at the sheriff's sale to satisfy the debt. In cases where the property has lost value since the loan was made, the lender is likely to protect itself by choosing judicial foreclosure.

The main advantage of nonjudicial foreclosure for the lender is that it is fairly quick and inexpensive compared to judicial foreclosure. It is because of this advantage that deeds of trust have almost completely replaced mortgages in about two-thirds of the states. And in many states where mortgages are still the dominant real estate security instrument, it's now common or even standard for a mortgage to have a power of sale clause.

The advantages and disadvantages of the two forms of foreclosure for the borrower correspond to those for the lender, but in reverse. From the borrower's point of view, the right to cure the default and reinstate the loan is an important advantage of nonjudicial foreclosure. Without that right, a home buyer who misses just a couple of loan payments may be faced with the prospect of having to pay off the debt completely in order to save the home. On the other hand, in a judicial foreclosure the borrower usually has a long time to get the money together to pay off the debt, because of the slow court proceedings and the statutory redemption period.

Alternatives to Foreclosure

A homeowner who can no longer make the payments on her mortgage may have alternatives to foreclosure, even if the property is worth less than the amount owed (making it impossible to sell the property for enough to pay off the mortgage). There are three basic alternatives to foreclosure: loan workouts, deeds in lieu of foreclosure, and short sales. A lender may agree to forego foreclosure and take one of these other paths in order to save on attorney fees and court costs, as well as to put an end to a money-losing situation with relative speed.

Loan Workouts. A borrower hoping to avoid foreclosure typically begins by requesting a loan workout from the lender or loan servicer. Some workouts involve a repayment plan—a simple adjustment in the timing of payments. The borrower gets extra time to make up a missed payment or is allowed to skip a few payments, with the skipped payments added on to the repayment period. This is all the relief that some borrowers need.

Homeowners in more severe financial distress should seek an actual modification in their loan terms. Typical loan modifications include switching an ARM to a fixed-rate mortgage (to prevent it from resetting to a higher rate), reducing the interest rate, and reducing the amount of principal owed.

Deed in Lieu of Foreclosure. If the borrower can't negotiate a satisfactory loan workout and must give up the property, he can offer the lender a deed in lieu of foreclosure (often simply called "a deed in lieu"). With a deed in lieu, the borrower deeds the property to the lender and this satisfies the debt.

Giving the lender a deed in lieu is a simpler and less public process than foreclosure. However, the borrower's credit rating will suffer nearly as much as with a foreclosure (this is also true of a short sale, discussed below). Typically, the borrower's credit record bears a notation such as "Settlement of Debt for Less than Full Amount" (as opposed to "Paid in Full").

Since the lender is typically receiving title to a property that is worth less than the outstanding balance on the loan, the lender may want the borrower to sign a promissory note to cover any shortfall that results when the lender later sells the property. Obviously, the borrower will want to negotiate a solution with the lender that avoids this.

A lender who accepts a deed in lieu of foreclosure takes title subject to any liens against the property (such as second mortgages). Thus, lenders almost never agree to accept a deed in lieu if there are junior liens of any significant dollar amount against the property. The lender would prefer to proceed with foreclosure, a process that extinguishes junior liens, rather than risk having to pay off the junior lienholders.

Loan workout:
- Repayment plan, or
- Modification of terms

Deed in lieu: borrower deeds property to lender to satisfy debt

Short Sales. As an alternative to a deed in lieu, an owner facing foreclosure may seek the lender's consent to a short sale. In a short sale, the owner sells the house for whatever it will bring (something "short" of the amount owed because the home's value has decreased). The lender receives the sale proceeds and, in return, releases the borrower from the debt. As when arranging a deed in lieu, the borrower will want to make sure that the lender doesn't have the right to sue for a deficiency following the sale.

The existence of secondary liens won't necessarily prevent a lender from approving a short sale. This is because—unlike with a deed in lieu—the lender isn't taking responsibility for the property or its liens. However, the presence of multiple liens will complicate matters, since all of the lienholders must consent to the sale. The junior lienholders (or creditors) aren't likely to get much if anything from a short sale and may not be willing to approve the transaction. In this situation, a foreclosure may be inevitable.

Let's look at the process of obtaining consent from a lender for one of these alternatives to foreclosure.

Obtaining Lender Consent. Homeowners seeking a loan workout, deed in lieu of foreclosure, or short sale will usually negotiate with their loan servicer, if there is one; otherwise, they will seek approval directly from the lender. The process can be challenging in the best of circumstances. Financial institutions often have various departments that must each give independent approval to a foreclosure alternative. If there is more than one lender, the situation becomes even more complex.

Some lenders won't consider any type of loan workout until the borrower is at least 90 days behind on the loan payments. In any case, the borrower will have to demonstrate financial hardship—that is, a genuine inability to meet the mortgage payments. The borrower will have to fill out an application and provide copies of pay stubs, bank statements, bills, and so on.

Borrowers who want help with what can be a lengthy and frustrating process can contact nonprofit housing counseling services. Alternatively, borrowers can hire a professional mortgage negotiator. A number of real estate licensees now provide this service. (Note that many states have recently passed legislation regulating distressed

> Short sale: lender agrees to accept proceeds of sale to satisfy debt, even if proceeds are less than amount owed

property consultants, entities who offer services to property owners who are on the brink of foreclosure.)

Unfortunately, sometimes a lender cannot agree to one of these foreclosure alternatives, even though it makes financial sense to do so. As we mentioned in Chapter 3, many mortgages have been securitized (that is, grouped together in a pool, with portions of the pool then sold off to investors). Many of the contracts governing the sale of these mortgage-backed securities to investors include guarantees promising that few (if any) of the pooled loans can be modified without investor consent. (Accepting a deed in lieu or a short sale constitutes modifying the terms of a loan.) Obtaining consent from all the investors for changes to each individual loan just isn't practical. Thus, the holder of a securitized mortgage that goes into default may have no legal choice but to foreclose. So far, neither the mortgage industry nor regulators have been able to figure out a complete solution to this problem.

Income Tax Implications. Loan workouts, deeds in lieu, and short sales all result in borrowers owing less money than they originally agreed to pay their lender. This reduction of debt is known as **debt relief**. Generally, the IRS treats debt relief as taxable income. In other words, the taxpayer will have to pay income tax on the amount of debt that was forgiven. This IRS treatment of debt relief may seem a little surprising, but keep in mind that the borrower had the use of the debt to buy or improve a house, and also got to deduct the interest paid on the debt from his income.

At any rate, many homeowners now qualify for an exception to this taxation rule. Under the Mortgage Forgiveness Debt Relief Act of 2007, a taxpayer's forgiven debt isn't treated as income provided the debt was:

- secured by the taxpayer's principal residence,
- used to improve the principal residence, and
- forgiven during the years 2007 through 2009.

Note that even if the taxpayer doesn't meet these requirements, some or all of the debt relief won't count as income if the borrower was insolvent at the time of the forgiveness. A person is insolvent if his liabilities exceed his assets. If a borrower was suffering financial distress severe enough to justify debt forgiveness, demonstrating insolvency may not be difficult.

Debt relief: a reduction of debt, as in a successful short sale; usually taxable as income

Finance Instrument Provisions

This section of the chapter covers a variety of important provisions that may appear in real estate finance instruments. Some of them are used only in certain types of transactions; others are virtually always used. Depending on the transaction, the rights and responsibilities of the borrower and the lender may be affected by:

- a subordination clause,
- a late charge provision,
- a prepayment provision,
- a partial release clause,
- an acceleration clause, and/or
- an alienation (due-on-sale) clause.

Clauses often found in finance instruments:
- Subordination
- Late charge
- Prepayment
- Partial release
- Acceleration
- Alienation

Subordination Clauses

Ordinarily, the priority among mortgages and deeds of trust is determined by the date of recording: the first one recorded has first lien position, the highest priority. In some situations, however, the parties may want to give an instrument that was recorded later priority over one that was recorded earlier.

This is particularly common in construction financing. In many cases a developer who applies for a construction loan has already borrowed money to purchase the land that's going to be built on, so a mortgage or deed of trust against the property has already been recorded. But because construction loans involve some extra risk, lenders usually refuse to make a construction loan unless they can be assured of first lien position. In order for the later construction loan mortgage or deed of trust to take priority over the earlier instrument, the earlier instrument must contain a subordination clause.

A **subordination clause** states that the security instrument in which it appears will be **subordinate** (junior) to another security instrument that is to be recorded later.

Subordination clause gives mortgage recorded earlier lower priority than another mortgage that will be recorded later

Lender agrees that this instrument shall be subordinate to a lien to be given by Borrower to secure funds for the construction of improvements on the Property, provided said lien is duly recorded and the amount secured by said lien does not exceed $125,000.

Inclusion of a subordination clause must be negotiated at the time of the earlier transaction (in our example, when the developer bought the land and the earlier security instrument was signed). If a subordination clause was not included in the earlier security instrument, the earlier lender might be willing to sign a separate subordination agreement later on. A prudent developer wouldn't count on that, however.

Subordination profoundly affects the strength of both lenders' security interests, so any subordination provision should be drafted or reviewed by a real estate lawyer.

Late Charge Provisions

In real estate loan transactions, the promissory note usually provides for late charges if the borrower doesn't make the payments on time. A lender typically allows for a grace period after the payment's actual due date, but if the payment hasn't reached the lender by the time the grace period expires, a late fee will be added to the amount overdue.

State laws protecting borrowers from excessive late charges and unfair collection practices may override provision in note

Many states have laws that protect borrowers by limiting excessive late charges and prohibiting unfair collection practices. For example, lenders generally aren't permitted to charge more than one late fee on a single overdue payment, even if the payment remains overdue for more than one month.

Prepayment Provisions

Some promissory notes have a provision that imposes a penalty on the borrower if she repays some or all of the principal before it is due. This is called **prepaying** the loan. Prepayment deprives the lender of some of the interest it expected to receive on its investment over the loan term. In effect, a prepayment penalty compensates the lender for the lost interest.

Prepayment charge imposed if loan repaid early, to compensate lender for lost interest

As an example, the following provision imposes a penalty if the borrower prepays more than 20% of the original loan amount in one of the first five years of the loan term. If the borrower's prepayment exceeds that limit, the borrower is required to pay the lender 3% of the original loan amount as a penalty.

> If, within five years from the date of this note, Borrower makes any prepayments of principal in excess of twenty percent of the original principal amount in any twelve-month period beginning with the date of this note or anniversary dates thereof ("loan year"), Borrower shall pay the Note Holder three percent of the original principal amount.

Prepayment penalties are no longer standard in residential loan agreements. The Fannie Mae/Freddie Mac promissory note used for most conventional loans specifically gives the borrower the right to prepay without penalty. Prepayment penalties are also prohibited in connection with FHA and VA loans.

Although prepayment penalties aren't standard, some lenders offer reduced loan fees or a lower interest rate in exchange for including a prepayment provision in the promissory note. While this can be a reasonable arrangement, the borrower should carefully consider the consequences before agreeing to a prepayment penalty.

In connection with a residential loan, a prepayment penalty (if any) is usually charged only if the loan is prepaid during the first few years of the loan term, as in the example above. The borrower should find out how many years the prepayment penalty provision will be in effect. He also needs to ask under what circumstances the penalty will be charged. Will he have to pay the penalty if the loan is paid off early because he has sold the property? What if he refinances? And how much will the penalty be?

Charging a heavy prepayment penalty or including other unreasonable terms is considered a predatory lending practice (see Chapter 14). Some states have laws limiting the amount of prepayment penalties and restricting how they can be imposed.

Unreasonable prepayment penalties are considered predatory

Partial Release Clauses

A partial release clause in a mortgage is often called a partial satisfaction clause; in a deed of trust, it's often called a partial reconveyance clause. This provision obligates the lender to release part of the property from the lien when part of the debt has been paid.

Example: The Harveys borrowed money to purchase five acres of land. Their mortgage includes a partial satisfaction clause. The clause states that when the borrowers have repaid 25% of the loan amount, the lender will release one acre of their land from the mortgage lien.

Partial release: part of the property is released from lien when part of debt is paid

A partial release clause is typically included in a mortgage or deed of trust covering a subdivision that is in the process of being developed and sold. When the developers find a buyer for a lot, they pay the lender a specified portion of the loan amount to have that lot released from the lien. The clause permits them to acquire clear title to that lot and convey it to the buyer, without having to pay off the whole loan.

> Upon payment of all sums due with respect to any lot subject to this lien, Lender shall release said lot from the lien at no cost to Borrower.

Acceleration Clauses

Almost all promissory notes, mortgages, and deeds of trust contain an acceleration clause. As we explained earlier, this provision allows the lender to accelerate the debt: that is, to declare the entire outstanding balance immediately due and payable if the borrower defaults.

Acceleration: upon default, lender may declare entire debt due immediately

This means that a borrower who misses even one payment might discover the next month that he owes not just two payments, but rather the entire remaining balance. In practice, though, most lenders wait until payments are at least 90 days delinquent before accelerating a loan. In an effort to aid distressed homeowners, several states have enacted laws requiring lenders to wait for various periods of time before accelerating a loan or taking other foreclosure steps.

Here is a typical acceleration clause:

> In case the Mortgagor [or Trustor] fails to pay any installment of principal or interest secured hereby when due or to keep or perform any covenant or agreement aforesaid, then the whole indebtedness hereby secured shall become due and payable, at the election of the Mortgagee [or Beneficiary].

Keep in mind that a lender's right to accelerate a loan is effectively limited when state law gives the borrower the right to cure the default and reinstate the loan.

Alienation Clauses and Assumptions

In the real estate context, **alienation** refers to transfer of ownership. An alienation clause (often called a **due-on-sale** clause) in a security instrument is designed to limit the borrower's right to transfer title to the property without the lender's permission, unless the loan is paid off first.

To understand the purpose of an alienation clause, let's look first at what happens if a borrower transfers the security property without paying off the loan. There are essentially three possibilities:

- the new owner may simply take title subject to the loan;
- there may be an assumption of the loan by the new owner without a release of the original borrower; or
- there may be an assumption and release.

Whenever ownership of real property is transferred, the new owner takes title **subject to** any existing liens, including an existing mortgage or deed of trust. The lender still has the power to foreclose on the property, in spite of the transfer of ownership.

The new owner may or may not agree to **assume** the loan. In an assumption, the new owner (the assumptor) takes on legal responsibility for repaying the loan. But unless the lender agrees to a release, the original borrower (the former owner) remains secondarily liable to the lender even after an assumption. If there is a foreclosure and the lender obtains a deficiency judgment, the original borrower can be forced to pay it if the assumptor does not.

Buyer who assumes loan takes on primary liability, but unreleased seller remains secondarily liable

Even though the original borrower is still liable to the lender after selling the property, the transfer of ownership may increase the lender's risk. The new owner could be a much worse credit risk than the original borrower, or might allow the security property to deteriorate. So the lender wants some control over transfer of the property, to ensure that any new owner is no more likely to default than the original borrower.

An alienation clause gives the lender that control. Most alienation clauses are triggered not only by a complete transfer of ownership, but also by the transfer of any significant interest in the property (including a long-term lease or any lease with an option to purchase). In the event of a transfer, the clause usually gives the lender the right to declare the entire loan balance due immediately—hence the name

Alienation clause allows lender to call in the loan if borrower transfers an interest in the property "due-on-sale" clause. This is acceleration of the loan triggered by transfer, instead of by default.

> If all or any part of the Property or an interest therein is sold or transferred by Borrower without Lender's prior written consent, Lender may, at Lender's option, declare all the sums secured by this instrument to be immediately due and payable.

If the lender is not satisfied with the person the borrower intends to sell the property to, the lender cannot forbid the sale; but it can require the borrower to pay off the loan rather than allowing the new owner to assume it.

If the proposed buyer is a good credit risk, the lender is likely to approve the assumption. The lender may reset the loan's interest rate, charging the buyer a rate between the loan's original rate and the current market rate. This is sometimes called a "blended rate." The lender will also charge an **assumption fee**, which may be as substantial as a loan origination fee—for example, 1.5% of the loan balance.

Alienation clauses are now standard in residential security instruments. They appear in the security instruments used by Fannie Mae and Freddie Mac for conventional loans, and also in the security instruments used in FHA and VA loan transactions. However, some recent loans and many older loans do not have alienation clauses. To find out whether a seller's loan can be assumed without the lender's approval or whether it contains an alienation clause, contact the lender.

When the lender's consent to a sale is required, it should be obtained in the form of an **estoppel letter**. An estoppel letter acknowledges the transfer of ownership and waives the lender's right to accelerate the loan on account of the transfer. By writing the letter, the lender is estopped (legally prevented) from later trying to enforce the alienation clause based on this sale.

An estoppel letter is often requested even in a transaction where the security instrument for the seller's existing loan does not contain an alienation clause. The lender is asked to state in the estoppel letter the amount of the outstanding principal balance, and also to acknowledge that the loan is not in default. The buyer then has written confirmation of the amount and the status of the obligation she is planning to assume or take title subject to.

Lender that allows assumption may raise interest rate

Estoppel letter:
- Acknowledges transfer and waives due-on-sale clause, or
- States balance and status of loan without any change in the existing loan's terms

122

When taking a listing, a real estate agent should ask the seller about the existing financing and consider whether offering assumption might be a good marketing tool. If the seller would like to offer assumption, the lender should be asked for an estoppel letter. (Note that many lenders charge a fee for preparation of an estoppel letter.) If an assumption of the seller's loan is eventually arranged, both parties—the seller and the buyer—should obtain legal advice, and the agreement should be drawn up by a lawyer.

Types of Real Estate Loans

Real estate finance terminology includes many terms for various types of mortgage loans—terms that describe the status, purpose, or function of different loans. We'll end this chapter with a review of some of the most common of these terms.

In accordance with general usage, we often use "mortgage" or "mortgage loan" to refer to any loan secured by real property, whether the security instrument actually used is a mortgage or a deed of trust. Keep in mind that in many states a deed of trust could be (and perhaps usually would be) used instead of a mortgage to make any of these types of loans.

Junior or Senior Mortgage. A **junior mortgage** is one that has lower lien priority than another mortgage (or deed of trust) against the same property. In relation to the junior mortgage, the mortgage with higher lien priority may be called a **senior mortgage**. A senior mortgage with first lien position is called a **first mortgage**; a junior mortgage may be referred to as a second mortgage or third mortgage, depending on its relative lien priority. And sometimes you'll hear a junior mortgage called a subordinate mortgage.

Senior mortgage has higher lien priority than junior mortgage

A property may become encumbered with two mortgages (or maybe even more than two) in a number of different situations. When property is purchased, a junior mortgage loan may provide secondary financing to supplement the primary loan that's secured by the first mortgage. (Secondary financing is discussed in Chapters 6 and 13.) A land purchase mortgage that has been subordinated to a construction mortgage is another example of a junior mortgage. And many junior mortgages secure home equity loans (see below).

As we discussed earlier, foreclosure of a mortgage affects any junior liens against the property. If a property has a senior mortgage and a junior mortgage against it and the senior lender forecloses, the foreclosure extinguishes the lien of the junior mortgage. The junior lender will be paid only after the senior lender has been paid in full. If the foreclosure sale proceeds aren't sufficient to pay off the senior lender and the other lienholders with higher priority, the junior lender receives no share of the proceeds. The junior lender could still sue the debtor, but the junior loan is now an unsecured loan.

If a junior mortgage is foreclosed on, the foreclosure sale purchaser takes title to the property subject to the lien of the senior mortgage. Foreclosure on the junior mortgage does not extinguish the senior mortgage.

Purchase Money Mortgage. This term is used in two ways. Sometimes it means any mortgage loan used to finance the purchase of the property that is the collateral for the loan. So when a buyer borrows money to buy property and gives the lender a mortgage on that same property to secure the loan, that may be referred to as a purchase money mortgage.

In other cases, "purchase money mortgage" is used more narrowly, to mean a mortgage that a buyer gives to a seller in a seller-financed transaction. Instead of paying the full price in cash at closing, the buyer gives the seller a mortgage on the property and pays the price off in installments.

> **Example:** The sales price is $180,000. The buyer makes a $20,000 downpayment and signs a promissory note and purchase money mortgage in favor of the seller for the remaining $160,000. The buyer will pay the seller in monthly installments at 7% interest over the next 15 years.

Purchase money mortgages used for seller financing are covered in Chapter 13.

Home Equity Loan. A property owner can obtain a mortgage loan using her equity in property that she already owns as collateral. This is called an **equity loan**; when the property is the borrower's residence, it's called a **home equity loan**.

A property owner's equity is the difference between the property's current market value and the liens against it. In other words, it's the portion of the property's value that the owner owns free and clear—the

Purchase money mortgage:
- Any mortgage loan used to purchase the security property, or
- Seller financing

Home equity loan: a loan secured by a mortgage against the borrower's equity in a home he already owns portion that is available to serve as collateral for another loan. With an equity loan, the lender agrees to loan a sum of money to the property owner in exchange for a second mortgage against the property.

> **Example:** The Hutchinsons bought their house six years ago for $260,000, making a $20,000 downpayment and borrowing $240,000 for the purchase. Naturally, the loan is secured with a mortgage against the house.
>
> The Hutchinsons' house has appreciated since they bought it, and it's worth about $280,000 in the current market. The balance due on the mortgage is now $223,000. So the Hutchinsons' equity is $57,000 ($280,000 – $223,000 = $57,000).
>
> When the Hutchinsons have some unexpected expenses, they apply to a lender for a $15,000 home equity loan. To provide security for the loan, they sign a deed of trust that gives the lender a junior lien against their property.

In some cases, a home equity loan is used to finance remodeling or other improvements to the property. In other cases, it's used for expenses unrelated to the property. It's not uncommon for a home equity loan to be used to pay off credit cards, for example. The interest rate on the home equity loan is often much lower than the rate on the credit cards, and the interest on the loan is usually deductible, whereas the credit card interest is not. (Mortgage interest is currently the only type of interest on consumer debt that is deductible.)

The interest rates charged on home equity loans are higher than the rates on home purchase loans. Since a home equity loan is a second mortgage, it represents a greater risk to the lender (see the discussion of junior mortgages, above). The higher interest rate compensates the lender for the additional risk.

Instead of having to apply for a home equity loan, some homeowners have a **home equity line of credit** (or **HELOC**) that they can draw on when the need arises. This works in much the same way as a credit card—with a credit limit and minimum monthly payments based on the amount borrowed—except that the debt is automatically secured by the borrower's home. The line of credit is a revolving credit account, in contrast to the home equity loan, which is an installment loan with regular payments made over a certain term.

Refinance Mortgage. Borrowers who refinance their mortgage loan are actually obtaining an entirely new loan to replace the existing one. Funds from the refinance loan are used to pay off the existing loan.

Refinancing: a new loan that's used to pay off an existing mortgage against the same property

Depending on the situation, refinancing may be arranged with the same lender that made the existing loan, or with a different lender.

Borrowers often choose to refinance when market interest rates drop; refinancing at a lower interest rate can result in substantial savings over the long run. However, they must take into account the loan fee, appraisal fee, and other expenses connected with the refinancing; these can add up to thousands of dollars. Refinancing to take advantage of lower interest rates may not make financial sense if it would take more than two or three years to recover the cost of the refinancing.

Another situation in which a borrower is likely to refinance is when the payoff date of the existing mortgage is approaching and a large balloon payment will be required. (See the discussion of partial amortization in Chapter 6.) Funds from the refinance loan will be used to make that balloon payment.

While a basic refinance loan is for no more than the amount needed to pay off the existing mortgage and cover the refinancing costs, borrowers who have a significant amount of equity when they refinance may have the option of a "cash-out" refinance loan. With cash-out refinancing, the loan amount is more than the amount of the existing mortgage balance plus the refinancing costs, so that the borrowers also receive some cash from the refinance lender. This is another way for homeowners to tap into their equity. As with a home equity loan, the cash from the refinancing may be used for remodeling or other improvements, or for expenses unrelated to the property.

Bridge Loan. It often happens that buyers are ready to purchase a new home before they've succeeded in selling their current home. They need funds for their downpayment and closing costs right away, without waiting for the proceeds from the eventual sale of the current home. In this situation, the buyers may be able to obtain a **bridge loan**. A bridge loan is secured by equity in the property that is for sale, and it will be paid off when that sale closes. In most cases, a bridge loan calls for interest-only payments (see Chapter 6), and the principal is due when the loan is paid off. A bridge loan may also be called a **swing loan** or a **gap loan**.

Bridge loan provides cash for purchase of a new home pending sale of the old home

Budget Mortgage. The monthly payment on a budget mortgage includes not just principal and interest on the loan, but one-twelfth of the year's property taxes and hazard insurance premiums as well.

Budget mortgage: monthly payments include property taxes and hazard insurance

The lender keeps these tax and insurance payments in an **impound account** (also called a reserve account or escrow account) and pays the taxes and the insurance premiums out of the account when they come due. Most residential loans are secured by budget mortgages. This is the safest and most practical way for lenders to make sure the property taxes and insurance premiums are paid on time.

The payments on a budget mortgage are often referred to as PITI payments. PITI stands for principal, interest, taxes, and insurance.

Package Mortgage. When personal property and real property are financed with a single mortgage loan, it's called a package mortgage.

> Package mortgage is secured by personal property as well as real property

> **Example:** A restaurant building on a city lot is being sold. The buyer also wants to purchase the restaurant equipment (ovens, freezers, and so on) that's in the building. The equipment is considered to be personal property, not fixtures. The buyer's purchase of this personal property along with the real property could be financed with a package mortgage.

Alternatively, a buyer may finance personal property separately from the real property, obtaining a separate loan either from the same lender or from a different lender. In that situation, in addition to executing a mortgage that creates a security interest in the real property, the buyer executes a **security agreement** that creates a security interest in the personal property. Under the Uniform Commercial Code, a lender with a security interest in personal property provides public notice and establishes the priority of that interest by filing a **financing statement** in the office of the Secretary of State in the state where the transaction takes place. The financing statement serves the same purpose in regard to personal property that a recorded mortgage or deed of trust serves for real property.

A key advantage of using a package mortgage, instead of financing the personal property separately, is that the mortgage term is usually much longer than the term of an ordinary loan for personal property. So the package mortgage allows the borrower to pay for the personal property over a longer period. In addition, the interest rate on the mortgage may be lower than the rate for a personal property loan, and the interest paid will be tax-deductible. (Normally, interest on a personal property loan is only deductible if the property is used in a trade or business or for investment.)

Blanket mortgage:
- Secured by more than one parcel of land
- Partial release clause

Blanket Mortgage. Sometimes a borrower mortgages two or more pieces of property as security for one loan. For example, a ten-acre parcel subdivided into twenty lots might be used to secure one loan made to the subdivider. Blanket mortgages usually have a partial release clause (also called a partial satisfaction clause, or in a deed of trust, a partial reconveyance clause). As we discussed earlier, this provision requires the lender to release some of the security property from the blanket lien when a specified portion of the overall debt has been paid off.

> **Example:** A ten-acre parcel subdivided into twenty lots secures a $500,000 loan. After selling one lot for $50,000, the subdivider pays the lender $45,000 and receives a release for the lot that is being sold. The blanket mortgage is no longer a lien against that lot, so the subdivider can convey clear title to the lot buyer.

The properties covered by a blanket mortgage do not have to be contiguous or neighboring parcels. A borrower who owns pieces of land in two different counties could offer both pieces of land as collateral for a single blanket mortgage loan. (To fully protect the lender's security interest, the blanket mortgage document would have to be recorded in both counties.)

Construction loan: temporary financing that provides funds for construction until project is completed

Construction Loan. A construction loan (sometimes called an **interim loan**) is a short-term loan used to finance the construction of improvements on land already owned by the borrower. The mortgage for this type of loan creates a lien against both the land and the improvements under construction.

Construction loans can be very profitable, but they are considered risky. Accordingly, lenders charge high interest rates and loan fees on construction loans, and they supervise the progress of the construction. There is always a danger that the borrower will overspend on the construction project and exhaust the loan proceeds before construction is completed. If the borrower cannot afford to finish, the lender is left with a security interest in a partially completed project.

Lenders have devised a number of plans for disbursement of construction loan proceeds that guard against overspending by the borrower. Perhaps the most common is the **fixed disbursement plan**. This calls for a series of predetermined disbursements, called **obligatory advances**, at various stages of construction. Interest begins to accrue with the first disbursement.

Example: The construction loan agreement stipulates that the lender will release 10% of the proceeds when the project is 20% complete, and thereafter 20% draws will be available whenever construction has progressed another 20% toward completion.

The lender will often hold back 10% or more of the loan proceeds until the period for claiming construction liens (mechanic's or materialmen's liens) has expired, to protect against unpaid liens that could affect the marketability of the property. The construction loan agreement usually states that if a valid construction lien is recorded, the lender may use the undisbursed portion of the loan to pay it off.

When the construction is completed, the construction loan is replaced by permanent financing that is called a **take-out loan**. The borrower then repays the amount borrowed, plus interest, over a specified term, as with an ordinary mortgage.

Nonrecourse Mortgage. A nonrecourse mortgage is one that gives the lender no recourse against the borrower. That means the lender's only remedy in the event of default is foreclosure on the collateral property; the borrower is not personally liable for repayment of the loan.

A loan may be a nonrecourse mortgage for one of two reasons. The loan contract itself may provide that the lender will have no recourse against the borrower in the event of default. Or, as we discussed earlier in this chapter, state law may prevent the lender from obtaining a deficiency judgment against the borrower. In either case, the loan may be considered a nonrecourse mortgage.

Participation Mortgage. A participation mortgage allows the lender to participate in the earnings generated by the mortgaged property, usually in addition to collecting interest payments on the principal. In some cases the lender participates by becoming a part-owner of the property. Participation loans are most common on large commercial projects where the lender is an insurance company or other large investor.

Shared Appreciation Mortgage. Real property usually appreciates (increases in value), given sufficient time. Appreciation normally benefits only the property owner, by adding to her equity. With a shared appreciation mortgage, however, the lender is entitled to a specified share of the increase in the property's value. This type of mortgage is rare, especially during times when home prices are flat or falling.

Nonrecourse mortgage:
- Lender can't sue borrower
- Foreclosure is lender's only remedy

Participation mortgage entitles lender to a share of the property's earnings

Shared appreciation mortgage entitles lender to a share of increases in property's value

Fig. 5.5 Types of mortgage loans

- **Junior or Senior**
  Refers to lien priority

- **Purchase Money**
  Used to buy security property

- **Home Equity**
  Secured by equity in property already owned

- **Refinance**
  New loan used to pay off old

- **Bridge**
  Provides cash for purchase of new home pending sale of old

- **Budget**
  Payments include share of taxes and insurance

- **Package**
  Secured by both personal and real property

- **Blanket**
  Secured by multiple parcels

- **Construction**
  Temporary loan funds project until completed

- **Nonrecourse**
  Foreclosure is lender's only remedy

- **Participation**
  Lender receives share of property's earnings

- **Shared Appreciation**
  Lender receives share of equity

- **Wraparound**
  Underlying loan is still being paid off

- **Reverse Equity**
  Elderly owner receives payments from lender

Nonetheless, some suggest that shared appreciation mortgages could play a role in helping to correct the housing market downturn. Analysts note that if the government provides direct financial aid to troubled homeowners, a shared appreciation arrangement might eventually provide a return to taxpayers in exchange for the tax dollars spent.

Wraparound mortgage is a form of seller financing

Wraparound Mortgage. A wraparound mortgage is a new mortgage that includes or "wraps around" an existing first mortgage on the property. Wraparounds are used almost exclusively in seller-financed transactions, and we will discuss them in detail in Chapter 13.

Reverse equity mortgage provides elderly homeowners with a source of income, without requiring them to sell their home

Reverse Equity Mortgage. A reverse equity mortgage, sometimes called a reverse annuity mortgage or simply a reverse mortgage, is designed to provide income to older homeowners. With this type of loan, a homeowner borrows against the home's equity but will receive a monthly check from the lender, rather than making monthly payments. This can make it possible for an elderly person who might otherwise have to sell his home (and invest the proceeds to obtain a source of income) to keep the home.

Typically, a reverse equity borrower is required to be over a certain age (for example, 62 or 65) and must own the home with little or no outstanding mortgage balance. The home usually must be sold when the owner dies in order to pay back the mortgage. The amount of the monthly payment from the lender depends on the appraised value of the home, the age of the homeowner, the interest charged, and the terms of repayment.

Outline: Finance Instruments

I. Promissory Notes

    A. A promissory note is basic evidence of a borrower's legal obligation to pay a debt.

        1. The debtor (usually a buyer) is the maker of the note; the creditor (the lender) is the payee.

        2. The note will specify the names of the parties, the amount of debt, the interest rate, and how and when the money will be repaid.

    B. The promissory notes used in real estate loans are negotiable, to facilitate resale of the loans on the secondary market.

        1. A negotiable instrument is freely transferable by the payee to a third party.

        2. If a promissory note is endorsed "without recourse," the original payee will not be liable if the maker fails to make payments to the third party.

        3. A third party purchaser who buys a promissory note from a payee in good faith is known as a holder in due course.

    C. Types of notes

        1. Straight note: required payments are interest only, with a balloon payment at the end of the term.

        2. Installment note: payments include part of the principal as well as interest.

II. Security Instruments

    A. A security instrument makes the borrower's property collateral for the loan and gives the lender the right to foreclose in the event of default.

        1. Originally, under the theory of hypothecation, a borrower would transfer title to the property as security for the duration of the loan term.

        2. Now, in most jurisdictions, a mortgage simply creates a lien against the borrower's property in favor of the lender.

    B. Types of security instruments

        1. Mortgage: a two-party security instrument where a borrower (the mortgagor) mortgages his property to the lender (the mortgagee).

        2. Deed of trust: a three-party security instrument between the borrower (grantor) and the lender (beneficiary) where a third party (the trustee) holds the power of sale.

III. Foreclosure

    A. Types of foreclosure

        1. Judicial foreclosure: a mortgagee must file suit against a defaulting borrower in order for the court to order the property to be sold at a sheriff's sale to the highest bidder.

        2. Nonjudicial foreclosure: with a deed of trust, the lender does not need to file a lawsuit in the event of default; the trustee will arrange for the sale of the property through a trustee's sale.

    B. Judicial foreclosure process

        1. In a judicial foreclosure, in some states the borrower may repay the delinquent amount and reinstate the loan at any point before the court hearing occurs.

        2. In other states, the borrower can't reinstate the loan but may pay off the entire loan balance before the sheriff's sale in order to stop the foreclosure; this is known as the equitable right of redemption.

        3. If the foreclosure action goes to trial, in most cases the judge will issue a court order called a writ of execution, ordering the sheriff to seize and sell the property.

        4. Proceeds from the sheriff's sale will be used to pay off the mortgage and other liens, with any surplus going to the debtor.

        5. If the proceeds do not pay off the mortgage and other liens, the lender may also get a deficiency judgment against the borrower for the amount of the shortfall.

        6. The debtor has an additional period of time after the sheriff's sale to redeem the property, known as the statutory right of redemption.

        7. At the end of the statutory redemption period, the purchaser at the sheriff's sale receives a sheriff's deed to the property.

    C. Nonjudicial foreclosure process

        1. The trustee will provide notice of default to the borrower and then give notice of a trustee's sale.

        2. In the period before the sale, the borrower may reinstate the loan by paying the delinquent amount plus costs.

        3. A deed of trust borrower does not have the right of redemption; the lender is typically not able to receive a deficiency judgment.

        4. When the property is sold at the trustee's sale, title immediately passes to the winning bidder.

D. Alternatives to foreclosure

 1. Loan workouts: the borrower may be able to convince the lender to arrange a repayment plan to pay off past due amounts; alternatively, the borrower may try to convince the lender to modify the terms of the loan.

 2. Deed in lieu of foreclosure: the borrower can deed the property to the lender to satisfy the debt; if the property is worth considerably less than the amount owed, the borrower may be required to sign a promissory note for the difference.

 3. Short sale: the borrower may obtain the lender's consent to sell the home for what it will bring on the open market (usually something "short" of the full amount owed); the lender receives the sale proceeds and releases the borrower from the debt.

 4. To obtain lender consent, the borrower may have to be at least 90 days behind on payments and prove financial hardship by filling out an application and providing copies of pay stubs, bank statements, bills, etc.

 5. Borrowers receiving a reduction of debt may be liable to the IRS for income taxes on this debt relief, unless they qualify for an exception under the Mortgage Forgiveness Debt Relief Act of 2007.

IV. Finance Instrument Provisions

 A. Subordination clause: allows an instrument recorded later to take priority over an earlier recorded instrument.

 B. Late charge provisions: adds a late fee to overdue payments.

 C. Prepayment provisions: may impose a penalty if the borrower repays some or all of the principal before it is due, in order to compensate the lender for lost interest.

 D. Partial release clause: in a security instrument covering multiple parcels, provides for the release of part of the security property when part of the debt has been paid.

 E. Acceleration clause: declares the entire loan balance immediately due in the event of a default.

 F. Alienation clause: limits the borrower's right to transfer the property without the lender's permission unless the loan is paid off first.

 1. If loan isn't paid off, the new owner may take title subject to existing liens; the lender will retain the power to foreclose on the property.

2. Alternately, the new owner may assume the loan; the new owner will take on responsibility for paying the loan while the former owner retains secondary liability.

3. The lender may charge an assumption fee if it approves an assumption.

V. Types of Real Estate Loans

   A. Junior or senior mortgage: a senior mortgage has first lien position, while a junior mortgage has lower lien priority.

   B. Purchase money mortgage: in its narrower sense, a mortgage that a buyer gives to a seller in a seller-financed transaction.

   C. Home equity loan: a loan using property that the borrower already owns as collateral.

   D. Refinance mortgage: a new mortgage used to replace an existing mortgage on the same property, often used by borrowers when interest rates drop.

   E. Bridge loan: a temporary loan used by buyers to purchase a new home before the sale of their old home closes.

   F. Budget mortgage: a mortgage where payments include not just principal and interest, but also property taxes and hazard insurance.

   G. Package mortgage: a mortgage that covers the purchase of both real property and personal property (such as fixtures or equipment).

   H. Blanket mortgage: a mortgage which contains a partial release clause that uses multiple properties as collateral.

   I. Construction loan: a short-term loan used to finance construction of improvements on land already owned by the borrower.

   J. Nonrecourse mortgage: a mortgage that does not allow for a deficiency judgment against the borrower; the lender's only remedy is foreclosure.

   K. Participation mortgage: a mortgage where the lender receives a percentage of earnings generated by the property as well as interest payments.

   L. Shared appreciation mortgage: a mortgage where a lender is entitled to a portion of any increase in the property's value.

   M. Reverse equity mortgage: a mortgage where a lender makes monthly payments to a homeowner (typically an older person); the home will typically be sold when the owner dies in order to pay back the mortgage.

Key Terms

Promissory note: A written, legally binding promise to repay a debt, which may or may not be a negotiable instrument.

Maker: In a promissory note, the party who promises to pay; the debtor or borrower.

Payee: In a promissory note, the party who is entitled to be paid; the creditor or lender.

Negotiable instrument: An instrument establishing a right to payment, which is freely transferable from one person to another, such as a promissory note or check.

Holder in due course: A third party purchaser of a promissory note who purchased the note for value and in good faith.

Straight note: A promissory note that calls for regular payments of interest only.

Installment note: A promissory note that calls for regular payments of principal and interest until the debt is paid off, as used in an amortized loan.

Security instrument: A document that creates a voluntary lien against real property to secure repayment of a loan.

Hypothecation: Making property security for a loan by transferring title to the lender, without surrendering possession.

Legal title: Title held as security, without the right to possess the property.

Equitable title: The property rights that a borrower retains while a lender or vendor holds legal title.

Lien: A nonpossessory interest in property giving the lienholder the right to foreclose if the owner does not pay a debt owed to the lienholder.

Mortgage: An instrument creating a voluntary lien on a property to secure repayment of a debt, consisting of two parties (a mortgagor/borrower and a mortgagee/lender).

Deed of trust: A security instrument similar to a mortgage giving power of sale to a third party; the parties are a grantor/borrower, a beneficiary/lender, and a trustee.

Judicial foreclosure: A court-supervised foreclosure, beginning with a lawsuit filed by a mortgagee (or beneficiary) to foreclose on property on which a borrower has defaulted.

Nonjudicial foreclosure: Foreclosure by a trustee under the power of sale contained in a deed of trust.

Power of sale: A clause in a deed of trust that gives the trustee the right to foreclose nonjudicially in the event of default.

Reinstatement: The right of a defaulting borrower to prevent foreclosure by curing the default plus costs.

Redemption: The right of a defaulting borrower to prevent foreclosure by paying off the entire loan balance plus costs.

Equitable right of redemption: A period prior to a sheriff's sale in which a mortgagor may avoid foreclosure by paying off the loan balance plus costs.

Statutory right of redemption: A period following the sheriff's sale in which a mortgagor may avoid foreclosure by paying off the loan balance plus costs.

Sheriff's sale: A public auction of property after a judicial foreclosure.

Deficiency judgment: A court judgment requiring the debtor to pay to the lender the difference between the amount of the debt and the proceeds of the foreclosure sale.

Trustee's sale: A nonjudicial foreclosure sale conducted by a trustee under the power of sale clause in a deed of trust.

Loan workout: When the lender adjusts the payment schedule or modifies the loan terms to help the borrower avoid foreclosure.

Deed in lieu of foreclosure: When a borrower deeds the property to the lender to satisfy the debt.

Short sale: When a borrower obtains the lender's consent to sell the home for less than the full amount owed; the lender receives the sale proceeds and releases the borrower from the debt.

Subordination clause: A provision in a security instrument that permits a later security instrument to have a higher lien priority than the instrument in which the clause appears.

Prepayment provision: A clause allowing a lender to charge borrowers for prepaying principal on a loan, to compensate for lost interest.

Partial release clause: A clause allowing one or more parcels under a blanket lien to be released from the lien while other parcels remain subject to it.

Acceleration clause: A provision in a security instrument allowing the lender to declare the entire debt due if the borrower breaches one or more provisions.

Alienation clause: A clause in a security instrument giving the lender the right to accelerate the loan if the borrower sells the property or transfers a significant interest in it without the lender's approval.

Assumption: When a buyer takes on responsibility for repaying an existing loan and becomes liable to the lender; the seller remains secondarily liable to the lender.

Estoppel letter: Letter from lender that either acknowledges transfer of ownership and waives due-on-sale clause, or states balance and loan status.

Junior mortgage: A mortgage that has lower lien priority than another mortgage against the same property (the senior mortgage).

Purchase money mortgage: Generally, any loan used to purchase the property that secures the loan; narrowly, a loan given to a buyer by a seller in a seller-financed transaction.

Home equity loan: A loan obtained by a borrower using property he already owns as collateral.

Refinance mortgage: A mortgage loan used to pay off an existing mortgage on the same property.

Budget mortgage: A mortgage where monthly payments include a share of the property taxes and insurance, in addition to principal and interest.

Package mortgage: A mortgage secured by items of personal property as well as real property.

Blanket mortgage: A mortgage that encumbers more than one parcel of property.

Construction loan: A loan used to finance the construction of a building, which remains in place only until construction is completed, at which point it is replaced with a take-out loan.

Reverse equity mortgage: An arrangement where a homeowner mortgages a home (usually owned free and clear) in exchange for a monthly payment from the lender.

Chapter Quiz

1. The purpose of a promissory note is to:
   a. give the lender the right to foreclose on the borrower's property in the event of default
   b. allow the lender to foreclose nonjudicially instead of judicially
   c. establish the borrower's legal obligation to repay the loan
   d. prevent the lender from accelerating the loan in the event of default

2. The equitable right of redemption:
   a. usually lasts until the sheriff's sale is held
   b. enables the mortgagor to redeem the property after the sheriff's sale
   c. allows the trustee to cure the default and reinstate the loan
   d. doesn't apply in a judicial foreclosure

3. If the proceeds of a foreclosure sale are not enough to pay off all the liens against the property:
   a. each lienholder receives a proportionate share of the proceeds
   b. the lien with the highest priority is paid off first, and the junior lienholders are paid only if there is money left over
   c. the sale is declared void, and the property is auctioned again
   d. clear title to the property will be transferred to the foreclosing lender

4. To redeem property after a sheriff's sale, the borrower is generally required to pay:
   a. only the amounts that were delinquent before the loan was accelerated, plus the costs of the sale
   b. the original principal amount of the loan, plus costs
   c. the amount paid for the property at the sheriff's sale, plus interest accrued from the time of the sale
   d. whatever the sheriff's sale purchaser asks for the property, as long as it is not more than the appraised value

5. The key difference between a mortgage and a deed of trust is that:
   a. the mortgage contains a power of sale clause
   b. the mortgage contains an acceleration clause
   c. the deed of trust contains an acceleration clause
   d. the deed of trust contains a power of sale clause

6. In a state where all of the following types of instruments are used, a lender who wants to be able to foreclose quickly and inexpensively probably should choose a:

   a. mortgage
   b. deed of trust
   c. bridge loan
   d. package mortgage

7. A buyer can assume a seller's existing loan without the lender's permission only if the mortgage or deed of trust does not contain:

   a. a prepayment clause
   b. a subordination clause
   c. an acceleration clause
   d. an alienation clause

8. In an estoppel letter:

   a. the buyer assumes legal responsibility for repayment of the seller's loan
   b. the lender acknowledges the transfer and waives the right to exercise the due-on-sale clause
   c. the seller agrees to pay a prepayment penalty
   d. the seller accepts secondary liability for repayment of the loan assumed by the buyer

9. Which of the following types of loans calls for the lender to make monthly payments to the borrower?

   a. Purchase money mortgage
   b. Wraparound mortgage
   c. Reverse equity mortgage
   d. Participation mortgage

10. A refinance loan:

   a. enables the borrower to pay off an existing mortgage
   b. is a modification of the existing mortgage, not a new loan
   c. must be arranged with the same lender as the existing mortgage
   d. All of the above

Answer Key

1 c. A promissory note is written evidence of a borrower's legal obligation to repay a loan.

2. a. The equitable right of redemption will usually last until the sheriff's sale has been held.

3. b. If foreclosure sale proceeds are inadequate to pay all creditors, the lienholder with the highest priority is paid first, followed by each junior lienholder in order of priority.

4. c. To redeem the property during the statutory redemption period, the debtor usually must pay the amount that was paid for the property at the sheriff's sale, plus any interest accrued since the time of the sale.

5. d. A deed of trust, unlike a mortgage, contains a power of sale clause that allows the trustee to foreclose nonjudicially.

6. b. A lender who wants a quick, inexpensive foreclosure would prefer to use a deed of trust as a security instrument.

7. d. If a mortgage contains an alienation clause, the entire loan balance must be paid off if the property is sold without the lender's approval, preventing the possibility of assumption without permission.

8. b. An estoppel letter is issued by a lender that wishes to acknowledge a transfer and waive a due-on-sale clause.

9. c. With a reverse equity mortgage, a lender makes monthly payments to a homeowner, typically an older homeowner who needs an income stream.

10. a. A refinance is a loan taken out to pay off an existing loan on the same property. It is a new loan, and does not need to be with the same lender.

Chapter 6
Basic Features
of a Residential Loan

Amortization

Repayment Period
- Monthly payment
- Total interest
- Repayment period and interest rate

Loan-to-Value Ratio

Mortgage Insurance or Loan Guaranty

Secondary Financing

Fixed or Adjustable Interest Rate
- How ARMs work
- ARM features
- Explaining ARMs

Loan Features and Financing Options

Introduction

The size of loan a home buyer can get depends on the buyer's income, net worth, and credit history, and on the value of the property in question. It also depends on the features of the loan and the way it's structured. How long does the buyer have to repay the loan? How much of a downpayment does the lender require? Is the interest rate fixed or adjustable? Lenders offer different financing options at different times, depending on the current condition of the mortgage finance market and the cost of housing. Lenders structure their loans to limit the risk of foreclosure loss while still enabling buyers to purchase homes.

To understand the financing options available to home buyers in your area at a given time, you first need to understand the basic features of a mortgage loan. Variations in these features distinguish one loan program from another and determine which type of loan is right for a particular buyer. The basic features of a mortgage loan include:

- how the loan is amortized,
- the length of the repayment period,
- the loan-to-value ratio,
- whether there is mortgage insurance or a guaranty,
- whether there is secondary financing, and
- whether the interest rate is fixed or adjustable.

Amortization

Loan amortization refers to how principal and interest are paid to the lender over the course of the repayment period. A loan is **amortized** if the borrower is required to make regular installment payments that include some of the principal as well as interest on the principal. The regular payments are usually made in monthly installments.

Most home purchase loans made by institutional lenders are **fully amortized**. With a fully amortized loan, the regular monthly payments are enough to pay off all of the principal and interest by the end of the loan term. Each payment includes both a principal portion and an interest portion. When a payment is made, the principal portion is applied to the debt, paying back some of the amount originally borrowed. The remainder of the payment, the interest portion,

Fully amortized loan: level payments (including principal and interest) pay off loan by end of term

144

is retained by the lender as earnings or profit. With each payment, the amount of the debt is reduced and the interest due with the next payment is calculated based on the lower principal balance. The total monthly payment remains the same throughout the term of the loan, but every month the interest portion of the payment is smaller and the principal portion is correspondingly larger. The final payment pays off the loan completely; the principal balance is zero and no further interest is owed.

In the early years of a fully amortized loan, the principal portion of the payment is quite small, so it takes several years for the borrower's equity in the property to increase significantly through debt reduction. But toward the end of the loan term, the borrower's equity increases more rapidly.

> **Example:** A fully amortized, 30-year $100,000 loan at 6% interest calls for monthly payments of $599.55. Only $99.55 of the first payment is applied to the principal (see Figure 6.1). But by the twentieth year of the loan term, $327.89 of the $599.55 payment is applied to the principal.

There are two alternatives to a fully amortized loan: a partially amortized loan or an interest-only loan. Like a fully amortized loan, a **partially amortized** loan requires regular payments of both principal and interest. However, the regular payments are not enough to completely pay off the debt by the end of the loan term. The regular payments have repaid only part of the principal, and the remaining

Partially amortized loan: balloon payment required at end of term

---

Fig. 6.1 How an amortized loan's payments are applied to principal and interest

Example: $100,000 loan, 6%, 30-year term, monthly payments *(Figures approximate)*					
Payment Number	**Principal Balance**	**Total Payment**	**Interest Portion**	**Principal Portion**	**Ending Balance**
1	$100,000.00	$599.55	$500.00	$99.55	$99,900.45
2	$99,900.45	$599.55	$499.50	$100.05	$99,800.40
3	$99,800.40	$599.55	$499.00	$100.55	$99,699.85
4	$99,699.85	$599.55	$498.50	$101.05	$99,598.80
5	$99,598.80	$599.55	$497.99	$101.56	$99,497.24

balance must now be paid off. This final principal payment is called a **balloon payment**, because it is much larger than the regular payments made during the loan term.

> **Example:** A partially amortized $100,000 loan at 6% interest might require monthly payments of $599.55 for 15 years. At the end of that period, the remaining principal balance will be about $71,000. The borrower will have to make a balloon payment of $71,000 to pay off the loan.

In most cases, the borrower comes up with the funds for the balloon payment by refinancing. (Refinancing means using the funds from a new mortgage loan to pay off an existing mortgage.)

With an **interest-only** loan, the regular payments the borrower is required to make during the loan term cover the interest accruing on the loan, without paying down the principal.

> **Example:** With a $100,000 interest-only loan at 6% interest, the borrower must pay the lender $500 in interest each month during the loan term. At the end of the term, the borrower will have to pay the lender the entire $100,000 originally borrowed.

Interest-only loan requires no principal payments during the loan term, or for a specified period at the beginning of the term

Alternatively, an interest-only loan may allow the borrower to make interest-only payments for a specified period at the beginning of the loan term; at the end of this period, the borrower must begin making amortized payments that will pay off all principal and interest by the end of the term. This type of interest-only loan (sometimes called an "interest-first mortgage") was popular prior to the financial crisis, especially in areas where housing prices were high; more stringent qualifying standards have made them a less common option now. These types of mortgages are discussed in greater detail in Chapter 10.

Repayment Period

A loan's **repayment period** is the number of years the borrower has to repay the loan. The repayment period is often called the **loan term**.

Until the 1930s, the repayment period for a home purchase loan was ordinarily only five years, and the payments were interest-only. At the end of the five-year period, if the lender didn't renew the loan, a balloon payment of the full principal amount was required. When the Federal Housing Administration was established to help home buyers during the Depression, it made loans with a 30-year term available. With this longer repayment period, the loans could be fully amortized while keeping the monthly payments at an affordable level. Lenders realized that this dramatically decreased the risk of default, and 30 years soon became the standard repayment period for all home purchase loans.

30-year loan term:
- Standard
- Affordable payments

While 30-year loans are still regarded as standard and are still the most common, many lenders also offer 15-year, 20-year, and even 40-year loans. In some cases a term as short as ten years is allowed.

The length of the repayment period affects two important aspects of a mortgage loan:

1. the amount of the monthly payment, and
2. the total amount of interest paid over the life of the loan.

To see the impact that the repayment period has on the monthly payment and the total interest paid, let's compare a 30-year loan with a 15-year loan.

Monthly Payment Amount

As mentioned above, the main reason that 30 years became the standard term for a residential mortgage is that a longer repayment period reduces the amount of the monthly payment. Thus, a 30-year loan is more affordable than a 15-year loan.

> **Example:** The monthly payment on a $100,000 30-year loan at 7% interest is $665.30. The monthly payment on the same loan amortized over a 15-year period is $898.83.

The higher monthly payment required for a 15-year loan means that the borrower will build equity in the home much faster. But the higher payment also makes it much more difficult to qualify for a 15-year loan than for the same size loan with a 30-year term. A buyer who wants a 15-year loan and has sufficient funds might decide to make a larger downpayment and borrow less money to make the monthly payment amount more affordable. Or the buyer might decide to buy a much less expensive home than he could afford with a 30-year loan.

Shorter loan term means higher payment amount:
- Equity builds faster
- But many buyers can't qualify for a loan as large as they could with a 30-year term

Total Interest

Probably the biggest advantage of a shorter repayment period is that it substantially decreases the amount of interest paid over the life

Shorter term means less total interest paid over loan term

of the loan. With a 15-year mortgage, a borrower will end up paying less than half as much interest over the life of the loan as required by a 30-year mortgage.

> **Example:** Let's look at the $100,000 loan at 7% interest again. By the end of a 30-year loan term, the borrower will pay a total of $239,508. But by the end of a 15-year term, the borrower will pay only $161,789. After deducting the original $100,000 principal amount, you can see that the 30-year loan will require $139,508 in interest, while the 15-year loan will require only $61,789 in interest.

Repayment Period and Interest Rate

To simplify our comparison of a 15-year loan and a 30-year loan, we applied the same interest rate (7%) to both loans. In fact, however, a lender is likely to charge a lower interest rate on a 15-year loan than it charges on a comparable 30-year loan. Since the 15-year loan ties up the lender's capital for a shorter period, the lender's risk is reduced.

Shorter term typically means a lower interest rate

The interest rate on a 15-year loan might be half a percentage point lower than the rate on a 30-year loan. If the interest rate on the 15-year loan in our example were only 6.5% instead of 7%, the monthly payment would be $871.11. The total interest paid over the life of the loan would be $56,799.

Thus, the 30-year mortgage has affordable payments, but requires the borrower to pay much more interest over the life of the loan. On the other hand, the 15-year loan has higher monthly payments, but allows the borrower to pay far less interest over the life of the loan. Figure 6.2 compares $100,000, $150,000, and $200,000 mortgages at 6.5% interest for 15-year terms and 7% for 30-year terms.

As you can see, for a relatively small additional monthly payment, a 15-year loan offers substantial savings over its 30-year counterpart. A 15-year loan also provides the borrower with free and clear ownership of the home in half the time.

15-year loan term
Advantages:
1. Lower interest rate
2. Total interest much less
3. Free and clear ownership in half the time
Disadvantages:
1. Higher monthly payments
2. Tax deduction lost sooner

On the other hand, the higher monthly payments make the 15-year loan more difficult to afford in the short run. A larger downpayment would make the payments more affordable, but that's not an option for many buyers, so a 15-year loan would sharply reduce their buying power. Another disadvantage of a shorter loan term is that the borrower loses the tax deduction on the mortgage interest payments sooner (because the mortgage is paid off sooner).

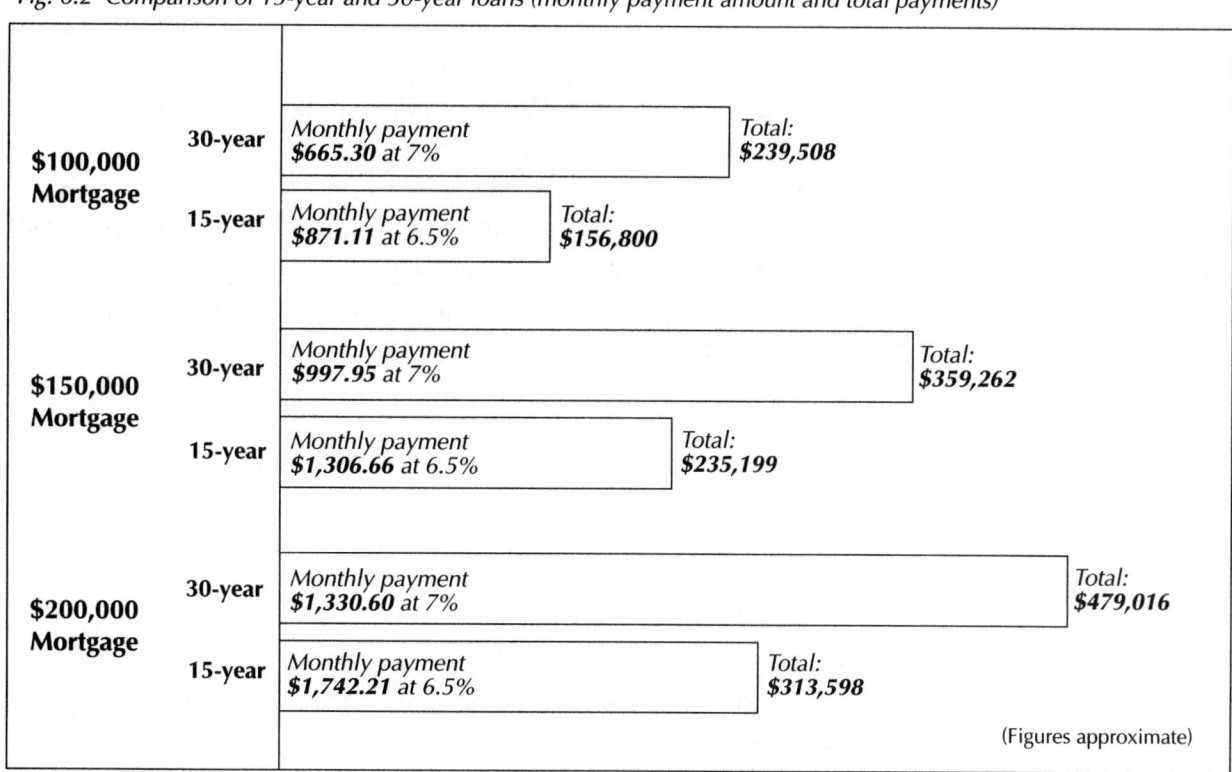

Fig. 6.2 Comparison of 15-year and 30-year loans (monthly payment amount and total payments)

$100,000 Mortgage

30-year — Monthly payment $665.30 at 7% — Total: $239,508

15-year — Monthly payment $871.11 at 6.5% — Total: $156,800

$150,000 Mortgage

30-year — Monthly payment $997.95 at 7% — Total: $359,262

15-year — Monthly payment $1,306.66 at 6.5% — Total: $235,199

$200,000 Mortgage

30-year — Monthly payment $1,330.60 at 7% — Total: $479,016

15-year — Monthly payment $1,742.21 at 6.5% — Total: $313,598

(Figures approximate)

20-year loans. A 20-year loan represents a compromise between the standard 30-year loan and the 15-year loan. Although the monthly payments for a 20-year loan are higher than the payments for a 30-year loan, they aren't as high as the payments for a 15-year loan. And yet the 20-year loan still provides significant interest savings over the life of the loan.

20-year loan is a compromise between a 15-year loan and a 30-year loan

Example: For purposes of comparison, suppose that a $200,000 loan at 7% interest is amortized over 15, 20, and 30 years (not even taking into account that 15-year and 20-year loans are offered at lower interest rates than 30-year loans).

The monthly payment for the 30-year loan would be $1,330.60, and the borrower would have to pay about $479,016 over the life of the loan. The monthly payment for the 15-year loan would be $1,797.66 (35% more than the 30-year payment), but the total payments would be only $323,579 (32% less than the total payments on the 30-year loan). The monthly payment for the 20-year loan would be $1,550.60 (only 17% more than the 30-year payment), and the total payments would be $372,144 (still 22% less than the total payments on the 30-year loan).

40-year loans. A 40-year loan is an option in areas where housing expenses are very high and a standard 30-year loan is unlikely to be adequate to purchase a desirable house. Payments are lower for a 40-year loan than for a 30-year loan. However, most 40-year borrowers aren't looking for lower payments; instead, they want to use the same-sized payment to buy a more expensive home.

The main disadvantage of the 40-year loan is that the amortization schedule unfolds even more slowly than with a 30-year loan. The monthly payments will remain mostly interest for a much longer time period, and the borrower will build up equity much more slowly. The total interest paid over the life of the loan will be much higher, as well.

Loan-to-Value Ratio

A loan-to-value ratio (LTV) expresses the relationship between the loan amount and the value of the home being purchased. If a buyer is purchasing a $100,000 home with an $80,000 loan and a $20,000 downpayment, the loan-to-value ratio is 80%. If the loan amount were $90,000 and the downpayment were $10,000, the loan-to-value ratio would be 90%. The higher the LTV, the larger the loan amount and the smaller the downpayment.

The higher the loan-to-value ratio, the smaller the downpayment

A loan with a low LTV is generally less risky than one with a high LTV. The borrower's investment in her home is greater, so she'll try harder to avoid defaulting on the loan and losing the home. And if the borrower does default, the outstanding loan balance is less, so it's more likely that the lender will be able to recoup the entire amount in a foreclosure sale.

Lenders use loan-to-value ratios to establish maximum loan amounts

Lenders use LTV limits to establish maximum loan amounts. For example, under the terms of a particular loan program, the maximum loan-to-value ratio might be 95% of the sales price or appraised value of the property, whichever is less. For a $100,000 home financed with a loan from that program, the maximum loan amount would be $95,000. The borrower would be required to make a downpayment of at least 5%, or $5,000.

As you can see, a loan program's maximum LTV determines not only the maximum loan amount for a transaction financed through that program, but also the minimum downpayment required. Thus, the maximum LTV is a key factor in determining how expensive a home a buyer can afford through a particular program.

> **Example:** The Allens have only $5,000 saved for a downpayment. They're hoping to buy a $100,000 house. If a particular loan program has a maximum LTV of 90%, the Allens won't be able to finance their purchase through that program unless they're able to come up with additional cash. Depending on the program's rules, they might be able to do that with gift funds (see Chapter 8) or secondary financing (discussed later in this chapter). Otherwise, they'll have to finance the purchase through a different loan program that has a higher LTV limit.

To protect themselves against foreclosure loss, residential lenders traditionally had low LTV limits. For example, many lenders had a maximum LTV of 80%, requiring borrowers to make a 20% downpayment—a very substantial investment in the property. High-LTV home loans were available only through special programs such as the FHA and VA loan programs. In recent years, however, high-LTV loans have become more readily available. This has made homeownership possible for considerably more people than it once was.

High-LTV loans help people buy homes when they don't have much money for a downpayment

There are various ways that lenders can reduce or compensate for the extra risk involved in making high-LTV loans. For instance, they can apply stricter qualifying standards or charge a higher interest rate. Probably the most effective way to minimize the risk of loss is with mortgage insurance or a loan guaranty. In fact, some form of mortgage insurance or guaranty is a requirement in almost all high-LTV home loan programs.

Mortgage Insurance or Loan Guaranty

Many home purchase loans are covered by a mortgage insurance policy or a loan guaranty. The purpose of the insurance or guaranty is to protect the lender from foreclosure loss. The coverage may be required by the lender or else offered as a feature of a particular loan program. (For example, the VA home loan program provides lenders with a guaranty on loans made to eligible veterans.) In either case, the insurance or guaranty serves as an incentive for lenders to make loans on terms that they would otherwise consider too risky. This may include not only high-LTV loans, as discussed above, but also loans to borrowers who represent extra risk (for example, a borrower with a high debt-to-income ratio or a mediocre credit score).

Mortgage insurance or loan guaranty often required for loan with high LTV or other increased risk factors

Mortgage Insurance

Mortgage insurance works basically like other types of insurance: in exchange for premiums, the insurer provides coverage for certain types of losses specified in the policy. Mortgage insurance premiums are ordinarily paid by the borrower. The policy protects the lender against losses that might result from the borrower's default on the mortgage and the subsequent foreclosure.

In the event that there is a default and foreclosure, the insurer will **indemnify** the lender. This means that if the proceeds of the foreclosure sale aren't enough to pay off the entire remaining amount that the borrower owes the lender, plus the lender's other expenses, the insurer will make up the shortfall. Depending on the policy, covered losses may include unpaid principal, interest, property taxes, and hazard insurance, attorney's fees, and the cost of preserving the property during the period of foreclosure and resale, as well as the cost of the foreclosure sale itself.

Because the mortgage insurer assumes most of the risk of loan default, the insurer also underwrites the loan. In other words, the borrower must meet the qualifying standards of the mortgage insurer as well as the standards of the lender.

We'll discuss mortgage insurance in more detail in Chapter 10 (private mortgage insurance policies for conventional loans) and Chapter 11 (the mutual mortgage insurance coverage offered through the FHA-insured loan program).

Loan Guaranty

With a loan guaranty, a third party (called the **guarantor**) agrees to take on secondary legal responsibility for a borrower's obligation to a lender. If the borrower defaults on the loan, the guarantor will reimburse the lender for resulting losses. Thus, although a loan guaranty is not technically a form of insurance, from a mortgage lender's point of view it serves the same purpose as mortgage insurance.

The guarantor for a mortgage loan might be a private party, a nonprofit organization, or a governmental agency. The guarantor's motive for providing the guaranty is usually to help the borrower, rather than to turn a profit. The guaranty encourages the lender to make a loan on special terms favorable to the borrower, making it easier for the borrower to purchase a home. For example, the VA-guaranteed loan program is intended to promote homeownership among veterans.

Loan guaranty: third party agrees to take on secondary responsibility for borrower's obligation

Like a mortgage insurer, a guarantor may be involved in underwriting the loan. This is true for the VA loan program, which we'll cover in Chapter 12.

Secondary Financing

Sometimes a home buyer obtains two mortgage loans at once: a primary loan for most of the purchase price, and a second loan to pay part of the downpayment or closing costs required for the first loan. This second loan is called **secondary financing**. Secondary financing may come from an institutional lender, from the seller, or from a private third party. When an institutional lender is the source of the secondary financing, it may be the same lender that is making the first mortgage loan, or it may be a different lender.

Secondary financing: loan to pay part of downpayment or closing costs

A lender making a primary loan will usually place restrictions on the type of secondary financing arrangement that the borrower may enter into. For example, the primary lender will make sure that the payments required for the second loan don't exceed the borrower's ability to pay. When qualifying ratios are applied to the borrower's stable monthly income, the payments for both the first loan and the second loan will be taken into account. Also, in most cases the primary lender will still require the borrower to make at least a minimum downpayment out of her own funds, even if the secondary lender would be willing to supply the entire downpayment needed for the first loan.

Buyer must qualify for combined payments on both loans

The basic point of these and other restrictions on secondary financing is to minimize the risk of default on the second loan, since both loans are going to be secured by the same property. A second mortgage with a high risk of default would impair the primary lender's security interest and make default on the first mortgage more likely.

The specific restrictions that a primary lender imposes depend in part on whether the primary loan is conventional, FHA-insured, or VA-guaranteed. We'll discuss the secondary financing rules for each of the major loan programs in Chapters 10, 11, and 12.

Fixed or Adjustable Interest Rate

The final basic loan feature that we're going to cover in this chapter is the interest rate. A loan's interest rate can be either fixed or adjustable (variable).

Fixed-rate mortgage: interest rate remains the same throughout loan term

With a **fixed-rate loan**, the interest rate charged on the loan remains constant throughout the entire loan term. If a borrower obtains a 30-year mortgage loan with a 7% fixed interest rate, the interest rate remains 7% for the whole 30-year period, no matter what happens to market interest rates during that time. If market rates increase to 10%, or if they drop to 5%, the interest rate charged on the loan will still be 7%.

The fixed-rate mortgage is regarded as the standard. It has been the cornerstone of residential financing since the Depression in the 1930s. In fact, through the end of the 1970s virtually all home purchase loans had fixed interest rates.

During the 1980s, however, market interest rates rose dramatically and also became more volatile—in other words, they changed more frequently. When mortgage interest rates are high, many potential home buyers can no longer afford financing. (Mortgage rates as high as 18% were not unheard of in the early 1980s.) And when rates are volatile, lenders are less willing to tie up their funds for a long period, such as 30 years, at a fixed rate.

For instance, suppose the current market rate for home mortgages is 10%, but economists are predicting much higher interest rates within the next year or so. A lender might hesitate to make a fixed-rate loan at 10% interest when it looks as though market rates might soon be up to 13%.

ARM: lender adjusts loan's interest rate from time to time to reflect changes in cost of money

To address both of these issues—affordability and volatility—the **adjustable-rate mortgage (ARM)** was introduced. An ARM allows the lender to periodically adjust the loan's interest rate to reflect changes in the cost of money. This transfers the risk of interest rate fluctuations to the borrower. If market rates climb, the borrower's interest rate and payment amount go up; if market rates decline, the borrower's rate and payment amount go down. Because ARMs shift this risk to the borrower, lenders have generally charged lower interest rates on ARMs than on fixed-rate loans—sometimes dramatically lower. For instance, under certain market conditions, a borrower who could get a fixed-rate loan at 6% might be able to get an ARM with an initial rate of 4.25%.

In the 1980s, when interest rates were at record highs, ARMs became a popular way to afford the financing needed to buy a home. When market rates are low, ARMs are less popular. But even when fixed-rate loans aren't very expensive, some buyers find ARMs attractive. For example, buyers who plan to own the property they're buying for only a few years might use an ARM with a low initial rate to buy "more house" than they otherwise could.

Recently, however, as part of the fallout from the mortgage crisis, most lenders have stopped offering ARMs at lower rates than fixed-rate loans. In fact, now a borrower may even have to pay a higher rate for an ARM than for a fixed-rate loan. And without the incentive of a lower initial interest rate, few borrowers choose ARMs over fixed-rate loans.

How ARMs Work

Next, let's look at how ARMs work and what their special features are. They're considerably more complicated than fixed-rate loans.

An ARM borrower's interest rate is determined initially by the cost of money (market interest rates) at the time the loan is made. Once the interest rate on the loan has been set, it is tied to one of several widely recognized indexes. Future interest rate adjustments are based on the upward and downward movements of that index. An **index** is a published statistical report that serves as a reliable indicator of changes in the cost of money.

ARM's interest rate tied to index that indicates changes in cost of money

When an ARM is made, the lender selects the index it prefers, and thereafter the loan's interest rate will be adjusted (increased or decreased) to reflect increases and decreases in the rates reported by that index. A change in the loan's interest rate will also result in an increase or decrease in the amount of the monthly payment the borrower is required to make.

ARM Features

To provide for interest rate and payment adjustments, adjustable-rate mortgages have a number of special features. Depending on the loan, an ARM may have all or only some of the following elements:

- a note rate,
- an index,
- a margin,
- a rate adjustment period,
- a mortgage payment adjustment period,
- a lookback period,
- an interest rate cap,
- a mortgage payment cap,
- a negative amortization cap, and
- a conversion option.

Note Rate. An ARM's initial interest rate is called the note rate because it is the rate stated in the promissory note. The note rate may also be referred to as the contract rate.

To attract borrowers, lenders sometimes offer ARMs with a discounted initial rate: an interest rate for the first year that is lower than the rate indicated by the index when the loan is made. This is often referred to as a "teaser rate."

Index. As we said above, an index is a statistical report that is used as an indicator of changes in the cost of money. There are several regularly published indexes that lenders use in connection with ARMs. Examples include the Treasury securities indexes (the weekly average yield on Treasury securities, adjusted to a constant maturity of one, three, or five years); the 11th District cost of funds index (an average of the interest rates paid by savings and loans for deposits and other borrowings with a certain range of maturities); and the LIBOR index (an international index based on the rate commercial banks pay for short-term loans from other commercial banks on the London market).

Some indexes are more responsive to changes in the cost of money than others. For example, the one-year Treasury securities index is very responsive to economic fluctuations, while the cost of funds index is more stable. Lenders tend to prefer the more responsive indexes. A borrower benefits from a more responsive index when interest rates are decreasing, but may prefer a more stable index if rates are increasing.

Margin. An ARM's margin is the difference between the index rate and the interest rate that the lender charges the borrower. Since the index is a reflection of the lender's cost of money, it's necessary to add a margin to the index to cover the lender's administrative expenses and provide a profit. In fact, between lenders who use the same index, it's the size of the margin that makes the difference in the interest rates they charge. Margins vary from 2% to 3%. The index plus the margin equals the interest rate on the loan.

Index
+ Margin
Interest Rate

Example:

3.25%	Current index value
+ 2.00%	Margin
5.25%	ARM interest rate

It is the index rate that fluctuates during the loan term and causes the borrower's interest rate to increase and decrease; the lender's margin remains constant.

Rate Adjustment Period. The interest rate on an ARM isn't adjusted every time the index rate changes. Instead, the ARM has a rate adjustment period that determines when the lender may adjust the interest rate on the loan. It could provide for a rate adjustment every six months, once a year, or every three years, for example. A rate adjustment period of one year is the most common, and ARMs with one-year rate adjustment periods are referred to as one-year ARMs.

ARM's interest rate adjusted only at specified intervals

At the end of each rate adjustment period, the lender checks what the index rate was on a specified date. If the index has increased or decreased, the lender makes a corresponding change in the loan's interest rate and notifies the borrower in writing of the change.

Some ARMs have a two-tiered rate adjustment structure. These loans are often called **hybrid ARMs**, because they're like a combination of an ARM and a fixed-rate loan. They provide for a longer initial period before the first rate adjustment, with more frequent adjustments after that.

Hybrid ARMs have an initial fixed-rate period

> **Example:** The borrowers are financing their home with a 30-year ARM that has an initial rate adjustment period of three years, with annual rate adjustments from then on. The interest rate charged on their loan won't change during the first three years of the repayment period, but it will change each year after that.

The loan in the example would be called a 3/1 ARM. There are also 5/1 ARMs, 7/1 ARMs, and 10/1 ARMs. In each case, the first number is the number of years in the initial rate adjustment period, and the second number means that subsequent rate adjustments will occur once a year. Some borrowers who choose a hybrid loan plan to sell or refinance their home before the end of the initial adjustment period. Originally, hybrids with longer initial adjustment periods had higher initial interest rates, but that's no longer necessarily true. For example, depending on market conditions, a lender might charge a higher initial interest rate on a 3/1 ARM than on a 7/1 ARM.

Mortgage Payment Adjustment Period. An ARM's mortgage payment adjustment period determines when the lender changes the amount of the borrower's monthly principal and interest payment to reflect a change in the interest rate charged on the loan. For most

ARMs, the mortgage payment adjustment period is the same as the rate adjustment period. As soon as the interest rate is adjusted, the lender also adjusts the mortgage payment.

With some ARMs, however, the payment adjustment period doesn't coincide with the rate adjustment period. Instead, the lender adjusts the interest rate more frequently than the mortgage payment. For example, the loan agreement might call for interest rate adjustments every six months, but changes in the amount of the mortgage payment only every two years. This arrangement can have undesirable consequences for the borrower. (See the discussion of negative amortization later in this section.)

Payment amount not necessarily adjusted every time interest rate is adjusted

Lookback Period. As we've just explained, how often the lender changes an ARM borrower's interest rate and payment amount depends on the loan's rate and payment adjustment period(s). You may also hear reference to an ARM's "lookback period." A typical lookback period is 45 days. That means that the loan's rate and payment adjustments will actually be determined by where the index stood 45 days before the end of the adjustment period (not on the date the adjustment period ends).

> **Example:** A one-year ARM has a 45-day lookback period. At the end of the one-year rate adjustment period, on July 2, the index that the ARM is tied to has risen 0.75%. But 45 days earlier, on May 18, the index had risen only 0.50%. Therefore the lender can raise the interest rate on the borrower's loan only by 0.50%, not 0.75%.

Interest Rate Cap. Not long after adjustable-rate mortgages were introduced, some ARM borrowers encountered a problem that came to be known as **payment shock**. Payment shock occurs when market interest rates rise very rapidly. As market rates go up, so do ARM indexes, and that results in sharp increases in the interest rates lenders charge ARM borrowers. Of course, a higher interest rate also translates into higher monthly payments. In some cases the payments can increase so dramatically that the borrowers can no longer afford them. Borrowers who fall victim to payment shock often have to sell their homes or face foreclosure.

Payment shock: sharp increase in payment due to rate increase

To protect borrowers from payment shock (and protect themselves from default), many lenders include interest rate caps in their ARMs. An **interest rate cap** limits how much the interest rate on the loan

Interest rate cap limits how much rate can increase

can increase, regardless of what the index does. By limiting interest rate increases, the rate cap prevents the monthly payment from increasing too much.

Some ARMs have two kinds of rate caps. One limits the amount that the interest rate can change in any single adjustment period. The other (and more rare) type of cap limits the amount that the interest rate can increase over the entire loan term. For example, a one-year ARM might have a 2% annual rate cap and a 5% life-of-the-loan cap. When the lender adjusts the loan's interest rate each year, the annual rate cap prevents the lender from increasing the rate more than 2% at one time. And because of the life-of-the-loan cap, the borrower knows from the outset that no matter how much the index increases over the course of the loan term, the interest rate charged on the loan can never be more than 5% higher than the note rate.

For most ARMs, the annual interest rate cap applies to rate reductions as well as rate increases.

> **Example:** A loan agreement provides that the loan's interest rate can't increase or decrease more than 2% per year. If the index rate rises 3% in one year, the lender can raise the loan's interest rate by only 2%; and if the index drops 3% in one year, the lender will reduce the loan's rate by only 2%.

In contrast, a life-of-the-loan cap typically limits only rate increases, not decreases.

Mortgage Payment Cap. A second way of limiting payment increases is with a mortgage payment cap. A **payment cap** directly limits how much the lender can raise the monthly mortgage payment. Typically, payment caps limit mortgage payment increases to 7.5% annually. (A 7.5% payment increase is considered to be approximately equivalent to a 1% interest rate increase.) Note that payment caps apply only to increases in the principal and interest portion of the loan payment; there is no limit to how much the payment can increase because of raising property taxes or hazard insurance premiums.

Some ARMs have only an interest rate cap and no mortgage payment cap. Some have both an interest rate cap and a payment cap, and still others have only a payment cap. Any of these arrangements will protect the borrower from payment shock if interest rates skyrocket. However, if a loan has a payment cap and no rate cap, the borrower may encounter the problem of negative amortization (see below).

Payment cap directly limits how much mortgage payment can increase

Over time, interest rate
increases may be offset by
rate decreases

While protections against payment shock are important, keep in mind that steadily rising interest rates and sharp payment increases are the worst case scenario for an ARM. Over the course of a 30-year loan term, the borrower's interest rate and payment will probably decrease from time to time, offsetting at least some increases.

Negative Amortization. When an adjustable-rate mortgage has certain features, changes in the loan's interest rate may result in negative amortization. Before we define negative amortization, let's look at an example.

> **Example:** The Walkers borrowed $190,000 to buy their home. Their mortgage is a one-year ARM with a 7.5% annual payment cap but no interest rate cap. Their initial interest rate was 4.5%, and their monthly payment during the first year has been $962.70. At the end of the first year, the index that the Walkers' ARM is tied to has risen 2.75%. So the lender adjusts the loan's interest rate up by 2.75% (from 4.5% to 7.25%). Without a payment cap, this rate increase would increase the monthly payment by $325, to $1,287.70. Out of that payment amount, approximately $1,129.40 would be interest.
>
> However, the payment cap limits the Walkers' payment increase to no more than 7.5% of the payment amount per year. In this case, that is $72.20:
>
> | | |
> |---|---|
> | $962.70 | Year 1 payment amount |
> | × 7.5% | Payment cap percentage |
> | $72.20 | Maximum payment increase for Year 2 |
>
> As a result, the monthly payment during the second year of the Walkers' loan term can be no more than $1,034.90:
>
> | | |
> |---|---|
> | $962.70 | Year 1 payment |
> | + 72.20 | 7.5% of the Year 1 payment |
> | $1,034.90 | Maximum Year 2 payment |
>
> In this situation, the payment cap has prevented the payment from increasing enough to cover all of the interest charged on the loan during the second year. Even if the Walkers' entire $1,034.90 monthly payment is applied only to interest (without paying down the principal balance at all), the interest accruing on the loan during the second year won't be fully covered. The shortfall will be about $94.50 per month, or $1,134 for the year.

Negative amortization:
unpaid interest added to
principal balance, increasing
the amount owed

The lender will handle the situation in the example by adding the unpaid interest to the loan's principal balance. When unpaid interest is added to the loan balance, it is called **negative amortization**.

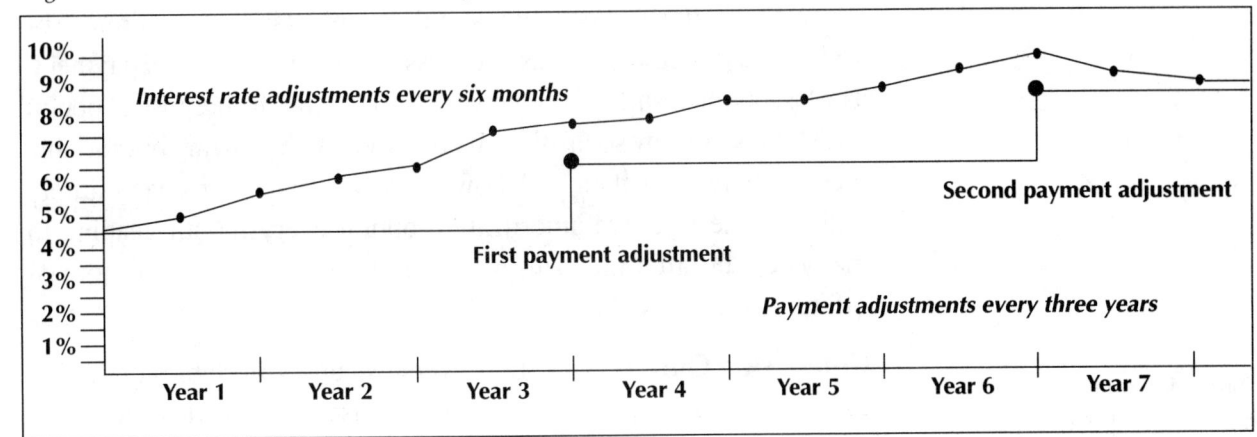

Fig. 6.3 When an ARM's interest rate changes more often than the payment amount, negative amortization may result

Ordinarily, a loan's principal balance declines steadily, although gradually. But negative amortization causes the principal balance to go up instead of down. The borrower may owe the lender more than she originally borrowed.

In the example, negative amortization occurred because there was a payment cap and no interest rate cap. Negative amortization can also occur when an ARM's interest rate adjustment period and mortgage payment adjustment period do not coincide. Suppose a borrower has an ARM with a six-month rate adjustment period and a three-year payment adjustment period. Over a three-year period, the loan's interest rate might increase five times while the payment amount stayed the same (see Figure 6.3). The borrower would be paying too little interest during that period, which would result in negative amortization.

Many adjustable-rate loans are structured to prevent negative amortization from occurring. But when negative amortization is a possibility, the loan may have a **negative amortization cap**: a limit on the amount of unpaid interest that can be added to the principal balance.

A negative amortization cap typically limits the total amount a borrower can owe to 125% of the original loan amount. When that point is reached, the loan is recast and the monthly payment is set to fully repay the loan over the remainder of the term.

Prior to the financial crisis that began in 2007, some ARMs were intentionally set up to allow negative amortization. Known as **option ARMs**, these loans allowed the borrower to choose one of several payment options every month. The various payment options included

ARM features that can lead to negative amortization:
- Payment cap but no rate cap; or
- Payments adjusted less often than interest rate

a traditional payment of principal and interest, based on a 15- or 30-year amortization period; interest-only payments; and a minimum (or limited) payment, which was even less than the interest-only payment. The last option resulted in negative amortization. The purpose of option ARMs was to allow sophisticated borrowers with growing but variable incomes to manage their cash flow. However, many borrowers simply relied on the negative amortization option every month, leading to many defaults after the loans were recast. Most lenders have stopped offering option ARMs.

Conversion Option. Some borrowers feel uncomfortable continuing to bear the risk of rate and payment increases that an ARM involves. Many ARMs allow the borrower to convert the loan to a fixed-rate mortgage at designated times during the loan term.

Conversion option: opportunity to switch from adjustable to fixed interest rate

A conversion option ordinarily involves a limited time to convert, and the borrower is usually required to pay a conversion fee. For example, a borrower with a convertible ARM might have the option of converting from an adjustable interest rate to a fixed rate between the 13th and 59th month of the loan term (only on one of the annual rate adjustment dates), for a conversion fee of $250. If the borrower chooses to convert the loan, the fixed rate will be the current market rate at the time of conversion.

Explaining ARMs

Clearly, adjustable-rate mortgages are a lot more complicated than fixed-rate mortgages. It's not surprising that many buyers have trouble understanding ARMs. To address that problem, the Truth in Lending Act requires lenders to make special disclosures to ARM loan applicants (see Chapter 14).

When you're working with buyers who are considering an ARM, it can be helpful to go over the lender's required disclosures with them. You may also find the question and answer sheet shown in Figure 6.4 and the ARM comparison worksheet in Figure 6.5 useful.

Loan Features and Financing Options

As a real estate agent, in addition to helping home buyers evaluate their financing options, you may occasionally be called upon to help design a financing option to fit a special situation. The loan features

Fig. 6.4 ARM questions and answers

What You Need to Know About ARMs

A real estate agent should be prepared to answer the following questions about adjustable-rate mortgages:

1. **What will my initial interest rate be?**

   It usually isn't necessary to break the rate down into index and margin. The buyer is concerned only with the total. The initial rate (note rate or contract rate) will be based on the cost of money when the loan is made.

2. **How often will my interest rate change?**

   The adjustment period will be stated in the loan agreement. Depending on the lender's preference, adjustments may occur every six months, annually, every three years, or every five years. Six-month and one-year intervals are most common.

3. **How often will my payment change?**

   Again, in order to give an accurate answer, you have to be familiar with the policies of the particular lender. Most lenders prefer simultaneous rate and payment changes.

4. **Is there any limit to how much my interest rate can be increased?**

   Most ARMs have interest rate caps. An annual cap is usually 1% or 2%; a life-of-the-loan cap is usually 5% or 6%.

5. **Is there any limit to how much my payment can be increased at any one time?**

   Some ARMs have payment caps, but most keep payment increases under control with interest rate caps. When there is a payment cap, payment increases are usually limited to 7.5% of the payment amount per year.

6. **Will my ARM involve negative amortization?**

   Most new ARMs don't allow negative amortization. However, it still is a possibility with some new ARMs, and also with some older ARMs (which a buyer might consider assuming). If negative amortization is a possibility, the loan should have a negative amortization cap.

7. **Can my ARM be converted to a fixed-rate loan?**

   Many ARMs contain a conversion option that permits the borrower to convert to a fixed interest rate at certain points in the loan term, for a fee. The fixed rate will usually be the market interest rate at the time of conversion.

Fig. 6.5 *ARM comparison worksheet*

ARM Comparison Worksheet

	Loan 1	Loan 2	Loan 3
Lender	_____	_____	_____
Loan amount	$ _____	$ _____	$ _____
Discount fee	$ _____	$ _____	$ _____
Origination fee	$ _____	$ _____	$ _____
Index	_____	_____	_____
Current index rate	_____ %	_____ %	_____ %
Margin	_____ %	_____ %	_____ %
Note rate	_____ %	_____ %	_____ %
Initial payment	$ _____	$ _____	$ _____
Rate adjustment period	_____	_____	_____
Payment adjustment period	_____	_____	_____
Interest rate cap			
• periodic	_____ %	_____ %	_____ %
• life of loan	_____ %	_____ %	_____ %
Payment cap			
• periodic	_____ %	_____ %	_____ %
• life of loan	_____ %	_____ %	_____ %
Negative amortization			
• possible?	_____	_____	_____
• cap	_____ %	_____ %	_____ %
Conversion option			
• conversion fee	$ _____	$ _____	$ _____
• restrictions	_____	_____	_____

that we've covered in this chapter—amortization, repayment period, loan-to-value ratio, a fixed or adjustable interest rate, and (in some cases) mortgage insurance or secondary financing—are the basic elements used to design financing. In combination with one another, they determine whether a particular loan will enable a particular buyer to buy a particular property. They determine how much money the buyer can borrow (the loan amount), how much money the buyer will need to close the loan (the downpayment), and how affordable the loan will be (the monthly payment amount). Those are the key issues that will come up again and again throughout the rest of the book.

Outline: Basic Features of a Residential Loan

I. Amortization

    A. An amortized loan involves regular payments of both principal and interest.

        1. Most home purchase loans are fully amortized.

        2. Alternatives to fully amortized loans are partially amortized loans and interest-only loans.

II. Repayment Period

    A. The repayment period or loan term is how long the borrower has to pay off the loan.

        1. A 30-year loan term is regarded as standard, but other terms such as 15, 20, and 40 years are available.

        2. A 30-year loan has a lower monthly payment than a 15-year loan, but a 15-year loan will require payment of much less interest over the life of the loan.

        3. A 15-year loan is likely to have a lower interest rate than a 30-year loan.

III. Loan-to-Value Ratio

    A. The loan-to-value ratio reflects the relationship between the loan amount and the value of the home being purchased.

    B. A loan with a lower LTV is less risky than one with a higher LTV.

IV. Mortgage Insurance or Loan Guaranty

    A. Mortgage insurance or a loan guaranty may be used to protect the lender from loss in the event of default.

    B. Mortgage insurance

        1. In exchange for mortgage insurance premiums, an insurer will indemnify a lender for any shortfall resulting from a foreclosure sale.

        2. Mortgage insurance is used in conventional and FHA loans.

    C. Loan guaranty

        1. In a loan guaranty (used in VA loans), a guarantor takes on secondary responsibility for a borrower's obligation.

        2. If the borrower defaults, the guarantor will reimburse the lender for any resulting losses.

V. Secondary Financing

    A. A buyer may obtain, in addition to a primary loan, a secondary loan to cover part of the downpayment and closing costs.

    B. Restrictions are placed on secondary financing, such as making sure that the borrower can afford payments on both loans.

VI. Fixed or Adjustable Interest Rate

    A. A loan's interest rate can be fixed for the entire loan term, or adjustable.

    B. Fixed-rate loans are regarded as the standard, and were used almost exclusively until high interest rates in the 1980s encouraged use of ARMs.

    C. An adjustable-rate mortgage (or ARM) allows a lender to adjust the loan's interest rate periodically to reflect changes in the cost of borrowing money.

    D. Adjustable-rate mortgage features

        1. Note rate: the initial rate stated in the promissory note is an ARM's note rate.

        2. Index: a statistical report indicating changes in the cost of money, which the lender will use in order to adjust the ARM's interest rate.

        3. Margin: the difference between an ARM's interest rate and the index rate, reflecting the lender's profit margin and administrative costs.

        4. Rate adjustment period: the period that determines how often a lender will adjust the interest rate on an ARM.

        5. Payment adjustment period: the period that determines how often a lender will adjust the payment amount on an ARM.

        6. Interest rate cap: a limit on how high the interest rate for an ARM can go, either limiting how high it can go in one adjustment or a maximum rate for the entire loan.

        7. Payment cap: a limit on how high the monthly payment for an ARM can go.

        8. Negative amortization: when monthly payments on an ARM don't cover all of the monthly interest, thus adding to the principal balance instead of subtracting from it (which might occur if an ARM has a payment cap but no interest rate cap).

        9. Conversion option: a feature allowing an ARM borrower to convert to a fixed-rate loan at certain points during the loan term.

Key Terms

Amortization: Gradually paying off a loan through installment payments that include both principal and interest.

Fully amortized loan: A loan with monthly payments that completely pay off the principal and interest by the end of the loan term.

Partially amortized loan: A loan with monthly payments that include both principal and interest, but don't pay off the entire principal amount by the end of the loan term; as a result, a balloon payment is necessary.

Interest-only loan: A loan that allows the borrower to pay only the interest due (with no principal) during the loan term, or during a specified period at the beginning of the term.

Repayment period: The number of years a borrower is given to repay a loan. Also called the loan term.

Loan-to-value ratio (LTV): The relationship between the loan amount and either the sales price or the appraised value of the property (whichever is less), expressed as a percentage.

Mortgage insurance: Insurance protecting a mortgage lender against losses resulting from default and foreclosure.

Loan guaranty: An arrangement in which a third party guarantor accepts secondary liability for a loan and will reimburse the lender for losses resulting from the borrower's default.

Secondary financing: Money borrowed to pay part of the required downpayment or closing costs for a first loan; this loan is secured by the same property as the first loan.

Fixed-rate loan: A mortgage loan in which the lender charges an unchanging interest rate throughout the loan term.

Adjustable-rate mortgage: A loan in which the interest rate is periodically increased or decreased to reflect changes in the cost of money; commonly called an ARM.

Note rate: The interest rate specified in a loan's promissory note; also called the coupon rate or contract rate.

Index: A published statistical report that indicates changes in the cost of money (market interest rates), used as the basis for the interest rate adjustments in an ARM.

Margin: The difference between an ARM's index rate and the interest rate charged on the loan.

Rate adjustment period: The minimum interval between adjustments of an ARM's interest rate.

Payment adjustment period: The minimum interval between adjustments of an ARM's monthly payment amount.

Interest rate cap: A provision in an ARM that limits the amount that the interest rate may be increased (or in some cases, decreased).

Mortgage payment cap: A provision in an ARM that limits the amount the monthly payment may be increased.

Negative amortization: When deferred interest on an adjustable-rate loan is added to the principal balance.

Conversion option: A provision in an adjustable-rate mortgage allowing the borrower to convert the interest rate to a fixed rate at certain points in the loan term.

Hybrid ARM: An adjustable-rate mortgage with an initial fixed-rate period; for example, a 3/1 hybrid ARM has a fixed interest rate for the first three years and is subject to annual rate adjustments after that.

Chapter Quiz

1. Unpaid interest added to the loan balance is referred to as:

    a. payment shock

    b. a conversion option

    c. negative amortization

    d. positive amortization

2. A limit placed on the amount an ARM interest rate can increase in any given year is:

    a. an index cap

    b. a margin cap

    c. a negative amortization cap

    d. an interest rate cap

3. All of the following are disadvantages of a 15-year mortgage, except:

    a. the interest rate is higher

    b. the monthly payments are higher

    c. the mortgage interest deduction (for income tax purposes) is lost sooner

    d. a larger downpayment may be needed

4. An ARM with a conversion option:

    a. has graduated payments

    b. may be converted to a fixed-rate loan

    c. may be converted to a GEM

    d. has a negative amortization feature

5. A loan involves monthly payments of both interest and principal, but the borrower must still make a balloon payment at the end of the loan term. This is a/an:

    a. fully amortized loan

    b. partially amortized loan

    c. interest-only loan

    d. adjustable-rate loan

6. Which loan repayment period would involve paying the least amount of total interest over the life of the loan?

    a. 15 years
    b. 20 years
    c. 30 years
    d. 40 years

7. Which loan-to-value ratio would represent the greatest risk to a lender?

    a. 80%
    b. 90%
    c. 95%
    d. 97%

8. Which of the following will protect a lender against the risk of loss in the event of a borrower's default?

    a. Negative amortization
    b. Mortgage insurance
    c. Secondary financing
    d. A high loan-to-value ratio

9. When would secondary financing be used?

    a. The borrower wishes to purchase more than one property
    b. The borrower is using a VA loan
    c. The borrower has inadequate cash to make the downpayment and closing costs on the primary loan
    d. The borrower plans to finance the purchase of personal property as well as real property

10. An adjustable-rate mortgage is structured so that its interest rate remains the same for the first five years, and then changes once every year for the remaining loan term. Five years and then one year would be the:

    a. payment adjustment period
    b. rate adjustment period
    c. monthly payment cap
    d. interest rate cap

Answer Key

1. c. If monthly payments for an ARM are insufficient to meet the interest charged in that particular month, the unpaid interest is added to the principal balance. This is known as negative amortization.

2. d. An interest rate cap prevents an ARM's interest rate from increasing over a particular limit, either in a given period or for the life of the loan.

3. a. The interest rate of a 15-year mortgage is typically lower, to reflect the lower risk to the lender.

4. b. An ARM with a conversion option may be converted to a fixed-rate loan at certain points in the loan term.

5. b. A partially amortized loan involves monthly payments of both principal and interest, but does not pay off the entire loan balance over the loan term, requiring a balloon payment at the end of the loan term.

6. a. Although it requires the highest monthly payments, a 15-year loan will require the lowest amount of total interest paid over the life of the loan.

7. d. The higher the loan-to-value ratio, the greater the risk to the lender. This is because a buyer who has made a larger downpayment will work harder to avoid default and, if default occurs, the lender is more likely to recover the entire loan amount in a foreclosure sale.

8. b. Mortgage insurance is used to protect a lender against the risk of loss in the event of a borrower's default, as it will reimburse a lender for some or all of a shortfall resulting from a foreclosure sale.

9. c. Secondary financing involves the use of a second loan to cover some of the downpayment and closing costs associated with a first loan secured by the same property.

10. b. The rate adjustment period of an ARM dictates how frequently the interest rate may be increased or decreased.

Chapter 7
The Financing Process

Shopping for a Loan

- Assessing the buyers' circumstances
- Choosing a lender
- Loan costs
- Evaluating financing options

Applying for a Loan

- Loan application form
- Required disclosures
- Locking in the interest rate

Application Processing

- Underwriting decision
  - Rejection
  - Conditional commitment
  - Preapproval letter
  - Firm commitment

Closing a Loan Transaction

- Closing agent
- Steps in the closing process

Introduction

Getting a mortgage loan can be a straightforward, painless experience, or it can turn into a complicated, time-consuming hassle that ends in disappointment. In most cases, of course, the process of getting a loan falls somewhere between those two extremes. How smoothly it goes depends on many factors, including the buyers' financial situation, how expensive a home they want, and the lender they choose. Helping buyers get through the process as easily as possible, given their particular circumstances, is part of a real estate agent's job.

The financing process can be broken down into these stages, and we'll look at each of them in turn:

1. shopping for a loan,
2. applying for a loan,
3. application processing, and
4. closing.

Shopping for a Loan

Home buyers should comparison shop for financing

There are many financing options available to home buyers, and buyers are encouraged to comparison shop: to find the best type of loan on the best possible terms. But understanding the advantages and disadvantages of different financing options can be complex and overwhelming.

For home buyers, shopping for a mortgage loan involves:

- assessing their own wants, needs, and finances;
- choosing a lender;
- comparing rates and fees; and
- evaluating financing options.

Although we'll be treating these as separate topics, keep in mind that they aren't really separate steps that take place in a certain order; instead, they overlap and influence one another. As a real estate agent, you can help buyers with all of these tasks, but they should also have the input of a financing expert: a mortgage lender.

Assessing the Buyers' Circumstances

For buyers, the day they begin thinking about mortgage shopping should be no later than the day they begin house hunting. It's a vital part of the task of deciding what kind of home they need, and learning what kind of home they can afford. It's much better for buyers if they have a realistic idea of their price range before they start house hunting in earnest.

Before shopping for a loan or a house, buyers need to assess their wants and needs and their financial situation

> **Example:** After talking about buying a home for a long time, the Morrisons have started driving through the neighborhood they like, keeping an eye out for "For Sale" signs. One day they find a house they love. It costs more than they planned to spend, but it's exactly what they want. They make a full-price offer, which the seller accepts.
>
> The Morrisons apply for a loan and start making arrangements to move into their new home. Then, to their surprise and embarrassment, their loan application is rejected. The sale, which was contingent on financing, terminates. The seller is inconvenienced and annoyed, and the Morrisons are so disappointed that they're reluctant to resume house hunting.

Because of the importance of financing to a transaction, today many sellers won't even consider a home buyer's offer until a lender has verified that the buyer will qualify for sufficient funding to purchase the home.

Prequalifying vs. Preapproval. There are two ways for home buyers to learn in advance how large a mortgage loan they'll qualify for. Either they can get prequalified for a loan, or they can get preapproved for one.

Prequalifying is an informal process that can be performed by a real estate agent, a lender, or via online mortgage calculators. Home buyers provide basic information about their income, assets, debts, and credit history, and then receive an estimate of an affordable price range for them, based on this data.

Prequalifying: informal process that may be done by a lender or a real estate agent

It's a fairly straightforward process to estimate the price range of homes the buyer should be able to afford. The maximum monthly mortgage payment the buyers qualify for, together with how much money they have for a downpayment and closing costs, determines their maximum loan amount—the largest mortgage a lender will give them. The maximum loan amount plus their downpayment sets the upper limit of their price range.

Preapproval is a more formal process than prequalifying, and it can be done only by either a mortgage broker or a lender. (Note that for simplicity's sake, we'll be using the term lender in most of this

Preapproval: formal process that can only be done by a lender discussion. Depending on the transaction, the person working with the prospective borrowers might be either a loan officer employed by the lender or an independent mortgage broker. See Chapter 4.)

To get preapproved, buyers must complete a loan application and provide the required documentation of their income, assets, debts, and credit history, just as if they were applying for a loan after finding a house. A lender evaluates an application for preapproval in the same way as an ordinary loan application, with this exception: there's no property appraisal or title report at this point, since the buyers haven't found the specific home they want to buy yet. If the buyers are creditworthy, the lender sets a maximum loan amount based on their income and net worth. The lender gives the buyers a **preapproval letter**, agreeing to loan them up to the specified amount when they find the home they want to buy, as long as the property meets the lender's standards. (Preapproval letters are discussed in more detail later in this chapter.)

The basic point of prequalifying and preapproval is the same. Both options let the buyers know in advance how expensive a home they can afford. But preapproval has important advantages over prequalifying.

The first advantage is that a preapproval letter can be an extremely valuable tool in negotiations with a seller. It provides assurance to the seller that the buyer's financing contingency shouldn't be a problem; the buyer is in fact ready, willing, and able to buy at the agreed price. (A financing contingency is a provision in a purchase and sale agreement that allows the buyer to withdraw from the contract without penalty if he can't obtain the specified financing.) Preapproval is especially important in an active real estate market, when lots of buyers are competing for desirable homes.

The second advantage of preapproval is that it helps streamline the closing process. The lender has already evaluated the buyers, so the parties can focus on inspections, the appraisal, and the title report. However, it is important to note that even a preapproval is subject to modification if new information comes to light or circumstances change. Because of the likelihood of changing circumstances, most preapproval letters are valid for only a predetermined period of time, such as 30 days. To extend a preapproval commitment beyond the initial time frame, home buyers would need to re-verify all the information previously submitted.

Preapproval letter states that lender will loan buyers up to a specified amount

Advantages of preapproval:
• Tool in negotiations
• Streamlines the closing process

Note that while a mortgage broker can issue a preapproval letter stating that the home buyer's financial information meets generally accepted underwriting standards for most lenders, it's better for the home buyer to have a preapproval letter issued directly by the lender who will ultimately fund the loan.

How to Prequalify Buyers. Prequalifying buyers for financing was once a routine procedure for real estate agents. Now, in places where preapproval by a lender has become a standard practice, agents are no longer called upon to prequalify buyers very often, if at all. Even so, it's worthwhile for agents to know how prequalifying works, because it provides some practical insight into the financing process.

Prequalifying is essentially a simplified version of a mortgage lender's underwriting procedure. After getting the necessary financial information from the buyers, the agent's next step is to apply the income ratios used by the secondary market agencies (see Chapters 8 and 10). A financial calculator or mortgage calculation software is useful at this stage. If neither of these is available in the agent's office, many websites have mortgage calculators for online use.

Real estate agent uses simplified version of underwriting procedures to prequalify buyers

Whatever calculation tool the real estate agent uses, this is the underlying process for prequalifying buyers:

1. Income ratios are applied to the buyers' monthly income to calculate the approximate maximum monthly mortgage payment they'll qualify for. The payment amount must cover principal, interest, taxes, and insurance, referred to as PITI. (Income ratios and PITI are covered in Chapter 8.)

PITI: Principal, interest, taxes, and insurance

2. A certain percentage representing property taxes and insurance is subtracted from the PITI figure to arrive at an estimate of the maximum principal and interest payment.

3. This maximum principal and interest payment, along with the interest rate that would probably be charged in the current market, is used to calculate the maximum loan amount.

4. The maximum loan amount is divided by an appropriate loan-to-value ratio to determine the highest price the buyers should plan on paying for a home.

In prequalifying, buyers' maximum mortgage payment determines the maximum loan amount and price range ceiling

You'll understand these steps more fully after reading Chapter 8, which explains underwriting in detail. Of course, in real life, prequalifying—and loan underwriting—is considerably more complicated than these steps imply. For instance, a lender's qualifying standards interact with a number of factors, including the borrower's credit or FICO scores, the loan-to-value ratio, loan term, loan program, interest rate, and the lender's fees.

Prequalifying will give the home buyer a general price range to work with, but while this may be useful for some buyers, formal preapproval is advisable as soon as the buyers feel ready to apply for it. Of course, in order to get preapproved for a loan the buyers will need to choose a lender, which is our next topic.

Choosing a Lender

To choose a mortgage lender wisely, buyers first need to identify promising prospects and then use the right criteria to evaluate them.

Identifying Prospects. There are two main ways to decide which lenders to talk to: research and referrals.

Research. For buyers who are willing to do some research, advertisements and articles in the business or real estate section of a local newspaper can provide leads. Many newspapers include a handy "Mortgage Comparison Chart" to help consumers see at a glance the various lenders and mortgage products available to them. Looking under "Mortgages" in the yellow pages of the local telephone directory can also be useful.

An Internet search can be a particularly good source of information about both local and online lenders. Many websites allow buyers to quickly compare the interest rates and fees of several different lenders.

Whether in print or online, lenders' ads—like any ads—should be viewed with a critical eye. However, they can be a reasonable starting point if followed up with emails or phone calls to loan originators. As we mentioned, loan originators are either the lender's employees (also known as loan officers) or independent contractors (known as mortgage brokers) who meet with loan applicants, discuss their financing needs, and help them submit their mortgage applications.

Referrals. Referrals are also a reasonable way to find a good lender, especially since many buyers don't have the time or inclination to do the kind of research suggested above. In addition to asking family members, friends, and co-workers who recently bought homes to recommend a lender, many buyers ask their real estate agent for referrals. In fact, many rely entirely on the agent's advice.

Research tools for finding lenders:
- Newspaper articles and ads
- Yellow pages
- Internet

Lender referrals may come from family, friends, co-workers, real estate agents

An experienced agent has typically worked with quite a few lenders and knows that some are more knowledgeable and dependable than others. A less experienced agent should ask her broker or others in the office for the names of lenders to refer clients and customers to. As we will discuss in Chapter 14, it's important to note that real estate agents should never accept fees or any other unearned compensation in exchange for making these referrals.

Mortgage brokers. A mortgage broker specializes in bringing buyers and lenders together (see Chapter 4). While consulting a mortgage broker might seem to solve the problem of choosing a lender, buyers have to rely on the same kind of research and referrals described above to find a good mortgage broker.

If buyers work with a mortgage broker rather than directly with a lender, the broker performs most or all of the same tasks that loan officers employed by lenders do. However, mortgage brokers usually work with multiple lenders, so they may be able to present buyers with a bigger variety of loan options. Keep in mind that mortgage brokers are not legally required to find the best loan for a buyer, unless the broker and the buyer have an agency relationship. Typically, mortgage brokers present the options that borrowers are qualified to pursue. It's up to the borrower to decide which option is the best.

Buyer's own bank. When shopping for a mortgage, home buyers shouldn't overlook the financial institution where they do their banking. There may be special financing offers for established customers, and some people prefer to have one institution handle all of their financial transactions.

Interviewing Prospective Lenders. Whether buyers find prospective lenders through research or through referrals, mortgage financing experts generally recommend talking to at least three or four lenders before making a choice. Buyers should call or email each lender's office and arrange to talk to a loan originator, asking each a similar set of questions in order to compare their products and costs.

Buyers are encouraged to talk to three or four lenders, if possible

Unfortunately, some buyers don't talk to three or four lenders because they feel too busy, or because they find the jargon too complex or confusing. Inexperienced buyers may find talking to a loan originator intimidating. Even for more experienced buyers, shopping for a mortgage loan is still a relatively infrequent experience, making it hard to develop expertise or negotiating skill in this arena. Some buyers may be embarrassed about their financial situation, or worried that they're asking stupid questions and taking up too much of the loan originator's time. Some buyers who are perfectly competent in everyday life can become strangely passive in this context, accepting everything the loan originator says about their financing options as factual and not open to question or negotiation. Other buyers may feel obligated to go ahead and apply for a loan with the first lender they contact, just to keep the loan process moving.

Of course, good mortgage professionals won't let any of that happen. They're aware that many buyers feel intimidated, and they know how to put buyers at ease. They don't take advantage of the situation and push buyers into submitting an application before they're ready. Other loan originators, however, may be more focused on getting business than advising consumers to shop around. As a result, federal and state regulators have developed a number of consumer publications and regulations that encourage home buyers to seek both the best lender and the best mortgage they can. We'll discuss these consumer protection regulations more in Chapter 14, but for now it's enough to know that the government advises home buyers to get three or four written good faith estimates from different lenders (with loan quotes for the same day) before committing to a formal loan application with just one lender.

Criteria for Choosing a Lender. Some buyers and even some real estate agents believe that one lender is much the same as another, and that the only real distinction between them is the interest rates and fees they charge. It's true that interest rates and fees are a very important consideration when choosing a lender, and in the next section we'll discuss how to compare the rates and fees that different lenders are offering. But rates and fees shouldn't be the only consideration when choosing a lender.

Look for expertise, efficiency, and honesty, not just low interest rates and fees

Buyers should also be concerned with a lender's expertise, efficiency, stability, and honesty. A lender might offer a low interest rate, but provide inaccurate or misleading information and slow, sloppy service. Loan originators who aren't really knowledgeable may not be aware of some financing options that would be well suited to certain buyers. Mistakes in loan processing can delay the closing of a real estate transaction, or even derail it altogether. And if a closing cost estimate is carelessly or deceptively prepared, the buyers may be surprised by unexpected fees at closing.

In the absence of a referral, it may be difficult to judge the competence and trustworthiness of a lender and its representatives. Asking the loan originator for references from recent customers may be worthwhile. Researching customer satisfaction websites may also be beneficial. To a certain extent, however, buyers have to rely on their own impressions and instincts when they meet with a loan originator. Growing public awareness of predatory lending practices (see Chapter 14) may lead buyers to be more assertive and cautious when they're choosing a lender. Plus, recent changes to RESPA, TILA, and other lending regulations should make it more likely that home buyers will receive accurate information about loan terms and costs throughout the financing process.

Loan Costs

For most buyers, the primary consideration in choosing a lender is how much their loan is going to cost. The interest rate is the major cost of borrowing money, but it's by no means the only one. Mortgage lenders also impose a variety of other charges that can make a big difference in the cost of a loan.

Types of Loan Fees. Most significant among these other charges are origination fees and discount points, which are often grouped together and referred to as "loan fees" or "points." The term "point" is short for "percentage point." One point is one percentage point (one percent) of the loan amount. For example, for a $100,000 loan, one point would be $1,000; six points would be $6,000.

Loan fees:
• Origination fee
• Discount points

One point =
1% of loan amount

Origination fee. An origination fee may also be called an administrative charge, a transaction fee, a service fee, or simply a loan fee. An origination fee is charged in almost every mortgage loan transaction, unless the loan is expressly designated as a "no fee" loan (discussed later in this section). Origination fees pay for the costs that a lender incurs in making loans, such as staff salaries, commissions, facilities costs, and other overhead expenses. A typical origination fee is usually around 1% of the loan amount. The fee is a closing cost, paid when the transaction closes, and it is usually paid by the buyer.

Origination fee covers lender's administrative costs

> **Example:** A home buyer is borrowing $325,000, and the lender is charging an origination fee of one point (one percentage point). That means the buyer must pay the lender a $3,250 origination fee at closing. ($325,000 × 1% = $3,250.)

Discount points. In some transactions, in addition to the origination fee, the lender charges discount points, also known as a loan discount, a discount fee, or simply as points. The term "points" may cause confusion. Some lenders use "points" to mean only discount points, but others use it to mean the discount points and the origination fee combined.

> **Example:** When Lender A says it's charging four points on a loan, that means four discount points. It doesn't include the origination fee that will be charged on top of the discount points.
>
> When Lender B says it's charging four points on a loan, that refers to the discount points and the origination fee combined. For instance, Lender B would refer to three discount points plus a 1% origination fee as four points. Lender B would also call two discount points plus a 2% origination fee four points.

Either usage is considered correct. So when loan fees are discussed, it's important to make sure everyone involved is using "points" in the same way.

Discount fee increases lender's upfront yield

Discount points are designed to increase the lender's upfront yield, or profit, on the loan. By charging discount points, the lender not only gets the interest on the loan throughout the loan term, but also collects a sum of money in the beginning, right when the loan is funded. As a result, the lender is willing to make the loan at a lower interest rate than it would have without the points. In effect, the lender is paid a lump sum now so that the borrower can avoid paying more interest later. Depending on how long the borrower stays in the home (and keeps making payments on the loan), the discount points paid to reduce the interest rate may or may not save the home buyer money in the long run.

Lenders with lower interest rates typically charge more points

Although discount points aren't charged in all transactions, they have become quite common. The number of points charged is usually related to how the lender's quoted interest rate compares to market interest rates; typically, lenders who offer below-market interest rates charge more points. One lender might quote an interest rate of 6.25% plus two points, while another lender quotes 6% interest with four points. Also, a given lender might offer different rates with different discounts (for example, 6% interest with four points, or 6.5% interest with no points). The choice is between paying more cash up front or more interest over the life of the loan.

The calculation of how many points it will take to reduce the interest rate is affected by a number of factors and varies with market conditions. As a result, it's difficult to come up with a set formula that tells borrowers how many points a lender might require them to pay to discount the quoted loan rate by 1%. In recent years the number of points required for a 1% reduction in the interest rate has ranged from four to six points.

Relationship between number of points and increase in yield varies with market conditions

To determine how much a loan discount will cost, multiply the loan amount by the number of discount points the lender requires.

Example: $250,000 sales price; $225,000 loan amount

$225,000	Loan amount
× 4%	Discount of four points
$9,000	Cost of loan discount

Either the buyer or the seller can pay the discount points. In a buyer's market, a seller may agree to pay points: this makes her home more attractive to buyers by making financing more affordable. When buyers or sellers pay points to reduce the loan's interest rate this arrangement is called a **buydown**, as the points are used to "buy down" the interest rate, making the buyer's monthly loan payments smaller and easier to qualify for. (Buydowns are discussed in more detail in Chapter 10.)

Discount points may be paid by buyer or seller

When the buyer pays the points, the lump sum must be paid to the lender in cash at closing. In contrast, when the seller pays the points, the lender deducts the cost of the points from the loan amount.

Example: The loan is for $170,000. The lender is charging four points, and the seller has agreed to pay the points on the buyer's behalf.

When the loan is funded, the lender deducts 4% of the loan amount ($6,800) for the points. The remainder, $163,200, is delivered to the buyer to finance the purchase. The buyer signs a promissory note and mortgage agreeing to repay the entire $170,000 at the stipulated rate of interest. Thus, the lender is advancing only $163,200 but will eventually be repaid $170,000.

At closing, the buyer transfers the loan funds ($163,200) to the seller without making up the difference, so the seller's net proceeds from the sale are reduced by the cost of the points. In effect, the seller paid the lender $6,800 so the buyer could get a loan at the lower quoted interest rate.

Lenders charge a variety of minor fees in addition to main loan fees

Other fees. In addition to interest, a loan origination fee, and discount points, mortgage lenders usually charge a variety of other fees. For example, a buyer might be required to pay the lender an application fee, a document preparation fee, or an underwriting fee.

In addition to these miscellaneous lender fees, borrowers will also incur loan charges that relate to the loan but are paid to third parties instead of the lender. For instance, the appraisal fee and the credit report fee are paid to the appraiser and the credit reporting agency, not to the lender.

The fees that lenders charge vary considerably from one lender to another. Although many of the fees tend to be for comparatively small amounts, they do add up. Buyers can ask the loan originator if one or more of the fees can be reduced or waived altogether. Mortgages are consumer products just like a car or household furnishings, and borrowers are encouraged to discuss price reductions whenever possible. Some lenders may be quite willing to negotiate with buyers, and not just about miscellaneous fees, but also about the interest rate and points. Other lenders may not be as open to this type of negotiation, but there's no harm in asking.

Mortgage broker's fee. Buyers who are working with a mortgage broker are ordinarily charged a mortgage broker's fee or commission. This may be stated as a separate fee or included in the points quoted for the loan. Buyers should ask their brokers about the compensation arrangement and the impact that fee has on other loan costs. For the majority of home mortgages, federal law requires the disclosure of mortgage broker fees in the good faith estimates and on the settlement statement. Some states have similar requirements.

Mortgage broker's compensation doesn't necessarily make loan more expensive for buyer

As a general rule, the mortgage broker's compensation shouldn't make a loan obtained through a mortgage broker more expensive than one obtained directly from a lender. Mortgage brokers deal with wholesale lenders (see Chapter 4) who offer their loans to brokers at wholesale prices. The brokers mark the loans up to retail prices and keep the "overage" as their compensation. The retail price that buyers pay should be close to the market rate they'd be paying if they had gotten their loan directly from a retail lender, without a mortgage broker's help.

However, some broker compensation arrangements have raised concerns because these arrangements encourage brokers to steer borrowers to loans with unnecessarily high interest rates. While subprime borrowers may be required to pay higher-than-market interest rates, most prime borrowers are not. Yet mortgage brokers may earn more money when their customers end up with high-rate loans. When a broker persuades a home buyer to purchase a mortgage with an interest rate that is "above par" or higher than the market rate quoted for that day, the lender calculates the broker's compensation using a formula that rewards the broker for the difference between the loan's rate and the current market rate. This form of broker compensation is called a **yield spread premium** or YSP. While not illegal, YSPs have been the subject of some controversy because of their potential for abuse. Recent changes to the Real Estate Settlement Procedures Act (RESPA, a federal law that we'll discuss in more detail in Chapter 14) include some new disclosure requirements concerning YSPs, to help borrowers understand the relationship between broker fees and total loan costs.

Comparing Loan Costs. Because different lenders charge different origination fees, loan discounts, and other fees, it can be difficult to accurately compare the cost of two or more loans. For example, if one lender is quoting a 5.75% interest rate with four points, and another lender is quoting a 6% rate with two points, which loan is less expensive? The first loan (5.75% with four points) happens to be slightly less expensive, but it isn't easy to tell that just by looking at the lenders' quotes. Different types of loan products add further complications: which would be less expensive, a fixed-rate or an adjustable-rate mortgage?

One law that's intended to help loan applicants with this type of problem is the **Truth in Lending Act** (TILA), one of the federal consumer protection laws covered in Chapter 14. Under TILA, lenders must make certain disclosures to consumer loan applicants to help them understand exactly how much they're paying for credit. This information enables loan applicants to compare loan costs and shop around for the best terms.

Truth in Lending Act requires loan costs to be disclosed to borrowers

The most important disclosure required by TILA is the **annual percentage rate** (APR). The APR expresses the relationship of the **total finance charge** to the total amount financed (that is, the amount borrowed) as an annual percentage. In addition to interest, all of the following would be included in the total finance charge: the origination fee; any discount points paid by the buyer; a mortgage broker's fee, finder's fee, or service fee; and mortgage guaranty or insurance fees. (Title insurance costs, credit report charges, the appraisal fee, and points paid by the seller would not be included in the total finance charge.)

Annual percentage rate (APR): relationship of total finance charge to loan amount

Because interest is rarely the only fee that a mortgage lender charges, the APR of a mortgage loan is almost always higher than the quoted interest rate. For example, a loan with an interest rate of 7% might have an APR of 7.32%, because the APR takes into account the origination fee and the mortgage insurance as well as the interest.

To help determine which of two or more loans is the least expensive, it's important to compare the APRs quoted by the lenders. A buyer who compares only the quoted interest rates can easily be misled. A lender might quote a very low interest rate, but charge an unusually large origination fee or several discount points. In that case, the total cost of the loan may in fact be much greater than the cost of a loan from a competitor who is quoting a higher interest rate. The APRs of the two loans will reveal this difference in cost.

Compare APRs, not just interest rates

While buyers don't have to be given a Truth in Lending Act disclosure statement before they actually apply for a loan, it's possible to get an estimate of a loan's APR by calling the lender. As long as the interest rate, origination fee, and discount fee are known, a chart like the one in Figure 7.1 can be used to estimate the APR. (Note that on this chart, "Points" refers to the origination fee and the discount fee combined.)

In addition to the TILA disclosure statement, lenders are also required to give loan applicants good faith estimates (GFEs) of all of the closing costs they will be expected to pay, including loan-related charges. (This is a RESPA requirement; see Chapter 14.) Although lenders don't have to provide GFEs until they have received a written loan application, buyers should ask for GFEs from multiple lenders as early in the process as possible. Lenders may only charge nominal fees for preparing these good faith estimates.

No-fee/low-fee Loans. Some lenders offer no-fee or low-fee loans. As the names suggest, the lender doesn't charge the usual loan fees a home buyer is typically expected to pay, such as an origination fee, discount points, or other lender fees. The interest on the loan is the only (or nearly only) finance charge. As a result, the APR is the same or close to the same as the interest rate.

A no-fee or low-fee loan can be very helpful for buyers who don't have much cash for closing. However, the interest rate on a no-fee or low-fee loan is likely to be significantly higher than the rate on a comparable loan with typical fees. As a result, the two loans might

No-fee loan reduces amount of money needed for closing

Fig. 7.1 Annual percentage rate chart

Annual Percentage Rates for 15-Year Mortgages with Points									
Points	**0**	**0.5**	**1.0**	**1.5**	**2.0**	**2.5**	**3.0**	**3.5**	**4.0**	**4.5**
5.00	5.08	5.15	5.23	5.31	5.39	5.47	5.55	5.63	5.71
5.25	5.33	5.40	5.48	5.56	5.64	5.72	5.80	5.88	5.96
5.50	5.58	5.66	5.73	5.81	5.89	5.97	6.05	6.13	6.22
5.75	5.83	5.91	5.99	6.06	6.14	6.23	6.31	6.39	6.47
6.00	6.08	6.16	6.24	6.32	6.40	6.48	6.56	6.64	6.73
6.25	6.33	6.41	6.49	6.57	6.65	6.73	6.82	6.90	6.98
6.50	6.58	6.66	6.74	6.82	6.90	6.99	7.07	7.15	7.24
6.75	6.83	6.91	6.99	7.07	7.16	7.24	7.32	7.41	7.49
7.00	7.08	7.16	7.24	7.33	7.41	7.49	7.58	7.66	7.75
7.25	7.33	7.41	7.50	7.58	7.66	7.75	7.83	7.92	8.00
7.50	7.58	7.66	7.75	7.83	7.92	8.00	8.09	8.17	8.26
7.75	7.83	7.92	8.00	8.08	8.17	8.25	8.34	8.43	8.52
8.00	8.08	8.17	8.25	8.34	8.42	8.51	8.59	8.68	8.77
8.25	8.33	8.42	8.50	8.59	8.67	8.76	8.85	8.94	9.03
8.50	8.58	8.67	8.75	8.84	8.93	9.02	9.10	9.19	9.28
8.75	8.83	8.92	9.01	9.09	9.18	9.27	9.36	9.45	9.54
9.00	9.09	9.17	9.26	9.35	9.43	9.52	9.61	9.70	9.79
9.25	9.34	9.42	9.51	9.60	9.69	9.78	9.87	9.96	10.05
9.50	9.59	9.67	9.76	9.85	9.94	10.03	10.12	10.21	10.31
9.75	9.84	9.93	10.01	10.10	10.19	10.29	10.38	10.47	10.56
10.00	10.09	10.18	10.27	10.36	10.45	10.54	10.63	10.72	10.82
10.25	10.34	10.43	10.52	10.61	10.70	10.79	10.89	10.98	11.07
10.50	10.59	10.68	10.77	10.86	10.95	11.05	11.14	11.24	11.33
10.75	10.84	10.93	11.02	11.11	11.21	11.30	11.40	11.49	11.59

Annual Percentage Rates for 30-Year Mortgages with Points									
Points	**0**	**0.5**	**1.0**	**1.5**	**2.0**	**2.5**	**3.0**	**3.5**	**4.0**	**4.5**
5.00	5.04	5.09	5.13	5.18	5.22	5.27	5.32	5.36	5.41
5.25	5.29	5.34	5.39	5.43	5.48	5.52	5.57	5.62	5.67
5.50	5.55	5.59	5.64	5.68	5.73	5.78	5.83	5.87	5.92
5.75	5.80	5.84	5.89	5.94	5.98	6.03	6.08	6.13	6.18
6.00	6.05	6.09	6.14	6.19	6.24	6.29	6.34	6.39	6.44
6.25	6.30	6.35	6.39	6.44	6.49	6.54	6.59	6.64	6.69
6.50	6.55	6.60	6.65	6.70	6.75	6.80	6.85	6.90	6.95
6.75	6.80	6.85	6.90	6.95	7.00	7.05	7.10	7.15	7.21
7.00	7.05	7.10	7.15	7.20	7.25	7.30	7.36	7.41	7.46
7.25	7.30	7.35	7.40	7.45	7.51	7.56	7.61	7.67	7.72
7.50	7.55	7.60	7.66	7.71	7.76	7.81	7.87	7.92	7.98
7.75	7.80	7.85	7.91	7.96	8.01	8.07	8.12	8.18	8.23
8.00	8.05	8.11	8.16	8.21	8.27	8.32	8.38	8.44	8.49
8.25	8.30	8.36	8.41	8.47	8.52	8.58	8.64	8.69	8.75
8.50	8.55	8.61	8.66	8.72	8.78	8.83	8.89	8.95	9.01
8.75	8.81	8.86	8.92	8.97	9.03	9.09	9.15	9.21	9.27
9.00	9.06	9.11	9.17	9.23	9.29	9.34	9.40	9.46	9.52
9.25	9.31	9.36	9.42	9.48	9.54	9.60	9.66	9.72	9.78
9.50	9.56	9.62	9.68	9.73	9.79	9.85	9.92	9.98	10.04
9.75	9.81	9.87	9.93	9.99	10.05	10.11	10.17	10.23	10.30
10.00	10.06	10.12	10.18	10.24	10.30	10.37	10.43	10.49	10.56
10.25	10.31	10.37	10.43	10.50	10.56	10.62	10.69	10.75	10.81
10.50	10.56	10.62	10.69	10.75	10.81	10.88	10.94	11.01	11.07
10.75	10.81	10.88	10.94	11.00	11.07	11.13	11.20	11.26	11.33

have very similar APRs. The choice for the borrower is between paying fees up front or paying additional interest over the long term.

The same is true with financed closing costs, another option for cash-strapped buyers. The lender charges loan fees, but the fees and certain other closing costs are added to the loan amount and paid over time (as part of the mortgage payments) rather than at closing. Of course, interest is charged on the financed costs as well as the loan principal.

Evaluating Financing Options

When it comes time for buyers to evaluate their financing options and choose the loan they want, loan costs—interest rates, origination fees, discount points, and other lender charges—will naturally be a key consideration. But buyers should also consider how each of the different financing options is structured, and how each would affect their overall financial situation in the short term and the long term. For instance, would they have enough cash left over for furniture or necessary remodeling? Would they be required to dip into their retirement or college savings to pay the closing costs? All of these issues are important considerations when choosing a loan.

Buyers should ask themselves the following questions in connection with any mortgage loan they consider:

- How much money would we have left in savings after the transaction closes?
- How much spending money would we have left over each month after paying the mortgage payment?
- At what pace do we anticipate that our income will grow?
- How long do we plan to stay in the home we're buying?
- How rapidly would our equity build, based on reasonable market projections?
- How soon would the mortgage be paid off?
- Are we more concerned with the short-term cost of financing or the long-term cost?
- What alternative investment opportunities are available for money we don't put into the house?

The answers to these questions can affect a buyer's financing decision in a variety of ways. For example, some buyers are planning to live in the house they're purchasing for only a few years. These buyers might be good candidates for a loan with an adjustable interest rate. They can take advantage of a low initial rate with fewer worries about how high the rate may be ten years from now. However this type of buyer must also consider whether market conditions will allow them to sell their house at a profit after only a few years.

Generally speaking, when buyers don't expect to own the house they're buying for very long, it doesn't make sense to pay a lot of discount points to get a lower interest rate. Only a fairly long period of ownership will enable the buyers to recoup the money paid up front with interest savings over the long run.

Buyers who hope to retire early or reduce their workload may be most concerned with building equity and paying off their mortgage as soon as possible. They might prefer a loan with a 15-year or 20-year term, rather than the standard 30-year term, even though it means they will qualify for a smaller loan amount and have to buy a less expensive home than they otherwise could.

Many first-time buyers with limited buying power want to purchase the largest, most expensive home they can possibly afford. They are interested in any and all financing arrangements that can boost their price range: a downpayment assistance program, an adjustable interest rate, a high loan-to-value ratio, a 40-year loan term, secondary financing, and so on.

On the other hand, some buyers don't want to borrow as much money for a house as lenders would allow them to. They may want to invest their money differently, or they may simply prefer to avoid the financial stress that the maximum monthly mortgage payment would represent for them.

In short, buyers must evaluate every financing option in light of their own circumstances, goals, and preferences, along with relevant trends and developments in the housing market. Through qualifying standards, a lender takes certain aspects of the buyers' situation into account before agreeing to make a loan. But only the buyers themselves can decide which financing alternative is most comfortable for them and fits in best with their own financial plans.

Home Buyer Counseling Programs. Borrowing money to buy a house is such a complicated decision that it overwhelms many buyers, especially first-time buyers. In addition to asking real estate agents and loan officers for information and guidance, first-time buyers may

Length of time buyers expect to own their new house may affect financing choices benefit from participating in home buyer counseling before they decide what financing option will be best for them.

The Department of Housing and Urban Development (HUD) has developed a Housing Counseling Assistance Program that's open to anyone who is going to be house hunting and applying for a mortgage. (It's also open to renters and people who already own a home.) The counseling is provided by HUD-approved housing counseling agencies around the country. It's intended to educate participants about the responsibilities of home ownership (or tenancy): making mortgage or rent payments, maintaining the home, avoiding foreclosure or eviction, and so on.

A buyer who enrolls in a counseling program starts off with a confidential interview with a housing counselor. Housing counselors are required to establish action plans with every client (except reverse mortgagees) to help them achieve their housing goals. Any additional services depend on the buyer's needs. As a general rule, participation in counseling is entirely voluntary, but eligibility for certain HUD programs may require a certificate from a housing counselor verifying that an approved counseling program has been completed.

Applying for a Loan

After shopping for a loan and choosing a lender, the next step is to apply for the loan. To apply for a mortgage loan (or to obtain preapproval), the home buyers talk with a loan originator. This discussion may be a face-to-face meeting between the buyers and the loan originator, or the discussion may take place over the phone, by fax, or online. We'll refer to these communications between a loan originator and the home buyer as the "loan interview."

Prequalifying During the Interview. In the loan interview, the buyers and the loan originator will discuss the financing options the buyers have been considering and the loan programs and products that the lender offers. The loan originator will help the buyers decide which program best suits their needs.

While talking with the buyers, the loan originator may enter some key information about their finances into an automated underwriting system or other computer program. The system can provide a

HUD-approved housing counseling may be helpful to first-time home buyers

In loan interview, buyers discuss financing options with loan officer and fill out application form preliminary evaluation of what kind of loan the buyers are likely to qualify for and can be used to try out financing alternatives: How large a loan could the buyers qualify for if they made a $20,000 downpayment? What if they put only $10,000 down? What if they chose an adjustable-rate mortgage instead of a fixed-rate loan?

However, even if the system indicates at this stage that the buyers would qualify for the loan they want, that doesn't mean they've been preapproved for the loan. Preapproval doesn't take place until the buyers' background information has been documented and verified.

Deposit. When the buyers apply for the loan, they may be required to make a deposit to cover certain expenses that must be paid up front. Depending on the lender, these may include an application fee, a credit report fee, and other preliminary charges.

Most lenders require buyers to make a deposit to cover initial costs when application is submitted

Contract and Closing Date. If the buyers have already found the home they want to buy and have entered into a purchase agreement with the sellers, the loan originator will ask for a copy of the agreement. In examining the agreement, the loan originator will pay particular attention to the terms of any financing contingency clause and the agreed-upon closing date. The agreement may set a closing date that's too soon to be realistic; the financing, inspections, or other arrangements may not be completed in time. If the loan originator feels the closing date should be changed, she will consult with the real estate agent, who will explain the problem to the parties. When everyone has agreed on a more suitable date, the agent will have the buyers and sellers sign an amendment to the purchase agreement.

Loan officer reviews purchase and sale agreement for financing terms and closing date

The Loan Application Form

Lenders want their loans to be repaid without collection problems, and they try to make loans only to borrowers who can be expected to repay on time, as agreed. The purpose of the loan application is to gather the information the lender needs to determine whether the applicants will be reliable borrowers. It focuses on employment stability, income, credit scores, and net worth. The real estate agent working with the buyers should make sure they know in advance what information will be needed for the loan application, to avoid unnecessary delays in the process.

Uniform Residential Loan Application form is used by virtually all mortgage lenders

Virtually all mortgage lenders use the Uniform Residential Loan Application form shown in Figure 7.2. We'll go through the form to give you an overview of the information it requires.

Type and Terms of Loan. The application begins with questions about the loan being applied for: the type of loan, loan amount, loan term, interest rate, whether the rate will be fixed or adjustable, and whether the loan will involve any special amortization arrangement.

Property Information and Purpose of Loan. The next section of the application asks for the address and legal description of the property and when the house was built. (If the applicants are applying for preapproval and haven't found a house yet, this part of the form is left blank for now.) It also asks the purpose of the loan (purchase, construction, or refinance; primary residence, secondary residence, or investment property); the manner in which the buyers will take title (for example, as tenants in common); and the source of the downpayment, settlement charges (closing costs), and any secondary financing. This information will be used to order an appraisal of the property and to determine the maximum loan amount.

Borrower and Co-Borrower Information. The next section of the form requests the following information about each applicant: name, social security number, phone number, date of birth, years of schooling, marital status, and address. The lender also wants to know how many dependents the applicants must support, since children and other dependents may add considerably to their financial obligations. If the applicants have lived at their present address for less than two years, information about previous residences must also be provided.

Although it's legal for a lender to ask about a loan applicant's marital status and dependents, it's illegal for the lender to use that information in a discriminatory fashion. (See the discussion of the Equal Credit Opportunity Act in Chapter 14.)

Lender uses application form to gather information about the applicant's employment stability, income, and net worth

Employment Information. Each applicant must fill in the name and address of her employer, the number of years employed at this job, and the number of years employed in this line of work. The position, title, type of business, and business phone number must also be included. If an applicant has been at her current job for less than two years, the same information should be given for previous employers.

Fig. 7.2 Uniform Residential Loan Application form

Uniform Residential Loan Application

This application is designed to be completed by the applicant(s) with the Lender's assistance. Applicants should complete this form as "Borrower" or "Co-Borrower," as applicable. Co-Borrower information must also be provided (and the appropriate box checked) when ☐ the income or assets of a person other than the Borrower (including the Borrower's spouse) will be used as a basis for loan qualification or ☐ the income or assets of the Borrower's spouse or other person who has community property rights pursuant to state law will not be used as a basis for loan qualification, but his or her liabilities must be considered because the spouse or other person has community property rights pursuant to applicable law and Borrower resides in a community property state, the security property is located in a community property state, or the Borrower is relying on other property located in a community property state as a basis for repayment of the loan.

If this is an application for joint credit, Borrower and Co-Borrower each agree that we intend to apply for joint credit (sign below):

Borrower	Co-Borrower

I. TYPE OF MORTGAGE AND TERMS OF LOAN

Mortgage Applied for:	☐ VA ☐ FHA	☐ Conventional ☐ USDA/Rural Housing Service	☐ Other (explain):	Agency Case Number	Lender Case Number
Amount $	Interest Rate %	No. of Months	Amortization Type:	☐ Fixed Rate ☐ GPM	☐ Other (explain): ☐ ARM (type):

II. PROPERTY INFORMATION AND PURPOSE OF LOAN

Subject Property Address (street, city, state & ZIP)		No. of Units
Legal Description of Subject Property (attach description if necessary)		Year Built

Purpose of Loan	☐ Purchase ☐ Construction ☐ Other (explain): ☐ Refinance ☐ Construction-Permanent	Property will be: ☐ Primary Residence ☐ Secondary Residence ☐ Investment

Complete this line if construction or construction-permanent loan.

Year Lot Acquired	Original Cost $	Amount Existing Liens $	(a) Present Value of Lot $	(b) Cost of Improvements $	Total (a + b) $

Complete this line if this is a refinance loan.

Year Acquired	Original Cost $	Amount Existing Liens $	Purpose of Refinance	Describe Improvements Cost: $	☐ made ☐ to be made

Title will be held in what Name(s)	Manner in which Title will be held	Estate will be held in: ☐ Fee Simple ☐ Leasehold (show expiration date)
Source of Down Payment, Settlement Charges, and/or Subordinate Financing (explain)		

III. BORROWER INFORMATION

Borrower	Co-Borrower
Borrower's Name (include Jr. or Sr. if applicable)	Co-Borrower's Name (include Jr. or Sr. if applicable)

Social Security Number	Home Phone (incl. area code)	DOB (mm/dd/yyyy)	Yrs. School	Social Security Number	Home Phone (incl. area code)	DOB (mm/dd/yyyy)	Yrs. School

☐ Married ☐ Unmarried (include ☐ Separated single, divorced, widowed)	Dependents (not listed by Co-Borrower) no. ages	☐ Married ☐ Unmarried (include ☐ Separated single, divorced, widowed)	Dependents (not listed by Borrower) no. ages
Present Address (street, city, state, ZIP) ☐ Own ☐ Rent ___No. Yrs.		Present Address (street, city, state, ZIP) ☐ Own ☐ Rent ___No. Yrs.	
Mailing Address, if different from Present Address		Mailing Address, if different from Present Address	

If residing at present address for less than two years, complete the following:

Former Address (street, city, state, ZIP) ☐ Own ☐ Rent ___No. Yrs.		Former Address (street, city, state, ZIP) ☐ Own ☐ Rent ___No. Yrs.	

IV. EMPLOYMENT INFORMATION

Borrower	Co-Borrower

Name & Address of Employer	☐ Self Employed	Yrs. on this job	Name & Address of Employer	☐ Self Employed	Yrs. on this job
		Yrs. employed in this line of work/profession			Yrs. employed in this line of work/profession
Position/Title/Type of Business	Business Phone (incl. area code)		Position/Title/Type of Business	Business Phone (incl. area code)	

If employed in current position for less than two years or if currently employed in more than one position, complete the following:

Freddie Mac Form 65 7/05	Page 1 of 5	Fannie Mae Form 1003 7/05

Borrower		IV. EMPLOYMENT INFORMATION (cont'd)		Co-Borrower	
Name & Address of Employer ☐ Self Employed		Dates (from – to)	Name & Address of Employer ☐ Self Employed		Dates (from – to)
		Monthly Income $			Monthly Income $
Position/Title/Type of Business		Business Phone (incl. area code)	Position/Title/Type of Business		Business Phone (incl. area code)
Name & Address of Employer ☐ Self Employed		Dates (from – to)	Name & Address of Employer ☐ Self Employed		Dates (from – to)
		Monthly Income $			Monthly Income $
Position/Title/Type of Business		Business Phone (incl. area code)	Position/Title/Type of Business		Business Phone (incl. area code)

V. MONTHLY INCOME AND COMBINED HOUSING EXPENSE INFORMATION

Gross Monthly Income	Borrower	Co-Borrower	Total	Combined Monthly Housing Expense	Present	Proposed
Base Empl. Income*	$	$	$	Rent	$	
Overtime				First Mortgage (P&I)		$
Bonuses				Other Financing (P&I)		
Commissions				Hazard Insurance		
Dividends/Interest				Real Estate Taxes		
Net Rental Income				Mortgage Insurance		
Other (before completing, see the notice in "describe other income," below)				Homeowner Assn. Dues		
				Other:		
Total	$	$	$	Total	$	$

* Self Employed Borrower(s) may be required to provide additional documentation such as tax returns and financial statements.

Describe Other Income   *Notice:* **Alimony, child support, or separate maintenance income need not be revealed if the Borrower (B) or Co-Borrower (C) does not choose to have it considered for repaying this loan.**

B/C		Monthly Amount
		$

VI. ASSETS AND LIABILITIES

This Statement and any applicable supporting schedules may be completed jointly by both married and unmarried Co-Borrowers if their assets and liabilities are sufficiently joined so that the Statement can be meaningfully and fairly presented on a combined basis; otherwise, separate Statements and Schedules are required. If the Co-Borrower section was completed about a non-applicant spouse or other person, this Statement and supporting schedules must be completed about that spouse or other person also.

Completed ☐ Jointly ☐ Not Jointly

ASSETS Description	Cash or Market Value	Liabilities and Pledged Assets. List the creditor's name, address, and account number for all outstanding debts, including automobile loans, revolving charge accounts, real estate loans, alimony, child support, stock pledges, etc. Use continuation sheet, if necessary. Indicate by (*) those liabilities, which will be satisfied upon sale of real estate owned or upon refinancing of the subject property.		
Cash deposit toward purchase held by:	$			
List checking and savings accounts below		LIABILITIES	Monthly Payment & Months Left to Pay	Unpaid Balance
Name and address of Bank, S&L, or Credit Union		Name and address of Company	$ Payment/Months	$
Acct. no.	$	Acct. no.		
Name and address of Bank, S&L, or Credit Union		Name and address of Company	$ Payment/Months	$
Acct. no.	$	Acct. no.		
Name and address of Bank, S&L, or Credit Union		Name and address of Company	$ Payment/Months	$
Acct. no.	$	Acct. no.		

VI. ASSETS AND LIABILITIES (cont'd)

Name and address of Bank, S&L, or Credit Union		Name and address of Company	$ Payment/Months	$
Acct. no.	$	Acct. no.		
Stocks & Bonds (Company name/ number & description)	$	Name and address of Company	$ Payment/Months	$
		Acct. no.		
Life insurance net cash value Face amount: $	$	Name and address of Company	$ Payment/Months	$
Subtotal Liquid Assets	$			
Real estate owned (enter market value from schedule of real estate owned)	$			
Vested interest in retirement fund	$			
Net worth of business(es) owned (attach financial statement)	$	Acct. no.		
Automobiles owned (make and year)	$	Alimony/Child Support/Separate Maintenance Payments Owed to:	$	
Other Assets (itemize)	$	Job-Related Expense (child care, union dues, etc.)	$	
		Total Monthly Payments	$	
Total Assets a.	$	Net Worth ▶ (a minus b) $		**Total Liabilities b.** $

Schedule of Real Estate Owned (If additional properties are owned, use continuation sheet.)

Property Address (enter S if sold, PS if pending sale or R if rental being held for income) ▼	Type of Property	Present Market Value	Amount of Mortgages & Liens	Gross Rental Income	Mortgage Payments	Insurance, Maintenance, Taxes & Misc.	Net Rental Income
		$	$	$	$	$	$
Totals		$	$	$	$	$	$

List any additional names under which credit has previously been received and indicate appropriate creditor name(s) and account number(s):

Alternate Name	Creditor Name	Account Number

VII. DETAILS OF TRANSACTION		VIII. DECLARATIONS				
		If you answer "Yes" to any questions a through i, please use continuation sheet for explanation.	**Borrower**		**Co-Borrower**	
			Yes No		Yes No	
a.	Purchase price	$	a. Are there any outstanding judgments against you?	☐ ☐		☐ ☐
b.	Alterations, improvements, repairs		b. Have you been declared bankrupt within the past 7 years?	☐ ☐		☐ ☐
c.	Land (if acquired separately)		c. Have you had property foreclosed upon or given title or deed in lieu thereof in the last 7 years?	☐ ☐		☐ ☐
d.	Refinance (incl. debts to be paid off)		d. Are you a party to a lawsuit?	☐ ☐		☐ ☐
e.	Estimated prepaid items		e. Have you directly or indirectly been obligated on any loan which resulted in foreclosure, transfer of title in lieu of foreclosure, or judgment?	☐ ☐		☐ ☐
f.	Estimated closing costs		(This would include such loans as home mortgage loans, SBA loans, home improvement loans, educational loans, manufactured (mobile) home loans, any mortgage, financial obligation, bond, or loan guarantee. If "Yes," provide details, including date, name, and address of Lender, FHA or VA case number, if any, and reasons for the action.)			
g.	PMI, MIP, Funding Fee					
h.	Discount (if Borrower will pay)					
i.	Total costs (add items a through h)					

Freddie Mac Form 65   7/05   Page 3 of 5   Fannie Mae Form 1003   7/05

VII. DETAILS OF TRANSACTION		VIII. DECLARATIONS				
			Borrower		Co-Borrower	
		If you answer "Yes" to any questions a through i, please use continuation sheet for explanation.	Yes	No	Yes	No
j. Subordinate financing						
k. Borrower's closing costs paid by Seller		f. Are you presently delinquent or in default on any Federal debt or any other loan, mortgage, financial obligation, bond, or loan guarantee? If "Yes," give details as described in the preceding question.	☐	☐	☐	☐
l. Other Credits (explain)		g. Are you obligated to pay alimony, child support, or separate maintenance?	☐	☐	☐	☐
		h. Is any part of the down payment borrowed?	☐	☐	☐	☐
m. Loan amount (exclude PMI, MIP, Funding Fee financed)		i. Are you a co-maker or endorser on a note?	☐	☐	☐	☐
		j. Are you a U.S. citizen?	☐	☐	☐	☐
n. PMI, MIP, Funding Fee financed		k. Are you a permanent resident alien?	☐	☐	☐	☐
		l. Do you intend to occupy the property as your primary residence? If "Yes," complete question m below.	☐	☐	☐	☐
o. Loan amount (add m & n)		m. Have you had an ownership interest in a property in the last three years?	☐	☐	☐	☐
p. Cash from/to Borrower (subtract j, k, l & o from i)		(1) What type of property did you own—principal residence (PR), second home (SH), or investment property (IP)?	_____		_____	
		(2) How did you hold title to the home—solely by yourself (S), jointly with your spouse (SP), or jointly with another person (O)?	_____		_____	

IX. ACKNOWLEDGEMENT AND AGREEMENT

Each of the undersigned specifically represents to Lender and to Lender's actual or potential agents, brokers, processors, attorneys, insurers, servicers, successors and assigns and agrees and acknowledges that: (1) the information provided in this application is true and correct as of the date set forth opposite my signature and that any intentional or negligent misrepresentation of this information contained in this application may result in civil liability, including monetary damages, to any person who may suffer any loss due to reliance upon any misrepresentation that I have made on this application, and/or in criminal penalties including, but not limited to, fine or imprisonment or both under the provisions of Title 18, United States Code, Sec. 1001, et seq.; (2) the loan requested pursuant to this application (the "Loan") will be secured by a mortgage or deed of trust on the property described in this application; (3) the property will not be used for any illegal or prohibited purpose or use; (4) all statements made in this application are made for the purpose of obtaining a residential mortgage loan; (5) the property will be occupied as indicated in this application; (6) the Lender, its servicers, successors or assigns may retain the original and/or an electronic record of this application, whether or not the Loan is approved; (7) the Lender and its agents, brokers, insurers, servicers, successors, and assigns may continuously rely on the information contained in the application, and I am obligated to amend and/or supplement the information provided in this application if any of the material facts that I have represented herein should change prior to closing of the Loan; (8) in the event that my payments on the Loan become delinquent, the Lender, its servicers, successors or assigns may, in addition to any other rights and remedies that it may have relating to such delinquency, report my name and account information to one or more consumer reporting agencies; (9) ownership of the Loan and/or administration of the Loan account may be transferred with such notice as may be required by law; (10) neither Lender nor its agents, brokers, insurers, servicers, successors or assigns has made any representation or warranty, express or implied, to me regarding the property or the condition or value of the property; and (11) my transmission of this application as an "electronic record" containing my "electronic signature," as those terms are defined in applicable federal and/or state laws (excluding audio and video recordings), or my facsimile transmission of this application containing a facsimile of my signature, shall be as effective, enforceable and valid as if a paper version of this application were delivered containing my original written signature.

Acknowledgement. Each of the undersigned hereby acknowledges that any owner of the Loan, its servicers, successors and assigns, may verify or reverify any information contained in this application or obtain any information or data relating to the Loan, for any legitimate business purpose through any source, including a source named in this application or a consumer reporting agency.

Borrower's Signature	Date	Co-Borrower's Signature	Date
X		X	

X. INFORMATION FOR GOVERNMENT MONITORING PURPOSES

The following information is requested by the Federal Government for certain types of loans related to a dwelling in order to monitor the lender's compliance with equal credit opportunity, fair housing and home mortgage disclosure laws. You are not required to furnish this information, but are encouraged to do so. The law provides that a lender may not discriminate either on the basis of this information, or on whether you choose to furnish it. If you furnish the information, please provide both ethnicity and race. For race, you may check more than one designation. If you do not furnish ethnicity, race, or sex, under Federal regulations, this lender is required to note the information on the basis of visual observation and surname if you have made this application in person. If you do not wish to furnish the information, please check the box below. (Lender must review the above material to assure that the disclosures satisfy all requirements to which the lender is subject under applicable state law for the particular type of loan applied for.)

BORROWER ☐ I do not wish to furnish this information	CO-BORROWER ☐ I do not wish to furnish this information
Ethnicity: ☐ Hispanic or Latino ☐ Not Hispanic or Latino	Ethnicity: ☐ Hispanic or Latino ☐ Not Hispanic or Latino
Race: ☐ American Indian or Alaska Native ☐ Asian ☐ Black or African American ☐ Native Hawaiian or Other Pacific Islander ☐ White	Race: ☐ American Indian or Alaska Native ☐ Asian ☐ Black or African American ☐ Native Hawaiian or Other Pacific Islander ☐ White
Sex: ☐ Female ☐ Male	Sex: ☐ Female ☐ Male

To be Completed by Interviewer This application was taken by: ☐ Face-to-face interview ☐ Mail ☐ Telephone ☐ Internet	Interviewer's Name (print or type)	Name and Address of Interviewer's Employer
	Interviewer's Signature Date	
	Interviewer's Phone Number (incl. area code)	

CONTINUATION SHEET/RESIDENTIAL LOAN APPLICATION		
Use this continuation sheet if you need more space to complete the Residential Loan Application. Mark **B** f or Borrower or **C** for Co-Borrower.	Borrower:	Agency Case Number:
	Co-Borrower:	Lender Case Number:

I/We fully understand that it is a Federal crime punishable by fine or imprisonment, or both, to knowingly make any false statements concerning any of the above facts as applicable under the provisions of Title 18, United States Code, Section 1001, et seq.

Borrower's Signature	Date	Co-Borrower's Signature	Date
X		X	

Freddie Mac Form 65   7/05   **Page 5 of 5**   **Fannie Mae Form 1003   7/05**

Income and Monthly Housing Expense Information. This section requests information about primary employment income, overtime, bonuses, commissions, dividends and interest, net rental income, and income from any other sources. Each applicant must list his current monthly housing expense—either the rent or the house payment (including principal and interest, hazard insurance, property taxes, mortgage insurance, and homeowners association dues).

Assets may include:
• Good faith deposit
• Money in bank
• Investments
• Life insurance policy
• Retirement account
• Automobile
• Personal property
• Real property

Liabilities may include:
• Student loan
• Car loan
• Real estate loan
• Other installment loan
• Charge accounts
• Credit cards
• Alimony or child support owed
• Job-related expenses

Assets and Liabilities. In the next section of the form, each loan applicant lists all of his assets and liabilities. Assets include the good faith deposit given to the seller (if a purchase agreement has been signed), money in checking and savings accounts, stocks and bonds, life insurance policies, retirement funds, automobiles, other personal property, and real estate already owned. (For real estate, a separate schedule in the application form must also be filled out.) If the applicants own a business, they must list its net worth and attach a financial statement to the application form.

The applicants' liabilities may include student loans, car loans, real estate loans, and other installment debts; revolving credit (charge accounts and credit cards); alimony and/or child support payments; child care expenses; and job-related expenses such as union dues. The applicants should also be prepared to list debts that have recently been paid off.

Details of Transaction. The next section asks for information on the real estate transaction itself. (Again, if the applicants are applying for preapproval and haven't found a house yet, this section will be left blank for the time being.) The applicants are to fill in the purchase price, the cost of alterations or improvements, the cost of the land (if the land is acquired separately), prepaid expenses, and closing costs. There are also blanks for the mortgage insurance or funding fee, discount fee, any secondary financing, any closing costs to be paid by the seller, and the loan amount. The lender will use these figures to calculate the cash the applicants will need to close the transaction.

Declarations. The loan applicants must answer several questions regarding outstanding judgments, bankruptcies, property foreclosures, lawsuits, loan defaults, and alimony or child support payments. Then the application asks whether any part of the downpayment is borrowed and whether each applicant is a co-maker or endorser on any promissory notes. Next, each applicant is asked whether she is a U.S. citizen or a permanent resident alien. Finally, the form asks if the applicants intend to occupy the property as a primary residence. If so, they are required to indicate whether they have owned any other property during the previous three years, what type of property it was (a principal residence, a second home, or an investment property), and how title was held. Applicants who haven't owned a home in the previous three years may be treated as first-time buyers for the purposes of certain loan programs.

Acknowledgment and Agreement. By signing and dating the application form, the applicants are agreeing to several provisions regarding the application and the loan. Among other things, the applicants agree to inform the lender if any of the information provided in the application changes before closing.

> Applicant agrees to correct or update information on the application if necessary

Information for Government Monitoring. One of the last sections of the application form sets forth optional questions regarding the applicants' ethnicity, race, and sex. If the applicants answer these questions, the federal government will use the information to evaluate the lender's compliance with fair lending laws.

Continuation Sheet. The last page of the loan application form is a continuation sheet, in case the applicants need more room to answer any of the questions on the previous pages. Note that the applicants must sign and date the continuation sheet in addition to the "Acknowledgment and Agreement" section on the previous page.

Application Checklist. Real estate agents can help buyers prepare for the application process by going over a checklist of required information and documentation with them. See the sample checklist in Figure 7.3.

> Agent should let buyer know information needed for loan application

Required Disclosures

In residential mortgage transactions, federal law requires lenders and mortgage brokers to meet four disclosures requirements. The first is the Truth in Lending Act disclosure, which provides information about the loan's financing costs, including the annual percentage rate, the total finance charge, and the total amount financed. The second disclosure is the good faith estimate of closing costs, required under the Real Estate Settlement Procedures Act. It lists estimates of all loan-related charges and all other costs the buyers will be expected to pay at closing. In addition, RESPA requires lenders and mortgage

Fig. 7.3 Checklist of application information and documentation

Loan Application Checklist

Purchase and sale agreement (if the applicant has already entered into one)

Social security number for each applicant

Residence history:
- ✓ Addresses where the applicant has lived during the past few years
- ✓ Name and address of the applicant's current landlord

Employment history:
- ✓ Names and addresses of the employers the applicant has worked for in the last two years; positions held; whether employment was full- or part-time; and the wage or salary at time of departure
- ✓ If the applicant was recently in school or the military, a copy of the diploma or discharge papers

Income information:
- ✓ W-2 forms for the previous two years and payroll stubs for the previous 30 days (showing current and year-to-date earnings)
- ✓ If commissions are a significant part of the applicant's income, tax returns for the past two years
- ✓ If the applicant is self-employed, business and personal tax returns for the past two years, plus a year-to-date income and expense statement
- ✓ If the applicant is a major stockholder in a corporation (owns 25% or more of the stock), three years of corporate tax returns
- ✓ Amount and sources of income, including wages and secondary sources (such as a pension, social security, or child support)
- ✓ Documentation for all sources of income; child support/alimony requires a copy of the divorce decree

List of assets:
- ✓ Names, addresses, and account numbers for all bank accounts
- ✓ Bank statements for the past three months
- ✓ Investment statements for the past three months
- ✓ Value of household goods and other personal property
- ✓ Make, model, year, and market value of automobiles
- ✓ Cash and face value of insurance policies
- ✓ Address, description, and value of any real estate owned; any lease agreements
- ✓ Gift letter, if a gift is the source of part of the funds for closing (see Chapter 8)
- ✓ If the applicant's present home is to be sold, the net amount from the sale after deducting all selling expenses
- ✓ If the applicant is being relocated by an employer who is paying some of the closing costs, a letter from the employer stating which costs will be paid by the company

List of liabilities:
- ✓ For each debt, the name, address, and phone number of the creditor, and the balance, monthly payment, and account number
- ✓ Copy of divorce decree, for child support or alimony obligation

Current or estimated property taxes for the home being purchased (if the home has been chosen)

Certificate of Eligibility for VA loans

brokers to give loan applicants a special information booklet, to help borrowers understand the homebuying and settlement process better. Finally, RESPA requires lenders to give loan applicants a mortgage servicing disclosure statement, to inform the borrower about the likelihood of their loan being transferred to another entity at any time during the loan term.

Lenders are required to provide these disclosures within three business days of receiving a written loan application, unless the loan application is declined before that. Most lenders give the disclosures to loan applicants at the time of application. If the disclosed information changes significantly over the course of the transaction, new disclosures should be made before closing. (Both the Truth in Lending Act and the Real Estate Settlement Procedures Act are discussed more fully in Chapter 14.)

Lender must provide TILA and RESPA disclosure statements within 3 days after application

Locking In the Interest Rate

One other issue that should be addressed during the loan application process is whether the buyers want to have the interest rate on the loan they're applying for **locked in**, or guaranteed, for a certain period. If the rate isn't locked in, it will **float**, which means that it will move up or down with market interest rates until shortly before the transaction closes. Naturally, a change in the interest rate will also cause a change in the monthly payment for the loan.

Lock-in: lender guarantees certain interest rate for specified period

> **Example:** When Jim Dawson applies for a loan, the loan officer says the interest rate will be 6.25%, and that's the figure filled in on the loan application form. Dawson doesn't ask to have the rate locked in, however.
>
> Market interest rates are going up, and by the time Dawson's loan closes (four weeks later) the rate on his loan has risen to 6.75%. Dawson is faced with the prospect of paying a higher interest rate and making a larger monthly mortgage payment than he anticipated. With the new interest rate, his monthly payment amount has increased from $1,231 to $1,297.

A situation like the one in the example could be a serious problem, especially for buyers who barely qualified for their loan in the first place. A sharp increase in the interest rate might increase the monthly payment so much that they no longer qualify. They could reduce the monthly payment back to an affordable level by putting more money down (to reduce the loan amount) or by paying discount points (to reduce the interest rate). However, many buyers would be unable or unwilling to take either of those steps. If market interest rates are likely to rise, locking in the loan's rate can be extremely important.

Real estate agents should keep in mind that a buyer's failure to lock in the interest rate can affect the home seller as well as the buyer. If an increased interest rate forces the buyer to choose between an increase in the monthly payment amount, the downpayment amount, or the points, the transaction could be seriously delayed or even terminated.

Lock-in Period. When a loan officer quotes an interest rate, the buyers should ask whether the rate can be locked in, and if so, starting when and for how long. (Common lock-in periods are 15, 30, or 45 days.) Some lenders are willing to lock in the interest rate when the application is submitted; others won't do it until the loan has been approved. Either way, the lock-in period should always extend beyond the expected loan processing time. A 15-day guarantee is worthless if there's little hope of closing the transaction in that time. The best arrangement is for the lock-in period to be extended automatically if the closing is delayed. Some lenders provide a free automatic extension; others will charge an extension fee.

Lock-in Fee. Locking in an interest rate may require a lock-in fee; for example, the lender might charge 1.5% of the loan amount. The fee is typically applied to the buyers' closing costs if the transaction closes. (If the loan application is rejected, the lock-in fee is refunded.)

Lock-in fee will be refunded if loan application is denied

Rate Decreases. If the buyers think market interest rates might drop in the next few weeks, it probably doesn't make sense to lock in the rate any sooner than necessary. (Lenders generally require the rate to be locked in 72 hours before closing, so that accurate settlement statements can be prepared.) A lender usually has the right to charge the locked-in rate even if market rates have gone down in the period before closing.

Written Agreement. As you can see, the details of interest rate lock-ins can have a significant impact on the total costs for a loan. Just like other details of the mortgage application process, it's a matter of contract between the lender and the buyers. A real estate agent should impress on her buyers the importance of having the lender put all of the details of the lock-in agreement in writing. A spoken commitment from the loan originator is not enough to protect the buyers' interests, and the consequences of a misunderstanding could be very significant.

Application Processing

Once a loan application has been filled out, the next step is to verify the information provided by the buyers. Verification forms are sent out to the buyers' employers, banks or other financial institutions, and previous mortgage lender, if any. Credit reports and credit scores are obtained from the major credit reporting agencies (see Chapter 8). If the buyers have already entered into a contract for the purchase of a particular property, the lender orders a title report from a title insurance company and sends an appraiser to appraise the property.

When the completed verification forms, reports, and other documentation have been received, a loan processor puts together a loan package and sends it to the underwriting department.

Verification forms and other documentation are used to check information on application

Loan officer submits loan package to underwriter

The Underwriting Decision

The loan underwriter first looks over the loan package to make sure it's complete. If necessary, the underwriter will ask the loan officer to have the buyers submit additional documentation, such as investment account records, pension plan documents, or tax returns.

The underwriter carefully examines the application, verification forms, credit reports, and other documentation, and applies the appropriate qualifying standards to the buyers. These steps may be carried out with or without the help of an automated underwriting system (see Chapter 8). At the end of the evaluation process, the underwriter approves the loan, rejects it, or approves it subject to certain conditions.

Rejection. When a loan application is denied, the lender is required by federal law to provide the applicants with a written statement explaining why. Applicants are entitled to receive this statement within 30 days after submitting their completed application. Depending on the reasons for the denial, the buyers might want to apply to a different lender, apply for a smaller loan or a different type of loan, or decide to wait until they can pay off some of their debts, improve their credit score, or save additional money for a larger downpayment.

When an application is denied, some of the fees the applicants paid up front may be refunded, but others won't be. For example, a lock-in fee is typically refunded, while the application fee and credit report fee are not.

Conditional Commitment. A conditional approval, often called a conditional commitment, requires fulfillment of specified conditions and submission of additional documentation. For example, if approval is conditioned on the sale of the buyers' current home, final approval will require the settlement statement from that sale.

Preapproval Letter. Preapproval for a loan is a form of conditional commitment; the approval is contingent on a satisfactory appraisal and title report once the buyers have found the home they want to buy.

After an underwriter decides that buyers should be preapproved for the loan they're seeking, a **preapproval letter** is prepared. As explained earlier, the preapproval letter states that the lender will loan the buyers up to a specified amount of money to buy a house that meets the lender's standards.

The preapproval letter will expire at the end of a specified period, such as 30 days. If the buyers still haven't found the house they want to purchase during that time, the lender may agree to an extension if the buyers' financial information is reverified.

Final Commitment. When all of the conditions for loan approval have been fulfilled, the lender will give the buyers a final commitment letter, confirming the exact terms on which the loan will be made. This is sometimes called a firm commitment, in contrast to the earlier conditional commitment. The commitment letter will specify a date on which the lender's commitment will expire.

Firm commitment letter states exact terms on which loan will be made

Closing the Loan

The last stage of the financing process is coordinated with the closing of the real estate transaction as a whole. We'll look at some aspects of closing that concern the buyer's financing.

The Closing Agent

Real estate closing procedures vary from one part of the country to another. In many areas, closings are handled through escrow. **Escrow** is an arrangement in which a neutral third party holds money and documents on behalf of the buyer and seller until their transaction is ready to close. When all of the conditions set forth in the purchase agreement have been fulfilled, the third party—known as an **escrow**

Escrow: neutral third party holds money and documents for buyer and seller

204

agent or **closing agent**—disburses the purchase price to the seller and delivers the deed to the buyer.

Depending on local practices, the closing agent may be an independent escrow agent, an employee of the buyer's lender or the title company, a lawyer, or a real estate broker.

Steps in the Closing Process

The closing agent is usually responsible for handling all of the details that must be taken care of before the transaction can close. Some of these details involve requirements imposed by the lender.

Clearing and Insuring Title. Since the property being purchased is going to serve as collateral for the new loan, the lender wants to make sure that the title is free of encumbrances that could interfere with the lender's security interest. Except for property tax liens and special assessment liens, any liens that would have higher priority than the new mortgage or deed of trust must be removed. These older liens are the seller's responsibility, and the closing agent will usually arrange for them to be paid off out of the seller's proceeds at closing. The appropriate lien releases will be recorded along with the other documents (the new deed, the new mortgage or deed of trust, and so on).

The lender's security interest will also be protected by an extended coverage title insurance policy, usually paid for by the buyer. Under the terms of the policy, if it turns out that there are liens against the property that weren't listed as exceptions from coverage, the title insurance company will reimburse the lender for resulting losses.

Inspections and Corrective Action. Another way for a lender to protect the value of its collateral is by requiring certain inspections to be carried out. For example, a pest control inspection, a soil percolation test, or a flood hazard inspection might be considered necessary, depending on the type of property and the area it's located in. Inspection reports will be submitted to the lender for review, and the lender may decide that specific repairs must be made or other corrective action must be taken. The repairs or corrective action may or may not have to be completed before closing.

Loan Documents and Buyer's Funds. Once the buyer's loan has been approved, the lender forwards the loan documents (promissory note,

Lender's closing concerns:
- Clearing liens from title
- Establishing condition of title
- Inspections and repairs
- Buyer's funds for closing
- Document preparation and recording

mortgage or deed of trust, and—if necessary—updated disclosure statements) to the closing agent. At this point, the buyer can complete his part of the transaction by depositing funds for the downpayment and closing costs into escrow and signing the loan documents. The signed documents are then returned to the lender.

Impound Account. In most transactions, the buyer is required to make a deposit into an impound account at closing. An impound account, also called a reserve account or escrow account, is a trust account set up by the lender to ensure that the buyer's property taxes and hazard and mortgage insurance premiums are paid on time. The buyer will pay the lender a portion of these expenses each month along with the principal and interest payment on the loan. The lender will deposit the tax and insurance payments into the impound account, and when taxes or insurance premiums become due, pay them out of the impound account. At closing, the lender usually has the buyer make an initial deposit into the impound account, to serve as a cushion for future expenses. Federal law caps out the amount buyers can be required to deposit to no more than two months worth of escrow payments.

Interim Interest. In the course of this chapter we've already mentioned most of the fees and charges connected with the loan that the buyer will pay as closing costs. They may include an origination fee, discount points, a mortgage broker's commission, a document preparation fee, and so on. One charge the buyer will encounter at closing that we haven't explained yet is interim interest, also called prepaid interest.

Interim interest arises in part because of a custom concerning the due date of the buyer's initial loan payment. As a general rule, a buyer's first monthly mortgage payment is not due on the first day of the month immediately following closing, but rather on the first day of the next month after that.

> **Example:** Closing takes place on January 23. The buyer is not required to make a mortgage payment on February 1. Instead, the first payment on the loan is due on March 1.

This practice gives the buyer a chance to recover from the financial strain of closing. However, even though the first loan payment isn't

Impound account ensures that taxes, hazard insurance, and mortgage insurance are paid on time

Interim interest covers period from closing date to end of month in which closing occurs

Buyer's first payment is due on the first day of the second month following the month in which closing occurs

due for an extra month, interest begins accruing on the loan starting with the day of closing.

Interest on a mortgage loan is paid in arrears. In other words, the interest that accrues during a given month is paid at the end of that month. So, to return to the example above, the March 1 payment will cover the interest that accrues during February. However, that first payment won't cover the interest that accrued between January 23 (the closing date) and January 31. The lender requires the interest for those nine days to be paid in advance, when the transaction closes. This advance payment of interest is called interim or prepaid interest and is one of the buyer's closing costs.

Mortgage interest is paid in arrears

Funding the Loan. When the loan documents have been executed and all of the lender's conditions have been satisfied, including final verification of the buyer's employment status and other financial information, the lender releases the buyer's loan funds to the closing agent. This is referred to as funding the loan.

Settlement Statements. Once precise figures for all of the closing costs have been determined, the closing agent prepares final settlement statements for the buyer and the seller in compliance with the Real Estate Settlement Procedures Act (see Chapter 14). RESPA requires the closing agent to provide a detailed list of each party's settlement charges and credits on a Uniform Settlement Statement Form (also known as a HUD-1). These itemized charges and credits will be taken into account for that party in closing the transaction and disbursing the funds. Under federal law, the buyer has a right to inspect this settlement statement, upon request, at least one day prior to closing.

Settlement statement is a detailed listing of each party's credits and debits at closing

Final Steps. The closing agent arranges for the deed, mortgage or deed of trust, lien releases, and other documents to be recorded, and disburses the appropriate funds to the seller, the real estate agent, and other parties entitled to payment. The title company issues the buyer's and lender's title insurance policies, the lender sends copies of the loan documents to the buyer, and the buyer provides a copy of the hazard insurance policy to the lender. The transaction has closed.

Outline: The Financing Process

I. Shopping for a Loan

    A. Loan consumers should engage in comparison shopping for a loan, which involves assessing their own needs and finances as well as comparing rates and fees.

    B. Prequalifying vs. preapproval

        1. Prequalifying: informal process performed by either a lender or a real estate agent, used to determine an affordable price range for a buyer.

        2. Preapproval: formal process performed by a lender, which results in a preapproval letter stating a maximum loan amount based on the buyer's income and net worth.

        3. Advantages of preapproval: can make a buyer's offer more appealing to a seller, and streamlines the closing process.

    C. Prequalification process

        1. First step is to apply an income ratio to buyers' monthly income to calculate maximum monthly mortgage payment.

        2. Second step is to subtract a percentage representing taxes and insurance, to calculate the maximum principal and interest payment.

        3. Third step is to use market interest rates to calculate the maximum loan amount.

        4. Final step is to divide the maximum loan amount by the appropriate loan-to-value ratio to determine the appropriate price a buyer should pay for a home.

    D. Choosing a lender

        1. A buyer should research lenders by comparing interest rates and fees.

        2. A buyer also may rely on referrals to find a reputable and competent lender.

        3. Buyers should be concerned with a lender's expertise and efficiency as well as its interest rates and fees.

    E. Loan costs

        1. Loan fees: usually described in terms of "points," where a point is one percentage point of the loan amount.

        2. Origination fee: a one-time service fee charged by the lender to cover administrative expenses associated with issuing the loan.

3. Discount points: an additional charge imposed by a lender to increase the lender's upfront yield on the loan.

4. A lender usually charges a lower interest rate in exchange for a buyer paying discount points upfront.

5. A seller may pay discount points on a buyer's behalf in order to "buy down" the buyer's interest rate.

6. Other fees: a lender may charge additional fees for application, underwriting, or document preparation.

7. Mortgage broker fees: a mortgage broker's fee may be a separate charge or part of the points quoted for the loan; the amount should be disclosed in the good faith estimate and settlement statement.

F. Comparing loan costs

1. The Truth in Lending Act (TILA) is a federal consumer protection act requiring certain disclosures to help borrowers understand the true cost of credit.

2. TILA requires disclosure of the annual percentage rate (APR), which is the relationship of the total finance charge to the loan amount, expressed as an annual percentage.

G. Evaluating financing options

1. Buyers need to weigh considerations other than the loan costs, such as financial priorities, how long they will live in the house, and other investment opportunities.

2. Buyers may use a home buyer counseling program for assistance in deciding which financing option is most appropriate.

II. Applying for a Loan

A. Loan interview and application

1. Buyers will provide financial information to the loan originator, which will be the basis for the loan approval or preapproval. Buyers may also need to pay certain expenses, such as a loan application fee.

2. The information provided to the originator includes information regarding employment, income, current monthly housing expense, assets and liabilities.

B. Disclosure statements

1. The lender will provide a Truth in Lending disclosure, which discloses the overall cost of the loan, including annual percentage rate and total finance charge.

2. The lender will also provide the good faith estimate of closing costs required under the Real Estate Settlement Procedures Act.

C. Locking in the interest rate

1. Buyers may lock in the interest rate on the application date, to avoid the risk of interest rates going up between the application date and the closing date.

2. A lender may charge a lock-in fee.

III. Application Processing

A. Underwriting decision

1. An underwriter will evaluate the loan application and decide whether to approve it, reject it, or approve it subject to conditions.

2. A conditional commitment may require additional documentation, such as proof of sale of the buyers' current home.

3. When all conditions for loan approval are met, the lender will issue a final commitment letter.

IV. Closing the Loan

A. Closing agent

1. A closing agent or escrow agent will act as a neutral third party who holds money and documents on behalf of the buyer and seller until the transaction is ready to close.

B. Steps in closing process

1. Clearing and insuring title: the lender will want to ensure that the property is free of encumbrances that could interfere with its security interest.

2. Inspections: a lender may require certain inspections of the property to be performed, to make sure that the property will continue to be adequate collateral.

3. Impound account: the buyer will make an initial deposit into the impound account; a portion of each monthly loan payment will be deposited into the account as well. Property taxes and insurance will be paid out of this account.

4. Interim interest: because mortgage interest is paid in arrears, but no payment is due in the month following closing, a buyer will need to pay interest up front to pay for the partial first month's interest.

5. Settlement statement: a closing agent will prepare settlement statements for both parties listing all charges and credits.

Key Terms

Prequalification: Informal approval from a lender or real estate agent suggesting the maximum amount a buyer could afford to spend on a home.

Preapproval: Formal loan approval from a lender stating a maximum loan amount that the lender is willing to issue, based on the borrower's income and assets.

PITI payment: The full monthly mortgage payment, including property taxes and hazard insurance as well as principal and interest.

Mortgage broker: An intermediary who brings lenders and borrowers together and negotiates loan agreements between them.

Loan fee: Any one-time fee that a lender charges at closing for a loan or an assumption, including origination fees and discount points.

Origination fee: A fee charged by a lender upon making a new loan, intended to cover the administrative cost of processing the loan.

Discount points: A fee a lender may charge at closing to increase its upfront profit on the loan.

Buydown: When a seller or third party pays the lender a lump sum at closing to lower the interest rate charged to the buyer.

Yield spread premium: A form of compensation to mortgage brokers based on a formula that rewards the broker for the difference between the loan's interest rate and the current market rate.

Truth in Lending Act: A federal law that requires lenders to make disclosures concerning loan costs (including the total finance charge and annual percentage rate) to consumer loan applicants.

Annual Percentage Rate: Under the Truth in Lending Act, the relationship between a loan's total finance charge and the total amount financed, expressed as an annual percentage.

Total finance charge: All charges associated with a loan, including the interest, any discount points paid by the borrower, the loan origination fee, and mortgage insurance.

Real Estate Settlement Procedures Act: A federal law that requires lenders to disclose certain information about closing costs to loan applicants; also known as RESPA.

Lock-in: When a lender guarantees a loan applicant a particular interest rate for a specific period of time.

Conditional commitment: A conditional approval of a loan that requires fulfillment of certain conditions.

Escrow agent: A third party who holds things of value (such as money and documents) on behalf of parties to a transaction until specified conditions are fulfilled.

Impound account: A bank account maintained by a lender for the payment of property taxes and insurance premiums on the security property; the lender requires the borrower to make regular deposits into the account, and then pays the expenses out of the account.

Interim interest: Interest on a new loan that must be paid at the time of closing; it covers the interest due for the first month of the loan term.

Chapter Quiz

1. The best way to compare the cost of loans is by using the:

   a. lender's yield

   b. annual interest rate

   c. combination of the origination fee and the loan discount

   d. annual percentage rate

2. A lender will want to know a loan applicant's:

   a. current rent or house payment

   b. employment history for the past ten years

   c. tax bracket for the past three years

   d. All of the above

3. The Masons are buying a house. The sales price is $163,500, and they're borrowing $139,000. They've agreed to pay a loan discount fee of two points, which amounts to:

   a. $3,270

   b. $2,780

   c. $1,635

   d. $1,390

4. The fee that pays for the lender's overhead is the:

   a. loan discount

   b. APR

   c. origination fee

   d. interest rate

5. When a lender guarantees a particular interest rate for a certain period of time, it is called:

   a. a discount fee

   b. a lock-in

   c. a float

   d. an annualized percentage rate

6. The portion of a borrower's monthly payment that goes toward property taxes and insurance will be held in a/an:

   a. trust fund
   b. recovery account
   c. impound account
   d. balloon payment

7. The charges payable by or to a party in a real estate transaction show up on the:

   a. settlement statement
   b. good faith estimate of closing costs
   c. lender disclosure statement
   d. Uniform Land Cost Disclosure Statement

8. Which of the following costs are reflected in a loan's APR?

   a. Interest, points paid by borrower, loan origination fee, mortgage insurance
   b. Interest, appraisal fee, loan origination fee, points paid by either party
   c. Appraisal fee, credit report fee, loan origination fee
   d. Points paid by borrower, origination fee, appraisal fee, credit report fee

9. The purpose of discount points is to:

   a. cover the administrative costs associated with issuing and servicing the loan
   b. increase the lender's upfront yield
   c. pay for costs associated with preparing the good faith estimate of costs
   d. increase the loan's interest rate in exchange for no loan fees

10. Formal approval by a lender, in the form of a letter stating the maximum loan amount the lender is willing to authorize, is:

    a. preapproval
    b. prequalification
    c. predetermination
    d. preauthorization

Answer Key

1. d. To compare loans costs, applicants should compare the various loans' annual percentage rates.

2. a. A lender will want to know a loan applicant's current housing expenses. The lender will not be concerned with the applicant's tax bracket, and will want to see employment information for only the previous two years.

3. b. The Masons' loan amount is $139,000 and two points of $139,000 is $2,780 ($139,000 × .02 = $2,780).

4. c. An origination fee pays for the lender's administrative costs.

5. b. With a lock-in, a lender guarantees a borrower's interest rate even if rates go up between the application date and the closing date.

6. c. An impound account is used to hold the portion of a borrower's monthly payments that are applied to property taxes and hazard insurance until those bills come due.

7. a. A settlement statement is used by a closing agent to show the charges and credits that will apply to each party during the closing process.

8. a. Interest, borrower-paid points, the origination fee, and mortgage insurance are all considered part of the total finance charge.

9. b. Discount points increase the lender's upfront yield, or profit. A lender charges a lower interest rate in exchange for the payment of discount points.

10. a. Preapproval is a formal approval process performed by a lender, which results in the lender agreeing to loan the buyer up to a specified amount when he finds a home he wishes to buy.

Chapter 8
Qualifying the Buyer

The Underwriting Process
- Qualifying standards
- Automated underwriting

Evaluating Creditworthiness

Credit Reputation
- Credit reports
- Length of credit history
- Payment record
- Major derogatory incidents
- Credit scores
- Obtaining credit information
- Explaining credit problems

Income Analysis
- Characteristics of income
- Stable monthly income
- Calculating stable monthly income
- Income ratios

Net Worth
- Funds for closing
- Assets
- Liabilities
- Gift funds

Other Factors in Underwriting

Subprime Lending

Risk-based Loan Pricing

Introduction

Before agreeing to make a real estate loan, a lender will evaluate both the buyer and the property to determine whether they **qualify** for the loan—that is, whether they meet the lender's minimum standards. This evaluation process is called **loan underwriting**; the person who performs the evaluation is called a loan underwriter or credit underwriter.

The primary purpose of the evaluation is to determine the degree of risk that the loan would represent for the lender. This determination hinges on the answers to two fundamental questions:

Loan underwriter evaluates:
1. Loan applicant's overall financial situation
2. Value of property

1. Does the buyer's overall financial situation indicate that he can reasonably be expected to make the proposed monthly loan payments on time?
2. Is there sufficient value in the property pledged as collateral to ensure recovery of the loan amount in the event of default?

The underwriter tries to make sure the buyer is someone who can afford the loan and who is unlikely to default. But since default always remains a possibility, the underwriter also tries to make sure that the property is worth enough so that the proceeds of a foreclosure sale would cover the loan amount.

Our discussion of underwriting is divided into two main parts: qualifying the buyer, covered in this chapter, and qualifying the property, covered in the next one. This chapter explains the factors that are taken into account in evaluating a home buyer's financial situation. The next chapter explains how a home is appraised and how the appraised value is used to set the loan amount. First, however, let's begin with some general information about the underwriting process.

The Underwriting Process

Underwriting a mortgage loan involves these basic tasks: reviewing the loan application; obtaining additional information about the applicant from other sources; applying the lender's qualifying standards; verifying information provided by the applicant; evaluating the property appraisal; and making a recommendation in favor of or against loan approval. How these tasks are carried out varies from one lender to another, of course. And the underwriting process changes over time, as new practices become established in the lending industry. In particular, the growing role of computer programs in underwriting has caused major changes, as we'll discuss shortly.

Qualifying Standards

The minimum standards used in underwriting—called **underwriting standards** or qualifying standards—draw a boundary line between acceptable risks and unacceptable risks. Loans that meet the standards are considered acceptable risks; loans that don't are considered unacceptable risks. Who sets those standards? In other words, who decides which loans are worth the risk of making them?

In theory, residential lenders are free to set their own qualifying standards. They can take virtually any risks they want to, as long as they don't violate the federal and state regulations that govern financial institutions. In practice, however, residential lenders usually apply qualifying standards set by the major secondary market agencies (Fannie Mae and Freddie Mac), by the FHA, or by the VA. If a conventional loan is going to be sold to Fannie Mae or Freddie Mac, their standards must be met. If the loan is going to be insured by the FHA or guaranteed by the VA, the FHA or VA standards must be met.

Each of these sets of qualifying standards (Fannie Mae, Freddie Mac, FHA, and VA) is different. The specific rules for the various loan programs are covered in Chapter 10, Conventional Financing; Chapter 11, FHA-Insured Loans; and Chapter 12, VA-Guaranteed Loans. But all of the different rules are based on the underlying principles and concepts that we'll be discussing in this chapter.

Underwriting standards:
- Most lenders use Fannie Mae/Freddie Mac standards for conventional loans
- FHA and VA standards must be used for FHA and VA loans

Automated Underwriting

Within the limits set by the qualifying standards they apply, underwriters often have to draw on their own experience and judgment in deciding whether to recommend that a particular loan be approved or denied. The qualifying standards guide them in evaluating various aspects of the loan application, but weighing the positive factors against the negative isn't always a simple matter. Underwriting has been described as an art, not a science.

However, **automated underwriting** (AU) has moved the underwriting process at least somewhat closer to the scientific end of the

Automated underwriting system: a computer program designed to analyze loan applications and recommend approval or rejection

spectrum. An **automated underwriting system** (AUS) is a computer program designed to perform a preliminary analysis of loan applications and make a recommendation for or against approval. Introduced in the 1990s, these systems are now in widespread use. AU systems don't completely replace traditional underwriting (now referred to as **manual underwriting**). Instead, the two types of underwriting are used in conjunction with one another.

AU and the Secondary Market. Some large lenders have their own proprietary automated underwriting systems, but the predominant systems are the ones developed by Fannie Mae (Desktop Underwriter®) and Freddie Mac (Loan Prospector®). Both Desktop Underwriter® and Loan Prospector® can be used to underwrite conventional, FHA, or VA loans, applying the appropriate qualifying standards for each loan program.

The primary purpose of Desktop Underwriter® and Loan Prospector® is to make loan purchase decisions for Fannie Mae and Freddie Mac. (See Chapter 2 for a discussion of how lenders sell their loans to the secondary market agencies.) However, a lender who plans to sell a loan to either agency isn't required to use automated underwriting. Both Fannie Mae and Freddie Mac are still willing to purchase loans that have been underwritten manually, in the traditional way. Nonetheless, both agencies favor automated underwriting and encourage lenders to use their AU systems.

Also, a lender may choose to use Desktop Underwriter® or Loan Prospector® to underwrite loans that it plans to keep in portfolio. Even though these loans don't have to meet Fannie Mae or Freddie Mac standards, the AU analysis can still be very useful to the lender's underwriters.

AU Programming. The programming of the secondary market agencies' AU systems is based on the performance of millions of mortgage loans. The term "loan performance" simply refers to whether the loan payments are made as agreed. Statistical analysis of the performance of millions of loans provides strong evidence of precisely which factors in a loan application make default more likely or less likely.

Loan performance: whether loan payments are made as agreed

For instance, it's generally understood that a home buyer who has funds left over (cash reserves) after making the downpayment and paying the closing costs is less likely to default than one who doesn't have anything left over. Accordingly, lenders prefer (and sometimes require) that borrowers have a specified amount in reserve after closing—for example, enough money to cover at least two months' mortgage payments, in case of emergency. What computerized statistical analysis of loan performance adds to this traditional, common-sense underwriting idea is greater precision. Exactly how much less likely to default is a borrower who has two months of reserves than one who has no reserves? What about a borrower with enough reserves for three months of payments, or six months? This type of information, along with computer analysis of all of the other factors that affect default risk, can be programmed into an automated underwriting system. The system will then be able to predict with considerable accuracy how likely it is that a particular loan applicant will default on the loan she is seeking.

This computer analysis of loan performance by the secondary market agencies is ongoing, and they use the latest information to adjust their automated underwriting systems and their qualifying standards. Because Fannie Mae and Freddie Mac are so influential in residential lending, these adjustments have a nationwide impact on underwriting.

How AU Works. The first step in submitting a loan application for automated underwriting is entering the information from the application form into the AU system. (This may be done by the loan officer, by an underwriter, or by someone else in the lender's underwriting department.) The system then obtains the applicant's credit information directly from the major credit agencies. After analyzing all of this data using statistical models and the appropriate qualifying rules, the AUS provides a report for an underwriter to review.

The recommendations in an automated underwriting report fall into three main categories:

- a risk classification,
- a recommended level of documentation, and
- a recommendation concerning the property appraisal or inspection.

Risk classification. The risk classification determines the level of underwriting scrutiny the loan application should receive. If the information submitted to the automated underwriting system meets

AU recommendation categories:
- Risk
- Documentation
- Appraisal

all of the applicable qualifying standards, the AUS will give the application a risk classification of "Approve" or "Accept." (The exact terminology depends on the system.) Another possible risk classification is "Approve/Ineligible," which means that the loan meets credit risk standards but doesn't meet mortgage eligibility criteria in some other way. (For example, a loan term longer than 30 years or a loan amount that exceeds the conforming loan limit might result in an Ineligible classification.)

An application that doesn't appear to meet all of the qualifying standards will receive a risk classification of "Refer" or "Caution." This doesn't necessarily mean that the loan should be denied, or that it can't be sold to Fannie Mae or Freddie Mac; instead, further review of the application is needed.

This further review will take the form of manual underwriting. In other words, the underwriter will now examine the loan application in the traditional way, to see if it can be approved even though it didn't receive a "passing grade" from the automated underwriting system. The AU report provides the underwriter with guidance, listing the main factors that led to the Refer or Caution classification and pointing out where additional information might make a difference. The underwriter looks for favorable information about the loan applicant's situation that the AUS has not already taken into account.

Note that some lenders have a policy of rejecting Refer or Caution loans without underwriting them manually. These lenders don't consider this extra step—and the extra cost—to be worth their while. Other lenders are willing to manually underwrite Refer or Caution loans, in the expectation that the extra cost will be covered by profits from the additional loans that are ultimately approved. This policy difference is one reason why a loan applicant who's been rejected by one lender may be accepted by another.

Fannie Mae or Freddie Mac may be willing to purchase a loan even though it was given a Refer or Caution classification by the AUS. However, instead of being treated as a prime loan, it will be considered an A-minus loan, and the borrower will have to pay additional fees and/or a higher interest rate.

Documentation. The AU report will also indicate the level of documentation the underwriter should obtain in order to verify the information provided by the applicant. The stronger the application, the lower the documentation requirement may be.

There used to be three basic documentation levels: standard, streamlined ("low-doc"), and minimal ("no-doc"). However, one consequence of the mortgage crisis has been a trend toward requiring more documentation. "No doc" loans, requiring virtually no documentation or verification of information provided by the applicant, appear to be a thing of the past.

As the name suggests, standard documentation is the full verification process used in traditional underwriting. An automated underwriting system generally requires standard documentation for loans that have been given a risk classification of "Refer" or "Caution" (and therefore must be manually underwritten).

Loans given an "Approve" or "Accept" classification are usually eligible for streamlined documentation. For example, if an applicant has a perfect credit reputation and is making a very large downpayment, a phone call to her employer might be sufficient verification of her employment. A verification of employment form signed by the employer isn't required. (Documentation requirements will be discussed in more detail later in the chapter.)

Appraisal or inspection. The third type of recommendation made in an AU report concerns the appraisal or inspection of the property. For example, the report might tell the underwriter that a full appraisal is appropriate, or that a drive-by inspection would be sufficient, or even that a report on the property's likely value (without an actual inspection) is all that's required. This recommendation is based on the overall strength of the application and on information about the property that was submitted to the automated underwriting system.

Advantages of AU. Automated underwriting has a number of advantages over traditional underwriting, with benefits for both lenders and borrowers. First, it can streamline the underwriting process for many mortgage loans, requiring significantly less paperwork and enabling lenders to make approval decisions more quickly.

Second, AU makes the underwriting process more objective and consistent, since it generally reduces reliance on the underwriter's experience and subjective judgment. This helps ensure fair, unbiased lending decisions.

Advantages of AU:
- Streamlines process
- Increases objectivity
- Improves underwriting accuracy

Third, AU improves the accuracy of underwriting, because it can weigh all of the risk factors more precisely. Lenders (and the secondary market agencies) can have greater confidence in a loan approval decision reached with the help of AU. This allows them to accept more loan applications and extend financing to more home buyers, while still managing risk.

In spite of these advantages, automated underwriting by no means eliminates the need for human underwriters. Both Fannie Mae and Freddie Mac emphasize that an AU system is only a tool. The final decision on whether to approve or deny a loan is made by the lender, not the computer.

Evaluating Creditworthiness

Now that you have some background information about the underwriting process, we'll look more closely at the factors that are taken into account in qualifying a buyer. As we said at the beginning of the chapter, a lender's fundamental question concerning a buyer is: "Does the buyer's overall financial situation indicate that she can reasonably be expected to make the proposed monthly loan payments on time?" If the answer is yes, the buyer is considered **creditworthy**.

To decide whether a buyer is creditworthy, the underwriter—with or without the aid of an automated underwriting system—must consider dozens of factors in the buyer's financial situation. These can be grouped into three main categories:

Qualifying the buyer involves evaluation of:
- Credit reputation
- Income
- Net worth

- credit reputation,
- income, and
- net worth (assets).

You can think of a good credit reputation, stable income, and adequate net worth as the basic components of creditworthiness. We'll be discussing each of these as separate topics, but you should keep in mind that underwriters don't look at any aspect of a loan application in isolation from the rest of it. Strength in one area may or may not be enough to offset weakness in another. The recommendation to approve or deny the loan is based on the buyer's financial situation as a whole.

Credit Reputation

A good credit reputation is the first major component of credit-worthiness. Many residential lending experts would say it's the most important.

To evaluate a loan applicant's credit reputation, lenders rely on credit reports obtained from credit reporting agencies. If a report reveals significant derogatory information, the loan application could be turned down for that reason alone. Or the loan could be approved on less favorable terms (at a higher interest rate, for instance). (See the discussion of risk-based pricing at the end of this chapter.)

Credit Reports

A personal credit report presents information about an individual's loans, credit purchases, and debt repayment for the previous **seven years**. It typically covers revolving credit accounts (credit cards and charge accounts), installment debts (such as car loans and student loans), and mortgages. Other bills, such as utility bills or medical bills, usually aren't listed unless they were turned over to a collection agency.

Personal credit report: individual's debts and repayment record

The credit reporting agencies (also called credit repositories or credit bureaus) are private companies, not government agencies. There are three major credit agencies in the U.S.: Equifax, Experian (formerly TRW), and TransUnion. Keeping track of credit information about millions of people is complicated, and the reports that these companies issue on a particular individual don't necessarily match perfectly. To underwrite a mortgage loan application, a lender may obtain reports from all three agencies, or else use a "tri-merge" report that combines the information provided by the three agencies.

The credit information that's important to an underwriter includes:

- the length of the credit history,
- the payment record,
- derogatory credit incidents, and
- credit scores.

Length of Credit History

The term "credit history" is generally used as a synonym for "credit reputation." In this broad sense, it refers to an individual's overall record of borrowing and debt repayment—how well she has handled credit. But "credit history" is also used in a narrower sense, to mean the length or duration of the applicant's experience with credit—how many years she has been borrowing money and paying it back.

As a general rule, a mortgage loan applicant should have at least a one-year history of credit use with three or more active accounts (loans or credit cards). Although this requirement doesn't present a problem for most applicants, it is an obstacle for some. Young adults who are potential home buyers may not have had a chance to establish a credit history yet. A low-income head of household applying for an affordable housing program might never have been offered credit. And some people deliberately steer clear of credit, preferring to stay out of debt and manage their budgets strictly on a cash basis. While staying out of debt is a sensible course, it can backfire when it's time to borrow money to buy a home. If an applicant doesn't have an established credit history, a key set of data is missing, and it's harder for the lender to evaluate the risk of default.

In recent years, with the encouragement of Fannie Mae and Freddie Mac, lenders have become more willing to work with loan applicants who don't have an established credit history. To take the place of or supplement a traditional credit report, the applicant may provide records showing reliable, timely payment of rent, utility bills, insurance premiums, medical bills, school tuition, child care costs, and other regular non-credit payments. Typically, at least four different items such as these must be provided to piece together an adequate picture of the borrower's credit history.

Payment Record

For each account that appears on a credit report, there's a payment record showing whether the payments have been made on time. Late payments are shown as 30 days, 60 days, or 90 days overdue.

If a loan applicant is chronically late in making payments, the underwriter will interpret that as a sign that the applicant tends to be financially overextended or fails to take debt repayment seriously (or both). Late payments on a previous mortgage are particularly damaging. However, a spotless payment record generally isn't required, and late payments that occurred more than two years ago won't usually affect the underwriter's decision.

Major Derogatory Incidents

Serious credit problems that may show up on an individual's credit report include charge-offs, debt collection accounts, repossessions, judgments, foreclosures, and bankruptcy.

- **Charge-offs.** When there has been no payment on an account for six months, the chances that it will ever be collected are low. The tax code allows the creditor to write off or "charge off" such a debt, treating it as a loss for income tax purposes.

  However, the charge-off doesn't relieve the debtor of legal responsibility for repaying the debt. The creditor may continue to try to collect the debt after it has been charged off. If the debtor pays off the debt—or the creditor is willing to settle for partial payment—the charge-off can still appear on the debtor's credit report unless the creditor agrees to have it removed.

- **Collections.** After several attempts to get a debtor to pay a bill, a frustrated creditor may turn the bill over to a collection agency. Once this happens, the debt will show up on the debtor's credit report, even if the original bill did not.

- **Repossessions.** If someone purchases an item on credit and fails to make the payments, the creditor may be able to repossess the item.

- **Judgments.** When an individual is sued and loses the lawsuit, the court may order him to pay a sum of money (damages) to the person who sued. This order is called a judgment.

- **Foreclosures.** As you might expect, mortgage lenders regard a real estate foreclosure on a loan applicant's credit report as a matter of special concern. Giving a lender a deed in lieu of foreclosure also is considered a derogatory incident.

- **Bankruptcy.** Not surprisingly, lenders also consider a bankruptcy on an applicant's credit report to be a very bad sign.

Negative information on credit report:
- Charge-offs
- Collections
- Repossessions
- Judgments
- Foreclosures
- Bankruptcies

Under the federal Fair Credit Reporting Act, all of these incidents may remain on a credit report for no more than seven years, with the exception of bankruptcy, which may remain for ten years.

An underwriter won't necessarily be concerned about an incident that occurred more than two years before the loan application, unless it was a foreclosure or a bankruptcy. These are taken very seriously; even after years have passed, a foreclosure or a bankruptcy will lead to an especially careful review of the application and may result in denial of the loan or less favorable terms.

Credit Scores

Most underwriters now use credit scores to help evaluate a loan applicant's credit history. A credit reporting agency calculates an individual's credit score using the information that appears in his credit report and a quantitative model developed by a national credit scoring company. Credit scoring models, which are based on statistical analysis of large numbers of mortgages, are designed to predict the likelihood of successful repayment or default on a mortgage. In general, someone with poor credit scores is much more likely to default than someone with good credit scores.

The most widely used type of credit score in residential lending is the FICO score. (FICO is an acronym for Fair Isaac and Company, which developed the predominant credit scoring model.) FICO scores range from under 400 to over 800. A relatively high FICO score (for example, over 700) is a positive sign. You may hear FICO scores referred to by other names; for example, Equifax calls the credit scores it bases on the FICO model Beacon scores.

Just as the three agencies' credit reports for a particular loan applicant won't always match perfectly, the applicant's credit scores typically vary a bit from one agency to another. Underwriting rules generally dictate that the underwriter use the lower of two scores or the middle of three.

Level of Review. An underwriter uses the applicant's credit scores to decide what level of review to apply to the applicant's credit history. For example, if the applicant has good credit scores, the underwriter might perform a basic review, simply confirming that the information in the credit report is complete and accurate without investigating further. Aside from a foreclosure or a bankruptcy, the underwriter probably won't question the applicant about derogatory information in the report, because it's already been taken into account in calculating the credit scores. On the other hand, if the applicant

Credit scores:
- Predict likelihood of default
- Determine appropriate level of review

has mediocre or poor credit scores, the underwriter will perform a more complete review, looking into the circumstances that led to the credit problems.

Maintaining Good Credit Scores. Almost any information that appears on a person's credit report may affect the credit score he receives from the agency that prepared that report. Credit activity within the previous two years has the greatest impact, however.

While most people would expect chronically late payments and collection problems to hurt someone's credit scores, some of the other factors that can lower scores might come as a surprise. For example, with a credit card, maintaining a balance near the credit limit ("maxing out" the card) will have a negative impact on the cardholder's credit scores, even if he always makes his payments on time.

Applying for too much credit can also have a negative effect. Each time a person applies for credit (a store charge card, a car loan, and so on), the creditor makes a "credit inquiry" that becomes part of the applicant's credit history. Occasional inquiries are fine, but too many within the past year can lower the applicant's credit scores. From a lender's point of view, a lot of inquiries may indicate that the applicant is in danger of becoming overextended.

Special rules apply to credit inquiries for mortgages and car loans. Someone who wants to buy a home or a car often applies to several lenders, intending to compare financing offers and accept the best one. This will result in multiple credit inquiries, even though the consumer is looking for only one loan. To allow for that type of comparison shopping, when a credit score is calculated, mortgage and car loan credit inquiries in the previous 30 days are ignored. Also, multiple inquiries for a mortgage or a car loan within any 45-day period (a typical shopping period) are counted as a single inquiry.

Obtaining Credit Information

It's a good idea for prospective home buyers to obtain their credit reports and find out their credit scores well before they apply for a mortgage. (Obtaining a copy of your own credit report does not count as a credit inquiry.) A credit report may contain incorrect information, and the Fair Credit Reporting Act requires credit reporting agencies to investigate complaints and make corrections. This process can take a month or more.

Also, even if the negative information that appears on a buyer's credit reports is correct, reviewing the reports in advance will help prepare the buyer to explain her credit problems to potential lenders.

Explaining Credit Problems

In some cases, negative credit reports and poor credit scores may not prevent a home buyer from obtaining a loan. Credit problems can often be explained. If the underwriter is convinced that the past problems don't reflect the loan applicant's overall attitude toward credit and that the circumstances leading to the problems were temporary and are unlikely to recur, the loan application may well be approved.

Most people try to meet their credit obligations on time; when they don't, there's usually a good reason. Loss of a job, divorce, hospitalization, prolonged illness, or a death in the family can create extraordinary financial pressures and adversely affect bill paying habits. If a loan applicant has poor credit scores, it may be possible to show that the credit problems occurred during a specific period of time for an understandable reason, and that the applicant has handled credit well both before and since that period. The applicant should put this explanation in writing and provide supporting documentation from a third party (such as hospital records).

When explaining credit problems to a lender, it's a mistake to blame the problems on misunderstandings or on the creditors. Underwriters hear too many explanations from loan applicants who refuse to accept responsibility for their own acts, insisting instead that the blame lies elsewhere. The reaction to these explanations is very predictable: skepticism, disbelief, and rejection. Underwriters reason that an applicant's reluctance to take responsibility for past credit problems is an indication of what can be expected from her in the future.

If a loan applicant's credit report is laced with problems over a period of years, there's little hope for approval of a prime loan, and even a subprime loan could be difficult to obtain. Perpetual credit problems are more likely to reflect an attitude than a circumstance, and it's reasonable to assume the pattern will continue in the future.

Most credit problems can be resolved with time, however. When buyers tell you they have had some credit problems in the past, it would be a mistake to leap to the conclusion that they can't qualify for a loan. Refer them to a lender and get an expert's opinion.

Letter explaining negative credit report:
- State reason for problem
- Problem occurred during specific period
- Problem no longer exists
- Good credit before and since
- Provide documentation from third party
- Don't blame creditors

Income Analysis

Of course, a loan applicant's credit reputation is only one element of her creditworthiness. The underwriter must analyze the buyer's income as well. Even if the buyer has excellent credit, the lender won't approve her loan unless she has sufficient income to make the mortgage payments each month.

Characteristics of Income

From an underwriter's point of view, income has three dimensions: quantity, quality, and durability.

Quantity. A key consideration in underwriting is whether the loan applicant's monthly income is enough to cover the proposed monthly mortgage payment in addition to all of his other expenses. So the underwriter wants to know how much income the applicant has. Not all income is equal in an underwriter's eyes, however. Only income that meets the tests of quality and durability is taken into account in deciding whether the applicant has enough income to qualify for the loan.

Income analysis:
- Quantity
- Quality
- Durability

Quality (Dependability). To evaluate the quality of a loan applicant's income, the underwriter looks at the sources from which it is derived. The income sources should be reasonably dependable, such as an established employer, a government agency, or an interest-yielding investment account.

> **Example:** Jeanne Ellington is applying for a mortgage. She works for a medium-sized company that manufactures machine parts. The company has been in business for 35 years and hasn't been subject to downsizing or periodic layoffs in recent memory. Because Ellington's employer is well-established and stable, the underwriter sees it as a very dependable source of income. Thus, Ellington's salary will be considered high-quality income.

The less dependable the source (a brand new company or a high-risk investment, for example), the lower the quality of the income.

> **Example:** Suppose instead that Jeanne Ellington works for a small graphic design company that was started less than a year ago. The underwriter might decide that the company isn't a very dependable source of income, and therefore conclude that Ellington's salary is relatively low-quality income. That will count

as a weakness in her loan application, although by itself it won't lead to denial of the loan.

Durability (Probability of Continuance). Income is considered durable if it can be expected to continue in the future—preferably for at least the **next three years**. Wages from permanent employment (as opposed to a temporary job), permanent disability benefits, and interest on established investments are all examples of durable income.

Stable Monthly Income

Income that meets the tests of quality and durability is generally referred to as the loan applicant's **stable monthly income**. Typically, stable monthly income is made up of earnings from one primary income source, such as a full-time job, plus earnings from acceptable secondary sources. Secondary income can take many forms, such as bonuses, commissions, social security payments, military disability and retirement income, interest on savings or other investments, and so on.

The following types of income generally meet the tests of quality and durability, so that lenders are willing to count them as part of the loan applicant's stable monthly income.

Employment Income. Permanent employment is the major income source for most home buyers. The underwriter will consider not only the loan applicant's current job and wage or salary level, but also her recent employment history. Not surprisingly, a history of steady, full-time employment is viewed favorably. Ideally, a loan applicant will have been employed by the same employer or in the same field continuously for **at least two years**.

If the applicant has held his current position for two years or more, the underwriter usually won't consider it necessary to look at the applicant's previous employment. Otherwise, the underwriter may want to check into the applicant's two previous jobs.

Frequent changes in employment don't necessarily count against the applicant. While persistent job-hopping might indicate a problem, changing jobs for career advancement is usually a good sign. The key issue for the underwriter is whether the job changes have hurt the loan applicant's ability to pay her financial obligations.

On the whole, job continuity isn't as important as continuity of earnings. As long as the applicant has consistently been able to find work that brings in a certain level of income, it may not matter that he hasn't stayed in the same line of work. But if the loan application reveals a period longer than 60 days with no employment income, the applicant may be asked to explain it.

Note that in some cases loan approval may be warranted even without an established two-year work history. For example, the applicant may have recently graduated from college or a vocational school. Training or education that has prepared the applicant for a specific kind of work can strengthen the loan application. Also, even in the absence of special training, an unimpressive employment history could be counterbalanced by other factors in the loan application.

Commissions, overtime, and bonuses. These forms of employment income are considered durable if they can be shown to have been a consistent part of the loan applicant's overall earnings pattern, usually for at least two years. (Some lenders count bonuses as stable income only if the applicant has received them for three years or more.)

The underwriter will calculate the average amount of overtime, bonus, or commission income, but will also consider the trend: Have these earnings been steady, or have they been increasing or decreasing? If they're decreasing, the underwriter may count less than the average amount as stable income.

Part-time and seasonal work. Earnings from part-time work can be counted as stable income if the loan applicant has held the job for at least two years. Seasonal or periodic earnings—wages from agricultural work or a construction job, for instance—may also be treated as stable income if there is an established earnings pattern.

> **Example:** Harold Jensen has worked as a deckhand on a fishing boat every summer for the past three years, and he intends to continue doing that. Although his summer income alone isn't enough to qualify him for a mortgage loan, an underwriter would be willing to treat it as stable income and add it to his earnings from the rest of the year.

Self-employment income. When a loan applicant owns a business, the income received from that business is self-employment income. (It isn't necessary to be the sole owner of the business;

lenders generally treat income from a business as self-employment income if the applicant has an ownership interest of 25% or more.) Income from freelance or consulting work is also considered to be self-employment income.

To lenders, self-employment adds an extra element of risk to a loan, because the borrower's income is often unpredictable, and small businesses often fail. So a loan applicant should expect some extra scrutiny if self-employment is his main source of income. If the applicant hasn't been self-employed for very long, the underwriter may hesitate to approve the loan. Lenders are wary of new businesses and generally want to see that a self-employed applicant has operated her business profitably for at least two years. The underwriter will consider the trend of the applicant's earnings, her training and experience, and the nature of the business.

For some self-employed loan applicants, a lender may be willing to avoid the issue of self-employment income altogether and focus instead on the applicant's assets and credit reputation. As a general rule, this is only an option for applicants who have a substantial net worth and excellent credit.

Verifying employment income. As we discussed earlier, the information provided in the loan application must be verified—that is, confirmed and documented. Generally, a lender will require either a standard or streamlined level of documentation, depending on the strength of the application. For applications submitted to an automated underwriting system, the AU report tells the underwriter what level of documentation is needed; in manual underwriting, the underwriter usually follows the documentation rules for the loan program in question.

The standard method of verifying a loan applicant's employment income is to send a "Request for Verification of Employment" form (see Figure 8.1) directly to the applicant's employer. The employer fills out the form and sends it directly back to the lender. To eliminate the possibility that the applicant might tamper with the verification form, the applicant isn't allowed to return the form to the lender. Note that the form asks the employer about the probability of continued employment.

For many mortgage loans, lenders now use a streamlined method of employment verification. The loan applicant can provide the lender with W-2 forms for the previous two years and payroll stubs

In addition to regular wages from a full-time job, stable monthly income may include:
• Bonuses
• Commissions
• Overtime
• Part-time earnings
• Self-employment income
• Retirement income
• Alimony or child support
• Public assistance
• Investment income

Positive employment history:
• Consistency, usually 2 years in same job or field
• Job changes have been for advancement
• Special training or education

Fig. 8.1 Request for Verification of Employment form

⚘ FannieMae

Request for Verification of Employment

Privacy Act Notice: This information is to be used by the agency collecting it or its assignees in determining whether you qualify as a prospective mortgagor under its program. It will not be disclosed outside the agency except as required and permitted by law. You do not have to provide this information, but if you do not your application for approval as a prospective mortgagor or borrower may be delayed or rejected. The information requested in this form is authorized by Title 38, USC, Chapter 37 (if VA); by 12 USC, Section 1701 et. seq. (if HUD/FHA); by 42 USC, Section 1452b (if HUD/CPD); and Title 42 USC, 1471 et. seq., or 7 USC, 1921 et. seq. (if USDA/FmHA).

Instructions: Lender — Complete items 1 through 7. Have applicant complete item 8. Forward directly to employer named in item 1.
Employer — Please complete either Part II or Part III as applicable. Complete Part IV and return directly to lender named in item 2.
The form is to be transmitted directly to the lender and is not to be transmitted through the applicant or any other party.

Part I — Request

1. To (Name and address of employer)	2. From (Name and address of lender)

I certify that this verification has been sent directly to the employer and has not passed through the hands of the applicant or any other interested party.

3. Signature of Lender	4. Title	5. Date	6. Lender's Number (Optional)

I have applied for a mortgage loan and stated that I am now or was formerly employed by you. My signature below authorizes verification of this information.

7. Name and Address of Applicant (include employee or badge number)	8. Signature of Applicant

Part II — Verification of Present Employment

9. Applicant's Date of Employment	10. Present Position	11. Probability of Continued Employment

12A. Current **Gross Base Pay** (Enter Amount and Check Period)
☐ Annual   ☐ Hourly
☐ Monthly   ☐ Other (Specify)
$ _____   ☐ Weekly

13. For Military Personnel Only		14. If Overtime or Bonus is Applicable, Is Its Continuance Likely?
Pay Grade		Overtime ☐ Yes ☐ No
Type	Monthly Amount	Bonus ☐ Yes ☐ No

12B. Gross Earnings

Type	Year To Date	Past Year 19____	Past Year 19____			15. If paid hourly — average hours per week
	Thru _____ 19__			Base Pay	$	
Base Pay	$	$	$	Rations	$	16. Date of applicant's next pay increase
				Flight or Hazard	$	
				Clothing	$	17. Projected amount of next pay increase
Overtime	$	$	$	Quarters	$	
Commissions	$	$	$	Pro Pay	$	18. Date of applicant's last pay increase
				Overseas or Combat	$	19. Amount of last pay increase
Bonus	$	$	$	Variable Housing Allowance	$	
Total	$	$	$			

20. Remarks (If employee was off work for any length of time, please indicate time period and reason)

Part III — Verification of Previous Employment

21. Date Hired	23. Salary/Wage at Termination Per (Year) (Month) (Week)
22. Date Terminated	Base _____ Overtime _____ Commissions _____ Bonus _____
24. Reason for Leaving	25. Position Held

Part IV — Authorized Signature - Federal statutes provide severe penalties for any fraud, intentional misrepresentation, or criminal connivance or conspiracy purposed to influence the issuance of any guaranty or insurance by the VA Secretary, the U.S.D.A., FmHA/FHA Commissioner, or the HUD/CPD Assistant Secretary.

26. Signature of Employer	27. Title (Please print or type)	28. Date
29. Print or type name signed in Item 26	30. Phone No.	

Fannie Mae
Form 1005   July 96

or vouchers for the previous 30-day period. The pay stubs must identify the applicant, the employer, and the applicant's gross earnings for both the current pay period and the year to date. The lender may then confirm the employment and earnings information with a phone call to the employer.

When commissions, overtime, bonuses, or seasonal earnings are a significant part of the applicant's employment income, the lender typically requires copies of the applicant's federal income tax returns for the previous two years to verify these earnings. (The lender may want to obtain these directly from the IRS, rather than from the applicant. This requires the applicant's written permission.) The lender will ask the employer if overtime or bonus income is likely to continue, and if the applicant has business expenses that will be deducted from commissions.

Self-employed loan applicants should be prepared to provide business and personal income tax returns for the two years prior to the loan application. (If the business is well-established and the applicant won't be using any funds from the business to close the loan, the requirement for business tax returns may be waived.) If the business is a sole proprietorship, the underwriter may also want to see a balance sheet covering the previous one or two fiscal years and a year-to-date profit and loss statement. This additional documentation is especially likely to be requested if the stability or durability of the applicant's self-employment income is in doubt.

Retirement Income. Pension and social security payments received by retired persons are usually dependable and durable, so they can be included in stable monthly income.

The federal Equal Credit Opportunity Act (see Chapter 14) prohibits age discrimination in lending. Nonetheless, it is not illegal for an underwriter to consider an elderly loan applicant's life expectancy when deciding whether or not to approve a loan.

Investment Income. Dividends or interest on investments may be counted as part of stable monthly income. The underwriter will calculate an average of the investment income for the previous two years. Of course, if the loan applicant is going to cash in an investment to raise the funds needed for closing, then the underwriter will not regard that investment as a durable source of income.

Employment verification:
- Verification form sent to employer, or
- W-2 forms for 2 years plus pay stubs for 30 days, with phone call to employer

Self-employed applicant needs financial records and income tax returns for 2 years

Rental Income. A lender will count income from rental properties as stable monthly income if a stable pattern of rental income can be verified. The applicant should be prepared to submit authenticated copies of the property's books showing gross earnings and operating expenses for the previous two years, along with her income tax returns.

There are many unpredictable factors connected with rental income, such as emergency repairs, vacancies, and tenants who don't pay. To leave a margin for error, the underwriter usually includes only a certain percentage (for example, 75%) of the verified rental income in the loan applicant's stable monthly income. (The percentage allowed varies, depending on the type of loan applied for.)

If the loan applicant has negative rental income—if property expenses add up to more than the rent that the property generates—it will be treated as a liability when the underwriter calculates the applicant's monthly obligations.

Separate Maintenance, Alimony, and Child Support. These types of income are considered part of stable monthly income only if it appears that the payments will be made reliably. That determination depends on whether the payments are required by a court decree, how long the loan applicant has been receiving the payments, the overall financial and credit status of the estranged or ex-spouse, and the applicant's ability to legally compel payment if necessary.

A copy of the court decree usually must be submitted to the lender. And unless the payments are made through the court, proof of receipt of payments is also required. Some lenders accept the loan applicant's bank statements (showing that the checks have been deposited) as proof of receipt; others require photocopies of the deposited checks.

The underwriter will examine the record of payment. If some payments in the preceding 12 months were missed or were significantly late, the underwriter will probably exclude the alimony, maintenance, or child support from the loan applicant's stable monthly income.

An ex-spouse's obligation to pay child support ordinarily ends when the child turns 18. As a result, whether an underwriter will include child support payments in a loan applicant's stable monthly income depends on the age of the applicant's child. The closer a child gets to age 18, the less durable child support becomes. If the child is over 15, it is unlikely that the underwriter will count the child support payments as stable monthly income.

In some situations, a loan applicant who receives (or is entitled to receive) alimony, maintenance, or child support might prefer not to list that income on the application. That might be the case, for example, if the ex-spouse is hostile or uncooperative. The Equal Credit Opportunity Act, which prohibits discrimination based on marital status in the underwriting process, prevents lenders from asking borrowers if they're divorced and from requiring them to disclose alimony or child support. Of course, if a particular source of income isn't listed on the loan application, the lender won't count it as part of the applicant's stable monthly income.

Public Assistance. The Equal Credit Opportunity Act prohibits lenders from discriminating against loan applicants because all or part of their income is derived from a public assistance program (such as welfare or food stamps). Public assistance payments will be counted as part of a loan applicant's stable monthly income only if they meet the test of durability. If the applicant's eligibility for the assistance program will terminate in the near future, the underwriter will not take the payments into account.

Unacceptable Types of Income. The following are some types of income that underwriters usually exclude from a loan applicant's stable monthly income.

Temporary employment. Income from any job (full- or part-time) that the employer classifies as temporary ordinarily does not count as stable monthly income. That's true even if there's no definite termination date.

> **Example:** A recent flood damaged a large section of an industrial complex. The property manager has hired several full-time workers to help clean up the debris and repair the damage. These jobs have no termination date, but they're temporary in nature. As a result, the workers' wages wouldn't be considered stable monthly income.

In some cases, however, when a loan applicant has supported himself through a particular type of temporary work for years, that income can be presented to the lender as income earned through self-employment.

Alimony & child support:
- Copy of court decree
- Proof of receipt
- Payments must be reliable
- Child support no longer counts when child reaches mid-teens

Unemployment compensation. Unemployment compensation is rarely treated as stable monthly income because eligibility usually lasts only for a specified number of weeks (for example, 26 weeks). However, in some cases a worker receives unemployment compensation during a certain period each year, because of the seasonal nature of her work. For example, a farm worker or resort employee who can't find other work during the off-season might collect some unemployment benefits every year. If a loan applicant's tax returns for the preceding two years establish that unemployment benefits have been a regular part of her income, and this pattern appears likely to continue, an underwriter may be willing to count the benefits as stable monthly income.

Income from unobligated family members. An underwriter will ordinarily consider only the earnings of the heads of the household—the loan applicants—when calculating stable monthly income. Contributions from other family members who are going to occupy the home, such as teenage children or an elderly parent, are usually voluntary rather than contractual. Since these other family members have no legal obligation to the lender or the borrower and may move out at any time, their contributions could stop without notice. As a result, they aren't regarded as durable.

However, if a primary borrower's family member is listed on the application as a co-borrower, that family member's income will be considered in the qualifying process. (See the discussion of cosigners later in this chapter.)

Income that usually doesn't count as stable monthly income:
- Wages from temporary job
- Unemployment compensation
- Contributions from family members

Calculating Stable Monthly Income

After deciding which portion of the loan applicant's income meets the tests of quality and durability, the underwriter returns to the question of quantity. The income from all the acceptable sources is added up to determine the applicant's stable monthly income.

Many types of income are paid to the recipient once a month, but others are paid weekly, every two weeks, quarterly, or annually. Since what matters for the purposes of underwriting is stable *monthly* income, all payments are converted to monthly figures.

To convert hourly wages to monthly earnings, multiply the hourly wage by the number of hours the loan applicant works per week, then multiply by 52 (weeks in a year) and divide by 12 (months in a year).

Example:

Hourly wage: $14.50

Hours per week: 40

Weekly income: $14.50 × 40 = $580

Annual income: $580 × 52 = $30,160

Monthly income: $30,160 ÷ 12 = $2,513

There's a shortcut. You can reach the same result by multiplying the hourly wage by 173.33 (as long as the buyer is being paid for a 40-hour week).

Example:

Hourly wage: $14.50

Hours per week: 40

Monthly income: $14.50 × 173.33 = $2,513

Notice that being paid every two weeks (26 payments per year) is not the same as being paid twice a month (24 payments per year). If the buyer is paid every two weeks, multiply the payment amount by 26 to get the annual total, then divide by 12 to get the monthly figure.

Nontaxable Income. To calculate a loan applicant's stable monthly income, an underwriter uses gross income figures—the full amount earned or received, without subtracting the taxes that have been withheld or that the applicant will have to pay. Qualifying standards have been set with the understanding that the applicant is required to pay taxes on most, if not all, of his stable monthly income, and only what's left over—the after-tax income—is actually available for personal use.

However, certain types of income, such as child support, disability payments, and some public assistance, are generally exempt from taxation. Since the recipient doesn't have to pay taxes on this income, 100% of it can be used for personal expenses, like paying the mortgage and other bills. An underwriter may take this into account when calculating a loan applicant's stable monthly income, by "grossing up" any nontaxable income. For instance, in the calculations, the underwriter might add 25% to the amount of child support a loan applicant actually receives, to approximate the equivalent amount of gross taxable income the child support payments represent.

Example: Each month, Cheryl Bowie earns $3,600 and receives $390 in child support from her ex-husband. When she applies for a mortgage, the underwriter grosses up the child support figure because Bowie won't have to pay income taxes on that part of her income. The underwriter estimates how much gross income the child support represents by adding 25% to it.

$390 + 25% = $487.50 (grossed up monthly child support)

$3,600	Employment income
+ 487.50	Child support
$4,087.50	Stable monthly income

Income Ratios

Once the underwriter has calculated the applicant's stable monthly income, the next step is to measure the adequacy of that income: Is it enough so that the applicant can afford the proposed monthly mortgage payment? To measure adequacy, underwriters use **income ratios**. The rationale behind the ratios is that if a borrower's expenses exceed a certain percentage of her monthly income, the borrower may have a difficult time making the payments on the loan.

There are basically two types of income ratios:

- A **debt to income ratio** (total obligations to income ratio) measures the proposed monthly mortgage payment plus any other regular installment debt payments against the monthly income.
- A **housing expense to income ratio** measures the monthly mortgage payment alone against the monthly income.

To measure adequacy of stable monthly income, underwriter uses income ratios:
- Debt to income ratio
- Housing expense to income ratio

For the purpose of income ratio calculations, the monthly mortgage payment includes principal, interest, property taxes, and hazard insurance—often abbreviated PITI. (When applicable, the monthly PITI payment will also include mortgage insurance and homeowners association or condominium association dues.) Each ratio is expressed as a percentage.

Example: Alice Cochrane's salary is $3,200 a month and her husband Eric's salary is $2,800, so their combined stable monthly income is $6,000. The mortgage they're applying for would require monthly PITI payments of $1,800. To calculate their housing expense to income ratio, divide the PITI payment by their monthly income:

$1,800 ÷ $6,000 = .30, or 30%

Their proposed housing expense represents 30% of their stable monthly income, so their housing expense to income ratio is 30%.

The Cochranes' other debt payments (credit cards, car loan, etc.) amount to $480 per month. To calculate their debt to income ratio, add the proposed housing expense and the other debt payments together, then divide by their monthly income:

$$\$1,800 + \$480 = \$2,280 \div \$6,000 = .38, \text{ or } 38\%$$

Their total monthly debt payments represent 38% of their stable monthly income, so their debt to income ratio is 38%.

Whether the income ratios in the example would be considered too high would depend on the lender and the type of loan the Cochranes were applying for. The specific income ratio limits used in each of the various financing programs—conventional, FHA, and VA—will be discussed in later chapters.

It's worth noting that in most loan programs, maximum income ratios are treated as guidelines rather than hard-and-fast limits. A loan may be approved in spite of a debt to income ratio or housing expense ratio that exceeds the recommended limit, as long as there are sufficient compensating factors—other strengths in the application that compensate for the weakness in income.

On the whole, lenders tend to be more concerned about the debt to income ratio than the housing expense to income ratio. The ratio that takes into account all of the monthly debt payments (including the housing expense) is a better predictor of default than the ratio that takes into account only the housing expense.

Cosigners. Sometimes a home buyer applies for a loan with a co-borrower who will not be occupying the property and will not have an ownership interest in it. This type of co-borrower is often referred to as a **cosigner**, because she will sign the promissory note along with the primary borrower. A primary borrower and a cosigner have **joint and several liability** for the loan, which means that a court can order either one of them to pay the entire loan balance, not just half of it. A cosigner may also be called a guarantor or surety.

By sharing responsibility for repayment, a cosigner helps the primary borrower qualify for the loan. For example, parents may use their established income and financial status to help a son or daughter who otherwise would be unable to purchase a house. The lender is

Cosigner helps borrower qualify by sharing responsibility for loan willing to make the loan because the borrower's parents will have to repay it if the borrower fails to do so.

Like a primary borrower, a cosigner must have income, assets, and a credit reputation that are acceptable to the lender. Marginal cosigners shouldn't be used; they may do more harm than good to the loan application.

To analyze an application involving a cosigner, the underwriter will combine the cosigner's stable monthly income with the primary borrower's, combine their housing expenses and other debts, and then calculate income ratios using these combined figures. In addition, the underwriter will calculate income ratios for the primary borrower alone, to make sure that they aren't too far over the standard limits. The primary borrower shouldn't be relying too heavily on the cosigner's income in order to qualify for the loan.

Exercise No. 1

Roy Cutter has recently been honorably discharged from the U.S. Air Force, where he received training as an airplane mechanic. After discharge, Roy and his wife Judy moved to a new city. Roy accepted a full-time job three months ago with an airline, with a starting position of apprentice mechanic; two weeks after that, Judy found a job with a local hospital as a vocational nurse. Roy's hourly wage is $26; Judy earns $685 a week.

1. What is the Cutters' stable monthly income?

2. Are there any special circumstances that might result in loan approval even though the Cutters have only been with their employers for a short time?

Net Worth

The third component of creditworthiness is net worth. An individual's net worth is determined by subtracting personal liabilities from total personal assets.

Someone who has built up a significant net worth from earnings, savings, and other investments clearly has the ability to manage financial affairs. Thus, lenders use net worth as a gauge of how well a loan applicant handles money.

Getting an idea of the applicant's financial management skills isn't the only reason for investigating his net worth, however. The underwriter also needs to make sure the applicant has sufficient liquid assets to close the purchase transaction.

Funds for Closing

Liquid assets include cash and any other assets that can be quickly converted to cash, such as stock. A loan applicant must have enough liquid assets to cover the cash downpayment, the closing costs, and other expenses incidental to the purchase of the property.

In addition, as we mentioned earlier in the chapter, the applicant may be required to have **reserves** left over after making the downpayment and paying the closing costs. Generally, these reserves must be enough cash or other liquid assets to cover a specified number of mortgage payments. This provides some assurance that the applicant could handle financial emergencies, such as unexpected bills or a temporary interruption of income, without defaulting on the mortgage.

Whether a loan applicant is required to have reserves—and if so, how many months of reserves—depends on the lender and the loan program. When reserves are required, the most common requirement is two or three months' worth of mortgage payments in reserve. Affordable housing programs (loan programs targeted at low-income and first-time buyers) often require only one month's payment in reserve. In any case, if the loan applicant will have more than the required amount in reserve after closing, that strengthens the application.

Assets

Almost any asset that a loan applicant has may help the application. Real estate, automobiles, furniture, jewelry, stocks, bonds, or cash value in a life insurance policy can all be listed on the application

Net worth: assets minus liabilities
- Indicates ability to manage financial affairs
- Applicant must have enough liquid assets to close transaction

Liquid assets: cash and other assets that can be easily converted into cash

Fig. 8.2 Request for Verification of Deposit form

FannieMae

Request for Verification of Deposit

Privacy Act Notice: This information is to be used by the agency collecting it or its assignees in determining whether you qualify as a prospective mortgagor under its program. It will not be disclosed outside the agency except as required and permitted by law. You do not have to provide this information, but if you do not your application for approval as a prospective mortgagor or borrower may be delayed or rejected. The information requested in this form is authorized by Title 38, USC, Chapter 37 (If VA); by 12 USC, Section 1701 et.seq. (If HUD/FHA); by 42 USC, Section 1452b (if HUD/CPD); and Title 42 USC, 1471 et.seq. or 7 USC, 1921 et.seq. (If USDA/FmHA).

Instructions: Lender — Complete Items 1 through 8. Have applicant(s) complete Item 9. Forward directly to depository named in Item 1.
Depository — Please complete Items 10 through 18 and return DIRECTLY to lender named in Item 2.
The form is to be transmitted directly to the lender and is not to be transmitted through the applicant(s) or any other party.

Part I — Request

1. To (Name and address of depository)	2. From (Name and address of lender)

I certify that this verification has been sent directly to the bank or depository and has not passed through the hands of the applicant or any other party.

3. Signature of lender	4. Title	5. Date	6. Lender's No. (Optional)

7. Information To Be Verified

Type of Account	Account in Name of	Account Number	Balance
			$
			$
			$

To Depository: I/We have applied for a mortgage loan and stated in my financial statement that the balance on deposit with you is as shown above. You are authorized to verify this information and to supply the lender identified above with the information requested in Items 10 through 13. Your response is solely a matter of courtesy for which no responsibility is attached to your institution or any of your officers.

8. Name and Address of Applicant(s)	9. Signature of Applicant(s)

To Be Completed by Depository

Part II — Verification of Depository

10. Deposit Accounts of Applicant(s)

Type of Account	Account Number	Current Balance	Average Balance For Previous Two Months	Date Opened
		$	$	
		$	$	
		$	$	

11. Loans Outstanding To Applicant(s)

Loan Number	Date of Loan	Original Amount	Current Balance	Installments (Monthly/Quarterly)		Secured By	Number of Late Payments
		$	$	$	per		
		$	$	$	per		
		$	$	$	per		

12. Please include any additional information which may be of assistance in determination of credit worthiness. (Please include information on loans paid-in-full in Item 11 above.)

13. If the name(s) on the account(s) differ from those listed in Item 7, please supply the name(s) on the account(s) as reflected by your records.

Part III — Authorized Signature - Federal statutes provide severe penalties for any fraud, intentional misrepresentation, or criminal connivance or conspiracy purposed to influence the issuance of any guaranty or insurance by the VA Secretary, the U.S.D.A., FmHA/FHA Commissioner, or the HUD/CPD Assistant Secretary.

14. Signature of Depository Representative	15. Title (Please print or type)	16. Date
17. Please print or type name signed in item 14	18. Phone No.	

Fannie Mae
Form 1006   July 96

form, and the underwriter will take whatever steps are necessary to verify the information provided. Liquid assets tend to be more helpful than non-liquid ones, and the asset that underwriters usually regard most favorably is the most liquid one of all: money in the bank.

Bank Accounts. When standard documentation procedures are followed, a "Request for Verification of Deposit" form (Figure 8.2) is used to verify the loan applicant's funds. The verification form is sent directly to the bank holding the account, and returned to the underwriter without passing through the applicant's hands.

In contrast, when streamlined documentation is allowed, the underwriter relies on bank statements to check how much money a loan applicant has in her bank account(s). The applicant is simply asked to submit original bank statements for the previous two or three months to show that there is sufficient cash for closing.

In reviewing either the applicant's bank statements or the completed Verification of Deposit form, the underwriter has these questions in mind:

Verification of funds in bank accounts:
- Verification of deposit form sent to bank, or
- Bank statements for 2 or 3 months

1. Does the verified information conform to the statements in the loan application?
2. Does the applicant have enough money in the bank to meet the expenses of the purchase?
3. Has the bank account been opened only recently (within the last three months)?
4. Is the present balance notably higher than the average balance?
5. If the applicant claims that this account was the source of the good faith deposit (the earnest money), is the average balance high enough to confirm that?

Recently opened accounts or higher-than-normal balances must be explained, because these strongly suggest that the applicant has resorted to borrowed funds for the downpayment and closing costs. As a general rule, a home buyer is not allowed to borrow from relatives, friends, or other sources to come up with either the funds needed for closing or the reserves. Borrowing the money would defeat the purpose of the lender's requirements: the buyer would have an additional debt instead of an investment in the property.

There are exceptions to this rule, however. A buyer may be allowed to use funds from a loan secured by an asset such as a car, stock, a certificate of deposit, a life insurance policy, or real estate other than the home being purchased. Of course, the payments on such a secured loan would be counted as part of the buyer's total obligations when the debt to income ratio is calculated.

Also, affordable housing programs often have more flexible policies than standard programs. The buyer may be allowed to borrow part of the funds needed for closing from a relative or certain other sources. (See Chapter 10 for more information.)

Note, too, that a buyer may obtain the money needed for closing from a relative or another source if the buyer won't be required to repay it—in other words, if the money is a gift rather than a loan. We'll discuss the issue of gift funds later in this chapter.

Real Estate for Sale. If a loan applicant is selling another property to raise cash to buy the subject property, the net equity in the property that is for sale can be counted as an asset available to be applied to the downpayment, closing costs, and required reserves. The **net equity** is the difference between the market value of the property and the sum of the liens against the property plus the selling expenses:

Market value
– Liens and selling expenses
Net equity in real estate to be sold

Net Equity = Market Value – (Liens + Selling Expenses)

In other words, the loan applicant's net equity is the amount of money that he can expect to receive from the sale of the property.

> **Example:** The Yamamotos put their home up for sale a month ago, and now they've found the home they want to buy. They've signed a purchase agreement for the new home that's contingent on the sale of the old home and also on their ability to obtain financing. When they apply for a loan to finance the purchase of their new home, the underwriter will count their net equity in the old home as a liquid asset.
>
> | | |
> |---|---|
> | $289,000 | Market value of old home |
> | –213,000 | First mortgage (to be paid off) |
> | – 10,000 | Home improvement loan (to be paid off) |
> | $66,000 | Gross equity |
> | – 29,000 | Estimated cost of selling old home |
> | $37,000 | Net equity in old home |
> | + 13,000 | In savings account |
> | $50,000 | Available for purchase of new home |

The underwriter's calculation of net equity may begin with the appraised value or the listing price of the old home or, if the loan applicant has already found a buyer for the old home, with the price that buyer has agreed to pay. Selling costs vary from one area of the country to another, but 10% of the listing or sales price is often used as a rough estimate.

If equity is the exclusive source or one of the main sources of money for the purchase of the new home, the lender will not actually fund the loan until it has been given proof that the old home has been sold and the borrower has received the sale proceeds. A copy of the final settlement statement from the sale of the old home is usually required. (Of course, the purchase of the new home may be ready to close before the buyer has succeeded in selling the old home. In that case, the buyer may want to apply for a swing loan to obtain the cash needed for closing. The swing loan will be secured by the buyer's equity in the old home, and it will be paid off out of the proceeds from the eventual sale of the old home.)

Other Real Estate. Often a loan applicant owns real estate that she is not planning to sell. Whether the real estate is income producing (e.g., rental property) or not (e.g., vacant land), it is an asset and should be considered in connection with the loan application.

Bear in mind, though, that it's the equity, not the value of the property, that contributes to net worth. Only the equity can be converted into cash in the event of need. When a loan applicant owns real estate with little or no equity in it, its impact as a liability cancels out its value as an asset.

Liabilities

Liabilities include:
- Credit card & charge account balances
- Installment debts
- Taxes owed
- Liens against real estate owned

All of the loan applicant's personal liabilities are subtracted from the total value of his assets to calculate net worth. The balances owing on credit cards, charge accounts, student loans, car loans, and other installment debts are subtracted; so are any other debts, such as income taxes that are currently payable. If the applicant owns real estate, the remaining balance on the mortgage will be subtracted, along with the amount of any other liens against the property.

Gift Funds

If a loan applicant lacks some of the funds needed to close a transaction, her relatives may be willing to make up the deficit. The underwriter will usually accept this arrangement, as long as the money is a gift to the applicant rather than a loan.

The rules concerning gift funds vary from one loan program to another and from one lender to another. In most cases, the rules limit how much of the downpayment and closing costs may be covered by gift funds; the loan applicant has to come up with the rest out of his own money, as a minimum investment. (A buyer who has made a significant investment of her own funds is less likely to default. See Chapter 6.) The rules typically also restrict who can provide gift funds. For example, one program might permit gift funds only from close relatives, while another program might also accept gift funds from the applicant's employer or a nonprofit organization.

Whatever the source, the gift should be confirmed by means of a "gift letter" signed by the donor. The letter should clearly state that the money is a gift and does not have to be repaid. Most lenders have forms for gift letters, and some require that their form be used.

Since gift funds have to be verified, the donor should actually give them (not just promise them) to the loan applicant as soon as possible. The applicant should deposit the gift funds in the bank so that they can be verified along with the rest of the money in his account.

Gift funds
- Gift letter states funds do not have to be repaid
- Funds should be deposited in applicant's account

Exercise No. 2

Mr. Able wants to buy a home. The downpayment would be $17,000, and his closing costs are estimated at $3,400; he would also be required to have reserves of $2,615 (two months' mortgage payments) left over after closing.

Able has been working at a large, established company for three years. He is paid $1,400 every two weeks. He is selling his current home for $162,500; the mortgage on the property has a principal balance of $133,250, and the estimated selling expenses are $14,500. Able has checking and savings accounts with a local bank and plans to draw on those accounts to close the transaction (refer to the Verification of Deposit form in Figure 8.3).

1. What is Able's stable monthly income?

2. What is Able's net equity in the home that he is selling?

3. Will Able have any problems closing the transaction? Explain.

4. Do you see any problems with his verification of deposit? If so, explain what they are.

5. List some possible solutions to Able's problems.

Other Factors in Underwriting

In addition to the main components of creditworthiness we've discussed, certain other aspects of a proposed loan affect whether or not it will be approved. These include:

- the loan type,
- the repayment period,
- owner-occupancy, and
- the property type.

These factors may either add risk, making approval of the loan less likely, or compensate for risk, making approval more likely. In a case where income, net worth, or credit reputation is somewhat marginal, one of these other factors can make a difference, for better or worse.

Fig. 8.3 Verification of Deposit for Exercise No. 2

FannieMae

Request for Verification of Deposit

Privacy Act Notice: This information is to be used by the agency collecting it or its assignees in determining whether you qualify as a prospective mortgagor under its program. It will not be disclosed outside the agency except as required and permitted by law. You do not have to provide this information, but if you do not your application for approval as a prospective mortgagor or borrower may be delayed or rejected. The information requested in this form is authorized by Title 38, USC, Chapter 37 (If VA); by 12 USC, Section 1701 et.seq. (If HUD/FHA); by 42 USC, Section 1452b (if HUD/CPD); and Title 42 USC, 1471 et.seq. or 7 USC, 1921 et.seq. (If USDA/FmHA).

Instructions: Lender — Complete Items 1 through 8. Have applicant(s) complete Item 9. Forward directly to depository named in Item 1.
Depository — Please complete Items 10 through 18 and return DIRECTLY to lender named in Item 2.
The form is to be transmitted directly to the lender and is not to be transmitted through the applicant(s) or any other party.

Part I — Request

1. To (Name and address of depository)
Seaside Savings
1919 Second Avenue
Anytown, USA

2. From (Name and address of lender)
Coastal Mortgage
332 Juniper Street
Anytown, USA

I certify that this verification has been sent directly to the bank or depository and has not passed through the hands of the applicant or any other party.

3. Signature of lender	4. Title	5. Date	6. Lender's No. (Optional)
Warren Carter	Loan Officer	April 19	

7. Information To Be Verified

Type of Account	Account in Name of	Account Number	Balance
Checking	Carl B. Able	11616-6	$ 482.00
Savings	Carl B. Able	61161-1	$ 3,100.00
			$

To Depository: I/We have applied for a mortgage loan and stated in my financial statement that the balance on deposit with you is as shown above. You are authorized to verify this information and to supply the lender identified above with the information requested in Items 10 through 13. Your response is solely a matter of courtesy for which no responsibility is attached to your institution or any of your officers.

8. Name and Address of Applicant(s)
Carl B. Able
1800 Mill Street
Anytown, USA

9. Signature of Applicant(s)
Carl B Able

To Be Completed by Depository
Part II — Verification of Depository

10. Deposit Accounts of Applicant(s)

Type of Account	Account Number	Current Balance	Average Balance For Previous Two Months	Date Opened
Checking	11616-6	$ 200.00	$ 215.00	2/20
Savings	61161-1	$ 3,600.00	$ 650.00	2/20
		$	$	

11. Loans Outstanding To Applicant(s)

Loan Number	Date of Loan	Original Amount	Current Balance	Installments (Monthly/Quarterly)		Secured By	Number of Late Payments
		$	$	$	per		
		$	$	$	per		
		$	$	$	per		

12. Please include any additional information which may be of assistance in determination of credit worthiness. (Please include information on loans paid-in-full in Item 11 above.) none

13. If the name(s) on the account(s) differ from those listed in Item 7, please supply the name(s) on the account(s) as reflected by your records.

Part III — Authorized Signature - Federal statutes provide severe penalties for any fraud, intentional misrepresentation, or criminal connivance or conspiracy purposed to influence the issuance of any guaranty or insurance by the VA Secretary, the U.S.D.A., FmHA/FHA Commissioner, or the HUD/CPD Assistant Secretary.

14. Signature of Depository Representative	15. Title (Please print or type)	16. Date
Julia G. Hedges	Assistant Vice President	April 23
17. Please print or type name signed in item 14 Julia G. Hedges	**18.** Phone No. 809-9696	

Fannie Mae
Form 1006   July 96

Loan Type

Loan type refers to whether the proposed loan is a fixed-rate mortgage, an adjustable-rate mortgage, or some other type, such as a balloon mortgage. Borrowers tend to default more often on ARMs and other loans that involve changes in the payment amount than they do on fixed-rate mortgages. So an application for an ARM generally receives closer scrutiny, and this could tip the balance toward denial of the loan.

Repayment Period

The length of a proposed loan's repayment period affects the qualifying process because of its impact on the size of the monthly mortgage payments. A 15-year loan requires much bigger monthly payments than a 30-year loan for the same amount (see Chapter 6), and therefore is considerably more difficult to qualify for. But the repayment period also has a positive aspect. A 15-year loan presents less risk for the lender (or a secondary market purchaser) than a 30-year loan, since the loan funds are committed for a shorter period. As a result, the fact that a buyer is applying for a 15-year loan often counts as a compensating factor in the qualifying process.

Owner-Occupancy

Most home buyers intend to occupy the property they're buying. If a loan applicant won't be occupying the home he wants to purchase, the loan is referred to as an **investor loan**. Investor loans have a much higher default rate than loans to owner-occupants, so an applicant's investor status is treated as an additional risk factor in the qualifying process. Because of the additional risk, investor loans are subject to higher LTV requirements, additional fees, and/or higher interest rates.

Property Type

The type of home to be purchased can have an impact on the process of qualifying the buyer. Manufactured homes, condominium units, and some other types of residential property tend not to appreciate as much or as reliably as site-built single-family homes. If the home that the loan applicant wants to buy isn't a regular single-family home, that may be treated as an additional risk factor. That's true even when the appraisal shows that the home meets the lender's standards for the type of property in question. Fannie Mae and Freddie Mac will not even purchase investor loans secured by certain types of property with an increased risk of default, such as manufactured housing.

Subprime Lending

Our discussion of qualifying the buyer has been focused on so-called "prime" lending: loans that meet the normal underwriting standards of the secondary market agencies. But the mortgage market has another important segment: **subprime lending**. You should understand the basics of subprime lending because it was the boom and bust of subprime loans over the last several years that precipitated the recent mortgage crisis, one of the most significant developments in the history of the U.S. lending industry.

What is Subprime Lending?

The term "subprime lending" does not have a precise definition, but it generally refers to making loans to borrowers who pose greater risks than those who meet standard underwriting guidelines. Without subprime lending, these potential buyers might not be able to purchase the home they want—or, in some cases, any home at all.

Subprime lending: making loans to borrowers who pose greater risks

Subprime lenders can often be distinguished from prime lenders by their advertisements: subprime ads are aimed at potential home buyers who would have trouble getting a standard loan, and they often place special emphasis on their flexibility and personalized service. According to HUD, subprime lenders are more likely than prime lenders to have words such as "acceptance" or "consumer" in their names. Refinancing and home equity loans for the purpose of debt consolidation make up a large part of the subprime market, but there are many subprime home purchase loans as well.

Subprime Borrowers

Many of the home buyers who get subprime mortgages have blemished credit histories and mediocre credit scores. Depending on how poor the credit history is, these loans may be categorized as B, C, or D loans. (Prime, or standard, financing is often referred to as A credit.)

However, subprime lenders also deal with other categories of buyers: buyers who have good credit, but present some other risk factor. For example, subprime financing may be necessary for buyers who:

- can't (or would rather not have to) meet the income and asset documentation requirements of prime lenders;
- are carrying more debt than prime lenders consider acceptable; or
- want to make a smaller downpayment than prime lenders would allow.

These buyers generally fall into the "A-minus" credit category. (Their credit is good—thus the "A" status—but the additional element of risk knocks the rating down to A-minus.) When Fannie Mae and Freddie Mac began buying some A-minus loans (see Chapter 3), it blurred the line between prime and subprime lending, leading some to argue that A-minus loans shouldn't be considered subprime loans at all. Nevertheless, an A-minus borrower will still pay higher fees or a higher interest rate than she would with a truly prime loan.

Subprime Rates and Fees

Subprime lenders can take on riskier borrowers and make riskier loans because they apply more flexible underwriting standards. In exchange, they typically charge much higher interest rates and fees than prime lenders charge.

> **Example**: The Gundersons want to buy a home. Because of some recent credit problems, they can't qualify for a prime loan. Their subprime lender classifies them as B-risk borrowers and charges them 9% interest for their loan, although the market rate for prime loans (A loans) is only 6%. If the Gundersons had an even worse credit history and were classified as C-risk borrowers, the lender would charge them 10.5% interest. And if they were D-risk borrowers, they'd have to pay 12%.

Subprime lenders charge higher interest rates and loan fees

Subprime lenders justify their higher rates and fees by pointing to their higher servicing costs and greater default rate. Subprime loans require more aggressive servicing because of higher delinquency rates. (Charging more for riskier loans is called risk-based pricing, and it's a key aspect of subprime lending. We'll discuss it in more detail in the next section.)

In addition to having high interest rates and fees, subprime loans are more likely than prime loans to have features such as prepayment penalties, balloon payments, and negative amortization (see Chapter 6). These features help subprime lenders counterbalance some of the extra risk involved in their loans, but they can also cause trouble for borrowers. Although the majority of subprime lenders are legitimate, there are some who profit by deliberately making burdensome loans to home buyers who are likely to have great difficulty repaying them. This problem of predatory lending, discussed in Chapter 14, is generally associated with the subprime market.

Subprime Lending and the Secondary Market

The subprime segment of the mortgage market is estimated to have increased from about $35 billion in 1994 to $332 billion in 2003, and then to $1.3 trillion at its peak in early 2007. This growth was fueled by the increasing number of Wall Street investors who bought subprime loans and used them as the basis for issuing private label mortgage-backed securities.

Subprime loans were purchased by investors and packaged into mortgage-backed securities

Traditionally, Fannie Mae and Freddie Mac participated very little in the subprime market. In fact, their underwriting standards were at one time thought to define prime mortgage lending. However, HUD encouraged Fannie Mae and Freddie Mac to enter the subprime market to help meet their affordable housing goals (see Chapter 3), and in the last few years, both GSEs started buying more subprime loans. This drew protests from those already involved in the subprime market. However, for the most part, the GSEs only purchased the very top layer of the subprime market, A-minus loans, leaving other investors with the riskier subprime loans.

End of the Boom. The GSEs' expansion into A-minus territory was one of several ways in which the line between prime and subprime mortgage lending began to blur. As enthusiasm grew for purchasing subprime loans and repackaging them as mortgage-backed securities, underwriting standards for all loans—including prime loans—became increasingly lax, and default rates soared. The ripple effects from this wave of foreclosures, and the resulting losses, led to the failure of not only many subprime lenders but several major investment banks as well. Lenders who were known for making prime loans also suffered during the mortgage crisis, because they too had participated in the race to make more (and riskier) mortgage loans.

Today, many subprime lenders are gone and most other lenders have lost their appetite for risky loans. Subprime lending is now a much smaller segment of the market than in previous years. For instance, subprime loans accounted for less than 10% of the total number of loans originated in 2007.

Risk-based Loan Pricing

Risk-based pricing: charging risky borrowers more for their loans

To end the chapter, we'll take a brief look at risk-based loan pricing. **Risk-based pricing** refers to charging mortgage borrowers different interest rates and loan fees depending on whether they're good credit risks or poor credit risks. Poor credit risks are charged higher rates and fees than good risks. Only applicants with exceptionally bad credit histories are denied loans altogether.

As we just discussed, risk-based pricing has long been the standard practice in subprime lending. It has only been used to a limited extent in prime lending, however. Instead, prime lenders have traditionally used what's known as **average cost pricing** or **par rate pricing**. With this type of pricing, all borrowers who are approved for a loan are charged the same interest rate and fees, without regard to whether they easily met the lender's underwriting standards or just barely squeaked over the approval threshold. Those who don't meet the lender's standards are denied a loan.

Prime lenders do charge higher rates and fees for certain types of loans that entail extra risk, such as loans with high loan-to-value ratios. But until recently, it was unusual for prime lenders to charge different rates based on the strength or weakness of a loan applicant's income, net worth, and credit reputation.

Now risk-based pricing is becoming established in prime lending. For instance, in 2007 Fannie Mae and Freddie Mac implemented fees known as **loan-level price adjustments** (LLPAs). These are one-time fees, paid upon the origination of the loan, that vary depending on the risks presented by the loan. (LLPAs will be discussed in more detail in Chapter 10.) Automated underwriting is one of the main reasons for this change. It's comparatively easy for an AUS to draw distinctions between strong and weak borrowers and price their loans accordingly.

Risk-based pricing means that more people may be able to obtain loans, albeit more expensive ones. Some claim that risk-based pricing is fairer than average cost pricing, since the best credit risks don't have to subsidize those who aren't quite as good.

On the other hand, with risk-based pricing, some buyers who don't qualify for the best rates may be priced out of the market. Risk-based pricing can also make loan shopping more confusing, since lenders can't advertise one interest rate (or annual percentage rate) for all borrowers.

Whatever the advantages and disadvantages of risk-based pricing, it has taken hold in the prime market. This is a significant change for the industry, one that's blurring the distinction between prime and subprime mortgage lending.

Outline: Qualifying the Buyer

I. The Underwriting Process

    A. Underwriting is the process of evaluating a proposed loan to assess whether the buyer and the property meet the lender's minimum standards.

    B. Qualifying standards

        1. Underwriting standards establish what a lender considers to be acceptable and unacceptable risks.

        2. Because most loans will be sold on the secondary market, most lenders use underwriting standards established by Fannie Mae, Freddie Mac, the FHA, or the VA.

    C. Automated underwriting

        1. Today, most underwriting is done using software that makes a preliminary analysis of information provided on the loan application.

        2. Automated underwriting is based on the performance of millions of existing mortgage loans, which provides evidence of the factors that make default more or less likely.

        3. An automated underwriting decision will take the form of a risk classification. An application classified as "Accept" can be approved, while one classified as "Refer" won't necessarily be denied but will require further scrutiny by an underwriter.

        4. The automated underwriting report will also state whether a "low-doc" loan is possible, and whether a drive-by inspection is possible instead of a full appraisal.

II. Evaluating Creditworthiness

    A. Creditworthiness can be divided into three basic categories: credit reputation, income, and net worth.

    B. Strength in one area can offset weakness in another aspect of creditworthiness.

III. Credit Reputation

    A. Credit report

        1. A credit report will contain information about an individual's loans, credit purchases, and repayments for the previous seven years.

        2. There are three credit reporting agencies, each of which can issue a separate credit report on an applicant.

B. Credit history

   1. Credit history refers to how long an individual has been borrowing money and paying it back.

   2. Applicants should have at least a one-year credit history, but lending options are available for applicants who don't.

C. Major derogatory incidents that will be listed on a credit report include charge-offs, collections, repossessions, judgments, foreclosures, and bankruptcies.

D. Credit scores

   1. Credit scores predict the likelihood that an individual will default on a loan, given her previous credit history.

   2. The most widely used credit scores are FICO scores.

IV. Income Analysis

A. Characteristics of income

   1. Income has three dimensions: quantity, quality (how dependable the source of income is), and durability (the likelihood the income will continue in the future).

   2. Income that meets tests for quality and durability is considered stable monthly income.

B. Stable monthly income

   1. If an applicant has held the same employment position for two years or more, it won't be necessary to investigate previous work history.

   2. Continuity of earnings is more important than job continuity, and education or training that will enhance earning power can substitute for a two-year work history.

   3. Commissions, overtime, bonuses, and part-time or seasonal work can be considered durable income if they have been earned consistently for two years or more.

   4. Self-employment income adds an extra level of risk; lenders will expect to see that the business has been operated profitably for at least two years.

   5. A lender may send a Request for Verification of Employment to the applicant's employer, or the applicant may be able to provide W-2 forms and payroll stubs.

   6. Retirement income (such as pensions and social security) are dependable so they are considered stable monthly income.

7. Dividends or interest from investment income may be counted as stable monthly income if they are earned reliably.

8. Rental property income may be considered stable monthly income, although a percentage for bad debts and vacancies will be deducted.

9. Alimony, maintenance, and child support will be included as stable monthly income if it appears payments have been made reliably.

10. Unacceptable income includes income from unemployment benefits and income from temporary employment or unobligated family members.

C. Calculating stable monthly income

1. All income payments paid on a weekly or biweekly basis must be converted to monthly income.

2. Qualifying standards assume that income will be taxed, so if some income is nontaxable (such as child support), it may be "grossed up."

D. Income ratios

1. Debt to income ratio: the relationship between the proposed monthly mortgage payment and all other regular installment debt payments, and the monthly income.

2. Housing expense to income ratio: the relationship between the proposed monthly mortgage payment alone, and the monthly income.

3. The income of a cosigner, who will accept joint liability for the debt but will not be occupying the property, may be added to the applicant's income to increase the likelihood a loan will be approved.

V. Net Worth

A. Funds for closing

1. An applicant must have adequate liquid assets to cover the downpayment, closing costs, and other associated expenses.

2. The applicant may also be required to have two or three months' reserves left over after making the downpayment, to cover unexpected expenses without risk of default.

B. Assets

1. An underwriter will send a Request for Verification of Deposit to the applicant's bank to verify funds.

2. An underwriter will be suspicious of recently opened accounts or higher-than-normal balances, which may indicate funds for the downpayment were borrowed.

3. If the borrower is selling property to generate cash to buy new property, the lender will be concerned with the equity in the prop-

erty (market value minus liens and selling expenses) rather than the property's market value alone.

    4. If a buyer is unable to sell an old home in time to use the funds toward the new home, the buyer may use a temporary swing loan.

C. Gift funds

    1. An underwriter will usually accept gift funds from friends or relatives, so long as it is specified that the money is a gift and not a loan.

    2. The donor should give a gift letter stating that the funds given do not need to be repaid.

VI. Other Factors in Underwriting

A. Loan type: an ARM is riskier than a fixed-rate loan, and may require closer scrutiny.

B. Loan term: a 15-year loan is less risky to a lender than a 30-year loan.

C. Owner-occupancy: if a borrower doesn't plan to live in the property being purchased, it is considered an investor loan and a higher risk.

D. Property type: loans for certain property types that don't appreciate as fast, such as condos and mobile homes, might be considered riskier.

VII. Subprime Lending

A. Subprime lenders make loans with higher degrees of risk, either to borrowers with poor credit histories or to borrowers with good credit histories but with additional risk factors.

B. Subprime lenders apply more flexible underwriting standards and charge higher interest rates and fees.

C. The recent boom and bust in subprime lending played an important role in the current mortgage foreclosure crisis.

VIII. Risk-based Pricing

A. Subprime lenders use risk-based pricing; they make loans to borrowers with poor credit histories and charge them higher rates and fees than they charge other borrowers.

B. Prime lenders have traditionally charged all borrowers who met their standards the same rates, and turned away loan applicants who didn't meet their standards.

C. Now prime lenders are beginning to use risk-based pricing, blurring the line between prime and subprime lending.

Key Terms

Underwriting: The process of evaluating the financial status of a loan applicant and the value of the property he hopes to buy, to determine the risk of default and risk of loss in the event of foreclosure.

Underwriter: The employee of an institutional lender who evaluates loan applications, deciding which loans to approve.

Qualifying standards: The rules (concerning income, net worth, credit history, loan-to-value ratios) that an underwriter applies in deciding whether or not to approve a loan application; also called underwriting standards.

Automated underwriting (AU): Underwriting using software that makes a preliminary analysis of a loan application and makes a recommendation for approval or additional scrutiny.

Automated underwriting system (AUS): A computer program designed to perform automated underwriting; widely used.

Stable monthly income: Gross monthly income (from primary and secondary sources) that meets the lender's tests of quality and durability.

Income ratio: A test applied in qualifying a buyer for a loan, to determine whether or not he has sufficient income; the buyer's proposed housing expense and other debt repayments should not exceed a specified percentage of his stable monthly income.

Debt to income ratio: A ratio describing the maximum percentage of total monthly income that may be taken up by the proposed housing expense plus all other installment debt payments.

Housing expense to income ratio: A ratio describing the maximum percentage of total monthly income that may be taken up by the proposed housing expense.

Cosigner: A co-borrower who agrees to share liability with a borrower but who will not be occupying the property or have an ownership interest, in order to help the borrower qualify for the loan.

Net worth: An individual's personal financial assets, minus total personal liabilities.

Asset: Anything of value an individual owns.

Net equity: The market value of a property, minus any liens against the property and all anticipated selling expenses.

Gift funds: Money given to a buyer who would otherwise not have enough cash to close the transaction.

Gift letter: A document in which a donor of gift funds states that money given is not a loan and does not have to be repaid; required by a lender when the borrower intends to use gift funds as part of the downpayment or closing costs.

Credit report: A report prepared by a credit reporting agency outlining the credit history of an individual, showing amounts of debt and record of repayment.

Credit score: A figure used in underwriting to evaluate a loan applicant's credit history, calculated by a credit reporting agency.

Chapter Quiz

1. To evaluate the quality of a loan applicant's income, an underwriter considers whether the income:

    a. is derived from a dependable source

    b. is taxable

    c. can be expected to continue for a sustained period

    d. can be treated as a liquid asset

2. As a general rule, a loan applicant should have been continuously employed in the same field for at least:

    a. one year

    b. two years

    c. three years

    d. five years

3. The loan applicant receives child support from her ex-husband. Their child is now 16 years old. Will the child support payments be counted as part of the applicant's stable monthly income?

    a. Yes

    b. Only if the ex-husband has made the payments reliably

    c. Only if the applicant can provide proof of receipt

    d. No

4. The Hendersons have applied for a mortgage loan. Which of these is the underwriter most likely to treat as part of their stable monthly income?

    a. Wages the Hendersons' teenage daughter earns at a part-time job

    b. Unemployment compensation the husband is collecting

    c. Overtime the wife has been earning at her permanent job

    d. Money the husband has earned through occasional freelance work

5. After determining the quantity of the loan applicant's stable monthly income, the underwriter measures the adequacy of the income using:

    a. the consumer price index

    b. income ratios

    c. gross multipliers

    d. federal income tax tables

6. One reason an underwriter looks at a loan applicant's net worth is to see how well the applicant manages her financial affairs. Another reason is to:

   a. determine if the applicant has enough liquid assets to cover the costs of purchase and the required reserves
   b. find out if the new mortgage will have first lien position
   c. verify the accuracy of the applicant's credit rating
   d. prevent the applicant from resorting to gift funds for part of the closing costs

7. The Stanleys are selling their old home, and they plan to use the sale proceeds as a downpayment in buying a new home. In adding up the Stanleys' liquid assets, an underwriter would be willing to include:

   a. the sales price of the old home
   b. the net equity of the old home
   c. the gross equity of the old home
   d. None of the above

8. Bronowski doesn't have enough money for closing, so his parents are going to give him $2,500. The underwriter will:

   a. reject the loan application
   b. deduct the amount of the gift from the maximum loan amount
   c. require the parents to sign the promissory note
   d. require the parents to sign a gift letter

9. A personal credit report generally includes information about an individual's debts and payment history for the preceding:

   a. fifteen years
   b. twelve years
   c. seven years
   d. five years

10. The Olsens have a proposed monthly housing expense of $1,800, a monthly student loan payment of $180, and a monthly credit card payment of $100. Their stable monthly income is $6,500. What is their debt to income ratio?

    a. 28%
    b. 32%
    c. 4%
    d. 312.5%

Answer Key

1. a. The quality of an applicant's income reflects the dependability of the source of the income.

2. b. An underwriter will prefer to see that an applicant has been employed in the same field for at least two years.

3. d. While child support is usually included as stable monthly income if it is regularly paid, if the child is 16 the child support isn't going to continue for three years, so it won't be counted as stable monthly income.

4. c. Overtime, commissions, or bonuses regularly earned for several years as part of a permanent job can be considered stable monthly income.

5. b. Income ratios are used to determine whether the applicant's income is adequate to support the proposed monthly mortgage payment.

6. a. Investigating an applicant's net worth is important because the applicant must not only be able to make the downpayment and closing costs, but may also be required to have reserves left over.

7. b. The loan applicants' net equity in the house they're selling (the property's market value, minus the amount of all liens and anticipated selling expenses) is considered to be a liquid asset.

8. d. If a loan applicant's parents are giving him funds for the downpayment or closing costs, the parents must provide a gift letter stating that the funds do not need to be repaid.

9. c. The information on a credit report generally covers the previous seven years.

10. b. To calculate the debt to income ratio, add the proposed housing expense and all other monthly debt payments. The total monthly payments the Olsens will make add up to $2,080, which divided by $6,500 is 32%.

Chapter 9
Qualifying the Property

The Lender's Perception of Value

- Appraisals and loan-to-value ratios

Appraisal Standards

The Appraisal Process

Appraisal Methods

- Sales comparison method
- Replacement cost method
- Income method
- Final value estimate

Dealing with Low Appraisals

- Preventing low appraisals
- Request for reconsideration of value

Introduction

Qualifying the property:
Is it worth enough to serve as
collateral for the loan?

After qualifying the buyer, the underwriter's second major task is to qualify the property. Qualifying a property involves an analysis of its features to determine whether it has sufficient value to serve as collateral for the proposed loan. An underwriter is concerned with both the present value of the property and whether it is likely to maintain its value in the years to come.

Lenders make loans in anticipation of being repaid (with interest), so a lender's willingness to make a loan depends on the likelihood that the borrower will be able to repay the loan as promised. But regardless of the borrower's financial status, it is the property that serves as security for the debt. Before approving the loan, the underwriter should make certain that the property is worth enough to protect the lender's investment.

The Lender's Perception of Value

Underwriter relies on
appraisal for estimate of
market value

An underwriter's evaluation of a property is based on an appraisal prepared by a qualified appraiser. An **appraisal** is an *estimate* of the value of a piece of real estate. For a loan transaction, an appraiser is asked to analyze the property thoroughly and to issue an objective estimate of its **market value**. Here is the most widely accepted definition of market value, one used by Fannie Mae and Freddie Mac:

> The most probable price which a property should bring in a competitive and open market under all conditions requisite to a fair sale, the buyer and seller each acting prudently and knowledgeably, and assuming the price is not affected by undue stimulus.

Notice that according to this definition, market value is the *most probable* price (not "the highest price") that the property *should* bring (not "will bring"). Appraisal is a matter of estimation and likelihood, not certainty.

An appraiser's estimate of market value will not necessarily coincide with the price agreed on by the buyer and seller. A purchase agreement often reflects emotional or subjective considerations that matter to the buyer and seller, but that aren't pertinent to the property's market value. It's the true market value that the lender cares about.

Fig. 9.1 Principles of value

Highest and Best Use: The use which, at the time of appraisal, is most likely to produce the greatest net return from the property over a given period of time.

Change: Property values are in a constant state of flux, increasing and decreasing in response to social, economic, and governmental forces.

Anticipation: Value is created by the expectation of benefits to be received in the future.

Supply and Demand: Value varies directly with demand and inversely with supply.

Substitution: The maximum value of property is set by how much it would cost to obtain another property that is equally desirable, assuming there would not be a long delay or significant incidental expenses involved in obtaining the substitute.

Conformity: The maximum value of property is realized when there is a reasonable degree of social and economic homogeneity in the neighborhood.

Contribution: The value of real property is greatest when the improvements produce the highest return commensurate with their cost (the investment).

Example: Jim thinks his property is worth $375,000 and lists the home for that amount. Sally is happy to pay that price, because she loves the home's quirky characteristics. They enter into a sales contract. However, an appraiser determines that the market value of the property is only $320,000. Sally's lender will agree to a loan based on the $320,000 appraised value, not the $375,000 sales price. The lender isn't interested in what Jim and Sally think the property is worth, only in the property's market value.

To estimate market value, appraisers take into account the fundamental appraisal concepts known as the "principles of value." Figure 9.1 summarizes some of these principles.

Appraisals and Loan-to-Value Ratios

A lender uses a property's appraised value to help determine how much money it can safely loan using that property as security. The **loan-to-value ratio (LTV)** expresses the relationship between the loan amount and the property's value. For example, if a lender

Lender uses appraised value to help determine how much money to loan with property as security makes an $80,000 loan secured by a home appraised at $100,000, the loan-to-value ratio is 80%; the loan amount is 80% of the property's value, and the buyer makes a 20% downpayment. A $75,000 loan on the same property would have a 75% LTV and a 25% downpayment. The lower the LTV, the smaller the loan amount and the bigger the downpayment.

LTVs and Risk. The loan-to-value ratio affects the degree of risk involved in the loan—both the risk of default and the risk of loss in the event of default. Borrowers are less likely to default on loans with low LTVs. A borrower who makes a large downpayment has a substantial investment in the property, and will therefore try harder to avoid foreclosure. And when foreclosure is necessary, the lender is more likely to recover the entire debt if the LTV is relatively low. Foreclosure sale proceeds are often less than the full market value of the property, but if the original loan amount was only 75% of the value (for example), it's much more likely that the sale's proceeds will cover the outstanding loan balance.

The higher the LTV, the greater the lender's risk. So lenders use loan-to-value ratios to set maximum loan amounts. LTV rules limit the maximum loan that a lender is willing to make in relation to the appraised value of the property. For example, if a lender's maximum loan-to-value ratio for a particular type of loan is 90%, and the property has been appraised at $100,000, then $90,000 is the maximum loan amount.

Loans with higher LTVs usually carry higher interest rates. Higher interest rates help offset the lender's increased risk when making high-LTV loans.

As with other underwriting standards, the LTV rules that lenders apply depend on whether the loan is conventional, FHA-insured, or VA-guaranteed. These different loan types will be discussed in more detail in Chapters 10, 11, and 12.

Loan Based on Sales Price or Appraised Value. Lenders actually base the maximum loan amount on the sales price or the appraised value, whichever is less. This is a universal policy.

> **Example:** Let's return to our previous example. Jim and Sally have agreed on a $375,000 sale price. However, Sally's lender will base the loan amount on the property's appraised value of $320,000, since that's less than the sales price.

Loan-to-value ratio (LTV) affects:
- Risk of default
- Risk of loss if foreclosure required

Lower LTV = Lower risk

Lenders use LTVs to set maximum loan amounts

Loan-to-value ratio based on:
- Sales price or
- Appraised value,
- Whichever is less

$320,000   Sales price
×   80%   Loan-to-value ratio
$256,000   Maximum loan amount

In the example, the maximum loan amount is based on the lower of the two figures, the appraised value. If the lender applied the LTV to the higher of the two figures (the sales price), the loan amount would be too high for the lender's risk tolerance. 80% of the sales price would equal a loan that is almost 94% of the appraised value ($375,000 × 80% = $300,000; $300,000 ÷ $320,000 = 93.75%). In the event of default, this lender would be very likely to lose money in the foreclosure sale.

Appraisal Standards

Because of the relationship between loan-to-value ratio and risk, an accurate appraisal is an essential element of the loan underwriting process. If the appraiser overvalues the property, the loan amount will be larger than it should be, and the lender's risk of loss in the event of foreclosure may be much greater.

The appraisal industry tends to come under scrutiny when mortgage foreclosures reach crisis level. The industry was closely examined during the 1980s, after a considerable increase in foreclosure losses. Many analysts concluded that unreliable appraisals were a significant part of the problem.

In 1989, the Financial Institutions Reform, Recovery, and Enforcement Act (FIRREA) was passed in response to this conclusion. FIRREA includes licensing and certification standards that states were required to implement. While FIRREA does not require all appraisers to be licensed or certified, only appraisals prepared by state-licensed or certified appraisers can be used in "federally related" loan transactions. The majority of residential real estate loans are federally related, since the category includes loans made by any bank or savings and loan association that is regulated or insured by the federal government. There's an exemption for some loans less than $250,000; the appraisals for these smaller loans may be prepared by an unlicensed appraiser. (It is worth noting that the major secondary market agencies generally require all the mortgages they purchase to

Appraisals used for most mortgages must be prepared by licensed or certified appraiser be based on appraisals by licensed or certified appraisers, no matter what the loan amount.)

Despite reforms brought about by FIRREA, inflated appraisals are thought to have been a large factor in the mortgage and foreclosure crisis that began in 2007. This has led to renewed scrutiny of the appraisal profession, as officials try to address the problem of falling home values and the wave of foreclosures. New laws and regulations have been put into place to reduce the number of faulty appraisals. For example, rules enacted in 2008 now require all FHA loan appraisals to be conducted by certified appraisers who are on an FHA-approved roster, regardless of the loan amount. Other laws, both state and federal, are designed to foster the appraiser's independence from the influence of lenders and brokers. Additional legislation is likely as the fallout from the foreclosure crisis continues.

The Appraisal Process

It isn't necessary for real estate agents to be able to appraise real estate, at least not with the sophistication of a professional appraiser. It is helpful, however, to know something about the mechanics of the appraisal process and the reasoning that underlies many of the appraiser's conclusions. If an agent understands how appraisers estimate market value, it makes arranging sales that will hold together much easier.

Real estate appraisers generally follow these steps when completing an appraisal:

1. **Define the problem.** This includes identifying the property to be appraised (referred to as the **subject property**), determining the purpose of the appraisal, and specifying the "as of" date. Since property values are constantly changing, an appraisal is only valid "as of" a particular date. For a standard residential appraisal, the "as of" date is the date the appraisal is performed. But property can also be appraised as of a specified date in the past (estimating the past value of property involved in a lawsuit, for example) or even a specified date in the future (estimating the future value of property that is going to be developed, for example).

2. **Determine the scope of work.** This refers to figuring out what's involved in solving the problem. The scope of work includes both the type and quantity of information needed, as well the type of analysis that will be used in the appraisal assignment. Finally, the scope of work may involve planning the tasks involved in completing the appraisal; complex assignments may require consulting additional experts, for example.

3. **Collect and verify data.** Appraisal data can be divided into two categories: general data and specific data. **General data** refers to information concerning factors outside the property itself that have a bearing on the property's value. In a residential appraisal, this includes information about the region's economy and information about the neighborhood where the home is located. **Specific data** refers to information concerning the property itself—the site, the house, and other improvements on the site. (See the list of Neighborhood Considerations and Property Features in Figure 9.2.) All of the data collected must be verified in some way, such as by inspection and in-person measurements or by cross-checking information with county records.

4. **Analyze data.** Analyzing the data requires the appraiser to judge the relevance of each piece of information that has been collected. For instance, the appraiser will consider what the data regarding market trends says about the subject property's value.

5. **Determine site value.** Site valuation is an estimate of the value of a property, excluding the value of any existing or proposed improvements. For vacant land, site valuation is the same as appraising the property. For improved property (such as property with a house on it), site valuation involves appraising the property as if vacant. A separate site valuation may be necessary depending on the method of appraisal that will be used (for example, the cost approach to value; see below).

6. **Apply the appropriate methods of appraisal.** The three methods of appraisal are explained in the next section of

The steps in the appraisal process are:
- Define the problem
- Determine scope of work
- Collect and verify data
- Analyze data
- Determine site value
- Apply appraisal method
- Reconciliation
- Issue appraisal report

this chapter. Each method that the appraiser applies results in a **value indicator**, a figure that the appraiser treats as an indication of the subject property's value.

7. **Reconcile the results to arrive at a final value estimate.** After taking into account the purpose of the appraisal, the type of property, and the reliability of the data gathered, the appraiser weighs the value indicators and decides on a final estimate of the subject property's market value.

8. **Issue the appraisal report.** The appraiser's last step is to prepare an appraisal report, presenting the value estimate and summarizing the underlying data for the client. When property is appraised to determine its value as collateral for a loan, the appraiser's client is the lender.

Appraisers usually—but not always—gather data about the subject property through an in-person inspection. When the property is a single-family home, the appraiser ordinarily walks through the rooms taking notes about the overall condition and about particular features, good and bad.

In some situations, a lender may allow a "drive-by appraisal" instead of an in-person inspection. To complete a drive-by appraisal, the appraiser first collects information about the subject property from online sources (such as the website of the multiple listing service), then pays a very brief visit to the property to get an idea of its general condition. The appraiser simply looks at the exterior of the house, without going inside; in fact, she might not even get out of her car. The USPAP requires appraisers to acquire adequate information about the subject property to make an informed estimate of value. If that's not possible using a drive-by inspection, the appraiser will tell the lender that an actual inspection is needed. A drive-by appraisal is generally appropriate only if the property is typical for the area.

Drive-by appraisals were relatively common in the years leading up to the mortgage crisis. However, some experts believe that these fairly casual appraisals led to overstated values and put many lenders at risk. It's likely that lenders will rely on drive-by appraisals much less in the future. Note that in some cases, an in-person inspection is always required; this is true for FHA loans.

Appraisal Methods

There are basically three ways to appraise real estate:

1. the sales comparison method,
2. the replacement cost method, and
3. the income method.

Three methods of appraisal:
• Sales comparison
• Replacement cost
• Income

All three methods, or only one or two, may be applied in valuing a particular property, depending on the purpose of the appraisal and the type of property in question. As described above, each method yields a value indicator. The appraiser will base the final estimate of value on these value indicators.

Sales Comparison Method

Of the three appraisal methods, the sales comparison method (also known as the market data method) is the one preferred by appraisers, especially for residential property. This technique involves comparing the subject property with similar properties in the same neighborhood that have sold recently. These similar properties are called **comparable sales** or **comparables**. Appraisers know that competitive forces influence prices. Under ordinary circumstances, an informed buyer will not pay more for a particular property than he would have to pay for an equally desirable substitute property, and an informed owner will not sell property for less than it's worth. Thus, recent sales prices of comparables give a good indication of their market values and can be used to estimate the probable market value of the subject property.

Sales comparison method: sales prices of comparables used to estimate market value of subject property

Sales Comparison Appraisal vs. CMA. Many real estate agents use a competitive market analysis (CMA) to help sellers set listing prices. A CMA is essentially a less formal version of the sales comparison method of appraisal, but it should not be referred to or treated as an appraisal. A real estate agent performing a CMA may make use of certain data that an appraiser would not rely on. For example, in addition to using actual sales as comparables, the real estate agent might use properties that are listed for sale but have not sold yet. In an appraisal, although the appraiser may analyze current listings as

CMA: informal version of sales comparison appraisal

CMA may use current and expired listings; appraisal is based on actual sales

supporting data (especially in a rapidly changing market), the main comparables must be actual sales.

Sales prices are excellent indicators of market value, because they represent actual agreements between buyers and sellers in a competitive marketplace. Listing prices, on the other hand, are less accurate indicators of market value. A home's listing price may be considerably higher than the price it eventually sells for.

Even so, current listings provide useful information about market conditions for a CMA. The seller's home will be competing with those other listings. Some CMAs also compare the subject property to homes that failed to sell before their listings expired; these homes apparently were priced too high.

Identifying Legitimate Comparable Sales. Sales make better comparables than listings, and some sales make better comparables than other sales. When evaluating a sale to see if it qualifies as a legitimate comparable, the appraiser is concerned with five issues:

Choosing comparables:
- Date of sale
- Location
- Physical characteristics
- Terms of sale
- Conditions of sale

- the date of the sale,
- the location of the property sold,
- the physical characteristics of the property,
- the terms of sale, and
- the conditions of the sale.

1. Date of comparable sale. The sale should be recent, within the past six months if possible. During times of rapid market change, however, sales within the last two or three months may be required. Recent sales give a more accurate indication of what's happening in the marketplace today, so appraisers will want to find the most recent sales possible.

At least three comps needed for sales comparison approach

An appraiser ordinarily needs at least three comparables to apply the sales comparison method. If the market has been inactive and there are not enough legitimate comparable sales from the past six months, the appraiser can go back farther. Comparable sales over one year old are generally not acceptable, however, even in a very stable market.

Comps should never be more than one year old

If the comparable sales are more than a few months old, it is often necessary to make adjustments for inflationary or deflationary trends or other forces that have affected prices in the area.

Fig. 9.2 Sales comparison considerations

Key Considerations in a Sales Comparison Appraisal

There are many things to consider during a residential appraisal; some of them are very important, others less so. Here's a list of some of the elements that matter most to appraisers in choosing comparables and valuing homes.

Neighborhood Considerations

Percentage of home ownership. Is there a high degree of owner-occupancy or do rental properties predominate? Owner-occupied neighborhoods are generally better maintained and less susceptible to deterioration.

Foreclosures/Vacant homes and lots. An unusual number of vacant homes or lots suggests a low level of interest in the area, which has a negative effect on property values. On the other hand, construction activity in a neighborhood signals current interest in the area.

Conformity. The homes in a neighborhood should be reasonably similar to one another in style, age, size, and quality. Strictly enforced zoning and private restrictions promote conformity and protect property values.

Changing land use. Is the neighborhood in the midst of a transition from residential use to some other type of use? If so, the properties are probably losing their value as residences (even though the change promises higher values overall because of the potential for more productive use of the land in the future).

Contour of the land. Mildly rolling topography is preferred to terrain that is either monotonously flat or excessively hilly.

Streets. Wide, gently curving streets are more appealing than narrow or straight streets. Streets should be hard surfaced and well maintained.

Utilities. Is the neighborhood adequately serviced by electricity, water, gas, sewers, and telephones?

Nuisances. Nuisances in or near a neighborhood (odors, eyesores, industrial noises or pollutants, or exposure to unusual winds, smog, or fog) hurt property values.

Prestige. Is the neighborhood considered prestigious, in comparison to others in the community? If so, that will increase property values.

Proximity. How far is it to traffic arterials and to important points such as downtown, employment centers, and shopping centers?

Schools. What schools serve the neighborhood? Are they highly regarded? Are they nearby? The quality of a school or school district can make a major difference to property values in a residential neighborhood.

Public services. Is the neighborhood properly serviced by public transportation, police, and fire units?

Government influences. Does zoning in and around the neighborhood promote residential use and insulate the property owner from nuisances? How do the property tax rates compare with those of other neighborhoods nearby?

(continued)

Property Features

Site. The appraiser will note the lot's size, shape, and topography, and how much street frontage it has. Rectangular lots are more useful than lots with irregular shapes; unusually steep lots may have problems with soil instability. Drainage and landscaping are important, and a view can add substantially to value. An easement or encroachment will be taken into account, as well as zoning and private restrictions.

Design and appeal. Is the home's overall appeal good, average, or poor? There are dozens of house styles: ranch (rambler), colonial, Victorian, etc. The appraiser will try to find comparables in the same general style as the subject property. Comparisons between one- and two-story houses generally are not valid, but a one-story house can be compared to a split-level with certain adjustments.

Construction quality. Is the quality of materials and workmanship good, average, or poor?

Age/condition. When the subject property and comparables are in similar condition, a difference in age up to five years is generally inconsequential. Is the property's overall condition good, average, or poor?

Size of house (square footage). The appraiser is concerned with the gross living area (GLA), which is the improved living area, excluding the garage, basement, and porches.

Basement. A functional basement, especially a finished basement, contributes to value. (In many cases, however, the amount a finished basement contributes to value is not enough to recover the cost of the finish work.)

Interior layout. Is the floor plan functional and convenient? It should not be necessary to pass through a public room (such as the living room) to reach other rooms, or to pass through one of the bedrooms to reach another.

Number of rooms. The appraiser will add up the total number of rooms in the house, excluding bathrooms and (usually) basement rooms. Usually the appraiser will try to find comparables with the same number of rooms as the subject.

Number of bedrooms. Differences in the number of bedrooms have a major impact on value. For instance, if all else is equal, a two-bedroom comparable is worth considerably less than a three-bedroom subject.

Number of bathrooms. A full bath is a lavatory (wash basin), toilet, and both a bathtub and a shower; a ¾ bath is a lavatory, toilet, and either a shower or a tub; a ½ bath is a lavatory and toilet only. The number of bathrooms can have a noticeable effect on value.

Air conditioning. The presence or absence of an air conditioning system is important in warm climates.

Energy efficiency. With spiraling energy costs, an energy-efficient home is more valuable than a comparable one that is not. Energy-efficient features include: double-paned windows; clock-controlled thermostats; insulated ducts and pipes in unheated areas; adequate insulation for floors, walls, and attic; weather stripping for doors and windows.

Garage/carport. An enclosed garage is generally better than a carport. How many cars can it accommodate? Is there work or storage space in addition to parking space? Is it possible to enter the home directly from the garage or carport, protected from the weather?

Example: A comparable residential property sold six months ago for $477,000. In general, local property values have fallen by 4% over the past six months. The comparable property, then, should be worth approximately 4% less than it was six months ago.

$477,000	Value six months ago
× 96%	Deflation factor
$457,920	Approximate present value

2. Location of comparable sale. Whenever possible, comparables should be selected from the neighborhood where the subject property is located. In the absence of any legitimate comparables in the neighborhood, the appraiser can look elsewhere, but the properties selected should at least come from comparable neighborhoods.

If a comparable selected from an inferior neighborhood is structurally identical to the subject property, it is probably less valuable; conversely, a structurally identical comparable in a superior neighborhood is probably more valuable than the subject property. It is generally conceded that location contributes more to the value of real estate than any other characteristic. A high-quality property cannot overcome the adverse effects on value that a low-quality neighborhood causes. On the other hand, the value of a relatively weak property is enhanced by a stable and desirable neighborhood.

3. Physical characteristics. To qualify as a comparable, a property should have physical characteristics (construction quality, design, amenities, etc.) that are similar to those of the subject property. When a comparable has a feature that the subject property lacks—or lacks a feature that the subject property has—the appraiser will adjust the comparable's price.

Comp's price adjusted to indicate value of subject:
- Down if subject lacks feature
- Up if subject has extra feature

Example: One of the comparables the appraiser is using is quite similar to the subject property overall, but there are several significant differences. The subject property has a two-car garage, while the comparable has only a one-car garage. Based on experience, the appraiser estimates that space for a second car adds approximately $2,400 to the value of a home in this area. The comparable actually sold for $223,500. The appraiser will add $2,400 to that price, to reflect the fact that the subject property has more garage space than the comparable.

On the other hand, the comparable has a fireplace and the subject property does not. The appraiser estimates a fireplace adds approximately $1,100 to the value of a home. She will subtract $1,100 from the comparable's price, to reflect the fact that the subject property has no fireplace.

After adjusting the comparable's price up or down for each difference in this way, the appraiser can use the resulting figure as an indication of the value of the subject property.

4. Terms of sale. The terms of sale can affect the price a buyer will pay for a property. Attractive financing concessions (such as seller-paid discount points or seller financing with an especially low interest rate) can make a buyer willing to pay a higher price than he would otherwise be willing to pay. These kinds of special terms become more common in a slow market. Sellers may also offer help with closing costs or even a free vacation to attract buyers.

An appraiser has to take into account the influence the terms of sale may have had on the price paid for a comparable property. If the seller offered the property on very favorable terms, there's an excellent chance that the sales price did not represent the true market value of the comparable.

Under the Uniform Standards of Professional Appraisal Practice, an appraiser giving an estimate of market value must state whether it is the most probable price in terms of cash, in terms of financial arrangements equivalent to cash, or in other precisely defined terms. (The Uniform Standards of Professional Appraisal Practice, or US-PAP, are guidelines adopted by the Appraisal Foundation, a nonprofit organization established to enhance the quality of appraisals.)

If the estimate is based on financing with special conditions or incentives, those terms must be clearly set forth, and the appraiser must estimate their effect on the property's value. Market data supporting the value estimate (that is, the selling prices of comparables) must be explained in the same way.

5. Conditions of sale. Finally, a comparable sale can be relied on as an indication of what the subject property is worth only if it occurred under normal conditions and the buyer and seller were typically motivated. This means the sale must meet these four criteria:

- the sale was between unrelated parties (an "arm's length transaction");
- both parties were acting free of unusual pressure;

Special financing can make buyer willing to pay more, so appraiser takes terms of sale into account when evaluating a comparable

Conditions of sale:
- Arm's length transaction
- No unusual pressure to act
- Both parties fully informed
- Property on open market for reasonable time

- both parties were informed of the property's attributes and deficiencies, and were acting in their own best interests; and
- the property was offered for sale on the open market for a reasonable length of time.

A property sold from one family member to another would not qualify as a comparable. Likewise, foreclosures and short sales should not be used as comparables, as the sellers are often acting under pressure and with little bargaining power. However, in some markets particularly hard hit by foreclosures, those may be the only types of comparables available. The appraiser will have to use experience and knowledge of the local market to judge which comparables are the most appropriate.

When appraising a property that is owned by a financial institution because of a mortgage default (referred to as an REO, for "real estate owned"), the appraiser should use only other REOs as comparables. REOs typically have lower market values than comparable properties owned by more typical homeowners or investors. There are various reasons for this. For one thing, REOs are usually vacant, which means an increased risk of vandalism or other deterioration. Further, there are often delays in the closing process, caused by institutional bureaucracy. Lengthy delays can jeopardize the buyer's financing and will certainly mean a later possession date. If an appraiser who is evaluating an REO is forced to use a non-REO as a comparable, she will usually have make a downward price adjustment to the comparable property.

Adjustments. An appraiser can rarely find three ideal comparables: three homes exactly like the subject property, in the same neighborhood, that all sold for cash within the previous month. So, as you've seen, the appraiser has to make adjustments, taking into account differences in time, location, physical characteristics, or terms of sale, in order to arrive at an **adjusted selling price** for each comparable.

Reconciliation. The appraiser bases his estimate of the subject property's value on the adjusted selling prices of the comparables. The appraiser reviews all the data regarding each comparable, then uses her judgment and experience to select a value within the range of the adjusted selling prices of the comparables. This process is referred to as **reconciliation**.

Reconciliation: the process of analyzing the adjusted selling prices of the comparables to arrive at a value indicator

Choosing an appropriate value for the subject property is not a mechanical process. The appraiser should never simply average the adjusted selling prices of the comparables. Instead, the appraiser considers the relative reliability of each comparable, and gives more weight to the ones that are the most reliable.

It stands to reason that the more adjustments an appraiser has to make, the less reliable the resulting estimate of value will be. In fact, if the necessary adjustments add up to a significant percentage of a comparable's sales price (for example, 25% of the price), then that property isn't sufficiently similar to the subject to make a good comparable.

Let's look at a simplified example of how reconciliation works.

Example: The appraiser found three comparables for the subject property:

Comparable	Adjusted Selling Price	Adjustments as Percentage of Sales Price
A	$365,000	9%
B	$342,700	18%
C	$359,000	6%

Comparables A and B had relatively modest adjustments to their prices. Comparable B had significant adjustments. Giving the least weight to Comparable B, the appraiser determines that the subject property's fair market value is $361,000.

Market Conditions. As of April 2009, appraisers are required to complete Form 1004MC, the Market Conditions Addendum to the Uniform Residential Appraisal Report (see Figure 9.4) for all federally regulated loans on one- to four-unit properties. This change, coming in the wake of the mortgage and foreclosure crisis, is intended to give lenders a more accurate picture of the subject property's local market. With this information, lenders will be able to better understand the complex market conditions and trends that support the appraiser's opinion of value.

The Market Conditions addendum requires appraisers to analyze supply and demand factors in the local housing market. In addition, appraisers are asked to analyze other trends, such as changes to median home prices, average number of days a listing is on the market, and changes in the listing-to-sales price ratios. There is a section for analyzing the local trend in seller concessions (such as seller-paid assistance with closing costs) within the previous 12 months. Finally, Form 1004MC asks appraisers to summarize the number and frequency of foreclosures in the subject property's local market and report on the impact of those foreclosures on value.

Replacement Cost Method

The replacement cost method of appraisal is based on the premise that the value of a house or other building is limited by the cost of building a new one just like it. (This is a version of the principle of substitution: a buyer won't pay more for a property than it would cost to obtain an equally desirable substitute. See Figure 9.1.) To use the cost method, appraisers must keep abreast of construction costs in their area. Here are the steps involved in the cost method:

Replacement cost method: a property's value won't exceed the cost of replacing it

Step 1: Estimate the cost of replacing the building(s) and any other improvements on the property.

Step 2: Estimate and deduct any accrued depreciation.

Step 3: Add the value of the lot to the depreciated value of the improvements.

Estimating Replacement Cost. A building's **replacement cost** is how much it would currently cost to construct a new building with equivalent utility—in other words, one that would have essentially the same features and could be used in essentially the same way. Replacement cost is not the same thing as **reproduction cost**, which is how much it would cost to construct an exact duplicate or replica of the building, at current prices. In most cases, the reproduction cost would be considerably higher than the replacement cost, and would not give an accurate indication of the property's current market value. For an ordinary appraisal, the appraiser is concerned with replacement cost, not reproduction cost.

There are a number of ways to estimate replacement cost. The simplest is **comparative-unit method**, also known as the square foot method. By analyzing the average cost per square foot of construction for recently built improvements comparable to the subject property's, the appraiser can estimate what the square foot cost of replacing the improvements under appraisal would be.

Comparative-unit method: using square foot cost of recently built comps to estimate cost of replacing subject property

To calculate the cost of replacing the building on the subject property, the appraiser multiplies the estimated cost per square foot by the number of square feet in the building. The number of square feet in a house is determined by measuring the dimensions of each floor of the structure, including the outer wall surfaces. The square footage refers only to the improved living area; the garage, basement, and porches are excluded.

> **Example:** The subject property is a ranch-style house with a wooden exterior, containing 1,800 square feet. Based on an analysis of the construction costs of three recently built homes of comparable size and quality, the appraiser estimates that it would cost $126.37 per square foot to replace the home.
>
> | | |
> |---:|:---|
> | 1,800 | Square feet |
> | × $126.37 | Cost per square foot |
> | $227,466 | Estimated cost of replacing improvements |

Of course, a comparable structure (or "benchmark" building) is unlikely to be exactly the same as the subject property. Variations in design, shape, and grade of construction will affect the square foot cost—moderately or substantially. The appraiser will make appropriate adjustments to take these differences into account.

When there aren't any recently built comparable homes available, the appraiser relies on current cost manuals to estimate the basic construction costs.

Estimating Depreciation. When the home being appraised is one that has been lived in, the presumption is that it is not as valuable as a comparable new home; it has depreciated in value. So, after estimating replacement cost, the appraiser's next step is to estimate the depreciation. This is the most difficult part of the replacement cost method of appraisal.

Depreciation is a loss in value due to any cause. Value can be lost as a result of:

Depreciation: loss in value from any cause
- Physical deterioration
- Functional obsolescence
- External obsolescence

- physical deterioration,
- functional obsolescence, or
- external obsolescence.

Physical deterioration refers to physical wear and tear, damage, and structural defects that reduce the value of the property.

Functional obsolescence, also called functional depreciation, is a loss in value due to inadequacies such as poor design or outmoded features. In older homes, not enough bathrooms in relation to the number of bedrooms is a common example of functional obsolescence.

External obsolescence (also called external inadequacy, external depreciation, or economic obsolescence) is a loss in value due to factors outside the property, such as a deteriorating neighborhood, declining market values, zoning changes, or poor access to schools, shopping, or employment centers.

Depreciation is considered **curable** if the cost of correcting it could be recovered in the sales price when the property is sold. Depreciation is **incurable** if it is impossible to correct, or if it would cost so much to correct that it would not make sense to do so. Physical deterioration and functional obsolescence may be either curable or incurable. (Curable physical deterioration may be referred to as deferred maintenance.) External obsolescence, on the other hand, is always incurable, because it's caused by factors beyond the property owner's control.

After estimating how much the depreciation in each of the three categories is reducing the subject property's value, the appraiser deducts the depreciation from the estimated replacement cost of the improvements.

Example:

$227,466	Estimated replacement cost
8,510	Physical deterioration (roof in need of repair; garage door should be replaced)
7,050	Functional obsolescence (living room too small; family room too far from kitchen)
– 3,000	External obsolescence (odors from nearby factory)
$208,906	Depreciated value of improvements

Because estimating depreciation is difficult, the older the property, the less reliable the replacement cost method is. In many cases, an appraiser will decide not to use the cost method in an appraisal of an older home. The cost method also isn't used for appraising a unit in a condominium.

Deferred maintenance and underwriting. An appraisal is submitted to the underwriter in one of two ways: "as is" or "subject to." An "as is" appraisal reports deferred maintenance (curable physical deterioration, such as broken windows, worn-out roof, drainage problems, damaged siding, etc.), but the final value estimate represents the market value of the property in its current condition. In a "subject to" appraisal, the final value estimate represents what the market value of the property would be if the deferred maintenance were corrected.

Appraisal may be "as is," or "subject to" repairs

In some cases the underwriter will make correction of the deferred maintenance a condition of loan approval. These "lender-required repairs" must be completed before the loan can be funded.

Adding Land Value. The last step in the replacement cost method is to add the value of the land to the depreciated value of the improvements, to arrive at an estimate of value for the property as a whole.

Example:

$208,906   Depreciated value of the improvements
+ 59,000   Land value
$267,906   Depreciated value of the property

The value of the land is estimated by the sales comparison method. Prices recently paid for vacant lots similar to the subject property's lot are compared and used as indications of what the subject property's lot is worth.

Income Method

The income method of appraisal is based on the idea that there is a relationship between the income that a property generates and its value to a potential investor (a potential buyer). To arrive at an estimate of the subject property's value, its annual net income is divided by a capitalization rate that represents the return an investor would expect from the property.

Residences generally aren't regarded as income-producing properties, so formal income analysis techniques don't apply when a home is being appraised. If a residential appraiser uses the income method at all, she will use a simplified version called the **gross income multiplier method** (also known as the gross rent multiplier method). As a rule, this is done only when the subject property is located in a neighborhood where most of the properties are rentals, not owner-occupied homes.

Gross income multiplier method: used to estimate value of rental home

In the gross income multiplier method, the appraiser looks at the relationship between a rental property's income and the price paid for the property.

Example:

Sales price: $246,000
Monthly rent: $2,000
Conclusion: Monthly rent is equal to 0.81% of the sales price; the sales price is approximately 123 times the monthly rent.

Monthly rents may run about one percent of selling prices in one market, and more or less in another. (A market exists where specific rental properties compete with each other for tenants.) For competitive reasons, rents charged for similar properties tend to be similar within the same market. As a result, if one rental property has a monthly income that is one percent of its sales price, comparable properties will have similar income-to-price ratios.

A monthly multiplier is calculated by dividing the sales price by the monthly rental income. An annual multiplier is calculated by dividing the sales price by the annual rental income.

Example:

Sales Price		Monthly Rent		Monthly Multiplier
$346,000	÷	$2,000	=	173

Sales Price		Annual Income		Annual Multiplier
$346,000	÷	$24,000	=	14.42

After locating a sufficient number of comparable residential rental properties, the appraiser determines their monthly or annual gross income multipliers (either is acceptable—it's a matter of the appraiser's preference) by dividing the rents into their respective selling prices.

Example:

Comp.	Sales Price	Monthly Rent	Monthly Multiplier
1	$337,500	$1,950	173.08
2	$345,000	$1,975	174.68
3	$350,000	$2,025	172.84
4	$353,500	$2,100	168.33

The appraiser uses the multipliers of the comparables to determine an appropriate multiplier for the subject property, taking into account the similarities and differences between the properties. Then the appraiser multiplies the rent that the subject property is generating by the chosen gross income multiplier for a rough estimate of its value as an income-producing property.

Note that the number of comparables necessary to develop an appropriate multiplier for the subject property will vary, depending on the size and type of the local market. In some cases, as few as three or four comparables will be sufficient (as in our example); in other markets, the appraiser may need more.

The principal weakness of the gross income multiplier method is that it's based on gross income figures and does not take into account vacancies or operating expenses. If two rental homes have the same rental income, the gross income multiplier method would indicate they are worth the same amount; but if one is older and has higher maintenance costs, the net return to the owner would be less, and so would its actual value.

If possible, the appraiser should use the subject property's **economic rent** or **market rent** (the rent the property could command in the current marketplace if it were available for lease today) as opposed to the **contract rent** (the rent the owner is actually receiving).

> **Example:** The owner leased the home two years ago for $1,850 a month and the lease contract has another year to go. Market rents have risen sharply over the past two years, so that the property could now command a much higher rent—probably about $2,175 a month. If the appraiser were to use the $1,850 contract rent in the gross income multiplier method, it would distort the estimate of value.

Final Value Estimate

If the appraiser has applied all three appraisal methods (sales comparison, replacement cost, and income), he must analyze and compare the three results in order to draw a conclusion about the property's value. That process of interpretation is known as **reconciliation** or **correlation**. (This is essentially the same process used to arrive at the value indicator for the sales comparison approach.)

Appraiser weighs results to arrive at final value estimate

The appraiser's experience and judgment play a critical role in the reconciliation process. The final estimate of value is not simply the average of the results yielded by the three approaches. The appraiser must weigh each result carefully, considering all the factors that affect its reliability for the type of property in question. From that analysis, the appraiser decides on a figure that represents his expert opinion of the subject property's market value.

Sales comparison method most important for residential property

For single-family homes not used as rental properties, the sales comparison method is far more reliable than the other methods. Appraisers frequently base the final value estimate for a single-family home on the result of the sales comparison method alone.

Once the appraiser arrives at a final estimate of value, she presents it to the client in an appraisal report. Typically—particularly for single-family residential real estate—the appraiser will use the

Uniform Residential Appraisal Report, shown in Figure 9.3. Reviewing this form will give you a clearer idea of what the appraiser must do before she can issue a responsible estimate of value.

Dealing with Low Appraisals

Understanding the appraisal process helps real estate agents eliminate or at least minimize a common selling problem, the low appraisal. No one gets through an entire real estate career without facing the low appraisal problem at least a few times, and in rapidly rising or falling markets, low appraisals may be even more common.

A low appraisal is an estimate of value that is below (perhaps way below) the price the buyer and seller agreed on. A sale is written, the parties are pleased, and then a week or so later the agent gets the bad news. A lower than expected appraisal puts the sale in serious jeopardy.

Low appraisal: value estimate below the price agreed on

If the transaction is contingent on financing, the buyer does not have to complete the sale if the appraisal comes in low. Buyers are understandably reluctant to pay more for a property than a professional appraiser says it is worth. And even when a buyer would like to go ahead with the purchase in spite of the low appraisal, he may not be able to afford to. Since the purchase loan is based on the sales price or the appraised value, whichever is less, a low appraisal means a smaller loan—and a bigger downpayment.

Example:
1. Buyer is prepared to make a 10% downpayment and obtain a 90% loan.
2. Sales price is $300,000.
3. Appraisal is issued at $291,000.
4. Maximum loan amount is 90% of $291,000.

$291,000	Appraised value
× 90%	Loan-to-value ratio
$261,900	Maximum loan amount

Because of the low appraisal ($9,000 less than the sales price), the loan amount is limited to $261,900. The buyer expected to make a $30,000 downpayment ($300,000 sales price × 90% = $270,000 loan). But the buyer would now have to make a $38,100 downpayment ($300,000 − $261,900 loan = $38,100) to pay the $300,000 price.

Fig. 9.3 Uniform Residential Appraisal Report form

Uniform Residential Appraisal Report File

The purpose of this summary appraisal report is to provide the lender/client with an accurate, and adequately supported, opinion of the market value of the subject property.

SUBJECT

Property Address		City		State	Zip Code
Borrower	Owner of Public Record			County	

Legal Description

Assessor's Parcel #   Tax Year   R.E. Taxes $

Neighborhood Name   Map Reference   Census Tract

Occupant ☐ Owner ☐ Tenant ☐ Vacant   Special Assessments $ ☐ PUD   HOA $ ☐ per year ☐ per month

Property Rights Appraised ☐ Fee Simple ☐ Leasehold ☐ Other (describe)

Assignment Type ☐ Purchase Transaction ☐ Refinance Transaction ☐ Other (describe)

Lender/Client   Address

Is the subject property currently offered for sale or has it been offered for sale in the twelve months prior to the effective date of this appraisal? ☐ Yes ☐ No

Report data source(s) used, offering price(s), and date(s).

CONTRACT

I ☐ did ☐ did not analyze the contract for sale for the subject purchase transaction. Explain the results of the analysis of the contract for sale or why the analysis was not performed.

Contract Price $ Date of Contract   Is the property seller the owner of public record? ☐ Yes ☐ No Data Source(s)

Is there any financial assistance (loan charges, sale concessions, gift or downpayment assistance, etc.) to be paid by any party on behalf of the borrower? ☐ Yes ☐ No

If Yes, report the total dollar amount and describe the items to be paid.

NEIGHBORHOOD

Note: Race and the racial composition of the neighborhood are not appraisal factors.

Neighborhood Characteristics			One-Unit Housing Trends				One-Unit Housing		Present Land Use %	
Location ☐ Urban ☐ Suburban ☐ Rural			Property Values ☐ Increasing ☐ Stable ☐ Declining				PRICE	AGE	One-Unit	%
Built-Up ☐ Over 75% ☐ 25–75% ☐ Under 25%			Demand/Supply ☐ Shortage ☐ In Balance ☐ Over Supply				$ (000)	(yrs)	2-4 Unit	%
Growth ☐ Rapid ☐ Stable ☐ Slow			Marketing Time ☐ Under 3 mths ☐ 3–6 mths ☐ Over 6 mths				Low		Multi-Family	%
Neighborhood Boundaries							High		Commercial	%
							Pred.		Other	%

Neighborhood Description

Market Conditions (including support for the above conclusions)

SITE

Dimensions		Area	Shape	View

Specific Zoning Classification   Zoning Description

Zoning Compliance ☐ Legal ☐ Legal Nonconforming (Grandfathered Use) ☐ No Zoning ☐ Illegal (describe)

Is the highest and best use of the subject property as improved (or as proposed per plans and specifications) the present use? ☐ Yes ☐ No If No, describe

Utilities	Public	Other (describe)		Public	Other (describe)	Off-site Improvements—Type	Public	Private
Electricity	☐	☐	Water	☐	☐	Street	☐	☐
Gas	☐	☐	Sanitary Sewer	☐	☐	Alley	☐	☐

FEMA Special Flood Hazard Area ☐ Yes ☐ No FEMA Flood Zone   FEMA Map #   FEMA Map Date

Are the utilities and off-site improvements typical for the market area? ☐ Yes ☐ No If No, describe

Are there any adverse site conditions or external factors (easements, encroachments, environmental conditions, land uses, etc.)? ☐ Yes ☐ No If Yes, describe

IMPROVEMENTS

General Description		Foundation		Exterior Description	materials/condition	Interior	materials/condition
Units ☐ One ☐ One with Accessory Unit		☐ Concrete Slab ☐ Crawl Space		Foundation Walls		Floors	
# of Stories		☐ Full Basement ☐ Partial Basement		Exterior Walls		Walls	
Type ☐ Det. ☐ Att. ☐ S-Det./End Unit		Basement Area sq. ft.		Roof Surface		Trim/Finish	
☐ Existing ☐ Proposed ☐ Under Const.		Basement Finish %		Gutters & Downspouts		Bath Floor	
Design (Style)		☐ Outside Entry/Exit ☐ Sump Pump		Window Type		Bath Wainscot	
Year Built		Evidence of ☐ Infestation		Storm Sash/Insulated		Car Storage ☐ None	
Effective Age (Yrs)		☐ Dampness ☐ Settlement		Screens		☐ Driveway # of Cars	
Attic ☐ None		Heating ☐ FWA ☐ HWBB ☐ Radiant		Amenities ☐ Woodstove(s) #		Driveway Surface	
☐ Drop Stair ☐ Stairs		☐ Other Fuel		☐ Fireplace(s) # ☐ Fence		☐ Garage # of Cars	
☐ Floor ☐ Scuttle		Cooling ☐ Central Air Conditioning		☐ Patio/Deck ☐ Porch		☐ Carport # of Cars	
☐ Finished ☐ Heated		☐ Individual ☐ Other		☐ Pool ☐ Other		☐ Att. ☐ Det. ☐ Built-in	

Appliances ☐ Refrigerator ☐ Range/Oven ☐ Dishwasher ☐ Disposal ☐ Microwave ☐ Washer/Dryer ☐ Other (describe)

Finished area **above** grade contains: Rooms   Bedrooms   Bath(s)   Square Feet of Gross Living Area Above Grade

Additional features (special energy efficient items, etc.)

Describe the condition of the property (including needed repairs, deterioration, renovations, remodeling, etc.).

Are there any physical deficiencies or adverse conditions that affect the livability, soundness, or structural integrity of the property? ☐ Yes ☐ No If Yes, describe

Does the property generally conform to the neighborhood (functional utility, style, condition, use, construction, etc.)? ☐ Yes ☐ No If No, describe

Freddie Mac Form 70 March 2005   Page 1 of 6   Fannie Mae Form 1004 March 2005

Uniform Residential Appraisal Report

File #

There are _____ comparable properties currently offered for sale in the subject neighborhood ranging in price from $ _____ to $ _____ .

There are _____ comparable sales in the subject neighborhood within the past twelve months ranging in sale price from $ _____ to $ _____ .

FEATURE	SUBJECT	COMPARABLE SALE # 1		COMPARABLE SALE # 2		COMPARABLE SALE # 3	
Address							
Proximity to Subject							
Sale Price	$		$		$		$
Sale Price/Gross Liv. Area	$ sq. ft.	$ sq. ft.		$ sq. ft.		$ sq. ft.	
Data Source(s)							
Verification Source(s)							
VALUE ADJUSTMENTS	DESCRIPTION	DESCRIPTION	+(-) $ Adjustment	DESCRIPTION	+(-) $ Adjustment	DESCRIPTION	+(-) $ Adjustment
Sale or Financing Concessions							
Date of Sale/Time							
Location							
Leasehold/Fee Simple							
Site							
View							
Design (Style)							
Quality of Construction							
Actual Age							
Condition							
Above Grade	Total Bdrms. Baths	Total Bdrms. Baths		Total Bdrms. Baths		Total Bdrms. Baths	
Room Count							
Gross Living Area	sq. ft.	sq. ft.		sq. ft.		sq. ft.	
Basement & Finished Rooms Below Grade							
Functional Utility							
Heating/Cooling							
Energy Efficient Items							
Garage/Carport							
Porch/Patio/Deck							
Net Adjustment (Total)		☐ + ☐ -	$	☐ + ☐ -	$	☐ + ☐ -	$
Adjusted Sale Price of Comparables		Net Adj. % Gross Adj. %	$	Net Adj. % Gross Adj. %	$	Net Adj. % Gross Adj. %	$

I ☐ did ☐ did not research the sale or transfer history of the subject property and comparable sales. If not, explain

My research ☐ did ☐ did not reveal any prior sales or transfers of the subject property for the three years prior to the effective date of this appraisal.

Data source(s)

My research ☐ did ☐ did not reveal any prior sales or transfers of the comparable sales for the year prior to the date of sale of the comparable sale.

Data source(s)

Report the results of the research and analysis of the prior sale or transfer history of the subject property and comparable sales (report additional prior sales on page 3).

ITEM	SUBJECT	COMPARABLE SALE # 1	COMPARABLE SALE # 2	COMPARABLE SALE # 3
Date of Prior Sale/Transfer				
Price of Prior Sale/Transfer				
Data Source(s)				
Effective Date of Data Source(s)				

Analysis of prior sale or transfer history of the subject property and comparable sales

Summary of Sales Comparison Approach

Indicated Value by Sales Comparison Approach $

Indicated Value by: Sales Comparison Approach $ _____ Cost Approach (if developed) $ _____ Income Approach (if developed) $ _____

This appraisal is made ☐ "as is", ☐ subject to completion per plans and specifications on the basis of a hypothetical condition that the improvements have been completed, ☐ subject to the following repairs or alterations on the basis of a hypothetical condition that the repairs or alterations have been completed, or ☐ subject to the following required inspection based on the extraordinary assumption that the condition or deficiency does not require alteration or repair:

Based on a complete visual inspection of the interior and exterior areas of the subject property, defined scope of work, statement of assumptions and limiting conditions, and appraiser's certification, my (our) opinion of the market value, as defined, of the real property that is the subject of this report is
$ _____ , as of _____ , which is the date of inspection and the effective date of this appraisal.

Freddie Mac Form 70   March 2005   Page 2 of 6   Fannie Mae Form 1004   March 2005

Uniform Residential Appraisal Report

File #

ADDITIONAL COMMENTS

COST APPROACH TO VALUE (not required by Fannie Mae)

Provide adequate information for the lender/client to replicate the below cost figures and calculations.

Support for the opinion of site value (summary of comparable land sales or other methods for estimating site value)

ESTIMATED ☐ REPRODUCTION OR ☐ REPLACEMENT COST NEW		OPINION OF SITE VALUE .... = $
Source of cost data		Dwelling Sq. Ft. @ $ .... =$
Quality rating from cost service	Effective date of cost data	Sq. Ft. @ $ .... =$
Comments on Cost Approach (gross living area calculations, depreciation, etc.)		Garage/Carport Sq. Ft. @ $ .... =$
		Total Estimate of Cost-New .... = $
		Less Physical Functional External
		Depreciation =$( )
		Depreciated Cost of Improvements............................ =$
		"As-is" Value of Site Improvements............................ =$
Estimated Remaining Economic Life (HUD and VA only) Years		Indicated Value By Cost Approach .... =$

INCOME APPROACH TO VALUE (not required by Fannie Mae)

Estimated Monthly Market Rent $ _____ X Gross Rent Multiplier _____ = $ _____ Indicated Value by Income Approach

Summary of Income Approach (including support for market rent and GRM)

PROJECT INFORMATION FOR PUDs (if applicable)

Is the developer/builder in control of the Homeowners' Association (HOA)? ☐ Yes ☐ No Unit type(s) ☐ Detached ☐ Attached

Provide the following information for PUDs ONLY if the developer/builder is in control of the HOA and the subject property is an attached dwelling unit.

Legal name of project

Total number of phases _____ Total number of units _____ Total number of units sold _____

Total number of units rented _____ Total number of units for sale _____ Data source(s) _____

Was the project created by the conversion of an existing building(s) into a PUD? ☐ Yes ☐ No If Yes, date of conversion

Does the project contain any multi-dwelling units? ☐ Yes ☐ No Data source(s)

Are the units, common elements, and recreation facilities complete? ☐ Yes ☐ No If No, describe the status of completion.

Are the common elements leased to or by the Homeowners' Association? ☐ Yes ☐ No If Yes, describe the rental terms and options.

Describe common elements and recreational facilities

Freddie Mac Form 70 March 2005   Page 3 of 6   Fannie Mae Form 1004 March 2005

Uniform Residential Appraisal Report

File #

This report form is designed to report an appraisal of a one-unit property or a one-unit property with an accessory unit; including a unit in a planned unit development (PUD). This report form is not designed to report an appraisal of a manufactured home or a unit in a condominium or cooperative project.

This appraisal report is subject to the following scope of work, intended use, intended user, definition of market value, statement of assumptions and limiting conditions, and certifications. Modifications, additions, or deletions to the intended use, intended user, definition of market value, or assumptions and limiting conditions are not permitted. The appraiser may expand the scope of work to include any additional research or analysis necessary based on the complexity of this appraisal assignment. Modifications or deletions to the certifications are also not permitted. However, additional certifications that do not constitute material alterations to this appraisal report, such as those required by law or those related to the appraiser's continuing education or membership in an appraisal organization, are permitted.

SCOPE OF WORK: The scope of work for this appraisal is defined by the complexity of this appraisal assignment and the reporting requirements of this appraisal report form, including the following definition of market value, statement of assumptions and limiting conditions, and certifications. The appraiser must, at a minimum: (1) perform a complete visual inspection of the interior and exterior areas of the subject property, (2) inspect the neighborhood, (3) inspect each of the comparable sales from at least the street, (4) research, verify, and analyze data from reliable public and/or private sources, and (5) report his or her analysis, opinions, and conclusions in this appraisal report.

INTENDED USE: The intended use of this appraisal report is for the lender/client to evaluate the property that is the subject of this appraisal for a mortgage finance transaction.

INTENDED USER: The intended user of this appraisal report is the lender/client.

DEFINITION OF MARKET VALUE: The most probable price which a property should bring in a competitive and open market under all conditions requisite to a fair sale, the buyer and seller, each acting prudently, knowledgeably and assuming the price is not affected by undue stimulus. Implicit in this definition is the consummation of a sale as of a specified date and the passing of title from seller to buyer under conditions whereby: (1) buyer and seller are typically motivated; (2) both parties are well informed or well advised, and each acting in what he or she considers his or her own best interest; (3) a reasonable time is allowed for exposure in the open market; (4) payment is made in terms of cash in U. S. dollars or in terms of financial arrangements comparable thereto; and (5) the price represents the normal consideration for the property sold unaffected by special or creative financing or sales concessions* granted by anyone associated with the sale.

*Adjustments to the comparables must be made for special or creative financing or sales concessions. No adjustments are necessary for those costs which are normally paid by sellers as a result of tradition or law in a market area; these costs are readily identifiable since the seller pays these costs in virtually all sales transactions. Special or creative financing adjustments can be made to the comparable property by comparisons to financing terms offered by a third party institutional lender that is not already involved in the property or transaction. Any adjustment should not be calculated on a mechanical dollar for dollar cost of the financing or concession but the dollar amount of any adjustment should approximate the market's reaction to the financing or concessions based on the appraiser's judgment.

STATEMENT OF ASSUMPTIONS AND LIMITING CONDITIONS: The appraiser's certification in this report is subject to the following assumptions and limiting conditions:

1. The appraiser will not be responsible for matters of a legal nature that affect either the property being appraised or the title to it, except for information that he or she became aware of during the research involved in performing this appraisal. The appraiser assumes that the title is good and marketable and will not render any opinions about the title.

2. The appraiser has provided a sketch in this appraisal report to show the approximate dimensions of the improvements. The sketch is included only to assist the reader in visualizing the property and understanding the appraiser's determination of its size.

3. The appraiser has examined the available flood maps that are provided by the Federal Emergency Management Agency (or other data sources) and has noted in this appraisal report whether any portion of the subject site is located in an identified Special Flood Hazard Area. Because the appraiser is not a surveyor, he or she makes no guarantees, express or implied, regarding this determination.

4. The appraiser will not give testimony or appear in court because he or she made an appraisal of the property in question, unless specific arrangements to do so have been made beforehand, or as otherwise required by law.

5. The appraiser has noted in this appraisal report any adverse conditions (such as needed repairs, deterioration, the presence of hazardous wastes, toxic substances, etc.) observed during the inspection of the subject property or that he or she became aware of during the research involved in performing this appraisal. Unless otherwise stated in this appraisal report, the appraiser has no knowledge of any hidden or unapparent physical deficiencies or adverse conditions of the property (such as, but not limited to, needed repairs, deterioration, the presence of hazardous wastes, toxic substances, adverse environmental conditions, etc.) that would make the property less valuable, and has assumed that there are no such conditions and makes no guarantees or warranties, express or implied. The appraiser will not be responsible for any such conditions that do exist or for any engineering or testing that might be required to discover whether such conditions exist. Because the appraiser is not an expert in the field of environmental hazards, this appraisal report must not be considered as an environmental assessment of the property.

6. The appraiser has based his or her appraisal report and valuation conclusion for an appraisal that is subject to satisfactory completion, repairs, or alterations on the assumption that the completion, repairs, or alterations of the subject property will be performed in a professional manner.

Uniform Residential Appraisal Report
File #

APPRAISER'S CERTIFICATION: The Appraiser certifies and agrees that:

1. I have, at a minimum, developed and reported this appraisal in accordance with the scope of work requirements stated in this appraisal report.

2. I performed a complete visual inspection of the interior and exterior areas of the subject property. I reported the condition of the improvements in factual, specific terms. I identified and reported the physical deficiencies that could affect the livability, soundness, or structural integrity of the property.

3. I performed this appraisal in accordance with the requirements of the Uniform Standards of Professional Appraisal Practice that were adopted and promulgated by the Appraisal Standards Board of The Appraisal Foundation and that were in place at the time this appraisal report was prepared.

4. I developed my opinion of the market value of the real property that is the subject of this report based on the sales comparison approach to value. I have adequate comparable market data to develop a reliable sales comparison approach for this appraisal assignment. I further certify that I considered the cost and income approaches to value but did not develop them, unless otherwise indicated in this report.

5. I researched, verified, analyzed, and reported on any current agreement for sale for the subject property, any offering for sale of the subject property in the twelve months prior to the effective date of this appraisal, and the prior sales of the subject property for a minimum of three years prior to the effective date of this appraisal, unless otherwise indicated in this report.

6. I researched, verified, analyzed, and reported on the prior sales of the comparable sales for a minimum of one year prior to the date of sale of the comparable sale, unless otherwise indicated in this report.

7. I selected and used comparable sales that are locationally, physically, and functionally the most similar to the subject property.

8. I have not used comparable sales that were the result of combining a land sale with the contract purchase price of a home that has been built or will be built on the land.

9. I have reported adjustments to the comparable sales that reflect the market's reaction to the differences between the subject property and the comparable sales.

10. I verified, from a disinterested source, all information in this report that was provided by parties who have a financial interest in the sale or financing of the subject property.

11. I have knowledge and experience in appraising this type of property in this market area.

12. I am aware of, and have access to, the necessary and appropriate public and private data sources, such as multiple listing services, tax assessment records, public land records and other such data sources for the area in which the property is located.

13. I obtained the information, estimates, and opinions furnished by other parties and expressed in this appraisal report from reliable sources that I believe to be true and correct.

14. I have taken into consideration the factors that have an impact on value with respect to the subject neighborhood, subject property, and the proximity of the subject property to adverse influences in the development of my opinion of market value. I have noted in this appraisal report any adverse conditions (such as, but not limited to, needed repairs, deterioration, the presence of hazardous wastes, toxic substances, adverse environmental conditions, etc.) observed during the inspection of the subject property or that I became aware of during the research involved in performing this appraisal. I have considered these adverse conditions in my analysis of the property value, and have reported on the effect of the conditions on the value and marketability of the subject property.

15. I have not knowingly withheld any significant information from this appraisal report and, to the best of my knowledge, all statements and information in this appraisal report are true and correct.

16. I stated in this appraisal report my own personal, unbiased, and professional analysis, opinions, and conclusions, which are subject only to the assumptions and limiting conditions in this appraisal report.

17. I have no present or prospective interest in the property that is the subject of this report, and I have no present or prospective personal interest or bias with respect to the participants in the transaction. I did not base, either partially or completely, my analysis and/or opinion of market value in this appraisal report on the race, color, religion, sex, age, marital status, handicap, familial status, or national origin of either the prospective owners or occupants of the subject property or of the present owners or occupants of the properties in the vicinity of the subject property or on any other basis prohibited by law.

18. My employment and/or compensation for performing this appraisal or any future or anticipated appraisals was not conditioned on any agreement or understanding, written or otherwise, that I would report (or present analysis supporting) a predetermined specific value, a predetermined minimum value, a range or direction in value, a value that favors the cause of any party, or the attainment of a specific result or occurrence of a specific subsequent event (such as approval of a pending mortgage loan application).

19. I personally prepared all conclusions and opinions about the real estate that were set forth in this appraisal report. If I relied on significant real property appraisal assistance from any individual or individuals in the performance of this appraisal or the preparation of this appraisal report, I have named such individual(s) and disclosed the specific tasks performed in this appraisal report. I certify that any individual so named is qualified to perform the tasks. I have not authorized anyone to make a change to any item in this appraisal report; therefore, any change made to this appraisal is unauthorized and I will take no responsibility for it.

20. I identified the lender/client in this appraisal report who is the individual, organization, or agent for the organization that ordered and will receive this appraisal report.

Freddie Mac Form 70   March 2005   Page 5 of 6   Fannie Mae Form 1004   March 2005

Uniform Residential Appraisal Report   File

21. The lender/client may disclose or distribute this appraisal report to: the borrower; another lender at the request of the borrower; the mortgagee or its successors and assigns; mortgage insurers; government sponsored enterprises; other secondary market participants; data collection or reporting services; professional appraisal organizations; any department, agency, or instrumentality of the United States; and any state, the District of Columbia, or other jurisdictions; without having to obtain the appraiser's or supervisory appraiser's (if applicable) consent. Such consent must be obtained before this appraisal report may be disclosed or distributed to any other party (including, but not limited to, the public through advertising, public relations, news, sales, or other media).

22. I am aware that any disclosure or distribution of this appraisal report by me or the lender/client may be subject to certain laws and regulations. Further, I am also subject to the provisions of the Uniform Standards of Professional Appraisal Practice that pertain to disclosure or distribution by me.

23. The borrower, another lender at the request of the borrower, the mortgagee or its successors and assigns, mortgage insurers, government sponsored enterprises, and other secondary market participants may rely on this appraisal report as part of any mortgage finance transaction that involves any one or more of these parties.

24. If this appraisal report was transmitted as an "electronic record" containing my "electronic signature," as those terms are defined in applicable federal and/or state laws (excluding audio and video recordings), or a facsimile transmission of this appraisal report containing a copy or representation of my signature, the appraisal report shall be as effective, enforceable and valid as if a paper version of this appraisal report were delivered containing my original hand written signature.

25. Any intentional or negligent misrepresentation(s) contained in this appraisal report may result in civil liability and/or criminal penalties including, but not limited to, fine or imprisonment or both under the provisions of Title 18, United States Code, Section 1001, et seq., or similar state laws.

SUPERVISORY APPRAISER'S CERTIFICATION: The Supervisory Appraiser certifies and agrees that:

1. I directly supervised the appraiser for this appraisal assignment, have read the appraisal report, and agree with the appraiser's analysis, opinions, statements, conclusions, and the appraiser's certification.

2. I accept full responsibility for the contents of this appraisal report including, but not limited to, the appraiser's analysis, opinions, statements, conclusions, and the appraiser's certification.

3. The appraiser identified in this appraisal report is either a sub-contractor or an employee of the supervisory appraiser (or the appraisal firm), is qualified to perform this appraisal, and is acceptable to perform this appraisal under the applicable state law.

4. This appraisal report complies with the Uniform Standards of Professional Appraisal Practice that were adopted and promulgated by the Appraisal Standards Board of The Appraisal Foundation and that were in place at the time this appraisal report was prepared.

5. If this appraisal report was transmitted as an "electronic record" containing my "electronic signature," as those terms are defined in applicable federal and/or state laws (excluding audio and video recordings), or a facsimile transmission of this appraisal report containing a copy or representation of my signature, the appraisal report shall be as effective, enforceable and valid as if a paper version of this appraisal report were delivered containing my original hand written signature.

APPRAISER

Signature_____
Name _____
Company Name _____
Company Address_____
_____
Telephone Number _____
Email Address _____
Date of Signature and Report_____
Effective Date of Appraisal _____
State Certification #_____
or State License #_____
or Other (describe) _____ State # _____
State _____
Expiration Date of Certification or License _____

ADDRESS OF PROPERTY APPRAISED
_____

APPRAISED VALUE OF SUBJECT PROPERTY $ _____
LENDER/CLIENT
Name _____
Company Name _____
Company Address_____
_____
Email Address _____

SUPERVISORY APPRAISER (ONLY IF REQUIRED)

Signature_____
Name_____
Company Name _____
Company Address_____
_____
Telephone Number _____
Email Address _____
Date of Signature _____
State Certification #_____
or State License #_____
State _____
Expiration Date of Certification or License _____

SUBJECT PROPERTY

☐ Did not inspect subject property
☐ Did inspect exterior of subject property from street
   Date of Inspection _____
☐ Did inspect interior and exterior of subject property
   Date of Inspection _____

COMPARABLE SALES

☐ Did not inspect exterior of comparable sales from street
☐ Did inspect exterior of comparable sales from street
   Date of Inspection _____

Freddie Mac Form 70   March 2005   Page 6 of 6   Fannie Mae Form 1004   March 2005

Fig. 9.4 Market Conditions Addendum to the Appraisal Report

Market Conditions Addendum to the Appraisal Report

File No.

The purpose of this addendum is to provide the lender/client with a clear and accurate understanding of the market trends and conditions prevalent in the subject neighborhood. This is a required addendum for all appraisal reports with an effective date on or after April 1, 2009.

Property Address	City	State	Zip Code

Borrower

Instructions: The appraiser must use the information required on this form as the basis for his/her conclusions, and must provide support for those conclusions, regarding housing trends and overall market conditions as reported in the Neighborhood section of the appraisal report form. The appraiser must fill in all the information to the extent it is available and reliable and must provide analysis as indicated below. If any required data is unavailable or is considered unreliable, the appraiser must provide an explanation. If data sources provide the required information as an average instead of the median, then the appraiser should report the available figure and identify it as an average. Sales and listings must be properties that compete with the subject property, determined by applying the criteria that would be used by a prospective buyer of the subject property. The appraiser must explain any anomalies in the data, such as seasonal markets, new construction, foreclosures, etc.

Inventory Analysis	Prior 7–12 Months	Prior 4–6 Months	Current – 3 Months	Overall Trend		
Total # of Comparable Sales (Settled)				☐ Increasing	☐ Stable	☐ Declining
Absorption Rate (Total Sales/Months)				☐ Increasing	☐ Stable	☐ Declining
Total # of Comparable Active Listings				☐ Declining	☐ Stable	☐ Increasing
Months of Housing Supply (Total Listings/Ab.Rate)				☐ Declining	☐ Stable	☐ Increasing
Median Sale & List Price, DOM, List/Sale Ratio	Prior 7–12 Months	Prior 4–6 Months	Current – 3 Months	Overall Trend		
Median Comparable Sale Price				☐ Increasing	☐ Stable	☐ Declining
Median Comparable Sales Days on Market				☐ Declining	☐ Stable	☐ Increasing
Median Comparable List Price				☐ Increasing	☐ Stable	☐ Declining
Median Comparable Listings Days on Market				☐ Declining	☐ Stable	☐ Increasing
Median List-to-Sale Price Ratio				☐ Declining	☐ Stable	☐ Increasing

Seller-(developer, builder, etc.)paid financial assistance prevalent? ☐ Yes ☐ No   ☐ Declining ☐ Stable ☐ Increasing

Explain in detail the seller concessions trends for the past 12 months (e.g., seller contributions increased from 3% to 5%, increasing use of buydowns, closing costs, condo fees, options, etc.).

Are foreclosure sales (REO sales) a factor in the market? ☐ Yes ☐ No If yes, explain (including the trends in listings and sales of foreclosed properties).

Cite data sources for above information.

Summarize the above information as support for your conclusions in the Neighborhood section of the appraisal report form. If you used any additional information, such as an analysis of pending sales and/or expired and withdrawn listings, to formulate your conclusions, provide both an explanation and support for your conclusions.

If the subject is a unit in a condominium or cooperative project , complete the following: **Project Name:**

Subject Project Data	Prior 7-12 Months	Prior 4-6 Months	Current – 3 Months	Overall Trend		
Total # of Comparable Sales (Settled)				☐ Increasing	☐ Stable	☐ Declining
Absorption Rate (Total Sales/Months)				☐ Increasing	☐ Stable	☐ Declining
Total # of Active Comparable Listings				☐ Declining	☐ Stable	☐ Increasing
Months of Unit Supply (Total Listings/Ab. Rate)				☐ Declining	☐ Stable	☐ Increasing

Are foreclosure sales (REO sales) a factor in the project? ☐ Yes ☐ No If yes, indicate the number of REO listings and explain the trends in listings and sales of foreclosed properties.

Summarize the above trends and address the impact on the subject unit and project.

Signature	Signature
Appraiser Name	Supervisory Appraiser Name
Company Name	Company Name
Company Address	Company Address
State License/Certification # State	State License/Certification # State
Email Address	Email Address

Freddie Mac Form 71 November 2008   Page 1 of 1   Fannie Mae Form 1004MC November 2008

Side labels: MARKET RESEARCH & ANALYSIS / CONDO/CO-OP PROJECTS / APPRAISER

The simplest solution to the problem of a low appraisal is for the seller to lower the sales price to the appraised value. But don't be surprised if your seller resists a price reduction. Once a seller has become accustomed to a certain sales price, she will be very reluctant to give it up.

Another possibility is a compromise price somewhere in between the appraised value and the original selling price. But this solution is likely to run up against both the seller's reluctance to lower the price and the buyer's reluctance (or inability) to pay more than the appraised value.

Because of these problems, when there's a significant gap between the sales price and the appraised value, the most likely result is termination of the sale. (According to some estimates, it happens more than two-thirds of the time.) But it's the real estate agent's job to help the parties avoid this outcome whenever possible.

In some cases the agent should ask the lender to reconsider the appraised value, in the hope that it will be increased to a figure more acceptable to the buyer and seller. This can work if it's handled properly. The correct way to request a reconsideration of value will be explained later in this chapter.

Of course, the best way to eliminate the problems that low appraisals create is to prevent them in the first place.

Possible solutions after low appraisal:
- Buyer pays over value
- Seller lowers price to appraised value
- Compromise price
- Request for reconsideration of value

Preventing Low Appraisals

A real estate agent can prevent most low appraisals by helping sellers price properties realistically. A seller should not be given an unrealistic estimate of the property's worth. Even if a buyer can be persuaded to pay the inflated price, the appraisal will come back low (reflecting the property's true market value) and the real struggle to keep the transaction together will begin.

If for some reason the property is not priced realistically when it's listed, at least try to correct the problem when you write the sale. No case can be made for overstating the value when property is listed or sold; sooner or later every sale that is dependent on financing must yield to the conclusions of a professional appraiser.

Prevent low appraisal by helping seller price property correctly
- Perform careful CMA
- Price personal property separately

CMA. The best way for an agent to help a seller price a home is to perform a competitive market analysis (CMA). As mentioned earlier in the chapter, a competitive market analysis is an informal version of a sales comparison appraisal. The agent suggests an appropriate price for the seller's home based on a careful evaluation of comparable homes that were recently sold or listed. Performing a reliable CMA takes patience and practice, but the results are worth the effort.

Sales comparison information can be obtained from a variety of sources, including real estate office files, multiple listing services, and appraisers' records. Acquaint yourself with the most comprehensive and accessible sources of information in your area. If you're doing your job, you will refer to them often.

Personal Property. One pitfall to avoid when writing a sale concerns the seller's personal property (such as furniture) that the buyer would like to buy along with the home. In this situation, some real estate agents include the personal property in the real property transaction: the sale is written so that the price covers both the real property (the land, the house, and other attachments) and the personal property that the buyer wants. This is always a mistake, and it can lead to a low appraisal.

Underwriting guidelines require residential appraisers to exclude the value of personal property from the final estimate of value for the real property. When the sales price includes personal property and the appraised value does not, the appraised value may be much lower than the sales price.

The sale of personal property to a home buyer should be treated as a separate transaction. The personal property should be priced and paid for separately from the home, and proper procedures for the transfer of title to personal property should be followed. (Those procedures vary from state to state, so you should be sure to check local requirements.)

On the other hand, an appraiser will include the value of fixtures (such as built-in appliances) in the final estimate of value, because fixtures are considered part of the real property. So the sales price of the home should reflect all of the fixtures that are going to be transferred to the buyer.

If you're not certain whether a particular item will be treated as personal property or as a fixture in the appraisal, check with local sources. The distinction between personal property and fixtures sometimes depends on local custom.

Request for Reconsideration of Value

Regardless of how objective an appraiser might try to be, subjective considerations and conclusions are a part of every appraisal. In the end the appraiser's finding is only an opinion of value. If you are affected by a low appraisal and sincerely believe the appraiser has made a mistake, there is a chance that you can appeal his decision and, with the proper documentation, get the appraisal increased—possibly to the figure the buyer and seller originally agreed on.

The sooner you find out about a low appraisal, the better. After the property has been inspected, ask the loan officer or the underwriter to call you with the results of the appraisal as soon as they are received. Don't try to get the results directly from the appraiser; the appraiser has a fiduciary relationship with the lender and is not allowed to disclose information about the appraisal to others without the lender's permission.

If the appraisal comes in low, ask the loan officer or underwriter for the following information:

1. the final value estimate,
2. the value indicated by the sales comparison method, and
3. the addresses of the three comparables the appraiser used.

This is the essential information, because the sales comparison analysis is the heart of a residential appraisal, the part that the lender really relies on in deciding whether to approve a loan.

Evaluate the appraiser's three comparables and update your competitive market analysis. Then decide if a request for reconsideration of value is a realistic option. You will have to support your request with at least three comparable sales that indicate a higher value estimate is in order. If you're going to convince the lender that your comparables are more reliable than the appraiser's, yours must be at least as similar to the subject property as the appraiser's are.

If you believe the lender is likely to grant a request for reconsideration, prepare the request and a cover letter as outlined below.

Preparing the Request. Some lenders have their own form for requests for reconsideration of value. If so, you should use their form (you may even be required to). Otherwise, you can prepare your

When appraisal comes in low:
- *Ask lender for information*
- *Evaluate appraisal*
- *Update CMA*
- *Submit request for reconsideration only if lender likely to grant it*

Fig. 9.5 A sample letter asking for a reconsideration of value

---

Request for Reconsideration of Value

Mr. Arthur Jewel
Hillside Bank

Dear Mr. Jewel:

Attached is a sales comparison analysis that supports this request for reconsideration of the value estimate for 412 Acme Drive, dated November 14. I believe the market data presented indicates that an estimate of value in the amount of $235,000 is justified.

Thank you for your attention to this matter.

Sincerely,
Thomas M. Crane

---

own. It makes sense to present your information in the same format that's used in the "Sales Comparison Analysis" section of the Uniform Residential Appraisal Report form. Make four columns for the properties, with the subject in the first column and three comparables to the right, as in the example shown in Figure 9.5.

Write a cover letter making your request and attach your sales comparison analysis to it. The cover letter should be simple and very polite; do not criticize the appraiser.

Sometimes appraisers don't use the best information available, and when they don't, their findings can be successfully challenged. If your request for reconsideration of value contains well-researched, properly documented information and is presented in a professional manner, your chances of success will improve. Make your request carelessly and the reverse is true.

Fig. 9.6 Data sheet supporting request for reconsideration of value

Item	Subject Property	Comparable 1	Comparable 2	Comparable 3
Sales Comparison Analysis 412 Acme Drive				
Address	412 Acme Drive	131 Skip Road	221 Sutter Street	168 Bow Road
Sales price	$235,000	$238,000	$234,500	$229,500
Data source	sales contract	present owner	MLS	Selling broker
Date of sale		8/29/08	9/14/08	10/17/06/08
Location	high quality suburb	same	same	same
Site/view	corner lot	inside lot	corner lot	inside lot
Design	rambler	same	same	same
Appeal	excellent	same	same	same
Construction	good	same	same	same
Age	7 years	6 years	8 years	8 years
Condition	good	same	same	same
No. of rooms	8	7	7	6
No. of bedrooms	4	4	3	3
Living area	2,400 sq. ft.	2,500 sq. ft.	2,350 sq. ft.	2,150 sq. ft.
Garage/carport	2-car attached garage	same	same	same
Patio	15' × 21' patio	15' × 26' patio	18' × 16' patio	15' × 17' patio
Additional features	2 fireplaces, range, oven, D/W, disposal, central air	2 fireplaces, range, oven, D/W central air	1 fireplace, range, oven, D/W central air	1 fireplace, range, oven D/W, disposal, central air
Comments	Subject is more energy-efficient than Comps 2 and 3, and is at least equal in this respect to Comp 1.			

Outline: Qualifying the Property

I. The Lender's Perception of Value

  A. An underwriter will evaluate the property based on an appraisal: an estimate of the value of a property, performed by a professional appraiser.

  B. An appraiser will focus on market value: the most probable price a property should bring in a competitive and open market where the parties act knowledgeably and without undue stimulus.

  C. The lender focuses on the loan-to-value ratio: the relationship between loan amount and the property's value.

    1. A higher LTV creates greater risk for a lender, since a buyer with a smaller downpayment is more likely to default.

    2. The LTV is based on either the sales price or the appraised value, whichever is lower.

    3. Lenders may be willing to make high-LTV loans but usually impose stricter qualifying standards and higher interest rates to compensate for the higher risk.

II. Appraisal Standards

  A. To prevent unreliable appraisals, the federal government requires states to license and certify appraisers who perform appraisals for "federally related" loan transactions.

  B. Some states require that all appraisers be licensed or certified.

  C. Inflated appraisals played a role in the mortgage and foreclosure crisis; as a result, appraisal standards have been strengthened at both the federal and state level.

III. Appraisal Process

  A. There are eight steps in the appraisal process: defining the problem, determining the scope of work, collecting and verifying data, analyzing data, determining the site value, applying the appropriate methods of appraisal, reconciling the results to arrive at a final value estimate, and issuing the appraisal report.

  B. In some situations, an appraiser may be able to perform a "drive-by appraisal" rather than performing a full inspection of the property.

IV. Appraisal Methods

  A. Sales comparison method

    1. Appraisers using the sales comparison method rely on the sales prices of comparable properties to estimate the value of the subject property.

2. The sales comparison method uses the same principles as a competitive market analysis, although a CMA can use data from current listings and expired listings.

3. To determine whether a recently sold property is comparable, an appraiser considers: the date of the sale, the location of the property, the physical characteristics of the property, the terms of sale, and the conditions of the sale.

4. The sale should have occurred within the previous six months, although the appraiser may have to adjust the sales price for changes in value if the property was sold more than a few months ago in a volatile market.

5. Comparable properties should be located in the same neighborhood and have similar size, design, and quality as the subject property.

6. Comparable properties must have sold under normal conditions: the buyer and seller are unrelated parties, acting free of unusual pressure, and are fully informed; and the property was on the open market for a reasonable period of time.

7. As of April 2009, appraisers must complete the Market Conditions Addendum to the Uniform Residential Appraisal Report for all federally regulated loans on one- to four-unit properties.

8. If there are differences between the subject property and comparables, the appraiser should adjust the sales price of the comparables to reflect what they would have sold for were they more similar to the subject property.

B. Replacement cost method

1. There are three steps in the replacement cost method: estimating the cost of replacing the improvements, deducting any depreciation, and adding the value of the land.

2. The appraiser usually relies on the replacement cost (the cost of constructing a new building with equivalent utility) rather than the reproduction cost (the cost of building an exact replica using the same materials and techniques).

3. The easiest way to estimate the construction cost is the square foot method, where the appraiser multiplies the estimated cost per square foot by square footage of the building.

4. There are three types of depreciation that must be estimated: physical deterioration, functional obsolescence, and external obsolescence.

5. Depreciation may be considered curable or incurable, depending on whether correcting the problem adds more value than the cost of the repair.

6. An appraisal may be "as is," which evaluates the property in current condition, or "subject to," which values the property as if all physical deterioration was cured.

C. Income method

1. Value under the income method is calculated by dividing a property's annual net income by the rate of return an investor would expect from the property.

2. For residential rental properties, an appraiser will use a simplified version of the income method called the gross income multiplier method.

3. The appraiser finds value by multiplying the property's rent by a multiplier indicated by the relationship between other properties' rents and values.

4. An appraiser should use the property's economic rent (the rent the owner would receive if the property were currently available) rather than contract rent (the rent the owner currently receives).

D. Final value estimate

1. The appraiser will reconcile the values indicated by the various appraisal methods to arrive at a final estimate of value.

2. The result is not an average of the figures; the appraiser may give weight to certain methods based on the type of property.

V. Dealing with Low Appraisals

A. A low appraisal can terminate a transaction, since the lender will adjust its loan amount based on the property's appraised value, requiring the borrower to come up with a larger downpayment.

B. A real estate agent can seek to prevent low appraisals.

1. An agent should help the seller to set a reasonable selling price, based on the agent's CMA.

2. The agent should avoid including personal property as part of the sales price.

C. If a low appraisal occurs, an agent may request a reconsideration of value, by providing the lender with alternate comparables that suggest a higher value for the subject property.

Key Terms

Appraisal: An expert's estimate of the value of a piece of real estate as of a particular date, based on a documented analysis of the property's features.

Appraiser: One who estimates the value of property, especially an expert qualified to do so by training and experience.

Market value: The most probable price a property should sell for if it is sold under normal conditions and the buyer and seller are typically motivated; also called objective value

Loan-to-value ratio (LTV): The relationship between the loan amount and either the sales price or the appraised value of the property (whichever is less), expressed as a percentage.

Sales comparison method: Method of appraisal in which the sales prices of comparable properties are used to estimate the value of the subject property.

Subject property: In an appraisal, the property being appraised.

Comparables: In the sales comparison approach, properties similar to the subject property that have recently been sold; the appraiser uses the sales prices of the comparables as an indication of the value of the subject property.

Competitive market analysis (CMA): A real estate agent's estimate of the value of a listed home, based on the sales prices or listing prices of comparable homes.

Normal conditions of sale: A sale in which both the buyer and seller are unrelated and fully informed of the property's attributes and deficiencies, neither is acting under unusual pressure, and the property has been offered on the open market for a reasonable period of time.

Replacement cost method: Method of appraisal in which an estimate of the subject property's value is arrived at by estimating the cost of replacing the improvements, then deducting estimated depreciation, and adding the estimated market value of the land.

Replacement cost: The current cost of constructing a building with the same utility as the subject property, using modern materials and construction methods.

Reproduction cost: The current cost of constructing a replica of the subject property, using the same materials and methods as originally used but at current prices.

Depreciation: Loss in value due to any cause.

Physical deterioration: Depreciation resulting from physical wear and tear.

Functional obsolescence: Depreciation resulting from functional inadequacies, such as poor or outmoded design.

External obsolescence: Depreciation resulting from factors outside the property itself and outside the owner's control.

Income method: A method of appraisal in which an estimate of the subject property's value is based on the net income it produces.

Gross income multiplier method: A method of appraisal used for residential rental property, in which an estimate of the subject property's value is based on the relationship between the sales prices and the rental income of comparable properties.

Economic rent: The rent a property could command in the current marketplace if it were available for lease today.

Contract rent: The rent an owner is currently receiving from a property.

Reconciliation: The final step in an appraisal, when the appraiser assembles and interprets the data in order to arrive at a final value estimate.

Low appraisal: An appraisal where the appraised value is lower than the agreed-upon sales price, which may affect financing and terminate the transaction.

Request for reconsideration of value: A request by an agent to a lender to increase the appraised value of a property, based on evidence provided by comparables other than those selected by the appraiser.

Chapter Quiz

1. A lender asks a residential appraiser to:
    a. estimate the book value of the home
    b. determine the assessed value of the home
    c. determine the subjective value of the home
    d. estimate the market value of the home

2. From the lender's point of view, a low-risk loan would be one that has:
    a. no downpayment
    b. a high loan-to-value ratio
    c. a low loan-to-value ratio
    d. a 100% loan-to-value ratio

3. For residential property, the most important method of appraisal is the:
    a. sales comparison method
    b. replacement cost method
    c. income method
    d. gross income multiplier method

4. A sales comparison appraisal is mainly based on:
    a. listing prices
    b. expired listings
    c. sales prices
    d. assessed values

5. An appraiser should not use a sale as a comparable unless it:
    a. occurred within the past six months
    b. was in the same neighborhood as the subject property
    c. involved financing concessions
    d. was an arm's length transaction

6. The most difficult step in the replacement cost method of appraisal is:
    a. finding benchmark buildings
    b. measuring square footage
    c. estimating depreciation
    d. calculating the gross income multiplier

7. If a home sold for $175,000 and rents for $1,150 per month, then its monthly gross income multiplier is:

   a. .079
   b. 12.68
   c. 66.0
   d. 152.17

8. A real estate agent is helping the Martins set a listing price for their home. The Martins have some furniture they would like to sell along with the home. The agent should advise the Martins:

   a. to include the value of the furniture in the price of the home
   b. to price the furniture separately from the home
   c. not to sell the furniture to the person who buys the home
   d. to treat the furniture as fixtures

9. In the event of a low appraisal, the listing agent should:

   a. always submit a request for a reconsideration of value
   b. submit a request for reconsideration only if the appraiser has made a significant mathematical error
   c. submit a request for reconsideration only if the loan officer recommends it
   d. evaluate the appraisal, update the CMA, and submit a request for reconsideration only if there is a good possibility that it will be granted

10. A property's value is diminished by its proximity to a paper mill. This would be considered:

   a. deferred maintenance
   b. functional obsolescence
   c. external obsolescence
   d. curable depreciation

Answer Key

1. d. An appraiser performing an appraisal for a residential lender is typically concerned with the property's market value.

2. c. A low loan-to-value ratio, such as 80% or lower, is considered a low-risk loan. A larger downpayment reduces the risk of default, and increases the likelihood the full loan amount can be recovered in a foreclosure sale.

3. a. The sales comparison method is the most relevant method in residential appraisal.

4. c. The sales comparison method relies on the recent sales prices of comparable properties. A CMA may include current and expired listings, but an appraisal may not.

5. d. An appraiser should not include a sale that was not an arm's length transaction. An appraiser may make adjustments for the date of sale, the location of the property, or financing terms.

6. c. The most difficult part of the cost approach to value is estimating depreciation.

7. d. To calculate the monthly gross income multiplier, divide the property's value by its monthly rent. In this case, the monthly multiplier is 152.17 ($175,000 ÷ $1,150 = 152.17).

8. b. Furniture and other personal property should be priced separately from the real estate. Including personal property can inflate the sales price and lead to a low appraisal.

9. d. If a low appraisal occurs, an agent should investigate the appraisal and see if other comparables can be found that indicate a higher value for the subject property. If that is the case, the agent should request a reconsideration of value.

10. c. Loss of value caused by factors outside of the property, such as a nearby nuisance like a paper mill, would be external obsolescence. External obsolescence is always incurable.

Chapter 10
Conventional Financing

Conforming and Nonconforming Loans

Conventional Loan Characteristics
- Property types and owner-occupancy rules
- Loan amounts
- Repayment periods
- Amortization
- Loan-to-value ratios
- Risk-based loan fees
- Private mortgage insurance
- Secondary financing

Qualifying Standards
- Evaluating risk factors
- Credit reputation
- Income analysis
- Available funds

Making Conventional Loans More Affordable
- Buydown plans
- Loans with lower initial payments
- Low-downpayment programs
- Accelerated payment plans

Introduction

Loans made by institutional lenders (such as banks, savings and loans, and mortgage companies) can be divided into two main categories: conventional loans and government-sponsored loans.

Conventional loan: not insured or guaranteed by government

A **conventional loan** is any institutional loan that isn't insured or guaranteed by a government agency. For example, a loan that's made by a bank and insured by a private mortgage company is a conventional loan. A loan that's made by a bank and insured by the FHA (Federal Housing Administration) or guaranteed by the VA (Department of Veterans Affairs) is not a conventional loan, because it is backed by a government agency.

The two main government-sponsored loan programs are covered in Chapters 11 and 12. In this chapter, we'll examine conventional loans.

Conforming and Nonconforming Loans

Conforming loan complies with Fannie Mae and/or Freddie Mac's guidelines

Fannie Mae and Freddie Mac are the major secondary market agencies that purchase conventional loans, and most conventional loans are made in compliance with their underwriting guidelines. The guidelines of the two agencies are similar in many respects, although they aren't identical. Loans that comply with (conform to) their guidelines are called **conforming loans**.

Nonconforming loan:
- Doesn't comply with the agencies' standards
- Fannie Mae and Freddie Mac won't buy it

Lenders making conventional loans aren't required to follow the guidelines of the secondary market agencies; they're free to apply their own underwriting standards instead. But if a loan isn't made in compliance with Fannie Mae or Freddie Mac's guidelines, it's considered **nonconforming** and can't be sold to either agency, except by special arrangement.

Conventional Loan Characteristics

Lenders like to have the option of selling their loans on the secondary market, and when they make conforming loans, they know that they'll be able to sell them to Fannie Mae or Freddie Mac at good prices. As a result, the two agencies' underwriting guidelines are widely followed by the mortgage industry. For that reason, our discussion of conventional loans generally focuses on those guidelines, particularly the rules governing owner-occupancy, loan amounts, loan-to-value ratios, mortgage insurance, and secondary financing. It's important to keep in mind, however, that not all conventional loans conform to the guidelines or have the characteristics we describe here.

Property Types and Owner-Occupancy Rules

Fannie Mae and Freddie Mac buy loans secured by residential properties, including detached site-built houses, townhouses, condominium units, cooperative units, and manufactured homes.

The borrowers may intend to occupy the security property either as their principal residence or as a second home. Generally, a principal residence may have up to four dwelling units, but a second home should have no more than one dwelling unit.

Fannie Mae and Freddie Mac are also willing to buy **investor loans** secured by property with up to four dwelling units. A loan is considered an investor loan if the borrower doesn't intend to occupy the property; in most cases, the borrower plans to rent it out to tenants instead. Investor loans are underwritten using different (and generally stricter) standards than loans for owner-occupied homes. We'll mainly be discussing owner-occupied homes, not investment properties.

Conventional loan may be secured by:
- Principal residence
- Second home
- Investment property

Loan Amounts

In order for a loan to be eligible for purchase by Fannie Mae or Freddie Mac, the loan amount must not exceed the applicable conforming loan limit. Conforming loan limits for dwellings with one, two, three, or four units are set by the Federal Housing Finance Agency (the agency that oversees the secondary market agencies) based on median housing prices nationwide. The limits may be adjusted annually to reflect changes in median prices.

Conforming loan limits may be adjusted annually

In most parts of the country, the 2009 conforming loan limit for single-family homes and other one-unit dwellings is $417,000. In **high-cost areas**—areas where housing is more expensive—the limit is 125% of the area median home price, up to a maximum of $729,750 (see Figure 10.1). There are higher limits for Alaska, Hawaii, Guam, and the Virgin Islands, where homes are exceptionally expensive.

Conventional loans that exceed the conforming loan limits are also available in many areas, although they're generally ineligible for

Fig. 10.1 Fannie Mae and Freddie Mac's conforming loan limits for 2009

2009 Conforming Loan Limits for single-family homes and other one-unit dwellings		
General Loan Limit	Limit in High-Cost Areas	Limits in Alaska, Guam, Hawaii, and the Virgin Islands
$417,000	125% of area median home price, up to $729,750	$625,500 generally, and up to $1,094,625 in high-cost areas in these locations

Jumbo loan: loan amount exceeds conforming loan limit

sale to the major secondary market agencies. For these larger loans, sometimes called **jumbo loans**, lenders generally charge higher interest rates and fees and apply stricter underwriting standards. For example, the maximum loan-to-value ratio for a jumbo loan may be lower, and the buyers may be required to have higher credit scores and more money in reserve than they would for a conforming loan.

Repayment Periods

Repayment periods for conventional loans can range from ten years to forty years. Thirty years is still the standard term, but fifteen-year loans are also popular. See the discussion of repayment periods in Chapter 6.

Amortization

Most conventional loans are fully amortized, meaning the payments are large enough to pay off the loan completely by the end of the term (see Chapter 6). However, partially amortized and interest-only loans are also available. We'll discuss those types of loans at the end of the chapter, when we cover special programs and payment plans for conventional loans.

Loan-to-Value Ratios

Conventional loans are often classified by loan-to-value ratio, with different rules applied to each category. For instance, a lender might have somewhat different standards for loans with LTVs of 80% or less, 80.01% to 85%, 85.01% to 90%, and 90.01% to 95%. As a kind of shorthand, the percentage that sets the upper limit of a particular category may be used to refer to all loans in that category. For example, all loans with LTVs between 85.01% and 90% may be called "90% loans," and all loans with LTVs between 90.01% and 95% may be called "95% loans." These categories seem to be falling out of use as manual underwriting plays less and less of a role; underwriting software uses complex algorithms that make these categories unnecessary.

Traditionally, the standard conventional loan-to-value ratio was 80%. A mortgage loan for 80% of the property's sales price or appraised value is generally regarded as a very safe investment. The 20% downpayment gives the borrower a substantial incentive to avoid default, and if foreclosure becomes necessary, the lender is likely to recover the full amount owed.

At one time, very few lenders were willing to make conventional loans with LTVs over 80%. That started changing in the 1980s. More and more lenders became comfortable making conventional loans with higher LTVs, and soon they were widely available. By the late 1990s they had become more common than 80% loans. Lenders routinely made conventional loans with LTVs up to 95%, requiring only a 5% downpayment.

Common conventional LTVs:
- 80%
- 90%
- 95%

Conventional loans with even higher loan-to-value ratios—97% or above—became widespread in the early 2000s. Some lenders even made 100% conventional loans, allowing the borrowers to put no money down.

Unfortunately, high LTV-loans are now playing a role in our mortgage foreclosure crisis. In 2007 and 2008, when home values began dropping around the country, many borrowers who had started out with very little equity suddenly had none. As values continued to decline, these borrowers soon had "negative equity"—in other words, they owed their lenders more than their homes were worth. When these borrowers could no longer afford to pay their mortgages and defaulted, their lenders incurred serious losses. As a result of the foreclosure crisis, conventional loans with LTVs over 95% are no longer common, although some lenders still offer them through special programs. (See the discussion of low downpayment programs later in the chapter.)

Less common conventional LTVs:
- 97%
- 100%

Applicants for conventional loans with LTVs over 90% are usually required to meet strict qualifying standards and can expect to pay higher interest rates and loan fees. Some lenders also require these loans to have a fixed interest rate, because the unpredictability of changes in the interest rate and monthly payment amount of an ARM makes default more likely than with a fixed-rate loan.

High-LTV loans:
- Higher interest rates and fees
- Stricter underwriting

Combined LTV ratio: the ratio of all loans to the value of the property

In the case of financing where there are junior mortgages, a lender will be concerned with the **combined loan-to-value ratio** (CLTV), which is the ratio of all loans to the value of the property. If the junior mortgage is a home equity line, it may be referred to as the home equity combined loan-to-value ratio (HCLTV). Generally, lenders treat CLTVs or HCLTVs the same as LTVs, but in some cases they may be allowed to go higher than LTVs alone.

Exercise No. 1

Rita Maynard would like to buy the Chandlers' house, which she would use as her primary residence. The sales price is $318,750, and the appraisal came in at $321,000. Maynard wants to make a $25,500 downpayment and obtain a conventional loan for the rest of the price.

1. What would Maynard's loan-to-value ratio be?

2. If Maynard decreased her downpayment amount to $19,125, what would the loan-to-value ratio be?

Risk-based Loan Fees

LLPAs shift some of the risk of default to borrower

Conventional borrowers are nearly always expected to pay an origination fee, and they may also agree to pay discount points. In addition, if their loan is going to be sold to Fannie Mae or Freddie Mac, they will probably be charged one or more **loan-level price adjustments** (LLPAs) that the lender will pass on to the secondary market agency. Loan-level price adjustments, which are also called **delivery fees**, shift some of the risk (that is, the cost) of mortgage defaults to borrowers. As a general rule, the riskier the loan, the more the borrower is required to pay in LLPAs. Subprime lenders have traditionally done the same sort of thing, charging riskier borrowers more for their loans (see the discussion of risk-based pricing in Chapter 8).

Nearly all loans sold to the secondary market agencies are subject to an LLPA that varies depending on the borrower's credit score and the loan-to-value ratio; the percentages charged can be found on tables issued by Fannie Mae and Freddie Mac.

For instance, a borrower with a credit score of 650 and an 80% LTV might be required to pay a fee of 2.75% of the loan amount at closing, while a borrower with a credit score of 710 and a 90% LTV might pay only a 0.50% fee. In fact, borrowers with high credit scores and very low LTVs may actually be assigned a negative loan-level price adjustment, resulting in a credit at closing. For example, if the LLPA for a borrower who has a 750 credit score and a 60% LTV is −0.25%, she'll be given a credit of 0.25% of the loan amount at closing. (Note that this credit would effectively cancel out the 0.25% adverse market delivery charge mentioned below.)

There are also LLPAs for certain types of loans that involve more risk, such as investor loans, loans with secondary financing, interest-only loans, and adjustable-rate mortgages. And there are LLPAs for certain types of properties, including condominiums and duplexes. When applicable, one or more of these LLPAs will be charged in addition to the one that's based on credit score and loan-to-value ratio. Fannie Mae and Freddie Mac have also opted to account for the greater risks associated with poor market conditions by imposing a flat rate charge on every borrower: the **adverse market delivery charge**. This is a fee of 0.25% and it is levied on all new loans.

Adverse market delivery charge: fee of .25% imposed to compensate for greater risks associated with poor market conditions

Private Mortgage Insurance

Another charge that many borrowers face is **private mortgage insurance** (PMI). Private mortgage insurance is called "private" because it's obtained from private insurance companies, not through the FHA's mortgage insurance program. Like FHA mortgage insurance, PMI is designed to protect lenders from the greater risk of high-LTV loans; the insurance makes up for the reduced borrower equity. Both Fannie Mae and Freddie Mac require PMI on conventional loans if the loan-to-value ratio is greater than 80%.

PMI:
- Protects lender
- Premium(s) paid by borrower

How PMI Works. When insuring a loan, a private mortgage insurance company actually assumes only a portion of the risk of default. Instead of covering the entire loan amount, the insurance just covers the upper portion of the loan. The amount of coverage varies depending on the loan term and loan-to-value ratio. Coverage of 25% to 30% is typical, but it may be as high as 35% for a 97% LTV with a 30-year term or as low as 6% for an 80% LTV with a 15-year term.

PMI typically covers 25% to 30% of the loan amount

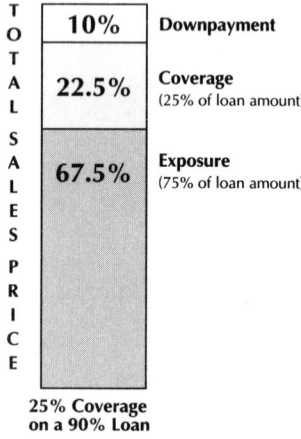

25% Coverage
on a 90% Loan

Example: 25% coverage

$200,000	Sales price
× 90%	LTV
$180,000	90% loan
× 25%	Amount of coverage
$45,000	Amount of policy

In the event of default and foreclosure, the lender, at the insurer's option, will either sell the property and make a claim for reimbursement of actual losses (if any) up to the policy's coverage amount, or else relinquish the property to the insurer and make a claim for actual losses up to the coverage amount.

As explained in Chapter 6, private mortgage insurance companies have their own underwriting standards. A company will insure only loans that meet its standards, since it's the company that will bear most of the risk of default and foreclosure loss. Like the underwriting standards of Fannie Mae and Freddie Mac, the standards set by the largest private mortgage insurance companies have been influential throughout the mortgage industry.

PMI Premiums. In return for insuring a loan, a mortgage insurance company charges insurance premiums, which are ordinarily paid by the borrower. Depending on the company, there are a variety of possible payment plans.

PMI premiums:
• Monthly premium,
• Initial premium at closing, plus renewal premiums, or
• Financed one-time premium

One of the most common arrangements is for the insurer to charge a flat monthly premium. The premium corresponds to the risk of the loan, based on factors such as the loan term, loan-to-value ratio, and the borrower's credit reputation. For example, for someone with good credit and a loan with a 95% loan-to-value ratio, the annual premium might be 0.67% of the loan amount. The same borrower with a 90% LTV might pay an annual premium of 0.52%. The lender will usually require the borrower to pay one-twelfth of the annual premium each month, as part of the monthly payment on the mortgage.

Example: $200,000 sales price; 90% loan

$180,000	Loan amount
× 0.52%	For 25% coverage
$936	Initial premium at closing
÷ 12	
$78	Monthly payment

Instead of paying monthly premiums, the borrower may pay more of the total cost upfront. With this kind of plan, the insurance company charges a large initial premium (paid at closing), plus smaller annual renewal premiums thereafter. These smaller annual renewal premiums are based on either the original loan amount or the declining loan balance. One-twelfth of the annual premium is charged to the borrower each month.

The final payment plan we will mention is a single life-of-the-loan premium. This can be paid at closing or financed over the loan term. To finance the single premium, the lender adds the premium to the loan amount before calculating the monthly payment. An advantage of this plan is that the borrower doesn't have to come up with cash at closing for the PMI.

With some payment plans, the borrower may be entitled to a refund of part of the initial premium or financed premium if the borrower pays the loan off early or the lender cancels the mortgage insurance. Premiums are lower for plans that don't provide for refunds, however.

Tax Deductibility. Private mortgage insurance premiums became tax deductible in 2007. This is a temporary economic stimulus measure and is set to expire in 2010. Private mortgage insurance premiums are fully deductible for families with an adjusted gross income of $100,000 or less. Families with an adjusted gross income up to $109,000 are eligible for a partial deduction.

Cancellation of PMI. As a loan is paid off by the borrower, the loan-to-value ratio decreases (as long as the market value of the property serving as collateral isn't decreasing). With a lower LTV, the risk of default and foreclosure loss is reduced, and eventually the private mortgage insurance has fulfilled its purpose.

Under the **Homeowners Protection Act**, a federal law passed in 1998, lenders must cancel a loan's PMI under certain conditions. The law requires the PMI to be canceled once the loan has been paid down to 80% of the property's original value, if the borrower formally

By law, lender must cancel PMI automatically when loan balance reaches 78% of property value

requests the cancellation. Automatic cancellation of the PMI, without a request from the borrower, is required once the loan balance reaches 78% of the property's original value.

The Homeowners Protection Act applies only to loans on single-family dwellings (including condominium and cooperative units, townhouses, and manufactured homes) occupied as the borrower's principal residence.

If a borrower's mortgage insurance payment plan involved an initial premium and renewal premiums, canceling the PMI means that the monthly loan payment will be reduced by the amount attributable to the renewal premium. If the PMI was financed, the borrower may receive a refund of part of the premium, but the monthly payment usually won't change.

Secondary Financing

Lenders generally allow secondary financing, whatever the source, in conjunction with a conventional loan. However, most lenders impose some restrictions when secondary financing is used. Secondary financing increases the risk of default on the primary loan, and the primary lender wants to minimize that additional risk as much as possible.

Primary lender sets rules for secondary financing

Restrictions on Secondary Financing. Here are some of the rules that a lender might apply in a transaction that involves secondary financing:

1. **The borrower must be able to qualify for the payments on both the first and second mortgages.** For qualifying purposes, the primary lender will include the payments on the second loan in the borrower's housing expense.

2. **The borrower must make a minimum 5% downpayment.** The primary lender might not allow the total of the first and second mortgages to exceed 95% of the appraised value or sales price, whichever is less. The borrower would be required to pay the remaining 5% of the purchase price out of his own funds. (Some lenders limit the combined LTV for the two loans to 90% and require a 10% downpayment.)

3. **Scheduled payments must be due on a regular basis.** The primary lender will almost certainly require the second loan

to have regularly scheduled payments. In some cases, quarterly, semi-annual, or annual payments might be acceptable, but usually the primary lender will insist that the second loan have monthly payments. The secondary loan payments can be designed to fully or partially amortize the debt, or to cover interest only. If the loan is partially amortized or interest-only, a balloon payment will be due at the end of the loan term.

4. **The second mortgage can't require a balloon payment sooner than five years after closing.** If the second loan isn't fully amortized, the primary lender is likely to set a minimum term for it (often five years). This prevents the second lender from requiring a large balloon payment from the borrower early in the term of the primary loan, when the risk of default is greatest.

5. **If the first mortgage has variable payments, the second mortgage must have fixed payments.** In other words, the primary lender may require the second mortgage to be a fixed-rate loan if the first mortgage is an adjustable-rate loan, or if the first mortgage is subject to a temporary buydown. (Buydowns are discussed later in this chapter.) Conversely, if the first mortgage is a fixed-rate loan without a buydown, the primary lender will usually allow the second mortgage to be an ARM.

6. **No negative amortization.** The primary lender may specify that the regular payments on the second mortgage must at least equal the interest due on the second mortgage.

7. **No prepayment penalty.** The second mortgage usually must be payable in part or in full at any time without a prepayment penalty.

Again, these are just examples of secondary financing rules. If you're working with a buyer who plans to use secondary financing, ask the buyer's primary lender what rules will apply.

Piggyback Loans. As you recall from our discussion in Chapter 4, the term piggyback loan refers to secondary financing: the second loan "rides piggyback" on a first loan. With a piggyback loan, the buyer can finance most or all of the downpayment instead of coming up with the cash.

Piggyback loan enables borrower to avoid paying for PMI, or paying a higher interest rate for a jumbo loan

In actual practice, piggybacking refers specifically to the use of secondary financing as a way to avoid paying private mortgage insurance or to avoid jumbo loan treatment. At least until fairly recently, using piggybacking to achieve these ends could result in real savings. Borrowers without much cash for a downpayment could still keep the loan-to-value ratio of their primary financing at 80% or less and avoid having to pay for mortgage insurance. And for buyers of expensive properties, who required loans greater than the conforming loan limit (see Figure 10.1), using a piggyback loan could shrink the size of their primary loan. Since lenders charge more for jumbo loans than they do for conforming loans, the borrower could save money by using two conforming loans rather than a single jumbo.

However, government policy changes have watered down or eliminated these advantages. Private mortgage insurance is at least temporarily tax deductible, effectively lowering the cost of the insurance. And a borrower who uses secondary financing to avoid a jumbo loan may have to pay a higher loan-level price adjustment, more or less eliminating the savings. For now, any advantages to piggyback financing are more theoretical than real, and piggyback financing has largely disappeared.

Exercise No. 2

A buyer is seeking conventional fixed-rate financing in order to purchase a home. The sales price is $289,500 and the property has been appraised at $291,500. The buyer is planning to make a 5% cash downpayment and finance the balance with two loans: an 80% conventional first mortgage at 7% interest for 30 years and a 15% second mortgage from the seller at 6.5% interest. Payments on the second mortgage would be based on a 30-year amortization schedule, with a balloon payment of $40,650 due five years after closing.

The first loan has a 1.5% loan origination fee and a 0.25% adverse market delivery charge. The buyer's credit score is 740; no LLPA is charged.

The first loan would require a monthly principal and interest payment of $1,540.84. The second loan would require a monthly principal and interest payment of $274.48. In addition, one-twelfth of the annual property taxes of $3,190 and one-twelfth of the annual hazard insurance premium of $720 would be included in the buyer's total monthly mortgage payment.

1. What would the loan amounts for the first and second loans be?

2. How much would the buyer pay at closing for the downpayment, loan origination fee, and adverse market delivery charge?

3. What would the buyer's total monthly payment for both loans come to, including principal, interest, taxes, and insurance (PITI)?

Qualifying Standards

Chapter 8 explained the general process of qualifying buyers for home purchase loans. Now we'll discuss the qualifying standards that apply to conventional loans. As explained earlier, the qualifying standards most lenders use for conventional loans are based on guidelines established by Fannie Mae and Freddie Mac.

Evaluating Risk Factors

Over the past few years, both Fannie Mae and Freddie Mac have made significant changes in how they evaluate the creditworthiness of loan applicants. They're still concerned with credit reputation, income, and net worth (available assets), but they use high-tech methods to weigh that information in order to decide whether or not to make a loan. These newer methods—automated underwriting systems and computer analysis of data about mortgage borrowers (see Chapter 8)—have dramatically decreased the prevalence of manual underwriting (underwriting carried out by human underwriters).

Fannie Mae uses a "comprehensive risk assessment" approach to evaluate the risk factors in a loan application. In this approach, there are two **primary risk factors**. The first is the applicant's credit reputation, as reflected by her credit score. The second is the cash investment the applicant will be making, measured by the loan-to-value ratio. Based on the credit score and the loan-to-value ratio, a proposed loan is ranked as having a low, moderate, or high primary risk, and that determines the level of review applied to the rest of the loan application.

Fannie Mae treats the other aspects of the application, such as the debt to income ratio and cash reserves, as **contributory risk factors** that may increase or decrease the risk of default. Each contributory risk factor is assigned a value depending on whether it "satisfies basic risk tolerances," increases risk, or decreases risk. In the comprehensive risk assessment, these factors are weighed along with the primary risk factors to determine whether to approve or reject the loan application.

Freddie Mac's approach involves a separate evaluation of each of the main components of creditworthiness—capacity to repay (income and net worth), and collateral (the value of the property)—and an evaluation of the "overall layering of risk." This means that strength in one component of the application may compensate for weakness in another. But even if each of the main components seems acceptable on its own, the combined risk factors in the application as a whole may amount to excessive layering of risk. In that case, the loan should be denied.

As we look at the rules generally used in qualifying buyers for conventional loans, keep in mind that Fannie Mae uses these rules in the context of its comprehensive risk analysis. Freddie Mac uses them in the context of an evaluation of layering of risk. The difference is largely one of terminology—both agencies consider the borrower's overall picture, with positive factors offsetting negative ones and vice versa.

Primary risk factors for comprehensive risk assessment:
- Credit score
- Loan-to-value ratio

Underwriter may evaluate overall layering of risk

Credit Reputation

Credit reputation is probably the most important factor in weighing a borrower's eligibility for a loan. Freddie Mac requires and Fannie Mae "generally expects" manual underwriters to use credit scores in evaluating loan applicants' credit reputation. In most cases, a borrower's credit reputation is determined by her credit score.

The credit scores (FICO scores) that the three main credit bureaus provide for a particular applicant usually vary somewhat from one another. In that situation, an underwriter picks one score to use as the basis for the underwriting. Both Fannie Mae and Freddie Mac's rules for manual underwriting require the underwriter to choose the lower of two scores, or the middle of three. The credit score used to establish credit reputation may be referred to as the indicator score, the representative score, or the underwriting score, depending on the context.

A credit score may not be usable unless the borrower has at least three open credit card accounts or "tradelines" (other forms of regular payment such as rent may be substituted in some cases). These accounts should be seasoned—that is, have been open for a certain amount of time (for example, six months). A borrower who opens several credit cards in a hurried attempt to establish or improve his credit reputation probably won't succeed; in fact, credit agencies tend to view numerous recent accounts as a sign of financial turmoil and downgrade the credit score as a result. Conversely, closing credit cards in the period before applying for a loan will probably result in lowered scores, so doing so should be approached with caution.

An excellent credit score can offset weaknesses in certain other aspects of the loan application, such as marginal income ratios, low reserves, or a high LTV. A poor credit score, on the other hand, can be determinative; Fannie Mae will no longer purchase loans made to borrowers with credit scores below 580. Depending on the type of loan and the LTV, Freddie Mac will consider borrowers with scores as low as 600, although many of their loan programs require minimum scores of 660 or higher.

When two people apply for a conventional loan together (as in the case of a married couple), the lender will obtain credit scores for both applicants. However, in most cases the lowest score is the one that the lender will use in qualifying the applicants. If the other applicant's score is very high, that might be treated as a compensating factor.

Credit scores have become a central factor in conventional underwriting

For couples, underwriter uses lowest credit score, not an average

Income Analysis

Stable monthly income is income that meets the lender's tests of quality and durability (see Chapter 8). Fannie Mae and Freddie Mac consider income durable if it is expected to continue for at least three years after the loan is made.

Once the lender determines how much stable monthly income the loan applicant has, the next step is to decide if the amount of stable monthly income is adequate to support the proposed monthly mortgage payment. This is where the income ratios come into play.

Total Debt to Income Ratio. Lenders generally consider a loan applicant's income adequate for a conventional loan if the applicant's **total monthly obligations** do not exceed **36%** of her stable monthly income. Total monthly obligations include the proposed housing expense plus the applicant's other recurring obligations. The **housing expense** includes PITI: principal, interest, taxes, hazard insurance, and—if applicable—mortgage insurance and homeowners association dues.

A loan applicant's **recurring obligations** include installment debts, revolving debts, and other obligations. **Installment debts** have a fixed beginning and ending date. A car loan is a good example. The monthly payments are a fixed amount and continue for a fixed number of months. An installment debt will be included when calculating the loan applicant's total debt to income ratio if there are more than ten months' worth of payments remaining. (A debt that will be paid off in ten months or less may also be included if the required payments are very large.) Having at least one installment debt in the borrower's record instead of only credit card debt may improve a credit score.

Revolving debts involve an open-ended line of credit, with minimum monthly payments. The most obvious examples are Visa, MasterCard, and department store charge accounts. Borrowers seeking a strong credit score should keep their balances relatively low—ideally using only 10% of their credit, but certainly no more than 50%.

Another category of recurring obligations includes alimony, child support, and similar ongoing financial obligations. At present, neither Fannie Mae nor Freddie Mac considers child care expenses as part of a loan applicant's recurring obligations. However, some individual lenders do take child care expenses into account, especially if they are planning to keep the loan in portfolio.

Benchmark for debt to income ratio: 36%

Total obligations include:
- Housing expense
- Installment debts
- Revolving debts
- Other obligations

Housing Expense to Income Ratio. The second ratio that lenders have traditionally used for conventional loans is the housing expense to income ratio. The proposed housing expense (PITI) generally should not exceed **28%** of the loan applicant's stable monthly income.

Lenders regard the housing expense ratio as less important than the total debt to income ratio, which takes all of the loan applicant's other recurring obligations into account as well as the housing expense. This means there's a good chance that a lender will approve a loan if the applicant's debt to income ratio is the standard 36%, even though her housing expense to income ratio is a little high.

Fannie Mae no longer applies a housing expense to income ratio; the agency now considers the monthly housing expense as only one of the components of the total debt to income ratio. However, we will use both ratios in our examples, since Freddie Mac and many lenders still use both.

Applying the Ratios. Using income ratios, it's a simple matter to determine how large a mortgage payment a buyer is likely to qualify for. Take the buyer's stable monthly income and multiply it by the 36% total debt to income ratio. The buyer's total monthly payments on all long-term obligations (including the proposed mortgage) should not exceed this amount. Take this figure and subtract the buyer's total monthly payments on long-term obligations other than the mortgage; the result is the largest mortgage payment allowed under the total debt to income ratio. Next, multiply the stable monthly income by the 28% housing expense to income ratio. This answer is the largest mortgage payment allowed under the second ratio.

> Benchmark for housing expense to income ratio: 28%
>
> Housing expense ratio is less important than debt to income ratio

Example:

$425	Car payment (18 installments remaining)
+ 250	Credit card payments
$675	Monthly obligations
$6,100	Stable monthly income
× 36%	Total debt to income ratio
$2,196	
– 675	Monthly obligations
$1,521	Maximum mortgage payment under the total debt to income ratio

$6,100 Stable monthly income
× 28% Housing expense to income ratio
$1,708 Maximum mortgage payment
under the housing expense ratio

As in the example, the mortgage payment determined by the total debt to income ratio is usually smaller than the payment determined by the housing expense to income ratio. This is because most buyers have significant recurring obligations besides the proposed mortgage payment. In any case, the smaller of the two results is the maximum allowable mortgage payment.

Example: Marianne Smith has a stable monthly income of $4,200. She has four long-term monthly obligations: a $310 car payment, a $65 personal loan payment, a $40 Sears credit card payment, and a $45 MasterCard payment. What is the largest mortgage payment she can qualify for?

Total debt to income ratio:

$4,200 Stable monthly income
× 36% Income ratio
$1,512 Maximum total obligations
− 310 Car payment
− 65 Personal loan payment
− 40 Sears credit card payment
− 45 MasterCard payment
$1,052 Maximum mortgage payment
under the total debt to income ratio

Housing expense to income ratio:

$4,200 Stable monthly income
× 28% Income ratio
$1,176 Maximum mortgage payment
under the housing expense ratio

The largest mortgage payment that Smith could probably qualify for is $1,052. Remember, after both ratios have been applied, the lower resulting figure is the one that counts. Of course, if Smith could pay off some of her debts and reduce her total obligations, she could qualify for a larger mortgage payment.

Higher Ratios and Compensating Factors. Although we've been referring to 36% and 28% as the "maximum" allowable income ratios for conventional loans, that isn't strictly accurate. Both Fannie Mae and Freddie Mac consider these income ratios to be benchmarks or guidelines rather than rigid limits. Both agencies will purchase a loan even though the borrower's ratios exceed 36% and/or 28%, as long as there are **compensating factors** that justify making the loan in spite of the higher ratios. The stronger the compensating factors, the higher the ratios are allowed to be. In this analysis, a lender could treat any of the following as a compensating factor:

- a large downpayment;
- substantial net worth;
- a demonstrated ability to incur few debts and accumulate savings;
- education, job training, or employment history that indicates strong potential for increased earnings;
- short-term income that doesn't count as stable monthly income (because it won't last for three years);
- a demonstrated ability to devote a greater portion of income to basic needs, such as the housing expense; or
- significant energy-efficient features in the home being purchased.

Compensating factors:
- Large downpayment
- Substantial net worth
- Savings and few debts
- Potential for increased earnings
- Short-term income
- More income devoted to basic needs
- Energy-efficient home

Let's look at an example to see how a lender might take some of these compensating factors into account.

Example: Walter Quinn and Lisa Porter have a stable monthly income of $5,200. Their only recurring obligation is a $342 monthly car payment. They've applied for a mortgage with monthly payments of $1,686 (including principal, interest, taxes, hazard insurance, and mortgage insurance).

When the underwriter calculates Quinn and Porter's income ratios, he finds that their total debt to income ratio is 39% and their housing expense ratio is over 32%. So the underwriter reviews their application for compensating factors, to see if loan approval would be justified in spite of income ratios that exceed the benchmarks.

First, the underwriter checks Porter and Quinn's credit scores. Both have good scores, in the mid-700s. Next, the underwriter notes that Porter and Quinn have been paying $1,575 a month for rent on their current home, so the proposed housing expense wouldn't represent a dramatic increase for them. They've demonstrated that they can devote a greater portion of income to basic needs than most people.

Quinn also receives $400 per month from his first wife, for the support of their 15-year-old daughter. The child support wasn't included in stable monthly income, because the payments will end in two and a half years, when the daughter turns 18. It can count as a compensating factor, however.

Finally, the underwriter notes that Quinn and Porter have few debts and they will have $16,000 in savings left over after meeting all the expenses of purchasing their home. He decides that Quinn and Porter's application is supported by sufficient compensating factors to justify loan approval.

Keep in mind that even when there are compensating factors to justify income ratios higher than the 36% and 28% benchmarks, lenders won't accept ratios that are too far over those limits. How much higher than the benchmark can the ratio be? If the loan application is manually underwritten, neither Fannie Mae nor Freddie Mac will accept a debt to income ratio over 45%, no matter how many compensating factors are present. If the application is submitted to an automated underwriting system, there's no set maximum; the software will determine whether the high ratio is acceptable in the context of the overall default risk that the application presents.

Factors that Increase Risk. Of course, instead of compensating factors, some loan applications present factors that represent increased risk for the lender. In that situation, income ratios in excess of the benchmarks would generally be unacceptable. For example, many lenders won't accept a high total debt to income ratio for a loan with a loan-to-value ratio over 90% or for an adjustable-rate loan.

Income Analysis for ARMs. Lenders evaluate applications for adjustable-rate mortgages very carefully, because the monthly payments for an ARM may increase significantly, sometimes in the first few years of the loan term. Fannie Mae and Freddie Mac generally accept ARMs underwritten using the standard income ratios, but they expect the lender to consider whether the loan applicant will be able to handle payment increases. An ARM borrower facing the possibility of a sharp increase should have strong potential for increased earnings, significant liquid assets (reserves), or a demonstrated ability to manage finances and apply a greater portion of income to housing expenses.

ARMs must be underwritten carefully, to make sure applicants can handle payment increases

Under certain market conditions, ARMs are offered at lower interest rates than fixed-rate loans. That can make it easier to qualify for an ARM than for a fixed-rate loan, since a lower interest rate means a lower monthly payment amount. However, that may be counteracted by the extra scrutiny an ARM application will receive. Also, in some cases a lender won't use the actual initial interest rate to qualify an ARM applicant. Instead, the applicant will be qualified using the maximum interest rate that could be in effect at the end of the introductory interest rate period.

ARM applicants may be qualified using a higher rate than the initial rate

> **Example:** The Conrads have applied for a $210,000 ARM from a lender that's offering an initial interest rate of 5.5%. The loan would have an LTV of 90%, a 30-year term, a one-year rate adjustment period, and a 2% annual rate cap.
>
> The lender will apply the standard 36% and 28% income ratios to qualify the Conrads. But their income ratios will be calculated using a proposed housing expense based on 7.5% interest (the maximum rate possible at the end of the first year) rather than the 5.5% they'll actually have to pay during the first year if the loan is approved. This means the Conrads will qualify only if their income is sufficient to handle a $1,468 principal and interest payment, as opposed to the $1,192 principal and interest payment they would actually be making during the first year.
>
> In addition, the lender won't approve the loan unless there is reason to believe the Conrads will be able to handle future payment increases. They must have strong potential for increased earnings, significant liquid assets, or the ability to devote an extra share of their income to housing expenses, if necessary.

This method of qualifying is generally used only for ARMs with features that permit substantial payment increases, such as the 2% annual interest rate cap in the example. If the Conrads had applied for an ARM with a 1% rate cap, then the lender would probably have qualified them using the 5.5% interest rate.

Available Funds

Lenders must determine whether the applicant has enough money available for the downpayment and closing costs, and also whether there will be any money left over in reserve after closing. As we noted earlier, a borrower's lack of reserves is considered a contributory risk factor.

Reserves. The more liquid assets borrowers have in reserve after closing, the more likely it is that they can weather financial emergencies without defaulting on their mortgage. Conventional loan applicants

Conventional borrower may be required to have 2 months' mortgage payments in reserve

generally should have the equivalent of at least two months of mortgage payments in reserve after making the downpayment and paying all closing costs. Not every loan requires this, but less than that in reserve will weaken an application, and more will strengthen it. And for a few types of loans, mostly investor loans, the borrower must have a full six months of reserves on hand at closing.

Reserves must be cash or liquid assets that could easily be converted to cash if necessary (for example, the cash value of a life insurance policy, or the vested portion of a retirement account).

Gift Funds. In regard to the resources that a borrower has available for closing, Fannie Mae and Freddie Mac set limits on the use of gift funds. First of all, the donor must be:

Gift funds
- Donor must be a relative, employer, city, or nonprofit organization
- Borrower usually still must make 5% downpayment from own funds

- the borrower's relative, fiancé, or domestic partner;
- the borrower's employer;
- a municipality or public agency; or
- a nonprofit religious or community organization.

Also, as a general rule the borrower must make a downpayment of at least 5% of the sales price out of her own resources.

> **Example:** Grace Wessel has agreed to buy a house for $200,000; the appraised value is $201,000. Wessel hopes to qualify for a 90% loan. Her mother is willing to give her $14,000 to close the transaction. But Wessel can use only $10,000 in gift funds toward the downpayment; she will be required to come up with the remaining $10,000 out of her own resources. (Wessel may use the additional $4,000 gift from her mother for closing costs or reserves.)
>
> If Wessel were trying to obtain a 95% loan, she could not use any gift funds for the downpayment, but she could use them for closing costs or reserves.

However, when the loan-to-value ratio is 80% or less, the 5% requirement does not apply. For example, if Wessel's mother were to supply a 20% downpayment, Wessel would not have to contribute any of her own money toward the purchase.

Gift funds may also count towards a borrower's reserves. However, if a particular loan imposes a reserve requirement, the borrower cannot meet this requirement solely by using gift funds. The borrower must also have some of her own funds left in reserve after closing.

Exercise No. 3

Mike and Barbara Tanaka want to buy a home. Mike makes $62,000 a year as a controller for a small electronics company. Barbara makes $4,750 a month as an administrator at a local community college. They have two car payments, one at $317 a month (21 payments left) and the other at $375 a month (13 payments left). They have a personal loan with a remaining balance of $2,400, which requires monthly payments of $250. The Tanakas make three credit card payments every month, with the following minimum payments: $55 a month to a department store, $42 a month to Visa, and $54 a month to MasterCard.

1. Suppose the Tanakas would like a fixed-rate 90% loan. Applying the benchmark income ratios, how large a mortgage payment would the Tanakas qualify for?

2. List two or three compensating factors that might allow the Tanakas to qualify for a somewhat larger payment, if these factors were present in their financial situation.

3. Even if there aren't any compensating factors in the Tanakas' financial situation that would lead the lender to accept income ratios higher than the standard limits, what can the Tanakas do to qualify for a larger payment?

Making Conventional Loans More Affordable

The traditional conventional mortgage loan had a 30-year term, an 80% loan-to-value ratio, a fixed interest rate, and fully amortized monthly payments. We've already discussed some of the basic alternatives to that traditional model that are now in widespread use, including loans with 15-year terms, with 90% and 95% loan-to-value ratios, and with adjustable interest rates. In this section of the chapter we'll discuss a variety of other ways to structure conventional financing, focusing mainly on alternatives that lower the monthly payments or otherwise make loans more affordable for borrowers.

Buydown Plans

Buydown:
- Seller or third party pays lump sum to lender at closing
- Increases lender's upfront yield
- Lowers buyer's payment
- May make it easier to qualify

One of the easiest ways to make a loan more affordable is a **buydown**. In a buydown arrangement, a property seller or a third party pays the lender a lump sum at closing to lower the interest rate on the buyer's loan. The lump sum payment increases the lender's upfront yield on the loan, and in return the lender charges a lower interest rate, which lowers the amount of the borrower's monthly payment. The lender will evaluate the borrower on the basis of a reduced payment, making it easier to qualify for the loan.

This is the equivalent of paying the lender discount points, but it's called a buydown when the seller or a third party pays the points on the buyer's behalf. Also, a buydown can be arranged even when the lender was quoting a specified interest rate without discount points.

> **Example:** Seaside Savings is offering fixed-rate 30-year loans at the market interest rate, 11%. In order to help buyers afford financing to purchase her home, Irene Glover is willing to pay for a 2% buydown, which would reduce the quoted interest rate to 9%.

Buydowns are generally used when interest rates are high, as in the example.

A buydown can be permanent or temporary. With a **permanent buydown**, the borrower pays the lower interest rate (and a lower payment) for the entire loan term. With a **temporary buydown**, the interest rate and monthly payment are reduced only during the first years of the loan term.

Permanent Buydowns. If a borrower's interest rate is bought down permanently (for the entire loan term), the buydown reduces the note rate—the interest rate stated in the promissory note.

> **Example:** Bowen needs to borrow $150,000 to buy Sanderson's property. The lender quoted a 12% interest rate for a 30-year fixed-rate loan, and Bowen can't quite afford the loan at that rate. Sanderson offers to buy down Bowen's interest rate to 11%. The lender agrees to make the loan to the buyer at this lower rate if Sanderson pays the lender $9,000.
>
> With this arrangement in place, the promissory note that Bowen signs sets the interest rate at 11%. The buyer will pay 11% interest for the life of the loan. At closing, the lender will withhold $9,000 from the loan funds, reducing Sanderson's proceeds from the sale.
>
> By reducing the interest rate from 12% to 11%, the buydown will lower Bowen's mortgage payment by $115 per month and enable her to qualify for the loan.

$1,543	Payment at quoted 12% rate
− 1,428	Payment at 11% after buydown
$115	Monthly savings resulting from buydown

The fee the lender charges for a permanent buydown is calculated in terms of points (percentage points) of the loan amount. The number of points required to increase the lender's yield by 1% (and decrease the borrower's interest rate by 1%) varies from one area to another. It's affected by current market conditions, including prevailing interest rates, and the average time that loans are outstanding before being paid off. As we noted in Chapter 7, lenders in recent years have generally required the payment of four to six points to buy a 1% reduction in the interest rate. To know the exact cost of a permanent buydown, you should ask the lender.

Permanent buydown rule of thumb: 4 to 6 points for 1% interest rate reduction

> **Example:** In the example above, the lender charged the seller six points for a 1% buydown.

$150,000	Loan amount
× 6%	Six points
$9,000	Cost of 1% buydown

Temporary Buydowns. A temporary buydown reduces the buyer's monthly payments in the early months or years of the loan term. Temporary buydowns appeal to buyers who feel they can grow into a larger payment, but need time to get established.

Fig. 10.2 Three-year temporary buydown with level payments

Year	Note Rate	Buydown	Effective Rate	Payment at 13%	Actual Payment	Monthly Subsidy	Annual Subsidy
1	13%	2%	11%	$2,046	$1,762	$284	$3,408
2	13%	2%	11%	$2,046	$1,762	$284	$3,408
3	13%	2%	11%	$2,046	$1,762	$284	$3,408
4	13%	- 0 -	13%	$2,046	$2,046	- 0 -	- 0 -

Total Buydown: $10,224

There are two types of temporary buydown plans: level payment plans and graduated payment plans.

Level payments. A level payment plan calls for an interest reduction that stays the same throughout the buydown period.

Temporary buydowns:
- *Level payment*
- *Graduated payment*

> **Example:** The lender agrees to make a 30-year loan of $185,000 at 13% interest. The property seller buys down the borrower's interest rate to 11% for three years by paying the lender $10,224 at closing.
>
> As shown in Figure 10.2, during the first three years of the loan term the buydown lowers the monthly payment on the loan by $284, from $2,046 to $1,762. At the beginning of the fourth year, the payment amount goes up to the unsubsidized level, $2,046, and stays at that level for the remaining 27 years of the loan term.

Graduated payments. A graduated payment buydown plan calls for the largest payment reduction in the first year, with progressively smaller reductions in each of the remaining years of the buydown period.

> **Example:** The lender agrees to make a 30-year loan of $185,000 at 13% interest. By paying the lender $10,188 at closing, the seller buys down the borrower's interest rate by 3% the first year, 2% the second year, and 1% the third year. Figure 10.3 shows how the monthly payment will change.

The graduated payment buydown in the example (in which the interest rate is bought down 3% the first year, 2% the second year, and 1% the third year) is called a 3-2-1 buydown. Probably the most common form of graduated payment buydown is the 2-1 buydown. In a 2-1 buydown, the interest rate is bought down 2% the first year and 1% the second year; the buyer starts paying the note rate in the third year.

Fig. 10.3 Three-year temporary buydown with graduated payments

Year	Note Rate	Buydown	Effective Rate	Payment at 13%	Actual Payment	Monthly Subsidy	Annual Subsidy
1	13%	3%	10%	$2,046	$1,624	$422	$5,064
2	13%	2%	11%	$2,046	$1,762	$284	$3,408
3	13%	1%	12%	$2,046	$1,903	$143	$1,716
4	13%	- 0 -	13%	$2,046	$2,046	- 0 -	- 0 -
						Total Buydown:	**$10,188**

Computing the cost of a temporary buydown. As with a permanent buydown, to get the exact cost of a temporary buydown, it's best to ask a lender for a quote. But the cost of a temporary buydown can be computed fairly accurately with a financial calculator.

1. Calculate the buyer's monthly principal and interest payment without the buydown, at the full rate of interest the lender is charging.

2. Calculate the buyer's monthly payment with the bought-down interest rate.

3. Subtract the bought-down payment from the actual payment and multiply by 12 for the annual buydown amount.

4. For a level payment buydown, multiply the annual buydown amount by the number of years in the buydown plan.

Estimating cost of temporary buydown:
- Calculate difference between unsubsidized and subsidized payments
- Multiply by 12 for annual cost
- Add up annual costs for total cost

Example: Three-year level payment buydown

$203,000	Loan amount
11.25%	Note rate
9.25%	Bought-down rate

1. Calculate the monthly principal and interest payment without the buydown: $1,971.66.

2. Calculate the payment with the buydown: $1,670.03.

3. Subtract the bought-down payment from the actual payment and multiply by 12 (months).

$1,971.66	Actual payment
− 1,670.03	Bought-down payment
$301.63	Monthly buydown amount
× 12	Months
$3,619.56	Annual buydown amount

4. Multiply the annual buydown amount by the number of years in the buydown plan.

$3,619.56	Annual buydown amount
× 3	Years in buydown plan
$10,858.68	Total buydown: lump sum required by lender

A graduated payment buydown is calculated in the same way, except that the amount of each year's buydown has to be calculated separately and then all the annual figures are added together. The sum is the total cost of the graduated payment buydown.

Buydowns and Qualifying Rules. As we said earlier, by lowering the monthly payment, a buydown can make it easier for the buyer to qualify for a loan. With a permanent buydown, the lender uses the bought-down interest rate to calculate the payment, and then determines if the buyer can qualify for that reduced payment. If the seller permanently buys down the loan's interest rate from 12% to 10%, the buyer only has to qualify for a payment at 10% interest.

It isn't that simple with a temporary buydown. Since the buydown is only going to last a few years, the buyer will eventually have to afford the larger payment based on the full note rate. So in some cases, instead of qualifying the buyer at the bought-down rate, the lender uses a higher rate for the qualifying calculations; for instance, the lender might use a rate only 1% below the note rate to qualify the buyer.

> **Example:** Refer back to the 3-2-1 graduated payment buydown shown in Figure 10.3. The note rate is 13%. In the first year, the interest rate will be bought down 3%—from 13% to 10%. Even so, the lender qualifies the buyer at 12%, only one percentage point below the note rate. The buyer has to qualify for a $1,903 payment (the payment calculated using 12% interest), even though the actual payments will be lower than that in the first two years of the loan term. This gives the lender some assurance the buyer will be able to handle the payment increases when the time comes.

Fannie Mae generally allows a buyer with a temporary buydown to be qualified using the bought-down rate, as long as the loan has a fixed interest rate or, if it is an ARM, it has an initial interest rate period of three years or more. In addition, the buyer's credit score must be 660 or higher and the loan has to be for the borrower's principal residence.

With permanent buydown, lender qualifies buyer at bought-down interest rate

With temporary buydown, lender may qualify buyer at:
- The bought-down rate,
- The note rate, or
- An intermediate rate

Freddie Mac has its own rules for temporary buydowns. The buyer can usually be qualified using the bought-down interest rate if the property will be the buyer's principal residence. (If the property is a second home, the note rate must be used.) The buydown rate can't be used for certain low-downpayment programs or cash-out refinances. Also, no buydown plan may extend for more than three years after the first scheduled payment date. ARMs with an initial period of five years or less aren't eligible for buydowns, except in special circumstances.

Both Fannie Mae and Freddie Mac expect lenders to evaluate loans subject to temporary buydowns with special care. As with an ARM, the buyer should have strong potential for increased income, or significant liquid assets, or the ability to apply an extra share of her income to the housing expense, if necessary.

Many lenders follow other policies of their own in regard to temporary buydowns. When you're handling a transaction in which the parties would like to arrange a temporary buydown, always ask the lender what interest rate and what income ratios will be used for qualifying, and what other rules apply.

Limits on Buydowns and Other Contributions. Fannie Mae and Freddie Mac limit the amount of a buydown to a percentage of the property's sales price or appraised value, whichever is less, as shown in Figure 10.4. The limits also apply to most other contributions the buyer accepts from the seller, or from another interested party, such as the builder or a real estate agent involved in the transaction. For example, if the seller agreed to pay closing costs that would ordinarily be paid by the buyer, these limits would apply.

If seller's contributions exceed limits, excess deducted from sales price in loan amount calculations

If the seller's contributions exceed these guidelines, the excess contribution must be deducted from the sales price before determining the maximum loan amount.

Fig. 10.4 Limits on contributions from sellers or other interested parties

Contribution Limits for Owner-Occupied Homes	
Loan-to-Value Ratio	*Maximum Contribution*
Over 90%	3%
76% to 90%	6%
75% or less	9%

Example:

> $300,000 sales price; $302,000 appraised value; 90% loan
> Maximum contribution: $18,000 (6% of the sales price)

For this transaction, any contribution in excess of $18,000 would be deducted from the sales price, which would result in a lower loan amount. For instance, if the seller were to contribute $19,000, the extra $1,000 would be subtracted from the sales price, and the maximum loan amount would be only $269,100 instead of $270,000.

$300,000	Sales price
– 1,000	Excess contribution
$299,000	
× 90%	LTV
$269,100	Loan amount

These limits on contributions from interested parties generally don't apply to contributions from someone who isn't participating in the transaction—for example, the buyer's employer, or a family member.

Exercise No. 4

Dan Johnson agrees to purchase Morris Callahan's home for $350,000, contingent on obtaining the necessary financing. But Johnson can afford to put only 10% down, and it turns out that he can't quite qualify for the monthly payment on a 90%, 30-year conventional loan at the market interest rate, 8.75%. Callahan offers to buy the interest rate down to 7.75% so that Johnson can qualify for the loan and go through with the purchase.

1. In this market, lenders estimate that it takes about six points to increase the yield on a loan by 1%. Approximately how much would a permanent buydown cost Callahan?

2. With the buydown, Johnson's monthly principal and interest payment would be $2,256.70, compared to $2,478.11 without the buydown. How much could the buydown save Johnson over the life of the loan?

Loans with Lower Initial Payments

Many first-time home buyers are just starting out in their careers. They expect their incomes to increase steadily, so they also expect to be able to afford a higher mortgage payment several years down the line. These buyers may be able to buy a more expensive home immediately, without waiting for their incomes to increase, if they get a loan that has lower payments at first and higher payments later on.

As we just discussed, a temporary buydown is one way of making a loan more affordable in the first years of the repayment period. In Chapter 6, we also discussed hybrid ARMs: adjustable-rate mortgages with two-tiered rate adjustment schedules. One example is the 5/1 ARM: the interest rate and payment amount start out lower than the rate and payment for a fixed-rate loan, and they don't change during the first five years; the lender makes annual adjustments after that. Other types of two-tiered conventional loans that offer lower payments in the initial years than a comparable fixed-rate loan include:

Loans with lower initial payments:
- Hybrid ARMs
- Two-step mortgages
- Balloon/reset mortgages
- Interest-only mortgages

- two-step mortgages,
- balloon/reset mortgages, and
- interest-only mortgages.

Two-step Mortgages. A two-step mortgage provides some of the advantages of an ARM, but less uncertainty for the borrower. A two-step mortgage is a 30-year loan that allows the lender to adjust the loan's interest rate at only one point during the loan term. The most common two-step programs are the 5/25 plan and the 7/23 plan.

The interest rate of a 5/25 loan is automatically adjusted after five years to the current market rate and the monthly payment is adjusted accordingly. (Usually the interest rate can't be raised more than a certain amount, for example 6%.) The interest rate and payment then stay at that level for the remaining 25 years of the loan term.

> **Example:** When Paul Jacoby obtained a loan, the current fixed interest rate was 6%. Jacoby was able to get a 5/25 two-step loan at a 5.5% initial interest rate. Five years later, the market rate has increased by 2%, so Jacoby's rate increases to 7.5%. He will continue to pay 7.5% interest for the remainder of the loan term, 25 years.

A 7/23 loan automatically adjusts after seven years to the current market rate (again, as limited by any interest rate cap), and then stays at that rate for the remaining 23 years of the loan term.

Because the lender will have an opportunity to adjust the loan's interest rate to reflect changes in the market rate, two-step mortgages are offered at a lower initial rate than fixed-rate loans. And while the borrower assumes the risk that interest rates will increase in the next five or seven years, he also gets to take advantage of lower rates without refinancing if market rates decrease during that five- or seven-year period. Because the interest rate on a two-step loan changes only once, many borrowers feel more comfortable with this type of loan than with an ARM.

Balloon/Reset Mortgages. Balloon/reset mortgages are similar to two-step mortgages, with some key differences. Like two-step mortgages, balloon/reset mortgages come in two versions, 5/25 and 7/23. (Note that Fannie Mae does not buy 5/25 balloon/reset loans.) With a balloon/reset mortgage, however, the initial five- or seven-year period is actually the term of the loan. Although the payment amount is based on a 30-year amortization schedule, the entire mortgage balance becomes due at the end of the five- or seven-year term. In other words, a balloon/reset mortgage is a partially amortized loan.

At the end of the five- or seven-year term, the borrowers may have to refinance in order to make the balloon payment. Alternatively, they may be allowed to "reset" the loan. Under the reset option, the loan stays in place and the interest rate is adjusted to the current market rate (limited by any interest rate cap). The rate and payment are then level for 25 or 23 years.

By exercising the reset option, the borrowers can avoid refinancing charges. To be entitled to reset the loan, the borrowers have to meet

Two-step or balloon/reset mortgage: interest rate adjusted only once (5 or 7 years into loan term)

certain conditions. For example, they must not have been delinquent on the mortgage payments during the preceding year, and they must not have placed other liens against the property.

Interest-Only Mortgages. As we said earlier in the chapter, some loans allow the borrower to make interest-only payments for a specified period at the beginning of the loan term. The borrower isn't required to start paying off the principal until that period expires. Let's look at an example of a typical interest-only plan.

Interest-only mortgage allows interest-only payments during first part of loan term, then is fully amortized for the remainder of the term

> **Example:** Ann's loan has a 30-year term, with a 10-year interest-only period. She won't have to begin paying off the principal until the 11th year. The interest rate will remain fixed throughout the 30-year term. When it's time for Ann to begin paying off the principal, the entire loan amount will be fully amortized over the remaining 20 years of the term.

The interest rate is fixed in the above example, but interest-only loans may also have adjustable rates.

Because the principal is amortized over the remainder of the term, the amount of the required monthly payment is likely to rise sharply at the end of the interest-only period, making payment shock a serious risk. However, the borrower is allowed to make prepayments of principal at any time during the initial interest-only period. Any prepayments will reduce the amount of the monthly payment later on.

Both Fannie Mae and Freddie Mac will buy fixed-rate loans with interest-only periods ranging from under three years to over fifteen years. They'll also buy hybrid ARMs with interest-only payments, as long as they have an initial fixed-rate period of three years or more. Other types of ARMs, as well as balloon/reset loans, cannot be interest-only.

Low-Downpayment Programs

For many potential home buyers, especially first-time buyers, coming up with enough cash is the biggest challenge in buying a home. They have a steady, reliable income, but they don't have the savings to cover the downpayment and closing costs required for a standard conventional loan. Even the 5% downpayment required for a 95% loan may be beyond their means. Buyers in this situation may want to consider special programs that have reduced cash requirements and allow them to draw on alternative sources for the cash they need.

The details of these programs vary, but here are two examples of the types of loans that buyers can look for:

- A loan with a 95% LTV that requires a 3% downpayment from the borrower's own funds, with 2% from alternative sources.
- A loan with a 97% LTV that requires a 3% downpayment from the borrower's own funds, plus a 3% contribution to closing costs that may come from alternative sources.

Depending on the program, the allowable alternative sources of funds may include gifts, grants, or unsecured loans. The funds may come from a relative, an employer, a public agency, a nonprofit organization, or a private foundation. More than one source may be tapped to get the necessary funds together.

Some of these programs don't require the borrower to have any reserves after closing. Others require one month's mortgage payment in reserve.

Affordable Housing Programs. Although some conventional low-downpayment programs are open to any prospective home buyer, many are specifically targeted at low- and moderate-income buyers. As a general rule, a buyer can qualify for one of these programs if his stable monthly income does not exceed the median income in the metropolitan area in question. (Increased income limits apply in high-cost areas.) To make it even easier for low- and moderate-income buyers to get a mortgage, these programs may allow a total debt to income ratio of 38% or even 40% without compensating factors, and may have no maximum housing expense to income ratio.

To encourage neighborhood revitalization, some affordable housing programs waive their income limits for buyers who are purchasing homes in low-income or rundown neighborhoods. Thus, buyers whose income is well above the area median could still qualify for a low-downpayment program targeted at low-income buyers if they're buying a home in a neighborhood that meets the program's standards.

Other conventional low-downpayment programs are offered to specific groups such as teachers, police officers, and firefighters. These programs are intended to enable the borrowers to purchase homes in the urban areas they serve, instead of being priced out of their community.

Affordable housing programs:
- Easier to qualify
- Cash requirements reduced
- Eligibility based on income, property location, or job

344

Accelerated Payment Plans

We'll end the chapter by describing two accelerated payment plans—the bi-weekly mortgage and the growing equity mortgage. These plans allow the borrower to repay a conventional loan in a shorter period than the loan's stated term (for example, a 30-year mortgage might be paid off in 15 years). This means that a borrower pays considerably less interest over the life of the loan, and he also acquires equity relatively rapidly. To some degree, buyers can achieve these same ends simply by getting a loan with a shorter term (for example, a 15-year mortgage instead of a 30-year mortgage), or else by paying off their 30-year loan more quickly (by sending in extra payments at their own discretion as they're able to afford them). However, the particular features of bi-weekly and growing equity mortgages make these plans the best choice for certain borrowers.

Bi-Weekly Mortgages. With a bi-weekly mortgage, both the interest rate and the payment amount are fixed, but payments are made every two weeks instead of every month. Each payment is equal to half of what the monthly payment would be for a fully amortized, 30-year, fixed-rate loan of the same amount at the same interest rate.

Bi-weekly loan:
- 26 half payments per year, equivalent to 13 monthly payments
- Loan paid off in 20 to 22 years

The attraction of the bi-weekly loan is the amount of interest the borrower can save. For example, a $90,000 loan at 8.5% interest paid on a bi-weekly basis saves almost $48,000 in interest compared to the monthly payment plan (see Figure 10.5). By paying every two weeks (26 payments a year), the borrower makes the equivalent of 13 monthly payments a year. As a result, bi-weekly loans are usually paid off in 20 to 22 years, instead of 30 years.

Most lenders require bi-weekly borrowers to authorize automatic transfers from their checking accounts to reduce the extra processing

Fig. 10.5 Comparison of bi-weekly loan payments to ordinary monthly payments

Example: $90,000 loan, 8.5% fixed rate, 30-year amortization			
Schedule	Payments	No. of Payments	Total Paid
Monthly	$692.02	360	$249,130
Bi-weekly	$346.01	582	$201,365
The bi-weekly loan would be paid off in a little over 22 years, with total interest payments of approximately $47,765 less than the loan with monthly payments.			

cost in handling 26 payments instead of the 12 required for a standard mortgage. The borrower may also be required to buy overdraft protection. Since many people get paid on a bi-weekly basis, setting up the mortgage payment on the same basis makes a certain sense. However, the borrower must make sure the funds are available for payment every two weeks.

Growing Equity Mortgages. As with other accelerated payment plans, a borrower with a growing equity mortgage (GEM) pays off the loan balance more quickly than the stated term. Though there are many variations, most GEMs share the following characteristics:

GEM:
- Fixed interest rate
- Initial payment based on 30-year amortization
- Annual payment increases
- Quick principal reduction
- Payoff in 15 years or less

- The interest rate is fixed over the life of the loan.
- The loan must be paid off in 15 years or less.
- First-year payments of principal and interest are based on a 15- or 30-year term.
- The borrower's payments increase at specified intervals (usually annually) for all or a portion of the loan term.
- Since the interest rate is fixed, 100% of the annual payment increases are used to reduce the principal balance.

There are a number of different ways of handling the annual payment adjustments for a GEM, but most commonly the payments are increased by a fixed percentage—typically 3% or 5% per year. Because the payment increases are used to reduce the principal balance, a borrower will pay off a GEM much sooner than a 30-year fixed-rate mortgage. If payments are increased 5% per year on a loan at 10% interest, the entire debt will be retired in just 13 years and 6 months. (A GEM's actual repayment period depends on the interest rate and the magnitude of the annual payment increases.)

However, GEM payments become substantially higher over time compared to fixed-rate payments. During periods of high inflation, this can work out fairly well. Borrowers can readily adjust to payment hikes because their wages are also rising. The reward is a relatively quickly retired mortgage. An $84,000, 30-year, fixed-rate mortgage shows a balance of $72,040.81 after 13 years and 4 months; at the end of the same period, the GEM loan is paid in full. However, when the inflation rate is low, or if the employment picture is bleak, GEM plans do not look so attractive, because the borrower can't rely on rising wages to offset the higher payments.

Outline: Conventional Financing

I. Conforming and Nonconforming Loans

   A. Conforming loans: loans that comply with Fannie Mae and Freddie Mac underwriting guidelines.

   B. Nonconforming loans: loans that don't follow secondary market agency guidelines, which can't be sold to either agency.

II. Conventional Loan Characteristics

   A. Property types and owner-occupancy

      1. Fannie Mae and Freddie Mac will purchase loans secured by residential properties, including site-built homes, manufactured homes, townhouses, condos, and co-ops.

      2. The loan may be for a principal residence (with up to four units) or a second home (with no more than one unit).

      3. Fannie Mae and Freddie Mac also buy investor loans, which are for properties that will be rented out to tenants; these loans are underwritten differently.

   B. Loan amounts

      1. Conforming loan limits are set annually; limits are higher in Alaska, Guam, Hawaii, the Virgin Islands, and other high-cost areas.

      2. Jumbo loans are loans that exceed conforming loan limits; they typically have higher interest rates and stricter qualifying standards.

   C. Repayment periods: can range from ten to forty years; thirty years is standard.

   D. Amortization: most conventional loans are fully amortized, but partially-amortized and interest-only loans are also available.

   E. Loan-to-value ratios

      1. The traditional loan-to-value ratio (LTV) for conventional loans is 80%, but borrowers can look for 90%, 95%, and 97% loans.

      2. Fannie Mae and Freddie Mac require private mortgage insurance on loans with LTVs over 80%.

      3. Lenders usually charge higher interest rates and fees for high-LTV loans and impose stricter qualifying standards.

F. Risk-based loan fees

    1. Loan-level price adjustment (LLPA) shifts risk of default to borrower; generally, the riskier the loan, the higher the LLPA.

    2. Varies based on borrower's credit score and proposed LTV.

    3. Certain types of riskier loans (investor, interest-only) may be charged an LLPA in addition to the one based on credit score and LTV.

    4. Adverse market delivery charge: .25% fee levied by Fannie Mae and Freddie Mac against every new loan, because of poor market conditions.

G. Private mortgage insurance (PMI)

    1. PMI is issued by private companies instead of a government agency. It protects lenders from the greater risk of high-LTV loans.

    2. PMI typically covers 25% to 30% of the loan amount rather than the whole amount.

    3. In the event of default, the lender may either foreclose on the property or relinquish it to the insurer, and then submit a claim for actual losses up to the policy amount.

    4. PMI premiums are paid by the buyer.

        a. There may be a flat monthly premium.

        b. Or there may be an initial premium (paid at closing) plus annual renewal premiums (usually paid on a monthly basis).

        c. Or there may be a one-time premium (which is paid at closing or financed over the loan term).

    5. Homeowners Protection Act requires lenders to cancel PMI at the borrower's request when the loan is paid down to 80% of the property's original value, or automatically when it reaches 78% of the original value.

H. Secondary financing

    1. Lenders typically allow secondary financing, regardless of the source, but impose a number of restrictions to reduce risk of default.

    2. Examples of rules concerning secondary financing:

        a. Borrower must be able to qualify for the payments on both the first and second mortgages.

        b. Borrower must make at least a 5% downpayment.

        c. Payments must be regularly scheduled.

        d. Second mortgage can't require a balloon payment until at least five years after closing.

  e. If the first mortgage has variable payments, the second mortgage must have fixed payments.

  f. Negative amortization and prepayment penalties are not allowed.

 3. Piggyback loans: Using secondary financing to avoid having to pay private mortgage insurance or to avoid the loan being designated a jumbo loan.

III. Qualifying Standards

 A. Evaluating risk factors

  1. Fannie Mae's comprehensive risk assessment approach uses primary risk factors and contributory risk factors.

  2. Two primary risk factors determine level of review applied to the rest of the application:

   a. credit reputation, and

   b. proposed loan-to-value ratio.

  3. Contributory risk factors include the other aspects of the application, such as income ratios and cash reserves.

 B. Credit reputation

  1. Credit reputation based on credit score from one or more of the three main credit agencies; also known as indicator score, underwriting score, or representative score.

  2. Good credit score can offset weaknesses in other areas, but a low score may prevent loan approval.

  3. Fannie Mae and Freddie Mac require manual underwriters to use lower of two scores, or middle of three.

  4. When two people apply for loan, lowest score used.

 C. Income analysis

  1. Debt to income ratio: total monthly obligations generally should not exceed 36% of stable monthly income.

  2. Recurring obligations include housing expense (PITI), installment debts (such as car loans), revolving debts (such as credit cards), and other debts (such as alimony and child support).

  3. Housing expense to income ratio: proposed housing expense (PITI) generally should not exceed 28% of stable monthly income.

  4. The smaller of the two ratios is usually the maximum allowable mortgage payment.

5. 36% and 28% aren't strict maximums; compensating factors such as a large downpayment or a substantial net worth may give the lender a reason to allow higher ratios.

6. For loans with an LTV over 90%, most lenders won't accept ratios higher than 36% or 28% without especially strong compensating factors.

7. ARM borrowers may receive greater scrutiny because of the risk of payment shock; lenders may require borrowers to qualify under the maximum interest rate that could be in effect at the end of the loan's introductory period.

D. Available funds

1. Gift funds can be used for most of downpayment and closing costs, but borrowers generally must pay at least 5% of the sales price out of their own resources, unless LTV is 80% or less.

2. Reserves

a. Fannie Mae and Freddie Mac no longer have specific reserve requirements, although reserves can be an important compensating factor.

b. Some lenders still require borrowers to have two months' payments in reserve after making the downpayment and closing costs; some lenders require more.

IV. Making Conventional Loans More Affordable

A. Buydown lowers interest rate permanently or temporarily.

1. Temporary buydown may have level or graduated payments.

2. Fannie Mae and Freddie Mac limit how much a seller or other interested party can contribute for buyer.

B. Loans with lower initial payments: hybrid ARMs, two-step loans, balloon/reset loans, interest-only loans.

C. Low downpayment programs: high-LTV conventional loans; affordable housing programs with eligibility based on income, property location, or job.

D. Accelerated payment plans: bi-weekly mortgages and growing-equity mortgages (GEMs).

Key Terms

Conventional loan: An institutional loan that is not insured or guaranteed by a government agency.

Conforming loan: A loan made in accordance with the standardized underwriting criteria of the major secondary market agencies, Fannie Mae and Freddie Mac, and which therefore can be sold to those agencies.

Nonconforming loan: A loan that does not meet the underwriting guidelines set by Fannie Mae and Freddie Mac, and therefore can't be sold to those agencies except by special arrangement.

Investor loan: A loan issued for the purchase of property that will be rented to tenants rather than owner-occupied.

Jumbo loan: A loan that exceeds the conforming loan limits set annually by Fannie Mae and Freddie Mac based on national median housing prices.

Loan-to-value ratio (LTV): The relationship between the loan amount and either the sales price or the appraised value of the property (whichever is less), expressed as a percentage.

Private mortgage insurance (PMI): Insurance used to diminish the risk of high-LTV conventional loans; provided by a private insurance company (instead of a government agency).

Homeowners Protection Act: A federal law that requires lenders to eliminate private mortgage insurance payments at the borrower's request when the loan balance reaches 80% of the original property value, or to automatically cancel the PMI when the loan balance reaches 78% of the original property value.

Secondary financing: Money borrowed to pay part of the required downpayment or closing costs for a first loan, when the second loan is secured by the same property that secures the first loan.

Piggyback loan: Secondary financing used to avoid the payment of private mortgage insurance by keeping the primary loan's loan-to-value ratio at 80% or less, or used to avoid the higher interest rate a jumbo loan would require.

Debt to income ratio: A figure used in loan underwriting to measure the adequacy of the applicant's income; states in percentage terms how much of the applicant's stable monthly income would be required to make all the monthly payments on the applicant's debts and other liabilities plus the proposed housing expense.

Recurring obligations: Financial obligations that a borrower must meet each month, including housing expense, installment debts, revolving debts, and other obligations.

Buydown: When the seller or a third party pays the lender a lump sum at closing to lower the interest rate charged on the buyer's loan.

Permanent buydown: A buydown that lowers the loan's interest rate for the entire term.

Temporary buydown: A buydown that lowers the loan's interest rate for only the first few years of the term; the monthly payments during the buydown period may be level or graduated.

Two-step mortgage: A loan that allows the lender to adjust the loan's interest rate to the market level at one point during the loan term, such as a 5/25 plan where the interest rate is adjusted once after five years.

Balloon/reset mortgage: A loan with an initial term of only five or seven years; at the end of the term, the loan may be reset, or a balloon payment will be required.

Interest-only mortgage: A loan that allows the buyer to pay only interest during the first part of the loan term.

Affordable housing program: A loan program that features easier qualifying standards and lower downpayment requirements, with eligibility limited to buyers who have low or moderate incomes or are purchasing property in a targeted neighborhood.

Bi-weekly mortgage: A loan that requires a payment every two weeks instead of once a month; the borrower makes the equivalent of 13 payments per year, and thus pays the loan off early and saves a considerable amount in interest.

Growing equity mortgage (GEM): A fixed-rate loan with annual payment increases that are used to reduce the principal balance, so that the loan is paid off much more quickly than it would be with ordinary level payments.

Chapter Quiz

1. A buydown plan:
    a. helps lower the buyer's initial monthly mortgage payments
    b. may help the buyer qualify for the loan
    c. is a plan in which a party pays a lump sum to the lender up front to reduce the loan's interest rate
    d. All of the above

2. One major advantage of a bi-weekly loan is that:
    a. the interest rate is usually higher
    b. equity builds more quickly
    c. payments are lower during the first two years
    d. interest costs are the same as for a fixed-rate loan

3. Private mortgage insurance is ordinarily required only if the loan-to-value ratio is:
    a. 75% or higher
    b. 90% or higher
    c. over 95%
    d. over 80%

4. As a general rule, a buyer who is seeking a 90% loan:
    a. must make a 10% downpayment from his own funds
    b. must make a 5% downpayment from his own funds
    c. may use secondary financing to come up with the additional 10% of the purchase price
    d. can expect to pay a higher interest rate than he would for a 95% loan

5. The Turinos are applying for an 80% loan. Unless there are compensating factors, their debt to income ratio should not exceed:
    a. 25%
    b. 28%
    c. 36%
    d. 33%

6. Jamison is applying for a 90% conventional loan. Which of the following is a compensating factor that might justify loan approval in spite of income ratios that are slightly higher than the standard limits?

   a. Jamison will have one month's mortgage payment in reserve at closing
   b. Her parents are providing gift funds for 5% of the downpayment
   c. She is a first-time home buyer
   d. She has strong potential for increased earnings and advancement at work

7. Shaw is applying for a 90% conventional loan. His stable monthly income is $2,950. His recurring monthly debts total $375. In the absence of any compensating factors, what is the maximum monthly mortgage payment he will qualify for?

   a. $826
   b. $687
   c. $784
   d. $912

8. A 2-1 buydown plan calls for:

   a. the interest rate to be bought down by 1% for two years
   b. the seller and the broker to buy down the interest rate by 1%
   c. the interest rate to be bought down by 2% the first year and 1% the second year
   d. the interest rate to be bought down by 1% the first year and 2% the second year

9. A conventional lender will take an installment debt into consideration when calculating income ratios:

   a. only if it has more than twelve payments remaining
   b. only if it has more than ten payments remaining
   c. no matter how many payments remain to be made
   d. only if the borrower has a poor credit history

10. Secondary financing used in conjunction with a conventional loan may be:
    a. partially amortized with a balloon payment
    b. fully amortized
    c. interest-only
    d. Any of the above

Answer Key

1. d. In a buydown, a seller or third party pays a lump sum to a lender to reduce the borrower's interest rate. This lowers the borrower's initial payment amount and makes it easier for the borrower to qualify.

2. b. A bi-weekly loan allows equity to build more quickly, since the borrower makes the equivalent of 13 monthly payments per year.

3. d. Private mortgage insurance is usually required for loans with an LTV over 80%.

4. b. A borrower seeking a 90% loan generally must make a downpayment of at least 5% out of her own funds, even if using gift funds.

5. c. For most conventional 80% loans, the maximum debt to income ratio will be 36%, absent any compensating factors.

6. d. A potential compensating factor for a person whose income ratio is slightly higher than allowable limits would be the potential for increased future earnings.

7. b. To calculate the maximum monthly mortgage payment, multiply the stable monthly income by the debt to income ratio ($2,950 × .36 = $1,062) and then subtract any recurring monthly obligations ($1,062 − $375 = $687).

8. c. The 2-1 buydown plan is a temporary buydown where the interest rate is reduced 2% in the first year and 1% in the second year.

9. b. An installment debt will be considered when calculating income ratios only if more than ten months' payments remain.

10. d. Secondary financing used in conjunction with a conventional loan may be fully or partially amortized, or interest-only. Certain restrictions may apply, such as requiring scheduled payments and not allowing a balloon payment within the first five years.

Case Study:
Conventional Financing

Rick and Teresa Cortina are thinking of buying their first home. Based on the financial information shown below, answer the questions that follow. There are worksheets at the end of the case study that you can use for the calculations.

Current housing expense

The Cortinas have lived in the same rental house for five years; for the past two years, their rent has been $2,300 per month.

Employment

Teresa has been a paralegal at Tarman & Andrews, a law firm, for two and a half years. Rick has been a sales manager at Acme Tire, Inc. for four years.

Income

Rick earns a monthly salary of $1,600, plus commissions. His commissions have averaged $1,990 per month for the past two years. Teresa earns $20.35 per hour for a full-time (40-hour) work week.

Taxes (monthly figures)

Rick's taxes:
- Federal income taxes: $380
- State income taxes: $145
- Social Security/Medicare: $204

Teresa's taxes:
- Federal income taxes: $375
- State income taxes: $141
- Social Security/Medicare: $218

Credit scores from the three major agencies

Rick: 669, 678, 682

Teresa: 730, 730, 738

Assets

- Savings account: $58,000
- Miscellaneous (cars, jewelry, etc.): $42,000

Liabilities (monthly payments)

- Car loan: $278 (30 payments remaining)
- Car loan: $215 (17 payments remaining)
- Installment contract: $122 (15 payments remaining)
- Credit cards: $110 (minimum payments)
- Student loan: $65 (8 payments remaining)
- Student loan: $103 (12 payments remaining)

Interest rates and fees (30-year conventional loans)

Lenders are typically charging the following rates and fees in the Cortinas' area:

Fixed-rate loans

LTV 90% or less: 5.50% interest

LTV over 90%: 6.00% interest

ARMs

LTV 90% or less: 5.70% interest

LTV over 90%: currently unavailable in the Cortinas' area

Discount points

With either a fixed-rate loan or an ARM, if discount points are paid, each point will reduce the interest rate by one-quarter of one percent (0.25%).

Loan fees

For a conventional loan, borrowers will pay an origination fee, an adverse market delivery charge, and one or more loan-level price adjustments.

1. Which of the Cortinas' credit scores will be treated as the indictor score (representative score) for underwriting purposes?

2. What's their stable monthly income? (Round the answer down to the next dollar.)

3. Suppose the Cortinas are getting preapproved for a conventional loan. What's the maximum monthly principal and interest payment they could expect to qualify for in each of the following cases? Assume that 15% of their total mortgage payment will go toward property taxes and hazard insurance. If mortgage insurance is required, assume that an additional 10% of their total mortgage payment will be used for that. (These percentages provide only a very rough approximation for the purposes of this exercise.)

   a) They're preapproved for Loan A, a fixed-rate loan with an 80% LTV.

  b) They're preapproved for Loan B, an ARM with a 90% LTV.

  c) They're preapproved for Loan C, a fixed-rate loan with a 95% LTV.

4. With the maximum principal and interest payments you calculated for Question 3, the Cortinas could qualify for the maximum loan amounts indicated below.

  For each loan, state the interest rate that would be charged, taking any discount points into account. (Refer back to the rates listed at the beginning of the case study; each point reduces the listed rate by 0.25%.)

  Then use the loan-to-value ratio to calculate an estimated house price: the sales price they could afford to pay with the maximum loan amount plus the corresponding minimum downpayment. For example, a $180,000 loan with a 90% LTV and a 10% downpayment would make it possible to buy a $200,000 house: $180,000 ÷ .90 = $200,000.

  a) Loan A: fixed rate, 80% LTV; no discount points will be paid.
    Maximum loan amount: $265,580

  b) Loan B: ARM, 90% LTV; two discount points will be paid.
    Maximum loan amount: $252,645

  c) Loan C: fixed rate, 95% LTV; three discount points will be paid.
    Maximum loan amount: $251,230

Credit Score/LTV Loan-Level Price Adjustments for Case Study				
	Loan-to-Value Ratio			
Indicator Credit Score	75.01% to 80%	80.01% to 85%	85.01% to 90%	90.01% to 95%
740 or above	0.00%	0.00%	0.00%	0.00%
720-739	0.25%	0.00%	0.00%	0.00%
700-719	0.75%	0.50%	0.50%	0.50%
680-699	1.50%	1.00%	0.75%	0.75%
660-679	2.50%	2.25%	1.75%	1.75%
	LLPAs are a percentage of the loan amount.			

5. Now calculate how much cash would be needed at closing for each of the transactions in Question 4. To determine the LLPA percentage(s) that apply in each case, use the chart above and the indicator score selected in Question 1.

Add together the downpayment, origination fee, adverse market delivery charge, and loan-level price adjustment(s). Use 3% of the sales price as an estimate of the rest of the closing costs; add that to the other charges. Also add two months of mortgage payments (PITI) as reserves. For each transaction, do the Cortinas have enough cash to qualify?

a) Loan A, the 80% fixed-rate loan, with no discount points.
- Origination fee: 1.50%
- Adverse market delivery charge: 0.25%
- Loan-level price adjustment based on credit score and LTV (see chart)

b) Loan B, the 90% ARM, with two discount points.
- Origination fee: 1.50%
- Adverse market delivery charge: 0.25%
- Loan-level price adjustments: LLPA based on credit score and LTV (see chart), plus 0.25% LLPA charged because the loan is an ARM

c) Loan C, the 95% fixed-rate loan, with three discount points.
- Origination fee: 2.00%
- Adverse market delivery charge: 0.25%
- Loan-level price adjustment based on credit score and LTV (see chart)

6. The Cortinas would rather not get an ARM; they don't want to be faced with interest rate and payment increases down the road. They also don't like the idea of a 95% fixed-rate loan; they'd rather make a larger investment in the property and spend less on loan costs. And the $265,580 fixed-rate loan with an 80% LTV requires too much cash at closing. So the Cortinas are looking for alternatives to the three loans we've been considering.

a) Suppose the Cortinas get a 90% fixed-rate loan instead of an ARM. How would that compare to the 90% ARM? (You can just consider this in general terms; it's not necessary to do specific calculations.) Assume that they will pay one discount point on the fixed-rate loan (compared to two points with the ARM), so the interest rate will be 0.25% below the ordinary fixed interest rate.

b) What if the Cortinas get an 80% fixed-rate loan, but purchase a house that costs considerably less than $331,975? For example, suppose they wanted to buy a house for $265,000. Could they qualify for an 80% fixed-rate loan to make that purchase? (You'll be able to answer this question just by calculating the downpayment and 3% of the sales price for an estimate of closing costs; calculations involving the monthly payment amount or the loan fees won't be necessary.)

7. Finally, suppose that the Cortinas have found a house they really want to buy. It's priced at $300,000. The sellers just put the property on the market, so they aren't willing to sell it for less than the listing price or negotiate about points or other financing concessions. If the Cortinas got a 90% fixed-rate loan at 5.25% with one discount point, their PITI payment would be $1,863.69 and they'd need about $55,000 in cash.

    a)   What are the Cortinas' income ratios with this PITI payment?

    b)   Are there any compensating factors in the Cortinas' financial circumstances that might help them qualify for the 90% loan and buy this house? Refer back to the information given at the beginning of the case study.

    c)   On the other hand, are there any risk factors in the Cortinas' situation that might make a lender reluctant to approve a conventional loan with a debt to income ratio over 36%?

    d)   If the lender won't approve this loan for the Cortinas, what steps could they take that might still make it possible for them to buy this house?

Income Qualifying—Conventional Loans
Loan A: Fixed Interest Rate, 80% Loan-to-Value Ratio

Stable Monthly Income

Base salary

    Wage earner 1 _____

    Wage earner 2 _____

Overtime _____

Commissions _____

Bonuses _____

Other   + _____

Total _____

Recurring Obligations

Car loans _____

Credit cards _____

Student loans _____

Other debts _____

Child support _____

Alimony _____

Other   + _____

Total _____

Debt to Income Ratio

_____   Stable monthly income

_____ x .36   Maximum ratio (36%)

_____   Maximum obligations

_____ −   Recurring obligations

_____   Maximum mortgage payment (PITI) under debt to income ratio

Housing Expense to Income Ratio

_____   Stable monthly income

_____ x .28   Maximum ratio (28%)

_____   Maximum mortgage payment (PITI) under housing expense ratio

Maximum Mortgage Payment (PITI) _____

_____   Maximum PITI payment

_____ ÷ 1.15   15% for taxes and hazard insurance

_____   Maximum principal and interest payment

Interest rate _____

Maximum Loan Amount _____

_____   Maximum loan amount

_____ ÷ .80   Loan-to-value ratio (80%)

_____   Sales price

Sales Price _____

Income Qualifying—Conventional Loans
Loan B: Adjustable Interest Rate, 90% Loan-to-Value Ratio

Stable Monthly Income

Base salary

    Wage earner 1 _____

    Wage earner 2 _____

Overtime _____

Commissions _____

Bonuses _____

Other   + _____

Total _____

Recurring Obligations

Car loans _____

Credit cards _____

Student loans _____

Other debts _____

Child support _____

Alimony _____

Other   + _____

Total _____

Debt to Income Ratio

_____   Stable monthly income

_____ x .36   Maximum ratio (36%)

_____   Maximum obligations

_____ −   Recurring obligations

_____   Maximum mortgage payment (PITI) under debt to income ratio

Housing Expense to Income Ratio

_____   Stable monthly income

_____ x .28   Maximum ratio (28%)

_____   Maximum mortgage payment (PITI) under housing expense ratio

Maximum Mortgage Payment (PITI) _____

_____   Maximum PITI payment

_____ ÷ 1.25   25% for taxes, hazard insurance, and PMI

_____   Maximum principal and interest payment

Interest rate _____

Maximum Loan Amount _____

_____   Maximum loan amount

_____ ÷ .90   Loan-to-value ratio (90%)

_____   Sales price

Sales Price _____

Income Qualifying—Conventional Loans
Loan C: Fixed Interest Rate, 95% Loan-to-Value Ratio

Stable Monthly Income

Base salary

Wage earner 1 _____

Wage earner 2 _____

Overtime _____

Commissions _____

Bonuses _____

Other + _____

Total _____

Recurring Obligations

Car loans _____

Credit cards _____

Student loans _____

Other debts _____

Child support _____

Alimony _____

Other + _____

Total _____

Debt to Income Ratio

_____ Stable monthly income

_____ x .36 Maximum ratio (36%)

_____ Maximum obligations

_____ − Recurring obligations

_____ Maximum mortgage payment (PITI) under debt to income ratio

Housing Expense to Income Ratio

_____ Stable monthly income

_____ x .28 Maximum ratio (28%)

_____ Maximum mortgage payment (PITI) under housing expense ratio

Maximum Mortgage Payment (PITI) _____

_____ Maximum PITI payment

_____ ÷ 1.25 25% for taxes, hazard insurance, and PMI

_____ Maximum principal and interest payment

Interest rate _____

Maximum Loan Amount _____

_____ Maximum loan amount

_____ ÷ .95 Loan-to-value ratio (95%)

_____ Sales price

Sales Price _____

Chapter 11
FHA-Insured Loans

An Overview of FHA Loans

- FHA mortgage insurance
- The role of FHA loans
- FHA loan programs

Rules for FHA-Financed Transactions

- Owner-occupancy requirement
- Local maximum loan amounts
- Minimum cash investment and LTV
- Loan charges and closing costs
- Sales concessions
- Secondary financing
- Property flipping prevention rules
- Assumption

FHA Insurance Premiums

- Upfront premium
- Annual premiums
- Risk-based premiums

FHA Underwriting Standards

- Credit reputation
- Income analysis
- Assets for closing

FHA Rehabilitation Loans and Reverse Mortgages (HECMs)

Introduction

In Chapter 10 we discussed conventional loans: institutional loans that are not insured or guaranteed by a government agency. Now we'll look at institutional loans that have government backing.

The federal government has two major home financing programs: the FHA-insured loan program and the VA-guaranteed loan program. These programs were established to encourage residential lending and make housing more affordable, and are available to eligible home buyers throughout the United States. This chapter covers the FHA program; we'll discuss VA-guaranteed loans in Chapter 12.

There are other federal programs that provide home financing, such as the Rural Housing Service loan program, but those are much more limited in scope than the FHA and VA programs. Also, many state, county, and city governments offer financing programs for their own residents. These local options are sometimes called "bond programs." Although we're only going to cover the two main federal programs here, you may want to take the time to find out whether there are other government-sponsored financing programs available to home buyers in your area.

An Overview of FHA Loans

The Federal Housing Administration (FHA) was created by Congress in 1934, during the Great Depression, with the passage of the National Housing Act. The purpose of the act, and of the FHA, was to generate new jobs through increased construction activity, to exert a stabilizing influence on the mortgage market, and to promote the financing, repair, improvement, and sale of residential real estate nationwide.

FHA:
- Insures loans
- Does not make loans itself

Today the FHA is part of the Department of Housing and Urban Development (HUD). The FHA's primary function is to insure mortgage loans; lenders who make loans through its programs are compensated for losses that result from borrower default. The FHA does not build homes or make loans.

FHA Mortgage Insurance

The FHA's insurance program, the Mutual Mortgage Insurance Plan, is funded with premiums paid by FHA borrowers. Under the plan, lenders who have been approved by the FHA to make insured loans either submit applications from prospective borrowers to the local FHA office for approval or, if authorized by the FHA to do so, perform the underwriting functions themselves. (Note that prospective borrowers always apply to an FHA-approved lender, not to the FHA itself.)

Lenders who are authorized to underwrite their own FHA loan applications are called **direct endorsement lenders**. Direct endorsement lenders are responsible for the entire lending process, from application through closing. When a direct endorsement lender has approved and closed a loan, the application for mortgage insurance is submitted to the FHA.

> Direct endorsement lenders: lenders authorized to handle entire underwriting process for FHA loans

As the insurer, the FHA is liable to the lender for the full amount of any losses resulting from default and foreclosure. After the FHA has compensated the lender, however, the borrower must reimburse the federal government for the amount paid. This liability is considered a delinquent federal debt, which means that the government can collect it out of any federal income tax refund owed to the borrower, or garnish any pay the borrower receives from the federal government. Unless the borrower enters into an agreement to repay the debt, he won't be eligible for another FHA-insured loan (or for a VA-guaranteed loan).

> If FHA borrower defaults:
> • FHA reimburses lender for full amount of loss
> • Borrower required to repay FHA

In exchange for insuring loans, the FHA requires lenders to follow certain procedures and dictates many of the terms and conditions on which the loans are made. Lenders must comply with FHA regulations, which have the force and effect of law. If the FHA pays a lender's claim after a borrower defaults, and it's later determined that the loan didn't actually meet FHA standards, the lender can be required to reimburse the government. The lender may also lose its authorization to make FHA loans and could face prosecution for fraud.

The Role of FHA Loans

FHA-insured loans are designed to help people with low or moderate incomes buy homes. The program doesn't have income restrictions, so eligibility isn't limited to borrowers whose incomes are under a certain limit. But it does have restrictions on loan amounts, and the maximum loan amounts are generally only enough to finance comparatively modest homes. In addition, the FHA has always had low downpayment requirements, lenient underwriting standards,

> FHA-insured loans are designed for low- and moderate-income buyers

and other policies that help first-time buyers and others who might otherwise have difficulty affording a home.

For much of the twentieth century, FHA loans were the main financing option for home buyers who didn't have a lot of savings or a substantial income. But in the first years of this century, during the subprime boom, buyers lost interest in FHA loans. Conventional underwriting standards were loosened, and buyers with very little cash for closing could get conventional loans. At the same time, home prices increased so dramatically in some parts of the country that FHA loans were no longer useful there; the maximum loan amount wasn't enough to finance the purchase of even a modest home.

These developments led to a sharp reduction in the use of FHA programs. FHA loans financed about 15% of existing home sales in the U.S. in fiscal year 2000, but only 3.5% in 2006.

Now, however, low-downpayment conventional loans are no longer widely available and easy to qualify for. Also, FHA maximum loan amounts for high-cost areas were significantly increased in 2008. As a result, buyers with tight budgets and limited funds for a downpayment have once again been turning to FHA-insured loans. In fiscal year 2008, the market share of FHA loans rebounded to nearly 12% of existing home sales.

FHA Loan Programs

FHA financing includes several specific loan programs that address different needs. These programs are commonly referred to by their section numbers, which are taken from the numbered provisions in the National Housing Act. Here are the FHA programs that are of the most interest to the average home buyer or owner:

Most FHA loans are 203(b) loans

- **Section 203(b): Standard FHA Loans.** The 203(b) program is the basic FHA mortgage insurance program; it accounts for a substantial majority of all FHA-insured loans. A loan made through the 203(b) program can be used to purchase or refinance a residential property with up to four dwelling units. The property must be the borrower's principal residence. The 203(b) program is our primary focus in this chapter.

- **Section 203(k): Rehabilitation Loans.** The 203(k) program insures loans that are used to purchase (or refinance) and then rehabilitate "fixer-uppers." We'll discuss 203(k) loans in more detail later in the chapter.

- **Section 234(c): Condominium Units.** The 234(c) program covers the purchase or refinancing of individual condominium units. It works in tandem with other programs, such as 203(b).

   Originally only units in FHA-approved condominium projects were eligible for FHA financing; developers who wanted approval would ordinarily apply for it when projects were built or converted. Later the "spot loan" procedure was developed, making it possible to get an FHA loan for a unit in a project that wasn't approved, as long as it met certain criteria. Based on a provision in the 2008 Housing and Economic Recovery Act, it appears that the FHA is planning to simplify the process of obtaining FHA financing for individual condominium units.

- **Section 251: ARMs.** Section 251 provides mortgage insurance for adjustable-rate loans. It's administered in conjunction with either the 203(b) or the 203(k) program, so an FHA ARM may be used to purchase, refinance, or rehabilitate a principal residence with up to four units. The loan must have a 30-year term; the FHA won't insure ARMs with shorter terms.

   An FHA ARM may be a one-year ARM, with annual interest rate adjustments from the outset. An FHA ARM may also be a hybrid ARM, with an initial fixed-rate period; 3/1, 5/1, 7/1, or 10/1 plans are allowed (see Chapter 6). One-year ARMs and 3/1 and 5/1 hybrids have a 1% annual interest rate cap and a 5% life-of-the-loan rate cap. For 7/1 and 10/1 hybrids, the annual cap is 2% and the life-of-the-loan cap is 6%.

   A special underwriting rule applies to one-year FHA ARMs with a loan-to-value ratio of 95% or above. For those loans, the applicant is qualified using the initial interest rate plus 1%—in other words, using the maximum possible second-year interest rate. (In contrast, applicants for hybrid ARMs are qualified using the initial interest rate.)

- **Section 255: Reverse Mortgages (HECMs).** Section 255 provides FHA insurance for home equity conversion mortgages (HECMs), also known as reverse mortgages (see Chapter 5). We'll take a closer look at the HECM program later in the chapter.

FHA loan programs:
- 203(b) – standard FHA loans
- 203(k) – rehab loans
- 234(c) – condos
- 251 – ARMs
- 255 – reverse mortgages

For the most part, we'll be discussing the rules for standard FHA purchase loans made through the 203(b) program. Many of those rules also apply to the other programs, which are largely based on 203(b).

Rules for FHA-Financed Transactions

When a home purchase is financed with an FHA-insured loan, the transaction must comply with the FHA's rules concerning owner-occupancy, the loan amount, the borrower's cash investment, sales concessions, secondary financing, property flipping, and assumption.

Owner-Occupancy Requirement

FHA borrowers must intend to occupy the property they're buying. As a general rule, the property must be used as the borrower's principal residence. If the property has more than one dwelling unit, the borrower is required to use one of the units as her principal residence.

A person can have only one principal residence at a time, so this requirement means that a borrower can ordinarily have only one FHA loan outstanding at a time. There are limited exceptions for situations involving relocation, divorce, or an increase in family size.

General rule: FHA borrower must intend to occupy home as principal residence

Secondary Residences. A secondary residence is a home the borrower occupies less than 50% of the time. An FHA loan can be used to buy a secondary residence only if denial of the loan would cause undue hardship. The secondary residence must be needed for employment-related reasons; it can't be a vacation home. And the borrower must show that there is no suitable rental housing available in the area.

Investor Loans. Although it did so at one time, the FHA generally does not insure investor loans—loans that allow the borrower to buy the property merely as an investment, not as a home. The FHA may make an exception for an investor who wants to purchase a property that HUD owns as a result of foreclosure.

Local Maximum Loan Amounts

As we said earlier, the FHA limits the size of loans that it will insure. FHA maximum loan amounts are based on local median house prices, so they vary from one area to another. Each area has local maximums for one-, two-, three-, and four-unit residences. The maximums are higher in areas where home prices are above average.

Fig. 11.1 Maximum loan amounts vary based on local median housing costs

2009 FHA Maximum Loan Amounts		
Number of Units	Basic Maximum Loan Amount	Maximum Loan Amount in High Cost Areas [†]
1	$271,050	125% of median price, up to $729,750
2	$347,000	125% of median price, up to $934,200
3	$419,400	125% of median price, up to $1,129,250
4	$521,250	125% of median price, up to $1,403,400

[†] In Alaska, Hawaii, Guam, and the Virgin Islands, the 2009 ceilings are $1,094,625 for one unit; $1,401,300 for two units; $1,693,875 for three units; and $2,105,100 for four units.

The FHA's maximum loan amounts are tied to the conforming loan limits—the maximum loan amounts set annually by the secondary market agencies for the conventional loans they buy (see Chapter 10). Like the conforming loan limits, the FHA local maximums are subject to annual adjustments, to reflect changes in housing costs.

Under current rules, the basic maximum for FHA loans is 65% of Freddie Mac's general conforming loan limit. In 2009, the general conforming loan limit for a one-unit property is $417,000. That means the FHA's basic maximum loan amount for a one-unit property is $271,050 ($417,000 × .65 = $271,050). This is the maximum FHA loan amount anywhere in the country that doesn't qualify as a high-cost area.

Local maximum loan amount:
- Based on local median housing costs
- Changes periodically

In places where housing is more expensive than average, the $271,050 limit doesn't apply. In a high-cost area, the FHA may increase the maximum loan amount up to 125% of the area median house price. Regardless of prices, however, the FHA may not set the maximum loan amount in any area higher than 175% of the conforming loan limit. The FHA refers to this as the "ceiling."

Thus, when Freddie Mac's conforming loan limit for one-unit properties is $417,000, the FHA ceiling for one-unit properties in high-cost areas is $729,750 ($417,000 × 1.75 = $729,750). A higher ceiling, $1,094,625, applies in Alaska, Hawaii, Guam, and the Virgin Islands. Figure 11.1 shows the FHA's basic and high-cost loan limits for 2009.

Fig. 11.2 Example illustrating the FHA's rules for local maximum loan amounts

Location	Median House Price	2009 Maximum FHA Loan for Single-family Homes
Lowood	$152,000	$271,050 (basic maximum)
Anytown	$268,400	$271,050 (basic maximum)
Midville	$314,700	$393,375 (125% of median price)
Highline	$529,300	$661,625 (125% of median price)
Goldenvale	$812,609	$729,750 (ceiling for high-cost areas)

Figure 11.2 shows how the rules for local maximum loan amounts would apply to hypothetical places with various median housing costs. In Lowood, where housing prices are comparatively low, the FHA's basic maximum loan amount (65% of the conforming loan limit) would apply. It would also apply in Anytown, where prices are somewhat higher but don't exceed the basic maximum. Midville and Highline are high-cost areas where the maximum is 125% of the median price in each area. In the most expensive location, Goldenvale, the maximum is set at the FHA's upper limit for high-cost areas. In Goldenvale, 125% of the median price would be $1,015,761, far above the FHA's ceiling ($729,750).

HUD usually sets maximum loan amounts on a county-by-county basis. As a result, if a county includes a large city where housing is expensive, the entire county is treated as a high-cost area, even if housing in its rural sections is relatively inexpensive. Sometimes an extensive metropolitan area will be treated as a single high-cost area, even if it overlaps county lines.

Check with a local lender for the current FHA maximum loan amount in your community. Keep in mind that the limit may be adjusted periodically to reflect changes in the cost of housing. To get the maximum loan amount for a particular area increased, lenders or other interested parties submit a request to HUD with recent sales price data supporting an increase.

Minimum Cash Investment and LTV

An FHA borrower is required to make a downpayment of at least 3.5% of the property's appraised value or sales price, whichever is less. This is called the borrower's **minimum cash investment**.

Because of this requirement, the maximum loan-to-value ratio for an FHA loan is 96.5%. There used to be more complicated LTV rules for FHA loans, but those have been eliminated.

Although certain closing costs paid by the borrower used to count toward the minimum cash investment, they no longer do. Discount points the borrower is paying also don't count; neither do "prepaid expenses," which include interim interest on the loan and impounds for property taxes and hazard insurance. The borrower must come up with the minimum cash investment in addition to the funds needed for closing costs, discount points, and prepaid expenses.

The borrower is not allowed to use secondary financing from the seller or a lender for the minimum cash investment, but may be allowed to use funds provided by a family member or certain other sources. We'll discuss these rules later in this chapter, in the section on secondary financing.

Exercise No. 1

Jerry Fletcher has agreed to pay $647,500 for a single-family home that he will occupy as his principal residence. It has been appraised at $648,700. Fletcher would like to finance the transaction with an FHA loan. He lives in a high-cost county where the area median house price is $540,000.

1. What's the 2009 maximum FHA loan amount for a one-unit property in Fletcher's area? (Refer to the chart in Figure 11.1.)

2. If Fletcher gets an FHA loan for this purchase, how much will the required minimum cash investment be?

3. What is the maximum FHA loan amount for Fletcher's transaction?

Loan Charges and Closing Costs

The FHA used to place significant restrictions on the charges that could be imposed on borrowers, but most of those restrictions have been eliminated over time. For example, years ago the FHA used to set a maximum interest rate, and borrowers were prohibited from paying discount points. (Any discount points charged had to be paid by the seller or a third party.) Now the interest rate for an FHA loan is freely negotiable between the lender and the borrower, just as it is with a conventional loan. Discount points, also negotiable, can be paid by any party.

Until quite recently, the FHA limited the origination fee for most loans to 1%, but now that restriction has been removed as well.

Also, at one time FHA borrowers could be charged only for those services and expenses that appeared on an FHA list of allowable closing costs. Now borrowers are permitted to pay whatever closing costs are "customary and reasonable" in their local area. A lender may not charge a borrower more for a service than it actually cost the lender.

The FHA's long-standing rule prohibiting prepayment penalties is still in force. FHA loans may be paid off at any time without penalty. However, unless the prepayment is made on or before the first of the month (the due date for ordinary payments), the lender can require the borrower to pay the full month's interest.

Sales Concessions and FHA Loans

As you know, sometimes a seller pays for a buydown, or pays all or part of the buyer's closing costs, or makes some other type of financial contribution to help the buyer afford the property. When a transaction is financed with an FHA loan, the FHA places certain restrictions on these sales concessions. The restrictions also apply if an interested party other than the seller—for example, the seller's real estate broker, or the subdivision developer—makes any contribution to help the buyer. The basic purpose of these restrictions is to prevent the parties from using contributions to defeat the FHA's maximum loan-to-value ratio and minimum cash investment rules.

FHA limits amount seller or other interested party can contribute to buyer in transaction

The FHA classifies contributions either as seller contributions or as inducements to purchase, and treats the two types differently.

Seller Contributions. The FHA considers it to be a seller contribution if the seller (or another interested party) pays for part or all of:

- the buyer's closing costs or prepaid expenses;
- any discount points;
- a temporary or permanent buydown;
- the buyer's mortgage interest; or
- the upfront premium for the FHA mortgage insurance.

Temporary buydowns are allowed in connection with fixed-rate FHA loans, but the buyer must qualify at the note rate. So even if a buydown brings the interest rate down from 8% to 6% in the first year, the buyer would still be required to qualify for the loan at 8%.

Seller contributions are limited to 6% of the sales price. Any contributions in excess of 6% are treated as inducements to purchase, and are deducted from the sales price in the loan amount calculations.

If seller contributions exceed 6% of sales price, excess is subtracted from sales price in base loan calculations

> **Example:** The Johanssons are buying a home for $254,000 and financing the purchase with an FHA loan. The seller has agreed to pay the lender $16,000 to buy down the interest rate on the Johanssons' loan. Six percent of the sales price is $15,240, so the buydown is $760 over the 6% limit on seller contributions ($16,000 − $15,240 = $760). The $760 excess seller contribution will be treated as an inducement to purchase.

Fees and closing costs that sellers typically pay as a matter of local custom aren't treated as seller contributions. For example, real estate commissions and pest inspection charges don't count toward the 6% limit if they're customarily paid by the seller.

Keep in mind that the 6% limit applies only to contributions from the seller or another interested party. FHA borrowers are allowed to pay discount points to their lenders to buy down their own interest rates. Points paid by the borrower may exceed 6% of the sales price without making it necessary to deduct the excess from the price.

Inducements to Purchase. In addition to seller contributions that exceed 6% of the sales price, other types of payments may also be deemed inducements to purchase. For example, the FHA considers it to be an inducement to purchase if the seller (or another interested party):

- gives the buyer a decorating or repair allowance;
- pays for the buyer's moving expenses;
- pays the buyer's agent a larger commission than is customary in the local area;
- pays the real estate agent's commission on the sale of the buyer's current home; or
- gives the buyer items of personal property other than those that are customarily included in the sale of a home.

Inducements to purchase are subtracted from sales price before LTV ratio is applied

The total value of any inducements to purchase is subtracted from the property's sales price, on a dollar-for-dollar basis, before the maximum loan-to-value ratio is applied. This reduces the loan amount available to the FHA borrower.

Example: Returning to the previous example, suppose that the seller has also agreed to give the Johanssons $1,000 toward their moving costs. This $1,000 and the $760 excess in seller contributions are considered inducements to purchase, and they're subtracted from the property's sales price before the maximum loan amount is calculated.

$254,000	Sales price
− 1,760	Inducements to purchase
$252,240	Adjusted sales price
× .965	Maximum loan-to-value ratio (96.5%)
$243,411	Maximum loan amount

The maximum loan amount based on the adjusted sales price is $243,411. That's $1,699 less than the $245,110 loan amount the Johanssons would have had without the inducements to purchase ($254,000 × .965 = $245,110), and they'll have to increase their downpayment by that same amount. As a result, they won't benefit much from the inducements to purchase. However, they will benefit from the $15,240 in seller contributions that didn't exceed the 6% limit.

Secondary Financing with FHA Loans

As you'll recall, secondary financing refers to a loan secured by a second mortgage against the same property that is being purchased with a first mortgage. The rules concerning secondary financing in conjunction with an FHA loan depend on whether the secondary financing is being used for the minimum cash investment, or simply as a supplement to make up the permitted maximum loan amount.

Secondary Financing and the Cash Investment. An FHA borrower generally is not allowed to use secondary financing from the seller, another interested party, or an institutional lender to pay the required minimum cash investment. However, secondary financing may be used to cover the minimum cash investment if it is provided by a member of the borrower's family (a child, parent, or grandparent of the borrower or of the borrower's spouse). Closing costs, prepaid expenses, and discount points may also be financed by a family member.

When a family member provides this kind of secondary financing, the total financing (the combined first and second mortgage loans) cannot exceed the property's value or sales price, plus closing costs, prepaid expenses, and discount points. If the family member's secondary financing provides for regular installment payments, the combined payments for the FHA loan and the secondary financing can't exceed the borrower's ability to pay. (In other words, the borrower is qualified based on the total of both payments.) And the secondary financing can't call for a balloon payment within five years after closing.

Government agencies and certain approved nonprofit agencies may also provide a borrower with secondary financing to cover the minimum cash investment. The secondary lien on the property must be held in the name of the agency. The total financing cannot exceed the property's value plus closing costs, prepaid expenses, and discount points, and the combined payments cannot exceed the borrower's ability to pay.

Older Borrowers. There are fewer restrictions on using secondary financing for the minimum cash investment if the borrower is 60 years old or older. In that case, the secondary financing may be provided by a relative (not necessarily a member of the borrower's immediate family), a close friend with a clearly defined interest in the borrower, the borrower's employer, or a humanitarian or welfare organization. The total financing cannot exceed the property's value plus prepaid expenses.

Secondary Financing for the Loan. FHA borrowers are permitted to use secondary financing to make up part of the maximum loan amount (as opposed to the minimum cash investment). This type of

> FHA may not use secondary financing from the seller or a lender for the minimum cash investment

> FHA borrower may use secondary financing from a close family member, or from a government or nonprofit agency, for minimum cash investment and other costs

secondary financing can come from anyone; it doesn't have to be a family member or a government agency.

When secondary financing is used for part of the loan amount, the following conditions must be met:

FHA rules for secondary financing from seller or lender:
- Not for minimum cash investment
- Combined loans can't exceed FHA base loan amount
- Borrower must qualify for combined payment
- Balloon payment allowed only after 10 years

1. The first and second loans together may not exceed the maximum loan amount for the transaction. In other words, the two loans together can't add up to more than 96.5% of the sales price or appraised value, and they also can't add up to more than the local maximum loan amount.

2. The combined total of the payments for the FHA-insured first mortgage and the non-FHA second mortgage may not exceed the borrower's ability to pay.

3. If the second loan has periodic installment payments, the payments must be collected on a monthly basis. Each payment must be substantially the same amount as the others.

4. The second loan can't have a balloon payment due sooner than ten years after closing without special FHA approval.

5. The second loan may not include a prepayment penalty (although the borrower may be required to give the second mortgagee 30 days' notice before prepaying).

Since the borrower will still have to come up with the same cash investment, why would anyone choose this arrangement? When market interest rates are high, a seller might be willing to offer a second mortgage at a lower rate than the FHA first mortgage (see Chapter 13). That would make the total payments on the two loans less than the payment on an FHA-insured mortgage for the full loan amount. In a marginal case, this might benefit a buyer whose income would otherwise be insufficient to qualify for an FHA loan.

Property Flipping Prevention Rules

Property flipping refers to reselling a property for a substantial profit shortly after purchasing it. This is considered a predatory practice when an appraiser, a lender, a mortgage broker, and/or a real estate agent collude to resell a home to an unsophisticated buyer at an inflated price. (See Chapter 14.) The FHA has rules designed to prevent FHA loans from being used to take advantage of buyers in this way. Here's a summary of the rules:

1. In any sale financed with an FHA loan, the seller must be the property owner of record; the transaction can't involve an assignment of the purchase agreement to a third party.

2. An FHA loan can't be used to finance a purchase unless more than 90 days have elapsed since the seller bought the property. (The days are counted from the closing date of that previous transaction to the date the new buyer signed the purchase agreement.)

3. If the seller bought the home within the previous 91 to 180 days and the new buyer will be paying more than twice the price the seller paid, the FHA will require additional documentation that supports the appraised value. This includes a second appraisal, and it might also include documentation of repairs and remodeling work. The borrower can't be charged for the second appraisal.

4. If the seller bought the home more than 90 days earlier but within the previous 12 months, the FHA has the option of examining the transaction and requiring additional evidence concerning the property value.

FHA's property flipping rules:
- Seller must be owner of record
- Restrictions on timing of resale
- Seller may have to justify price

There are several exemptions from these rules. For example, they don't apply if the home is being sold by an employer or a relocation company that acquired it when the previous owner relocated for employment reasons. Also exempt are sales of inherited property; sales of newly built homes; sales of homes in federal disaster areas; sales involving government agencies or government-sponsored enterprises; and sales by state or federally chartered financial institutions.

Assumption of FHA Loans

FHA loans contain due-on-sale clauses, and various limitations on assumption apply. Generally, the buyer must intend to occupy the property as his primary residence. Also, the lender will review the creditworthiness of the buyer before agreeing to the assumption This review is very similar to the process of qualifying a buyer for a new FHA loan. If the buyer assuming the loan is creditworthy,

FHA loans:
- Contain due-on-sale clause
- Limit assumptions

FHA loans originated before 12/15/89 can be assumed:
- Without FHA or lender approval
- By investor (non-occupant)

the lender is required to release the original borrower from liability automatically.

However, the assumption rules are slightly different for older FHA loans. An FHA loan that was originated before December 15, 1989 can be assumed by any buyer, including an investor who won't occupy the property. The buyer need not be approved by the lender or the FHA, unless the original borrower wants to be released from liability. If the assuming buyer is creditworthy, the original borrower will be released from liability upon written request.

For loans originated before January 27, 1991, if the original borrower was an owner-occupant and the buyer is an investor, and the borrower requests a release of liability from the lender, the investor must pay the loan down to a certain LTV (either 75% or 85%, depending on the age of the loan).

Exercise No. 2

Alison Lee is buying a house with an FHA loan. The property's appraised value is the same as the sales price, $170,000. In addition to the minimum cash investment, Lee will pay closing costs and prepaid expenses totaling $12,700; she isn't going to pay discount points.

1. Suppose the seller agreed to pay Lee's lender $12,000 to buy down her interest rate. How would that affect her loan amount?

2. Suppose instead that Lee's parents are loaning her $20,000 for her purchase, and their loan will be secured by a second mortgage on the house. How would that affect Lee's FHA loan? Would she still have to make the minimum cash investment out of her own funds? What FHA requirements would apply to the second loan?

3. It's July 1. Lee and the seller signed their purchase agreement on June 20. Now the lender has discovered that the seller has only owned the property since April 12. How will this information affect Lee's FHA loan?

FHA Insurance Premiums

Mortgage insurance is required on every FHA loan, regardless of the loan-to-value ratio. The premiums for FHA mortgage insurance are referred to as MMI (mutual mortgage insurance premiums) or MIP (mortgage insurance premiums). For most programs, an FHA borrower must pay both an upfront premium and annual premiums, as described below.

FHA insurance premiums:
- Upfront (one-time) MIP
- Annual premiums

Upfront MIP

The upfront mortgage insurance premium (UFMIP) is also called the one-time mortgage insurance premium (OTMIP). For purchase loans, the UFMIP is currently 1.75% of the loan amount.

> **Example:** John Rubino is buying a house with a $350,280 FHA loan. His upfront premium will be $6,129.90.
>
> | $350,280 | Loan amount |
> |---|---|
> | × 1.75% | Premium percentage |
> | $6,129.90 | UFMIP |

Paying the UFMIP. As the name suggests, the upfront premium may be paid up front—in other words, at closing, before the loan term begins—by either the borrower or the seller. Or, despite the name, the upfront premium can be financed over the loan term instead. When the UFMIP is financed, the amount of the premium is simply added to the base loan amount. (Note: base loan amount is defined as the loan amount excluding the upfront premium.)

Upfront MIP
- Paid in cash, or financed
- Percentage of base loan amount

Base loan
+ Financed UFMIP
_____
Total amount financed

Example: Rubino has chosen to finance his upfront MIP instead of paying it in cash at closing.

$350,280.00   Loan amount
+   6,129.90   UFMIP
_____
$356,409.90   Total amount financed

The total amount financed (or the base loan amount, if the upfront MIP is paid in cash) is rounded down to the next dollar. So if the base loan and the MIP add up to $356,409.90, the total amount financed will be rounded down to $356,409.

Financing the upfront MIP increases the borrower's monthly payment amount, of course, so that the total amount financed, plus interest accruing on the total, will be paid off by the end of the loan term.

FHA buyer may borrow maximum loan amount plus UFMIP

Financed UFMIP and loan amount. When the maximum loan amount rules are applied to a transaction, the financed upfront MIP is not considered part of the loan amount. The borrower can borrow the maximum loan amount allowed in the community plus the full amount of the upfront MIP. However, the total amount financed is not permitted to exceed the property's appraised value.

Financed UFMIP and loan fees. The loan origination fee paid by the borrower is a percentage of the base loan amount, so the upfront MIP is not included. In the example above, if the lender were charging a 1% origination fee, the fee would be $3,502.80 ($350,280 × .01 = $3,502.80). Discount points, however, are based on the total amount financed, including the upfront MIP. If the lender in the example were charging discount points, each point would be $3,564.09 ($356,409 × .01 = $3,564.09).

UFMIP Refund. If an FHA loan that was made before December 8, 2004 is paid off early (because the borrower is selling the property or refinancing, for example), the borrower may be entitled to a refund of part of the upfront MIP. The refund is prorated based on the number of years that have passed since the loan was made.

UFMIP refunds have been eliminated for loans made on or after December 8, 2004. There's an exception if the borrower refinances the property with another FHA-insured loan within the first three years of the original loan's term. In that case, the borrower will be entitled to receive a prorated refund of part of the UFMIP. (The borrower may choose to have the refund applied to the UFMIP for the new loan.)

Annual Premiums

In addition to the upfront premium, most FHA borrowers are required to pay annual premiums (also called periodic premiums) for a number of years. One-twelfth of each year's premium is added to the borrower's monthly payment.

The annual premium is 0.25%, 0.50%, or 0.55% of the loan balance (not including any financed UFMIP), depending on the loan term and the loan-to-value ratio, as shown in Figure 11.3.

If the loan term is longer than 15 years and the LTV is 95% or less, the annual premium is 0.50% of the loan balance; if the LTV is over 95%, the premium is 0.55%.

If the loan term is 15 years or less and the LTV is over 90%, the annual premium is 0.25%; if the LTV is 90% or less, no annual premium is charged.

The loan-to-value ratio is calculated by dividing the base loan amount (not including any financed upfront MIP) by the sales price or appraised value, whichever is less.

Cancellation of Annual MIP. FHA borrowers used to be required to pay the annual MIP for a period ranging from four to thirty years, depending on the loan term and the loan-to-value ratio. (The higher

Annual premium:
- 0.25% or 0.50% of base loan balance
- Paid during first several years of loan term
- Included in monthly loan payments

Fig. 11.3 An FHA borrower pays an upfront premium plus annual premiums

Upfront Premium:		
1.75% of the loan amount, at closing or financed		
Annual Premiums:		
Percentage varies depending on loan term and loan-to-value ratio		
Loan Term	**LTV**	**Annual Premium** (percentage of loan balance)
15 years or less	90% or less	No annual premium
	Over 90%	0.25% of loan balance
Over 15 years	LTV 95% or less	0.50% of loan balance, for at least five years*
	LTV over 95%	0.55% of loan balance, for at least five years*

*Annual premiums may be canceled when the LTV reaches 78% of the original sales price or value, but they must be paid for at least five years if the loan term is longer than 15 years.

the LTV, the greater the risk and the longer the annual premium had to be paid.) That changed in 2001; for loans closed since then, the annual MIP is canceled automatically once these conditions have been met:

1. The loan-to-value ratio has been paid down to 78% of the property's original sales price or appraised value.

2. In addition, if the loan term is longer than 15 years, the borrower must have paid the premium for at least five years.

Annual MIP canceled when LTV reaches 78%

If the loan's term is 15 years or less, the annual premium will be canceled once the LTV reaches 78% without regard to how long the borrower has paid the premium.

The FHA determines when the 78% threshold has been reached based on the loan's amortization schedule. However, if the borrower prepays the loan and thus reaches the threshold ahead of schedule, she can request cancellation of the annual MIP.

Even after the annual premium is canceled, the mortgage insurance policy will remain in force for the full term of the loan.

Risk-based Premiums

Annual premiums introduced an element of risk-based pricing into FHA financing. (See Chapter 8 for a general discussion of risk-based pricing.) As you've seen, annual premiums vary depending on two factors that affect risk: the length of the loan term and the loan-to-value ratio. In contrast, the upfront premium traditionally hasn't varied with the risk factors in particular transactions; everyone who qualifies for a certain type of FHA loan in a given year pays the same percentage of their loan amount as the upfront premium.

Risk-based pricing based on credit score and LTV

In July 2008, however, the FHA extended risk-based pricing to upfront premiums. It began charging borrowers different percentages for the upfront premium depending on their credit score and the loan-to-value ratio. For example, the upfront premium for a 30-year loan ranged from 1.25% of the loan amount for borrowers with high credit scores and low LTVs, up to 2.25% for borrowers with low credit scores and high LTVs.

But shortly after the new system was implemented, the Housing and Economic Recovery Act was passed, and it called for a one-year moratorium on the FHA's risk-based premiums. There was concern that risk-based premiums would be counterproductive during the mortgage crisis, by making FHA loans more costly for many borrowers. The moratorium is due to expire in October 2009, unless Congress decides to extend it.

Exercise No. 3

Diane Skillin is buying a home for $374,000, and she's applying for a 30-year FHA loan. The home is in an area where the maximum FHA loan amount for a single-family home is $364,800. The appraised value of the property is $373,000.

1. Assuming that Skillin is going to get the largest FHA loan she can, calculate her upfront premium amount for this transaction. Also, what percentage will be used to calculate her annual premium?

2. If Skillin finances the upfront premium, what will the total amount financed be? Does it matter that the total amount financed exceeds the maximum FHA loan amount for the area where the property is located? Is there another rule that can limit the loan amount for an FHA-insured loan when the upfront premium is financed?

FHA Underwriting Standards

As with any institutional loan, the underwriting for an FHA-insured loan involves analysis of the applicant's credit reputation, income, and net worth (see Chapter 8). But the FHA's underwriting standards are less strict than the Fannie Mae/Freddie Mac standards for conventional loans, which were described in Chapter 10. The FHA standards make it easier for low- and moderate-income home buyers to qualify for a mortgage.

FHA underwriting standards are less strict than Fannie Mae and Freddie Mac standards

385

Credit Reputation

If a loan applicant's credit report and credit scores are available, the FHA requires the lender to consider those in the underwriting evaluation. Mediocre credit scores won't necessarily rule out loan approval, but the FHA does set a lower limit: an applicant whose credit score is below 500 isn't eligible for an FHA loan unless the loan-to-value ratio is under 90%. That's not a very high hurdle to clear, however. (In comparison, Fannie Mae's lower limit is 580; Freddie Mac's cutoff is 600 or 660, depending on the loan program. See Chapter 10.)

If the three main credit agencies provide different scores for an applicant, the underwriter must select one score (known as the "decision credit score") to use. The FHA has essentially the same rules as Fannie Mae and Freddie Mac for making this selection: the middle of three scores are used (or the lower of two). When two or more people are applying for an FHA loan together, one score is selected for each applicant, and the lowest of those scores will be used as the decision score.

Although most prospective FHA buyers have an established credit history, some do not. For example, low-income first-time buyers may never have used credit before; the same may be true of younger buyers or recent immigrants to the United States. As part of its efforts to help underserved borrowers, the FHA has issued detailed rules for "nontraditional credit analysis." These rules allow a lender to manually underwrite an FHA loan application even when a standard credit report and credit scores aren't available. For example, the underwriter may ask the applicant to provide documentation showing how reliably he has paid rent, utility bills, or other obligations over the past twelve months.

Income Analysis

The income analysis for an FHA loan is based on the applicant's monthly **effective income**, which is essentially the same thing as stable monthly income (see Chapter 8). The FHA defines effective income as the applicant's gross income from all sources that can be expected to continue for the first three years of the loan term.

The underwriter applies two income ratios to determine the adequacy of the applicant's effective income: a debt to income ratio and a housing expense to income ratio. (The FHA's official term for

---

Margin notes:

Lowest credit score is used when:
- Multiple scores available
- Two or more applicants

Lender may manually underwrite FHA loan if no credit history available

Effective income:
- Gross income from all sources
- That is expected to continue for 3 years

the debt to income ratio is "total fixed payment to effective income ratio.") As a general rule, an FHA borrower's debt to income ratio should not exceed **43%**. In addition, the housing expense to income ratio should not exceed **31%**. The applicant should qualify under both tests.

The applicant's proposed housing expense (which is used in both income ratios) includes principal and interest (based on the total amount financed), property taxes, hazard insurance, one-twelfth of the annual premium for the FHA mortgage insurance, and any dues owed to a homeowners association.

To calculate the debt to income ratio, the proposed housing expense is added to the applicant's **recurring charges**: the monthly payments on any debt with ten or more payments remaining. (A debt with fewer payments remaining will also be considered if it is a large debt.) Alimony and child support payments, installment debt payments, and payments on revolving credit accounts are all counted.

> **Example:** Helen Crowder wants to buy a home using FHA financing. In the area where she lives, the maximum FHA loan amount is $271,050 and lenders are generally charging about 5.5% interest for 30-year fixed-rate FHA loans. She'd like to get preapproved for the maximum loan amount. The monthly payment (including principal, interest, taxes, hazard insurance, and mortgage insurance) for a loan that size would be approximately $1,693.
>
> Crowder's monthly salary is $4,500. Her ex-husband reliably sends her a child support payment each month for their four-year-old daughter. The child support is tax-exempt, so the lender "grosses up" the payment, and concludes that it's the equivalent of $650 in taxable income. Thus, Crowder's effective income is $5,150.
>
> Crowder has to pay the following recurring charges every month:
>
> | | |
> |---:|---|
> | $253 | Car payment (11 payments remaining) |
> | 65 | Furniture store payment (15 payments remaining) |
> | 55 | Minimum Visa payment |
> | 29 | Minimum MasterCard payment |
> | 125 | Student loan (63 payments remaining) |
> | + 60 | Average payment on Texaco credit card |
> | $587 | Total recurring charges |
>
> To calculate Crowder's debt to income ratio, first add the proposed housing expense to her recurring charges to determine

her total fixed payments. Then divide that figure by her effective income.

$1,693   Proposed housing expense
+   587   Recurring charges
$2,280   Total fixed payments

$2,280   Total fixed payments
÷ 5,150   Effective income
0.4427   Debt to income ratio (44%)

With the $1,693 proposed monthly payment, Crowder's housing expense to income ratio would be approximately 33%:

$1,693   Proposed housing expense
÷ 5,150   Effective income
0.3287   Housing expense to income ratio (33%)

So with the maximum loan amount and a $1,693 monthly payment, both of Crowder's income ratios would slightly exceed the FHA's limits. Her debt to income ratio would be about 44% instead of 43%, and her housing expense to income ratio would be about 33% instead of 31%.

A loan applicant whose income ratios exceed the 43% and/or 31% limits won't qualify for an FHA loan unless there are compensating factors that reduce the risk of default. The FHA lists the following compensating factors:

Compensating factors for an FHA loan:
- 10% downpayment
- Savings and conservative attitude toward credit
- Ability to devote extra income to housing expenses
- Short-term income
- Small increase over current housing expense
- Three months' payments in reserve
- Potential for increased earnings

- Over the past 12 to 24 months, the loan applicant's housing expenses have been at least equal to the proposed housing expenses under the new mortgage.

- The applicant plans to make a large downpayment (at least 10%).

- The applicant has demonstrated an ability to accumulate savings and a conservative attitude toward the use of credit.

- The applicant's credit history demonstrates an ability to devote a greater portion of income to housing expenses than most people can manage.

- The applicant receives income that was not counted as effective income (for example, because it will not continue for at least three years), but which directly affects the applicant's ability to pay the mortgage.

- The proposed housing expense represents only a small increase (10% or less) over the applicant's current housing expense.

- The applicant would have substantial reserves after closing (at least three months' mortgage payments).

- The applicant's job training or professional education indicates potential for increased earnings.

This list isn't exclusive—these are only examples. There may be other aspects of the loan applicant's financial situation that the lender and the FHA would accept as compensating factors that justify loan approval in spite of income ratios over 43% and 31%.

Also, when an FHA inspection has determined that the home in question is an energy-efficient home (EEH), the income ratios can be exceeded by 2%. In other words, buyers with a debt to income ratio of 45% and a housing expense to income ratio of 33% can qualify for an FHA loan if they're buying an energy-efficient home.

Exercise No. 4

The Herrons are applying for an FHA loan. Maggie Herron works for the Northshore Boat Company as a bookkeeper, earning $2,300 a month. Her husband, Bob, earns $510 a week as a customer service representative for Garner Industries. They have two personal loans from a local bank. The first loan has a monthly payment of $114 and a balance of $1,254. The second loan calls for monthly payments of $135, with $1,655 still owing. Their Visa card requires a minimum payment of $47; the balance is $1,460.

1. What is the Herrons' effective income?

2. Applying both the debt to income ratio and the housing expense ratio (and assuming there are no compensating factors that would allow higher-than-standard ratios), what's the maximum housing expense the Herrons could qualify for under the FHA's rules?

3. How does the answer to Question 2 compare to the maximum housing expense the Herrons could qualify for if they were applying for a conventional loan?

Assets for Closing

At closing, an FHA borrower will need to have enough cash to cover:

Cash required for closing:
- Minimum cash investment
- Prepaid expenses
- Discount points
- Closing costs or repair costs that can't be financed
- Difference between sales price and appraised value, if sales price is greater

- the minimum cash investment;
- the prepaid expenses;
- any discount points the borrower has agreed to pay;
- the upfront MIP, if it isn't being financed; and
- any closing costs, repair costs, or other expenses (e.g., all or part of a buyer's agent's fee) that aren't eligible for financing.

If the borrower has agreed to pay a sales price higher than the property's appraised value, then she has to come up with the difference in cash, in addition to the minimum cash investment. Ordinarily, no reserves are required for an FHA loan (although as you saw, reserves may be used as a compensating factor if the borrower's income ratios exceed the FHA limits).

FHA generally does not require reserves

The borrower may use gift funds for part or even all of the cash required for closing. The donor must be the borrower's employer or labor union, a close relative, a close friend with a clearly defined interest in the borrower, a charitable organization, or a government agency. The funds must be deposited in the borrower's bank account or with the closing agent, and a gift letter will be required (see Chapter 8).

Borrowers may use other sources of cash besides gift funds. As we discussed earlier, under certain circumstances a borrower may use secondary financing to cover the minimum cash investment and other funds needed for closing. Alternatively, a close family member may simply loan the funds to the borrower without requiring a second mortgage or any other form of security in return.

Also, the borrower may be permitted to borrow the cash needed for closing from someone other than a close family member, as long as the loan is secured by collateral other than the home being purchased with the FHA mortgage. For example, if the applicant can borrow money against his car or vacation property, the loan funds may be used to close the sale. This loan must be from an independent third party, not from the seller or a real estate agent involved in the transaction. (Of course, a loan requiring more than ten payments will be taken into account when qualifying the borrower.)

Sources of cash for closing:
- Gift funds
- Secondary financing from family member
- Unsecured loan from family member
- Loan secured by collateral other than home

FHA Rehabilitation Loans and Reverse Mortgages

We'll end this chapter with a closer look at two specific FHA programs—those insuring rehabilitation loans and reverse mortgages. In recent years, these types of loans have become increasingly popular with FHA borrowers.

FHA Rehabilitation Loans

The 203(k) program insures mortgages used to purchase (or refinance) and rehabilitate principal residences with up to four units. A portion of the loan proceeds are used to purchase the property or refinance an existing mortgage, and the remaining funds are deposited into a Rehabilitation Escrow Account to be released as the work progresses.

203(k) loan: used to purchase or refinance and rehabilitate principal residence

A home financed under this program must be at least a year old, and the FHA imposes certain structural and energy-efficiency standards on all rehabilitation work. The range of improvements that qualify as rehabilitation is fairly wide, although the costs of upgrade work must total at least $5,000 to be eligible for 203(k) financing. Luxury or temporary improvements are not eligible.

The basic rules of 203(b) (such as those governing minimum investment, loan term, and loan limits) apply to mortgages insured under Section 203(k). In some cases, however, lenders may charge a supplemental origination fee, and 203(k) borrowers do not pay an up-front mortgage premium (mortgage premiums were discussed earlier in the chapter). The property's value (for determining the maximum loan amount) is the least of:

1. the property's current value, plus the costs of rehabilitation;
2. the existing debt to be refinanced, plus the costs of rehabilitation; or
3. 110% of the property's value after rehabilitation.

203(k) improvements must:
- Total at least $5,000
- Not be temporary or luxury improvements

FHA Home Equity Conversion Mortgages (HECMs)

The FHA calls its reverse mortgages "home equity conversion mortgages," or HECMs. A reverse mortgage offers an elderly home owner a way to convert equity into income (see Chapter 5). It was the FHA that first popularized reverse mortgages, and they've represented a growing segment of FHA business in recent years.

Home equity conversion mortgage (HECM) = reverse mortgage

This program allows older homeowners to convert the equity in their homes into either a source of monthly income or a line of credit. Repayment is not required as long as the property remains the owner's principal residence. To qualify for an FHA HECM, a homeowner must be at least 62 years old. The property may have up to four dwelling units or be a condominium unit. It must be owned free and clear, or have only a small balance remaining on the mortgage. Homeowners are required to consult a HUD-approved HECM counselor to help decide if this type of mortgage would suit their needs.

HECM applicant must:
- Be at least 62 years old
- Own property free and clear, or with small balance only

The loan amount will depend on the local FHA maximum loan amount, the appraised value of the home, the current interest rate, and the age of the borrower. (If there's more than one borrower, the age of the youngest is the one that counts.) The more valuable the property, the lower the interest rate; and the older the borrower, the larger the loan amount can be, up to the FHA maximum. There are no income requirements or credit qualifications.

The lender recovers the amount borrowed, plus interest, when the property is sold. If the sale proceeds exceed the amount owed, the excess goes to the owner (the seller) or his heirs. If the proceeds don't cover the amount owed, the FHA will make up the difference to the lender.

HECMs for Purchase. Until recently, it was possible to use an HECM to purchase a new principal residence, but it was a two-step process: first, the senior had to obtain financing to buy the new home; then, she used the HECM to pay off the first mortgage. However, the Housing and Economic Recovery Act simplified this process: effective January 1, 2009, the proceeds from an FHA HECM can now be used to purchase a one- to four-unit principal residence.

Proceeds from FHA HECM can be used to purchase a one- to four-unit principal residence

> **Example:** The Garcias are empty-nesters who want to downsize from their current home to a nearby condominium. The condominium's asking price is $210,000. They anticipate that they will net $190,000 from the sale of their current home, but this won't be enough to purchase the new condo outright.
>
> The Garcias decide to use an FHA HECM to buy the condo. The HECM loan amount is $120,000. That amount, plus $90,000 of their own funds (out of the sale proceeds from their current home), is enough for the condo purchase price ($120,000 + $90,000 = $210,000).

An HECM for purchase can't be used for a second home or an investment property, and the borrower must occupy the purchased property within 60 days of closing. Certain types of property are ineligible for this program, including cooperative units and manufactured homes built before June 15, 1976 (as well as newer manufactured homes that don't meet HUD's permanent foundation guidelines).

HECM for purchase cannot be used for:
- *Second home*
- *Investment property*
- *Cooperative units*
- *Some manufactured homes*

Like a regular HECM, the loan amount is based on the local FHA maximum, the home's appraised value, the current interest rate, and the borrower's age. If the HECM loan amount is less than the purchase price, the remaining balance must come from the borrower's own funds (typically, this money comes from the sale of the borrower's current residence). The borrower can't use any other sort of financing, such as a bridge loan, seller financing, or a personal loan, to make up the difference.

Outline: FHA-Insured Loans

I. FHA Mortgage Insurance

   A. The Federal Housing Administration (FHA) is part of the Department of Housing and Urban Development (HUD). The purpose of the FHA is to promote the financing, improvement, and sale of residential real estate.

   B. The primary function of the FHA is insuring mortgage loans. It does not build homes or provide mortgage loans.

      1. A borrower applies to an FHA-approved lender who either underwrites the loan application directly or submits it to the FHA for approval.

      2. The borrower is liable to the federal government for any compensation the FHA must pay a lender as a result of the borrower's default.

   C. FHA loans are designed to help people with low and moderate incomes buy homes.

   D. FHA Loan Programs

      1. Section 203(b) is the standard FHA loan program. It provides insurance for loans used to purchase or refinance one- to four-unit properties.

      2. Section 234(c) insures loans used to purchase or refinance individual units in condominiums that have been approved by the FHA. A 234(c) loan may also be available to buy a unit in a non-approved condominium, if the unit meets certain criteria. This is called a "spot loan."

      3. Section 251 insures 30-year adjustable-rate mortgages (ARMs) used to purchase or refinance owner-occupied properties with up to four units.

         a. An FHA ARM can have an initial fixed interest rate period of one, three, five, seven, or ten years. After the initial period, rate increases occur annually.

         b. Depending on the length of the initial period, the annual interest rate adjustment is limited to 1% or 2%, and the total rate increase over the life of the loan is limited to 5% or 6%.

II. Rules for FHA-Financed Transactions

   A. A home purchased with an FHA loan is generally required to be an owner-occupied principal residence.

B. The FHA's local maximum loan amounts are based on median housing costs in the area. There are different maximums for one-, two-, three-, and four-unit residences.

    1. The FHA's maximum loan amounts are tied to the conforming loan limits set by Fannie Mae and Freddie Mac.

    2. Local maximums are adjusted annually to reflect changes in housing costs.

C. An FHA borrower must make a minimum cash investment of 3.5% of the appraised value or sales price, whichever is less. Borrower-paid closing costs no longer count toward the minimum cash investment.

D. Loan charges and closing costs

    1. FHA used to limit interest rates, origination fees, and loan costs, but now these items are negotiable and can vary from one lender to the next.

    2. FHA loans may not have a prepayment penalty.

E. The FHA restricts sales concessions from the seller or other interested parties, to prevent circumvention of the FHA's LTV rules. Sales concessions are classified either as seller contributions or as inducements to purchase.

    1. Seller contributions include payments towards the borrower's closing costs, prepaid expenses, mortgage interest, UFMIP, discount points, or a buydown.

       a. Seller contributions are limited to 6% of the sales price.

       b. Contributions in excess of 6% are considered inducements to purchase.

    2. Inducements to purchase are deducted from the property's sales price before the LTV is applied, lowering the allowable maximum loan amount.

       a. In addition to seller contributions in excess of 6%, inducements to purchase include funds given to the buyer for decorating, repairs, moving expenses, and buyer's agent fees, as well as personal property.

F. Secondary financing may be used with an FHA loan, if the primary and secondary loans don't add up to more than the maximum loan amount for the transaction and the borrower qualifies for the combined payment.

    1. As a general rule, secondary financing cannot be used for the borrower's minimum cash investment, but there are significant exceptions.

      a. Secondary financing provided by a close family member or a government agency may be used to cover the minimum cash investment, if the total financing doesn't exceed the property's value or sales price plus closing costs, prepaid expenses, and discount points.

      b. A borrower 60 years or older may cover the minimum cash investment with secondary financing from a relative, a close friend, an employer, or a charitable organization. The total financing cannot exceed the property's value plus prepaid expenses.

G. Property Flipping Prevention Rules

H. Assumption of FHA Loans

    1. Generally, an FHA loan can only be assumed by a creditworthy buyer who intends to occupy the property as a principal residence. Older FHA loans (closed before December 15, 1989) can be assumed by anyone, unless the seller wants to be released from liability.

    2. If the buyer assuming the loan is creditworthy, the lender must release the original borrower from liability automatically. With older loans, the lender must release the original borrower upon written request.

III. FHA Insurance Premiums

A. The mortgage insurance premiums (MIP) for most FHA programs include an upfront premium (UFMIP) and annual premiums.

B. The UFMIP is 1.75% of the base loan amount. It may be paid in cash at closing by the buyer or the seller, or it may be financed.

    1. A financed UFMIP is not included in the base loan amount used to calculate the maximum loan amount and loan origination fee.

    2. If an FHA loan made before December 8, 2004 is paid off early, the borrower may be eligible for a prorated refund of part of the UFMIP.

C. The annual MIP is 0.25%, 0.50%, or 0.55% of the loan balance, depending on the loan term and LTV.

    1. No annual premium is charged if the LTV is under 90%.

    2. For loans that closed on or after January 1, 2001, the annual premium is canceled once certain conditions are met. The mortgage insurance remains effective for the full loan term.

      a. If the loan term is over 15 years, the annual MIP is automatically canceled when the LTV reaches 78%, as long as the borrower has paid the premium for at least five years.

        b. If the loan term is 15 years or less, the annual MIP is automatically canceled when the LTV reaches 78%, regardless of how long the borrower has paid the premium.

        c. If the 78% threshold is reached early, the borrower may request cancellation.

  D. Risk-based premiums

     1. Annual premiums take into account loan term and LTV (and are therefore risk-based).

     2. In July, 2008, FHA extended risk-based pricing to upfront premiums, based on credit score and LTV.

     3. However, the 2008 Housing and Economic Recovery Act placed a one-year moratorium on the risk-based pricing plan (set to expire in October, 2009, unless Congress extends).

IV. FHA Underwriting Standards

  A. FHA underwriting standards are less strict than Fannie Mae and Freddie Mac standards for conventional loans.

  B. FHA requires lenders to consider a loan applicant's credit report and credit scores when available.

     1. Mediocre score won't rule out loan approval, but score cannot be lower than 500 unless LTV is under 90%.

     2. If there's more than one score available, underwriter must use middle of three (or lower of two).

     3. If two or more people are applying for a loan, the lowest score is used.

     4. FHA allows manual underwriting for applicants with little or no available credit reputation.

  C. In FHA loan underwriting, the applicant's monthly effective income is measured against the applicant's fixed payment and proposed housing expense.

     1. Effective income is the total amount of income from all sources that can be expected to continue for the first three years of the loan term.

     2. Fixed payments include the proposed monthly housing expense (principal, interest, property taxes, hazard insurance, one-twelfth of the annual MIP, and any homeowners or condominium association dues), plus recurring charges (monthly payments on any debt with ten or more payments remaining).

3. A borrower's debt to income ratio should not exceed 43%, and the housing expense to income ratio should not exceed 31%.

4. An applicant whose income ratios exceed these limits may still qualify for an FHA loan if compensating factors reduce the risk of default.

5. Compensating factors include a demonstrated ability to save money and meet financial obligations, a large downpayment, good credit history, and substantial reserves left over after closing.

V. Assets Required for Closing

A. At closing, an FHA borrower must have enough cash to cover the minimum cash investment, prepaid expenses, any borrower-paid discount points, the upfront MIP (if it isn't being financed), and any other closing costs that are not being financed or paid for by the seller.

B. Allowable sources for the cash required for closing:

1. Gift funds from an employer, labor union, relative, close friend, charitable organization, or government agency may be used to cover these costs.

2. Secondary financing (secured by a lien against the home being purchased) in compliance with certain rules.

3. An unsecured loan from a family member.

4. A loan from any independent third party (not the seller or a real estate agent involved in the transaction), as long as it is not secured by the home being purchased with the FHA loan.

VI. FHA Rehabilitation Loans and Reverse Mortgages (HECMs)

A. Section 203(k) insures mortgages used to purchase (or refinance) and rehabilitate one- to four-unit properties.

1. All loan proceeds used for the upgrade work must be put into an escrow account and released as the work progresses.

2. Rehabilitation work must meet HUD standards. The work must cost at least $5,000, and cannot include temporary or luxury improvements.

B. Section 255 insures home equity conversion mortgages (HECMs), also known as reverse mortgages.

1. Allows older homeowners to convert their equity into either a source of monthly income or a line of credit.

2. Repayment is not required as long as the property remains the owner's principal residence.

3. The homeowner must be at least 62 years old.

4. The property may have up to four units or be a condominium unit.

5. The property must be owned free and clear, or have only a small balance remaining on the existing mortgage.

6. The loan amount depends on the FHA local maximum loan amount, the home's appraised value, the current interest rate, and the age of the borrower.

7. The lender recovers the amount borrowed, plus interest, when the property is sold. The FHA will make up any shortfall in the sale proceeds.

8. Effective January 1, 2009, the proceeds from an FHA HECM can be used to purchase a one- to four-unit principal residence (but cannot be used to purchase a second home, investment property, cooperative unit, or some manufactured homes).

Key Terms

HUD: The Department of Housing and Urban Development, a cabinet-level department of the federal government.

Federal Housing Administration (FHA): An agency within the Department of Housing and Urban Development that provides mortgage insurance to encourage lenders to make more affordable home loans.

FHA-insured loan: A loan made by an institutional lender with mortgage insurance provided by the Federal Housing Administration, protecting the lender against losses due to borrower default.

MMI: The Mutual Mortgage Insurance program, the formal name of the FHA insurance program.

Direct endorsement lender: A lender authorized to underwrite its own FHA loan applications, rather than having to submit them to the FHA for approval.

Minimum cash investment: A downpayment of at least 3.5% of the sales price or appraised value, whichever is less, required of FHA borrowers; closing costs do not count toward the minimum.

Effective income: In FHA underwriting, the loan applicant's gross monthly income from all sources that can be expected to continue; the FHA equivalent of stable monthly income.

MIP: The fee charged for FHA insurance coverage. The initial FHA premium is referred to as the upfront MIP (UFMIP) or the OTMIP (one-time MIP).

Recurring charges: The monthly payments on any debt with ten or more payments remaining; used along with the applicant's proposed housing expense to determine an FHA borrower's debt to income ratio.

Home Equity Conversion Mortgage (HECM): The FHA's term for a reverse equity mortgage, which allows elderly homeowners to convert equity into income.

Chapter Quiz

1. The FHA:
   a. makes loans
   b. insures loans
   c. buys and sells loans
   d. All of the above

2. Bill Zelinski is buying a duplex. He can finance the transaction with an FHA loan if he intends to:
   a. occupy one of the units as his principal residence
   b. occupy one of the units as a secondary residence
   c. rent out both of the units
   d. Any of the above

3. The appraised value of a single-family home is $365,000, and it's selling for $364,000. The local maximum FHA loan amount is $362,790. The maximum loan amount available for this transaction is:
   a. $350,092
   b. $351,260
   c. $352,225
   d. $362,790

4. FHA local maximum loan amounts are based on local:
   a. median income
   b. debt to income ratios
   c. median housing costs
   d. mortgage insurance costs

5. All of the following statements about FHA loans are true *except*:
   a. points must be paid by the borrower
   b. the seller or an institutional lender is not allowed to provide secondary financing for the minimum cash investment
   c. mortgage insurance is required on all loans
   d. the government does not set a maximum interest rate

6. The Howells are buying a house worth $315,000 with a 30-year FHA 203(b) loan. The local maximum FHA loan amount is $307,913. If the Howells borrow that amount and also decide to finance the upfront MIP:

    a. the maximum loan amount will be reduced by the amount of the MIP
    b. the total amount financed, including the MIP, cannot exceed $307,913
    c. the total amount financed will be $307,913 minus the MIP
    d. the total amount financed will be $307,913 plus the MIP

7. Returning to the previous question, if the Howells obtain a 30-year loan for $307,913, they will be required to pay an annual premium of:

    a. 0.25% of the loan balance
    b. 0.50% of the loan balance
    c. 0.55% of the upfront MIP
    d. None of the above; an annual premium is not required if the MIP is financed

8. The buyer is obtaining a $187,000 FHA loan. The seller agrees to pay $3,000 toward the buyer's closing costs. The seller also agrees to pay the buyer's upfront MIP. Which of the following statements is correct?

    a. The seller contributions will total $3,273
    b. The seller contributions will total $6,273
    c. The seller contributions will exceed the 6% limit
    d. The $3,000 will be treated as an inducement to purchase

9. Secondary financing may be used to cover the borrower's minimum cash investment:

    a. only if the second loan comes from the seller
    b. only if the second loan comes from an institutional lender
    c. only if the two loans do not add up to more than the property's value
    d. under no circumstances

10. The Munnimans bought their house in 1986 with an FHA loan. Now they're selling it. The loan:

    a. could be assumed by an investor
    b. could only be assumed by a buyer who intends to occupy the property as her principal residence
    c. could only be assumed by a buyer who is found creditworthy
    d. cannot be assumed

Answer Key

1. b. The FHA insures mortgage loans made by FHA-approved lenders in accordance with FHA rules.

2. a. An FHA loan generally must be used to finance an owner-occupied principal residence.

3. c. Multiply the property's sales price or appraised value, whichever is less, by 96.5% (the maximum LTV ratio after the required 3.5% minimum cash investment downpayment). $364,000 × 96.5% = $351,260. Since this doesn't exceed the local FHA loan limit ($362,790), $351,260 is the maximum loan amount for the transaction.

4. c. FHA local maximum loan amounts are based on local median housing costs.

5. a. Discount points may be paid by the borrower or by another party, such as the seller.

6. d. The borrower can obtain a loan for the maximum amount allowed for the area, plus the amount of the upfront MIP.

7. b. For a loan with a term longer than 15 years and an LTV of over 95%, the annual premium is 0.55% of the loan balance.

8. b. The upfront MIP is 1.75% of the loan balance, or $3,273. With the upfront MIP added to the $3,000 in closing costs, the seller's contributions come to $5,805.

9. c. Secondary financing may be used to pay the borrower's required minimum cash investment, but it cannot come from the seller, another interested party, or an institutional lender. The total amount financed cannot exceed the property's value.

10. a. FHA loans that were originated before December 15, 1989 may be assumed by any buyer. The buyer may be an investor, and does not need to be approved by the lender or the FHA unless the original borrower wants a release from liability.

Case Study:
FHA-Insured Loans

After considering conventional loans, Rick and Teresa Cortina want to know whether an FHA-insured loan might work for them. They live in an area where the maximum FHA loan amount for single-family homes is $271,050. Refer back to the case study at the end of Chapter 10 for the information about the Cortinas' financial situation that you'll need to answer the questions below. There's a worksheet at the end of this case study that you can use for the calculations.

Interest rates and fees (30-year FHA loans)

In the Cortinas' area, lenders are typically charging the following interest rates and fees for FHA loans (regardless of the loan-to-value ratio):

- Fixed-rate FHA loans: 5.50% interest

- FHA ARMs: 5.7% interest

- 1% origination fee for either type of loan

- Discount points: each point paid reduces the interest rate by 0.25%

1. The Cortinas' effective income is $7,117 and their recurring charges add up to $828. (Those are the same figures as the stable monthly income and recurring obligations that you calculated for conventional loans in the Chapter 10 case study.) Apply the FHA income ratios to find the maximum housing expense the Cortinas can expect to qualify for.

2. Suppose the Cortinas want to get preapproved to borrow as much as FHA rules concerning maximum loan amounts would allow in the area where they live. They're planning to finance the upfront MIP. What's the largest base loan amount an FHA borrower can get in the Cortinas' area, if the upfront MIP is being financed? What would the total amount financed be? Round the total amount financed down to the next dollar.

3. Now determine whether the Cortinas could qualify for the total amount financed (from Question 2) if they choose a fixed-rate FHA loan and don't pay discount points. The principal and interest payment would be $1,565.92. To calculate the PITI payment, add 15% to the principal and interest payment to cover estimated property taxes and hazard insurance. Also add the monthly share of the FHA annual mortgage insurance premium. (When calculating the annual premium, assume that the loan-to-value ratio is over 95%.)

4. Suppose the Cortinas are borrowing the maximum FHA loan amount (and the upfront premium) calculated for Question 2. Apply the FHA's maximum loan-to-value ratio. How much would the Cortinas' minimum cash investment be? What home price could they afford with the FHA financing plus the minimum cash investment?

5. For the transaction in Question 4, how much cash would the Cortinas be required to have at closing? They'll need enough for the minimum cash investment and the origination fee, plus other closing costs. Use 3% of the sales price as an estimate of the other closing costs, including the prepaid expenses (impound account deposits). It isn't necessary to include cash reserves, since those generally aren't required in FHA transactions.

6. What if the Cortinas want to buy a house that costs more than the sales price you arrived at in Question 4? Could they use FHA financing for that purchase?

7. For the Cortinas, would there be any advantage to getting an FHA loan instead of a conventional loan? (Compare the results of your FHA calculations to your answers to the questions in the case study for conventional loans at the end of Chapter 10.)

Income Qualifying—FHA-Insured Loans

Effective Income

Base salary
 Wage earner 1 _____
 Wage earner 2 _____
Overtime _____
Commissions _____
Bonuses _____
Other + _____
Total _____

Recurring Charges

Car loans _____
Credit cards _____
Student loans _____
Other debts _____
Child support _____
Alimony _____
Other + _____
Total _____

Debt to Income Ratio

_____ Effective income
_____ x .43 Maximum ratio (43%)
_____ Maximum fixed payments
− _____ Recurring charges
_____ Maximum mortgage payment (PITI) under debt to income ratio

Housing Expense to Income Ratio

_____ Effective income
_____ x .31 Maximum ratio (31%)
_____ Maximum mortgage payment (PITI) under housing expense ratio

Maximum Mortgage Payment (PITI) _____

Maximum Loan Amount _____

_____ Loan amount
x _____ .0175 1.75% of base loan
_____ Upfront MIP
+ _____ Loan amount
_____ Total amount financed

_____ 1/12 of taxes, insurance
_____ 1/12 of annual MIP
+ _____ P&I payment
_____ PITI payment for loan with financed UFMIP

Total Amount Financed _____

_____ Maximum loan amount
_____ ÷ .965 Loan-to-value ratio (96.5%)
_____ Sales price
− _____ Loan amount
_____ Minimum cash investment

Sales Price _____

Chapter 12
VA-Guaranteed Loans

Characteristics of VA Loans

Eligibility for VA Loans
- Service requirements
- Eligibility of spouse

VA Guaranty
- Guaranty amount
- Restoration of guaranty entitlement
- Guaranty and veteran's liability
  - Liability after default
  - Liability after assumption
- Substitution of entitlement
- Remaining entitlement
- Entitlement and co-ownership
- Refinancing with a VA loan

VA Loan Amounts
- Making a downpayment
- Secondary financing

Underwriting Guidelines
- Income ratio analysis
- Residual income analysis
- Compensating factors
- Income ratio exceptions

Introduction

The VA home loan program was established to help veterans finance the purchase of their homes with affordable loans. For the eligible veteran, a VA-guaranteed loan is an excellent financing choice, especially in the wake of the mortgage crisis. Now that lending standards for conventional loans have been tightened, VA financing offers many advantages over conventional financing and has few disadvantages. In this chapter, we'll discuss the characteristics of VA loans, eligibility requirements, and the underwriting standards used to qualify VA loan applicants.

Characteristics of VA Loans

VA-guaranteed loans are made by institutional lenders, just like conventional loans and FHA-insured loans. However, when a VA-guaranteed loan is approved by the lender, a portion of the loan amount is guaranteed by the Department of Veterans Affairs (the VA). The loan guaranty serves the same purpose as mortgage insurance—it protects the lender against a large loss if the borrower defaults and the foreclosure sale proceeds fail to cover the full amount owed.

VA guaranty protects lender against losses from default

The term "VA-guaranteed loan" causes some confusion. You may occasionally encounter buyers who believe that, as eligible veterans, they are guaranteed to receive a VA home loan, no matter what their financial circumstances are. But a veteran has to qualify for a VA loan, just as for any other kind of mortgage loan; there are specific underwriting standards the veteran has to meet for the loan to be approved. The VA guaranty refers only to the lender's protection against loss.

Here are the key characteristics of VA-guaranteed loans:

- A VA loan can be used to finance the purchase or construction of a single-family home, or a multifamily residential property with up to four dwelling units.

- The VA doesn't guarantee investor loans, so the veteran borrower must intend to occupy the home (or one of the units, in the case of a multifamily property).

- Unlike most home loans, a typical VA loan doesn't require a downpayment; the loan-to-value ratio can be 100%. In other words, the loan amount can be as large as the appraised value of the property. This is probably the most important advantage of VA financing. It's particularly helpful to first-time home buyers, who usually have less cash to invest in their home.

- The VA does not set a maximum loan amount. (However, as we'll discuss later, lenders generally follow some rules of their own concerning VA loan amounts.)

- There are no maximum income limits; VA loans aren't restricted to low- or middle-income buyers.

- VA underwriting standards are less stringent than conventional underwriting standards, so it's generally easier for a veteran to qualify for a VA loan.

- VA loans have traditionally been 30-year fixed-rate loans, but currently ARMs, hybrid ARMs (3/1, 5/1, 7/1, or 10/1), graduated payment mortgages (GPMs), and growing equity mortgages (GEMs) are also available to VA borrowers.

- VA loans don't require mortgage insurance or reserves after closing.

- Lenders aren't allowed to charge VA borrowers standard origination fees. Instead, a lender may charge a flat fee of no more than 1% of the amount financed to cover costs. The lender may also charge reasonable discount points, which can be paid by the borrower, the seller, or a third party.

- VA loans cannot have prepayment penalties.

- A VA loan may be assumed by any buyer who meets the VA's underwriting standards—it doesn't have to be a veteran. The interest rate on the loan won't be increased, and the VA strictly limits the fees the lender can charge for an assumption.

- Forbearance is extended to VA borrowers who are experiencing temporary financial difficulties resulting from problems such as unemployment, disability, large medical bills, or the death of a spouse. The VA has loan officers who can help borrowers and lenders negotiate repayment plans for delinquent loans.

Characteristics of VA loans:
- Used to buy or build residence with up to four units
- Vet must occupy property
- No downpayment required
- VA doesn't set maximum loan amount
- No maximum income limits
- Less stringent qualifying standards
- Fixed-rate or ARM
- No mortgage insurance
- No reserves required
- 1% flat fee for lender
- No prepayment penalty
- Can be assumed by creditworthy buyer, veteran or non-veteran
- Forbearance for vet in financial difficulties

Funding Fees. While VA borrowers don't have to pay a mortgage insurance premium, they do have to pay a **funding fee**, which the VA uses to defray the administrative costs of the guaranteed loan program. The funding fee for a transaction may be paid at closing or financed along with the loan amount.

Funding fee: 2.15% of loan amount, unless veteran makes downpayment of 5% or more

For a member of the regular military obtaining a no-downpayment loan, the funding fee is 2.15% of the loan amount. If the borrower makes a downpayment of 5% or more, the funding fee is reduced. When the downpayment is at least 5% but less than 10%, the funding fee is 1.5%. When the downpayment is 10% or more, the funding fee is 1.25%.

For a member of the Reserves or the National Guard obtaining a no-downpayment loan, the funding fee is 2.4%. If the downpayment is between 5% and 10%, the funding fee is 1.75%; if the downpayment is 10% or more, the fee is 1.5%.

In cases where the borrower has had a VA-guaranteed loan before, the funding fee for the second (or subsequent) loan is 3.3% if less than a 5% downpayment is made.

When a VA loan is assumed, a funding fee of 0.5% of the loan balance is charged.

Certain parties are exempt from the funding fee requirement:

- veterans entitled to receive VA compensation for service-related disabilities (including those still on active duty and awaiting discharge);
- veterans who would be entitled to receive compensation for service-related disabilities if they weren't already receiving retirement pay;
- veterans who are rated by the VA as eligible to receive compensation as a result of pre-discharge examination and rating; and
- surviving spouses of veterans who died in service or from service-related disabilities.

Eligibility for VA Loans

Eligibility for VA-guaranteed loans is based on length of active duty service in the U.S. armed forces. The minimum requirement varies depending on when the veteran served, as follows:

90 days of active duty, any part of which occurred during one of these wartime periods:

1. World War II (September 16, 1940 through July 25, 1947),
2. the Korean War (June 27, 1950 through January 31, 1955),

3. the Vietnam War (August 5, 1964 through May 7, 1975), or

4. the period that began with the Persian Gulf War (which started August 2, 1990) and continues through the present.

181 days of continuous active duty during one of these peacetime periods:

1. July 26, 1947 through June 26, 1950

2. February 1, 1955 through August 4, 1964

3. May 8, 1975 through September 7, 1980

For service that began on or after September 8, 1980 (or for service as an officer that began on or after October 17, 1981):

- **24 months** of continuous active duty, or

- for a Reservist, the full period for which he was called to active duty, as long as it was at least 90 days during wartime, or at least 181 continuous days during peacetime.

A shorter period of service may be sufficient for veterans who are suffering from a compensable service-connected disability, or who were discharged for the convenience of the government, for hardship, or because of certain medical conditions that are not service-connected.

For veterans who were discharged for a service-connected disability, there is no minimum active duty service requirement. They are eligible for VA-guaranteed loans no matter how brief their period of service was—even if it was just a single day.

If an individual applies for a VA loan while still on active duty, she is eligible after serving at least 181 days of continuous active duty (regardless of when the period of service began), or after at least 90 days of active duty service, any part of which occurred during wartime.

Someone who has served in the Reserves or the National Guard for at least six years is eligible even without meeting the minimum active duty service requirement.

Veterans who received a dishonorable discharge are not eligible. Veterans whose discharge was neither honorable nor dishonorable are eligible, however.

The VA determines a veteran's eligibility for a VA loan. If a veteran is eligible, the VA will issue a **Certificate of Eligibility**, which the veteran then uses to apply for a VA loan. To get a Certificate of

Eligibility for VA loan:
1. Minimum active duty service requirement
2. Other than dishonorable discharge
3. Unremarried surviving spouse may be eligible

Eligibility, the veteran must complete and sign an application form, which is available from VA lenders or on the VA website. The veteran must also provide a photocopy of his most recent discharge or separation papers (usually form DD-214). If the veteran is currently on active duty, a statement of service on military letterhead signed by the appropriate military personnel is required.

In many cases, the lender can now instantly obtain a Certificate of Eligibility for a VA loan applicant through an online system.

Eligibility of a Spouse. A veteran's surviving spouse may be eligible for a VA loan if he or she has not remarried and the veteran was killed in action or died of service-related injuries. A veteran's spouse may also be eligible if the veteran is listed as missing in action or is a prisoner of war.

The VA Guaranty

An essential feature of VA loans is that they are guaranteed by the U.S. government. This significantly reduces the lender's risk of loss in case the borrower defaults. It's because of the government guaranty that lenders are willing to make no-downpayment loans through the program. VA regulations determine the guaranty amount available for a transaction, how a veteran's guaranty entitlement can be restored after use, and how the guaranty affects a veteran's liability.

Guaranty Amount

Like private mortgage insurance, the VA guaranty covers only a portion of the loan amount. The amount of coverage is referred to as the **guaranty amount**.

VA guaranty amount:
- Depends on loan amount
- Covers only part of loan amount
- May be tied to area median house price

Under current rules, the guaranty amount available in a particular transaction depends on the loan amount. It also depends on the maximum guaranty amount that applies in the county where the home being purchased is located. We'll discuss maximum guaranty amounts first, and then explain how the guaranty amount varies depending on the loan amount.

Maximum Guaranty Amounts. The guaranty amount has always been increased periodically to keep pace with rising housing costs. Just as a matter of historical interest, the increases made since the program began are shown in Figure 12.1.

Fig. 12.1 Increases in the VA guaranty amount since the program began

World War II guaranty amount: $4,000	
September 1951	$7,500
May 1968	$12,500
December 1974	$17,500
October 1978	$25,000
October 1980	$27,500
February 1988	$36,000
January 1990	$46,000 maximum
August 1995	$50,750 maximum
July 2003	$60,000 maximum
2005	$89,912 maximum
2006 through July 29, 2008	$104,250 maximum
July 30, 2008 through December 31, 2008	$104,250 maximum in most counties; higher maximums in high-cost counties, up to a ceiling of $182,437
2009	$104,250 maximum in most counties; higher maximums in high-cost counties, up to a ceiling of $319,265*

Since 2005, the VA maximum guaranty amount has been tied to conforming loan limits for conventional loans (see Chapter 10). Specifically, the maximum guaranty amount is ordinarily 25% of Freddie Mac's annual conforming loan limit for one-unit properties.

Also, as of July 30, 2008, the VA sets higher maximum guaranty amounts for counties designated as high-cost areas. In 2009, a high-cost county's maximum guaranty is 25% of 125% of the area median price for a single-family house; but it can't exceed 25% of 175% of Freddie Mac's conforming loan limit for one-unit properties in that county.

Here's how those complicated rules apply in 2009. Freddie Mac's 2009 loan limit for one-unit properties in most areas is $417,000. Therefore, the 2009 maximum VA guaranty amount in most areas is 25% of $417,000, or $104,250.*

In a high-cost county in 2009, the maximum guaranty will depend on the county's median house price. However, no matter how high the median house price is, the county's maximum guaranty can't exceed a ceiling of 25% of $1,277,060, or $319,265.* (The $1,277,060 figure is approximate; it's roughly 175% of $729,750, the 2009 conforming

* Note that Alaska, Hawaii, Guam, and the Virgin Islands have higher maximums. For those areas, in 2009 the maximum VA guaranty in most counties is 25% of $729,750, or $182,438. In high-cost counties, the ceiling is 25% of $1,094,625, or $273,656.

loan limit for conventional loans in high-cost areas. $729,750 × 1.75 = $1,277,062.50.)

The following example illustrates how the maximum guaranty amount is set for different counties.

> **Example:** In 54 of Colorado's 64 counties, including Denver County, the 2009 maximum VA guaranty is 25% of $417,000, or $104,250.
>
> The other ten counties are high-cost areas. Each of the high-cost counties has its own maximum guaranty that depends on the area median house price there. For instance, in Boulder County, the median house price is $437,500, so the 2009 maximum VA guaranty is 25% of $437,500, or $109,375. Pitkin County, which includes Aspen, is one of the most expensive places in the U.S. (the median house price is well over a million dollars). So in Pitkin County the 2009 maximum VA guaranty is at the ceiling: it's 25% of $1,277,060, or $319,265.

Guaranty Based on Loan Amount. So far we've been discussing the maximum VA guaranty amount that applies depending on the county where the property is located. But a county's maximum doesn't apply to all VA loan transactions that take place there. As we said earlier, the amount of the guaranty available in a particular transaction depends on the loan amount. Figure 12.2 shows the guaranty amounts for different loan amounts. Let's look at some examples.

Examples:

1. $75,000   Loan amount between $56,251 and $144,000
    × 40%   Guaranty: 40% of loan amount, up to $36,000
    $30,000   Guaranty amount in any county

Fig. 12.2 *The VA guaranty amount for a transaction depends on the loan amount*

Loan Amount	Guaranty Amount
Up to $45,000	50% of loan amount
$45,001 – $56,250	$22,500
$56,251 – $144,000	40% of loan amount, up to a maximum of $36,000
$144,001 – $417,000	25% of loan amount
Over $417,000	25% of loan amount, up to county maximum

2. | | |
    |---|---|
    | $125,000 | Loan amount between $56,251 and $144,000 |
    | × 40% | Guaranty: 40% of loan amount, up to $36,000 |
    | $50,000 | 40% of loan amount (exceeds $36,000) |
    | $36,000 | Guaranty amount in any county |

3. | | |
    |---|---|
    | $300,000 | Loan amount between $144,001 and $417,000 |
    | × 25% | Guaranty: 25% of loan amount |
    | $75,000 | Guaranty amount in any county |

4. | | |
    |---|---|
    | $450,000 | Loan amount over $417,000 |
    | × 25% | Guaranty: 25% of loan amount, up to county maximum |
    | $112,500 | 25% of loan amount (exceeds $104,250) |
    | $104,250 | Guaranty amount in most counties |
    | $110,750 | Guaranty in a county where the maximum is $110,750 |
    | $112,500 | Guaranty in a county where the maximum is $123,000 |

5. | | |
    |---|---|
    | $1,300,000 | Loan amount over $417,000 |
    | × 25% | Guaranty: 25% of loan amount, up to county maximum |
    | $325,000 | 25% of loan amount (exceeds $319,265 ceiling) |
    | $104,250 | Guaranty amount in most counties |
    | $180,500 | Guaranty in a county where the maximum is $180,500 |
    | $319,265 | Guaranty in a county where the maximum is at the ceiling |

Restoration of Guaranty Entitlement

The guaranty amount available to a particular veteran is called the veteran's **entitlement**. A veteran's guaranty entitlement doesn't expire. The entitlement is available until it is used by the veteran or by his or her unremarried surviving spouse.

If a veteran borrower sells the property that he financed with a VA loan, and is able to repay the loan in full from the proceeds of the sale, his full guaranty entitlement is **restored**. (Restoration of entitlement is sometimes referred to as reinstatement.)

Restoration of entitlement is also available if the prior VA loan is paid off and the same property is then used as security for a new VA loan (for example, if the veteran uses a VA loan to refinance an existing VA loan).

VA rules also allow for a one-time restoration of entitlement to a veteran who pays off a VA loan without selling the property. So the veteran could keep the first property and use her restored entitlement to obtain a second VA loan to buy a new home. (The veteran would have to occupy the newly purchased home, because of the VA's owner-occupancy requirement.) This is permitted only once, however; after

Entitlement: guaranty amount available to particular veteran

Full entitlement restored when vet pays off loan

that, if the veteran wants to obtain another VA loan, entitlement won't be restored without selling the property.

The Guaranty and the Veteran's Liability

The VA guaranty doesn't necessarily relieve a veteran of personal liability for his loan. Under limited circumstances, a veteran may be liable after default or (with older loans) after the loan has been assumed.

Liability After Default. The VA requires lenders to take certain steps to help VA borrowers avoid default. But if those efforts fail, the lender can foreclose on the property, just as with any other mortgage loan. If the foreclosure sale results in a loss, the lender can demand reimbursement from the VA to cover the loss, up to the guaranty amount. In some cases, a defaulting veteran may be held liable to the VA, to the lender, or both.

If VA pays lender's claim:
- Veteran is required to reimburse VA only if guilty of fraud or bad faith
- But vet's entitlement isn't restored unless VA is reimbursed

Liability to VA. After the VA pays a lender's claim, the veteran may be required to reimburse the VA for the amount paid. However, for loans closed on or after January 1, 1990, reimbursement is required only if the veteran was guilty of fraud, misrepresentation, or bad faith.

When the VA requires reimbursement, the amount that the veteran owes constitutes a delinquent federal debt. The veteran's income tax refunds can be applied to it, and any federal pay owed to the veteran can be garnished. The veteran isn't eligible for any further federal loans until arrangements to repay the debt are made.

Even if a veteran isn't required to reimburse the VA (because the case didn't involve fraud or bad faith), his guaranty entitlement won't be restored unless he does so.

Vet may be liable to lender for uncovered loss

Liability to lender. If the lender's foreclosure loss isn't fully covered by the guaranty amount, the veteran may be liable to the lender for the uncovered amount. (State law concerning deficiency judgments would apply.) In that situation, a veteran who was guilty of fraud or bad faith could be liable to the VA for the claim paid and also to the lender for the uncovered amount.

Liability After Assumption. As we said earlier, a VA loan can be assumed by either a veteran or a non-veteran. Unless the loan was made before March 1, 1988, the parties must obtain prior approval for the assumption from the VA or the lender.

Approval of an assumption will be granted if:

1. the buyer assuming the loan can meet the same underwriting standards an applicant for a new VA loan has to meet;

2. the loan payments will be current on the closing date; and

3. the buyer agrees to assume all of the original borrower's loan obligations.

When an assumption is approved, the original borrower is released from liability for the loan.

Different rules apply when a VA loan made before March 1, 1988 is assumed. The parties aren't required to obtain approval from the VA or the lender. However, the original borrower will remain liable unless a release of liability is requested and granted. A release will be granted only if the buyer is an acceptable credit risk, the payments are current, and the buyer assumes all of the original borrower's obligations.

Assumption requires prior approval
- *Buyer must meet VA underwriting standards*
- *Original borrower is released from liability*

Exception for assumption of older loans:
- *Prior approval not required*
- *But original borrower remains liable unless release requested*

Substitution of Entitlement

After an assumption, even if the veteran (the original borrower) is released from liability, the veteran's entitlement isn't automatically restored. Guaranty entitlement is only restored—making it possible for the veteran to obtain another VA loan—under certain conditions. The buyer who assumes the original loan must be an eligible veteran with entitlement equal to (or greater than) the loan's guaranty amount, and must agree to substitute her entitlement for the original borrower's. A substitution of entitlement must be requested from the VA.

Vet's full entitlement restored after assumption only if buyer is also veteran and agrees to substitution of entitlement

Remaining Entitlement

A veteran who arranges for his VA loan to be assumed by a non-veteran can't have full entitlement restored. Even so, the veteran may still have **remaining entitlement** (also called partial entitlement) that can be used to get another VA loan. Someone who obtained a VA loan years ago may have remaining entitlement now, because of increases in the maximum guaranty amount (see Figure 12.1).

The amount of remaining entitlement the veteran can use for a new loan depends on the loan amount. If the new loan amount is $144,000 or less, the remaining entitlement is determined by subtracting the amount of entitlement used on the earlier loan from $36,000. If the new loan amount is over $144,000, then the amount of entitlement used on the earlier loan is subtracted from the maximum guaranty

After VA loan assumed by non-veteran, veteran may have remaining entitlement

Amount of remaining entitlement depends on amount of new loan and guaranty amount used on prior loan

amount in the county where the property is located. In 2009, in most areas, that means it's subtracted from $104,250.

> **Example:** Andrea Jordan obtained a VA loan in 1987 and used the maximum guaranty then available, $27,500. Jordan sold her old home and allowed the non-veteran buyer to assume her VA loan. Now she wants another VA loan to buy a new home in a county where the maximum guaranty is $104,250.
>
> If Jordan wants to borrow $144,000 or less, her remaining entitlement is $8,500.
>
> | | |
> |---|---|
> | $36,000 | Basis for calculation of remaining entitlement |
> | − 27,500 | Guaranty on existing loan |
> | $8,500 | Remaining entitlement to be used for new loan |
>
> If Jordan wants to borrow more than $144,000, her remaining entitlement is $76,750.
>
> | | |
> |---|---|
> | $104,250 | Basis for calculation of remaining entitlement |
> | − 27,500 | Guaranty on existing loan |
> | $76,750 | Remaining entitlement to be used for new loan |
>
> Keep in mind that even though Jordan has up to $76,750 in remaining entitlement for a loan amount over $144,000, the guaranty for these larger loans can't exceed 25% of the loan amount. (See the guaranty chart earlier in the chapter, Figure 12.2.) For instance, Jordan's guaranty for a $200,000 loan would be $50,000.

Remaining entitlement is generally used only when the veteran has sold the property for which the earlier loan was obtained without paying that loan off, since VA loans require owner occupancy. A veteran who had a previous VA loan and isn't certain whether he has any remaining entitlement should call the local VA office. The veteran will need the VA's identifying numbers for the original loan.

Entitlement and Co-Ownership

Co-ownership:
- Even if buyers are both eligible veterans, maximum guaranty is not increased
- If veteran buys home with non-veteran other than spouse, guaranty only covers vet's half of the loan

If both a husband and a wife are veterans with guaranty entitlements, they can't combine their entitlements to increase the guaranty amount for their VA loan when they buy a home together. For example, if they're buying a $360,000 home, the guaranty is still only $90,000 (25% of $360,000). Either spouse can use his or her entitlement for the loan, or they can each contribute part of their entitlement.

If a veteran uses a VA loan to buy a home with a non-veteran who isn't his or her spouse, the guaranty is based only on the veteran's portion of the loan. The guaranty doesn't cover the non-veteran's portion. For example, suppose two brothers are purchasing a home together. Only one brother is a veteran. If they're borrowing $160,000, the amount of the guaranty will be $36,000—the guaranty amount for an $80,000 loan.

Refinancing with a VA Loan

A VA loan can be used to refinance an existing conventional, FHA, or VA loan, or seller financing. It can even be used to pay off other liens, such as tax or judgment liens. (The veteran may also receive cash from the proceeds of the new loan.) The VA loan may not exceed 100% of the appraised value of the property, plus the usual funding fee for a no-downpayment loan and the cost of energy-efficient improvements. Normal VA underwriting standards apply. If the VA loan is used to refinance an existing loan that is not a VA loan, guaranty entitlement must be used.

VA loan can be used to refinance any existing loan

If the new VA loan is used to refinance an existing VA loan solely to take advantage of lower interest rates, or to replace an ARM with a fixed-rate loan, the loan amount is limited to the balance of the old loan plus the closing costs, up to two discount points, a 0.5% funding fee, and the cost of energy-efficient improvements. Use of additional entitlement isn't required. This type of refinancing (sometimes referred to as streamline refinancing) is advantageous for the borrower because underwriting generally isn't required: neither the borrower nor the property has to meet VA underwriting standards.

Exercise No. 1

John Woods, a U.S. Navy Reservist, served 12 months on active duty, the full period he was called up for. He left the Navy with an honorable discharge. Woods now wants to buy his first home, and he's applying for a $325,000 VA-guaranteed loan.

1. Is Woods eligible for a VA loan? Why or why not? Based on the 2009 rules concerning guaranty amounts, what would the amount of his entitlement be?

2. If Woods gets a $325,000 loan, how much of it will be covered by the VA guaranty? Suppose the house he wants is in a high-cost county. How would that affect the guaranty amount?

VA Loan Amounts

Although the VA doesn't set a maximum loan amount, a VA loan may not exceed the appraised value of the property. The appraisal must be performed by a VA-approved appraiser, and the VA issues a **Notice of Value**, or NOV, stating the appraised value. (An NOV used to be called a Certificate of Reasonable Value, or CRV, and that term is also still in use.) If the sales price is greater than the appraised value, the difference must be made up with a cash downpayment out of the borrower's own funds.

The only other restrictions on the loan amount come from the lender, not the VA. Most lenders require the veteran's guaranty entitlement to equal at least 25% of the loan amount. In other words, they won't make a no-downpayment loan that's more than four times the guaranty amount. A loan that exceeds that limit will be more difficult to sell on the secondary market.

Since the maximum guaranty amount in most counties is 25% of the conforming loan limit, lenders in those counties typically won't loan more than the conforming loan limit without a downpayment.

> VA loan amount:
> - VA doesn't set maximum, but loan amount can't exceed appraised value
> - Lenders generally require guaranty to equal 25% of loan amount
> - So maximum amount for no-downpayment loans is usually four times the county maximum guaranty

$104,250   Maximum guaranty amount in most counties
÷   25%   Percentage of loan amount
$417,000   Maximum loan amount with no downpayment

Lenders generally follow the 25% rule in high-cost counties as well, making correspondingly larger loans in those places. For example, in a high-cost county where the maximum guaranty amount is $319,265, lenders are likely to be willing to make no-downpayment loans of up to $1,277,060 ($319,265 ÷ 25% = $1,277,060).

Making a Downpayment

A veteran who wants a VA loan larger than $417,000 (or larger than the corresponding limit in a high-cost county) can still get one, as long as he makes a downpayment. Lenders usually require the downpayment plus the guaranty amount to equal 25% of the loan amount.

If guaranty is less than 25% of loan amount, lender requires downpayment

Example: Robert Mendez wants to buy a home that has been valued at $450,000. He has full entitlement, and the maximum guaranty for his area is $104,250. His lender won't make a loan for more than $417,000 unless Mendez makes a downpayment.

$450,000	Sales price
× 25%	Desired ratio of guaranty + downpayment to price
$112,500	25% of loan amount
− 104,250	Maximum guaranty
$8,250	Downpayment required by lender

$450,000	Sales price
− 8,250	Downpayment
$441,750	Loan amount

Guaranty + downpayment should equal 25% of sales price

If the veteran has only partial entitlement left, making a downpayment is even more important.

Example: Marcia Riggs wants to buy a home for $215,000; the appraised value is $216,000. Her remaining entitlement is $32,000.

$215,000	Sales price
× 25%	Desired ratio of guaranty + downpayment to price
$53,750	
− 32,000	Remaining entitlement
$21,750	Downpayment required by lender

$215,000	Sales price
− 21,750	Downpayment
$193,250	Loan amount

Secondary Financing

If a veteran doesn't have enough cash for a downpayment required by the lender, she can finance part or all of it if the following conditions are met:

For a lender-required downpayment, veteran may use secondary financing
- Combined loans may not exceed value on NOV
- Buyer must qualify for combined payment
- Second loan must be assumable

1. the total financing doesn't exceed the appraised value of the property (established by the NOV);
2. the borrower has enough income to qualify based on the payments required for both loans; and
3. the second loan doesn't restrict the borrower's ability to sell the property more than the VA loan does (in other words, the second loan must be assumable by a creditworthy buyer).

Secondary financing can be used to generate enough cash for a lender-required downpayment and/or for closing costs. It can also be helpful when the interest rate on the second loan is lower than the rate on the VA loan. Here's an important limitation, however: secondary financing can't be used to cover a downpayment that's required by the VA because the sales price exceeds the appraised value (as opposed to one required by the lender because of the 25% rule).

Exercise No. 2

In each of the following cases, assume that it's 2009, the property isn't in a high-cost area, the prospective borrower is an eligible veteran, and the lender follows the 25% rule explained above.

1. Jeffrey Bates has never had a VA loan before. He wants to buy a home with an appraised value of $259,000. What is the largest loan the lender will offer him? How much of a downpayment would he have to make for that loan? How much would the guaranty be?

2. Helen Moreau wants to buy a home for $425,000 (the appraised value is $426,500). What is the largest VA loan the lender will offer her? How much of a downpayment would she be required to make for that loan? How much would the guaranty be?

3. Ben Jessell bought a home with a VA loan in 1994. He recently sold the home, and the non-veteran buyer assumed the loan. The guaranty on that loan is $46,000. Now Jessell wants to buy a new home for $382,000. How much remaining entitlement does he have if he chooses to finance this transaction with a VA loan? How much of a downpayment will the lender require Jessell to make?

Underwriting Guidelines

When making a VA loan, the lender analyzes the veteran's credit-worthiness using VA underwriting guidelines. Many of the guidelines are identical to the general qualifying principles discussed in Chapter 8. However, the guidelines for analyzing income are quite different from those used for conventional or FHA loans.

A VA loan applicant's income is analyzed using two different methods: the income ratio method and the residual income method. The veteran must qualify under both methods.

Two methods of income analysis for VA loans:
• Income ratio
• Residual income (cash flow)

Income Ratio Analysis

Like conventional and FHA underwriting, underwriting for VA loans involves an income ratio method of analysis. But instead of using both a housing expense to income ratio and a debt to income ratio, the VA uses only a debt to income ratio (sometimes formally referred to as the total obligations to income ratio). As a general rule, unless there are compensating factors, a VA borrower's debt to income ratio should not exceed **41%**. Installment debts with ten or more payments remaining are taken into account in calculating the ratio, along with the borrower's other recurring obligations.

Debt to income ratio generally should not exceed 41%

> **Example:** Robin Young is eligible for a VA loan. She and her husband, Mike Appleton, have a combined income of $6,000 per month. Their monthly obligations, not including their housing expense, add up to $1,030.
>
> | | |
> |---|---|
> | $6,000 | Monthly income |
> | × 41% | Maximum debt to income ratio |
> | $2,460 | |
> | − 1,030 | Monthly recurring obligations |
> | $1,430 | Maximum housing expense (PITI) |
>
> Young and Appleton could qualify for a $1,430 monthly housing expense under the VA's debt to income ratio rule.

Residual Income Analysis

The second method used to analyze a VA loan applicant's income is residual income analysis, which is also called cash flow analysis. For this analysis, the proposed housing expense (principal, interest, taxes, and insurance), all other recurring obligations, and certain taxes are subtracted from the veteran's gross monthly income to determine

Residual income: gross monthly income minus taxes, recurring obligations, and housing expense

his **residual income**. (The taxes include federal income tax, any state or local income tax, social security tax, Medicare tax, and any other taxes deducted from the veteran's paychecks.) The veteran's residual income usually should be at least one dollar more than the VA's minimum requirement. The minimum requirement varies based on the region of the country where the veteran lives, family size, and the size of the proposed loan, as shown in Figure 12.3.

> **Example:** Continuing with the previous example, suppose Young and Appleton have two children and live in the VA's Midwest region. They're planning to buy a home that costs more than $80,000. To meet the VA's guidelines, they should have at least $1,003 in residual income (see Figure 12.3).

$6,000	Gross monthly income
1,100	Federal income tax withheld
250	State income tax withheld
460	Social security and Medicare withheld
1,030	Recurring obligations
− 1,430	Maximum housing expense (from 41% ratio)
$1,730	Residual income

Fig. 12.3 Minimum residual income requirements for VA loan applicants

**Table of Residual Incomes by Region
For loan amounts of $79,999 and below**

Family Size	Northeast	Midwest	South	West
1	$390	$382	$382	$425
2	$654	$641	$641	$713
3	$788	$772	$772	$859
4	$888	$868	$868	$967
5	$921	$902	$902	$1,004
Over 5: Add $75 for each additional member up to a family of 7.				

**Table of Residual Incomes by Region
For loan amounts of $80,000 and above**

Family Size	Northeast	Midwest	South	West
1	$450	$441	$441	$491
2	$755	$738	$738	$823
3	$909	$889	$889	$990
4	$1,025	$1,003	$1,003	$1,117
5	$1,062	$1,039	$1,039	$1,158
Over 5: Add $80 for each additional member up to a family of 7.				

Since Young and Appleton's residual income is well above the $1,003 requirement, they can easily qualify for a VA loan with a $1,430 monthly payment. In fact, because their residual income exceeds the required minimum by so much, they may be able to qualify for a larger payment than that (see below).

Compensating Factors

The VA emphasizes that the 41% income ratio and the figures on the residual income chart are only guidelines, and failure to meet them shouldn't automatically result in rejection of the loan application. For instance, although residual income is a very important factor in evaluating a VA loan application, the loan may still be approved even if the applicant's residual income is slightly less than the minimum shown on the chart, if there are compensating factors. The chart merely helps the underwriter judge the applicant's relative strength or weakness in regard to residual income.

VA underwriting standards are merely guidelines, not hard and fast rules

The VA lists all of the following as examples of compensating factors which can help an application that is weak in certain respects:

Compensating factors may allow loan approval in spite of marginal income or other weakness

1. an excellent long-term credit history,
2. conservative use of consumer credit,
3. minimal consumer debt,
4. long-term employment,
5. significant liquid assets,
6. a sizable downpayment,
7. little or no increase in the housing expense,
8. military benefits,
9. satisfactory previous experience with home ownership,
10. high residual income,
11. a low debt to income ratio,
12. tax credits for child care,
13. tax benefits of home ownership, and
14. (for refinancing) significant equity in the property.

The VA points out that a particular compensating factor helps only if it's relevant to the particular weakness in the loan application. For example, if the applicant's residual income is slightly below the VA's minimum, significant liquid assets are a relevant compensating factor, because the family could draw on the liquid assets to supplement their income. On the other hand, long-term employment isn't relevant. The fact that the applicant has an exceptionally stable employment history strengthens the application in a general sense, but it doesn't specifically address the issue of marginal residual income—whether the applicant's family will have enough money to live on after paying all the bills. Without any compensating factors that are relevant to marginal income, the underwriter should probably reject the application, in spite of the applicant's good employment history.

Income Ratio Exceptions. The VA has specific rules for approving the loan of an applicant whose debt to income ratio is over 41%. The lender is generally required to submit a detailed statement to the VA listing the relevant compensating factors that justify loan approval in spite of the high income ratio, such as significant liquid assets, a substantial downpayment, or more residual income than the minimum requirement.

If residual income exceeds minimum by 20% or more, loan can be approved even though vet's income ratio is over 41%, without any other compensating factors

Extra residual income is especially helpful. If the applicant's residual income is at least 20% over the required minimum, the lender can approve the loan (in spite of a high income ratio) without any other compensating factors, and without submitting a statement of justification to the VA.

> **Example:** Refer back to the previous example involving Young and Appleton. This time assume that they want to buy a house that costs $218,000. Their monthly housing expense would be $1,570. With this housing expense added to their monthly recurring obligations ($1,030), their total monthly obligations come to $2,700. This gives them a 45% debt to income ratio ($2,700 ÷ $6,000 = 45%). Even though the ratio is higher than 41%, the lender may approve the loan if there are compensating factors that justify approval. But no other compensating factors are necessary if the couple's residual income exceeds the minimum by 20% or more. Let's see whether Young and Appleton have enough residual income to bring the 20% rule into play.
>
> | | |
> |---:|:---|
> | $6,000 | Gross monthly income |
> | 1,100 | Federal income tax withheld |
> | 250 | State income tax withheld |
> | 460 | Social security and Medicare withheld |
> | 1,030 | Recurring obligations |
> | − 1,570 | Maximum housing expense (45% ratio) |
> | $1,590 | Residual income |
>
> When the $1,570 housing expense is subtracted from their gross income along with their taxes and other obligations, it leaves Young and Appleton with $1,590 in residual income. However, the VA requires only $1,003 in residual income for a

family of four in the Midwest region. Now let's see if the couple's residual income exceeds the minimum by 20% or more.

$1,590	Residual income (with $1,570 housing expense)
− 1,003	Required minimum residual income
$587	Residual income in excess of required minimum

$1,003	Required minimum residual income
× 20%	
$201	20% of required minimum

Young and Appleton's extra $587 in residual income exceeds the minimum by much more than 20%, so the lender may well approve their loan—even though their debt to income ratio is significantly higher than 41%, and even if there are no other compensating factors in the couple's financial situation.

Overall, the VA's qualifying rules are much less stringent than the Fannie Mae/Freddie Mac rules. A borrower who would be considered marginal for a conventional loan might easily qualify for a VA loan. Eligible veterans should always keep VA financing in mind.

Exercise No. 3

Vince Martin, a former marine, is eligible for a VA loan; he hasn't used any of his entitlement yet. He and his wife, Cheryl, have four children, and they live in the VA's Western region.

The Martins have found a house they'd like to buy. They apply for a VA loan, and the NOV establishes the appraised value of the property as $207,500. The Martins' gross monthly income is $5,200. The withheld taxes come to $1,325 per month. Their recurring obligations (not counting their housing expense) come to $807 per month.

The Martins aren't planning to make a downpayment. Their interest rate would be 6%, and their monthly housing expense would be about $1,430 ($1,244 for principal and interest, plus 15% for estimated taxes and hazard insurance; mortgage insurance isn't required).

1. What would the Martins' debt to income ratio be?

2. Could the Martins qualify for this VA loan? Why or why not?

Outline: VA-Guaranteed Loans

I. Characteristics of VA Loans

    A. VA loan is made by institutional lender, but a portion of loan amount is guaranteed by the Department of Veterans Affairs.

        1. Loan guaranty functions like mortgage insurance, protecting the lender against a loss in the event of buyer default.

    B. VA loan can be used for purchase or construction of residence with up to four units.

        1. Veteran must occupy the home (or one of the units in a multifamily residence).

    C. Key characteristics of a VA loan:

        1. No downpayment required, as long as loan does not exceed home's appraised value.

        2. No maximum loan amount; no maximum income limits.

        3. Less stringent qualifying standards

        4. No mortgage insurance required.

        5. 1% flat fee for lender.

        6. No reserves required.

        7. No prepayment penalty allowed.

        8. Forbearance extended to borrowers with temporary financial difficulties.

        9. May be assumed by a veteran or a non-veteran.

    D. VA borrowers pay a funding fee ranging from 1.25% to 3.3% of the loan amount, depending on the downpayment, the type of service, and whether the veteran is a first-time VA borrower.

II. Eligibility for VA Loans

    A. Eligibility depends on the length of active duty in the U.S. armed forces.

    B. Minimum requirements:

        1. 90 days of active duty during a wartime period; or

        2. 181 days of continuous active duty during a peacetime period; *otherwise*

        3. 24 continuous months or the full period of time called to active duty; *or*

        4. six years of service in the Reserves or National Guard even without fulfilling the minimum active duty requirement.

C. Shorter period of service required for disabled veterans or veterans discharged early for government, hardship, or medical reasons.

D. An eligible veteran is issued a Certificate of Eligibility, which the veteran uses to apply for a VA loan.

E. The spouse of a veteran who was killed in action, died of service-related injuries, or is listed as missing in action or as a prisoner of war, may be eligible for a VA loan.

III. VA Guaranty

A. Guaranty available to a particular veteran is known as the veteran's "entitlement."

1. Guaranty available for a particular loan depends on size of loan.

2. Maximum guaranty (for loan amounts over $144,000)

a. In most counties, maximum guaranty is 25% of the current Freddie Mac conforming loan limit.

b. Each high-cost county has its own maximum guaranty amount based on the area median house price; but regardless of median price, maximum guaranty can't exceed a ceiling that's based on the conforming loan limit.

B. Entitlement may be restored (and then reused) if veteran pays off loan in full.

C. VA loan may be assumed by a veteran or non-veteran.

1. Generally, VA will issue release as long as loan is current and buyer is acceptable credit risk.

2. If loan is assumed by a veteran, the original borrower's entitlement is restored.

D. If spouses are both veterans, they cannot combine their entitlements to increase the guaranty amount for a single VA loan.

E. If a veteran buys a home with a non-veteran, the guaranty only applies to the veteran's portion of the loan.

F. VA loan may be used to refinance an existing VA loan without using additional entitlement.

1. If used to refinance a non-VA loan, entitlement must be used. Veteran may receive cash from the proceeds of the new loan.

IV. VA Loan Amounts

A. No maximum VA loan amount, but the loan may not exceed the property's appraised value.

1. VA-approved appraiser appraises the property; VA issues a Notice of Value (NOV).

B. Most lenders require the guaranty to equal at least 25% of the loan amount. In other words, they won't make a no-downpayment loan for more than four times the guaranty amount.

　1. In most areas, with the current maximum guaranty amount of $104,250, lenders generally won't make VA loans for more than $417,000 without a downpayment.

　2. In high-cost areas, lenders generally won't make VA loans for more than four times the county maximum guaranty.

C. If a VA loan amount is larger than four times the guaranty amount, borrower must make a downpayment to make up the difference between the maximum guaranty amount and 25% of the loan amount.

D. Borrower can finance part or all of a lender-required downpayment, as long as:

　1. total financing doesn't exceed property's appraised value;

　2. buyer's income is enough to qualify based on payments for both loans; and

　3. second loan is assumable by creditworthy buyer.

V. Underwriting Guidelines

A. Applicant must qualify under both methods of income analysis: income ratio and residual income.

B. In the income ratio method, the borrower's total obligations are measured against income. The debt to income ratio should be 41% or less.

C. In the residual income method, the borrower's proposed housing expense, recurring obligations, and certain taxes are subtracted from the gross monthly income to determine the residual income. The residual income should exceed the VA's minimum requirement, which is determined by the borrower's location, family size, and proposed loan size.

D. The income ratio and residual income methods of analysis are only guidelines; if a borrower does not qualify under one of them, the loan may still be approved.

　1. Compensating factors include: good credit history, minimal debt, long-term employment, significant liquid assets, downpayment, high residual income, and a low income ratio.

　2. If the applicant's debt to income ratio exceeds 41% but the residual income is at least 20% over the required minimum, the lender may approve the loan without any compensating factors.

Key Terms

VA: The U.S. Department of Veterans Affairs.

VA-guaranteed loan: A home loan to an eligible veteran made by an institutional lender and guaranteed by the Department of Veterans Affairs, protecting the lender against losses resulting from default.

VA guaranty: The portion of a VA loan guaranteed by the Department of Veterans Affairs; the maximum amount that the VA will pay the lender for a loss resulting from the borrower's default.

Funding fee: A charge paid by a VA borrower at closing, which the lender submits to the VA.

Certificate of Eligibility: A document issued by the Department of Veterans Affairs, indicating a veteran's eligibility for a VA-guaranteed loan.

VA entitlement: The guaranty amount to which a particular veteran is entitled.

Substitution of entitlement: When a VA borrower sells the security property to another eligible veteran, who agrees to substitute her guaranty entitlement for the seller's, so that the seller's entitlement is restored.

Notice of Value (NOV): A document issued by the Department of Veterans Affairs, setting forth a property's current market value, based on a VA-approved appraisal. Previously referred to as a Certificate of Reasonable Value.

Residual income: The amount of income that an applicant for a VA loan has left over after taxes, recurring obligations, and the proposed housing expense have been deducted from his gross monthly income.

Chapter Quiz

1. Because the VA guarantees the loan:
   a. the veteran borrower is not obligated to repay it
   b. lenders are willing to make no-downpayment loans
   c. a VA loan cannot be assumed by a non-veteran
   d. the veteran is entitled to at least two such loans

2. If a veteran allows her VA loan to be assumed, the veteran's entitlement can be restored only if the:
   a. buyer is a veteran with entitlement
   b. loan payments are current
   c. original borrower formally requests a substitution of entitlement
   d. All of the above

3. Which of the following is *not* true of a VA loan?
   a. A small prepayment penalty is allowed
   b. Owner occupancy is required
   c. The loan amount can't exceed the appraised value of the property
   d. No mortgage insurance is required

4. If a veteran with full entitlement wanted to obtain a $325,000 loan, how much would the required downpayment be?
   a. No downpayment is required
   b. $3,250
   c. $2,479
   d. $1,112

5. A veteran may obtain a VA-guaranteed loan on a:
   a. single-family residence only
   b. four-plex, as long as all units are rented out
   c. residence with up to two units, as long as the veteran occupies one unit
   d. one- to four-unit residence, as long as the veteran occupies one unit

6. Martha Jones served in the army on active duty for 120 days in 1989. Jones is:

   a. eligible for full VA entitlement
   b. eligible for partial VA entitlement
   c. eligible for a VA loan only if she meets the underwriting standards
   d. not eligible for a VA loan

7. If Ryan Spar gets a $132,000 VA loan, how much of the loan will the VA guaranty cover?

   a. $24,800
   b. $32,800
   c. $36,000
   d. $5,500

8. The VA allows secondary financing to be used in conjunction with a VA-guaranteed loan only if the:

   a. total amount financed does not exceed the appraised value
   b. buyer's income is sufficient to qualify for the payments on both loans
   c. second loan allows assumption by a creditworthy buyer
   d. All of the above

9. In 1994, Sam Walters obtained a VA loan with a $46,000 guaranty. A few years ago he sold his house and allowed a non-veteran to assume the VA loan. Now Sam wants to borrow $260,000 to buy a new home in a county where the maximum guaranty is $104,250. How much remaining entitlement does he have?

   a. None
   b. $58,250
   c. $65,000
   d. $104,250

10. Unless there are compensating factors, a VA loan applicant's debt to income ratio usually should not exceed:

   a. 36%
   b. 33%
   c. 41%
   d. 53%

Answer Key

1. b. The government's guaranty reduces the lender's risk of loss in case of default by the borrower. Because of this, lenders are willing to make VA loans without requiring the borrower to make a downpayment.

2. d. If a VA loan is assumed by another veteran, the new borrower may agree to substitute her entitlement for the original borrower's entitlement. If the loan's payments are current, the new borrower is qualified, and the parties obtain a substitution of entitlement from the VA, the original borrower's entitlement will be restored.

3. a. No prepayment penalties are allowed with VA loans.

4. a. Currently, lenders in most areas will lend up to $417,000 without a downpayment. As long as the loan doesn't exceed the property's appraised value, the veteran won't need to make a downpayment.

5. d. A VA loan must be used for a one- to four-unit residence, and the veteran must occupy one of the units.

6. d. For service that began after September 8, 1980 but before August 2, 1990 (when the Persian Gulf War period began), eligibility requires a minimum of 181 days of continuous active duty service. Since Jones only served 120 days in 1989, she isn't eligible for a VA loan, even if that was the full period for which she was called to active duty.

7. c. For a loan amount between $56,251 and $144,000, the VA guaranty amount is 40% of the loan amount, up to a maximum of $36,000. Forty percent of $132,000 is $52,800, so the guaranty amount would be $36,000.

8. d. A VA borrower may finance a downpayment if the total financing doesn't exceed the appraised value, the buyer's income is enough to qualify for payments on both loans, and the second loan is assumable. This applies only to a downpayment required by the lender, however; secondary financing can't be used for a downpayment required by VA rules.

9. b. Sam's remaining entitlement is calculated by subtracting the previously used entitlement, $46,000, from $104,250, the current maximum guaranty amount in the county. Sam's remaining entitlement is $58,250.

10. c. A VA loan applicant's debt to income ratio generally shouldn't exceed 41% unless there are compensating factors, such as more residual income than the minimum required.

Case Study:
VA-Guaranteed Loans

Once again, let's return to Rick and Teresa Cortina. This time we'll assume that they're thinking of buying their first home with a VA loan. (Rick was in the Army; his service included more than 24 months of continuous active duty, and he received an honorable discharge.) The Cortinas live in the VA's Southern region, and they have no children. The maximum VA guaranty amount in their area is $104,250.

Refer back to the case study at the end of Chapter 10 for the information you will need about the Cortinas' financial situation. There's a worksheet at the end of this case study that you can use for the calculations.

Interest rates and fees:

Lenders in the Cortinas' area are generally charging the following interest rates and fees for VA loans:

Fixed rate: 5.50% interest, 1% origination fee, no discount points

ARM: 5.625% interest, 1% origination fee, no discount points

1. Using the same figures for the Cortinas' monthly income and recurring charges that you used for the case studies in Chapters 10 and 11, apply the standard VA income ratio to determine a maximum mortgage payment figure (PITI). Round that figure up to the next dollar for Question 2.

2. Calculate how much residual income the Cortinas would have if they had the monthly housing expense you arrived at in Question 1. (You'll need the Cortinas' payroll tax figures, which are listed at the beginning of the Chapter 10 case study.) Check the residual income chart in this chapter, Figure 12.3, and compare the Cortinas' residual income to the VA's required minimum. (Assume that they'll be borrowing over $80,000.) Do the Cortinas have enough residual income to qualify for this monthly housing expense?

3. Now consider whether the Cortinas can qualify for a larger VA loan payment than the one from Question 1. What's the largest PITI payment they could qualify for if they were allowed a 45% debt to income ratio? With that larger payment, what would their residual income be? Do the Cortinas have enough extra residual income so that the lender could approve a loan with that larger payment even if there were no other compensating factors in their financial situation?

4. If 15% of the larger PITI payment from Question 3 would go toward property taxes and hazard insurance, how much would the principal and interest portion of the payment be? With that principal and interest payment, the maximum VA loan that the Cortinas could qualify for at 5.50% interest is approximately $363,692. Using 2009 limits, how much would the VA guaranty for this loan amount be?

5. For this loan, would the lender require the Cortinas to make a downpayment? How much cash would the Cortinas need at closing? They would have to pay the origination fee and the funding fee; assume that they'd also have to pay other closing costs adding up to about 3% of the sales price. No reserves are required.

6. Are the Cortinas likely to choose a VA loan over a conventional loan or an FHA loan? Why or why not?

Income Qualifying—VA-Guaranteed Loans

Taxes (per month)

	Wage earner 1
_____	Federal income tax
_____	State income tax
_____	Social Security/Medicare
	Wage earner 2
_____	Federal income tax
_____	State income tax
+ _____	Social Security/Medicare
_____	Total taxes withheld

Recurring Charges

Car loans	_____
Credit cards	_____
Student loans	_____
Other debts	_____
Child care	_____
Child support	_____
Alimony	_____
Other	+ _____
Total	_____

Gross Monthly Income

Base salary	
Wage earner 1	_____
Wage earner 2	_____
Overtime	_____
Commissions	_____
Bonuses	_____
Other	+ _____
Total	_____

Obligations to Income Ratio

_____	Gross monthly income	_____	Gross monthly income
_____ x .41	Standard ratio (41%)	_____ x .45	Higher ratio (45%)
_____	Maximum obligations	_____	Maximum obligations
− _____	Recurring obligations	− _____	Recurring obligations
_____	Maximum PITI payment with standard 41% ratio	_____	Maximum PITI payment with a 45% ratio

Income Qualifying—VA-Guaranteed Loans

Residual Income Analysis

Required minimum residual income _____

_____	Gross monthly income
_____	Taxes
_____	Recurring obligations
− _____	Proposed housing expense (from 41% ratio)
_____	**Residual Income**

_____	Gross monthly income
_____	Taxes
_____	Recurring obligations
− _____	Proposed housing expense (from 45% ratio)
_____	**Residual Income**

Income ratio over 41% acceptable with compensating factors.

If residual income exceeds the minimum by more than 20%, a ratio over 41% is acceptable even without any other compensating factors.

PITI Payment with 45% ratio _____

_____	Maximum PITI payment
_____ ÷ 1.15	15% for property taxes and hazard insurance
_____	Maximum principal and interest payment
	Interest rate _____

Maximum Loan Amount _____

_____	Loan amount
_____ × .25	Guaranty percentage for VA loan from $144,001 to $417,000
_____	Guaranty amount

Loan Amount = Sales Price
(unless downpayment required because
guaranty is less than 25% of loan amount)

Chapter 13
Seller Financing

How Seller Financing Works

When and Why Seller Financing is Used

Seller Seconds
- Supplementing a new loan
- Supplementing an assumption

Seller Financing as Primary Financing
- Unencumbered property
  - Protecting seller's security
  - Seller financing plus institutional second
  - Land contracts
- Encumbered property: wraparound financing
  - Wraparound vs. assumption plus seller second
  - Protecting a wraparound buyer

Alternatives to Seller Financing
- Buydowns
- Contributions to closing costs
- Equity exchanges
- Lease arrangements

Agent's Responsibilities in Seller-Financed Transactions
- Disclosures
- Liability

Introduction

Institutional lenders are not the only source of residential financing; home sellers are another important source. The wide variety of ways in which a seller can finance a buyer's purchase is the subject of this chapter.

We will begin with a basic explanation of how seller financing works and why it is used. Then we'll examine the forms seller financing can take, looking first at how it can function as secondary financing, and then at how it can function as primary financing. After that, we will briefly consider a few alternatives to seller financing—ways a seller can help the buyer without actually financing the purchase. In the last section of the chapter, we'll discuss the real estate agent's responsibilities in a seller-financed transaction.

How Seller Financing Works

Just like a bank or a savings and loan, a seller can use a promissory note accompanied by a mortgage or deed of trust to finance the buyer's purchase. The buyer takes title to the property and makes regular payments to the seller; the seller is the mortgagee or beneficiary, with the right to foreclose if the buyer defaults. This kind of transaction, where a mortgage or deed of trust is given by a buyer to a seller (instead of a third-party lender), is commonly called a **purchase money loan**.

A purchase money loan differs from an institutional loan in that the seller is simply extending credit to the buyer, rather than actually supplying loan funds. The seller finances the purchase by allowing the buyer to pay the price in installments over time, instead of requiring payment in full at closing.

For certain transactions, a seller has an alternative that institutional lenders do not have: the land contract. With a **land contract**, the buyer (vendee) takes possession of the property, but the seller (vendor) retains title until the contract price has been paid in full. Like a purchase money loan, a land contract represents an extension of credit from the seller to the buyer. We'll discuss land contracts in more detail later in this chapter.

In some transactions, seller financing is secondary financing: a "seller second" that supplements an institutional first mortgage. In

Purchase money loan:
- Seller extends credit to buyer
- Buyer gives seller mortgage or deed of trust

Land contract: alternative to purchase money loan in certain situations other cases, the seller provides primary financing, serving as the buyer's main source or only source of financing for the purchase.

Seller financing can be secondary financing or primary financing

In a transaction that involves both institutional financing and seller financing, the seller probably will not be allowed to use a land contract. As a general rule, an institutional lender is not willing to make a loan to someone who does not have title to the security property (which is the case with the vendee in a land contract).

Aside from that consideration, a seller will usually decide which type of finance instrument to use based on the various remedies each one allows in the event of default (see Chapter 5). For instance, in many states, if the seller wants to be able to foreclose without going to court, he would choose a deed of trust. Foreclosure laws are generally the same for a purchase money mortgage or deed of trust as for any other mortgage or deed of trust, but there may be important exceptions. For example, in some states a seller cannot obtain a deficiency judgment after foreclosure of a purchase money loan, even if it was a judicial foreclosure.

The finance instruments used in a seller-financed transaction should be prepared by a real estate lawyer, or at least reviewed by a lawyer before the parties sign them. If the seller uses a deed of trust, she will have to appoint a trustee when the loan documents are executed. Institutional lenders, title insurance companies, and lawyers often serve as trustees.

When and Why Seller Financing Is Used

What's the point of seller financing? In a tight money market (when institutional loans are hard to get), sometimes the only way a seller can find a buyer is to finance part of the purchase price himself. When prevailing market interest rates are very high, many potential home buyers cannot qualify for institutional financing. Others decide not to buy because they aren't willing to take on an expensive institutional loan. In this situation, a seller can attract buyers by offering financing at an interest rate significantly below the market rate. Even if the seller isn't in a position to finance the entire transaction, a seller second at a lower interest rate can offset the high rate charged on the institutional loan and enable the buyer to qualify.

Although seller financing is important when interest rates are high, it can also be used as a marketing tool at other times. In some cases,

Seller financing can:
- Attract buyers when interest rates are high
- Help buyers qualify for institutional loan
- Enable sellers to charge higher price
- Provide tax benefits to sellers

buyers are willing to pay more for a home if the seller offers financing. It may allow the buyers to avoid or reduce certain loan costs (such as the origination fee and discount fee), enabling them to close with less cash. A seller could set up a payment plan that might not be available from local lenders: graduated payments, biweekly payments, partial amortization with a balloon payment, or an interest-only loan with a balloon. Or the seller might be willing to extend credit to buyers who can't qualify for a conventional loan even though market interest rates are low.

> **Example:** Grandma Perkins owns her house free and clear. She has decided to move to her sister's farm, so she wants to sell her house. The Jarrells, a young couple from Grandma's church, are interested in buying it. They couldn't qualify for conventional financing, but Grandma believes they are honest and reliable people who can be trusted to pay off a loan.
>
> She offers them the following deal: a sales price of $120,000, with $5,000 down and the balance in the form of a purchase money loan, secured by a deed of trust with Grandma as the beneficiary. Interest will accrue at the rate of 3% for the first year, and increase 0.5% per year until it reaches 6%, where it will stay for the balance of the 30-year loan term. Payments are to be interest-only for the first five years, with the principal then fully amortized over the balance of the term.

In the post-financial crisis environment, seller financing may become more common. Today, a borrower with less-than-perfect credit or little cash for a downpayment may well be rejected by a conventional lender. However, a seller eager to sell her house might decide that such a buyer is an acceptable risk. (Bear in mind, though, that seller financing is most useful when the seller has a cushion of significant home equity. It is not going to be a good option for a seller with little or negative equity, who would need to be cashed out of her mortgage immediately.)

Flexibility is the keynote; the seller isn't bound by institutional policies regarding yields, loan-to-value ratios, or qualifying standards. There are risks involved in setting those standards aside, and these risks should be carefully weighed. (The unusual financing arrangement in the example above could turn out badly for both parties. See the "Agent's Responsibilities" section at the end of this chapter.)

Seller must evaluate risks, but is not bound by institutional lending rules

But a little extra risk may be justified if the financing arrangement allows the sale to proceed or enables the seller to get a higher price for the home.

In addition to making it easier to sell the home, seller financing can have tax benefits for the seller. Because the buyer is paying in installments over a period of years, the seller is not required to report the full profit from the sale on her federal income tax return in the year of the sale. Only the amount of profit actually received in a given year is considered taxable income for that year. Not only is the seller allowed to defer payment of part of the taxes, the profit from the sale may be taxed at a lower rate. (If it had been received in one lump sum, it could have pushed the seller into a higher tax bracket.)

Of course, seller financing is not an option for a seller who needs to be fully cashed out right away—for example, a seller who is planning to use all of his net equity from this home to buy a new one. But in many circumstances a downpayment is enough to satisfy the seller's need for cash at closing.

Now that you have a general understanding of how seller financing works and why it is used, we'll look more closely at the different forms it can take. First we'll focus on secondary financing from the seller, used in conjunction with an institutional loan. Then we'll discuss seller financing as primary financing.

Seller Seconds

Seller financing is often secondary financing. The buyer is paying most of the purchase price with an institutional loan—either by taking out a new loan, or by assuming the seller's existing loan. But instead of requiring the buyer to pay the difference between the loan amount and the purchase price in cash, the seller accepts a second mortgage for part of the remainder.

Seller second can supplement new institutional loan or assumption

In this section of the chapter, we will show how a seller second can help a buyer qualify for an institutional loan. We'll also discuss the factors that shape a seller second for a particular transaction—how much of the price the seller will finance, and on what terms. At the end of this section, we'll look at how a seller second can supplement an assumption.

Fig. 13.1 Summary of common secondary financing rules

Secondary Financing
with a Conventional First Loan

1. Total financing (the combined LTV) may not exceed 95%.

2. The second loan must have regularly scheduled payments.

3. The second loan can't require a balloon payment less than five years after closing.

4. If the first loan has variable payments, the second loan may be required to have fixed payments.

5. The second loan can't permit negative amortization.

6. The second loan can't have a prepayment penalty.

7. The buyer must qualify for both loan payments.

Supplementing a New Loan

Seller second supplementing new loan must comply with lender's rules

When it supplements a new institutional loan, a seller second has to meet certain standards applied by the lender. If the new loan is conventional, the lender will usually apply secondary financing rules similar to the ones discussed in Chapter 10, which are summarized in Figure 13.1. There are also specific rules for secondary financing in conjunction with FHA and VA loans (see Chapters 11 and 12).

Although the secondary financing rules impose significant limitations, many different kinds of seller seconds can comply with them. The seller second in the following example meets the requirements for secondary financing with a conventional loan on a single-family home. In the example, the institutional loan combined with a seller second is compared to an institutional loan without seller financing. This comparison demonstrates how a seller second can help a buyer qualify for an institutional loan.

> **Example:** The Bukowskis are selling their home; its appraised value is $101,000. The Fulbrights have offered to buy the house for $100,000. Setting aside enough cash for closing costs and reserves, they have about $10,000 left over for a downpayment. Market interest rates are high; the Fulbrights will have to pay 10.5% interest for a fixed-rate mortgage.
>
> If the Fulbrights applied for a 30-year, 90% conventional loan from an institutional lender, they would have to qualify

for a monthly payment of approximately $945. That includes principal, interest, taxes, and hazard insurance, and also private mortgage insurance, since the LTV is over 80%.

However, the Fulbrights' stable monthly income is only $3,600, and their monthly debt payments (other than their housing expenses) add up to $400. There aren't any compensating factors in their financial situation that would lead the lender to accept an income ratio higher than the standard 36%. That means the highest monthly mortgage payment the Fulbrights can qualify for is $896.

$3,600	Stable monthly income
× 36%	Maximum total obligations ratio
$1,296	
– 400	Monthly debt payments
$896	Maximum allowable monthly housing expense

Thus, the 90% conventional loan is out of the Fulbrights' reach at current market rates. But suppose the Bukowskis are willing to finance part of the purchase price in order to close the sale. They agree to finance $15,000 at 8% interest; there will be monthly interest-only payments, with a balloon payment of $15,000 (the entire principal amount) due in seven years. Now the Fulbrights will only need to borrow $75,000 from an institutional lender, instead of $90,000. Here's how the transaction would work:

Downpayment: $10,000

Conventional first mortgage:
$75,000, 30-year term, 10.5% fixed interest rate
$768 monthly payment (PITI, but no mortgage insurance)

Seller second mortgage:
$15,000, 7-year term (no amortization)
8% fixed interest rate
$100 monthly interest payment
$15,000 balloon payment due after 7 years

Total monthly payment for both loans: $868

The total monthly payment for both loans will be $868, which is $77 a month less than the payment on the $90,000 conventional loan. That's enough of a difference so that the Fulbrights should be able to qualify for this combination of an institutional loan and a seller second.

The $15,000, 8%, interest-only seller second in the example is by no means the only one that would comply with the rules for secondary financing in conjunction with a conventional loan. The sellers could have financed a larger share of the price, charged a different

Loan structuring: combining a
first mortgage with secondary
financing

interest rate, partially amortized the loan, provided for interest rate adjustments, and so on. In combining a conventional loan with a seller second (a process sometimes called "loan structuring"), several different elements can be manipulated: the relative amounts of the two loans; the downpayment amount; and the amortization, term, payment schedule, and interest rate of the seller second. Taken altogether, there are dozens of combinations for financing a $100,000 single-family home with a conventional first mortgage and a seller second.

Of course, all combinations are not created equal. Only certain combinations will fit the financial circumstances of a particular buyer and a particular seller.

The Buyer's Situation. As the previous example suggests, two factors in a prospective buyer's financial situation shape the design of a seller second. The first is how much money the buyer has for a downpayment (after setting aside enough cash for the closing costs and the required reserves). The second factor is the total monthly payment that the buyer can qualify for.

Buyer's evaluation of
first loan + seller second:
• Downpayment amount
• Combined monthly
  payment for both loans
• Balloon payment

In evaluating a seller second, the buyer will naturally focus on these two factors. But many seller seconds have another feature that the buyer should consider carefully: the balloon payment.

Look at the example again. This interest-only seller second has a low monthly payment. However, after seven years the buyers will have to come up with $15,000 to pay off the sellers. If the buyers aren't planning to keep the house that long, the balloon payment doesn't present much of a problem; they will pay it when they sell the property. Otherwise, the buyers will have to save up the amount of the balloon payment, or else refinance the property when the time comes.

> **Example:** Nearly seven years have passed, and it's almost time for the Fulbrights to make their $15,000 balloon payment to the Bukowskis. The house the Fulbrights bought is now worth about $121,000, and their equity in the property is about $34,000.
>
> The Fulbrights apply to an institutional lender for refinancing. The lender loans them $86,000 and accepts a new mortgage against the home. The Fulbrights use part of this refinance loan to make the balloon payment on the seller second, and they pay off their old conventional loan with the rest.

In many situations, it's easy to refinance, especially when the property has appreciated substantially. (In the example, the LTV for the refinance loan is only 71%.) And if interest rates have fallen, refinancing can result in lower mortgage payments. Under other circumstances, however, such as declining property values or increasing interest rates, refinancing may be difficult to obtain or may increase the mortgage payments. Also, refinancing usually costs at least a few thousand dollars (for loan fees, an appraisal, and so forth).

Seller financing arrangements that require a large balloon payment can work out fine, so a buyer should not always be frightened away from them. But the buyer should give careful thought to where the money for the balloon payment will come from.

The Seller's Situation. When a seller evaluates possible secondary financing arrangements, she should consider cash flow and yield. How much cash is needed at closing? Will the monthly payment on the seller second be an adequate addition to her income? How soon does she need the balloon payment (if any)? Does the interest rate on the second loan represent a reasonable return?

The seller also has to consider the tax consequences of each possible arrangement, preferably with expert advice. Although seller financing often has tax benefits for the seller, some arrangements will backfire. For instance, a seller who offers financing at an exceptionally low interest rate may run up against the "imputed interest" rules in the federal tax code. Under those rules, if the stated interest rate on seller financing is below a specified minimum, the Internal Revenue Service will treat a portion of the principal received each year as if it were interest. In effect, the IRS treats the sale as if the seller had charged a lower price for the home, but a higher interest rate on the financing. This can have an impact on the seller's income taxes, since all of the interest on an installment sale is taxed, while only part (if any) of the principal payments are taxed. (For instance, if the seller took a loss on the sale, the principal wouldn't be taxed at all.)

Lien priority is another important consideration for a seller who offers secondary financing. Purchase money mortgages are subject to the same priority rules as institutional mortgages. In the event of foreclosure, the first mortgage must be paid in full from the sale proceeds before any proceeds are allocated to the second mortgage (see Chapter 5). The seller should keep this in mind when negotiating the amount of a seller second. Is the property worth enough so that the proceeds of a foreclosure sale would be likely to cover both the

Seller's evaluation of second:
- Cash at closing
- Monthly income
- Timing of payoff (balloon payment)
- Yield on investment
- Tax consequences
- Lien priority

first and second mortgages? The seller should be especially careful when there is a possibility that property values will decline in the next few years.

Supplementing an Assumption

In some cases, a seller second can supplement the buyer's assumption of an existing mortgage on the property. The buyer will make a monthly payment to the seller, and also take over responsibility for the monthly payment the seller has been making to the lender.

> **Example:** The current market interest rate for a fixed-rate loan is 9%. The Rainwaters' property has an existing mortgage with a $125,500 balance and a 6% interest rate. The mortgage has 240 payments of $899.12 remaining.
>
> Ray McCarthy is interested in buying the Rainwaters' property and assuming their mortgage, but he does not have the $36,500 cash needed to meet the $162,000 sales price. McCarthy can make a $10,000 downpayment if the Rainwaters will take back a second deed of trust for the remaining $26,500. The Rainwaters agree to accept the second deed of trust at 8% interest (partially amortized, with a balloon payment due in ten years), and the sale closes. Each month, McCarthy sends $899.12 to the Rainwaters' lender for the first loan, and $194.45 to the Rainwaters themselves for the second loan.

Assumption + seller second: when existing mortgage has low interest rate and no due-on-sale clause

Assumption is attractive to buyers whenever the interest rate on the seller's existing mortgage is significantly lower than market rates at the time of the sale. But an assumption is only possible if the existing mortgage does not include a due-on-sale clause, or if the lender agrees to the assumption (see Chapter 5).

Whether or not there is a due-on-sale clause, the lender's consent is always necessary if the seller wants to be released from liability on the existing mortgage. When the assumption is going to be supplemented by a seller second, the lender will scrutinize the second loan before releasing the seller from the first loan. The lender will generally apply the same standards to a seller second supplementing an assumption as it would to a seller second supplementing a new loan (see above). For example, the lender will make sure that the buyer can afford the payments on both loans before agreeing to the release—or, if there is a due-on-sale clause, before agreeing to the assumption at all.

Exercise No. 1

The Pengs have listed their house for $179,000; it's been on the market for quite awhile. Mary Underwood and Joe Schirmer have offered to buy the property for $174,000, its appraised value. The current market interest rate for a fixed-rate mortgage is 7.5%. Underwood and Schirmer have $15,000 in cash; they will need approximately $4,700 for closing costs and reserves, and will be able to use the remainder ($10,300) as a downpayment. Their combined stable monthly income is $5,500, and their debt payments (not including housing expenses) total $540 per month.

Suppose that the Pengs accept the $174,000 offer and are willing to finance 5% of the purchase price at 6% interest. This seller second would be amortized over 30 years, so the monthly principal and interest payment would be only $52.16, but a balloon payment of the remaining principal balance would be due after five years. (The remaining principal balance after five years would be approximately $8,136.) Underwood and Schirmer apply to an institutional lender for a conventional loan at 7.5% interest, with a monthly principal and interest payment of $1,083.78.

1. What percentage of the purchase price would a $10,300 downpayment represent? With that downpayment and a 5% seller second, what would the loan-to-value ratio of the institutional loan be?

2. Calculate the loan amounts for the institutional loan and the seller second. What is the combined loan amount?

3. Does this loan arrangement comply with the typical rules for secondary financing in conjunction with a conventional loan that are listed in Figure 13.1?

4. In addition to the principal and interest for both loans, the monthly housing expense payment will include $150 for property taxes and $25 for hazard insurance, plus $110 for private mortgage insurance on the institutional loan. Will Underwood and Schirmer be able to qualify for this conventional loan combined with the seller second?

Seller Financing as Primary Financing

Seller financing is most flexible when it is the buyer's main source or only source of financing. We'll look first at financing arrangements for unencumbered property, including land contracts, and then at wraparound financing, a technique used for property that is subject to an existing mortgage.

Unencumbered Property

Seller financing is very flexible when property is not encumbered by an existing loan

When the seller has clear title to the property, free of any mortgages or other liens, seller financing is straightforward. The buyer and seller simply negotiate the sales price and the terms of their financing arrangement and have the appropriate documents drawn up. Of course, they still have to consider how much of a downpayment the buyer can make, how much cash the seller needs, and whether the buyer can afford the monthly payments; but they are not constrained by any institutional rules.

Even if the seller requires a substantial downpayment, the buyer is likely to need less cash for seller financing than for a comparable institutional loan. The buyer won't have to pay discount points or an origination fee, and in some cases other closing costs will be lower.

Protecting the Seller's Security. Lien priority does not present the same problem here that it does with a seller second. As long as the finance instruments are recorded at closing, the seller is assured of first lien position. The seller's security interest will not be threatened by the foreclosure of most other liens. If a junior lienholder were to foreclose, the purchaser at the foreclosure sale would take title subject to the seller's lien.

However, the seller should still be concerned about protecting her security interest. Even a mortgage in first lien position has lower lien priority than the lien for general property taxes and any special assessment liens. If the buyer fails to pay the taxes or assessments, the government can foreclose, and the seller may take a loss at the foreclosure sale. Also, if the buyer fails to keep the property insured, the seller's security interest could become worthless if the property is damaged or destroyed.

Of course, failure to pay the taxes or insure the property is a default under the terms of virtually all finance instruments (see Chapter 5). But the seller can help prevent this type of default by setting up an impound account for taxes and hazard insurance, just as many institutional lenders do (see Chapter 8). The seller may choose to have a loan servicer handle the buyer's payments, in exchange for a servicing fee. Many banks, savings and loans, and mortgage companies service loans on behalf of private parties; so do many certified public accountants. Each month, the servicer will deposit part of the buyer's payment into the impound account and pass the remainder on to the seller.

Seller can require impound account to protect security interest

Seller Financing Plus an Institutional Second. Sometimes a seller is willing to finance a good part of the purchase price, but also needs a substantial amount of cash at closing. For example, the seller may need the funds to make a downpayment on another property. If the buyer does not have enough cash, it may be possible to bridge the gap between the seller financing and the downpayment with a second mortgage from an institutional lender.

Institutional second can supplement seller financing if seller needs cash

Example: Linda Stanford has agreed to buy Charlotte Halvorsen's house for $160,000. Halvorsen is willing to accept a purchase money mortgage for $141,000 (at 7% interest, partially amortized with a balloon payment due in ten years), but she needs at least $19,000 at closing.

Stanford can only afford an $11,000 downpayment, so she applies to an institutional lender for an $8,000 loan. The lender agrees to make the loan at 9% interest (fully amortized over a ten-year term), accepting second lien position for its mortgage. Stanford will pay $938 per month to Halvorsen and $101 per month to the institutional lender.

This is the mirror image of the financing arrangements we looked at earlier, where a seller second made up the difference between an institutional loan and the downpayment. Like an institutional lender, a seller offering primary financing should find out where the buyer is going to get the rest of the purchase price. If a second mortgage is involved, the seller should investigate the terms of the proposed second before agreeing to the transaction. Can the buyer afford the monthly payment on both loans? Does the second have any provisions that make default likely? For example, a second that requires a large balloon payment 18 months after closing is quite risky; the buyer could end up defaulting on the seller's loan as well as the second.

Land Contracts. A seller who is providing primary financing for the buyer might choose to use a land contract instead of a mortgage or deed of trust. Land contracts are still a popular form of seller financing in some parts of the country, especially rural areas. They are known by several different names in different states; they may be called contracts for deed, bonds for deed, conditional sales contracts, installment sales contracts, installment land contracts, or real estate contracts.

Like a mortgage or deed of trust, a land contract is used to secure repayment of a debt. But while either a seller or a third-party lender can finance a buyer's purchase with a mortgage or deed of trust, only a seller can use a land contract. And a land contract works in quite a different way than those other instruments.

When the purchase of property is financed with either a mortgage or a deed of trust, the buyer takes title to the property immediately. Under a land contract, however, the seller (referred to as the **vendor**), retains legal title to the property until the buyer (the **vendee**) pays off the entire purchase price in installments. While paying off the contract—which

Land contract: when seller is financing whole transaction, or for wraparound

may take many years—the vendee has the right to possess and enjoy the property, but is not the legal owner. (The vendee's interest in the property is sometimes called equitable title, in contrast to the vendor's legal title.) The vendor typically delivers the deed to the vendee only after the contract price has been paid in full.

In a land contract:
- Vendee has equitable title
- Vendor has legal title

A land contract should always be recorded. A mortgage or a deed of trust is recorded to protect the lender by establishing lien priority, but a land contract is recorded to protect the vendee. It gives public notice of the vendee's interest in the property and establishes the priority of his interest.

Unlike a mortgage or a deed of trust, a land contract is generally not accompanied by a promissory note. The contract states all of the terms of the sale and the financing arrangement between the vendor and vendee: the price, the interest rate, and the monthly payment amount; when the vendee can take possession; when the vendor will be required to deliver the deed to the vendee; and what action the vendor can take if the vendee breaches the contract by failing to pay as agreed.

Remedies for breach of contract. Land contracts sometimes provide that if the vendee defaults on the contract obligation, all of the vendee's rights in the property are terminated, all payments made may be retained by the vendor as liquidated damages, and the vendor may retake possession of the property immediately. This severe penalty for breach of a land contract is called **forfeiture**. Unfortunately for vendors and fortunately for vendees, courts do not always enforce land contracts exactly the way they are written.

If the contract has been recorded, or if the vendee is in possession and refuses to leave, the vendor will usually have to take some legal action to clear title and/or remove the vendee from possession. As with a judicial foreclosure, the delay in reaching trial may be a matter of months or years, depending on court congestion in the county where the property is located. Once the case finally goes to trial, the judge may have a wide range of discretion in fashioning a remedy for the vendor. Depending on state law and on the circumstances of the case, a judge may:

Forfeiture:
- Vendee's rights terminated
- Payments are liquidated damages
- Vendor retakes possession

- enforce the contract as written, allowing the seller to retain all payments received, terminating the vendee's rights, and ordering the vendee to vacate the property;
- give the vendee a certain amount of time (anywhere from one month to one year) to pay off the entire contract balance;

- allow the vendee to simply reinstate the contract by paying delinquent payments plus interest; or
- order a sheriff's sale of the property with any surplus to go to the vendee, as would occur with a mortgage foreclosure.

In some states, the vendee's rights depend on how far along in the contract term it is when the vendee defaults. If the vendee has been making payments to the vendor for a long time, forfeiture would be especially harsh. In that situation, the law might not allow a forfeiture.

Some states do not allow forfeiture as remedy in certain circumstances

Advantages and disadvantages. For the vendor, one advantage of a contract sale may be the sense of security that can come from remaining the legal owner and not giving the vendee a deed until the entire purchase price has been paid. As our discussion of the forfeiture remedy suggests, however, this feeling of security may be largely illusory.

When forfeiture is allowed, the vendor may reacquire the property—which may have appreciated in value—instead of having to sell it and give any surplus to the debtor (as would be required in a mortgage or deed of trust foreclosure). This can be a substantial advantage for the vendor.

The main disadvantage for the vendor under a land contract is the delay and expense involved in court proceedings, which are frequently necessary in the event of breach. In many states, this disadvantage is increased by the uncertainty concerning the result after the case gets to trial.

For the vendee, the slow court proceedings can be an advantage, although the uncertainty is undesirable. A serious disadvantage for the vendee under a land contract (one that is not a problem with a mortgage or deed of trust) is that the vendor remains the legal owner of the property. This could create a variety of problems for the vendee. For example, in some states, a court judgment entered against the vendor might cloud the vendee's interest in the property, since the vendor is still the legal owner. And it might be difficult or even impossible for the vendee to obtain bank financing for construction or improvements. As we're about to discuss, banks are very reluctant to lend to someone who does not have legal title.

Using a land contract. A seller who is financing the entire transaction is free to use a land contract if she prefers it to a mortgage or deed of trust. But if the buyer wants to combine primary financing from the seller with institutional secondary financing, it will be hard to find a lender to make the second loan if the seller is using a land contract.

> **Example:** In an earlier example, Linda Stanford agreed to buy Charlotte Halvorsen's house for $160,000. Halvorsen was willing to accept a purchase money mortgage for $141,000, but she needed at least $19,000 at closing. Stanford could only afford an $11,000 downpayment, so she applied to an institutional lender for an $8,000 second mortgage.
>
> Now suppose Halvorsen offers to sell Stanford the property on those same terms, but she wants to use a land contract instead of a purchase money mortgage. Stanford still needs to pay Halvorsen $19,000 at closing, and she still has only $11,000 in cash. When she applies to a lender for an $8,000 mortgage, the lender turns her down.
>
> The problem is that under the contract, Stanford will not have legal title to the property. For that reason, she cannot use the property as security for the loan.

In theory, there are two possible solutions to this dilemma. Halvorsen (the vendor, who still has title) could agree to let the property stand as security for a loan to Stanford, without assuming personal responsibility for repayment. If Stanford were to default on the institutional second, the lender could foreclose on the property, but could not sue Halvorsen for a deficiency judgment. This might be acceptable to the lender, but it would present an additional risk for the vendor.

The other solution would be for Stanford to mortgage her equitable interest in the property. In a foreclosure, the lender would merely acquire Stanford's contract rights; the lender could not force the sale of the property. To obtain title, the lender would still have to pay Halvorsen the remainder of the contract price. Very few lenders regard a vendee's equitable interest as an acceptable form of collateral.

Neither of these solutions is particularly serviceable. So as a practical matter, a land contract only works in three situations. It works when the seller is able to provide all the financing the buyer needs. It works when the seller is supplementing an assumption, as long as the mortgagee's consent is not required; then the seller can use a contract for the secondary financing. And a land contract can also work for wraparound financing, which is our next topic.

Encumbered Property: Wraparound Financing

It's relatively rare to find a seller whose property is not encumbered by some form of mortgage lien. The seller of encumbered property generally cannot afford to offer primary financing to the buyer and also pay off the existing mortgage at closing.

> **Example:** Hank Ellison is selling his home for $202,000. Ellison would prefer to sell the property on an installment basis, receiving payments over a long period. But there is a mortgage against the property that has a 6.25% interest rate and a $152,600 balance. With an installment sale, Ellison would not have enough money at closing to pay off that balance.

As you saw earlier in the chapter, Ellison might be able to arrange for the buyer to assume the existing mortgage, then finance the rest of the purchase price himself with a seller second. But there is another alternative that might appeal to Ellison: wraparound financing.

Wraparound:
- Seller accepts mortgage for most of purchase price
- Property remains subject to underlying loan

With a wraparound, the property remains subject to the seller's existing mortgage after the sale. The amount of the seller financing is larger than the balance owed on the existing mortgage, so the seller financing "wraps around" the existing mortgage. The buyer does not take on responsibility for the existing mortgage, which is usually referred to as the **underlying loan**. The seller remains responsible for making the payments on the underlying loan. Each month, the buyer makes a payment to the seller on the wraparound loan, and the seller uses a portion of that payment to make the payment on the underlying loan.

> **Example:** Continuing with the example above, suppose Ellison sells his house to Janet Kingman for $202,000, accepting $20,000 down and financing the balance of the purchase price ($182,000) with a deed of trust at 8.5%.
>
> Kingman takes title to the property subject to the $152,600 underlying mortgage, but she does not assume that loan. Her monthly payment to Ellison is $1,400. Out of that amount, $1,115 goes to the underlying mortgagee and Ellison gets to keep $285. The underlying mortgage will be paid off in 20 years, and at that point Kingman will be required to make a balloon payment to Ellison for the remaining balance on the wraparound loan.

For a wraparound, the seller can use a mortgage, a deed of trust, or a land contract. When a deed of trust is used for a wrap, it is often referred to as an **all-inclusive trust deed**.

A wrap only works when the underlying loan does not have a due-on-sale clause. (In states where due-on-sale clauses are the norm, wraparound financing can be very rare.) Occasionally a seller will try to get around a due-on-sale clause by using a wraparound land contract and failing to notify the lender of the transaction; this is called a "silent wrap." But even though a contract sale does not involve an immediate transfer of title, it still gives the lender the right to accelerate the underlying loan pursuant to the due-on-sale clause. So if the lender finds out about the secret transaction, both the seller and the buyer will be in jeopardy. A real estate agent should never get involved in a silent wrap.

Wraparound works only if underlying loan does not have due-on-sale clause

Wraparound financing is attractive because it enables the buyer to finance the purchase at a below-market interest rate while still providing a market rate of return (or better) for the seller. To clarify this apparent contradiction, let's continue with the example given above.

Example: Although Ellison has received a $182,000 deed of trust from Kingman, he has actually extended only $29,400 in credit to her:

$202,000	Sales price
20,000	Downpayment
−152,600	Underlying mortgage balance
$29,400	Credit extended — net owed to seller

Yet Ellison will receive 8.5% interest on the entire $182,000 wraparound, while paying only 6.25% interest on the $152,600 underlying loan balance. This means that in the first year he will pay out $9,538 in interest on the underlying mortgage, but will receive $15,470 in interest on the wrap from the buyer. That gives him a net gain of $5,932. Since he extended only $29,400 in credit, he is earning $5,932 on $29,400, which represents a 20% annual return.

Here are the steps for determining the seller's yield in the first year of the loan term:

Calculating seller's yield on wraparound:

1. Calculate the interest the seller will receive in the first year on the wraparound loan.

$182,000	
× 8.5%	
$15,470	

2. Calculate the interest the seller will pay the same year on the underlying loan.

$152,600	
× 6.25%	
$9,538	

$$\frac{\text{Interest seller will receive}}{- \text{Interest seller will pay}}$$
Net interest to seller

$$\text{Credit extended} \overline{\left) \begin{array}{l} \underline{\text{Seller's yield}} \\ \text{Net interest} \\ \text{to seller} \end{array}\right.}$$

3. Determine the net interest to the seller in the first year.

$$\begin{array}{r} \$15,470 \\ -9,538 \\ \hline \$5,932 \end{array}$$

4. Divide the net interest by the amount of credit actually extended.

$$\begin{array}{r} 20\% \\ \$29,400\overline{)5,932} \end{array}$$

If the market interest rate is currently 9.5%, the seller is receiving more than double the market rate, while the buyer is paying 1% below the market rate.

Even when the interest rate that the seller charges on the wrap is not below the market rate, the arrangement may still be attractive to the buyer because of the greater flexibility of seller financing and lower closing costs. The seller's yield on the transaction depends in part on the difference between the interest rate on the wrap and the rate on the underlying loan, and in part on the amount of credit extended. The more credit extended by the seller, the lower the return.

Exercise No. 2

Compute the seller's first-year yield in the following situations. You may want to use the worksheet below.

1. Sales price $75,000; $8,000 downpayment; all-inclusive trust deed at 9% interest; underlying mortgage with a $39,700 balance at 7% interest.

Wraparound Worksheet

Sales price	_____		
– Downpayment	_____		
Wraparound	_____	x _____ % = _____	Interest received
– Underlying loan	_____	x _____ % = _____	– Interest paid
Credit extended	_____		_____ Net interest
		_____	÷ Credit extended
		_____	Seller's yield

2. Sales price $187,000; $28,000 downpayment; wraparound contract at 10% interest; underlying deed of trust with a $142,000 balance at 8% interest.

Wraparound vs. Assumption plus Seller Second. When the seller's existing loan has no due-on-sale clause, the parties can choose between a wraparound and an assumption plus a seller second. In either case, the actual amount of credit extended by the seller is the same; but the two arrangements have different benefits for the parties.

In an assumption, the buyer receives the benefit of an existing loan with a low interest rate. On the other hand, if the transaction is structured with a wraparound loan at the market rate, the seller receives the benefit of the existing low interest rate loan and a very attractive rate of return on the portion of the financing actually extended to the buyer.

> **Example:** A home is sold for $100,000, with the buyer making a $20,000 downpayment. The seller's existing loan with a balance of $60,000 carries an interest rate of 6%. The prevailing market interest rate at the time of the sale is approximately 9%.

	Wraparound	Assumption + Second
Sales price:	$100,000	$100,000
Downpayment:	$20,000	$20,000
Balance financed:	$80,000 @ 9% Wrap	$60,000 @ 6% Assumption $20,000 @ 9% Second
Credit extended by seller:	$20,000	$20,000
Yield to seller on credit extended:	18%	9%
Overall interest rate to buyer on $80,000 financed:	9%	6.75%

As you can see from this example, if a wraparound loan is made at the market rate, the seller enjoys a high yield on the credit he extends to the buyer. If the transaction is structured with an assumption and a second mortgage to the seller at the market rate, the buyer enjoys financing at a very low overall rate.

A wraparound can also be structured so that the seller receives an above-market rate on the credit actually extended and, at the same time, the buyer pays a below-market rate on the total amount financed. Then both of them are getting a good deal. In the example just given, if the wraparound loan were made at an interest rate of 7.5%, the buyer would be paying an overall rate 1.5% less than the prevailing market rate of 9%. The seller would be receiving a yield of approximately 12% on the $20,000 of credit that he extended to the buyer.

Protecting a Wraparound Buyer. From the buyer's point of view, the obvious problem with a wraparound is how to make sure that the seller makes the payments on the underlying loan. The buyer may have made every wrap payment to the seller on time, yet if the seller defaults on the underlying loan and the underlying lender forecloses, the buyer will lose the property.

One solution is to include in the finance instruments a provision requiring the seller to make timely payments on the underlying loan, and allowing the buyer to make those payments directly to the lender if the seller fails to do so.

> Seller shall maintain the existing mortgage in good standing; in the event that Seller fails to make any payment when due, or in any other way causes or allows the loan to go into default, Buyer shall be entitled to cure the default, and deduct all costs from the amounts next falling due to Seller on this note [or this contract].

In order for a provision like this to be effective in preventing fore-closure, the buyer needs some way of finding out when the seller has fallen behind in the payments on the underlying loan. In most states, the buyer can send the lender a "Request for Notice of Delinquency" when the wraparound transaction closes. (The seller's consent is usually necessary.) Then if the seller stops paying the lender, the lender

Wrap can offer:
- *Below-market rate for buyer*
- *Above-market yield for seller*
- *In some cases, both of the above*

Escrow Instructions

1. The buyer shall make all payments into an escrow account to be maintained by the escrow agent.

2. Upon receipt of each monthly payment, the escrow agent shall immediately make all payments due on the seller's underlying mortgage.

3. The escrow agent shall maintain a balance in the account equal to two monthly mortgage payments; all funds in excess of this minimum balance shall be disbursed to the seller, after compliance with provision 2 of these instructions.

---

will notify the buyer, and the buyer can take the necessary steps to cure the default.

Even with these safeguards in place, the best protection for the wraparound buyer is an escrow account for the loan payments, with a third party appointed to manage the wrap. Each month, the buyer will make the wrap payment into the escrow account, and the escrow agent will send part of the payment to the underlying lender and the remainder to the seller. Property taxes and hazard insurance can also be handled through this account (see the discussion of impound accounts, earlier in this chapter). The parties may appoint a certified public accountant or some other qualified person to manage their wrap; in some cases, they'll find that the loan servicer for the underlying loan is willing to take on this task.

Protection for wrap buyer:
- Request for Notice of Delinquency
- Escrow account

Exercise No. 3

In one of the examples given earlier in this chapter, the Rainwaters sold their house to Ray McCarthy for $162,000. They allowed him to assume their mortgage and accepted a second deed of trust for part of the remainder of the price. The existing mortgage had a balance of $125,500, a 6% interest rate, and 240 payments remaining. The seller second was for $26,500, at 8% interest (compared to the market rate of 9%); it was amortized over 30 years, with a balloon payment due in 10 years. McCarthy was going to make a $10,000 downpayment, and each month he would pay $899.12 to the lender on the assumed mortgage, and $194.45 to the Rainwaters on the seller second.

Now suppose that instead of that arrangement, the Rainwaters offered McCarthy a $152,000 wraparound mortgage at 7% interest, amortized over 30 years, with a balloon payment due after 20 years. (McCarthy would still make a $10,000 downpayment.) McCarthy's monthly payment on the wraparound would be $1,011.26.

1. Compare McCarthy's monthly payment on the wraparound to the total monthly payment for the assumption plus seller second.

2. What would the Rainwaters' yield on the wraparound loan be during the first year? Compare this to their yield on the seller second.

3. With the assumption plus second, what overall interest rate would McCarthy pay on the total amount financed? To determine the approximate overall rate, calculate the annual interest paid on each of the two loans, add those two figures together, and then divide that result by the total amount of financing. Compare this answer to the interest rate McCarthy would pay on the wraparound, and compare both of those rates to the market rate.

Alternatives to Seller Financing

Short of financing purchase, seller can help buyer with:
- Buydown
- Contribution to closing costs
- Equity exchange
- Lease/option

As you have seen, with a mortgage, deed of trust, or land contract, the seller can play the role of a lender by extending credit to the buyer. But in these seller financing arrangements, the seller often has to wait several years to collect the full profit from the sale. Not every seller is in a position to do that. In this section of the chapter, we will discuss some ways that a seller can help a buyer purchase his property without financing the transaction.

Buydowns

One popular way for a seller to assist a buyer is a buydown. Buydowns were explained in detail in Chapter 10. To buy down the interest rate on the buyer's institutional loan, the seller does not actually have to pay the lender a lump sum at closing. However, the seller's proceeds from the sale will be reduced by the amount of the buydown. From the seller's point of view, it's as if she had agreed to lower the sales price; but the buydown can have greater benefits for the buyer than a straight price reduction would have (see Chapter 10).

Contributions to Closing Costs

Occasionally, after coming up with the required downpayment and reserves for an institutional loan, the buyer doesn't have quite enough cash left over to pay for closing costs. The seller may be willing to make up the shortfall. Depending on the circumstances, this type of cash contribution from the seller may be more helpful than a price reduction for the same amount.

However, there are limits on how much a seller can contribute to the buyer's closing costs for a conventional loan. If the seller's contribution exceeds those limits, the loan amount will be reduced (see Chapter 10). Because of these rules, in some cases a large contribution from the seller doesn't really help the buyer.

Equity Exchanges

When a buyer can't come up with enough cash for a purchase, the seller may be willing to accept other assets and reduce the cash sales price. Maybe the buyer has equity in some vacant land, or in personal property such as a recreational vehicle or a boat. If the seller wants the property and the buyer is ready to part with it, they can work out an exchange.

> **Example:** Ellen Jarvis has decided to sell a rental house she owns. She lists the house for $225,000.
>
> Frank Tillman would like to buy the house. He has $22,000 for a downpayment, which would be enough if he could obtain an institutional loan for $203,000. But Tillman can't qualify for a loan that large.
>
> However, Tillman has meticulously restored a vintage sports car and is planning to sell it. The appraised value of the car is $27,500. In the course of a conversation with Jarvis, Tillman

discovers that she happens to be a sports car buff. He shows her the car he restored, and after long negotiations, Jarvis agrees to reduce the sales price on her house to $200,000 if Tillman will give her the car.

With the sales price reduced to $200,000, Tillman applies for an 80% conventional loan ($160,000). He easily qualifies for this smaller loan, and the transaction closes.

Lease Arrangements

In some cases, a prospective buyer is interested in leasing a home before actually buying it. The buyer may need additional time to acquire enough cash for a downpayment or closing costs—by saving, or by selling other property, for instance. Or perhaps the buyer is currently unable to qualify for a large enough loan, but has reason to believe that circumstances will change before long.

If the seller is willing, the property can be leased to the prospective buyer in one of two ways: with a lease/option (a lease agreement that includes an option to purchase) or with a lease/purchase contract (a purchase contract that allows the buyer to lease the property for an extended period before closing). Although the two arrangements are related, there are important differences between them.

Lease/Options. A lease/option is made up of a lease and an option to purchase. A seller leases her property to a prospective buyer for a specific term (often six months or one year), and grants the buyer an option to purchase the leased property at a specified price during the term of the lease. The seller is the landlord and optionor, and the prospective buyer is the tenant and optionee. The tenant/optionee is under no obligation to buy the property, but the landlord/optionor is not supposed to sell the property to anyone else during the option period.

A lease/option is by no means the equivalent of a sale. A seller considering this type of arrangement should be warned that in the majority of cases, the tenant/optionee decides not to buy. However, a carefully structured lease/option may keep a possible sale alive until the buyer is in a position to close.

Because the failure rate is high, a seller generally only grants a lease/option when it seems unlikely that other offers will be forthcoming in the near future, or when the arrangement allows the seller to ask a higher price for the property. Of course, a lease/option won't

Lease/option:
• Lease with option to buy
• Limited time period
• Option money
• Rent credit

work for residential property unless the seller has somewhere else to live. But the lease provides the seller with some income from the property, which can be used to make mortgage payments on a new house until the old house is sold, or to cover payments on an existing mortgage on the old house.

Note that unlike wraparound financing, a lease/option can be used with a property where there is a due-on-sale clause on the seller's loan. The due-on-sale clause is not triggered until the option is exercised.

How a lease/option works. The prospective buyer pays the seller a sum of money in exchange for the option. This **option money** is the consideration that makes the option binding on the seller. Once paid, the option money is not refundable, whether or not the optionee goes through with the purchase. Many lease/option agreements provide that the option money will be applied to the purchase price, much like the good faith deposit (earnest money) in an ordinary purchase and sale agreement.

A lease/option may also provide that part of the rental payments will be applied to the purchase if the tenant/optionee decides to buy. This is called a **rent credit** provision.

> **Example:** John Caldwell is selling a house for $315,000. Mark Bettelheim is interested in the property, but he will not be able to qualify for a loan until he receives a raise that he's expecting this year. The parties execute a lease/option, and Bettelheim pays Caldwell $6,000 as option money.
>
> Under the terms of their agreement, Bettelheim will lease the house for six months, paying $2,200 per month in rent. Bettelheim has the right to purchase the property at the agreed price at any time until the lease expires. If Bettelheim exercises his option, the option money and $1,100 out of each rental payment will be applied to the sales price.
>
> So if Bettelheim decides to buy at the end of six months, he will pay $302,400, the amount owed after deducting the option money and $6,600 in rental payments from the original price. If Bettelheim decides not to buy, Caldwell will keep the option money and all of the rent.

The rent charged in a lease/option is often considerably higher than the rent that would be charged for the property under an ordinary lease. This gives the optionee an incentive to exercise the option as soon as possible, and also provides additional compensation to the seller for the uncertainty and inconvenience of the option.

Option money:
- Consideration for option
- Not refundable
- Applied to purchase

Lease/option rent:
- Often higher than market rent
- Partial rent credit applied to purchase

There are two ways a rent credit can be applied toward the purchase: the amount of the credit can be deducted from the sales price (as it was in the example above), or the credit can be treated as part of the downpayment. A buyer who is short of cash might prefer to treat the credit as part of the downpayment. However, most institutional lenders will only accept a rent credit as part of the downpayment to the extent that the credit represents an extra amount paid above the fair market rent for the property. For instance, if the fair market rent was $1,500 and the lease/option rent was $1,800, no more than $300 out of each month's rent could be applied to the downpayment.

Provisions of a lease/option agreement. A lease/option should include all the terms of the lease, and in addition, all the terms of the potential purchase contract. That way, a binding purchase contract will be formed immediately if the optionee exercises the option to purchase.

The lease/option agreement should state that if the tenant/optionee defaults in connection with the lease (by failing to pay the rent, for example), the option rights will be forfeited.

The agreement should also make it clear that the option money is not a security deposit. (In most states, a tenant's security deposit must be kept in a trust account and refunded at the end of the lease. The seller can require a security deposit in a lease/option arrangement, but the deposit must be separate from the option money.) The agreement should specify that the option money may be disbursed to the seller/optionor as soon as the tenant/optionee moves into the home.

The amount of option money is negotiable, but it should be at least enough to pay the real estate brokerage fee. In some cases, the broker arranges to collect part of her fee out of the option money, and the remainder if the optionee goes through with the purchase. Keep in mind that the more option money the prospective buyer pays, the more likely it is that the option will be exercised.

Before signing the lease/option, the seller—like any other landlord—should review a copy of the prospective tenant's credit report, to make sure that he is a good credit risk.

Buyers should be wary of using lease/option agreements in markets where home values are poised to decline. If values go down, the buyer will be left with the choice of buying the property for more than its current value, or losing the previously paid option money.

Lease/option includes:
- All terms of lease
- All terms of potential purchase contract

Lease/Purchase Contract. A number of variations on the lease/option have been used by sellers attempting to improve the chances that a sale will eventually take place. One of these variations is the lease/purchase contract.

For a lease/purchase contract, instead of signing an option, the seller and the prospective buyer actually sign a purchase contract along with the lease. The buyer usually gives the seller a substantial good faith deposit, and the closing date is set quite far off—six months or a year away. In the meantime, the buyer leases the property.

The practical effect of a lease/purchase contract is very similar to that of a lease/option. If the tenant/buyer decides not to buy the property, he simply forfeits the deposit—which isn't very different from losing option money, in practical terms. But there is a significant psychological difference; the buyer tends to feel more committed with a lease/purchase contract. Deciding not to go through with the purchase means breaching a contract, as opposed to merely choosing not to exercise an option. Many real estate agents believe a lease/purchase contract is much more likely to result in a sale than a lease/option.

A lease/purchase contract should have many of the same provisions as a lease/option. There may be a rent credit provision, and the contract should clearly state that the good faith deposit is not a security deposit. Again, the seller should be sure the buyer has a satisfactory credit history before signing the contract.

The Agent's Responsibilities in Seller-Financed Transactions

The old saying "Where there's a will, there's a way" could be used as a slogan for seller financing. Open-minded negotiation between the buyer and the seller (and the lender, when applicable) closes many transactions that otherwise would not make it. An imaginative real estate agent can be the catalyst, showing the parties that they have many alternatives.

However, there are risks in any seller financing arrangement, even if it's straightforward and carefully planned. An extension of credit always involves the risk of default. In a badly planned transaction without adequate safeguards, default may be more likely than repayment, and may result in a devastating financial loss for the seller. The

Lease/purchase contract:
- Parties sign purchase agreement, not option
- Closing date far off
- Eventual sale more likely than with lease/option

risks affect the buyer, too. Suppose a seller offers graduated payment financing with very low initial payments; if the buyer can't afford the payment increases when the time comes, he may lose the home and everything he's put into it.

A real estate agent negotiating a seller-financed transaction should make sure that both the seller and the buyer understand all the terms and implications of their agreement. The agent should always suggest—and in most cases should strongly recommend—that the parties get legal and tax advice from real estate lawyers and/or certified public accountants. At the very least, the finance instruments should be prepared or reviewed by a lawyer. The real estate agent should not prepare these documents, even using standard forms; in most states that would be considered the unauthorized practice of law.

Disclosures

Some states require special disclosure forms to be used when a third party (such as a real estate agent) helps arrange seller financing. The agent is usually supposed to fill out the disclosure form and give a copy to both the seller and the buyer before they commit themselves. As an example, a form that meets the requirements of California's seller financing disclosure law is shown in Figure 13.2. The form details all the terms of the financing agreement, from the interest rate to the late payment charge.

Notice that the form also has a section for information concerning the buyer's creditworthiness. In a seller-financed transaction, the seller should always check into the buyer's financial situation—income, net worth, and credit history. After obtaining this information, the seller doesn't have to apply the same standards to it that an institutional lender would. For example, a seller might decide to finance the transaction even though the buyers have a 45% debt to income ratio. But the seller should at least have a clear picture of the buyers' circumstances.

Even when state law doesn't require a specific disclosure form, it's a good idea for a real estate agent handling a seller-financed transaction to prepare a disclosure statement. A local real estate organization (such as a multiple listing association or a Board of Realtors®) might have a form available for this purpose. Otherwise, an agent could have a local real estate lawyer draw up a form that accurately reflects state law concerning the rights of the parties.

Real estate agent should:
- Make sure both parties understand seller financing arrangement
- Encourage both parties to consult lawyers or CPAs

Seller financing disclosure statement:
- Discloses all financing terms
- Informs seller of buyer's financial situation
- Required in some states

Fig. 13.2 Seller financing disclosure statement

SELLER FINANCING ADDENDUM AND DISCLOSURE
(California Civil Code §§2956-2967)
(C.A.R. Form SFA, Revised 10/02)

CALIFORNIA ASSOCIATION OF REALTORS®

This is an addendum to the ☐ California Residential Purchase Agreement, ☐ Counter Offer, or ☐ Other _____
_____, ("Agreement"), dated _____,
On property known as _____ ("Property"),
between _____ ("Buyer"),
and _____ ("Seller").
Seller agrees to extend credit to Buyer as follows:

1. **PRINCIPAL; INTEREST; PAYMENT; MATURITY TERMS:** ☐ Principal amount $ _____, interest at _____%
    per annum, payable at approximately $ _____ per ☐ month, ☐ year, or ☐ other _____,
    remaining principal balance due in _____ years.

2. **LOAN APPLICATION; CREDIT REPORT:** Within 5 (or ☐ _____) **Days** After Acceptance: **(a)** Buyer shall provide Seller a completed
    loan application on a form acceptable to Seller (such as a FNMA/FHLMC Uniform Residential Loan Application for residential one to four
    unit properties); and **(b)** Buyer authorizes Seller and/or Agent to obtain, at Buyer's expense, a copy of Buyer's credit report. Buyer shall
    provide any supporting documentation reasonably requested by Seller. Seller, after first giving Buyer a Notice to Buyer to Perform, may
    cancel this Agreement in writing and authorize return of Buyer's deposit if Buyer fails to provide such documents within that time, or if
    Seller disapproves any above item within **5 (or ☐ _____) Days** After receipt of each item.

3. **CREDIT DOCUMENTS:** This extension of credit by Seller will be evidenced by: ☐ Note and deed of trust; ☐ All-inclusive
    note and deed of trust; ☐ Installment land sale contract; ☐ Lease/option (when parties intend transfer of equitable title);
    OR ☐ Other (specify) _____

**THE FOLLOWING TERMS APPLY ONLY IF CHECKED. SELLER IS ADVISED TO READ ALL TERMS, EVEN THOSE NOT
CHECKED, TO UNDERSTAND WHAT IS OR IS NOT INCLUDED, AND, IF NOT INCLUDED, THE CONSEQUENCES THEREOF.**

4. ☐ **LATE CHARGE:** If any payment is not made within _____ **Days** After it is due, a late charge of either $ _____,
    or _____% of the installment due, may be charged to Buyer. **NOTE:** On single family residences that Buyer intends to occupy,
    California Civil Code §2954.4(a) limits the late charge to no more than 6% of the total installment payment due and requires a
    grace period of no less than 10 days.

5. ☐ **BALLOON PAYMENT:** The extension of credit will provide for a balloon payment, in the amount of $ _____,
    plus any accrued interest, which is due on _____ (date).

6. ☐ **PREPAYMENT:** If all or part of this extension of credit is paid early, Seller may charge a prepayment penalty as follows (if
    applicable): _____. Caution: California Civil Code
    §2954.9 contains limitations on prepayment penalties for residential one-to-four unit properties.

7. ☐ **DUE ON SALE:** If any interest in the Property is sold or otherwise transferred, Seller has the option to require immediate
    payment of the entire unpaid principal balance, plus any accrued interest.

8.* ☐ **REQUEST FOR COPY OF NOTICE OF DEFAULT:** A request for a copy of Notice of Default as defined in California Civil
    Code §2924b will be recorded. **If Not**, Seller is advised to consider recording a Request for Notice of Default.

9.* ☐ **REQUEST FOR NOTICE OF DELINQUENCY:** A request for Notice of Delinquency, as defined in California Civil Code §2924e,
    to be signed and paid for by Buyer, will be made to senior lienholders. **If not**, Seller is advised to consider making a Request for
    Notice of Delinquency. Seller is advised to check with senior lienholders to verify whether they will honor this request.

10.* ☐ **TAX SERVICE:**
    A. If property taxes on the Property become delinquent, tax service will be arranged to report to Seller. **If not**, Seller is
    advised to consider retaining a tax service, or to otherwise determine that property taxes are paid.
    B. ☐ Buyer, ☐ Seller, shall be responsible for the initial and continued retention of, and payment for, such tax service.

11. ☐ **TITLE INSURANCE:** Title insurance coverage will be provided to **both** Seller and Buyer, insuring their respective interests
    in the Property. **If not,** Buyer and Seller are advised to consider securing such title insurance coverage.

12. ☐ **HAZARD INSURANCE:**
    A. The parties' escrow holder or insurance carrier will be directed to include a loss payee endorsement, adding Seller to
    the Property insurance policy. **If not**, Seller is advised to secure such an endorsement, or acquire a separate
    insurance policy.
    B. Property insurance **does not** include earthquake or flood insurance coverage, unless checked:
    ☐ Earthquake insurance will be obtained; ☐ Flood insurance will be obtained.

13. ☐ **PROCEEDS TO BUYER:** Buyer will receive cash proceeds at the close of the sale transaction. The amount received will be
    approximately $_____, from _____ (indicate source of
    proceeds). Buyer represents that the purpose of such disbursement is as follows: _____.

14. ☐ **NEGATIVE AMORTIZATION; DEFERRED INTEREST:** Negative amortization results when Buyer's periodic payments are
    less than the amount of interest earned on the obligation. Deferred interest also results when the obligation does not
    require periodic payments for a period of time. In either case, interest is not payable as it accrues. This accrued interest
    will have to be paid by Buyer at a later time, and may result in Buyer owing more on the obligation than at its origination.
    The credit being extended to Buyer by Seller will provide for negative amortization or deferred interest as indicated below.
    (Check A, B, or C. CHECK ONE ONLY.)
    ☐ **A.** All negative amortization or deferred interest shall be added to the principal _____
    (e.g., annually, monthly, etc.), and thereafter shall bear interest at the rate specified in the credit documents (compound interest);
    OR ☐ **B.** All deferred interest shall be due and payable, along with principal, at maturity;
    OR ☐ **C.** Other _____.

*(For Paragraphs 8-10) In order to receive timely and continued notification, Seller is advised to record appropriate notices and/or to
notify appropriate parties of any change in Seller's address.

SFA REVISED 10/02 (PAGE 1 OF 3) Print Date

Buyer's Initials (_____)(_____)
Seller's Initials (_____)(_____)

Reviewed by _____ Date _____

EQUAL HOUSING OPPORTUNITY

SELLER FINANCING ADDENDUM AND DISCLOSURE (SFA PAGE 1 OF 3)

Reprinted with permission, California Association of Realtors®. Endorsement not implied-.

Property Address: _____ Date: _____

15. ☐ **ALL-INCLUSIVE DEED OF TRUST; INSTALLMENT LAND SALE CONTRACT:** This transaction involves the use of an all-inclusive (or wraparound) deed of trust or an installment land sale contract. That deed of trust or contract shall provide as follows:

    A. In the event of an acceleration of any senior encumbrance, the responsibility for payment, or for legal defense is: _____ _____ ; OR ☐ **Is not** specified in the credit or security documents.

    B. In the event of the prepayment of a senior encumbrance, the responsibilities and rights of Buyer and Seller regarding refinancing, prepayment penalties, and any prepayment discounts are: _____ ; OR ☐ **Are not** specified in the documents evidencing credit.

    C. Buyer will make periodic payments to _____ (Seller, collection agent, or any neutral third party), who will be responsible for disbursing payments to the payee(s) on the senior encumbrance(s) and to Seller. **NOTE:** The Parties are advised to designate a neutral third party for these purposes.

16. ☐ **TAX IDENTIFICATION NUMBERS:** Buyer and Seller shall each provide to each other their Social Security Numbers or Taxpayer Identification Numbers.

17. ☐ **OTHER CREDIT TERMS** _____ _____

18. ☐ **RECORDING:** The documents evidencing credit (paragraph 3) will be recorded with the county recorder where the Property is located. **If not,** Buyer and Seller are advised that their respective interests in the Property may be jeopardized by intervening liens, judgments, encumbrances, or subsequent transfers.

19. ☐ **JUNIOR FINANCING:** There will be additional financing, secured by the Property, junior to this Seller financing. Explain: _____

20. SENIOR LOANS AND ENCUMBRANCES: The following information is provided on loans and/or encumbrances that will be **senior** to Seller financing. **NOTE:** The following are estimates, unless otherwise marked with an asterisk (*). If checked: ☐ A separate sheet with information on additional senior loans/encumbrances is attached

	1st	2nd
A. Original Balance	$ _____	$ _____
B. Current Balance	$ _____	$ _____
C. Periodic Payment (e.g. $100/month)	$ _____	$ _____/_____
Including Impounds of:	$ _____	$ _____/_____
D. Interest Rate (per annum)	_____ %	_____ %
E. Fixed or Variable Rate:	_____	_____
If Variable Rate: Lifetime Cap (Ceiling)	_____	_____
Indicator (Underlying Index)	_____	_____
Margins	_____	_____
F. Maturity Date	_____	_____
G. Amount of Balloon Payment	$ _____	$ _____
H. Date Balloon Payment Due	_____	_____
I. Potential for Negative Amortization? (Yes, No, or Unknown)	_____	_____
J. Due on Sale? (Yes, No, or Unknown)	_____	_____
K. Pre-payment penalty? (Yes, No, or Unknown)	_____	_____
L. Are payments current? (Yes, No, or Unknown)	_____	_____

21. BUYER'S CREDITWORTHINESS: (CHECK EITHER A OR B. Do not check both.) In addition to the loan application, credit report and other information requested under paragraph 2:

    A. ☐ No other disclosure concerning Buyer's creditworthiness has been made to Seller;

OR **B.** ☐ The following representations concerning Buyer's creditworthiness are made by Buyer(s) to Seller:

Borrower _____	Co-Borrower _____
1. Occupation _____	1. Occupation _____
2. Employer _____	2. Employer _____
3. Length of Employment _____	3. Length of Employment _____
4. Monthly Gross Income _____	4. Monthly Gross Income _____
5. Other _____	5. Other _____

22. ADDED, DELETED OR SUBSTITUTED BUYERS: The addition, deletion or substitution of any person or entity under this Agreement or to title prior to close of escrow shall require Seller's written consent. Seller may grant or withhold consent in Seller's sole discretion. Any additional or substituted person or entity shall, if requested by Seller, submit to Seller the same documentation as required for the original named Buyer. Seller and/or Brokers may obtain a credit report, at Buyer's expense, on any such person or entity.

Buyer's Initials (_____)(_____)
Seller's Initials (_____)(_____)

SFA REVISED 10/02 (PAGE 2 OF 3)

| Reviewed by _____ Date _____ |

SELLER FINANCING ADDENDUM AND DISCLOSURE (SFA PAGE 2 OF 3)

Property Address: _____ Date: _____

23. CAUTION:

    A. If the Seller financing requires a balloon payment, Seller shall give Buyer written notice, according to the terms of Civil Code §2966, at least 90 and not more than 150 days before the balloon payment is due if the transaction is for the purchase of a dwelling for not more than four families.

    B. If **any** obligation secured by the Property calls for a balloon payment, Seller and Buyer are aware that refinancing of the balloon payment at maturity may be difficult or impossible, depending on conditions in the conventional mortgage marketplace at that time. There are no assurances that new financing or a loan extension will be available when the balloon prepayment, or any prepayment, is due.

    C. If **any** of the existing or proposed loans or extensions of credit would require refinancing as a result of a lack of full amortization, such refinancing might be difficult or impossible in the conventional mortgage marketplace.

    D. In the event of default by Buyer: (1) Seller may have to reinstate and/or make monthly payments on any and all senior encumbrances (including real property taxes) in order to protect Seller's secured interest; (2) Seller's rights are generally limited to foreclosure on the Property, pursuant to California Code of Civil Procedure §580b; and (3) the Property may lack sufficient equity to protect Seller's interests if the Property decreases in value.

If this three-page Addendum and Disclosure is used in a transaction for the purchase of a dwelling for not more than four families, it shall be prepared by an Arranger of Credit as defined in California Civil Code §2957(a). (The Arranger of Credit is usually the agent who obtained the offer.)

_____

Arranger of Credit - (Print Firm Name)   By   Date

Address _____ City _____ State _____ Zip _____

Phone _____ Fax _____

> BUYER AND SELLER ACKNOWLEDGE AND AGREE THAT BROKERS: (A) WILL NOT PROVIDE LEGAL OR TAX ADVICE; (B) WILL NOT PROVIDE OTHER ADVICE OR INFORMATION THAT EXCEEDS THE KNOWLEDGE, EDUCATION AND EXPERIENCE REQUIRED TO OBTAIN A REAL ESTATE LICENSE; OR (C) HAVE NOT AND WILL NOT VERIFY ANY INFORMATION PROVIDED BY EITHER BUYER OR SELLER. BUYER AND SELLER AGREE THAT THEY WILL SEEK LEGAL, TAX AND OTHER DESIRED ASSISTANCE FROM APPROPRIATE PROFESSIONALS. BUYER AND SELLER ACKNOWLEDGE THAT THE INFORMATION EACH HAS PROVIDED TO THE ARRANGER OF CREDIT FOR INCLUSION IN THIS DISCLOSURE FORM IS ACCURATE. BUYER AND SELLER FURTHER ACKNOWLEDGE THAT EACH HAS RECEIVED A COMPLETED COPY OF THIS DISCLOSURE FORM.

Buyer _____ Date _____
              (signature)

Address _____ City _____ State _____ Zip _____

Phone _____ Fax _____ E-mail _____

Buyer _____ Date _____
              (signature)

Address _____ City _____ State _____ Zip _____

Phone _____ Fax _____ E-mail _____

Seller _____ Date _____
              (signature)

Address _____ City _____ State _____ Zip _____

Phone _____ Fax _____ E-mail _____

Seller _____ Date _____
              (signature)

Address _____ City _____ State _____ Zip _____

Phone _____ Fax _____ E-mail _____

SURE TRAC
The System for Success™

Published by the
California Association of REALTORS®

| Reviewed by _____ Date _____ |

EQUAL HOUSING OPPORTUNITY

SFA REVISED 10/02 (PAGE 3 OF 3)

SELLER FINANCING ADDENDUM AND DISCLOSURE (SFA PAGE 3 OF 3)

Liability

A disclosure statement protects the parties by helping them understand the financing transaction. It can also protect the real estate agent, by documenting that certain information was provided to the parties. However, the agent should not regard the disclosure statement as a shield against liability. With or without disclosures, an agent who suggests or encourages a financing arrangement that is plainly imprudent could be held liable for breach of fiduciary duty if his principal later suffers a loss. This is especially true when an unsophisticated party relies on the real estate agent alone instead of consulting another professional (such as a lawyer or a CPA).

In a seller-financed transaction, a court could hold that a seller's agent also had fiduciary duties to the buyer. An inadvertent dual agency may arise if the buyer believes the agent is representing his interests in negotiating the financing arrangement with the seller. In that case, the agent could be held liable for breach of duties owed to the buyer/debtor as well as to the seller/creditor. And even without a finding of dual agency, a seller's agent who persuaded a buyer to enter into an extremely unwise transaction might be held liable for fraud.

So use your imagination, but don't lose touch with reality. While seller financing can close a sale, what happens after closing matters too. The buyer must be able to pay as agreed, and the seller must be well protected in case of default. Make sure both parties get good professional advice and understand every aspect of their transaction.

Outline: Seller Financing

I. How Seller Financing Works

    A. A seller can use a promissory note and security instrument to finance the buyer's purchase; such a loan is known as a purchase money loan.

    B. A seller may also use a land contract, where the buyer takes possession of the property but the seller retains legal title until the price has been paid in full.

    C. Seller financing is usually secondary financing, where a "seller second" supplements an institutional first mortgage.

II. When and Why Seller Financing is Used

    A. If interest rates are high and buyers have difficulty qualifying for loans, the only way a seller may be able to sell the property is by financing part of the purchase price.

    B. Sellers may use seller financing as a marketing tool; buyers may pay more for a house if they can get favorable seller financing terms.

    C. Seller financing may have tax advantages: if payments are made over a period of years, the seller doesn't have to report the full profit from the sale in the first year.

III. Seller Seconds

    A. Often, seller financing is secondary financing, where the seller accepts a second mortgage (a "seller second") for the difference between the loan amount and the purchase price.

    B. Supplementing a new loan

        1. The seller second must meet lender requirements; for instance, for a conventional loan, the total financing may not exceed 95% of the sales price, and the second loan may not require a balloon payment within less than five years after closing.

        2. A buyer considering a seller second needs to consider how much he has for a downpayment, the total monthly payment he can qualify for, and how large the balloon payment for the seller second will be.

        3. A seller considering a seller second needs to think about whether cash flow and yield will be adequate, possible negative tax consequences (such as the imputed interest rule), and lien priority.

    C. Supplementing an assumption

        1. A seller second can supplement a buyer's assumption of an existing loan; the buyer will make a monthly payment to the seller as well as making the monthly payment the seller has been making to the lender.

2. If the loan has a due-on-sale clause, an assumption isn't possible unless the lender agrees to it.

3. Regardless of whether there is a due-on-sale clause, the lender's consent is necessary for the seller to be released from liability.

IV. Seller Financing as Primary Financing

   A. Unencumbered property

      1. Seller financing is straightforward if the seller owns the property free and clear.

      2. While lien priority is not as much of a concern with primary seller financing, the seller must make sure that taxes and special assessment liens are paid so that the government doesn't foreclose.

      3. Escrow account can be set up to handle the buyer's tax and hazard insurance payments.

      4. If a seller is willing to provide substantial financing but needs cash at closing, a possibility is seller financing with an institutional second mortgage.

   B. Land contracts

      1. A seller providing primary financing might choose to use a land contract (also known as a conditional sales contract or installment sales contract) instead of a mortgage.

      2. Under a land contract, the seller (or vendor) retains legal title to the property until the buyer (or vendee) pays off the entire purchase price in installments.

      3. A land contract is not accompanied by a promissory note; the contract describes the terms of sale and the financing arrangements.

      4. For some land contracts, if a vendee defaults on the contract obligation, the vendee's rights in the property are terminated and the vendor retains all payments made so far; this remedy is known as forfeiture.

      5. Courts won't necessarily allow forfeiture, depending on how long the vendee has been making payments.

      6. The expense and delay of court proceedings in the event of breach of a land contract is the main disadvantage.

      7. Lenders are not likely to offer institutional secondary financing if the primary financing is through a land contract.

C. Encumbered property: Wraparound financing

1. With a wraparound, the property remains subject to the existing mortgage (or underlying loan), and the seller continues to make payments.

2. Each month, the buyer makes a payment to the seller, and the seller uses a portion of that payment to make the payment on the underlying loan.

3. A wraparound can use a mortgage, deed of trust (called an all-inclusive deed of trust), or land contract.

4. The underlying loan cannot have a due-on-sale clause. It is never a good idea to use a "silent wrap," where the lender isn't informed of the sale of the property.

5. Wraparound financing can be attractive since it allows the buyer to finance a purchase at a below-market rate on the total amount financed while the seller receives an above-market rate on the credit extended.

6. The buyer's concern with a wraparound is to make sure that the seller makes payments on the underlying loan. The buyer may request a provision where the buyer can make the payment directly to the lender if the seller fails to do so, or make payments directly to an escrow account.

V. Alternatives to Seller Financing

A. Buydowns: The seller may assist a buyer with a buydown, by paying discount points to reduce the buyer's interest rate.

B. Contributions to closing costs: The seller may pay some of the buyer's closing costs, which can be more helpful than a price reduction for the same amount.

C. Equity exchanges: A seller may accept other assets from a buyer in addition to cash.

D. Lease arrangements: A seller may lease a property to a buyer for a time before the buyer purchases it, either through a lease/option or a lease/purchase.

1. A lease/option involves a lease for a specific term and then the option to purchase the property at a specified price.

2. The rental payments may be applied toward the purchase price in a lease/option, either deducted from the sales price or treated as part of the downpayment.

3. In a lease/purchase, buyer and seller sign a purchase contract along with the lease, so that deciding not to purchase at lease's end means a breach of the contract.

VI. Agent's Responsibilities in Seller-Financed Transactions

A. An agent should recommend that both parties get legal and tax advice, and have documents reviewed by a lawyer, before proceeding with seller financing.

B. A real estate agent should not prepare seller financing documents; this would be considered the unauthorized practice of law.

C. Disclosures: Some states require disclosure forms when a third party (such as a real estate agent) helps arrange seller financing.

D. Liability: A disclosure statement does not limit an agent's liability.

1. An agent who encourages an unwise financial arrangement might be liable for breach of fiduciary duties.

2. An agent who arranges seller financing might create an inadvertent dual agency.

Key Terms

Purchase money loan: A mortgage or deed of trust given by a buyer to a seller.

Seller financing: When a seller extends credit to a buyer to finance the purchase of the property, as opposed to having the buyer obtain a loan from a third party, such as an institutional lender.

Secondary financing: Money borrowed to pay part of the required downpayment or closing costs for a first loan, when the second loan is secured by the same property that secures the first loan.

Seller second: Secondary financing from the seller, when a purchase money loan is used to supplement an institutional first mortgage.

Land contract: A contract for the sale of property in which the buyer (vendee) pays the seller (vendor) in installments, taking possession of the property immediately but not taking legal title until the purchase price has been paid in full. Also called a contract for deed, conditional sales contract, installment sales contract, or real estate contract.

Wraparound financing: A seller financing arrangement in which the seller uses part of the buyer's payments to make the payments on an existing loan (called the underlying loan); the buyer takes title subject to the underlying loan, but does not assume it.

Buydown: When the seller or a third party pays the lender a lump sum at closing to lower the interest rate charged to the buyer, either for the life of the loan or during the first years of the loan term.

Equity exchange: When a buyer gives a seller real or personal property in addition to or instead of cash for the purchase price.

Lease/option: A lease that includes the option to purchase the leased property during the term of the lease.

Lease/purchase: A variation on the lease/option, in which the parties sign a purchase contract (instead of an option) and the prospective buyer leases the property for a specified period before closing.

Chapter Quiz

1. A seller can finance a buyer's purchase with:
   a. an all-inclusive trust deed
   b. a purchase money mortgage
   c. a land contract
   d. Any of the above

2. A seller second is most likely to be used to supplement a new institutional loan when:
   a. market interest rates are high
   b. the seller needs an exceptionally high yield on her investment
   c. the buyer has no cash for a downpayment at all
   d. negative amortization is a possibility

3. The Kramers are applying for a conventional loan that would be combined with a seller second. The monthly payment (PITI) on the institutional loan would be $1,838, and the payment on the seller financing would be $520; the Kramers' other debts add up to $490 per month. Applying a 36% maximum debt service to income ratio, the lender will make the loan if the Kramers' stable monthly income is at least:
   a. $5,106
   b. $6,467
   c. $6,550
   d. $7,911

4. Which of the following statements regarding balloon payments is true?
   a. A large balloon payment usually results in default
   b. In some cases, the buyer raises the cash for the balloon payment by refinancing
   c. A real estate agent should never suggest a seller financing arrangement that involves a balloon payment
   d. A new conventional loan cannot be combined with a seller second that requires a balloon payment

5. Which of the following instruments generally couldn't be used for a seller second supplementing a new institutional loan?
   a. Deed of trust
   b. Mortgage
   c. Land contract
   d. None of these could be used

6. The buyer made a downpayment, assumed the seller's mortgage, and gave the seller a deed of trust for the balance of the purchase price. The buyer defaults and the mortgagee forecloses on the assumed loan. If the foreclosure sale proceeds are not sufficient to cover the outstanding balance on the assumed mortgage:
   a. the seller will not be paid
   b. the mortgagee will not be paid
   c. the seller will be paid before the mortgagee is paid
   d. the mortgagee and the seller will each receive a prorated share of the sale proceeds

7. With wraparound financing:
   a. the buyer assumes the underlying loan
   b. the balance owed on the underlying loan is larger than the wraparound loan amount
   c. the seller remains responsible for making the payments on the underlying loan
   d. the more credit the seller extends to the buyer, the higher the seller's yield

8. The chief advantage of wraparound financing is that:
   a. it complies with the secondary financing rules that institutional lenders apply
   b. the seller can get an exceptionally high yield on the credit extended
   c. the due-on-sale clause on the underlying loan is not triggered, as it would be by an assumption
   d. the seller retains title to the property until the buyer has paid the full price

9. The remaining balance on the underlying loan is $230,000, and the interest rate is 8%. The seller offers a $260,000 wraparound at 10% interest. What would the seller's approximate yield be?

    a. 8%
    b. 12%
    c. 17%
    d. 25%

10. In a lease/option arrangement, the rent charged:

    a. is usually refunded if the tenant exercises the option to buy
    b. cannot be applied toward the purchase price
    c. cannot exceed the fair market rent for the property
    d. is often higher than the fair market rent for the property

Answer Key

1. d.   A seller may use an all-inclusive trust deed, a purchase money mortgage, or a land contract to finance a buyer's purchase.

2. a.   A seller second is likely to be used when market interest rates are high. If interest rates are high, few buyers may be able to qualify for a loan large enough to afford the full purchase price, so a seller may offer secondary financing as an incentive.

3. d.   To calculate the required stable monthly income, add all of the monthly debt payments ($1,838 + $520 + $490 = $2,848) and then divide that figure by the maximum debt to income ratio ($2,848 ÷ .36 = $7,911).

4. b.   When a balloon payment comes due, a borrower may be able to refinance the amount due rather than having to pay the full amount in cash.

5. c.   A land contract generally cannot be used for a seller second that supplements an institutional loan.

6. a.   If a lender forecloses on an assumed loan, and the foreclosure sale proceeds are not sufficient to cover the balance on the assumed loan, then the seller will not be paid any of the proceeds.

7. c.   A seller who uses wraparound financing will remain responsible for making payments on the underlying loan.

8. b.   With wraparound financing, a seller can get an above-market yield on the credit extended.

9. d.   To determine the seller's yield, first calculate the amount of credit extended ($260,000 – $230,000 = $30,000). Calculate the interest received on the wraparound ($260,000 × .1 = $26,000) and the interest received on the underlying loan ($230,000 × .08 = $18,400). Subtract the interest received on the underlying loan from the interest received on the wraparound, in order to calculate the net interest received by the seller ($26,000 – $18,400 = $7,600). Finally, divide the net interest by the total amount of credit extended to find the seller's yield ($7,600 ÷ $30,000 = .25, or 25%).

10. d.   The rent in a lease/option arrangement is usually higher than the market rate, since the tenant is receiving an additional benefit in having the possibility of purchase.

Case Study:
Seller Financing

Let's return to the Cortinas once more. This time, suppose that neither Rick nor Teresa is eligible for a VA loan. They've decided against FHA financing because they want a more expensive house than the FHA maximum loan amount in their area would enable them to buy. Also, they can qualify for a larger conventional loan PITI payment ($1,992.76, instead of $1,734.12) because they aren't carrying so much debt. Based on that payment amount, they've been preapproved for a 90% fixed-rate loan at 5.5% interest for up to $280,775, which will enable them to buy a house for about $312,000.

Although the Cortinas have seen several houses that would meet their needs, they haven't felt enthusiastic about any of them—until now. This afternoon they looked at a house they really want. Unfortunately, at $330,000, the property is beyond their price range.

The seller, Bonnie Wellman, was recently widowed and is about to retire. She plans to use part of the sale proceeds as a downpayment on a condominium, and to invest the rest to supplement her income. She'll have to pay off her mortgage, which has a due-on-sale clause; the current balance is about $94,000.

Wellman's home has been listed for almost four months; the market is very slow. Several people have looked at the property, but the only offer so far was for $310,000—$18,500 less than the appraised value, $328,500—and Wellman turned it down. She might accept $325,000 for the property, but at this point she's not willing to go any lower than that.

The Cortinas tell Wellman how much they like her house, and they explain that they can't qualify for a bank loan large enough to buy it. They ask if she would consider accepting a second deed of trust for part of the price. If so, they'd be willing to pay her full asking price, $330,000. Wellman says she's willing to discuss it. She estimates that she needs to take away at least $140,000 in cash from the closing. She would like to be paid at least 6% interest on any financing she provides, since that's about the rate of return she expects she could get on some other secure investment.

Answer the following questions to determine whether the Cortinas could qualify for a conventional loan supplemented by a seller second that would meet Wellman's needs.

Interest rates for fixed-rate 30-year conventional loans
      LTV 80% or less: 5.375%
      LTV 80.01% to 90%: 5.50% interest
      LTV over 90%: 5.75% interest

1. Assume that the Cortinas will get their primary financing from a lender with these secondary financing rules: the primary loan may not exceed 75% of the property's value, and the buyers must make at least a 10% downpayment. If the Cortinas buy Wellman's home for $330,000, what is the largest conventional loan they could supplement with a seller second? If they get a conventional loan for that amount, what is the largest amount of financing Wellman could provide? How much would the total amount financed be?

2. Suppose that the Cortinas obtain a 30-year fixed-rate conventional loan for the maximum amount (determined in Question 1) at the market interest rate, and Wellman finances her maximum share at 6% interest. If both the conventional loan and the seller second are amortized over a 30-year term, the monthly principal and interest payment for the conventional loan would be $1,379.63, and the monthly principal and interest payment for the seller second would be $295.43. To find the monthly housing expense, add 15% to the combined principal and interest payment to cover property taxes and hazard insurance. (Since the loan-to-value ratio of the primary loan is 80% or less, the lender won't require mortgage insurance.) Could the Cortinas qualify for this combined housing expense?

3. The primary lender would require the Cortinas to pay a 1.5% origination fee, the 0.25% adverse market delivery charge, a 2.00% loan-level price adjustment based on their indicator credit score, plus other closing costs estimated at 3% of the sales price. The lender will also require them to have two months of combined PITI payments as reserves. And, of course, they'll have to make the downpayment. How much cash would they need at closing for this transaction? Will their $58,000 in savings be enough?

4. Not surprisingly, Wellman isn't willing to wait 30 years to collect her full profit from the sale; she would like it in five years. How could this be arranged, without preventing the Cortinas from qualifying for the institutional loan?

5. If her selling costs came to 10% of the sales price, how much cash would Wellman receive at closing in this transaction? Remember that she would have to pay off her mortgage.

Chapter 14
Fair Lending and Consumer Protection

Fair Lending Laws
- Equal Credit Opportunity Act
- Fair Housing Act
- Community Reinvestment Act
- Home Mortgage Disclosure Act

Consumer Protection Laws
- Truth in Lending Act
- Real Estate Settlement Procedures Act

Predatory Lending
- Predatory lending practices
- Targeted victims
- Predatory lending laws
  - Home Ownership and Equity Protection Act
  - State laws

Introduction

In this chapter we'll discuss several federal laws that are intended to promote fairness, clarity, and honesty in residential mortgage lending. Some of these are fair lending laws, which make it illegal for lenders to discriminate when they evaluate loan applications and make loan approval decisions. Others are consumer protection laws designed to help buyers understand the lending process and make informed borrowing decisions. In spite of these laws, unscrupulous lenders and mortgage brokers often manipulate vulnerable and unsophisticated borrowers into taking out loans that are not in the borrowers' best interests. This problem of predatory lending is discussed at the end of this chapter.

Fair Lending Laws

Residential mortgage loan transactions are subject to federal anti-discrimination laws, including the Equal Credit Opportunity Act, the Fair Housing Act, the Community Reinvestment Act, and the Home Mortgage Disclosure Act.

Equal Credit Opportunity Act

The Equal Credit Opportunity Act (ECOA), which became law in 1974, applies to both individuals and businesses seeking credit. However, our discussion of ECOA will be limited to consumer credit. Consumer credit is credit that is extended to an individual (not a corporation or other business) for personal, family, or household purposes. This includes residential mortgage loans.

Equal Credit Opportunity Act prohibits discrimination based on:
- Race
- Color
- Religion
- National origin
- Sex
- Marital status
- Age
- Public assistance

ECOA prohibits discrimination against loan applicants based on race, color, religion, national origin, sex, marital status, or age (as long as an applicant is old enough to have contractual capacity under the laws of his state). In addition, the act prohibits discrimination against applicants who receive all or part of their income from a public assistance program, such as welfare. ECOA also prohibits discrimination against applicants who have exercised their rights under federal credit laws (for example, by requesting corrections to a credit report).

Lenders have to comply with ECOA when interviewing and communicating with loan applicants, and when analyzing the applicants' financial situation. The credit terms lenders offer applicants must also comply with ECOA.

Lenders must not discourage anyone from applying for a loan, and they must apply their credit guidelines to every loan applicant in the same manner, based on amount and stability of income, net worth, and credit reputation. Under ECOA, it's illegal for lenders to base lending decisions on assumptions about the creditworthiness of members of particular racial, ethnic, and religious groups; women or men; unmarried couples, divorced people, or single people; or elderly people or young adults.

Note that the law permits lenders to ask about a loan applicant's age or marital status, provided the information isn't used as a basis for discrimination. Inquiries about marital status must be limited to asking whether an applicant is married, unmarried, or separated (divorced, widowed, and single people are all categorized as unmarried) and whether the applicant prefers to be addressed as Mr., Ms., Mrs., or Miss.

Applicants may be asked about the number and age of their dependents and about expenses related to the dependents. However, lenders aren't allowed to ask whether loan applicants are planning to bear, adopt, or raise children (or more children in addition to the ones they already have). It's also illegal for a lender to assume that applicants who belong to certain groups are more likely to bear or raise children (which could result in diminished or interrupted income).

> Lenders aren't allowed to ask loan applicants about their childbearing plans

Under ECOA, credit applicants must be informed within 30 days of submitting a completed application whether their application was accepted or rejected. If the application is rejected, the creditor must give the applicant a notice informing her of the specific reason for the denial, or her right to inquire further within 60 days.

Fair Housing Act

The Federal Fair Housing Act, a 1968 law, includes provisions that address lending discrimination. The act applies to transactions involving residential properties with one to four dwelling units, and it prohibits discrimination based on race, color, national origin, religion, sex, disability, or familial status (a legal term that refers to families with minor children).

> Fair Housing Act prohibits discrimination based on:
> - Race
> - Color
> - National origin
> - Religion
> - Sex
> - Disability
> - Familial status

Under the Fair Housing Act, it is illegal for lenders to do any of the following for discriminatory reasons:

- refuse to provide information about mortgage loans,
- refuse to make a mortgage loan, or
- impose different terms or conditions on a loan.

Redlining: refusing to make loans in certain neighborhoods based on the race or ethnic background of the residents

The Fair Housing Act also prohibits **redlining**. Redlining is the refusal to make loans secured by property located in a certain neighborhood because the people who live in that neighborhood belong to a particular racial or ethnic group. At one time lenders routinely refused to make loans in minority neighborhoods because it was assumed that property values in those areas were declining. (The term "redlining" originates from the practice of using red ink to mark off these neighborhoods on a community map; mortgages weren't available for properties inside the red lines.) Redlining can turn discriminatory assumptions into self-fulfilling prophecies. When it isn't possible to obtain purchase or renovation loans in a redlined neighborhood, it's difficult to sell, maintain, or improve homes there, and then property values actually will decline as a result. While redlining is not as widespread as it once was, the problem remains.

Note, however, that a lender may legally refuse to make a loan if, in fact, property values in the neighborhood are declining. But the refusal has to be based on objective economic criteria about the condition and value of the neighborhood surrounding the property, without regard to the neighborhood's racial or ethnic composition. It is illegal for lenders to automatically assume that certain neighborhoods have declining property values.

Community Reinvestment Act

Community Reinvestment Act encourages lenders to serve low- and moderate-income people

In 1977, Congress decided to address their continuing concern about redlining and other forms of discrimination by passing a law that encourages certain lenders to serve low- and moderate-income people living in the communities where the lenders do business. Under the provisions of the Community Reinvestment Act (CRA), all depository institutions (commercial banks and savings institutions) must regularly report on the number of home and business loans they have provided to low- and moderate-income consumers living in their market neighborhoods. The law doesn't require lenders to modify their traditional underwriting standards to originate these loans; in fact lenders are encouraged to apply "safe and sound" lending practices. The main goal of the law is to illustrate to lenders that negative assumptions about certain neighborhoods (and the people living in those neighborhoods) are unfounded, and that lenders can serve these groups without incurring any additional risks.

Data reported under this law is considered during bank examinations, and is particularly important when a bank seeks to expand its operations. Regulators also consider input from community groups when determining whether a bank has met its CRA obligations.

As a result of the CRA, those who were underserved by lenders in the past are now better able to get home and business loans. Because CRA has been so successful in increasing access to loans, there have been discussions about expanding the law to cover nondepository lenders, including independent mortgage companies.

Home Mortgage Disclosure Act

The Home Mortgage Disclosure Act (HMDA) was enacted in 1975. It provides a way for the government to monitor whether lenders are fulfilling their obligation to serve the full spectrum of housing needs in their communities. (For example, institutions covered by the Community Reinvestment Act would include their CRA data in their HMDA reports.) The law also facilitates enforcement of the Fair Housing Act's prohibition of lending discrimination (including redlining).

Home Mortgage Disclosure Act helps the government spot redlining and predatory lending

HMDA applies to a broad range of mortgage lenders doing business in metropolitan areas, including banks, thrifts, credit unions, and independent mortgage companies. Depending on their asset size and level of mortgage activity, lenders must submit an annual report to the government describing the residential mortgage loans—purchase loans, home improvement loans, and refinancing—that they originated or purchased from other lenders during the fiscal year. A home improvement loan is a loan secured by a lien on property, when the purpose of any part of the loan is to repair, rehabilitate, remodel, or improve the dwelling located on the property. Home equity loans that are used for other purposes, such as to consolidate credit card debt or pay education expenses, are not included. The reporting of an open-ended home equity line of credit is optional.

Among other information, a lender has to furnish all of the following for each loan or loan application:

- the dollar amount of the loan;
- the type of loan (FHA, VA, or other);
- the purpose of the loan;
- whether the application was a request for preapproval and whether it was denied or approved;
- the race, ethnicity, sex, and gross annual income of the borrower;
- the type of property; and
- the geographic location of the property.

The information contained in these reports is used to detect redlining. If a lender's report reveals areas where few or no home loans have been made, government investigators are alerted that there may be a problem.

HMDA is implemented by the Federal Reserve Board's Regulation C. Amendments to Regulation C that went into effect in 2004 and 2008 require lenders to report additional information that may help the government address predatory lending issues. For example, a lender's report must now provide important information concerning a loan's costs and terms, to discourage the use of high-cost mortgages.

Consumer Protection Laws

Federal consumer protection laws that apply to mortgage loan transactions include the Truth in Lending Act and the Real Estate Settlement and Procedures Act. Many states have enacted similar consumer protection laws on a state level as well.

Truth in Lending Act

Truth in Lending Act is implemented by Regulation Z

The Truth in Lending Act (TILA) was passed in 1968. It's implemented by the Federal Reserve Board's **Regulation Z**. While Regulation Z does not set limits on interest rates or other finance charges, it does regulate the content and timing for the disclosure of these charges.

Loans Covered by TILA. A loan is a consumer loan if it is used for personal, family, or household purposes. A consumer loan is covered by the Truth in Lending Act if it is to be repaid in more than four installments, or is subject to finance charges, and is either:

- for $25,000 or less, or
- secured by real property.

Thus, any mortgage loan is covered by TILA as long as the proceeds are used for personal, family, or household purposes (such as buying or remodeling a home, consolidating personal debt, or sending children to college).

TILA applies to any mortgage loan used for personal, family, or household purposes

Loans Exempt from TILA. The Truth in Lending Act applies only to loans made to natural persons, so loans made to corporations or organizations aren't covered. Loans for business, commercial, or agricultural purposes are also exempt. So are loans in excess of $25,000, unless the loan is secured by real property. (Mortgage loans for personal, family, or household purposes are covered regardless of the loan amount.) Most seller financing is exempt, because extending credit isn't in the seller's ordinary course of business.

Disclosure Requirements. As we discussed in Chapter 7, a lender is required to give a loan applicant a disclosure statement with estimates of the loan costs within three business days after receiving the written application.

The two most important disclosures required under TILA are the total finance charge and the annual percentage rate (APR). Although TILA doesn't require a specific form for disclosures, all information should be presented "clearly and conspicuously in writing, in a form that the consumer may keep." The total finance charge and the annual percentage rate, along with the lender's name, must be presented even more conspicuously than the rest of the information. The total finance charge should be labeled "the dollar amount your credit will cost you," and the APR should be labeled "the cost of your credit as a yearly rate."

APR shows relationship of total finance charge to total amount financed

Lenders are expected to use the best information available to them in preparing a TILA disclosure statement and calculating the total finance charge and annual percentage rate. They are allowed to use "banker's months" with 30 days, rather than the exact number of days in each month in the calculations. The disclosures are considered adequate if the total finance charge is accurate to within $100 and

Fig. 14.1 Sample Truth in Lending Act disclosure statement form

	TRUTH-IN-LENDING DISCLOSURE STATEMENT REQUIRED BY FEDERAL RESERVE REGULATIONS Z	
		LOAN NUMBER
	DATE 19	
BORROWER(S)	TYPE OF LOAN	LOAN TERM YEARS
	PROPERTY LOCATION	

ANNUAL PERCENTAGE RATE The cost of your credit as a yearly rate	FINANCE CHARGE The dollar amount your credit will cost you	AMOUNT FINANCED The amount of credit provided to you or on your behalf	TOTAL OF PAYMENTS The amount you will have paid after you have paid all payments as scheduled
%	$	$	$

Notice to Borrower(s):   In compliance with Truth-In-Lending Law you are receiving a Good Faith Estimate of Settlement Charges in lieu of an itemization statement.

Your Payment Schedule will be:

Monthly Beginning

_____
Date

Number of Payments	Amount of Payments	When Payments Are Due	Number of Payments	Amount of Payments	When Payments Are Due
	$			$	
	$			$	
	$			$	
	$			$	

☐   This loan has a **Demand Feature.**

☐   Your loan contains a **Variable Rate Feature.** Disclosures about the Variable Rate have been provided to you earlier.

Your ARM Loan   ☐ has   ☐ does not have a **Conversion Feature.** (The option to convert your ARM loan to a Fixed Rate Mortgage loan.) If choose to convert to a Fixed Rate mortgage loan, your new interest rate will not be higher than _____ %, which is the Maximum Rate.

☐   **Variable Rate not applicable.**

☐   **Insurance:** The following insurance is required: ☐ Property Insurance   ☐ Flood Insurance

You may obtain insurance from an agent of your choice, provided they are acceptable to this lender.

☐   Property Insurance is available through the lender at a cost of $_____ for a one year term.

☐   Flood Insurance is available through the lender at a cost of $_____ for a one year term.

☐   Credit Life Insurance or Disability Insurance are not required.

☐   Credit Life Insurance and/or Disability Insurance are not provided.

☐   Credit Life Insurance and/or Disability Insurance are not available through this lender.

☐   Credit Life is available at a cost of $_____ for a _____ term. (X _____)

☐   Disability Insurance is available at a cost of $_____ for a _____ term. (X _____)

Security: You are giving a Security Interest   ☐ in the property being purchased   ☐ other accounts you have with us other (describe) _____

Late Charge: If your payment is _____ days late, you will be required to pay a Penalty charge of _____% of your payment.

Prepayment: If you pay this loan early, you   ☐ will   ☐ will not have to pay a penalty

and you   ☐ may   ☐ will not   be entitled to a refund of a part of the finance charge.

Assumption: Someone buying your property   ☐ may, subject to conditions   ☐ may not assume the remainder of your loan on the Original terms.

☐   This is an assumption of an existing loan. The interest rate for the term of the loan will not exceed _____%, which is the maximum rate.

☐   Filing Fees $_____

☐   This is an **Early Disclosure** and all dates and numerical disclosures are estimates except for late payment disclosures.

☐   This is your **Final Disclosure**

NOTE: See your contract documents for any additional information about nonpayment. default, any required repayment in full before the scheduled date and prepayment refunds and penalties.

(e) means an-estimate

I/we acknowledge receipt of a completed copy of this disclosure statement.

X _____ Date _____ 19 ____ X _____
    Borrower   Co-Borrower

the APR is accurate to within one-eighth of one percent. But if their initial calculations are later found to be incorrect, lenders are required to give revised information to borrowers in a timely fashion.

Total finance charge. Let's take a slightly more detailed look at the finance charge. The total finance charge is the sum of all fees and charges the borrower will pay in connection with the loan. It includes the interest, and it also may include an origination fee, discount points, a finder's fee, service charges, mortgage insurance premiums or guaranty fees, and a mortgage broker's fee or commission.

> Total finance charge may include:
> • Interest
> • Origination fee
> • Points paid by borrower
> • Finder's fee
> • Service charge
> • Mortgage insurance premium or guaranty fee
> • Mortgage broker's compensation

However, it's important to note that the law specifically excludes these charges from the calculation:

- application fee,
- appraisal fee,
- document preparation or notary fee,
- credit report fee,
- title report fee,
- title insurance premium,
- survey fee,
- pest inspection fee,
- flood hazard inspection fee,
- impounds for taxes and insurance,
- any points paid by the seller,
- late payment fees, or
- fees charged in the event of default.

Also, the total finance charge doesn't include any charges that would be incurred if the transaction were being carried out entirely in cash.

An escrow or closing agent's fee and the borrower's hazard insurance premiums may be included in the total finance charge if the lender requires a particular closing agent or insurance company to be used, rather than letting the borrower choose. In most transactions, however, the closing agent's fee and hazard insurance premiums are not part of the total finance charge.

Other disclosures. In addition to the total finance charge and annual percentage rate, all of the following must appear on a TILA disclosure statement: the identity of the lender; the amount financed; a payment schedule, with the number, amounts, and timing of payments; the total amount those payments will add up to; the prepayment fee

> In addition to APR and total finance charge, TILA disclosure statement must also show:
> • Lender's identity
> • Total amount financed
> • Payment schedule
> • Prepayment fee
> • Late charges
> • Assumption policy

(if any); late charges; and whether and under what terms the loan can be assumed by another person if the property is sold.

ARM disclosures. In addition to the disclosures already listed, the Truth in Lending Act requires a number of special disclosures for adjustable-rate mortgages. (We explain ARMs in Chapter 6.) Because the total amount of interest that will be collected over the loan term can't be calculated (because it will fluctuate based on market changes), the disclosure requirements for the APR and other related financing figures are different for an ARM than for a fixed-rate loan.

For ARMs secured by a principal dwelling, lenders must give applicants a booklet published by the Federal Reserve Board called the "Consumer Handbook on Adjustable-Rate Mortgages" (sometimes called the CHARM booklet). In addition, the borrower must be given a loan program disclosure for each ARM program that she expresses interest in, including descriptions of the ways the interest rate, payment, or loan terms may change, as well as information about the specific index that would be used.

In addition, the lender is required to give the loan applicant a hypothetical example showing how the monthly payments on a $10,000 ARM loan with the same features that the applicant is considering could be affected by interest rate changes in the future.

For fixed-rate mortgage loans, TILA's requirements end when the loan is funded. However, when an ARM is secured by the borrower's principal dwelling, the lender's disclosure requirements continue. When the loan's interest rate is adjusted, the lender must send the borrower an adjustment notice that describes the effects of the rate adjustment on the payment amount, the loan balance, and other aspects of the loan. If the payment amount is going to change, the adjustment notice must be sent at least 25 days, but not more than 120 calendar days, before the new payment is due. If the new interest rate doesn't change the payment amount, the notice must be sent at least once each year.

Right of Rescission. TILA provides a right of rescission in connection with certain types of mortgage loans. When the security property is the borrower's principal residence, the borrower may rescind the loan agreement within three days of: 1) signing the loan documents, 2) receiving a disclosure statement, or 3) receiving notice of the right of

TILA requires special disclosures for ARM programs

ARM's APR is subject to change after closing

TILA's three-day right of rescission applies only to home equity loans and refinancing with a new lender

rescission, whichever happens latest. The notice of the right to rescind can't be part of other TILA disclosures or loan documents; it must be a separate document. If the borrower never receives the statement or the notice, the right of rescission does not expire for three years.

The right of rescission applies only to home equity loans and to some refinancing, not to purchase or construction loans. With refinancing, the borrower has a right of rescission if the new loan is from a new lender. If the new loan is from the same lender that made the loan it's replacing, only an increase in the amount owed can be rescinded.

Advertising Under TILA. In addition to the disclosure requirements, TILA also has rules regulating the advertising of credit terms. These rules apply to anyone who advertises consumer credit, not just lenders. For example, a real estate broker advertising financing terms for a listed home must also comply with TILA and Regulation Z.

The purpose of TILA's advertising rules is to make sure consumers don't receive—and act on—misleading financing information. For example, the law prohibits lenders from using "bait and switch" tactics: advertising products that aren't really available as a way to draw in prospective borrowers. TILA also forbids lenders from advertising only their most attractive financing terms, a practice that disguises the true costs of the loan.

It is always legal under TILA to include the cash price or the APR in a consumer ad, as these are not subject to misinterpretation. However, if an ad contains other loan terms (such as the downpayment, the note's interest rate, or the monthly payment amount) then all additional financing terms must also be included, to make sure the consumer has enough information to understand the true cost of the loan product.

APR and cash price can be advertised without triggering TILA's full disclosure requirement

> **Example:** A newspaper ad says, "Assume VA loan at 5% interest." Because it mentions the interest rate, the ad will violate the Truth in Lending Act if it doesn't go on to reveal the APR, the downpayment, and all the other terms of repayment.

In this example, the reference to the interest rate triggered the full disclosure requirement. However, general statements such as "low downpayment," "easy terms," or "affordable interest rate" would not trigger the full disclosure requirement.

As you might expect, TILA has special requirements that apply to advertisements for ARM loans and other loans that involve variable

Fig. 14.2 An actual flyer that violates the Truth in Lending Act's advertising rules

> # GET THAT DREAM HOME...
> ## ...NOW!!!
>
> ### $400,000 HOME LOAN FOR
> ### *$958/MONTH*
>
> ### PURCHASE/REFINANCE
>
> ### 1-800-555-4321
>
> ### FREE $400 APPRAISAL

terms. For these loans, the ad must contain language alerting consumers to the fact that the rates or other terms quoted are subject to change. It is also a violation of TILA to refer to a loan as "fixed" when in fact the interest rate can change over the life of the loan.

An example of a flyer that violates the Truth in Lending Act is shown in Figure 14.2.

Real Estate Settlement Procedures Act

The Real Estate Settlement Procedures Act (RESPA), which is enforced by HUD, affects how closing is handled in most residential transactions financed with mortgage loans. Any professional involved in the settlement process (including a real estate agent, mortgage broker, lender, or employee of a title company) is regulated by the consumer protection provisions in this law.

RESPA has two main goals:

RESPA's main goals:
• Informing borrowers about closing costs
• Eliminating kickbacks

- to provide borrowers with information about their financing fees and closing costs; and
- to keep closing costs as low as possible, by eliminating kickbacks and referral fees that unnecessarily increase the borrower's costs.

Over the last few years, HUD has been working on new rules that would reduce closing costs and provide even more protections for consumers. In January of 2009, a number of new regulations were enacted. However, there is a one-year transition period for some of the new requirements. We'll begin by discussing current RESPA requirements and follow that with a discussion of the new requirements that will be mandatory for all transactions starting January, 2010.

Transactions Covered by RESPA. RESPA applies to all "federally related" loan transactions. A loan is federally related if:

1. it will be secured by a mortgage or deed of trust against:
    *   property on which there is (or on which the loan proceeds will be used to build) a dwelling with four or fewer units;
    *   a condominium unit or a cooperative apartment;
    *   a lot with (or on which the loan proceeds will be used to place) a mobile home; and

    RESPA applies to federally related loans, which include most mortgage loans made by institutional lenders

2. the lender is federally regulated, has federally insured accounts, is assisted by the federal government, makes loans in connection with a federal program, sells loans to Fannie Mae, Ginnie Mae, or Freddie Mac, or makes real estate loans that total more than $1,000,000 per year.

In short, the act applies to almost all institutional lenders and to most residential loans.

Exemptions. RESPA doesn't apply to the following transactions:
*   a loan used to purchase 25 acres or more;
*   a loan primarily for a business, commercial, or agricultural purpose;
*   a loan used to purchase vacant land, unless there will be a one- to four-unit dwelling built on it or a mobile home placed on it;
*   temporary financing, such as a construction loan;
*   an assumption for which the lender's approval is neither required nor obtained.

Note that RESPA also does not apply to seller-financed transactions, since they are not federally regulated.

Fig. 14.3 Good faith estimate of closing costs form

OMB Approval No. 2502-0265

Good Faith Estimate (GFE)

US DEPARTMENT OF HOUSING AND URBAN DEVELOPMENT

Name of Originator		Borrower	
Originator Address		Property Address	
Originator Phone Number			
Originator Email		Date of GFE	

Purpose

This GFE gives you an estimate of your settlement charges and loan terms if you are approved for this loan. For more information, see HUD's *Special Information Booklet* on settlement charges, your *Truth-in-Lending Disclosures*, and other consumer information at www.hud.gov/respa. If you decide you would like to proceed with this loan, contact us.

Shopping for your loan

Only you can shop for the best loan for you. Compare this GFE with other loan offers, so you can find the best loan. Use the shopping chart on page 3 to compare all the offers you receive.

Important dates

1. The interest rate for this GFE is available through _____. After this time, the interest rate, some of your loan Origination Charges, and the monthly payment shown below can change until you lock your interest rate.

2. This estimate for all other settlement charges is available through _____.

3. After you lock your interest rate, you must go to settlement within ☐ days (your rate lock period) to receive the locked interest rate.

4. You must lock the interest rate at least ☐ days before settlement.

Summary of your loan

Your initial loan amount is	$
Your loan term is	years
Your initial interest rate is	%
Your initial monthly amount owed for principal, interest, and any mortgage insurance is	$ per month
Can your interest rate rise?	☐ No ☐ Yes, it can rise to a maximum of %. The first change will be in .
Even if you make payments on time, can your loan balance rise?	☐ No ☐ Yes, it can rise to a maximum of $
Even if you make payments on time, can your monthly amount owed for principal, interest, and any mortgage insurance rise?	☐ No ☐ Yes, the first increase can be in and the monthly amount owed can rise to $. The maximum it can ever rise to is $.
Does your loan have a prepayment penalty?	☐ No ☐ Yes, your maximum prepayment penalty is $.
Does your loan have a balloon payment?	☐ No ☐ Yes, you have a balloon payment of $ due in years.

Escrow account information

Some lenders require an escrow account to hold funds for paying property taxes or other property-related charges in addition to your monthly amount owed of $ _____ .

Do we require you to have an escrow account for your loan?

☐ No, you do not have an escrow account. You must pay these charges directly when due.

☐ Yes, you have an escrow account. It may or may not cover all of these charges. Ask us.

Summary of your settlement charges

A	Your Adjusted Origination Charges *(See page 2.)*	$
B	Your Charges for All Other Settlement Services *(See page 2.)*	$
A + B	Total Estimated Settlement Charges	$

Good Faith Estimate (HUD-GFE) 1

Understanding your estimated settlement charges

Your Adjusted Origination Charges

1. Our origination charge This charge is for getting this loan for you.	
2. Your credit or charge (points) for the specific interest rate chosen ☐ The credit or charge for the interest rate of ⬚ % is included in "Our origination charge." (See item 1 above.) ☐ You receive a credit of $⬚ for this interest rate of ⬚ %. This credit **reduces** your settlement charges. ☐ You pay a charge of $⬚ for this interest rate of ⬚ %. This charge (points) **increases** your total settlement charges. The tradeoff table on page 3 shows that you can change your total settlement charges by choosing a different interest rate for this loan.	
A Your Adjusted Origination Charges	$

Some of these charges can change at settlement. See the top of page 3 for more information.

Your Charges for All Other Settlement Services

3. Required services that we select These charges are for services we require to complete your settlement. We will choose the providers of these services. *Service* *Charge*	
4. Title services and lender's title insurance This charge includes the services of a title or settlement agent, for example, and title insurance to protect the lender, if required.	
5. Owner's title insurance You may purchase an owner's title insurance policy to protect your interest in the property.	
6. Required services that you can shop for These charges are for other services that are required to complete your settlement. We can identify providers of these services or you can shop for them yourself. Our estimates for providing these services are below. *Service* *Charge*	
7. Government recording charges These charges are for state and local fees to record your loan and title documents.	
8. Transfer taxes These charges are for state and local fees on mortgages and home sales.	
9. Initial deposit for your escrow account This charge is held in an escrow account to pay future recurring charges on your property and includes ☐ all property taxes, ☐ all insurance, and ☐ other ⬚ .	
10. Daily interest charges This charge is for the daily interest on your loan from the day of your settlement until the first day of the next month or the first day of your normal mortgage payment cycle. This amount is $⬚ per day for ⬚ days (if your settlement is ⬚).	
11. Homeowner's insurance This charge is for the insurance you must buy for the property to protect from a loss, such as fire. *Policy* *Charge*	
B Your Charges for All Other Settlement Services	$
A + **B** Total Estimated Settlement Charges	$

Good Faith Estimate (HUD-GFE) 2

Instructions

Understanding which charges can change at settlement

This GFE estimates your settlement charges. At your settlement, you will receive a HUD-1, a form that lists your actual costs. Compare the charges on the HUD-1 with the charges on this GFE. Charges can change if you select your own provider and do not use the companies we identify. (See below for details.)

These charges **cannot increase** at settlement:	The total of these charges **can increase up to 10%** at settlement:	These charges **can change** at settlement:
■ Our origination charge ■ Your credit or charge (points) for the specific interest rate chosen *(after you lock in your interest rate)* ■ Your adjusted origination charges *(after you lock in your interest rate)* ■ Transfer taxes	■ Required services that we select ■ Title services and lender's title insurance *(if we select them or you use companies we identify)* ■ Owner's title insurance *(if you use companies we identify)* ■ Required services that you can shop for *(if you use companies we identify)* ■ Government recording charges	■ Required services that you can shop for *(if you do not use companies we identify)* ■ Title services and lender's title insurance *(if you do not use companies we identify)* ■ Owner's title insurance *(if you do not use companies we identify)* ■ Initial deposit for your escrow account ■ Daily interest charges ■ Homeowner's insurance

Using the tradeoff table

In this GFE, we offered you this loan with a particular interest rate and estimated settlement charges. However:

- If you want to choose this same loan with **lower settlement charges,** then you will have a **higher interest rate.**
- If you want to choose this same loan with a **lower interest rate,** then you will have **higher settlement charges.**

If you would like to choose an available option, you must ask us for a new GFE.

Loan originators have the option to complete this table. Please ask for additional information if the table is not completed.

	The loan in this GFE	The same loan with lower settlement charges	The same loan with a lower interest rate
Your initial loan amount	$	$	$
Your initial interest rate[1]	%	%	%
Your initial monthly amount owed	$	$	$
Change in the monthly amount owed from this GFE	No change	You will pay $ **more** every month	You will pay $ **less** every month
Change in the amount you will pay at settlement with this interest rate	No change	Your settlement charges will be **reduced** by $	Your settlement charges will **increase** by $
How much your total estimated settlement charges will be	$	$	$

[1] *For an adjustable rate loan, the comparisons above are for the initial interest rate before adjustments are made.*

Using the shopping chart

Use this chart to compare GFEs from different loan originators. Fill in the information by using a different column for each GFE you receive. By comparing loan offers, you can shop for the best loan.

	This loan	Loan 2	Loan 3	Loan 4
Loan originator name				
Initial loan amount				
Loan term				
Initial interest rate				
Initial monthly amount owed				
Rate lock period				
Can interest rate rise?				
Can loan balance rise?				
Can monthly amount owed rise?				
Prepayment penalty?				
Balloon payment?				
Total Estimated Settlement Charges				

If your loan is sold in the future

Some lenders may sell your loan after settlement. Any fees lenders receive in the future cannot change the loan you receive or the charges you paid at settlement.

 Good Faith Estimate (HUD-GFE) 3

RESPA Requirements. RESPA imposes a number of requirements for most home mortgage transactions:

1. Within three days after receiving a written loan application (unless the loan application is denied), the lender must give all loan applicants:

   - a copy of a **booklet about settlement procedures**, which explains the home buying process, RESPA, closing costs, and the settlement statement;

   - a **good faith estimate of closing costs** (see Figure 14.3), which include accurate estimates of all expected expenses a borrower is likely to incur, including payments made outside of the closing process; and

   - a **mortgage servicing disclosure statement**, informing the borrower about the likelihood of the lender transferring the loan or its servicing duties to another entity at any time during the loan term.

2. If any settlement provider refers a borrower to another settlement provider in which the referring provider has an ownership or other beneficial interest of more than 1%, the referring provider must give the borrower an **affiliated business arrangement disclosure** within three days of the referral.

3. The closing agent must itemize all loan settlement charges on a **Uniform Settlement Statement** form.

4. If the lender requires the borrower to make deposits into an impound account to cover taxes, insurance, and other recurring costs, the lender cannot require **excessive deposits**—more than those necessary to cover the expenses when they come due. (According to RESPA, an excessive deposit is more than two months' worth of payments for recurring costs.)

5. A lender or any other provider of settlement services (such as a title company, mortgage broker, or real estate agent) may not:

   - pay or receive **kickbacks** or **referral fees** for referring customers;

   - accept **unearned fees**—that is, fees for settlement services that were not actually provided; or

RESPA requires lender to give loan applicant:
- HUD booklet
- Good faith estimate of closing costs
- Mortgage servicing disclosure statement

Closing agent must itemize all settlement costs on a Uniform Settlement Statement

Fig. 14.4 Uniform Settlement Statement form

OMB Approval No. 2502-0265

A. **Settlement Statement (HUD-1)**

B. Type of Loan

| 1. ☐ FHA 2. ☐ RHS 3. ☐ Conv. Unins. | 6. File Number: | 7. Loan Number: | 8. Mortgage Insurance Case Number: |
| 4. ☐ VA 5. ☐ Conv. Ins. | | | |

C. Note: This form is furnished to give you a statement of actual settlement costs. Amounts paid to and by the settlement agent are shown. Items marked "(p.o.c.)" were paid outside the closing; they are shown here for informational purposes and are not included in the totals.

D. Name & Address of Borrower:	E. Name & Address of Seller:	F. Name & Address of Lender:
G. Property Location:	H. Settlement Agent:	I. Settlement Date:
	Place of Settlement:	

J. Summary of Borrower's Transaction		K. Summary of Seller's Transaction	
100. Gross Amount Due from Borrower		**400. Gross Amount Due to Seller**	
101. Contract sales price		401. Contract sales price	
102. Personal property		402. Personal property	
103. Settlement charges to borrower (line 1400)		403.	
104.		404.	
105.		405.	
Adjustment for items paid by seller in advance		Adjustments for items paid by seller in advance	
106. City/town taxes to		406. City/town taxes to	
107. County taxes to		407. County taxes to	
108. Assessments to		408. Assessments to	
109.		409.	
110.		410.	
111.		411.	
112.		412.	
120. Gross Amount Due from Borrower		**420. Gross Amount Due to Seller**	
200. Amounts Paid by or in Behalf of Borrower		**500. Reductions In Amount Due to Seller**	
201. Deposit or earnest money		501. Excess deposit (see instructions)	
202. Principal amount of new loan(s)		502. Settlement charges to seller (line 1400)	
203. Existing loan(s) taken subject to		503. Existing loan(s) taken subject to	
204.		504. Payoff of first mortgage loan	
205.		505. Payoff of second mortgage loan	
206.		506.	
207.		507.	
208.		508.	
209.		509.	
Adjustments for items unpaid by seller		Adjustments for items unpaid by seller	
210. City/town taxes to		510. City/town taxes to	
211. County taxes to		511. County taxes to	
212. Assessments to		512. Assessments to	
213.		513.	
214.		514.	
215.		515.	
216.		516.	
217.		517.	
218.		518.	
219.		519.	
220. Total Paid by/for Seller		**520. Total Reduction Amount Due Seller**	
300. Cash at Settlement from/to Borrower		**600. Cash at Settlement to/from Seller**	
301. Gross amount due from borrower (line 120)		601. Gross amount due to seller (line 420)	
302. Less amounts paid by/for borrower (line 220)	( )	602. Less reductions in amount due seller (line 520)	( )
303. Cash ☐ From ☐ To Borrower		**603. Cash** ☐ To ☐ From Seller	

The Public Reporting Burden for this collection of information is estimated at 35 minutes per response for collecting, reviewing, and reporting the data. This agency may not collect this information, and you are not required to complete this form, unless it displays a currently valid OMB control number. No confidentiality is assured; this disclosure is mandatory. This is designed to provide the parties to a RESPA covered transaction with information during the settlement process.

Previous editions are obsolete   Page 1 of 3   HUD-1

L. Settlement Charges

700. Total Real Estate Broker Fees		Paid From Borrower's Funds at Settlement	Paid From Seller's Funds at Settlement
Division of commission (line 700) as follows:			
701. $	to		
702. $	to		
703. Commission paid at settlement			
704.			

800. Items Payable in Connection with Loan			
801. Our origination charge	$ (from GFE #1)		
802. Your credit or charge (points) for the specific interest rate chosen $	(from GFE #2)		
803. Your adjusted origination charges	(from GFE A)		
804. Appraisal fee to	(from GFE #3)		
805. Credit report to	(from GFE #3)		
806. Tax service to	(from GFE #3)		
807. Flood certification	(from GFE #3)		
808.			

900. Items Required by Lender to Be Paid in Advance			
901. Daily interest charges from to @ $ /day	(from GFE #10)		
902. Mortgage insurance premium for months to	(from GFE #3)		
903. Homeowner's insurance for years to	(from GFE #11)		
904.			

1000. Reserves Deposited with Lender			
1001. Initial deposit for your escrow account	(from GFE #9)		
1002. Homeowner's insurance months @ $ per month $			
1003. Mortgage insurance months @ $ per month $			
1004. Property taxes months @ $ per month $			
1005. months @ $ per month $			
1006. months @ $ per month $			
1007. Aggregate Adjustment –$			

1100. Title Charges			
1101. Title services and lender's title insurance	(from GFE #4)		
1102. Settlement or closing fee $			
1103. Owner's title insurance	(from GFE #5)		
1104. Lender's title insurance $			
1105. Lender's title policy limit $			
1106. Owner's title policy limit $			
1107. Agent's portion of the total title insurance premium $			
1108. Underwriter's portion of the total title insurance premium $			

1200. Government Recording and Transfer Charges			
1201. Government recording charges	(from GFE #7)		
1202. Deed $ Mortgage $ Releases $			
1203. Transfer taxes	(from GFE #8)		
1204. City/County tax/stamps Deed $ Mortgage $			
1205. State tax/stamps Deed $ Mortgage $			
1206.			

1300. Additional Settlement Charges			
1301. Required services that you can shop for	(from GFE #6)		
1302. $			
1303. $			
1304.			
1305.			

1400. Total Settlement Charges (enter on lines 103, Section J and 502, Section K)			

Comparison of Good Faith Estimate (GFE) and HUD-1 Charges		Good Faith Estimate	HUD-1
Charges That Cannot Increase	**HUD-1 Line Number**		
Our origination charge	# 801		
Your credit or charge (points) for the specific interest rate chosen	# 802		
Your adjusted origination charges	# 803		
Transfer taxes	#1203		

Charges That in Total Cannot Increase More Than 10%		Good Faith Estimate	HUD-1
Government recording charges	# 1201		
	#		
	#		
	#		
	#		
	#		
	#		
Total			
Increase between GFE and HUD-1 Charges		$ or	%

Charges That Can Change		Good Faith Estimate	HUD-1
Initial deposit for your escrow account	#1001		
Daily interest charges	# 901 $ /day		
Homeowner's insurance	# 903		
	#		
	#		
	#		

Loan Terms

Your initial loan amount is	$
Your loan term is	years
Your initial interest rate is	%
Your initial monthly amount owed for principal, interest, and any mortgage insurance is	$ includes ☐ Principal ☐ Interest ☐ Mortgage Insurance
Can your interest rate rise?	☐ No. ☐ Yes, it can rise to a maximum of %. The first change will be on and can change again every after . Every change date, your interest rate can increase or decrease by %. Over the life of the loan, your interest rate is guaranteed to never be **lower** than % or **higher** than %.
Even if you make payments on time, can your loan balance rise?	☐ No. ☐ Yes, it can rise to a maximum of $.
Even if you make payments on time, can your monthly amount owed for principal, interest, and mortgage insurance rise?	☐ No. ☐ Yes, the first increase can be on and the monthly amount owed can rise to $. The maximum it can ever rise to is $.
Does your loan have a prepayment penalty?	☐ No. ☐ Yes, your maximum prepayment penalty is $.
Does your loan have a balloon payment?	☐ No. ☐ Yes, you have a balloon payment of $ due in years on .
Total monthly amount owed including escrow account payments	☐ You do not have a monthly escrow payment for items, such as property taxes and homeowner's insurance. You must pay these items directly yourself. ☐ You have an additional monthly escrow payment of $ that results in a total initial monthly amount owed of $. This includes principal, interest, any mortgage insurance and any items checked below: ☐ Property taxes ☐ Homeowner's insurance ☐ Flood insurance ☐ ☐

Note: If you have any questions about the Settlement Charges and Loan Terms listed on this form, please contact your lender.

- charge a **document preparation fee** for the Uniform Settlement Statement, an impound account statement, or the disclosure statement required by the Truth in Lending Act.

6. The property seller may not require the buyer to use a particular **title company**.

RESPA's prohibition on referral fees (listed in number 5 above) is designed to help curb practices that generate unearned compensation for real estate agents, lenders, and other settlement service providers at the expense of home buyers.

Uniform Settlement Statement. The closing agent must provide completed Uniform Settlement Statement forms to the buyer, the seller, and the lender on or before the closing date. Although the same form is used for both the buyer and the seller, in most cases a separate statement is prepared for each party. The one given to the buyer usually presents only the buyer's closing information, and the one given to the seller usually presents only the seller's closing information.

A copy of the Uniform Settlement Statement form is shown in Figure 14.4. The second page of the form is used to itemize each party's closing costs (settlement charges). The buyer's statement will show the buyer's costs in the left column. The seller's statement will show the seller's costs in the right column. On each statement, the costs are added up and the total is transferred to the front of the form. On the buyer's statement, the buyer's total costs are entered on line 103. On the seller's statement, the seller's total costs are entered on line 502.

On the front of the buyer's statement, lines 101 through 120 list the buyer's debits, and 201 through 220 list the buyer's credits. On the front of the seller's statement, lines 401 through 420 list the seller's credits, and 501 through 520 list the seller's debits. The amount of cash the buyer must bring to closing appears on line 303, and the amount of cash the seller will receive at closing is shown on line 603.

Additional RESPA Requirements. Starting in 2010, lenders and mortgage brokers must provide good faith estimates (GFEs) on a standardized form developed by HUD. (See Figure 14.3.) Prior to 2010, no particular form is required. The new GFE form correlates more closely with the Uniform Settlement Form (which has also been

RESPA prohibits lenders and service providers from:
- Requiring excessive impound deposits
- Paying or receiving kickbacks or referral fees
- Collecting unearned fees
- Charging for preparation of Uniform Settlement Statement, impound account statement, or TILA disclosure

modified; see Figure 14.4). HUD believes these forms will provide consumers with more accurate information about their transaction costs, making it easier to shop for the least costly loans.

To that end, the new provisions:

New RESPA rules require more accurate cost estimates and explanations about how settlement costs affect the interest rate.

- Encourage lenders and brokers to give the GFE to borrowers as early in the process as possible, so borrowers are better able to obtain multiple GFEs for comparison purposes. (Lenders may charge only for the cost of the credit report and a minor administrative fee at the time of application.)
- Impose limits or "tolerances" on the amount certain good faith estimates can increase from the time of the estimate up to closing, and give loan originators 30 days after closing to make corrections and issue refunds to borrowers. (If corrections are made after 30 days, the lender may incur penalties.)
- Add new explanations about the effects or "tradeoffs" certain settlement costs have on a borrower's interest rate, including a new emphasis on helping consumers understand the relationship between mortgage broker payments ("yield spread premiums") and interest rates.
- Encourage "volume discounts" resulting from the packaging of various settlement services, so long as those discounts are passed on to the consumer.

Predatory Lending

Over the years, as the subprime mortgage market expanded, policy makers and concerned citizens focused their attention on the problem of predatory lending. **Predatory lending** refers to practices that unscrupulous mortgage lenders and mortgage brokers use to take advantage of (prey upon) unsophisticated borrowers for their own profit. Real estate agents, appraisers, and home improvement contractors sometimes participate in predatory lending schemes; in some cases, a buyer or seller may participate in deceiving the other party, too.

Predatory lending became a widespread problem during the mortgage and foreclosure crisis.

For a variety of reasons, predatory lending is especially likely to occur in the subprime market. Also, it tends to be common in refinancing and home equity lending. Many people believe that predatory lending practices played a major role in the recent mortgage and foreclosure crisis (discussed in Chapter 4).

We'll examine some of the tactics and loan terms predatory lenders use, describe the buyers they tend to target, and consider the laws and regulatory efforts that have been implemented to address the problem.

Predatory Lending Practices

Some predatory lending practices involve tactics that are always abusive; others involve ordinary lending practices and loan terms that can be misused for a predatory purpose. The following list doesn't separate those two categories, but you should keep the distinction in mind.

Predatory Steering. Steering a buyer toward a more expensive loan (one with a higher interest rate and/or fees) when the buyer could qualify for a less expensive loan.

Fee Packing. Charging interest rates, points, or processing fees that far exceed the norm and are not justified by the cost of the services provided. This includes charges for unnecessary products that increase the cost of the borrower's loan.

Equity Stripping. "Stripping away" a homeowner's equity by charging high fees on repeated refinancings.

Loan Flipping. Encouraging a homeowner to refinance repeatedly in a short period, when there's no real benefit in doing so. This is another form of equity stripping.

Property Flipping. Purchasing property at a discount (because the seller needs a quick sale) and then rapidly reselling it to an unsophisticated buyer for an inflated price. This isn't illegal in and of itself, but it is illegal when a real estate agent, appraiser, and/or lender commit fraud to make the buyer believe the property is worth substantially more than it's actually worth.

Disregarding Buyer's Ability to Pay. Making a loan based on unverified income information or only on the property's value, without considering the borrower's ability to afford the loan payments.

Impound Waivers. Not requiring a borrower to make monthly deposits for property taxes and insurance into an impound account, even though the borrower is unlikely to be able to pay the taxes and

Predatory lending practices and loan provisions:
- Steering
- Fee packing
- Loan flipping/equity stripping
- Property flipping
- Disregarding buyer's capacity to repay
- Unaffordable payments
- Impound waivers
- Loans in excess of value
- Negative amortization/balloon payment abuses
- Fraud
- High-pressure sales tactics
- Advance payments from loan proceeds
- Excessive prepayment penalties and default interest rates
- Discretionary acceleration clauses
- Single-premium credit life insurance

insurance when they're due. Waiving the impound requirement encourages a home buyer or owner to borrow more because it reduces the monthly payment. Predatory brokers or lenders use this tactic when they are planning to sell the loan, and they won't be affected by any default and foreclosure.

Loan in Excess of Value. Loaning a home buyer or owner more than the appraised value of the property. This usually involves a fraudulent appraisal. It may occur when a lender and an appraiser collude in a property flipping scheme, or when a mortgage broker and an appraiser collude to deceive a lender, victimizing both the lender and the borrower.

Negative Amortization Schemes. Deliberately making a loan with payments that don't cover the interest. The unpaid interest will be added to the outstanding principal balance and the loan will become very difficult to pay off. When adjustable-rate mortgages were a new type of loan, negative amortization was an unfortunate side effect of the way some ARMs were structured. Legitimate lenders now generally structure loans to avoid negative amortization, but predatory lenders may not.

Balloon Payment Abuses. Making a partially amortized or interest-only loan that has low monthly payments, without properly disclosing to the borrowers that a large balloon payment will be required after a short period. When the time comes, the borrowers will be told that their only alternative to foreclosure is an expensive refinancing loan from the same lender.

Fraud. Misrepresenting or concealing unfavorable loan terms or excessive fees, falsifying documents, or using other fraudulent means to induce a prospective borrower to enter into a loan agreement.

High-pressure Sales Tactics. Telling prospective borrowers that they must decide on a loan immediately, and that no other lender will loan them the money they need. This includes pressuring borrowers to accept higher-risk loans, such as balloon loans or loans with interest-only payment arrangements, by making borrowers think that the higher-risk loan is their only option for financing.

Advance Payments from Loan Proceeds. Requiring a series of the borrower's mortgage payments to be paid at closing, out of the loan proceeds.

Excessive or Unfair Prepayment Penalties. Imposing an unusually large penalty, failing to limit the penalty period to the first few years of the loan term, and/or charging the penalty even if the loan is prepaid because the property is being sold. Prepayment penalties can also be used to prevent refinancing by borrowers who were steered into an unfavorable loan.

Unfair Default Interest Rate. Increasing a loan's interest rate by an excessive amount when the borrower defaults, in a way that isn't justified by the additional risk involved in the situation.

Discretionary Acceleration Clause. Including an acceleration clause in the loan documents that allows the lender to accelerate the loan at any time, not just because the payments are delinquent or the property is being sold.

Single-premium Credit Life Insurance. A credit life insurance policy will pay off a mortgage if the borrower dies. Some borrowers choose to purchase credit life insurance with reasonable premiums that are paid in installments, but predatory lenders often require their victims to purchase a credit life policy with a single large premium due at closing.

In addition to predatory lenders and brokers, there are predatory loan servicers. They charge improper late fees, fail to credit payments the borrower has made, and sometimes even institute foreclosure proceedings against borrowers who are not in default.

Targeted Victims

As you read through the list of predatory practices, you may have wondered how borrowers can possibly be persuaded to agree to some of the arrangements and terms described. The unfortunate explanation is that predatory lenders and brokers deliberately target prospective borrowers who:

Targeted victims of predatory lending tend to be uninformed and vulnerable

- aren't able to understand the transaction they're entering into, and/or
- don't know that better alternatives are available to them.

Potential borrowers are especially likely to be targeted if they are elderly, have a limited education, speak limited English, have a low income, are deeply in debt, have a poor credit history or no credit history, or live in redlined neighborhoods.

Predatory lending concerns overlap with fair lending issues, because racial and ethnic groups are disproportionately represented in the ranks of predatory lending victims.

Elderly people who are cognitively impaired and who have a lot of equity in their homes are the most frequent victims of predatory refinancing and equity stripping schemes.

Here is some of the advice that experts offer borrowers to help them avoid being victimized by predatory lenders:

Elderly people with lots of equity are frequently targeted by predatory lenders

1. Don't let a real estate agent, a mortgage broker, or anyone else steer you to one particular lender. It's best to shop around and compare costs.
2. Don't assume that you won't be able to qualify for a loan on reasonable terms from a legitimate lender.
3. Don't let anyone persuade you to make false statements on a loan application or regarding other aspects of the transaction.
4. Don't let anyone persuade you to borrow more money than you can afford to repay.
5. Don't let anyone convince you that you've committed yourself to a transaction before you actually have. For example, signing a disclosure form does not obligate you to proceed with the loan.
6. Don't sign documents that have blanks that haven't been filled in. If provisions don't apply in the current transaction, the blank lines should have "N/A" (for "not applicable") written in them.
7. Don't sign documents without reading them first and asking questions about provisions you don't understand.
8. If you don't speak English fluently, try to arrange for a translator to accompany you to the loan interview and help you review documents before signing.
9. Even if you are fluent in English, get the assistance of a lawyer, a housing counselor, a trusted real estate agent, or even a trusted friend or relative who has some experience in financial matters. Two pairs of eyes are better than one.

Many borrowers believe they can't afford to have a lawyer review their loan documents before they sign them. However, it's a precaution that typically costs only a few hundred dollars, and it could save borrowers thousands of dollars by helping them avoid a predatory lending scheme. Also, by calling the local bar association, low-income loan applicants may be able to find a free legal clinic where they can get legal advice.

Predatory Lending Laws

There are statutes and regulations designed to curb predatory lending at the federal level and also at the state level.

Federal Law. Although often discussed as a separate law, the Home Ownership and Equity Protection Act (HOEPA) is actually a group of provisions that were added to the Truth in Lending Act in 1994, in response to concerns about predatory lending. Up to that point, TILA had been primarily a disclosure law. It required disclosure of loan costs and certain loan terms, but it didn't restrict the types of loans lenders could offer or the terms they could impose. The HOEPA provisions went further. When a loan is covered by HOEPA, it can't have certain features or include certain types of provisions.

> HOEPA: provisions in Truth in Lending Act that address predatory lending

However, HOEPA is limited in scope. It applies only to home equity and refinance loans (not purchase loans) that are secured by the borrower's principal residence and that have high interest rates and loan fees. The rules for HOEPA loans are in Section 32 of TILA's Regulation Z, so HOEPA loans are sometimes called "Section 32 mortgages." They're also called **high-cost loans**.

> HOEPA restrictions:
> - Apply to high-cost home equity and refinance loans
> - Don't apply to home purchase loans

A loan is classified as high-cost (so that HOEPA applies) if either its APR or the total points and fees exceed particular thresholds. The APR threshold is based on the yield on certain Treasury securities; a first-lien loan is high-cost if its APR is more than 8% above that yield. The points and fees threshold is either 8% of the loan amount, or else a specified dollar amount ($583 in 2009), whichever is greater.

These thresholds are actually quite high, so it's easy for lenders to make sure their loans don't trigger the HOEPA restrictions. As a result, HOEPA applies to very few loans and has only been of limited use in combating predatory lending.

To provide consumers with greater protection, in 2008 Congress and the Federal Reserve added new provisions to TILA and Regulation Z. These provisions established another category of mortgage loans that, like HOEPA loans, are subject to special rules. Loans in this new category are referred to as **higher-priced loans**. (The term is somewhat confusing. Higher-priced loans are higher-priced compared to loans in general, not compared to high-cost loans. High-cost loans—HOEPA loans—are even more expensive than higher-priced loans.)

The new higher-priced category is much broader than HOEPA's high-cost category. First, the higher-priced category includes not just home equity and refinance loans, but also purchase loans. (As with HOEPA, the loan must be secured by the borrower's principal residence.) Second, the threshold for higher-priced loans is much lower than the HOEPA thresholds. A loan is classified as higher-priced if its APR exceeds a specified limit that's related to average rates and fees for prime loans. The Federal Reserve set the limit so that virtually all subprime loans would be included in the higher-priced category.

The following new rules will apply to both higher-priced loans and HOEPA loans. (Their effective date is October 2009, except for the escrow account rule, which won't go into effect until April 2010.)

- The lender may not make the loan without regard to the applicant's ability to repay it, and may not consider unverified income or assets during the underwriting process.
- A prepayment penalty can't be charged if the loan payment can change during the first four years of the loan.
- The prepayment penalty period may not exceed two years.
- For a first-lien loan, the lender must establish an escrow (impound) account and require the borrower to make deposits to cover payment of property taxes and insurance.

HOEPA loans also remain subject to several existing rules that won't apply to higher-priced loans. For example, if a HOEPA loan has a term of less than five years, it can't be structured so that a balloon payment will be necessary. Negative amortization isn't allowed with a HOEPA loan, and the interest rate can't be raised after default.

State Predatory Lending Laws. While TILA is the primary federal consumer protection law that addresses predatory lending, a majority of the states now have their own predatory lending laws, and other states are in the process of adopting one. Of course, the coverage and provisions of these state laws vary. Some apply only to home equity and refinance loans; others also apply to purchase loans.

One of the most recent concerns addressed by state laws is the need for consumer protection during the loan modification process, which takes place after a borrower has defaulted on her loan. Homeowners who are facing foreclosure are particularly vulnerable to predatory

More recent TILA amendments target predatory practices for a broader range of loans:
- Purchase loans as well as other home loans
- Threshold set to include almost all subprime loans

companies seeking to take advantage of them. In their confusion and distress, owners may fall prey to fraudulent schemes, paying high fees and ending up in no better position than they were in when they started. To address this problem, many states have passed distressed property laws that strictly regulate all activities related to loan modifications, including penalties for predatory practices.

Outline: Fair Lending and Consumer Protection

I. Fair Lending Laws

   A. Equal Credit Opportunity Act

      1. The Equal Credit Opportunity Act applies to all consumer credit, including residential mortgages.

      2. ECOA prohibits discrimination against loan applicants based on race, color, religion, national origin, sex, marital status, age, or whether income comes from public assistance.

      3. Lenders may not base lending decisions on assumptions about the creditworthiness of racial, ethnic, or religious groups.

   B. Fair Housing Act

      1. The Fair Housing Act applies to transactions involving residential properties and prohibits discrimination based on race, color, national origin, religion, sex, disability, or familial status.

      2. Under the act, a lender may not refuse to provide information about loans, refuse to make a loan, or impose different terms or conditions on a loan for discriminatory reasons.

      3. The act also prohibits redlining: refusing to make loans secured by property in particular neighborhoods because persons of a particular racial or ethnic group live there.

      4. A lender may refuse to make a loan in a neighborhood where property values are declining, but the decision must be based on objective economic criteria.

   C. Community Reinvestment Act

      1. The Community Reinvestment Act (CRA) requires depository institutions to collect information on loans made to low- and moderate-income borrowers living in the communities where these institutions do business.

      2. These lenders submit CRA data to the government as part of their annual examination process and required HMDA disclosures.

   D. Home Mortgage Disclosure Act

      1. The Home Mortgage Disclosure Act requires lenders in metropolitan areas to make disclosures to the federal government regarding all loans they originate or purchase (certain smaller lenders may be excluded from this requirement).

      2. The intent is for the government to monitor whether lenders are engaging in redlining or other discriminatory lending practices.

II. Consumer Protection Laws

A. Truth in Lending Act

1. The Truth in Lending Act requires disclosure of interest rates and other finance charges; it is implemented through the Federal Reserve Board's Regulation Z.

2. TILA covers many consumer loans, including those secured by real property.

3. TILA applies only to loans made to natural persons (not corporations), and excludes loans made for business or agricultural purposes; seller financing is also exempt, since it doesn't originate with a commercial lender.

4. The two most important TILA disclosures are the total finance charge and the annual percentage rate (i.e., the cost of credit as a percentage of the amount financed).

5. The total finance charge may include interest, origination fee, borrower-paid points, finder's fee, service charges, and mortgage insurance; it doesn't include appraisal, credit report, or inspection fees, title insurance, or seller-paid points.

6. TILA disclosures must also include the lender's identity, the total amount financed, the payment schedule, any prepayment fee, late charges, and the assumption policy.

7. Additional disclosures are required for ARMs, including a general brochure; the APR may be based on the initial interest rate but must state that it is subject to change, and also describe the index used for rate adjustments.

8. Home equity loan borrowers have a right of rescission within the three days following signing the loan agreement, receiving the disclosure statement, or receiving the notice of the right to rescind.

9. If certain loan terms are stated in an advertisement, then TILA requires that all loan terms must be stated; APR and cash price can be stated without triggering the requirement; slightly different rules apply for advertising ARMs.

10. TILA bans "bait and switch" advertising and advertising loan terms that provide a false picture of the lender's product.

B. Real Estate Settlement Procedures Act

1. The Real Estate Settlement Procedures Act provides borrowers with information about closing costs and prohibits kickbacks that increase settlement costs.

2. RESPA applies to federally related loan transactions, which includes almost all residential loans made by institutional lenders; all professionals involved in the settlement process are covered by the law, including real estate agents, mortgage brokers, lenders, and title companies.

3. RESPA doesn't apply to loans used to purchase 25 acres or more, loans for business or agricultural purposes, loans to purchase vacant land, temporary financing, or assumptions where lender's approval isn't required.

4. Within three days of a loan application, a lender must give the borrower a booklet about settlement procedures, a good faith estimate of closing costs, and a mortgage servicing disclosure statement. Also, an affiliated business arrangement disclosure may be required.

5. The closing agent must itemize all closing costs on a Uniform Settlement Statement.

6. The lender cannot require excessive deposits, accept unearned fees, charge a document preparation fee, or pay kickbacks to anyone for referring customers.

III. Predatory Lending

A. Predatory lending refers to practices in the lending business that take advantage of uninformed and vulnerable borrowers for profit.

B. Predatory lending practices include predatory steering, fee packing, loan flipping, equity stripping, property flipping, disregarding buyer's capacity to pay, requiring unaffordable payments, issuing loans in excess of value, waiving impound accounts, negative amortization schemes, and balloon payment abuses.

C. Predatory lenders tend to target persons who aren't able to understand the transaction they're entering into and aren't aware of better alternatives.

D. Home Ownership and Equity Protection Act

1. The Home Ownership and Equity Protection Act applies to high-cost home equity loans secured by a primary residence.

2. A lender making a loan covered by HOEPA must make certain disclosures and may not engage in certain practices.

E. Many states also have predatory lending laws that require disclosures and prohibit predatory practices. Recently, some states have added laws protecting borrowers from predatory practices that occur during the loan modification process.

Key Terms

Equal Credit Opportunity Act (ECOA): A federal law prohibiting discrimination by lenders against loan applicants on the basis of race, color, religion, national origin, sex, marital status, age, or whether income comes from public assistance.

Fair Housing Act: A federal law prohibiting discrimination in residential property transactions, including lending, on the basis of race, color, national origin, religion, sex, disability, or familial status.

Community Reinvestment Act (CRA): A federal law requiring banks and other depository institutions to serve low- and middle-income borrowers and to report these loans to the government.

Redlining: Refusing to make loans for the purchase or rehabilitation of property in a certain neighborhood because of its racial or ethnic composition.

Home Mortgage Disclosure Act (HMDA): A federal law requiring institutional lenders to report on residential loans they originated or purchased from other lenders; the law's intent is to detect redlining and other discriminatory lending practices.

Truth in Lending Act (TILA): A federal law that requires lenders to make disclosures concerning loan costs (including the total finance charge and the annual percentage rate) to consumer loan applicants.

Total finance charge: Under the Truth in Lending Act, the total finance charge on a mortgage loan includes the interest, any discount points paid by the borrower, the loan origination fee, and mortgage insurance costs.

Annual percentage rate (APR): Under the Truth in Lending Act, the relationship between a loan's total finance charge and the total amount financed, expressed as an annual percentage.

Real Estate Settlement Procedures Act (RESPA): A federal law that requires lenders to disclose certain information about closing costs to loan applicants.

Uniform Settlement Statement: A settlement statement required for any transaction involving a loan that is subject to the Real Estate Settlement Procedures Act.

Predatory lending: Lending practices where lenders or mortgage brokers take advantage of borrowers for their own profit.

Fee packing: Charging points or processing fees that are higher than usual and not justified by the services provided.

Equity stripping: Stripping away a homeowner's equity by charging high fees for repeated refinancings.

Home Ownership and Equity Protection Act (HOEPA): A federal law applicable to high-cost home equity loans that requires certain disclosures and prohibits certain predatory lending practices.

Chapter Quiz

1. The federal legislation that prevents discrimination against loan applicants on the basis of race is:

   a. RESPA
   b. the Truth in Lending Act
   c. the Equal Credit Opportunity Act
   d. Regulation Z

2. All of the charges payable by or to a party in a real estate transaction show up on the:

   a. settlement statement
   b. financial statement
   c. TILA disclosure statement
   d. impound account statement

3. Under the Real Estate Settlement Procedures Act, lenders:

   a. may pay real estate agents a fee for referring loan applicants to them
   b. are prohibited from paying kickbacks or referral fees
   c. must require borrowers to use a particular title insurance company
   d. must disclose the APR of the loan they are offering to make

4. RESPA requires a lender to give the loan applicant a good faith estimate of the closing costs:

   a. at the time of application
   b. within three days of application
   c. within seven days of application
   d. before closing

5. The purpose of the Home Mortgage Disclosure Act is to:

   a. require that lenders provide good faith estimates of all closing costs
   b. require that lenders disclose the total finance charge and annual percentage rate
   c. require that lenders disclose information that may provide evidence of redlining
   d. prohibit discrimination against individuals whose income is derived from public assistance

6. Which of the following phrases in an advertisement would NOT trigger the requirement, under TILA, that the annual percentage rate and total finance charge must be disclosed?

    a. "Low monthly payments of $1,200"
    b. "Great financing terms for borrowers with good credit"
    c. "Own with a downpayment of just $10,000"
    d. "Act now and get a 6% interest rate"

7. Which of the following practices is prohibited under the Real Estate Settlement Procedures Act?

    a. Kickbacks
    b. Redlining
    c. Equity stripping
    d. Loan flipping

8. Which of the following predatory lending practices involves charging processing fees or points that are higher than normal and not justified by the services provided?

    a. Property flipping
    b. Predatory steering
    c. Impound waivers
    d. Fee packing

9. Which federal law requires certain disclosures and prohibits predatory practices by lenders making high-cost home equity loans?

    a. Equal Credit Opportunity Act
    b. Home Mortgage Disclosure Act
    c. Real Estate Settlement Procedures Act
    d. Home Ownership and Equity Protection Act

10. Which of the following loans would be covered by the Truth in Lending Act?

    a. An unsecured loan for $35,000
    b. A loan secured by a farm property used to purchase farm equipment
    c. A loan issued by a savings and loan to purchase a four-unit residential property
    d. A second mortgage offered by a seller to cover part of the downpayment

Answer Key

1. c. The Equal Credit Opportunity Act prevents discrimination against loan applicants on the basis of race, color, religion, national origin, sex, marital status, age, or whether income is received from public assistance.

2. a. A Uniform Settlement Statement is used to show all closing costs payable by or to a party in a real estate transaction.

3. b. Under RESPA, lenders may not pay kickbacks or referral fees to any other service provider for referring customers.

4. b. Under RESPA, a lender must provide a good faith estimate of closing costs to an applicant within three days of receiving the loan application.

5. c. The Home Mortgage Disclosure Act requires large lenders to disclose information about all loans that they purchase or originate so that patterns suggesting redlining or other prohibited lending practices may be observed.

6. b. If an advertisement doesn't specifically disclose any loan terms but contains only general statements, it does not trigger the TILA requirement of disclosure of the total finance charge and annual percentage rate.

7. a. Kickbacks and other referral fees paid by lenders are prohibited under the Real Estate Settlement Procedures Act.

8. d. Fee packing is a predatory practice involving points or processing fees that are much higher than usual and not justified by the services provided.

9. d. The Home Ownership and Equity Protection Act applies to high-cost home equity loans and prohibits certain predatory practices.

10. c. The Truth in Lending Act excludes consumer loans for over $25,000 that aren't secured by real property; loans made for business or agricultural purposes; and seller financing.

Answer Key for Exercises

Chapter 8, Qualifying the Buyer

Chapter 8, Exercise No. 1

1.
$26	Roy's hourly wage
× 40	Hours in a work week
$1,040	Weekly income
× 52	Weeks in a year
$54,080	Annual income
÷ 12	Months in a year
$4,507	Roy's monthly income

Shortcut:

$26	Roy's hourly wage
× 173.33	(Result of 40 × 52 ÷ 12)
$4,507	Roy's monthly income

$685	Judy's weekly income
× 52	Weeks in a year
$35,620	Annual income
÷ 12	Months in a year
$2,968	Judy's monthly income
+ 4,507	Roy's monthly income
$7,475	Total stable monthly income

2. Yes, there are special circumstances in this case that may persuade the lender to approve the loan. Roy had special training in the Air Force, and Judy is a vocational nurse, which implies special training. They've been at their jobs for only a short time because they are new to the area. The lender will want to know whether Judy was employed as a nurse while Roy was in the Air Force.

Chapter 8, Exercise No. 2

1.
$1,400	Received every two weeks
× 26	Number of paychecks per year
$36,400	Annual income
÷ 12	Months in a year
$3,033	Able's stable monthly income

2.

	$162,500	Sales price for old home
−	133,250	Mortgage to be paid off
	$29,250	Gross equity
−	14,500	Estimated selling expenses
	$14,750	Net equity in old home

3. Yes, Able will have problems closing the transaction. He doesn't even have enough cash and other liquid assets to cover the downpayment and closing costs, much less the required reserves.

	$3,600	In savings account
	200	In checking account
+	14,750	Net equity in old home
	$18,550	Liquid assets available

	$17,000	Required downpayment
+	3,400	Closing costs
	$20,400	Needed at closing
+	2,615	Required reserves
	$23,015	Total liquid assets needed
−	18,550	Liquid assets available
	$4,465	Shortfall

4. The savings account was opened quite recently, and the current balance in the account is significantly higher than its average balance. These facts would lead an underwriter to wonder where the money in the account came from: Did Able borrow it?

5. Able might be able to sell some personal property to raise more cash, or his relatives might be willing to give him some money with a gift letter. If he has a life insurance policy, he might consider tapping into its cash value. Or perhaps the seller would be willing to pay part of Able's closing costs.

Able will also have to explain where the money in his savings account came from. Maybe he recently sold his old car, or received a bonus at work, or closed an account at another bank and transferred the funds. (Of course, if the money was in fact borrowed, it won't count as money available to close the transaction, which will make Able's cash problem even worse.)

Chapter 10, Conventional Financing

Chapter 10, Exercise No. 1

1. Maynard's LTV would be 92%. To determine this, first divide the downpayment by the sales price to find out what percentage of the sales price the downpayment represents. (Remember that the LTV is based on the sales price or the appraised value, whichever is less. In this problem, the sales price, $318,750, is less than the appraised value, $321,000.)

$$\$25,500 \div \$318,750 = 8\%$$

Since the downpayment is 8% of the sales price, a loan for the remainder would be 92% of the sales price:

$$100\% - 8\% = 92\%$$

2. The new downpayment amount would be 6% of the sales price.

$$\$19,125 \div \$318,750 = 6\%$$

The new LTV would be 94%.

$$100\% - 6\% = 94\%$$

Chapter 10, Exercise No. 2

1.

$289,500	Sales price (less than appraised value)
× 80%	LTV for first mortgage
$231,600	First mortgage loan amount

$289,500	Sales price
× 15%	LTV for second mortgage
$43,425	Second mortgage loan amount

2.

$289,500	Sales price
× 5%	
$14,475	Downpayment

$231,600	Amount of first mortgage
× 1.5%	
$3,474	Loan origination fee

$231,600	Amount of first mortgage
× .25%	
$579	Adverse market delivery charge

3. The total monthly payment for both loans would be $2,141.15.

$1,540.84	Principal and interest for first loan
274.48	Principal and interest for second loan
265.83	Share of property taxes ($3,190 ÷ 12)
+ 60.00	Share of insurance premium ($720 ÷ 12)
$2,141.15	Total monthly payment for both loans

Chapter 10, Exercise No. 3

1. For a 90% loan, the Tanakas could qualify for a $2,477 payment.

Stable monthly income: $9,917

$62,000	Mike's annual salary
÷ 12	Months in a year
$5,167	Mike's monthly income
+ 4,750	Barbara's monthly income
$9,917	Stable monthly income

Recurring obligations: $1,093

$317	Car payment
375	Car payment
250	Payment on personal loan
55	Store charge card payment
42	Visa payment
+ 54	MasterCard payment
$1,093	Total recurring obligations

Total debt to income ratio calculation:

$9,917	Stable monthly income
× 36%	
$3,570	Maximum total obligations
− 1,093	Recurring obligations
$2,477	Maximum housing expense under debt to income ratio

Housing expense to income ratio calculation:

$9,917	Stable monthly income
× 28%	
$2,777	Maximum housing expense under housing expense ratio

The result of the total debt to income ratio calculation will be the maximum housing expense for the Tanakas (since that's less than the result of the housing expense ratio calculation). Thus, the maximum mortgage payment they could qualify for would be $2,477.

2. The Tanakas might be able to qualify for a larger payment if they have excellent credit scores, if their current housing expense represents an unusually large share of their income (demonstrating that they can devote a greater portion of their income to basic needs than most people can), or if either of them has a strong potential for increased earnings, or if they have a substantial net worth. They could also qualify for a larger payment if the home they choose is energy-efficient.

3. If the Tanakas can afford to pay off their personal loan, or pay off one or more of their charge accounts, that would enable them to qualify for a larger mortgage payment.

Chapter 10, Exercise No. 4

1.
$350,000	Sales price
× 90%	LTV
$315,000	Loan amount
× 6%	Six points (= 1% interest)
$18,900	Approximate cost of buydown

2. The buydown could save Johnson as much as $79,708. (The savings would be less if he paid the loan off before the end of the 30-year term.)

$2,478.11	Monthly P&I payment at 8.75% (without buydown)
− 2,256.70	Monthly P&I payment at 7.75% (with buydown)
$221.41	Monthly savings
× 360	Months (30 years)
$79,708	Savings over 30 years

Chapter 11, FHA-Insured Loans

Chapter 11, Exercise No. 1

1. In 2009, the maximum FHA loan amount for a one-unit property in a high-cost area is 125% of the area median house price, up to a ceiling of $729,750. So the maximum loan amount for a one-unit property in Fletcher's area is 125% of $540,000, or $675,000 ($540,000 × 1.25 = $675,000).

2. The required minimum cash investment for an FHA transaction is 3.5% of the appraised value or sales price, whichever is less. In this case, Fletcher's minimum cash investment is 3.5% of the $647,500 sales price, or $22,663 ($647,500 × .035 = $22,662.50).

3. If you subtract the $22,663 minimum cash investment from the $647,500 sales price, the result is $624,837. This is the maximum FHA loan amount for Fletcher's transaction. (You would get the same result by multiplying the sales price by 96.5%, the maximum loan-to-value ratio for an FHA loan.)

Chapter 11, Exercise No. 2

1. With a $170,000 sales price, Lee's maximum loan amount would ordinarily be $164,050 (96.5% of the price), and she'd be required to make a minimum cash investment of $5,950 (3.5% of the price).

$170,000 Sales price
× .965 Maximum LTV (96.5%)
$164,050 Loan amount

$170,000 Sales price
− 164,050 Maximum loan amount
$5,950 Minimum cash investment

To determine how the seller's contribution of $12,000 would affect the transaction, start by multiplying the sales price by 6%. That's the limit on seller contributions in an FHA transaction.

$170,000 Sales price
× .06 Seller contribution limit (6%)
$10,200 Maximum seller contribution

The seller's $12,000 contribution exceeds the limit by $1,800. That excess amount will be treated as an inducement to purchase and subtracted from the sales price before the maximum loan amount is calculated.

$170,000 Sales price
− 1,800 Seller contribution in excess of 6% limit
$168,200 Adjusted sales price
× .965 Maximum loan-to-value ratio (96.5%)
$162,313 Maximum loan amount after seller contribution

Lee's loan amount would be $1,737 less with the $12,000 contribution than without it ($164,050 − $162,313 = $1,737). Any amount that the seller contributes over $10,200—the maximum allowed in this case under the 6% limit—reduces the amount that Lee is able to borrow, increasing her required downpayment. (Of course, in the long run, the reduced interest rate from the seller buydown will benefit Lee significantly.)

2. Lee is allowed to use secondary financing from her parents to pay her minimum cash investment, closing costs, and prepaid expenses. The two loans combined can't exceed the sales price/appraised value plus Lee's closing costs and prepaid expenses. If the FHA loan amount is $164,050 (96.5% of $170,000—see #1 above), the amount of the second loan can be no more than $17,650:

$170,000	Sales price/value
+ 11,700	Closing costs and prepaids
$181,700	Maximum total financing
− 164,050	FHA loan amount
$17,650	Maximum second loan from parents

Because of this rule, Lee's parents can't loan her the full $20,000 they were planning to unless the FHA loan amount is reduced by $2,350, to $161,700 ($20,000 + $161,700 = $181,700). Lee and her parents can decide whether she should borrow only $17,650 ($2,350 less than planned) from them, or whether she should borrow $2,350 less from the institutional lender who's making the FHA loan.

If Lee's parents expect her to make regular installment payments on the second loan, Lee must be able to afford the combined payments for both loans. The second loan can't call for a balloon payment within the first five years of the loan term.

3. Since the seller acquired the home less than 90 days before the buyer signed the purchase agreement, this transaction can't be financed with an FHA loan unless one of the exemptions from the property flipping rules applies. For example, if the seller had inherited the home, the transaction would be exempt, so Lee would be able to use an FHA loan to buy it.

Chapter 11, Exercise No. 3

1. To calculate the amount of Skillin's upfront premium, it's first necessary to determine her maximum loan amount. Her loan-to-value ratio can't exceed 96.5% of the appraised value (because that's less than the sales price).

$373,000	Appraised value
× .965	Maximum LTV
$359,945	Maximum loan amount
× .0175	1.75% upfront premium
$6,299.04	UFMIP amount

Since Skillin's loan term is longer than 15 years and the LTV is over 95%, the annual premium will be 0.55% of the loan balance.

2. If Skillin were to finance the upfront MIP, the total amount financed would be $366,244.

$359,945	Base loan
+ 6,299	UFMIP
$366,244	Total amount financed (rounded down to next dollar)

It doesn't matter that the total amount financed exceeds the local maximum loan amount ($364,800), as long as the base loan is under the limit (which it is in this case).

The other rule that can limit the amount of an FHA loan with a financed UFMIP is that the total amount financed (the base loan plus the upfront premium) can't exceed the appraised value of the property. That rule won't affect Skillin's transaction, since the total amount financed is less than the $373,000 appraised value.

Chapter 11, Exercise No. 4

1. The Herrons' effective income is $4,510.

$510	Bob's weekly income
× 52	Weeks in a year
$26,520	Bob's annual income
÷ 12	Months in a year
$2,210	Bob's monthly income
+ 2,300	Maggie's monthly income
$4,510	Effective income

2. With an FHA loan, the Herrons could qualify for a maximum housing expense of $1,398.

$114	Personal loan payment
135	Personal loan payment
+ 47	Visa payment
$296	Total recurring charges

$4,510	Effective income
× 43%	
$1,939	Maximum fixed payments
− 296	Recurring charges
$1,643	Maximum housing expense under the debt to income ratio

$4,510	Effective income
× 31%	
$1,398	Maximum housing expense under the housing expense ratio

The maximum housing expense would be $1,398, the result of the housing expense to income ratio calculation, since that's less than the result of the debt to income ratio calculation.

3. If the Herrons were applying for a conventional loan, the lender would apply a 36% debt to income ratio and a 28% housing expense ratio. Under these ratios, the Herrons could only qualify for a mortgage payment of $1,263. That's $135 less than the FHA payment they could qualify for.

$4,510	Stable monthly income
× 36%	Conventional debt to income ratio
$1,624	Maximum total obligations
− 296	Recurring obligations
$1,328	Maximum housing expense under conventional debt to income ratio

$4,510	Stable monthly income
× 28%	Conventional housing expense ratio
$1,263	Maximum housing expense under conventional housing expense ratio

Chapter 12, VA-Guaranteed Loans

Chapter 12, Exercise No. 1

1. Yes, Woods is eligible for a VA-guaranteed loan. Even assuming his active duty service occurred occurred after 1981 (when the service requirements were raised), he exceeded the minimum requirement. Since he served for the full period he was called to active duty, the applicable minimum requirement would be 181 continuous days during peacetime, or only 90 days during wartime.

It's clear that Woods hasn't used up any of his entitlement; he's buying his first home. So his entitlement is the same as the 2009 maximum guaranty amount for the county where the property is located. That's $104,250 in most areas; but a higher maximum would apply in a high-cost county, and his entitlement would be correspondingly greater.

2. For a $325,000 loan, the VA guaranty will cover $81,250. The 2009 guaranty for loan amounts between $144,001 and $417,000 is 25% of the loan amount, up to a maximum of $104,250. $325,000 × .25 = $81,250. That's the guaranty amount for this transaction even if the house is in a high-cost county. A county's maximum guaranty amount only comes into play for loans over $417,000.

Chapter 12, Exercise No. 2

1. The lender would offer Bates a loan for as much as $259,000, the full price of the home, with no downpayment necessary. Since the guaranty is 25% of the loan amount for a loan between $144,001 and $417,000, the guaranty amount would be $64,750.

$$
\begin{array}{ll}
\$259,000 & \text{Loan amount} \\
\underline{\times\ 25\%} & \\
\$64,750 & \text{Guaranty for \$259,000 loan}
\end{array}
$$

2. The lender would be willing to loan Moreau up to $423,000 and require a $2,000 downpayment. The downpayment plus the guaranty amount would cover 25% of the cost of the home.

$$
\begin{array}{ll}
\$425,000 & \text{Sales price (less than appraised value)} \\
\underline{\times\ 25\%} & \text{Ratio of guaranty + downpayment to price} \\
\$106,250 & 25\% \text{ of sales price} \\
\underline{-\ 104,250} & \text{Guaranty (maximum in a county that isn't high-cost)} \\
\$2,000 & \text{Downpayment required by lender}
\end{array}
$$

3. Since the loan amount will be over $144,000, the lender will use the county maximum guaranty ($104,250) as the basis for calculating Jessell's remaining entitlement. His remaining entitlement for this transaction will be $58,250.

$$
\begin{array}{ll}
\$104,250 & \text{Basis for calculating remaining entitlement} \\
\underline{-\ 46,000} & \text{Guaranty on existing loan} \\
\$58,250 & \text{Remaining entitlement}
\end{array}
$$

Applying the 25% rule, the lender will require a $37,250 downpayment. The loan amount will be $344,750.

$$
\begin{array}{ll}
\$382,000 & \text{Sales price} \\
\underline{\times\ 25\%} & \text{Ratio of guaranty + downpayment to price} \\
\$95,500 & 25\% \text{ of sales price} \\
\underline{-\ 58,250} & \text{Remaining entitlement} \\
\$37,250 & \text{Downpayment required by lender}
\end{array}
$$

$$
\begin{array}{ll}
\$382,000 & \text{Sales price} \\
\underline{-\ 37,250} & \text{Downpayment} \\
\$344,750 & \text{Loan amount}
\end{array}
$$

Chapter 12, Exercise No. 3

1. With a $1,430 housing expense, the Martins would have a 43% debt to income ratio.

$1,430	Housing expense
+ 807	Other recurring obligations
$2,237	Total obligations
÷ 5,200	Monthly income
0.43	Debt to income ratio (43%)

2. It's likely that the Martins could qualify for a VA loan with a $1,430 payment, even though their debt to income ratio would be over 41%, because their residual income is considerably higher than the required minimum. If a VA loan applicant's residual income is at least 20% above the minimum, the lender can approve the loan in spite of a debt to income ratio over 41%, even if there are no other compensating factors, and without submitting a statement justifying the decision to the VA.

To apply this 20% rule, first calculate how much residual income the Martins would have with the proposed housing expense.

$5,200	Monthly income
1,325	Taxes withheld
807	Recurring obligations
− 1,430	Proposed housing expense
$1,638	Residual income

Next, check to see if the Martins' residual income exceeds the VA's minimum requirement by at least 20%. The minimum residual income for a family of six in the Western region is $1,238 if they're borrowing $80,000 or more (see Figure 12.3 in Chapter 12).

$1,238	Minimum residual income
× 20%	
$248	20% of the required minimum

Add $248 to $1,238 to find that the Martins need a residual income of $1,486 in order to be at least 20% over the minimum. Their residual income of $1,638 exceeds $1,486, so a lender could accept an income ratio over 41% without other compensating factors.

Chapter 13, Seller Financing

Chapter 13, Exercise No. 1

1. A $10,300 downpayment would be 5.92% of the $174,000 purchase price.

    $$\$10,300 \div \$174,000 = 0.592 = 5.92\%$$

    The 5.92% downpayment plus the 5% seller second would make up about 11% of the price, so Underwood and Schirmer would need an institutional loan with an 89% loan-to-value ratio.

2. The loan amount for the seller second would be $8,700. To determine the amount of the institutional loan, subtract the amount of the seller second and the amount of the downpayment ($10,300) from the purchase price. The amount of the institutional loan would be $155,000. The combined loan amount would be $163,700.

$174,000	Purchase price
× 5%	Loan-to-value ratio for seller second
$8,700	Loan amount for seller second
$174,000	Purchase price
8,700	Seller second
− 10,300	Downpayment
$155,000	Loan amount for institutional loan
$155,000	Institutional loan
+ 8,700	Seller second
$163,700	Combined loan amount

3. Yes, this arrangement complies with the rules for secondary financing in conjunction with a conventional loan listed in Figure 13.1. The combined LTV for the first and second loans does not exceed 95%; the second loan does not require a balloon payment in less than five years; and there is no possibility of negative amortization on the second.

    $155,000 (first loan) + $8,700 (seller second) = $163,700 (total financing)

    $163,700 (financing) ÷ $174,000 (purchase price) = 94%

4. Yes, the couple should be able to qualify for this combination of a conventional loan and a seller second. The total monthly payment (PITI) will be about $1,421, and the conventional income ratios would allow them a payment of up to $1,440.

$1,083.78	Principal and interest for institutional loan
52.16	Principal and interest for seller second
150.00	Property taxes
25.00	Hazard insurance
+ 110.00	PMI
$1,420.94	Proposed monthly housing expense

$5,500	Stable monthly income
× 28%	Housing expense to income ratio
$1,540	Maximum housing expense under the 28% housing expense ratio

$5,500	Stable monthly income
× 36%	Debt to income ratio
$1,980	Maximum total obligations
– 540	Monthly debt payments
$1,440	Maximum housing expense under the 36% debt to income ratio

The buyers' maximum housing expense is the result of the debt to income ratio calculation ($1,440), since that's less than the result of the housing expense to income ratio calculation ($1,540).

Chapter 13, Exercise No. 2

1. The seller's first-year yield will be approximately 12%.

Wraparound Worksheet

Sales price	$75,000					
– Downpayment	$8,000					
Wraparound	$67,000	x	9%	=	$6,030	Interest received
– Underlying loan	$39,700	x	7%	=	– 2,779	– Interest paid
Credit extended	$27,300				$3,251	Net interest
					$27,300	÷ Credit extended
					12%	Seller's yield

2. The seller's first-year yield would be about 26.7%.

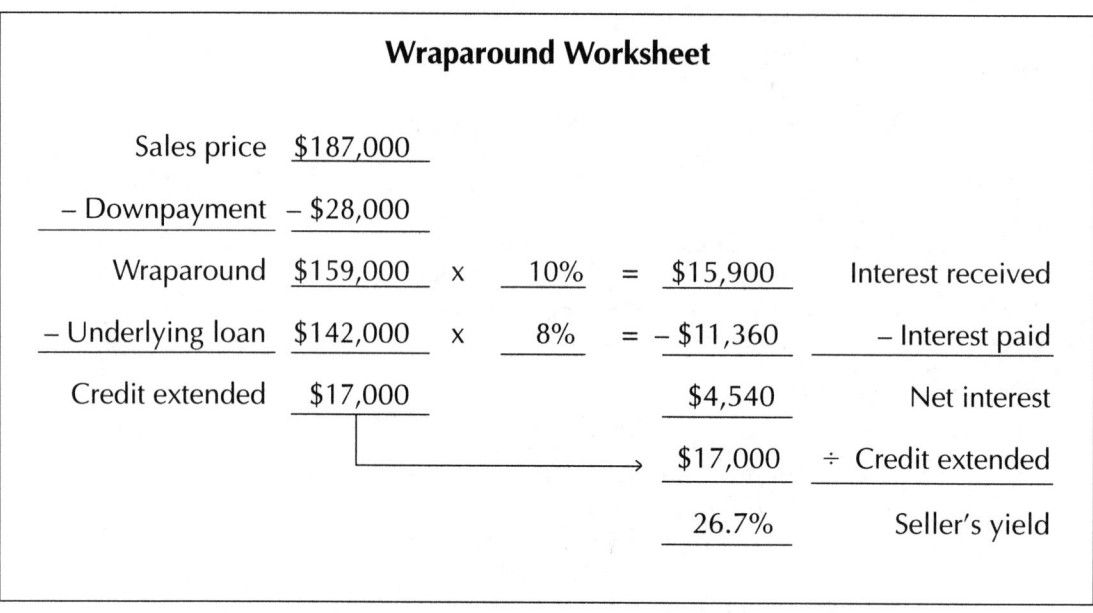

Chapter 13, Exercise No. 3

1. The total monthly payment for the assumption plus seller second would be $1,093.57. The monthly payment for the wraparound ($1,011.26) is significantly less.

    $899.12   Payment on assumed loan
 + 194.45   Payment on seller second
$1,093.57   Total monthly payment for assumption plus seller second

2. The Rainwaters' yield on the wraparound would be approximately 11.7%, compared to their 8% yield on the seller second.

  $152,000   Wraparound loan
 − 125,500   Underlying loan
   $26,500   Credit extended

  $152,000   Wraparound
  ×   7%   Interest rate
  $10,640   Annual interest received

  $125,500   Underlying loan
  ×   6%   Interest rate
   $7,530   Annual interest paid

$10,640   Interest received on wraparound
– 7,530   Interest paid on underlying loan
$3,110   Net interest earned

Divide the net interest by the credit extended to find the yield.

$$\$3,110 \div \$26,500 = 11.7\% \text{ yield}$$

The Rainwaters would have an 11.7% yield on the wraparound arrangement, compared to an 8% yield on the seller second.

3. With the assumption plus seller second, McCarthy would pay approximately 6.35% interest on the total amount financed, which is 2.65% below the current market rate of 9%. On the wraparound, he would pay 7% interest, which is higher than the rate on the assumption plus seller second, but still below the market rate.

$125,500   Assumed loan
× 6%   Interest rate
$7,530   Annual interest paid

$26,500   Seller second
× 8%   Interest rate
$2,120   Annual interest paid

$7,530   Interest on assumed loan
+ 2,120   Interest on seller second
$9,650   Total annual interest paid

$125,500   Assumed loan
+ 26,500   Seller second
$152,000   Total amount financed

Divide the total annual interest paid by the total amount financed to find the approximate overall interest rate on the assumption plus seller second.

$$\$9,650 \div \$152,000 = 6.35\% \text{ overall interest rate}$$

Case Study Answers

Case Study for Chapter 10, Conventional Financing

Question 1

Rick's middle credit score (678) will be used as the indicator score in underwriting the Cortinas' loan application. For each applicant, the indicator score is the lower of two scores or the middle of three scores. For Rick that's 678, and for Teresa it's 730. When there's more than one applicant, the indicator scores of the applicants are compared, and the lowest of those is used for underwriting. Thus, the indicator score for the Cortinas' application is 678.

Question 2

The Cortinas' stable monthly income is $7,117.

$20.35	Teresa's hourly wage
× 173.33	Factor for translating hourly wage into monthly income
$3,527.27	Teresa's monthly income
1,600.00	Rick's monthly salary
+ 1,990.00	Rick's average monthly commissions
$7,117.27	Stable monthly income

Question 3

If they apply for Loan A, which has an 80% LTV, the Cortinas should qualify for a principal and interest payment of approximately $1,507.93. For either Loan B (90% LTV) or Loan C (95% LTV), the maximum principal and interest payment would be approximately $1,387.30. The Cortinas qualify for a larger maximum principal and interest payment with Loan A because it doesn't require private mortgage insurance. (PMI is required only when the loan-to-value ratio is above 80%.) Without PMI, a larger portion of the maximum housing expense can be devoted to principal and interest.

The first step in calculating the maximum principal and interest payments is to add up the Cortinas' monthly recurring obligations (aside from their housing expense).

$278	Car payment
215	Car payment
122	Installment contract payment
110	Credit card payment
+ 103	Student loan payment
$828	Recurring obligations

(The $65 student loan payment shouldn't be counted, since only eight payments remain to be made.)

Next, calculate the Cortinas' maximum housing expense using the 36% and 28% conventional income ratios.

$7,117	Stable monthly income
× .36	Total debt to income ratio
$2,562.12	Maximum total obligations
− 828.00	Recurring obligations
$1,734.12	Maximum housing expense under the 36% debt to income ratio

$7,117	Stable monthly income
× .28	Housing expense to income ratio
$1,992.76	Maximum housing expense under the 28% housing expense ratio

Their maximum housing expense would be $1,734.12, the result of the debt to income ratio calculation, since that's less than the result of the housing expense to income ratio calculation. The next step is to set aside 15% for taxes and insurance, plus another 10% for mortgage insurance if required, to determine their maximum principal and interest payment.

$1,734.12	Maximum housing expense
÷ 1.15	15% for taxes and hazard insurance
$1,507.93	Maximum P&I payment if PMI isn't required (LTV 80% or less)

$1,734.12	Maximum housing expense
÷ 1.25	15% for taxes and hazard insurance, plus 10% for mortgage insurance
$1,387.30	Maximum P&I payment if PMI is required (LTV over 80%)

Question 4

a) The interest rate on an 80% fixed-rate loan with no discount points would be 5.50%. A $265,580 loan could buy a $331,975 house, with a downpayment of $66,395.

$265,580	Loan amount
÷ .80	80% LTV
$331,975	Sales price
− 265,580	Loan amount
$66,395	Downpayment

b) The interest rate on a 90% ARM with two discount points would be 5.20%. (5.70 − 0.25 = 5.20). A $252,645 loan could buy a $280,717 house, with a downpayment of $28,072.

$252,645	Loan amount
÷ .90	90% LTV
$280,717	Sales price
− 252,645	Loan amount
$28,072	Downpayment

c) The interest rate on a 95% fixed-rate loan with three discount points would be 5.25%. (Three points would reduce the interest rate by 0.75%, from 6.00% to 5.25%. 0.25 × 3 = 0.75.) A $251,230 loan could buy a $264,453 house, with a downpayment of $13,223.

$251,230	Loan amount
÷ .95	95% LTV
$264,453	Sales price
− 251,230	Loan amount
$13,223	Downpayment

Question 5

For the 80% fixed-rate loan, the Cortinas would need about $91,000 in cash. For the 90% ARM, they'd need about $54,500. For the 95% fixed-rate loan, about $42,200.

a) 80% fixed-rate loan at 5.50% interest, with a 1.50% origination fee, a 0.25% adverse market delivery charge, and a 2.50% LLPA (based on the 678 indicator score).

Sales price: $331,975   Loan amount: $265,580
Downpayment: $66,395   Monthly mortgage payment (PITI): $1,734.12

$265,580	Loan amount
× .015	Origination fee percentage (1.50%)
$3,983.70	Origination fee

$265,580	Loan amount
× .0025	Adverse market delivery charge percentage (0.25%)
$663.95	Adverse market delivery charge

$265,580	Loan amount
× .025	LLPA percentage (2.50%)
$6,639.50	Loan-level price adjustment based on credit score and LTV

Note: Since all of the loan fees are based on the loan amount, they can all be calculated together to save time, as long as you don't need to know the individual figures. Add together the percentages and multiply the result by the loan amount: 1.50% + 0.25% + 2.50% = 4.25% × $265,580 = $11,287.15.

$331,975	Sales price
× .03	Closing cost percentage (3.00%)
$9,959.25	Closing costs

$1,734.12	PITI payment
× 2	Months
$3,468.24	Reserves

$66,395	Downpayment
11,287	Total loan fees
+ 9,959	Closing costs
$87,641	Cash for closing
+ 3,468	Reserves
$91,109	Total cash requirement

b) 90% ARM at 5.20% interest, with two discount points, a 1.50% origination fee, a 0.25% adverse market delivery charge, a 0.25% LLPA because this is an ARM, and a 1.75% LLPA based on the 678 indicator score.

Sales price: $280,717   Loan amount: $252,645
Downpayment: $28,072   Monthly mortgage payment (PITI): $1,734.12

$252,645	Loan amount
× .02	Two points (2.00%)
$5,052.90	Two discount points

$252,645	Loan amount
× .015	Origination fee percentage (1.50%)
$3,789.68	Origination fee

$252,645	Loan amount
× .0025	Adverse market delivery charge percentage (0.25%)
$631.61	Adverse market delivery charge

$252,645	Loan amount
× .0025	LLPA percentage (0.25%)
$631.61	Loan-level price adjustment for ARMs

$252,645	Loan amount
× .0175	LLPA percentage (1.75%)
$4,421.29	Loan-level price adjustment based on credit score and LTV

(Total loan fees, including two discount points: 5.75% × $252,645 = $14,527.09)

$280,717	Sales price
× .03	Closing cost percentage (3.00%)
$8,421.51	Closing costs

$1,734.12	PITI payment
× 2	Months
$3,468.24	Reserves

$28,072	Downpayment
14,527	Total loan fees
+ 8,422	Closing costs
$51,021	Cash for closing
+ 3,468	Reserves
$54,489	Total cash requirement

c) 95% loan at 5.25% interest, with three discount points, a 2.00% origination fee, a 0.25% adverse market delivery charge, and a 1.75% LLPA based on the 678 indicator score.

Sales price: $264,453   Loan amount: $251,230
Downpayment: $13,223   Monthly mortgage payment (PITI): $1,734.12

$251,230   Loan amount
×   .03   Three discount points (3.00%)
$7,536.90   Discount points

$251,230   Loan amount
×   .02   Origination fee percentage (2.00%)
$5,024.60   Origination fee

$251,230   Loan amount
×   .0025   Adverse market delivery charge percentage (0.25%)
$628.08   Adverse market delivery charge

$251,230   Loan amount
×   .0175   LLPA percentage (1.75%)
$4,396.53   Loan-level price adjustment based on credit score and LTV

(Total loan fees, including three discount points: 7.00% × $251,230 = $17,586.10)

$264,453   Sales price
×   .03   Closing cost percentage (3.00%)
$7,933.59   Closing costs

$1,734.12   PITI payment
×   2   Months
$3,468.24   Reserves

$13,223   Downpayment
17,586   Total loan fees
+   7,934   Closing costs
$38,743   Cash for closing
+   3,468   Reserves
$42,211   Total cash requirement

The Cortinas have $58,000 in savings, so they have enough cash to buy a $280,717 house with Loan B, the 90% ARM (requiring about $54,500 in cash), or to buy a $264,453 house with Loan C, the 95% fixed-rate loan that requires about $42,200 in cash.

They don't have nearly enough in savings to buy a $331,975 house with Loan A, the 80% fixed-rate loan, which would require over $90,000 in cash.

Question 6

a) With a 90% fixed-rate loan, the Cortinas' interest rate will be slightly higher than the rate they'd pay with the 90% ARM (5.25% with two discount points, as opposed to 5.20% for the ARM). With the same principal and interest payment, the higher rate will result in a smaller loan amount. So they'll either have to buy a slightly less expensive house, or else make a slightly larger downpayment to make up the difference.

   Here are the specifics: With the 5.25% fixed interest rate and two discount points, the Cortinas could get a $251,230 loan, compared to $252,645 with the ARM. If they still wanted to buy a $280,717 house, they would need $55,200 in cash, compared to $54,500 with the ARM for the larger loan amount. (By the way, note that they won't have to pay the additional 0.25% loan-level price adjustment that applies to the ARM.)

   Those are small differences. There is one big difference, however: the Cortinas wouldn't have to worry about future interest rate and payment increases with the fixed-rate loan. Unless they plan to own this house for only a short period, that's a substantial advantage. It's true that an ARM's interest rate may go down as well as up in the future, and rate decreases may balance out the increases over the loan term. But when market interest rates are generally low and ARMs aren't being offered at lower rates than fixed-rate loans, most buyers would choose a fixed-rate loan over an ARM.

b) Even though the $265,000 sales price is almost $67,000 less than the $331,975 price the Cortinas were considering with Loan A, they still don't have enough cash to qualify for an 80% loan. The loan amount would be $212,000, with a $53,000 downpayment. Just by adding the 3% closing costs ($265,000 × .03 = $7,950), you can see that their savings aren't enough. They'd need $60,950 for the downpayment and closing costs alone. The loan fees (4.25%, or $9,010) and reserves would put the loan even further out of reach. (The PITI payment would be $1,384.27, so they'd need $2,769 for reserves.)

$265,000   Sales price
×   .80   80% LTV
$212,000   Loan amount

$265,000   Sales price
− 212,000   Loan amount
$53,000   Downpayment

$265,000   Sales price
×   .03   Closing cost percentage (3.00%)
$7,950   Closing costs

$53,000   Downpayment
7,950   Closing costs
9,010   Loan fees
+ 2,769   Reserves
$72,729   Total cash requirement

Notice that the $265,000 price tag the Cortinas can't afford with an 80% fixed-rate loan is essentially the same price they could afford with a 95% fixed-rate loan (Loan C—see Question 4c).

Question 7

a) With a $1,863.69 PITI payment, the Cortinas' income ratios are 37.8% and 26.2%.

$1,863.69 PITI
+ 828.00 Recurring obligations
$2,691.69 Total monthly obligations
÷ 7,117 Stable monthly income
0.378 Debt to income ratio (37.8%)

$1,863.69 PITI
÷ 7,117 Stable monthly income
0.262 Housing expense to income ratio (26.2%)

b) The Cortinas have been paying $2,300 a month in rent, considerably more than the $1,863.69 housing expense they'd have if this loan were approved. Their rent is 32.3% of their monthly income, so they've demonstrated that they can devote more of their income to housing than most people. A lender might be willing to treat that as a compensating factor to help offset the high debt to income ratio. How much it would help would depend on the "overall layering of risk" presented by their whole application.

Other considerations that can be treated as compensating factors include substantial net worth; a demonstrated ability to incur few debts and accumulate savings; education or employment history indicating strong potential for increased earnings; short-term income not counted as stable monthly income; or significant energy-efficient features in the house being purchased. None of these appears to apply in the Cortinas' case, with the possible exception of the last one. If the house they want has special energy-efficient features, they should bring that to the lender's attention.

c) The risk factor that will probably concern the lender most is the Cortinas' indicator credit score. (Remember that Fannie Mae regards a borrower's credit score as one of two primary risk factors, along with the loan-to-value ratio.) While Rick's 678 score isn't terrible, it's weak enough so that the lender might decide that a 37.8% debt to income ratio would be one layer of risk too many. Teresa's scores are much better than Rick's, but not so stellar that they cancel out the mediocre indicator score.

Another problem is that the Cortinas have quite a lot of debt. The proposed housing expense is only 26.2% of their income, yet their other obligations are enough to push their debt to income ratio up to 37.8%.

d) Depending on the financial circumstances of their families, the Cortinas might be able to use gift funds to make a larger downpayment, reducing the loan amount and the monthly payment without increasing their debts or expenses. There are other ways gift funds could be applied; for example, they could be used to pay discount points and reduce the loan's interest rate and monthly payment.

If the Cortinas paid off one or more of their debts (like the student loan with only 12 payments left), that could also help them qualify for the mortgage and buy this house. They should consult the lender before they do that, however, to make sure it would make a difference.

Case Study for Chapter 11, FHA-Insured Loans

Question 1

Applying the FHA's 43% and 31% income ratios, the maximum housing expense the Cortinas qualify for is $2,206.27 (the result of the housing expense to income ratio calculation, which is lower than the result of the debt to income ratio calculation).

$7,117	Effective income
× .43	FHA maximum debt to income ratio
$3,060.31	Maximum fixed payments
− 828.00	Recurring charges
$2,232.31	Maximum housing expense under the debt to income ratio

$7,117.00	Effective income
× .31	FHA maximum housing expense to income ratio
$2,206.27	Maximum housing expense under the housing expense ratio

Question 2

FHA borrowers are permitted to borrow enough to cover the upfront MIP in addition to the local maximum loan amount, as long as the total doesn't exceed the property's appraised value. So the Cortinas could be preapproved to borrow the maximum base loan amount for their area ($271,050), plus the upfront MIP (1.75% of the base loan amount, or $4,743). The total amount financed would be $275,793. However, if the Cortinas ultimately decided to buy a house appraised for less than that amount, their loan amount (and premium amount) would have to be adjusted.

$271,050	Maximum base loan amount
× .0175	Upfront MIP percentage (1.75%)
$4,743.38	Upfront MIP

$271,050.00	Loan amount
+ 4,743.38	Upfront MIP
$275,793.38	Total amount financed

Question 3

The Cortinas should easily qualify for a $271,050 FHA loan with the upfront MIP financed ($275,793 total amount financed). A fixed-rate FHA loan at 5.50% interest would have PITI payments of approximately $1,925, considerably less than the Cortinas' $2,206 maximum FHA housing expense.

First calculate the estimated monthly share of the property taxes and hazard insurance.

$1,565.92	Principal and interest payment for loan at 5.5% interest
× .15	15% for taxes and hazard insurance
$234.89	Monthly share of property taxes and hazard insurance

Next, calculate the monthly share of the annual premium, which will be 0.55% of the base loan amount if the loan-to-value ratio is over 95%.

$271,050	Base loan amount
× .0055	Annual premium percentage (.55%)
$1,490.78	Annual premium
÷ 12	Months in a year
$124.23	Monthly share of annual premium

Now add those two figures to the principal and interest payment.

$234.89	Monthly share of property taxes and hazard insurance
124.23	Monthly share of annual premium
+ 1,565.92	P&I payment
$1,925.04	PITI payment for $271,050 FHA loan at 5.5% with financed UFMIP

Question 4

The loan-to-value ratio for an FHA loan can't exceed 96.5% of the appraised value or sales price, whichever is less. The minimum cash investment (3.5%) would be $9,831. With the maximum loan amount plus the minimum cash investment, the Cortinas could pay about $280,880 for a house (assuming that the appraised value isn't less than the price).

$271,050	Base loan amount
÷ .965	LTV percentage (96.5% of sales price or value)
$280,881	Sales price
− 271,050	Loan amount
$9,831	Minimum cash investment (3.5% of sales price or value)

Note that the financed upfront premium isn't involved in these calculations, as long as the total amount financed doesn't exceed the property's appraised value. That's not a problem in this case: the total amount financed ($275,793—see Question 2) is less than the value.

Question 5

For this transaction, the Cortinas would need approximately $21,000 at closing.

$271,050	Loan amount
× .01	Origination fee percentage (1.00%)
$2,710.50	Origination fee

$280,880	Sales price
× .03	Closing cost percentage (3.00%)
$8,426.40	Closing costs

$9,831	Minimum cash investment (from Question 4)
2,711	Origination fee
+ 8,426	Closing costs
$20,968	Total cash needed at closing

Question 6

Even though the Cortinas' $280,880 price is based on the maximum FHA loan amount in their area, they could use their FHA financing to buy a more expensive house if they wanted to. They'd simply have to make a larger downpayment than the required 3.5% minimum cash investment.

For example, if they wanted to buy a house for $290,000, they'd have to make an $18,951 downpayment. That's the minimum cash investment ($9,831) plus the difference between $290,000 and $280,880 ($9,120). That would bring their total cash requirement to about $30,000 ($9,120 + $20,968 = $230,088).

Question 7

For home buyers, an FHA loan has two chief advantages over a comparable conventional loan: they may qualify for a significantly larger monthly payment, and they'll probably need significantly less cash for closing.

As you saw in the Chapter 10 case study (Question 6a), the Cortinas could qualify for a 90% fixed-rate conventional loan large enough to buy a house worth $280,000, and they'd need around $55,200 in cash for that transaction. Although that figure includes about $3,500 in reserves that they wouldn't actually have to relinquish to the lender, they would be left with only $6,300 in savings.

In comparison, the FHA loan we've been considering would allow them to buy the same $280,000 house with only about $21,000 in cash, leaving $37,000 in their savings account. They would qualify for the FHA loan more easily, too.

However, the Cortinas' monthly payment for the FHA loan ($1,925) would be larger than the payment for the conventional loan ($1,734). That's because they would be borrowing considerably more with the FHA financing. The downpayment required for the FHA loan is much less than the conventional downpayment (3.5% instead of 10%), so the FHA loan amount is correspondingly larger. Also, the Cortinas are planning to finance the upfront MIP for the FHA loan. That brings their total amount financed to $275,793, compared to the $247,745 conventional loan amount.

Qualifying for a larger payment sounds good to prospective buyers, since it generally means they can buy a more expensive house. However, the Cortinas should keep in mind that if they go through with the FHA transaction we've described, they're going to have to actually pay that larger payment month after month, year after year. And they would have a lot less equity in the property than they would with the 90% conventional loan. With any type of financing, borrowing the maximum amount that the lender and the underwriting rules will allow isn't necessarily the best course.

Of course, the Cortinas could use FHA financing to buy a less expensive house; or they could make a larger downpayment than the minimum required, decreasing the loan amount and the monthly payment. In any event, an FHA loan is likely to cost them less in loan fees than a conventional loan and give them the option of holding on to more of their savings.

Case Study for Chapter 12, VA-Guaranteed Loans

Question 1

Under the VA's standard 41% debt to income ratio, the Cortinas could have a maximum housing expense of $2,089.97, which we'll round up to $2,090.

$7,117	Monthly income
× .41	Maximum debt to income ratio (41%)
$2,917.97	
– 828.00	Recurring obligations
$2,089.97	Maximum housing expense

Question 2

With a $2,090 housing expense, the Cortinas' residual income would be $2,736. To calculate that figure, start by adding up all of the taxes that are withheld from their paychecks. Then subtract the taxes, the recurring obligations, and the proposed housing expense from monthly income.

$380	Federal income tax (Rick)
145	State income tax (Rick)
204	Social Security/Medicare (Rick)
375	Federal income tax (Teresa)
141	State income tax (Teresa)
+ 218	Social Security & Medicare (Teresa)
$1,463	Total taxes

$7,117	Monthly income
1,463	Taxes
828	Recurring obligations
– 2,090	Proposed housing expense
$2,736	Residual income

The Cortinas' residual income is far more than the $738 minimum required for a two-person family in the Southern region borrowing $80,000 or more. As long as other aspects of their application (such as their credit reputation) meet VA standards, they can easily qualify for a $2,090 payment.

Question 3

If the lender allowed them to have a 45% ratio, the Cortinas' maximum housing expense would be $2,375. Their residual income would be $2,451.

$7,117	Monthly income
× .45	Debt to income ratio (45%)
$3,202.65	Maximum total obligations
– 828.00	Recurring obligations
$2,374.65	Maximum housing expense (PITI)

$7,117   Monthly income
1,463   Taxes
828   Recurring obligations
– 2,375   Proposed housing expense
$2,451   Residual income

When a VA loan applicant's residual income exceeds the required minimum by more than 20%, the lender can approve the loan even if the debt to income ratio is over 41%, without other compensating factors. For the Cortinas, 20% of the minimum requirement ($738) is $147.60. Even with the $2,375 payment, their residual income would exceed the minimum requirement by much more than 20%.

$738   Minimum residual income
× 20%
$147.60   20% of required minimum

$2,451   Residual income (with $2,375 housing expense)
– 738   Minimum residual income
$1,713   Amount by which residual income exceeds required minimum

That means the lender could approve a VA loan with that larger payment for the Cortinas without having to submit a statement justifying the decision to the VA.

Question 4

With 15% of the payment going toward taxes and insurance, a $2,375 PITI payment translates into a maximum principal and interest payment of $2,065.

$2,375   Maximum housing expense
÷ 1.15   15% for property taxes and hazard insurance
$2,065.22   Maximum principal and interest payment

In 2009, the VA guaranty for a $363,692 loan would be $90,923, which is 25% of the loan amount.

$363,692   Loan amount
× .25   Guaranty percentage for VA loan between $144,001 and $417,000
$90,923   Guaranty amount

Question 5

The lender would not require a downpayment, since the guaranty amount is 25% of the loan amount. (In the Cortinas' area, a downpayment would typically be required if the loan amount was over $417,000, since the maximum guaranty, $104,250, would be less than 25% of the loan amount.)

With no downpayment, the sales price would be the same as the loan amount ($363,692). The 1% origination fee, 2.15% funding fee, and 3% closing costs add up to 6.15% of the loan amount/sales price. The Cortinas would need only about $22,370 in cash to close this VA loan.

$363,692	Loan amount
× .0615	Origination fee, funding fee, and closing costs (6.15%)
$22,367.06	Cash needed for closing

Question 6

The Cortinas might very well choose a VA loan over a conventional loan or an FHA loan, because it would allow them to buy a considerably more expensive house without a lot of cash.

Of course, they'd be taking on a much larger monthly mortgage payment in order to buy a $363,692 house, and they might not want to do that, even though they'd qualify for it. But they could buy a house in the price range they were considering for a conventional or FHA loan (for example, around $280,000) with a lot less money.

Case Study for Chapter 13, Seller Financing

Question 1

The lender doesn't allow a conventional loan that's supplemented with secondary financing to exceed 75% of the sales price or appraised value, whichever is less (in this case, it's the appraised value, $328,500). As a result, the amount of the primary loan will be $246,375.

$328,500   Appraised value (less than $330,000 sales price)
×   .75   Maximum LTV for primary loan (75%)
$246,375   Maximum conventional loan amount

This lender's secondary financing rules also require the Cortinas to make at least a 10% downpayment, so the loan-to-value ratio of Wellman's seller second can't exceed 15% of the appraised value. That means she can finance no more than $49,275. The total amount financed would be $295,650.

$328,500   Appraised value
×   .15   Maximum LTV for secondary financing (15%)
$49,275   Maximum seller second
+ 246,375   Conventional loan amount
$295,650   Total amount financed

Question 2

The monthly housing expense for this combination of a conventional loan and a seller second would be $1,926.32. Since the Cortinas are preapproved for a $1,992.76 PITI payment, they shouldn't have a problem qualifying for this combined payment.

$1,379.63   Principal and interest for first loan
+ 295.43   Principal and interest for seller second
$1,675.06   Combined principal and interest payment
×   1.15   15% for taxes and hazard insurance
$1,926.32   Combined PITI payment (total monthly housing expense)

Question 3

The Cortinas would need about $53,489 to close, plus $3,853 in reserve, for a total cash requirement of approximately $57,342. Their $58,000 in savings is just enough.

$330,000   Sales price
− 295,650   Total amount financed
$34,350   Downpayment

$246,375   Conventional loan amount
×   .015   Origination fee percentage (1.50%)
$3,695.63   Origination fee

$246,375	Conventional loan amount
× .0025	Adverse market delivery charge percentage (0.25%)
$615.94	Adverse market delivery charge

$246,375	Conventional loan amount
× .02	LLPA percentage (2.00%)
$4,927.50	Loan-level price adjustment based on credit score and LTV

(Total loan fees: 3.75% × $246,375 = $9,239.06)

$330,000	Sales price
× .03	Closing cost percentage (3.00%)
$9,900	Closing costs

$1,926.32	Combined loan payment
× 2	Months
$3,852.64	Reserves

$34,350	Downpayment
9,239	Total loan fees
+ 9,900	Closing costs
$53,489	Cash for closing
+ 3,853	Reserves
$57,342	Total cash requirement

Question 4

The seller second can be amortized over 30 years (so that the monthly payment is only $295.43), but require a balloon payment of the entire unpaid principal balance after five years. At that point, the remaining balance would be approximately $45,850. The Cortinas should plan ahead regarding the balloon payment. If all goes well—in terms of their own financial situation, property values, and the economy in general—refinancing will be an option when the time comes. But that isn't guaranteed.

Question 5

Wellman would receive approximately $153,725 at closing.

$330,000	Sales price
× .10	Selling costs percentage (10%)
$33,000	Selling costs

$330,000	Sales price
33,000	Selling costs
94,000	Mortgage payoff
− 49,275	Credit extended to the buyers
$153,725	Cash to seller at closing

Income Qualifying—Conventional Loans
Loan A: Fixed Interest Rate, 80% Loan-to-Value Ratio

Stable Monthly Income

Base salary	
Wage earner 1	$1,600
Wage earner 2	$3,527
Overtime	
Commissions	$1,990
Bonuses	
Other	+
Total	$7,117

Recurring Obligations

Car loans	$493
Credit cards	$110
Student loans	$103
Other debts	$122
Child support	
Alimony	
Other	+
Total	$828

Debt to Income Ratio

$7,117	Stable monthly income
x .36	Maximum ratio (36%)
$2,562.12	Maximum obligations
− 828.00	Recurring obligations
$1,734.12	Maximum mortgage payment (PITI) under debt to income ratio

Housing Expense to Income Ratio

$7,117	Stable monthly income
x .28	Maximum ratio (28%)
$1,992.76	Maximum mortgage payment (PITI) under housing expense ratio

Maximum Mortgage Payment (PITI) $1,734.12

$1,734.12	Maximum PITI payment
÷ 1.15	15% for taxes and hazard insurance
$1,507.93	Maximum principal and interest payment
Interest rate	5.50%

Maximum Loan Amount $265,580

$265,580	Maximum loan amount
÷ .80	Loan-to-value ratio (80%)
$331,975	Sales price

Sales Price $331,975

Income Qualifying—Conventional Loans
Loan B: Adjustable Interest Rate, 90% Loan-to-Value Ratio

Stable Monthly Income

Base salary	
Wage earner 1	$1,600
Wage earner 2	$3,527
Overtime	
Commissions	$1,990
Bonuses	
Other	+
Total	$7,117

Recurring Obligations

Car loans	$493
Credit cards	$110
Student loans	$103
Other debts	$122
Child support	
Alimony	
Other	+
Total	$828

Debt to Income Ratio

$7,117	Stable monthly income
x .36	Maximum ratio (36%)
$2,562.12	Maximum obligations
− 828.00	Recurring obligations
$1,734.12	Maximum mortgage payment (PITI) under debt to income ratio

Housing Expense to Income Ratio

$7,117	Stable monthly income
x .28	Maximum ratio (28%)
$1,992.76	Maximum mortgage payment (PITI) under housing expense ratio

Maximum Mortgage Payment (PITI) $1,734.12

$1,734.12	Maximum PITI payment
÷ 1.25	25% for taxes, hazard insurance, and PMI
$1,387.30	Maximum principal and interest payment
Interest rate	5.20% (with two points)

Maximum Loan Amount $252,645

$252,645	Maximum loan amount
÷ .90	Loan-to-value ratio (90%)
$280,717	Sales price

Sales Price $280,717

Income Qualifying—Conventional Loans
Loan C: Fixed Interest Rate, 95% Loan-to-Value Ratio

Stable Monthly Income			Recurring Obligations	
Base salary			Car loans	$493
Wage earner 1	$1,600		Credit cards	$110
Wage earner 2	$3,527		Student loans	$103
Overtime			Other debts	$122
Commissions	$1,990		Child support	
Bonuses			Alimony	
Other	+		Other	+
Total	$7,117		Total	$828

Debt to Income Ratio

$7,117	Stable monthly income
x .36	Maximum ratio (36%)
$2,562.12	Maximum obligations
− 828.00	Recurring obligations
$1,734.12	Maximum mortgage payment (PITI) under debt to income ratio

Housing Expense to Income Ratio

$7,117	Stable monthly income
x .28	Maximum ratio (28%)
$1,992.76	Maximum mortgage payment (PITI) under housing expense ratio

Maximum Mortgage Payment (PITI) $1,734.12

$1,734.12	Maximum PITI payment
÷ 1.25	25% for taxes, hazard insurance, and PMI
$1,387.30	Maximum principal and interest payment
Interest rate	5.25% (with three points)

Maximum Loan Amount $251,230

$251,230	Maximum loan amount
÷ .95	Loan-to-value ratio (95%)
$264,453	Sales price

Sales Price $264,453

Income Qualifying—FHA-Insured Loans

Effective Income

Base salary	
Wage earner 1	$1,600
Wage earner 2	$3,527
Overtime	
Commissions	$1,990
Bonuses	
Other	+
Total	$7,117

Recurring Charges

Car loans	$493
Credit cards	$110
Student loans	$103
Other debts	$122
Child support	
Alimony	
Other	+
Total	$828

Debt to Income Ratio

$7,117	Effective income
x .43	Maximum ratio (43%)
$3,060.31	Maximum fixed payments
− 828.00	Recurring charges
$2,232.31	Maximum mortgage payment (PITI) under debt to income ratio

Housing Expense to Income Ratio

$7,117	Effective income
x .31	Maximum ratio (31%)
$2,206.27	Maximum mortgage payment (PITI) under housing expense ratio

Maximum Mortgage Payment (PITI) $2,206.27

Maximum Loan Amount $271,050

$271,050	Loan amount
x .0175	1.75% of base loan
$4,743	Upfront MIP
+ 271,050	Loan amount
$275,793	Total amount financed

$234.89	1/12 of taxes, insurance
124.23	1/12 of annual MIP
+ 1,565.92	P&I payment at 5.5%
$1,925.04	PITI payment for $271,050 loan with financed UFMIP

Total Amount Financed $275,793

$271,050	Maximum loan amount
÷ .965	Loan-to-value ratio (96.5%)
$280,881	Sales price
− $271,050	Loan amount
$9,831	Minimum cash investment

Sales Price $280,881

Income Qualifying—VA-Guaranteed Loans

Taxes (per month)

	Wage earner 1
$380	Federal income tax
$145	State income tax
$204	Social Security/Medicare
	Wage earner 2
$375	Federal income tax
$141	State income tax
+ $218	Social Security/Medicare
$1,463	Total taxes withheld

Recurring Charges

Car loans	$493
Credit cards	$110
Student loans	$103
Other debts	$122
Child care	
Child support	
Alimony	
Other +	
Total	$828

Gross Monthly Income

Base salary	
Wage earner 1	$1,600
Wage earner 2	$3,527
Overtime	
Commissions	$1,990
Bonuses	
Other +	
Total	$7,117

Obligations to Income Ratio

$7,117	Gross monthly income	$7,117	Gross monthly income
x .41	Standard ratio (41%)	x .45	Higher ratio (45%)
$2,917.97	Maximum obligations	$3,202.65	Maximum obligations
− 828.00	Recurring obligations	− 828.00	Recurring obligations
$2,089.97	Maximum PITI payment with standard 41% ratio	$2,374.65	Maximum PITI payment with a 45% ratio

Income Qualifying—VA-Guaranteed Loans

Residual Income Analysis

Required minimum residual income _____ $738 _____

$7,117	Gross monthly income
1,463	Taxes
828	Recurring obligations
− 2,090	Proposed housing expense (from 41% ratio)
$2,736	**Residual Income**

$7,117	Gross monthly income
1,463	Taxes
828	Recurring obligations
− 2,375	Proposed housing expense (from 45% ratio)
$2,451	**Residual Income**

Income ratio over 41% acceptable with compensating factors.

If residual income exceeds the minimum by more than 20%, a ratio over 41% is acceptable even without any other compensating factors.

PITI Payment with 45% ratio _____ $2,375 _____

$2,375	Maximum PITI payment
÷ 1.15	15% for property taxes and hazard insurance
$2,065.22	Maximum principal and interest payment

Interest rate _____ 5.5% _____

Maximum Loan Amount _____ $363,692 _____

$363,692	Loan amount
× .25	Guaranty percentage for VA loan from $144,001 to $417,000
$90,923	Guaranty amount

Loan Amount = Sales Price
(unless downpayment required because guaranty is less than 25% of loan amount)

Glossary

The definitions given here explain how the listed terms are used in the field of real estate finance. Some of the terms have additional meanings, which can be found in a standard dictionary.

Acceleration—Declaring a loan's entire balance immediately due and payable, because the borrower has defaulted or (if the loan includes an alienation clause) sold the security property without the lender's approval. Also referred to as calling the loan.

Acceleration Clause—A provision in a security instrument that allows the lender to declare the entire debt due immediately if the borrower breaches one or more provisions of the agreement. Also called a call provision.

Accrued Items of Expense—Expenses that have been incurred but are not yet due or payable; in a settlement statement, the seller's accrued expenses are credited to the buyer.

Acknowledgment—When a person who has signed a document formally declares to an authorized official (usually a notary public) that he signed voluntarily. The official can then attest that the signature is voluntary and genuine.

Acquisition Cost—The amount of money a buyer was required to expend in order to acquire title to a piece of property; in addition to the purchase price, this ordinarily includes a variety of closing costs, and may also include other expenses.

Adjustable-Rate Mortgage (ARM)—A loan with an interest rate that is periodically increased or decreased to reflect changes in the cost of money. *Compare:* Fixed-Rate Loan.

Age, Actual—The age of a structure from a chronological standpoint (as opposed to its effective age); how many years it has actually been in existence.

Age, Effective—The age of a structure indicated by its condition and remaining usefulness (as opposed to its actual age).

Alienation—The transfer of ownership or an interest in property from one person to another, by any means.

Alienation Clause—A provision in a security instrument that gives the lender the right to accelerate the loan if the borrower sells the property or transfers a significant interest in it without the lender's approval. Also called a due-on-sale clause.

All-Inclusive Trust Deed—A deed of trust used for wraparound financing.

Amortization—The gradual reduction of a debt through installment payments that include principal as well as interest.

Annual Percentage Rate (APR)—Under the Truth in Lending Act, a figure that expresses the relationship between a loan's total finance charge and loan amount as an annual percentage.

Anticipation, Principle of—An appraisal principle which holds that value is created by the expectation of benefits to be received in the future.

Anti-Deficiency Rules—Laws that prohibit a secured lender from suing the borrower for a deficiency judgment after foreclosure, in certain circumstances.

Appraisal—An expert's estimate of the value of a piece of real estate as of a particular date, based on a documented analysis of the property's features. Also called a valuation.

Appraiser—One who estimates the value of property, especially an expert qualified to do so by training and experience.

Appreciation—An increase in the value of an asset over time, as a result of economic forces; the opposite of depreciation.

APR—*See:* Annual Percentage Rate.

ARM—*See:* Adjustable-Rate Mortgage.

Arm's Length Transaction—A sale in which the buyer and the seller are unrelated parties with no preexisting personal or business relationship.

Asset—Anything of value owned by a person or other entity.

Assets, Liquid—Cash or other assets that can be readily turned into cash (liquidated), such as stock.

Assign—To transfer rights (especially contract rights) or interests to another.

Assignee—One to whom rights or interests have been assigned.

Assignment—A transfer of contract rights from one person to another.

Assignment of Contract and Deed—The instrument used to substitute a new vendor for the original vendor in a land contract.

Assignor—One who has assigned her rights or interests to another.

Assumption—When a buyer takes on personal responsibility for repayment of the seller's existing mortgage loan, becoming liable to the lender. The seller remains secondarily liable unless released by the lender.

Assumption Fee—A fee charged by the lender when a buyer assumes a seller's loan.

Assumptor—One who assumes a mortgage or deed of trust, usually when buying the property that secures the debt.

Audit—An examination and verification of records, particularly the financial accounts of a business or other organization.

Automated Underwriting (AU)—*See:* Underwriting, Automated.

Average Cost Pricing—Charging all borrowers who are approved for a particular type of loan the same interest rate and fees, without regard to the borrowers' varying degrees of creditworthiness. Also called par rate pricing. *Compare:* Risk-Based Pricing.

Bad Debt/Vacancy Factor—In the income approach to appraisal, a percentage deducted from a property's potential gross income, estimating the income that's likely to be lost because of vacancies and tenants who don't pay.

Balance Sheet—*See:* Financial Statement.

Balloon Mortgage—A mortgage loan (partially amortized or interest-only) that requires the borrower to make a balloon payment.

Balloon Payment—1. The payment of the remaining principal balance due at the end of the term of a partially amortized or interest-only loan; so called because it is much larger than the regular payments made during the loan term. 2. Any loan payment that is larger than the regular payments.

Balloon/Reset Mortgage—A loan with an initial term of only five or seven years; at the end of the term, the loan may be reset to the current market interest rate, or a balloon payment will be required.

Basis—A figure used in calculating a gain on the sale of real estate for federal income tax purposes. Also called cost basis.

Basis, Adjusted—A property owner's initial basis in the property, plus capital expenditures for improvements, and minus any allowable cost recovery (depreciation) deductions.

Basis, Initial—The amount of a property owner's original investment in the property; what it cost to acquire the property, which may include closing costs and certain other expenses, as well as the purchase price.

Bearer—Whoever has possession of a negotiable instrument.

Beneficiary—1. A person on whose behalf a trust is established and administered. 2. A person who receives money or property through a will. 3. In a deed of trust transaction, the lender. *Compare:* Mortgagee.

Bill of Sale—A document used to transfer title to personal property from one person to another.

Bi-Weekly Loan—A fixed-rate loan that requires a payment every two weeks instead of once a month, so that the borrower makes 26 half payments per year, the equivalent of 13 monthly payments.

Blanket Mortgage—A mortgage that encumbers more than one parcel of real property.

Bond—A certificate of indebtedness issued by a governmental body or a corporation; the bondholder typically receives a return in the form of periodic payments of interest until the principal is repaid in a lump sum.

Bonus—An extra payment, over and above what is strictly due; especially an extra payment an employer gives to an employee, as an incentive or in recognition of good performance.

Breach—Violation of an obligation, duty, or law; especially an unexcused failure to perform a contractual obligation.

Brokerage Fee—The commission or other compensation charged for a real estate broker's services.

Budget Mortgage—A mortgage with monthly payments that include a share of the property taxes and insurance, in addition to principal and interest. The tax and insurance portions are kept in an impound account maintained by the lender until payment is due.

Buydown—When the seller or a third party pays the lender a lump sum at closing to lower the interest rate charged to the buyer, either for the life of the loan (permanent buydown) or during the first years of the loan term (temporary buydown); essentially the same thing as paying discount points on the buyer's behalf.

Call Provision—*See:* Acceleration Clause.

Capital Expenditures—Money spent on property improvements and modifications that add to the property's value or prolong its life.

Capital Improvement—Any improvement to real property that is designed to become a permanent part of the property or that will have the effect of significantly prolonging the property's life.

Capitalization—Estimating a property's value by dividing its annual net income by a percentage that represents the rate of return an investor would expect from the property (the capitalization rate).

Capitalization Method—*See:* Income Approach to Value.

Carryback Loan—*See:* Purchase Money Loan.

Certificate of Deposit (CD)—A savings arrangement in which a depositor agrees to leave money on deposit for a specified period, or pay a penalty for early withdrawal.

Certificate of Eligibility—A document issued by the Department of Veterans Affairs, indicating a veteran's eligibility for a VA-guaranteed loan.

Certificate of Reasonable Value (CRV)—*See:* Notice of Value.

Certificate of Sale—The document that a purchaser of foreclosed property at a sheriff's sale is given instead of a deed; it is replaced with a sheriff's deed only after the statutory redemption period expires.

Charge-Off—When a creditor writes off a delinquent debt for tax purposes, because no payment has been received for six months or more and the debt will probably never be collected.

Charter—An instrument that grants a power or a right of franchise.

Chattel Mortgage—An instrument that makes personal property (chattels) security for a loan. In the U.S., the Uniform Commercial Code has replaced the chattel mortgage with the security agreement.

Closed Mortgage—A mortgage loan that cannot be paid off early.

Closing—The final stage in a real estate transaction, when the loan funds are disbursed, the seller is paid the purchase price, and the buyer receives the deed. Also called settlement.

Closing Costs—Expenses incurred in a transfer of real estate, aside from the purchase price; for example, the appraisal fee, title insurance premiums, brokerage fee, and transfer taxes. Also called settlement costs.

Closing Statement—*See:* Settlement Statement.

CMA—*See:* Competitive Market Analysis.

Co-Borrower—Someone (often a member of the borrower's family) who accepts responsibility for the repayment of a mortgage loan along with the primary borrower, to help the borrower qualify for the loan. Also called a co-mortgagor or cosigner.

Collateral—Property (personal or real) accepted by a lender as security for a loan. If the borrower fails to repay the loan, the lender has the right to keep or sell the collateral.

Commercial Bank—A financial institution that holds deposits and makes loans, which emphasizes commercial lending but also makes many residential mortgage loans. *Compare:* Investment Bank.

Commission—The compensation paid to a real estate broker for services in connection with a real estate transaction; usually a percentage of the sales price.

Commitment—A lender's promise to make a loan. A loan commitment may be either firm or conditional.

Commitment, Conditional—A lender's promise to make a loan if specified conditions are fulfilled.

Commitment, Firm—A lender's approval of a loan without any conditions.

Co-Mortgagor—*See:* Co-Borrower.

Comparables—In a sales comparison appraisal, properties similar to the subject property that have recently been sold; the appraiser uses the sales prices of the comparables as an indication of the value of the subject property.

Competition, Principle of—An appraisal principle which holds that profits tend to encourage competition, and excess profits tend to result in ruinous competition.

Competitive Market Analysis (CMA)—A real estate agent's estimate of the value of a listed home, based on the sales prices or listing prices of comparable homes.

Compound Interest—*See:* Interest, Compound.

Condition—A provision in an agreement that makes the parties' rights and obligations depend on the occurrence (or nonoccurrence) of a particular event. Also called a contingency clause.

Conditional Commitment—*See:* Commitment, Conditional.

Conforming Loan—A loan made in accordance with the underwriting criteria of the major secondary market agencies, Fannie Mae and Freddie Mac, and which therefore can be sold to those agencies without special negotiations. A loan that does not meet Fannie Mae or Freddie Mac standards is called a nonconforming loan.

Conforming Loan Limit—The maximum conventional loan amount that Fannie Mae and Freddie Mac will purchase.

Conformity, Principle of—An appraisal principle which holds that property achieves its maximum value when there is a reasonable degree of social and economic homogeneity in the neighborhood.

Consideration—Something of value given to induce another to enter into a contract. An agreement is not a legally binding contract unless the parties exchange consideration.

Construction Loan—A loan to finance the construction of a building; when construction is completed, it is replaced by a take-out loan. Also called an interim loan.

Consumer Price Index—An index that tracks changes in the cost of goods and services for a typical consumer. Formerly called the cost of living index.

Contingency Clause—*See:* Condition.

Contract Rate—*See:* Note Rate.

Contract Rent—The rent a property owner is currently receiving for the property. *Compare:* Economic Rent.

Contribution, Principle of—An appraisal principle which holds that the value of real property is greatest when the improvements produce the highest return commensurate with their cost. Some improvements add more to the property's value than they cost, and others cost more than they add.

Conventional Loan—An institutional loan that is not insured or guaranteed by a government agency.

Convertible ARM—An adjustable-rate mortgage that includes a conversion option.

Conversion Option—A provision in an adjustable-rate mortgage that gives the borrower the option of converting to a fixed interest rate at one or more specified points during the loan term.

Cosigner—*See:* Co-Borrower.

Cost, Replacement—In appraisal, the current cost of constructing a building with the same utility as the subject property, using modern materials and construction methods. *Compare:* Cost, Reproduction.

Cost, Reproduction—In appraisal, the cost of constructing a replica (an exact duplicate) of the subject property, using the same materials and construction methods that were originally used, but at current prices. *Compare:* Cost, Replacement.

Cost Approach to Value—One of the three main methods of appraisal (along with the income approach and the sales comparison approach), in which an estimate of the subject property's value is arrived at by estimating the cost of replacing the improvements, then deducting the estimated accrued depreciation and adding the estimated market value of the land. Also called the replacement cost method.

Cost Basis—*See:* Basis.

Cost Recovery Deductions—Tax deductions allowed to owners of income property and property used in a trade or business, for the cost of assets that will wear out and eventually have to be replaced. Also called depreciation deductions.

Coupon Rate—*See:* Note Rate.

Credit—On a settlement statement, a payment receivable (owed to one of the parties), as opposed to a debit, which is a payment due (owed by one of the parties).

Creditor—One who is owed a debt.

Creditor, Secured—A creditor with a lien on specific property, which enables her to foreclose and collect the debt from the sale proceeds if the debtor does not pay.

Credit Report—A report prepared by a credit reporting agency that outlines the credit history of an individual or entity, listing current and past debts and records of repayment.

Credit Score—A figure used in underwriting that encapsulates the likelihood that a loan applicant will default, calculated using a credit scoring model and the information from the applicant's credit report.

Credit Union—A type of financial institution that serves only the members of a particular group, such as a professional organization or a labor union. Credit unions make consumer loans, including residential mortgage loans.

CRV—*See:* Notice of Value.

Cure—To remedy a default, by paying money that is overdue or by fulfilling other obligations.

Debit—On a settlement statement, a payment owed by one of the parties.

Debtor—One who owes money to another.

Debt Investment—*See:* Investment, Debt.

Debt Service—The amount of money required to make the periodic payments of principal and interest on an amortized debt such as a mortgage.

Debt Service Ratio—*See:* Debt to Income Ratio.

Debt to Income Ratio—A figure used in underwriting, calculated by dividing total monthly obligations (including the housing expense and other debts) by monthly income. Also called a total obligations to income ratio or a total debt service ratio. *Compare:* Housing Expense to Income Ratio.

Deduction—An amount a taxpayer is allowed to subtract from his income before the tax on the income is calculated.

Deed in Lieu of Foreclosure—A deed given by a borrower to a lender, transferring title to the security property to the lender to satisfy the debt and avoid foreclosure.

Deed of Reconveyance—A document which acknowledges that a deed of trust has been paid in full, releasing the security property from the lien. *Compare:* Satisfaction of Mortgage.

Deed of Trust—A real property security instrument that is similar to a mortgage, but which gives a third party the power to foreclose and sell the property in the event of default. The parties are the grantor or trustor (the borrower), the beneficiary (the lender), and the trustee (the neutral third party).

Default—Failure to fulfill an obligation, duty, or promise, as when a borrower fails to make payments, or a tenant fails to pay rent.

Deferred Interest—*See:* Interest, Deferred.

Deferred Maintenance—Curable depreciation resulting from physical wear and tear.

Deficiency Judgment—A court judgment against a debtor requiring the debtor to pay the creditor the shortfall between the amount of the debt and the proceeds of the foreclosure sale.

Delivery Fee—*See:* Loan-Level Price Adjustment.

Demand—Desire to own, coupled with the ability to afford.

Demand Deposit—A deposit in a financial institution that the depositor can withdraw on demand (at any time, without notice), such as a deposit in a checking account. *Compare:* Time Deposit.

Deposit—Money that is offered as an indication of commitment or as a protection against default, and that must be refunded under certain circumstances; for example, a buyer's earnest money deposit or a tenant's security deposit.

Depreciation—A loss in value due to any cause.

Depreciation, Curable—Depreciation (resulting from deferred maintenance or functional obsolescence) that a prudent property owner would ordinarily correct, because the cost of correction could be recovered in the sales price when the property is sold.

Depreciation, Incurable—Depreciation that is either impossible to correct, or not economically feasible to correct, because the cost could not be recovered in the sales price when the property is sold.

Depreciation Deductions—*See:* Cost Recovery Deductions.

Direct Endorsement Lender—A lender authorized to underwrite its own FHA loan applications, rather than having to submit them to the FHA for approval.

Discount—1. In the origination of a loan, to charge discount points. 2. In the purchase of a loan, to pay less than the face value of the promissory note.

Discount Fee—*See:* Discount Points.

Discount Points—A fee (stated as a percentage of the loan amount) that a lender may charge at closing to increase its upfront yield on the loan. Also called a discount fee.

Discount Rate—The interest rate that a Federal Reserve Bank charges on short-term loans to member banks. *Compare:* Federal Funds Rate.

Disintegration—In a property's life cycle, the period of decline when the property's present economic usefulness is near an end and constant upkeep is necessary.

Disintermediation—When depositors withdraw their savings from financial institutions and put the money into other types of investments with higher yields.

Diversification—The practice of investing in a variety of different sectors of the economy, to make a portfolio safer.

Dividend—A share of a company's profits paid to a stockholder as a return on the investment.

Double-Entry Bookkeeping—An accounting technique in which an item is entered in the ledger twice, once as a credit and once as a debit; used for settlement statements.

Downpayment—The part of the purchase price of property that the buyer is not borrowing; the difference between the purchase price and the financing.

Due-on-Sale Clause—*See:* Alienation Clause.

Earnest Money—A deposit that a prospective buyer gives the seller when the purchase agreement is signed, as evidence of her good faith intention to complete the transaction. Also called a good faith deposit.

Economic Life—The period during which improved property yields a return over and above the rent due to the land itself; also called the useful life. *Compare:* Physical Life.

Economic Obsolescence—*See:* External Obsolescence.

Economic Rent—The rent a property could command in the current marketplace if it were available for lease today. Also called market rent. *Compare:* Contract Rent.

Effective Income—In FHA underwriting, the loan applicant's gross monthly income from all sources that can be expected to continue; the FHA equivalent of stable monthly income.

Elements of Comparison—In the sales comparison approach to appraisal, considerations taken into account in selecting comparables and comparing them to the subject property; they include the date of sale, location, physical characteristics, and terms of sale.

Encumber—To place a lien or other encumbrance against the title to a property.

Encumbrance—A nonpossessory interest in real property; a right or interest held by someone other than the property owner; it may be a lien, an easement, or a restrictive covenant.

Endorsement—When the payee of a negotiable instrument (such as a check or a promissory note) assigns the right to payment to another, usually by signing the back or the face of the instrument.

Entitlement—*See:* VA Entitlement.

Equal Credit Opportunity Act (ECOA)—A federal law prohibiting discrimination by lenders against loan applicants on the basis of race, color, religion, national origin, sex, marital status, age, or whether income comes from public assistance.

Equilibrium—In the life cycle of a property, a period of stability, during which the property undergoes little, if any, change.

Equitable Title—*See:* Title, Equitable.

Equity—1. The difference between a property's value and the liens against it; an owner's unencumbered interest in his property. 2. Fairness.

Equity Exchange—When a buyer gives a seller real or personal property in addition to or instead of cash for the purchase price.

Equity Stripping—A predatory loan practice in which a lender eats into a homeowner's equity by charging high fees for repeated and unnecessary refinancing.

Escalation Clause—A clause in a contract or mortgage that provides for payment or interest increases if specified events occur, such as a change in the property taxes or in the prime interest rate. Also called an escalator clause.

Escrow—A system in which the parties to a transaction can have a disinterested third party hold things of value (such as money or documents) until specified conditions have been fulfilled.

Escrow Agent—A third party who holds things of value on behalf of the parties to a transaction in an escrow arrangement.

Estoppel—A legal doctrine that prevents a person from asserting rights or facts that are inconsistent with her earlier conduct or statements, when someone else has taken action in reliance on that earlier conduct.

Estoppel Letter—A document signed by a lender when property is sold subject to an existing mortgage. It either acknowledges the transfer and waives the right to accelerate the loan pursuant to a due-on-sale clause, or else merely states the balance due and the status of the loan.

Exclusion of Gain on Sale of Home—Under the federal income tax code, a gain of up to $250,000 (or $500,000 for a married couple filing jointly) on the sale of a principal residence may be excluded from taxation.

Execute—1. To sign an instrument and take any other steps (such as acknowledgment) that may be necessary to its validity. 2. To perform or complete.

Execution, Order of—A court order directing a public officer (such as the sheriff) to seize and sell property to satisfy a debt; also called a writ of execution.

Expenses, Fixed—Recurring property expenses that have to be paid at set times, such as property taxes and insurance.

Expenses, Maintenance—Cleaning, supplies, utilities, tenant services, and administrative costs for income-producing property.

Expenses, Operating—For income-producing property, the fixed expenses, maintenance expenses, and reserves for replacement; does not include debt service.

Expenses, Variable—Expenses incurred in connection with property that do not occur on a set schedule, such as the cost of repairing a roof damaged in a storm.

External Obsolescence—Depreciation resulting from factors outside the property itself and outside the owner's control. Also called economic obsolescence.

Fair Housing Act—A federal law prohibiting discrimination in residential property transactions, including lending, on the basis of race, color, national origin, religion, sex, disability, or familial status.

Fannie Mae—The Federal National Mortgage Association (FNMA), a government-sponsored enterprise supervised by the Federal Housing Finance Agency; one of the three major secondary market agencies, along with Freddie Mac and Ginnie Mae.

Farmers Home Administration (FmHA)— *See:* Rural Housing Service.

Federal Deficit—A shortfall in funds that occurs when the federal government spends more money than it collects in a particular year.

Federal Funds Rate—The interest rate that banks charge one another for overnight loans; a target for the rate is set by the Federal Reserve. *Compare:* Discount Rate.

Federal Home Loan Mortgage Corporation (FHLMC)—*See:* Freddie Mac.

Federal Housing Administration (FHA)—An agency within the Department of Housing and Urban Development that provides mortgage insurance to encourage lenders to make more affordable home loans.

Federal Housing Finance Agency—An independent federal agency that oversees Fannie Mae and Freddie Mac.

Federal National Mortgage Association (FNMA)—*See:* Fannie Mae.

Federal Open Market Committee—A board that makes decisions regarding the Federal Reserve's open market operations (its purchase and sale of government securities).

Federal Reserve Bank—An entity that performs a variety of functions for commercial banks in one of the 12 Federal Reserve Districts.

Federal Reserve Board—The seven-member Board of Governors that controls the Federal Reserve System and sets monetary policy.

Federal Reserve System—The system that regulates commercial banks and implements U.S. monetary policy. Often referred to as "the Fed."

Fee Packing—A predatory loan practice in which a lender charges points or processing fees that are higher than usual and not justified by the services provided.

FHA—*See:* Federal Housing Administration.

FHA-Insured Loan—A loan made by an institutional lender with mortgage insurance provided by the Federal Housing Administration, protecting the lender against losses due to borrower default.

FHLMC—*See:* Freddie Mac.

FICO Score—A credit score calculated using the credit scoring model developed by Fair Isaac and Company; the type of credit score most widely used in residential mortgage lending.

Finance Charge—Any charge a borrower is assessed, directly or indirectly, in connection with a loan. *See also:* Total Finance Charge.

Financial Institutions Reform, Recovery & Enforcement Act (FIRREA)—A federal law enacted in 1989 in response to the savings and loan crisis; it reorganized the federal agencies that oversee financial institutions.

Financial Statement—A summary of facts showing the financial condition of an individual or a business, including a detailed list of assets and liabilities. Also called a balance sheet.

Financing Statement—A brief instrument that is recorded to establish and give public notice of a creditor's security interest in an item of personal property.

FIRREA—*See:* Financial Institutions Reform, Recovery, & Enforcement Act.

First Lien Position—The position of lien priority held by a mortgage or deed of trust that has higher priority than any other mortgage or deed of trust against the property.

First Mortgage—The mortgage (or deed of trust) against a property that has first lien position; the one with higher lien priority than any other mortgage against that property.

Fiscal Policy—Actions taken by the federal government to raise revenue through taxation, spend tax revenues, and finance budget deficits. *Compare:* Monetary Policy.

Fiscal Year—Any twelve-month period used as a business year for accounting, tax, and other financial purposes, as opposed to a calendar year. For example, the federal government's fiscal year runs from October 1 through September 30.

Fixed-Rate Loan—A mortgage loan in which the lender charges an unchanging interest rate throughout the loan term. *Compare:* Adjustable-Rate Mortgage.

Fixture—An item that was originally personal property, but which has been attached to or closely associated with real property in such a way that it has legally become part of the real property.

Flip—*See:* Property Flipping.

FmHA—*See:* Rural Housing Service.

Foreclosure—When a lienholder forces property to be sold, so the unpaid debt secured by the lien can be satisfied from the sale proceeds.

Foreclosure, Judicial—A court-supervised foreclosure proceeding that begins when a mortgagee or other lienholder files a lawsuit against a property owner who has defaulted on the debt secured by the mortgage or lien.

Foreclosure, Nonjudicial—Foreclosure by a trustee pursuant to the power of sale clause in a deed of trust.

Forfeiture—Loss of a right or something of value as a result of failure to perform an obligation or fulfill a condition.

FNMA—*See:* Fannie Mae.

Freddie Mac—The Federal Home Loan Mortgage Corporation (FHLMC), a government-sponsored enterprise supervised by the Federal Housing Finance Agency; one of the major secondary market agencies, along with Fannie Mae and Ginnie Mae.

Free and Clear Ownership—Ownership of real property completely free of any mortgage liens.

Fully Amortized Loan—A loan structured so that regular installment payments pay off all of the principal and interest owed by the end of the loan term. *Compare:* Interest-Only Loan; Partially Amortized Loan.

Functional Obsolescence—Depreciation of property resulting from functional inadequacies, such as those caused by poor or outmoded design.

Funding Fee—A charge paid by a VA borrower at closing, which the lender submits to the VA.

Garnishment—A legal process by which a creditor gains access to a debtor's funds or personal property held by a third party. For example, if a debtor's wages are garnished, the employer is required to turn over part of each paycheck to the creditor.

Gift Funds—Money given (usually by a family member) to a buyer who otherwise would not have enough cash to close the transaction.

Gift Letter—A document in which a donor of gift funds states that the money given is not a loan and does not have to be repaid; required by the lender when the borrower intends to use gift funds as part of the downpayment or closing costs.

Ginnie Mae—The Government National Mortgage Association (GNMA), a government agency within HUD; one of the major secondary market agencies, along with Fannie Mae and Freddie Mac.

GNMA—*See:* Ginnie Mae.

Good Faith Deposit—*See:* Earnest Money.

Good Faith Estimate of Closing Costs—A disclosure statement that lenders are required to give loan applicants in transactions subject to the Real Estate Settlement Procedures Act.

Government-Sponsored Enterprise (GSE)—An entity that is privately owned and functions as a private corporation, but is created, chartered, and supervised by the government.

Graduated Payment Mortgage (GPM)—A loan in which the payments are increased periodically during the first years of the loan term, usually according to a fixed schedule.

Grantor—1. In a deed of trust transaction, the borrower, also called the trustor. 2. One who deeds title to real property to another.

Gross Income—An individual's income before payroll taxes have been deducted.

Gross Income Multiplier (GIM)—A figure used to estimate the value of residential rental property, determined by dividing the sales price by the rental income. Also called a gross rent multiplier.

Growing Equity Mortgage (GEM)—A fixed-rate loan with annual payment increases that are used to reduce the principal balance, so that the loan is paid off much more quickly than it would be with ordinary level payments.

Guarantor—*See:* Guaranty.

Guaranty—An arrangement in which one party (the guarantor) accepts liability to another party for the payment of a third party's obligations, if the third party fails to pay them. *See also:* Loan Guaranty; VA Guaranty Amount.

Hard Money Mortgage—A mortgage given to a lender in exchange for cash, as opposed to one given in exchange for credit.

Hazard Insurance—Insurance against damage to property caused by fire, flood, or other mishaps. Also called casualty insurance.

HECM—*See:* Reverse Equity Mortgage.

Highest and Best Use—The use which, at the time of appraisal, is most likely to produce the greatest net return from the property over a given period of time.

HOA—*See:* Homeowners Association.

HOEPA—*See:* Home Ownership and Equity Protection Act.

Holder in Due Course (HDC)—A third party purchaser of a promissory note who purchased the note for value and in good faith. An HDC is entitled to payment by the maker of the note, even if the maker has a defense that would defeat a claim by the original payee.

Home Equity Conversion Mortgage—*See:* Reverse Equity Mortgage.

Home Equity Loan—A loan obtained by the borrower using a home he already owns as collateral.

Home Mortgage Disclosure Act—A federal law requiring large institutional lenders to submit reports concerning the residential loans they've originated or purchased from other lenders; regulators use the reports to detect redlining.

Home Mortgage Interest Deduction—The federal income tax code allows a taxpayer to deduct interest paid on mortgage loans secured by her home or homes, up to certain limits.

Homeowners Association (HOA)—A nonprofit association made up of all of the homeowners in a subdivision, which is responsible for enforcing the restrictive covenants and managing other community affairs.

Homeowner's Insurance—Insurance that covers loss of or damage to a homeowner's personal property and real property, and also provides some liability protection.

Home Ownership and Equity Protection Act (HOEPA)—A federal law concerning high-cost home equity loans that requires certain disclosures and prohibits certain predatory lending practices.

Housing Expense to Income Ratio—A figure used in underwriting, calculated by dividing the monthly housing expense by monthly income. *Compare:* Debt to Income Ratio.

HUD—The Department of Housing and Urban Development, a cabinet-level department of the federal government that includes agencies such as the FHA and Ginnie Mae.

Hybrid ARM—An adjustable-rate mortgage with an initial fixed-rate period; for example, a 3/1 hybrid ARM has a fixed interest rate for the first three years and is subject to annual rate adjustments after that.

Hypothecation—Making property security for a loan by transferring title to the lender without surrendering possession. *Compare:* Pledge.

Impound Account—An escrow account maintained by a lender for paying property taxes and insurance premiums for the security property; the lender requires the borrower to make regular deposits, and pays the expenses out of the account when they come due. Also called a reserve account.

Improvements—Man-made additions to real property.

Income Approach to Value—A method of appraisal in which an estimate of the subject property's value is based on the net income it produces. Also called the income method or the capitalization method.

Income Property—Property that generates rent or other income for the owner, such as an apartment building.

Income Ratio—A figure used in underwriting to determine whether a loan applicant's income is adequate for the monthly payments on the proposed loan; a percentage calculated by dividing monthly housing expense or total monthly debt payments by monthly income.

Index—A published statistical report that indicates changes in the cost of money (market interest rates), used as the basis for interest rate adjustments in an ARM.

Inflation—A trend of general price increases throughout the economy.

Installment Land Contract—*See:* Land Contract.

Installment Note—*See:* Note, Installment.

Institutional Lender—A bank, savings and loan, or similar regulated lending institution; in some contexts, the term also includes private companies that are in the business of loaning money (such as mortgage companies), in contrast to individual private lenders.

Institutional Loan—A loan made by an institutional lender.

Instrument—A legal document; especially one that transfers title, creates a lien, or establishes a right to payment.

Integration—In a property's life cycle, the earliest stage, when the property is being developed. Also called the development stage.

Interest—A periodic charge a lender requires a borrower to pay for the temporary use of the borrowed funds, until the loan is repaid; usually expressed as an annual percentage of the principal balance. *Compare:* Principal.

Interest, Compound—Interest calculated as a percentage of both the principal and any accumulated interest that has not yet been paid. *Compare:* Interest, Simple.

Interest, Deferred—Interest that accumulates over the course of one or more payment periods but is not payable until some later time; a feature of some adjustable-rate loans.

Interest, Interim—*See:* Interest, Prepaid.

Interest, Prepaid—Interest on a new loan that must be paid at closing; it covers the interest that will accrue for the month in which the loan term begins. Also called interim interest.

Interest, Simple—Interest calculated as a percentage of the principal balance only. *Compare:* Interest, Compound.

Interest-Only Loan—A loan that requires only payments of the interest due (with no principal) during the loan term, or during a specified period at the beginning of the loan term. Sometimes referred to as an I/O Loan. *Compare:* Fully Amortized Loan; Partially Amortized Loan.

Interest Rate Cap—A provision in an ARM that limits how much the interest rate may be increased (and in some cases, decreased) during a single rate adjustment period or over the life of the loan.

Interest Rate Risk—The risk that, after a loan is made for a specified term at a fixed interest rate, market interest rates will rise and the lender will miss the opportunity to invest the loaned funds at a higher rate.

Interest Rates, Market—The rates that are generally being paid on particular types of investments or charged for particular types of loans under current economic conditions.

Interest Shortfall—When more interest accrues on a loan than the lender collects during a particular period. This can occur with ARMs that have certain features.

Interim Loan—*See:* Construction Loan.

Intermediary—1. An individual or entity who originates and/or services loans on behalf of another. 2. Any type of go-between.

Investment—When a person (an investor) makes a sum of money (investment capital) available for use by another person or entity, in the expectation that it will generate a return (a profit) for the investor.

Investment, Debt—An investment in which temporary use of an investor's funds is exchanged for interest payments, under an agreement that requires repayment of the funds or allows withdrawal of the funds.

Investment, Liquid—An investment that can be quickly and easily converted into cash.

Investment, Ownership—An investment in which the investor's funds are used to purchase an asset or a property interest in an asset.

Investment, Return of—*See:* Return of Investment.

Investment, Return on—*See:* Return on Investment.

Investment Bank—A firm that handles corporate finances, arranges for the issuance of government and corporate bonds, and provides investment advice to clients. Also called a securities firm or stock brokerage. *Compare:* Commercial Bank.

Investment Capital—Accumulated wealth made available to fund business enterprises or other ventures or projects.

Investor Loan—A loan for the purchase of residential property that will be rented to tenants rather than owner-occupied.

I/O Loan—*See:* Interest-Only Loan.

Judicial Foreclosure—*See:* Foreclosure, Judicial.

Jumbo Loan—A conventional loan with a loan amount that exceeds the conforming loan limit set by Fannie Mae and Freddie Mac.

Junior Lienholder—A secured creditor whose lien is lower in priority than another lien against the same property.

Junior Mortgage—A mortgage that has lower lien priority than another mortgage against the same property. Also called a second mortgage or secondary mortgage.

Land Contract—A contract for the sale of property in which the buyer (vendee) pays the seller (vendor) in installments, taking possession of the property immediately but not taking title until the purchase price has been paid in full. Also called a contract for deed, conditional sales contract, installment sales contract, or real estate contract.

Law of Supply and Demand—*See:* Supply and Demand, Law of.

Lease—A contract in which one party (the tenant) pays the other (the landlord) rent in exchange for the possession of real estate.

Lease/Option—A lease that includes an option to purchase the leased property during the term of the lease.

Lease/Purchase—A variation on the lease/option, in which the parties sign a purchase contract (instead of an option) and the prospective buyer leases the property for an extended period before closing.

Legal Title—*See:* Title, Legal.

Level Payment Loan—A loan that is repaid with equal periodic (usually monthly) payments; the payment amount does not change during the loan term. *Compare:* Graduated Payment Mortgage; Growing Equity Mortgage.

Leverage—The effective use of borrowed money to finance an investment, such as a real estate purchase.

Liability—1. A debt or obligation. 2. Legal responsibility.

Liable—Legally responsible.

Lien—A nonpossessory interest in real property giving the lienholder the right to foreclose if the property owner does not pay a debt owed to the lienholder; a financial encumbrance on the owner's title.

Lienholder—A secured creditor who has a lien against a debtor's real property.

Lien Priority—The order in which liens will be paid off out of the proceeds of a foreclosure sale.

Lien Theory—The legal theory holding that a mortgage or a deed of trust does not involve a transfer of title to the lender, but merely creates a lien against the borrower's property in the lender's favor. *Compare:* Title Theory.

Liquid Investment—*See:* Investment, Liquid.

Listing—A contract between a real estate broker and a seller, in which the seller appoints the broker as his agent in order to put the property up for sale.

LLPA—*See:* Loan-Level Price Adjustment.

Loan Correspondent—An intermediary who originates or arranges loans on behalf of a wholesale lender or a large investor, and may also service the loans.

Loan Fee—Any one-time fee that a lender charges a borrower at closing for making the loan (or for making it on certain terms), such as an origination fee, discount points, a loan-level price adjustment, or an assumption fee; usually a percentage of the loan amount.

Loan Guaranty—An arrangement in which a third party guarantor accepts secondary liability for a loan and will reimburse the lender for losses resulting from the borrower's default.

Loan-Level Price Adjustment (LLPA)—A loan fee charged in a transaction that involves a riskier borrower, type of loan, or type of property, to compensate for the additional risk. Also called a delivery fee.

Loan Officer—A loan originator who works for a particular lender. *Compare*: Mortgage Broker.

Loan Origination—The process of making a new loan: processing the application, deciding whether to approve or reject it, and funding the loan if approved. *Compare:* Loan Servicing.

Loan Origination Fee—A fee charged by a lender upon making a new loan, intended to cover the administrative costs involved. Also called an origination fee or a loan fee.

Loan Originator—The person who helps prospective borrowers apply for a loan; either a loan officer (who works for a particular lender) or a mortgage broker (who arranges loans with more than one lender).

Loan Servicing—Administering a loan after it has been made; collecting the payments, keeping payment records, and handling defaults. *Compare:* Loan Origination.

Loan Term—*See:* Repayment Period.

Loan Workout—When a lender adjusts a loan's payment schedule or modifies the loan terms to help the borrower avoid foreclosure.

Loan-to-Value Ratio (LTV)—The relationship between the loan amount and either the sales price or the appraised value of the property (whichever is less), expressed as a percentage; the loan amount divided by the sales price or the appraised value.

Lock-In—When a lender guarantees a loan applicant a particular interest rate if the transaction closes within a specified period.

Lock-In Clause—A clause in a promissory note or land contract that prohibits prepayment before a specified date, or prohibits it altogether.

LTV—*See:* Loan-to-Value Ratio.

Low Appraisal—An appraisal with a value estimate lower than the agreed-upon sales price, which may affect financing and lead to the termination of the transaction.

Maker—In a promissory note, the party who promises to pay; the debtor or borrower. *Compare:* Payee.

Margin—The difference between an ARM's index rate and the interest rate charged on the loan.

Market Data Approach—*See:* Sales Comparison Approach.

Market Interest Rates—*See:* Interest Rates, Market.

Market Price—The price for which a property actually sold; the final sales price.

Market Value—The most probable price a property should sell for if it is sold under normal conditions and the buyer and seller are typically motivated; also called objective value.

MBS—*See:* Securities, Mortgage-Backed.

Minimum Cash Investment—The minimum downpayment required for an FHA-insured loan.

Minimum Property Requirements—A lender's requirements concerning the physical condition of a building, which must be met before a loan can be approved.

MIP—Mortgage insurance premium. Most often used to refer to the fee charged for FHA insurance coverage. The initial FHA premium is referred to as the UFMIP (upfront MIP) or the OTMIP (one-time MIP).

MMI—The Mutual Mortgage Insurance program, the formal name of the FHA insurance program. Also, FHA mortgage insurance premiums are sometimes called the MMI.

Monetary Policy—Actions taken by the Federal Reserve to control the money supply and the cost of borrowing money, to keep the economy running smoothly. *Compare:* Fiscal Policy.

Mortgage—1. An instrument creating a voluntary lien on a property to secure repayment of a debt; the two parties involved are the mortgagor (borrower) and the mortgagee (lender). 2. A mortgage loan.

Mortgage-Backed Securities—*See:* Securities, Mortgage-Backed.

Mortgage Banker—*See:* Mortgage Company.

Mortgage Broker—An intermediary who brings real estate lenders and borrowers together and negotiates loan agreements between them; a loan originator who doesn't work for a particular lender and may help borrowers apply to a number of different lenders. *Compare:* Loan Officer.

Mortgage Company—A type of real estate lender that originates residential mortgage loans on behalf of large investors or for sale on the secondary market, and may also service the loans; not a depository institution. Also called a mortgage banking company or a mortgage banker.

Mortgagee—The one who is given a mortgage by the mortgagor; the lender.

Mortgage Insurance—Insurance coverage protecting a mortgage lender against losses resulting from default and foreclosure.

Mortgage Loan—A loan secured by a mortgage or a deed of trust against property owned by the borrower.

Mortgage Payment Cap—A provision in an ARM that limits the amount the monthly payment can be increased, either during a given period, or over the entire life of the loan.

Mortgaging Clause—A clause in a mortgage that describes the security interest given to the mortgagee.

Mortgagor—A property owner (usually a borrower) who gives a mortgage against the property to another (usually a lender) as security for payment of an obligation.

MPRs—*See:* Minimum Property Requirements.

Mutual Fund—A company that invests its capital in a diversified portfolio of securities on behalf of its investors, who own shares in the fund.

Mutual Savings Bank—A savings bank originally organized as a mutual company, owned by and operated for the benefit of its depositors (as opposed to stockholders).

Negative Amortization—When deferred interest on an adjustable-rate loan is added to the principal balance, increasing the amount owed.

Negative Amortization Cap—In an ARM, a limit on the amount of deferred interest that can be added to the principal balance.

Negotiable Instrument—An instrument establishing a right to payment, which is freely transferable from one person to another. It can be a check, a promissory note, a bond, a draft, or stock.

Net Equity—The market value of a property, minus any liens against the property and all anticipated selling expenses.

Net Worth—An individual's personal financial assets, minus total personal liabilities.

Nonconforming Loan—A loan that does not meet underwriting guidelines set by Fannie Mae or Freddie Mac and therefore can't be sold to those agencies, except by special arrangement.

Nonjudicial Foreclosure—*See:* Foreclosure, Nonjudicial.

Note—*See:* Note, Promissory.

Note, Demand—A promissory note that is due whenever the holder of the note demands payment.

Note, Installment—A promissory note that calls for regular payments of principal and interest until the debt is paid off; used for an amortized loan.

Note, Joint—A promissory note signed by two or more persons with equal liability for payment.

Note, Promissory—A written, legally binding promise to repay a debt; may or may not be a negotiable instrument.

Note, Straight—A promissory note that calls for regular payments of interest only.

Note Rate—The interest rate specified in a loan's promissory note. Also called the coupon rate or contract rate.

Notice of Default—A notice sent by a lender (mortgagee or deed of trust beneficiary) to the borrower, informing the borrower that she has breached the terms of the loan agreement and warning that the lender is going to begin the foreclosure process.

Notice of Sale—A notice stating that foreclosure proceedings have been commenced against a property.

Notice of Value (NOV)—A document issued by the Department of Veterans Affairs, setting forth a property's current market value, based on a VA-approved appraisal. Formerly called a Certificate of Reasonable Value (CRV).

NOV—*See:* Notice of Value.

Obligatory Advances—Disbursements of construction loan funds that the lender is obliged to make (by prior agreement with the borrower) when the borrower has completed certain phases of construction.

Obsolescence—*See:* External Obsolescence; Functional Obsolescence.

Open End Loan—A loan that permits the borrower to reborrow the money he has repaid on the principal, usually up to the original loan amount, without executing a new loan agreement; similar to a line of credit.

Open Market Operations—The purchase and sale of government securities by the Federal Reserve to adjust the money supply; purchases increase and sales reduce the amount of money in circulation.

Option—A contract that gives one party the right to do something (such as purchase a property or renew a lease), without obligating her to do it.

Optionee—The person to whom an option is given.

Option Money—The consideration paid by a buyer/optionee that makes an option to purchase binding on the seller/optionor.

Optionor—The person who gives an option to the optionee.

Option to Purchase—An option giving the optionee the right to buy property owned by the optionor at an agreed price during a specified period.

Origination—*See:* Loan Origination.

OTMIP—*See:* MIP.

Overimprovement—An improvement that is more expensive than the value of the land justifies.

Ownership Investment—*See:* Investment, Ownership.

Package Mortgage—A mortgage secured by items of personal property (such as appliances) in addition to the real property.

Par Rate Pricing—*See:* Average Cost Pricing.

Partial Reconveyance—*See:* Partial Release Clause.

Partial Release Clause—A clause in a security instrument allowing one or more of the parcels of property under a blanket lien to be released from the lien while other parcels remain subject to it. Also called a partial reconveyance clause (in a deed of trust) or a partial satisfaction clause (in a mortgage).

Partial Satisfaction—*See:* Partial Release Clause.

Partially Amortized Loan—A loan with monthly payments that include both principal and interest, but aren't sufficient to fully pay off the loan balance by the end of the loan term. *Compare:* Fully Amortized Loan; Interest-Only Loan.

Participation Loan—A loan that gives the lender a share of the earnings generated by the property, usually in addition to interest payments on the principal; the lender may also participate by becoming a part owner of the property.

Payee—In a promissory note, the party who is entitled to be paid; the creditor or lender. *Compare:* Maker.

Payment Adjustment Period—The minimum interval between adjustments of the monthly payment amount on an ARM.

Permanent Buydown—*See:* Buydown.

Personal Property—Any property that is not real property; movable property not affixed to land. Also called chattels or personalty.

Physical Life—An estimate of the time a building will remain structurally sound and capable of being used. *Compare:* Economic Life.

Piggyback Loan—Secondary financing used to avoid the payment of private mortgage insurance by keeping the primary loan's loan-to-value ratio at 80% or less, or used to avoid the higher interest rate a jumbo loan would require.

PITI Payment—A mortgage borrower's full monthly payment, including principal, interest, property taxes, and hazard or homeowner's insurance, and also, if applicable, mortgage insurance and homeowners association dues.

Pledge—When a debtor transfers possession of property to the creditor as security for repayment of the debt, as when an item of personal property is pawned. *Compare:* Hypothecation.

PMI—*See:* Private Mortgage Insurance.

Point—One point is one percent of the loan amount.

Points—1. Discount points. 2. All of the loan fees paid to a lender at closing; for example, the origination fee as well as discount points.

Portfolio—The collection of investments and cash reserves that are held by an investor.

Portfolio Loan—A mortgage loan that the lender keeps in its own investment portfolio until the loan is repaid (as opposed to selling it on the secondary market).

Power of Sale—A provision in a deed of trust that gives the trustee the right to foreclose nonjudicially (sell the property without court supervision) in the event of default.

Preapproval—Formal loan approval (based on a full evaluation of a prospective buyer's creditworthiness, including verification of income and assets) given before the buyer has chosen property to purchase, establishing the maximum loan amount that the lender is willing to provide. *Compare:* Prequalification.

Predatory Lending—Lending practices that unscrupulous lenders and mortgage brokers use to take advantage of unsophisticated borrowers for their own profit.

Prepayment—Paying off part or all of a loan before payment is due.

Prepayment Penalty—A penalty some lenders charge a borrower who prepays a loan, to compensate for the lost interest that the lender would have received if the borrower had continued paying off the loan over its entire term.

Prepayment Provision—A clause in a loan agreement allowing the lender to charge the borrower a prepayment penalty.

Prepayment Risk—The risk that a loan will be paid off sooner than expected, reducing the lender's anticipated yield.

Prequalification—An informal evaluation of a prospective buyer's financial situation, performed by a lender or a real estate agent, to estimate the maximum amount the buyer can afford to spend on a home. *Compare*: Preapproval.

Primary Market—The market in which real estate loans are originated, where lenders make loans to borrowers. *Compare:* Secondary Market.

Prime Rate—The interest rate a bank charges its most creditworthy customers.

Principal—1. The original amount of a loan, or the remainder of that amount after part of it has been paid. *Compare:* Interest. 2. The person an agent is representing. 3. One of the parties to a transaction (such as a buyer or a seller), as opposed to those who are involved in the transaction as agents or employees (such as a real estate broker or an escrow agent).

Principal Residence Property—Real property that is the owner's main dwelling. Under the federal income tax laws, a taxpayer can only have one principal residence at a time.

Priority—*See:* Lien Priority.

Private Mortgage Insurance (PMI)—Mortgage insurance provided by a private insurance company instead of a government agency; required for conforming conventional loans with loan-to-value ratios over 80%.

Progression, Principle of—An appraisal principle which holds that a property of lesser value tends to be worth more when it is located in an area with properties of greater value than it would be if located elsewhere. The opposite of the principle of regression.

Promissory Note—*See:* Note, Promissory.

Property Flipping—1. Reselling property at a substantial profit soon after buying it. 2. Buying property at a discount (because the seller needs a quick sale or is unaware of the property's true value) and then rapidly reselling it to an unsophisticated buyer for an inflated price.

Proration—The process of dividing or allocating something (especially a sum of money or an expense) proportionately, according to time, interest, or benefit.

Purchase Agreement—A contract in which a seller promises to convey title to real property to a buyer in exchange for the purchase price. Also called a purchase and sale agreement, earnest money agreement, deposit receipt, sales contract, purchase contract, or contract of sale.

Purchase Money Loan—1. Generally, any loan used to purchase the property that secures the loan. 2. More narrowly, a loan given to a buyer by a seller in a seller-financed transaction; also called a carryback loan.

Purchaser's Assignment of Contract and Deed—The instrument used to assign the vendee's equitable interest in a contract to another.

Qualifying—*See:* Underwriting.

Qualifying Standards—The rules (concerning credit reputation, income, net worth, loan-to-value ratios, etc.) that are applied in the underwriting process to determine whether a loan should be approved. Also called underwriting standards.

Piggyback loan—Secondary financing used to avoid the payment of private mortgage insurance by keeping the primary loan's loan-to-value ratio at 80% or less, or used to avoid the higher interest rate a jumbo loan would require.

Rate Adjustment Period—The minimum interval between adjustments of an ARM's interest rate.

Real Estate Contract—*See:* Land Contract.

Real Estate Cycles—Ups and downs in the level of activity in a real estate market, where a boom may be followed by a slump, or vice versa.

Real Estate Investment Trust (REIT)—A real estate investment business that is organized as a trust and receives tax benefits in exchange for compliance with certain rules.

Real Estate Settlement Procedures Act (RESPA)—A federal law that requires lenders to disclose certain information about closing costs to loan applicants.

Reamortization—Recalculating the monthly payment amount for a loan, either because the loan term has been changed or because the loan balance has increased (due to negative amortization). Also called recasting the loan.

Recapture—*See:* Return of Investment.

Recasting—*See:* Reamortization.

Reconciliation—The final step in an appraisal, when the appraiser assembles and interprets the data in order to arrive at a final value estimate. Also called correlation.

Reconveyance—*See:* Deed of Reconveyance.

Redeem—*See:* Redemption.

Redemption—The right of a defaulting borrower to avoid losing his property to foreclosure by paying the full amount of the debt, plus costs. This is called redeeming the property.

Redemption, Equitable Right of—In a judicial foreclosure, the mortgagor's (borrower's) right to redeem the property before the sheriff's sale takes place.

Redemption, Statutory Right of—In a judicial foreclosure, the mortgagor's (borrower's) right to redeem the property during a specified period following the sheriff's sale.

Redlining—When a lender refuses to make loans secured by property in a certain neighborhood because of the racial or ethnic composition of the neighborhood, in violation of fair lending laws.

Refinancing—Obtaining a new mortgage loan that will be used to pay off an existing mortgage on the same property.

Regression, Principle of—An appraisal principle which holds that a valuable property surrounded by properties of lesser value tends to be worth less than it would be worth in a different location; the opposite of the principle of progression.

Regulation Z—The Federal Reserve Board's regulation that implements the Truth in Lending Act.

Reinstatement—The right of a defaulting borrower to prevent foreclosure by curing the default (paying the delinquent amount, plus costs). The loan is reinstated and repayment resumes.

Release—1. To give up a legal right. 2. A document in which a legal right is given up.

Rent—A tenant's payment to a landlord in exchange for the possession and use of the leased property.

Rent Credit Provision—A provision in a lease/option or lease/purchase contract that allows part of the rent paid by the tenant to be applied to the purchase of the property.

Repayment Period—The number of years a borrower is given to repay a loan, usually with regularly scheduled installment payments. Also called the loan term.

Replacement Cost—*See:* Cost, Replacement.

Replacement Cost Method—*See:* Cost Approach to Value.

Request for Reconsideration of Value—A request that a real estate agent submits to a lender after a low appraisal, asking the lender to consider a higher value for the property based on evidence provided by different comparables than the ones the appraiser selected.

Reserve Account—*See:* Impound Account.

Reserve Requirements—The Federal Reserve requires commercial banks to hold a certain portion of their deposits on reserve for immediate withdrawal by depositors.

Reserves—Cash or other liquid assets that a borrower will have left over after closing (after making the downpayment and paying the closing costs) and could use to pay the mortgage in the event of a financial emergency.

Reserves for Replacement—For income-producing property, allowances set aside on a regular basis to pay for the replacement of structures and equipment that will eventually wear out.

Residual Income—The amount of income that an applicant for a VA loan has left over after taxes, recurring obligations, and the proposed housing expense have been deducted from her gross monthly income.

RESPA—*See:* Real Estate Settlement Procedures Act.

Retail Lending—Loan transactions in which the borrower applies directly to the lender, rather than to a loan correspondent or mortgage broker. *Compare:* Wholesale Lending.

Return of Investment—When an investment generates enough money for the investor to replace the amount she invested in it. Also called recapture.

Return on Investment—The profit an investment generates for an investor, over and above the amount of money she invested in it.

Reverse Equity Mortgage—An arrangement in which a homeowner mortgages her home to a lender in exchange for a monthly payment from the lender. Also called a home equity conversion mortgage (HECM).

RHS—*See:* Rural Housing Service.

Risk Analysis—*See:* Underwriting.

Risk-Based Loan Pricing—Charging borrowers different interest rates and loan fees based on their creditworthiness. *Compare:* Average Cost Pricing.

Rural Housing Service—A federal agency within the Department of Agriculture that subsidizes or guarantees loans for the purchase, development, or rehabilitation of property located in rural areas.

Sale-Leaseback—A financing arrangement in which the owner of industrial or commercial property sells the property and leases it back from the buyer, instead of mortgaging the property in exchange for a loan.

Sales Comparison Approach to Value—A method of appraisal in which the sales prices of comparable properties are used to estimate the value of the subject property. Also called the sales comparison method or the market data approach.

Satisfaction of Mortgage—A document which acknowledges that a mortgage has been paid in full, releasing the security property from the mortgage lien. *Compare:* Deed of Reconveyance.

Savings and Loan Association—*See:* Thrift Institution.

Savings Bank—*See:* Thrift Institution.

Seasoned Loan—A loan with an established record of timely payment by the borrower.

Second Mortgage—A mortgage that does not have first lien position. Also called a junior mortgage.

Secondary Financing—Money that is borrowed to pay part of the required downpayment or closing costs for a first loan, and that is secured by the same property as the first loan.

Secondary Liability—Liability that arises only in the event that the person who has primary liability for a debt fails to pay it.

Secondary Market—The market in which investors (including Fannie Mae, Freddie Mac, and Ginnie Mae) purchase real estate loans from lenders. *Compare:* Primary Market.

Secondary Market Agency—One of the three government-created entities that purchase loans and issue mortgage-backed securities: Fannie Mae, Freddie Mac, and Ginnie Mae.

Securities—Investment instruments, such as stocks and bonds, that confer an interest or a right to payment, without allowing direct managerial control over the enterprise invested in.

Securities, Mortgage-Backed (MBS)—Investment instruments that have pools of mortgage loans as collateral, and which are primarily issued by the major secondary market agencies (Fannie Mae, Freddie Mac, and Ginnie Mae).

Securitization—When a secondary market agency creates mortgage-backed securities by buying a large number of mortgage loans, "pooling" them together, and pledging the pool as collateral for the securities.

Security Agreement—Under the Uniform Commercial Code, a document that establishes a security interest in personal property that is serving as collateral for a loan.

Security Instrument—A document that creates a voluntary lien against real property, to secure repayment of a loan; either a mortgage or a deed of trust.

Security Interest—A secured creditor's interest in property owned by the debtor, which entitles the creditor to have the property seized and sold if the debtor does not pay as agreed.

Security Property—Property owned by a borrower that is serving as collateral (the lender's security) for a loan.

Seller Financing—When a seller extends credit to a buyer to finance the purchase of the property; as opposed to having the buyer obtain a loan from a third party, such as an institutional lender.

Seller Second—Secondary financing from the seller, when a purchase money loan is used to supplement an institutional first mortgage.

Servicing—*See:* Loan Servicing.

Servicing Fee—A fee paid by a secondary market agency or other investor to the entity that is servicing a mortgage loan.

Settlement—*See:* Closing.

Settlement Statement—A document that presents a final, detailed accounting for a real estate transaction, listing each party's debits and credits and the amount each will receive or be required to pay at closing. Also called a closing statement.

Sheriff's Deed—The deed that is given to someone who purchases property at a foreclosure sale, after the statutory redemption period has expired.

Sheriff's Sale—A public auction of property after judicial foreclosure.

Short Sale—When a borrower obtains the lender's consent to sell the home for less than the full amount owed; the lender receives the sale proceeds and releases the borrower from the debt.

Stable Monthly Income—Gross monthly income (from primary and secondary sources) that meets the lender's tests of quality and durability.

Stock—A share of a corporation's stock represents a fractional ownership interest in the corporation; a shareholder may receive a return on the investment in the form of dividends and/or appreciation of the share's value.

Straight Note—*See:* Note, Straight.

Subject Property—In an appraisal, the property that is being appraised.

Subject To—When a borrower sells the security property without paying off the mortgage or deed of trust, and the purchaser takes title "subject to" the lien, but does not assume the loan.

Subordination—When a mortgagee or deed of trust beneficiary agrees to accept lower lien priority than she would otherwise have, allowing a lender with a lien recorded later to have higher priority.

Subordination Clause—A provision in a security instrument that permits a later security instrument to have higher lien priority than the one in which the clause appears.

Subprime Lending—Making riskier loans to borrowers who might otherwise be unable to qualify for a loan, often requiring higher interest rates and fees to make up for the increased risk of default.

Substitution, Principle of—A principle of appraisal holding that the maximum value of a property is set by how much it would cost to obtain another property that is equally desirable, assuming that there would not be a long delay or significant incidental expenses involved in obtaining the substitute.

Substitution of Entitlement—When a VA borrower sells the security property to another eligible veteran, who agrees to substitute his guaranty entitlement for the seller's, so that the seller's entitlement is restored.

Supply and Demand, Law of—A basic rule of economics holding that prices rise when supply decreases or demand increases, and that prices fall when supply increases or demand decreases.

Take-Out Loan—Long-term financing used to replace a construction loan (an interim loan) when construction has been completed. Also called a permanent loan.

Temporary Buydown—*See:* Buydown.

Term—A prescribed period of time; especially the length of time allotted to a borrower in which to pay off a loan.

Thrift Institution—A type of depository institution that has traditionally focused on providing financial services to individuals, with an emphasis on residential mortgage lending; it may be a savings and loan association or a savings bank.

Tight Money Market—A real estate market in which loan funds are scarce and lenders are charging high interest rates and loan fees.

TILA—*See:* Truth in Lending Act.

Time Deposit—A deposit in a financial institution that can't be withdrawn without penalty unless the depositor gives prior notice to the financial institution, or until a certain period has elapsed. A certificate of deposit is an example. *Compare:* Demand Deposit.

Title Theory—The legal theory holding that a mortgage or deed of trust gives the lender legal title to the security property while the debt is being repaid. *Compare:* Lien Theory.

Title, Equitable—The interest of the vendee under a land contract, including the right to possession of the property and the right to acquire legal title by paying off the contract according to its terms. *Compare:* Legal Title.

Title, Legal—Title held as security, without the right to possess the property. *Compare:* Equitable Title.

Total Finance Charge—Under the Truth in Lending Act, all charges associated with a loan that the lender requires the borrower to pay, including the interest, any discount points paid by the borrower, the origination fee, other loan fees, and mortgage insurance costs. *See also:* Annual Percentage Rate.

Total Obligations to Income Ratio—*See:* Debt to Income Ratio.

Trust—A legal arrangement in which title to property is vested in one or more trustees who manage the property for the benefit of one or more beneficiaries, in accordance with instructions provided by the person who established the trust.

Trust Account—A bank account in which funds held in trust on behalf of another person are kept separate from the holder's own money.

Trust Deed—*See:* Deed of Trust.

Trustee—1. In a deed of trust transaction, a neutral third party appointed by the lender to handle nonjudicial foreclosure (if necessary) or reconveyance after the loan has been repaid. 2. The person appointed to administer a trust on behalf of the beneficiary.

Trustee's Deed—The deed given to the purchaser at a trustee's sale.

Trustee's Sale—A nonjudicial foreclosure sale conducted by a trustee under the power of sale clause in a deed of trust.

Trustor—In a deed of trust transaction, the borrower. Also called the grantor.

Truth in Lending Act (TILA)—A federal law that requires lenders to make disclosures concerning loan costs (including the total finance charge and the annual percentage rate) to consumer loan applicants.

Two-step mortgage—A loan that allows the lender to adjust the loan's interest rate to the market level at one point during the loan term, such as a 5/25 plan where the interest rate is adjusted once after five years.

UCC—*See:* Uniform Commercial Code.

UFMIP—*See:* MIP.

Underimprovement—An improvement that is not the most profitable use of the land.

Underlying Loan—*See:* Wraparound Financing.

Underwriter—The employee of an institutional lender who evaluates loan applications to determine which loans should be approved.

Underwriting—The process of evaluating the financial status of a loan applicant and the value of the property he hopes to buy, to determine the risk of default and the risk of loss in the event of default and foreclosure. Also called risk analysis or qualifying.

Underwriting, Automated (AU)—Underwriting using software that performs a preliminary analysis of a loan application and makes a recommendation for approval or additional scrutiny.

Underwriting Standards—*See:* Qualifying Standards.

Uniform Commercial Code (UCC)—A body of law that has been adopted in slightly varying versions in all states, intended to standardize commercial law dealing with matters such as negotiable instruments and sales of personal property.

Uniform Settlement Statement—A settlement statement required for any transaction involving a loan that is subject to the Real Estate Settlement Procedures Act (RESPA).

Uniform Standards of Professional Appraisal Practice—Guidelines for appraisers adopted by the Appraisal Foundation, a nonprofit organization of professional appraiser associations.

Usury—Charging an interest rate that exceeds legal limits.

VA—The U.S. Department of Veterans Affairs.

VA Entitlement—The VA guaranty amount that a particular veteran is entitled to.

VA-Guaranteed Loan—A home loan to an eligible veteran made by an institutional lender and guaranteed by the Department of Veterans Affairs, protecting the lender against losses resulting from default.

VA Guaranty Amount—The portion of a VA loan guaranteed by the Department of Veterans Affairs; the maximum amount that the VA will pay the lender for a loss resulting from the borrower's default.

Valuation—*See:* Appraisal.

Vendee—The buyer in a transaction financed with a land contract.

Vendor—The seller in a transaction financed with a land contract.

Verification of Deposit—A form a lender sends to a financial institution for confirmation that a loan applicant has the funds on deposit that she claims to have.

Verification of Employment—A form a lender sends to a loan applicant's employer to confirm that the applicant is actually employed as claimed, and to verify the amount of the applicant's salary.

Wholesale Lending—Loans made by large lenders or investors through loan correspondents or mortgage brokers. *Compare:* Retail Lending.

Wraparound Financing—A seller financing arrangement in which the seller uses part of the buyer's payments to make the payments on an existing loan (called the underlying loan); the buyer takes title subject to the underlying loan, but does not assume it.

Writ of Execution—*See:* Execution, Order of.

Yield—The rate of return a lender or other investor receives on an investment, usually stated as an annual percentage of the amount loaned or invested.

Yield Spread Premium (YSP)—Compensation that a lender may pay a mortgage broker for originating a loan, based on the difference between the loan's interest rate and the current market rate.

Index

Y